Trekking in the
Karakoram &
Hindukush

a Lonely Planet walking guide

John Mock
Kimberley O'Neil

SWAEn 1995

Trekking in the Karakoram & Hindukush

1st edition

Published by

Lonely Planet Publications

Head Office: PO Box 617, Hawthorn, Vic 3122, Australia
Branches: 155 Filbert St, Suite 251, Oakland, CA 94607, USA
             10 Barley Mow Passage, Chiswick, London W4 4PH, UK
             71 bis rue du Cardinal Lemoine, 75005 Paris, France

Printed by

Craft Print Pte Ltd, Singapore

Photographs by

All photographs by John Mock except for the snow leopard by Lindsay Brown
Front cover: Apricot blossom near Birmogh Lasht, Chitral (John Mock)
Title page: Woodblock print of a Marco Polo sheep by the Sherqila Women's Art Group (SWAG)

This Edition

November 1996

Although the authors and publisher have tried to make the information as accurate as possible, they accept no responsibility for any loss, injury or inconvenience sustained by any person using this book.

National Library of Australia Cataloguing in Publication Data

Mock, John (John Howard), 1949-
   Trekking in the Karakoram & Hindukush

   1st ed.
   Includes index.
   ISBN 0 86442 360 8.

   1. Hiking - Hindu Kush Mountains (Afghanistan and Pakistan) -
   Guidebooks 2. Hiking - Karakoram Range - Guidebooks.
   3. Karakoram Range - Guidebooks. 4. Hindu Kush Mountains
   (Afghanistan and Pakistan) - Guidebooks.
   I. O'Neil, Kimberley, 1960- . II. Title (Series : Lonely Planet
   walking guide).

915.46

John Mock

John first trekked in the Karakoram and Hindukush in 1977. Since then, he has spent most of his time in Pakistan, India, and Nepal studying, working, and trekking (which are not mutually exclusive). During that time John also earned MA and PhD degrees in South Asian Studies from the University of California at Berkeley, specialising in language and literature. His main research, for which he was awarded a Fulbright fellowship, has been in the Wakhi community in Gojal. He has worked as a consultant on the Khunjerab National Park for the Worldwide Fund for Nature (WWF), on Hunza for the National Geographic Society USA, and on ecotourism for The World Conservation Union (IUCN – Pakistan).

Kimberley O'Neil

Kimberley first visited South Asia in 1984 and has trekked and travelled throughout Pakistan, India, and Nepal. She has over 10 years experience in the adventure travel industry. As a former Director of Asian Operations for a North American tour operator, she designed and operated trekking and mountaineering trips throughout the Himalaya and Karakoram. She has worked as a consultant on ecotourism for IUCN – Pakistan, as a computer software instructor, and is active in women's issues. Kimberley and John were married in Kathmandu in 1991 and live in California.

From the Authors

We would like to acknowledge and thank the many people and organisations without whose friendship, support, and cooperation this guide book would still be a gleam in Tony Wheeler's eye; they are listed at the back of the book.

Mushkil Baba first showed us the way. We can follow in his tracks, but can never fill his boots.

From the Publisher

This book was edited in Melbourne, Australia, by Frith Luton. Thanks also to Lyn McGaurr and Linda Suttie for proofing. Andrew Smith did the layout and design, and prepared the maps with assistance from Geoff Stringer, Michael Signal and Paul Piaia.

The cover was designed by David Kemp with cartography by Adam Mc Crow. Thanks also to Trudi Canavan, Reita Wilson and Margaret Jung for the illustrations; to Dan Levin for the fonts; to Chris Love for help with the climate charts; and Lou Callan and Nicola Daly for help with the language section.

Trekking Disclaimer

Although the authors and publisher have done their utmost to ensure the accuracy of all information in this guide, they cannot accept any responsibility for any loss, injury or inconvenience sustained by people using this book. They cannot guarantee that the tracks and routes described here have not become impassable for any reason in the interval between research and publication.

The fact that a trip or area is described in this guidebook does not necessarily mean that it is safe for you and your trekking party. You are ultimately responsible for judging your own capabilities in the light of the conditions you encounter.

Piracy

Piracy is very common in Pakistan. When a book is pirated it is stolen property and neither the authors nor the publisher receive any payment. To avoid buying a pirated book check the page alignment and quality of the black and white photos, illustrations and colour pages. If the black and white images look like poor photocopies or the colour photographs have lines around the edges due to poor reproduction, the book is pirated. Pirated copies may also have thinner paper and ink bleed-through. Authentic books are available through the authorised Lonely Planet distributor.

Warning & Request

Things change – prices go up, schedules change, good places go bad and bad places go bankrupt – nothing stays the same. So if you find things better or worse, recently opened or long since closed, please write and tell us and help make the next edition better.

Your letters will be used to help update future editions and, where possible, important changes will also be included in an Update section in reprints.

We greatly appreciate all information that is sent to us by travellers. Back at Lonely Planet we employ a hard-working readers' letters team to sort through the many letters we receive. The best ones will be rewarded with a free copy of the next edition or another Lonely Planet guide if you prefer. We give away lots of books, but, unfortunately, not every letter/postcard receives one.

Contents

Map Legend

BOUNDARIES

.... International Boundary

.... Province Boundary

.... Disputed Boundary

ROUTES

.... Freeway

.... Highway

.... Major Road

.... Unsealed Road or Jeep Road

.... City Road

.... City Street

.... Railway

.... Underground Railway

.... Walking Track

.... Route

.... Ridge

.... Ferry Route

AREA FEATURES

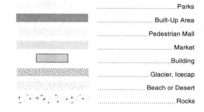

.... Parks

.... Built-Up Area

.... Pedestrian Mall

.... Market

.... Building

.... Glacier, Icecap

.... Beach or Desert

.... Rocks

HYDROGRAPHIC FEATURES

.... Coastline

.... River, Creek

.... Intermittent River or Creek

.... Rapids, Waterfalls

.... Lake, Intermittent Lake

.... Canal, Swamp

.... River flow

SYMBOLS

○ CAPITAL		.... National Capital
◉ Capital		...... Province or Regional Capital
◍ CITY		.... Major City
● City		.... City
● Town		.... Town
● Village		.... Village
■	▼	.... Place to Stay, Place to Eat
☲	▼	.... Cafe, Pub or Bar
✉	☎	.... Post Office, Telephone
❶	❺	.... Tourist Information, Bank
◒	◓	Bus Station or Terminal, Bus Stop
�benefitmuseum	✿	.... Museum, Youth Hostel
⌖	◮	Caravan Park, Camping Ground
✚	➕	.... Church, Cathedral
◪	◙	.... Mosque, Synagogue
◪	◎	.... Temple, Hospital
★		...... Police Station or Check Post

◔	◳	.... Embassy, Petrol Station
✈	✝	.... Airport, Airfield
▭	✿	.... Swimming Pool, Gardens
❖	🐘	.... Shopping Centre, Zoo
✣	▣	... Winery or Vineyard, Picnic Site
←	A25	One Way Street, Route Number
⛪	▲	.... Stately Home, Monument
✠	▣	.... Castle, Tomb
◠	⌂	.... Cave, Hut or Chalet
▲	☀	.... Mountain or Hill, Lookout
🜊	⚓	.... Lighthouse, Shipwreck
)(	◎	.... Pass, Spring
🦅	🏄	.... Beach, Surf Beach
∴		...... Archaeological Site or Ruins
		.... Ancient or City Wall
		... Cliff or Escarpment, Tunnel
		.... Railway Station

Note: not all symbols displayed above appear in this book

Introduction

The Karakoram and Hindukush mark the western end of the great mountain system of South and Central Asia. The main Hindukush and its offshoot, the Hindu Raj, extend from Afghanistan to the Ishkoman River valley. From here the Karakoram range runs east into India. These ranges form the greatest concentration of high peaks on the planet, and in the valleys beneath the summits lies the greatest expanse of glaciers outside the subpolar zones. The snows and glaciers of the Karakoram and Hindukush are the source for an extensive network of rivers, all of which flow into the Indus River. Older than the mountains themselves, it is the only river to transit these mountains, descending from its source in Tibet. Just south of the Karakoram, above the southern

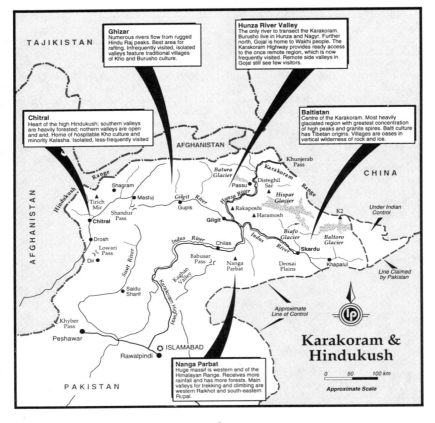

Ghizar
Numerous rivers flow from rugged Hindu Raj peaks. Best area for rafting. Infrequently visited, isolated valleys feature traditional villages of Kho and Burusho culture.

Hunza River Valley
The only river to transect the Karakoram. Burusho live in Hunza and Nagyr. Further north, Gojal is home to Wakhi people. The Karakoram Highway provides ready access to the once remote region, which is now frequently visited. Remote side valleys in Gojal still see few visitors.

Chitral
Heart of the high Hindukush; southern valleys are heavily forested; nothern valleys are open and arid. Home of hospitable Kho culture and minority Kalasha. Isolated, less-frequently visited

Baltistan
Centre of the Karakoram. Most heavily glaciated region with greatest concentration of high peaks and granite spires. Balti culture has Tibetan origins. Villages are oases in vertical wilderness of rock and ice.

Nanga Parbat
Huge massif is western end of the Himalayan Range. Receives more rainfall and has more forests. Main valleys for trekking and climbing are western Raikhot and south-eastern Rupal.

Karakoram & Hindukush

0   50   100 km

Approximate Scale

bank of the Indus, the Nanga Parbat massif marks the western end of the Greater Himalaya range. These peaks and glaciers have drawn mountaineers and expeditions since their discovery by the European explorers in the 19th century.

Although most trekkers first visit the region for the mountains, many often return for the people they meet there. The diversity and uniqueness of the people who live in the Karakoram and Hindukush offer a personal counterpoint to the immensity of the physical terrain.

This guidebook covers the trekking possibilities in this mountain region within the borders of Pakistan. The trekking areas in the Karakoram and Hindukush lie in Pakistan's Northwest Frontier Province (NWFP) and the Northern Areas. The primary trekking routes in NWFP are in Chitral district. Those in the Northern Areas are in all five districts: Ghizar, Gilgit, Diamir, Skardu, and Ghanche. In these trekking areas, unlike other popular trekking regions in South Asia, you can walk for days and never meet another foreigner.

The majority of travellers who visit the villages and valleys of the Karakoram and Hindukush do so by road. Relatively few foreigners go trekking, and most who do go up the famous Baltoro Glacier to Concordia for views of K2, the Trango Towers, the Gasherbrums, and the other towering peaks. Whenever you venture off these few well-travelled paths, you can find yourself in a trackless wilderness or on routes that see only handfuls of trekkers each year.

Trekking in the Karakoram and Hindukush encompasses more than just walking or backpacking along trails. Trekking is not mountaineering either, but trekking in this mountain region typically requires a greater level of fitness, self-sufficiency and competence than say trekking in the Nepal or Indian Himalaya. In the Karakoram and Hindukush routefinding, glacier travel and high-pass crossings are often required. Plenty of day hikes and short, easier treks can also be enjoyed with no glaciers involved. This guidebook will help you choose routes that suit your interest and abilities.

The information and route descriptions are based on our combined 26 years of experience travelling and trekking in Pakistan and over 32 years of visiting the mountains of South Asia. We have crossed more than 30 passes, traversed or crossed over 35 glaciers, and visited more valleys throughout the Karakoram and Hindukush than anyone else we know. This knowledge and experience is what we want to share with our readers.

We have found that trekking through Pakistan's northern mountains calls for an open spirit of adventure and a sense of humour, and brings the rewards of perhaps the most spectacular mountain scenery in the world, the gracious warmth and hospitality of the people met, and a feeling of accomplishing something remarkable.

Facts about the Region

HISTORY
General History

The Karakoram and Hindukush have always been rather porous barriers, offering shorter, seasonal routes between South and Central Asia. Over 4000 years ago, the people whose language was the common ancestor of all Indo-European languages travelled these routes. Some of them settled in the Hindukush, and others moved on to greater glory in India. Alexander the Great and his army crossed the Hindukush in 327 BC to reach the Indus River.

Alexander left behind Greek rulers, who founded the Bactrian Greek kingdoms south and west of the Hindukush. Buddhism, which had become the religion of most of India during the reign of Ashoka (272-235 BC), became the religion of the Bactrian kingdoms, and under a kind of *pax*

Alexander the Great (356-323 BC) and his army crossed the Hindukush in 327 BC.

Buddhica, trade between the Mediterranean and Asia flourished. Silk from China and spices from India flowed west, and the great overland trade routes known as the Silk Route blossomed. From India, Buddhism spread outward reaching Tibet, China, Korea, and Japan. Pulled by the wealth of the prosperous kingdoms of South Asia, and pushed by Chinese efforts to protect the silk trade, Scythians and Kushans came over the high passes from Central Asia and, displacing the Bactrian Greek rulers, established their rule over the Buddhist kingdoms.

Under the Kushans, Mahayana Buddhism flowered intellectually and artistically, producing an extraordinary fusion of Greek and Indian traditions, resulting in the first representation of Buddha in human form. From 100 AD, when Kanishka, the greatest of the Kushans, was emperor, they controlled the trade routes for several hundred years from the Gandharan capital at what is now Peshawar. But the empire gradually declined, and the successors to the Kushans, the Guptas, were pillaged by Huns from Central Asia, coming through the high passes.

The Chinese monks Fa-Hsien and Hsuan-Tsang journeyed through this area on their way to India in search of the sources of Buddhism in the 5th and 7th centuries. Their accounts tell us that Buddhism was active in the area. But although the courts were cosmopolitan and learned, the local mountain people retained their shamanistic beliefs coupled with a strong belief in magically endowed female spirit beings. It no doubt made for a strange mix, and Hsuan-Tsang reports that Buddhism had degenerated much in the area.

Even today, there is a popular belief in magical female spirit beings, called *peri* and *rui*. The peris are the owners of wild goats (ibex and markhor), and live on the high peaks.

The Chinese exerted considerable effort to

protect the trade routes, controlling forts in Chitral and Gilgit. Chinese power collapsed in the mid-8th century, but not without a struggle. Chinese and Tibetan annals record that Tibetans vied with China over Balur during the 7th and 8th centuries. From the 8th century until the coming of Islam, Tibetan influence remained a factor throughout this area.

As Islam's influence entered the Hindukush and Karakoram, the rulers of the small kingdoms of the area began to accept Islam. Yet the old religion remained part and parcel of popular belief. The last resistance to Islam was made by Hindu kings of Gilgit around the 13th century. The great Silk Route between the Mediterranean, India, and China, hard-hit by the power struggles in Central Asia, experienced one last resurgence around the same time. Chenghiz (Ghengiz) Khan ruthlessly subdued all the land between China and the Mediterranean, and under the harsh power of the Mongol dynasty, trade once again flowed freely.

The ruthless ruler Chenghiz Khan (1162-1227) controlled the land between China and the Mediterranean in the early 13th century.

Marco Polo and his uncles passed just north of the Karakoram and Hindukush on their way to the Mongol court in China.

However, the small states of the Karakoram and Hindukush remained remote from direct political domination, and the war-like chiefs held fast in their mountain strongholds over the centuries. The Sikh empire, which controlled Kashmir in the early 19th century, attempted to extend power to Gilgit and Baltistan. But in 1846, growing British power annexed the Sikh mountain territories. Calling them the State of Jammu and Kashmir, they sold it to one Gulab Singh and declared him the Maharaja of Kashmir. This territory included all of what are now Pakistan's Northern Areas and Azad Kashmir, plus the Indian-controlled Jammu, Kashmir and Ladakh. This newly created Kashmir functioned as a dependent border state against Russian expansion from the north-west. In what became known as 'The Great Game', Britain dispatched military and diplomatic missions to the mountainous no-man's land to counter Russian influence. The fiercely independent mountain chiefs of Chitral and Hunza fought the British, but by the early 20th century, British power was secure in the area.

When Britain finally left India, Pakistan and India divided Kashmir. India claimed territory all the way to the Chitral border, but Muslim troops in the Northern Areas secured the territory for Pakistan. A United Nations-supervised cease-fire has been in effect since 1949, but shelling and firing is a regular occurrence along the line. In the far east, the line was never demarcated. Taking advantage of this indeterminacy, Indian troops in 1984 moved onto the Siachen Glacier, seizing control of territory Pakistan had claimed. The Siachen's two western tributary glaciers, the Kondus and Bilafond, are still held by Pakistani troops. The Siachen and the Baltoro glaciers are separated by a line of high peaks with Pakistan troops stationed on the Baltoro side and Indian forces on the Siachen. More soldiers die from altitude and avalanches than from bullets in this high-altitude war.

History of Exploration

Pilgrims, traders, and other travellers traversed the Karakoram and Hindukush for millennia, but the area remained largely unknown. The ancient Greek and Roman geographers, working from the accounts of Alexander the Great's journey, compiled long lists of people living in the mountains at the head of the Indus River. So when British explorers began probing the region in the 19th century, they found there the people the classical geographers led them to expect to find. They also found a bewildering landscape of high mountains, deep river valleys and enormous glaciers. Driven by the need to protect the north-west flank of their Indian empire from Russian expansion, they set out from Kashmir to explore and map these great ranges.

The first to reach Skardu was GT Vigne in 1835. With a shotgun in hand and a kettle always ready to brew tea, he made four explorations into the Karakoram, giving the first description of its vastness and height. In 1847 lieutenants Vans Agnew and Young were first to reach Gilgit. Thereafter, a steady stream of explorers sounded out the passes and routes through the mountains. Notable among them were Frederic Drew, George Robertson, Francis Younghusband, George Cockerill, and Reginald CF Schomberg. Drew, a keen and systematic observer, explored the Ishkoman, Shimshal, and Basha valleys between 1862 and 1871. He also had the task of burying the less fortunate George Hayward, who was murdered in Darkot in 1870. Robertson during 1890 and 1891 was the first and only European to visit the Afghan Hindukush people before their conversion to Islam. In 1889 Younghusband visited the Shimshal Pass, then crossed the Mintaka Pass and entered Hunza from the north. Cockerill, in a flying survey of the borders of Chitral, saw in 1892 and 1894 more of that country than anyone else of the time. Schomberg, who travelled for British intelligence in the 1930s, is still remembered today by village greybeards in Bagrot, Chapursan and Shimshal. Less known are the travels of native secret agents, the 'pundits',

Francis Younghusband was one of the notable 19th-century explorers of the Karakoram region.

who went in disguise where British officers could not.

The first scientific explorers, interested not in potential chinks in the British empire's borders, but in a wide range of natural and anthropological phenomenon, were the Schlagintweit brothers, Hermann, Adolf, and Robert. Recommended to the British East India Company by Alexander von Humboldt, they travelled the Karakoram in 1855 and 1856. Among their achievements were the description of the Deosai Plains; the Nanga Parbat glaciers; and the Chogo Lungma, Biafo, Baltoro, and Bilafond glaciers. Adolf reached Concordia and was first to explore the Muztagh Pass.

The scientist-explorers of the Survey of India continued to map the region, establishing a triangulation network from Ladakh to Hunza by 1863. TG Montgomerie in 1856 recognised K2 as the highest Karakoram peak and HH Godwin-Austen advanced knowledge of the Karakoram glaciers, travelling up the Panmah, Biafo, and Baltoro glaciers in 1860 and 1861. The final step, to link the British survey with that of Russia, was begun in 1913 supervised by Kenneth Mason.

The only scientist to surpass the work of the Schlagintweits in the Karakoram was Giotto Dainelli, whose 12-volume report in Italian has never been translated into English. Dainelli first came to the Karakoram with Fillipo de Fillipi's 1913-14 expedition. Much of the exploration of the Karakoram and Hindukush was accomplished by such expeditions to high peaks and glaciers. The Conway expedition to the Central Karakoram, which, in 1892, first crossed the Hispar La, was like this, as were the Workman's seven expeditions to the Chogo Lungma, Biafo, Hispar, Aling,

Masherbrum, Gondogoro, Bilafond, Siachen, and Kondus glaciers between 1899 and 1912. The Vissers made three expeditions between 1922 and 1935, on one of which they made the first crossing of the Chapchingol Pass into Ghujerab. The Shipton-Tilman expedition to Shaksgam and Shimshal in 1935 and to the Biafo and Hispar glaciers in 1939 provided the basis for our current maps of the area. The Baltoro was accurately mapped by Norman Dyrenfurth's 1935 and 1939 expeditions and Ardito Desio's expedition in 1954, which made the first ascent of K2. And, it is fair to say,

PEAKS & ASCENTS

Peak	Height (metres)	First Ascent	Nationality	Route
Hindukush Range				
Noshaq	7492	1960	Japanese	south ridge
Tirich Mir	7706	1950	Norwegian	south ridge
Istor-o-nal	7403	1969	Spanish	south-west ridge
Saragrahr	7349	1959	Italian	north-east ridge
Udren Zom	7108	1964	Austrian	north face
Akher Chhīsh	7020	1966	Austrian	east ridge
Himalayan Range				
Nanga Parbat	8125	1953	Austrian-German	west ridge
Karakoram Range				
Batura Muztagh				
Batura I	7795	1976	German	south face/east ridge
Shishpar	7611	1974	Polish-German	south-east ridge from north
Passu Sar	7476	no record		
Muchu Chhīsh	7453	no record		
Ultar I	7388			
Bojohagur-Duanasir	7329	1984	Japanese	south-west ridge
Passu Diar	7295	1978	Japanese-Pakistani	south-west ridge
Hachindar Chhīsh	7163	1982	Japanese	east face
Kampir Dior	7143	1975	Japanese	south and west ridges
Pamri Sar	7016	1986	Italian	north ridge from west
Rakaposhi – Haramosh Muztagh				
Rakaposhi	7788	1958	British-Pakistani	south-west spur
Malubiting W	7458	1971	German	north-east ridge
Haramosh	7409	1958	Austrian	east ridge
Malubiting C	7291	1975	Japanese	west wall
Diran	7257	1968	German	north face/west ridge
Spantik	7027	1955	German	south-east ridge

today's scholars continue this exploration of a part of the planet still in many ways terra incognita for most of humanity.

GEOGRAPHY

Mountaineers and explorers describe a wilderness of pristine peaks and untravelled glaciers north and west of the Greater Himalaya Range, but the Karakoram and Hindukush have an enduring human presence.

Much of the region is really part of the steppes of Central Asia unaffected by the South Asian monsoon. In the north of Chitral, Hunza, and Baltistan, the southern forests vanish and trees appear only along stream beds and in sheltered places. This gives the landscape a harsh and desolate aura in contrast to the green oasis of each village. Glacier-fed rivers cut deeply through these mountains and devastating events have left their mark here. Sudden surging advances of glaciers and landslides caused by earthquakes have dammed rivers, causing destructive outburst floods. Yet on this inhospitable land live hospitable people, who use the rivers, the rocks, and the flowered summer meadows along the margins of ice and snow to maintain their cultures.

PEAKS & ASCENTS *continued*

Peak	Height (metres)	First Ascent	Nationality	Route
Hispar Muztagh				
Disteghil Sar	7885	1960	Austrian	south face/west ridge
Kunyang Chhīsh	7852	1971	Polish	south face/south ridge
Kanjut Sar	7760	1959	Italian	south ridge
Trivor	7728	1960	British-US	north-west ridge
Yukshin Garden	7530	1984	Austrian	south ridge
Pumari Chhīsh W	7492	1979	Japanese	north ridge
Momhil Sar	7343	1964	Austrian	south-east face/south ridge
Jutmo Sar	7330	1980	Japanese	west and north ridges
Lupgar Sar C	7200	1979	Japanese	traverse west ridge
Kunyang Chhīsh N	7108	1979	Japanese	north ridge
Mulungutti Sar	7025	1985	Japanese	
Biafo Glacier				
Baintha Brak	7285	1977	British	west ridge
Latok I	7151	1979	Japanese	south face
Baltoro Glacier				
K2	8611	1954	Italian	Abruzzi ridge
Gasherbrum I (Hidden Peak)	8068	1958	US	south face
Broad Peak	8047	1957	Austrian	alpine style, west face
Gasherbrum II	8035	1956	Austrian	south side
Gasherbrum III	7952	1975	Polish	east face
Gasherbrum IV	7925	1958	Italian	north-east ridge
Masherbrum NE	7821	1960	US-Pakistani	south-east face
Chogolisa I (Bride Peak)	7665	1975	Austrian	west ridge
Muztagh Tower	7273	1956	British	west ridge
		1956	French	south-east ridge
Sia Kangri	7422	1934	Dyrenfurth's International Expedition	Conway Saddle
Baltoro Kangri	7280	1963	Japanese	east ridge

The topography is a bewildering array of ridges and valleys. From Afghanistan, the Hindukush, crowned by Tirich Mir (7706m), reaches across Chitral, and, under the name Hindu Raj, continues east to the Indus and Ishkoman valleys. The Chitral and upper Ghizar rivers drain its glaciers and snows. From the Ishkoman River and stretching along Pakistan's border with China into India lies the Karakoram (which means 'black rock' in Turkish), with its four 8000m giants above the Baltoro Glacier. The Hunza, Shyok and Indus rivers drain this heavily glaciated region. The glaciers from Nanga Parbat (8126m), at the western end of the Great Himalaya, flow into the Indus River, which separates this massif from the Karakoram to its north.

GEOLOGY

The Karakoram and Hindukush, as well as the Pamir and Himalaya ranges, are a result of the still ongoing collision of the Indian land mass with that of Eurasia. Over 100 million years ago, the Indian land mass separated from the African land mass and began its inexorable drift northward. Some 50 million years ago, it collided with the Eurasian continent and the most spectacular period of mountain building in earth's history began. The Indian mass buckled and slid under the Eurasian, which crumpled and heaved upward, forming the Karakoram and Hindukush. Between the two, an area of what once were islands has been compressed and raised. Geologists term this area the Kohistan Arc. It includes Chilas, upper Swat, Gilgit, and Skardu. The main suture line between the Indian and Eurasian continents roughly corresponds with the Indus River. This river originates on the older upraised sea bed of the Tibetan plateau and has carved its gigantic canyon through the rising Karakoram range. The great massif of Nanga Parbat represents the prow of the Indian continent, and is still rising by seven mm every year. Across from Nanga Parbat, separated by the Indus River and the Kohistan Arc, lies Rakaposhi, the prow of the Eurasian land mass. Between these two lies the area where continents collide.

The inexorable force of this collision resulted in enormous pressures and temperatures deep in the earth. Rocks melted, ran together and cooled. Over millions of years, crystalline pockets have risen to the surface, and over the last 25 years, Pakistan has become famous as a major producer of mineral specimens and rough gems. Trekkers may meet villagers offering gem crystals mined high in the mountains. Fine aquamarine comes from Dassu village in the Braldu Valley of Baltistan and Sumayar village in Nagyr. Tourmaline comes from Stak Nala, garnet from Shengus village along the Indus River, topaz from Dassu and Nyet in the Braldu Valley, and tanzanite from Alchuri in the Shigar Valley.

CLIMATE

Far from the moderating influence of the ocean, the climate of the Karakoram and Hindukush is typified by extreme seasonal heat and cold. Most precipitation comes in the late winter and early spring, though southern regions and higher elevations get summer precipitation.

Chitral and the Northern Areas lie between 35° and 37° north latitude and 71° and 77° east longitude. Being north of and in the rain shadow of the Himalaya, there is just one trekking season, starting in late spring, peaking in summer, and tapering off with early autumn.

Seasons

The Karakoram and Hindukush have four seasons: a pleasant spring (March to May); a hot summer (June to mid-September); a cool autumn (mid-September to November); and a cold winter (December to February). Spring is a pleasant time in the lower valleys. Fields turn bright green with new wheat and fruit blossoms decorate the trees. In this season, most passes remain closed, except a few low-elevation passes in Chitral.

Around late May or early June, enough snow has melted high up for villagers to move flocks to alpine pastures. During late

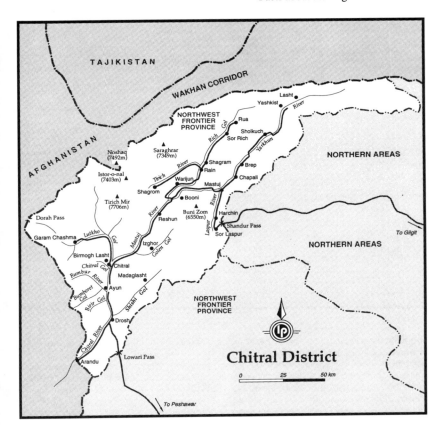

Chitral District

0   25   50 km

spring and summer, the snow line recedes by about 10m per day, and on southern slopes it rises to about 5500m by the end of summer. Passes open between April and July, depending upon their elevation and aspect. Summers are intensely hot in valleys below 2500m. Above, sunny areas warm quickly each day, while shaded spots remain cool. By mid-September, daytime temperatures fall and villagers move their flocks down close to the village. Any snow fall up high does not melt after September, and high passes close for the winter then. Autumn brings pleasant daytime temperatures, colourful leaves, and

cool nights, often dipping below freezing point. Winter nights are long, and in January and February, clouds hang over the mountains and snow falls, making it a bleak and colourless time of year. (See When to Go in the Facts for the Trekker chapter.)

Precipitation

The monsoon moves west across India and usually begins in Pakistan by the end of June, continuing through September. Since the Karakoram and Hindukush lie north of the main Himalaya range, most trekking areas receive little of the monsoon rains, which dominate the weather in the rest of Pakistan. However, southern Chitral, Swat Valley, Kaghan Valley and Rupal Valley on the southern flanks of Nanga Parbat get some monsoonal rain, as do all areas above 5000m. The monsoon strongly affects air and road travel between northern Pakistan and down-country cities, such as Islamabad, Rawalpindi, and Peshawar.

Precipitation in Chitral and the Northern Areas occurs primarily in late winter and spring from January to May. Chitral town receives about 450 mm of precipitation per year, with 270 mm from February to April. Gilgit receives about 165 mm per year, with 95 mm March to May. Skardu receives about 100 mm per year with most from March to May. What are just high clouds down low are often storm clouds in the mountains. Above 5000m annual precipitation is between 1000 and 2000 mm. Up to a third of the annual Karakoram snow pack comes from the monsoon.

When the monsoon first breaks in Pakistan, it is usually stormy in the high mountains. The Karakoram also experiences a curious precipitation peak around the end of August.

Temperature

In all seasons, there is a big day-night temperature difference. Temperature also varies with altitude. The temperature generally falls 6.2°C for each 1000m rise. During the peak trekking season, Gilgit and Chitral are hot in the daytime, reaching around 40°C during midsummer, but dry. Skardu, 1000m higher, is about 5°C cooler and also very dry.

The many rivers rise dramatically during the summer, carrying 20 times more water than in winter. This is not due to rainfall, but rather to melting glaciers and snow. The key factor is not air temperature, but rather the duration of sunshine on the ice and snow. This accounts for the dramatic rise and fall in some streams and rivers on sunny or

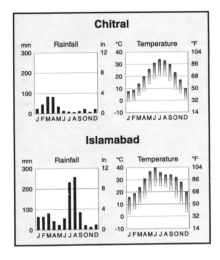

cloudy days. The silt from melting glaciers and riverbank erosion turns most rivers a grey-brown colour. Only snowmelt streams remain blue.

In Islamabad, Rawalpindi and Peshawar it is often very hot and humid.

ECOLOGY

Land use in the Karakoram and Hindukush is a result of adaptation to the extremes of climate and terrain. No more than 1% of the land is cultivated. In this arid climate, cultivation is made possible only by intensive irrigation using water from the high snows and glaciers, and control of irrigation has proved the key to political power. Villages are located on alluvial fans of side streams and on terraces above the main rivers. Village life follows a pattern of subsistence agriculture combined with animal husbandry, utilising all the different altitude zones of seasonal vegetation up to the permanent snow line at about 4800m to support livestock.

Up to a maximum altitude of 2400m, growing two crops is possible. Winter-sown wheat is followed closely by corn, buckwheat or millet. Above this elevation only a

single crop, almost always wheat, is grown. In the highest villages, those above 3000m, wheat ripens with difficulty. Soil fertility is maintained by the application of carefully collected animal dung and in some areas, human waste.

Trees are carefully tended. Apricots are probably the trees most trekkers remember; but walnuts, apples, mulberries, peaches, plums, pears, and cherries as well as grapes are also grown. The sweet, tasty apricot kernels are a valuable oil source. Tall quick-growing Lombardy poplars are also distinctive, and provide timber for house construction.

In Gojal, the introduction of potatoes in the early 1970s radically altered life for the people there. Before this, they barely subsisted on a single wheat crop per year. Now Gojal is producing bumper crops of virus-free seed potatoes to meet the insatiable down-country demand. With the money earned from potatoes, they buy all the wheat they need and still have money left over for education, travel, and consumer goods.

Most households grow their own green vegetables, which is why they are rare in bazaars. In some areas, especially the Yarkhun Valley, cannabis and opium are cultivated in small plots. These used to be major trade commodities, but now the demand has dwindled and the production has reduced to meet the low-level local demand. Opium and cannabis are not actually legal, of course.

Sheep and goats are the most numerous livestock; poor indeed is the household that doesn't have a few goats. Milking cows are also kept and bulls are essential for ploughing the small terraced plots where tractors are impractical. Bulls are sometimes still used for threshing in roadless areas. In the high-altitude regions, especially among the Wakhi, yaks are prized. In Baltistan, crosses of cows and yaks, called *dzo* are favoured.

Conservation

Pakistan has been making determined steps to address environmental issues within the country and in the broader global context. To this end, a high-level Environmental Protection Council has been set up and the Environment & Urban Affairs Division of the government has devised a National Conservation Strategy (NCS).

Provincial conservation strategies are under way for NWFP and the Northern Areas. To revitalise the conservation ethic and community spirit *(qannat* and *haqūq ul-ibād* in Arabic), the NCS calls for cooperation with community organisations and non-governmental organisations (NGOs). The main organisations below are directly involved with the Karakoram and Hindukush.

The Worldwide Fund for Nature (WWF)

WWF – Pakistan (☎ 586-2354; Internet:user @wwflhr.lhe.imran.pk), PO Box 5180, Lahore, is the national branch of the well-known international organisation. In the Karakoram and Hindukush, it works to protect migratory birds in Chitral, and is the main NGO for the Khunjerab National Park.

The World Conservation Union (IUCN)

The local group, IUCN – Pakistan (☎ 586 1540-2; fax 587 0287; Internet:mail@iucn-isb.sdnpk.undp.org), 1 Bath Island Rd, Karachi 75530, is the national branch of the world's largest alliance of conservation authorities and interest groups. IUCN – Pakistan is the driving force behind the NCS and the provincial conservation strategies. In the NWFP and Northern Areas, it works closely with the Aga Khan Rural Support Program (AKRSP), is actively involved with conserving biodiversity, and is working to establish the Central Karakoram National Park.

The Aga Khan Foundation (AKF)

The Aga Khan Foundation operates a highly regarded group of service organisations in the Northern Areas and Chitral: Aga Khan Educational Services (AKES), Aga Khan Health Services (AKHS), and AKRSP.

Recognising the need for community involvement with conservation, most international NGOs work through AKF's network of village-level organisations.

Protected Areas

Pakistan currently recognises just three categories of protected areas: national parks, wildlife sanctuaries, and game reserves. These now outdated categories and the equally outdated legislation behind them severely restrict how Pakistan manages its unique wilderness resources. Current United Nations-sanctioned categories number six, with a wide range of management options.

Almost all of Pakistan's protected areas in the Karakoram and Hindukush were once the property of local princes. When the princely states were absorbed into Pakistan, the government assumed ownership of these areas. Local people, who had traditionally used the areas for pasturing and wood gathering saw themselves as the inheritors of the high mountain valleys and grasslands. The resulting disputes are still with the courts.

Also these mountain areas have now also become the object of desire of competing interests – resort hotels, polo tournaments, adventure tourism, big-game hunting, and the military. Pakistan's understaffed, under-equipped, and undertrained wildlife officers are unable to handle the growing complexity of management. With the government as owner, and others as users, no one has sufficient control over resources, and effective management seems impossible. Whether the government can revise legislation and resolve park conflicts resulting from multiple users remains to be seen.

National Parks There are three officially gazetted national parks in the Karakoram and Hindukush: Chitral Gol, Khunjerab, and Central Karakoram. Three other parks, Shandur-Hundrup, Fairy Meadows, and Deosai Wilderness, were declared national parks by the Chief Commissioner of the Northern Areas in 1993. They are currently under review for the official gazetting process by the federal government. Trekkers who visit these three new parks will find no indication of their park status. National parks are administered by the government Forestry Division.

The National Council for the Conserva-

A trek sign at the boundary of the 7750 hectare Chitral Gol National Park, along the jeep road below Birmogh Lasht.

tion of Wildlife (NCCW), of the Ministry of Food, Agriculture & Cooperatives, has the major responsibility for park development.

Chitral Gol National Park This 7750 hectare former hunting preserve of the ex-Mehtar of Chitral has one of the few remaining viable populations of markhor, currently several hundred in number (see Endangered Species below). Chitral Gol's ownership is tied up in a three-way dispute between the ex-Mehtar, who claims it is still his private property, the government and local people. The case has been in litigation for more than 20 years. Hopefully, these parties will decide to work together to manage and conserve this beautiful ecosystem for future generations.

Khunjerab National Park This 2269 sq km area is in the Gojal region of northern Hunza. It lies on either side of the Karakoram Highway (KKH) from Dih to the China border at the Khunjerab Pass. Most of Shimshal's Pamir and Ghujerab regions are also included, but currently, only the area along the KKH is being actively managed.

The famous wildlife biologist George Schaller recommended the establishment of this park in 1975 to the then prime minister, Zulfikar Ali Bhutto. The prime minister then declared it done but following this almost

nothing actually was done. Marco Polo sheep, a magnificent species once abundant in the Khunjerab Pass region, were almost wiped out. They are now recovering thanks to efforts by WWF – Pakistan to develop sound management practices respecting the rights of local communities and involving them in decision making. The Directorate of Khunjerab National Park (DKNP) is responsible for management of the Khunjerab National Park. DKNP operates more as a bureaucracy with administrative headquarters in Gilgit. Wildlife protection is the responsibility of villagers living near the park.

Central Karakoram National Park Established in 1993 in response to growing environmental pressure on Baltistan's once pristine Baltoro Glacier, this park also includes the Biafo and Hispar glaciers and their tributaries. The crown jewel, of course, is K2 (8611m). Pakistan intends to nominate the park for World Heritage status. On the Baltoro Glacier, the accumulation of military hardware and debris from the long-simmering conflict with India remains a problem. Management plans have yet to be developed and time will tell if the park can avoid repeating problems that have plagued other parks.

Shandur-Hundrup National Park This park includes two separate areas in the Northern Areas' Ghizar district: the 996 sq km Hundrup River valley up to the Dadarelli An and the 644 sq km Shandur Pass area. The Hundrup River is a world-class trout stream and the Shandur Pass is the site of an annual polo tournament (see Cultural Festivals in Facts for the Trekker.) The area was declared a park in an attempt to control the merrymakers at the polo tournament, who were not inclined to clean up their mess. Now, tour operators are cleaning up after the tournament, but garbage still fills ravines in the high meadows beside Shandur Lake.

Fairy Meadows National Park This alpine area in the Raikhot Valley on the western slopes of Nanga Parbat was long-coveted by the Shangrila Resorts, which constructed the jeep road to Tato, logged the forests and planned to build a hotel there. Since the death of the Shangrila founder and the declaration of the area as a park, it now seems that Fairy Meadows may remain a natural area.

Deosai Plateau Wilderness Park The Deosai Plateau is a 3464 sq km high-altitude plain bordering on Indian Kashmir. Uninhabited and little used, the area has the largest brown bear population in Pakistan, numerous marmots, and clear streams with unusual snow trout.

Wildlife Sanctuaries These are all remote former hunting grounds of local rulers and for each sanctuary there is at least one desig-nated game watcher – your best guide to the land and the wildlife. There is no visible indication of the sanctuary status of these areas. In theory, hunting is banned. Wildlife sanctuaries include:

Agram-Besti Wildlife Sanctuary covers 30,000 hectares in the high valleys of Agram and Besti in the Lutkho district of Chitral.

Naltar Wildlife Sanctuary covers 273 sq km of the Naltar Valley to its juncture with the Hunza River, and is contiguous with the Pakora and Sherqila Game Reserves.

Kargah Wildlife Sanctuary covers 445 sq km of the Kargah Valley five km north-west of Gilgit.

Astor Wildlife Sanctuary covers 416 sq km on the north side of the Astor Valley from the junction with the Indus River to the confluence with the Parashing Gah. It is contiguous with the Baltistan Wildlife Sanctuary.

ENDANGERED SPECIES

In the Karakoram and Hindukush little is actually known about the current status of most wildlife. Some species, such as brown bear and blue sheep, appear endangered although globally they are not. IUCN attempts to track the status of species worldwide and classifies the following species as endangered.

Marco Polo Sheep As recently as 1968, hundreds of Marco Polo sheep *(Ovis ammon polii)*, with their enormous curly horns, could be seen in the Khunjerab Pass. But during the construction of the KKH they were slaughtered to feed workers and soldiers and hunted by visiting bigwigs. This magnificent species is now strictly protected. They can still be found in remote Khunjerab valleys, now closed to for-eigners.

Kashmir Markhor These mountain mon-archs, Kashmir markhor (*Capra falconeri cashmiriensis*), typically are found on cliffs at lower elevations than the more common ibex. They belong to the goat family, but are a far cry from the common domestic variety. The males weigh up to 90 kg and have unique long, spiral-ling horns and a flowing white ruff at the neck. Chitral has perhaps the largest population of these magnificent animals left on the planet.

Baltistan Wildlife Sanctuary covers 415 sq km in Baltistan, contiguous with the Astor Wildlife Sanctuary. It lies south of the Indus River, between Rondu and Shengus villages.

Satpara Wildlife Sanctuary lies 35 km south of Skardu in Baltistan. It includes Satpara Nala and lake, and borders the Deosai Plains.

Game Reserves These, too, were former hunting grounds, or *shikar gah*. Most of the game now is scarce and hard to find, but trekkers may encounter herds of ibex when descending a pass. Villagers report snow leopard in most reserves which include:

Drosh Gol Game Reserve covers 2000 hectares of the small Drosh Gol, above Drosh village, east of the Chitral River.

Chinar/Purit Gol Game Reserve, 6500 hectares, covers the Purit Gol, a southern tributary of the Shishi Gol close to Drosh.

Tooshi Game Reserve, along the paved road to Garam Chashma in Chitral's Lutkho district, covers 1000 hectares and is proposed to be reclassified as a wildlife sanctuary, as it has a large (about 160) and readily viewable markhor population, best seen from the road at dusk. The jeep ride is just 20 minutes from Chitral town and costs Rs 250 return.

Ghariet Gol Game Reserve covers 4800 hectares of the Ghariet Gol, east of the Chitral River in southern Chitral.

Golen Gol Game Reserve in Chitral, covering 50,000 hectares, is one of the most beautiful and extensive areas, with numerous side valleys. With its fantastic variety of ecosystems, it is a trekker's delight.

Chassi/Bahushtaro Game Reserve includes 37,000 hectares of the rugged territory of the Bahushtaro Gol and is contiguous with the Naz Bar Game Reserve.

Naz Bar Nala Game Reserve covers 33,000 hectares of the upper Naz Bar in Yasin.

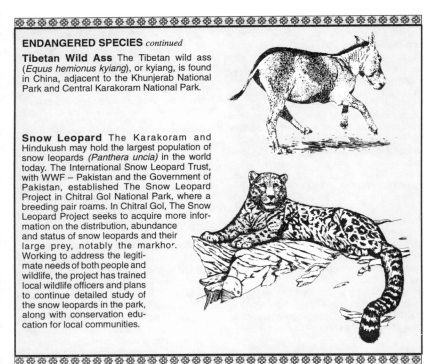

ENDANGERED SPECIES *continued*

Tibetan Wild Ass The Tibetan wild ass (*Equus hemionus kyiang*), or kyiang, is found in China, adjacent to the Khunjerab National Park and Central Karakoram National Park.

Snow Leopard The Karakoram and Hindukush may hold the largest population of snow leopards *(Panthera uncia)* in the world today. The International Snow Leopard Trust, with WWF – Pakistan and the Government of Pakistan, established The Snow Leopard Project in Chitral Gol National Park, where a breeding pair roams. In Chitral Gol, The Snow Leopard Project seeks to acquire more information on the distribution, abundance and status of snow leopards and their large prey, notably the markhor. Working to address the legitimate needs of both people and wildlife, the project has trained local wildlife officers and plans to continue detailed study of the snow leopards in the park, along with conservation education for local communities.

Pakora Game Reserve includes 7500 hectares of the Pakora Valley in Ishkoman and is contiguous with the Naltar Wildlife Sanctuary.

Sherqila Game Reserve, in Ghizar district 48 km west of Gilgit, covers 17,000 hectares of Sherqila Valley above Sherqila village.

Dainyor Game Reserve is six km east of Gilgit and covers 44,000 hectares.

Kilik/Mintaka Game Reserve lies along the border with China, east of the KKH and the Khunjerab National Park. It includes 65,000 hectares of important Marco Polo sheep habitat, and is closed to foreigners.

Stak Nala Game Reserve covers 13,000 hectares north of the Indus River in Baltistan.

Nar/Ghoro Game Reserve covers the 7000 hectare area of two small valleys that run north of the Indus River between the Shigar and Shyok rivers, east of Skardu.

FLORA

In the arid Karakoram and Hindukush, where there is plenty of sunlight, moisture is the key factor for plant growth. Precipitation increases with elevation, with near desert-like conditions on lower valley floors and dense forest on shaded higher slopes. Dry sage brush (*artemisia*) steppes start as low as 1500m and continue to 2400m on north slopes and up to 3400m on south slopes. In relatively moist southern Chitral, dry oak forest predominates below 2400m. In areas where moist monsoon air reaches, notably southern Chitral, the southern bank of the Ghizar and Gilgit rivers, south of Rakaposhi and Haramosh, and around Nanga Parbat, conifer forests of pine, cedar, and fir are found from 2400m to 3400m.

Where accessible by road, these forests have been heavily cut down over the last 20 years. In the drier northern areas, magnificent juniper stands are found. The treeline roughly corresponds with a 10 to 12°C midday summer temperature. Above the timberline are scattered stands of birch, willow, and juniper bent by snow and wind. Higher still and reaching to the snowline are alpine sedge meadows. As the snowline recedes, colourful flowers appear, literally carpeting these areas for the short intense summer.

Trees

Some of the most common trees are fir (*Abies pindrow*), birch (*Betula utilis*), cedar (*Cedrus deodara*), juniper (*Juniperus macropoda*), spruce (*Picea smittiana*), chilgoza pine (*Pinus gerardiana*), Himalayan chir pine (*Pinus roxburghii*), blue pine (*Pinus walenchia*), oak (*Quercus ilex*), willow (*Salix* spp), and sycamore (*Acer pseudoplatanus*).

The cedar *(Cedrus deodara)* grows between 2400m and 3400m altitude in forests around the Nanga Parbat massif.

Bushes & Shrubs

Among the more frequent short woody plants are ephedra (*Ephedra gerardiana*), rose (*Rosa webbiana*), tamarisk (*Myricaria elegans*), sage (*artemisia*), and viburnum (*Viburnum cotonifolium*).

Wildflowers & Herbs

Wildflower-lovers will recognise many familiar species. Some of the most common alpine flowers and their botanical family are asters and daisies (*Asteracae*), gentians (*Gentianacae*), geraniums (*Geraniaceae*), snapdragons (*Scrophulariaceae*), mint (*Lamiaceae*), potentillas (*Rosaceae*), poppies (*Papaveracae*), delphiniums and buttercups (*Ranunculaceae*), and mustards (*Brassicaceae*).

FAUNA

Although the wildlife species of the mountains are known, little is known about their distribution and status. For example, a previously unrecognised species, the woolly flying squirrel, was located south of Gilgit in 1995. Large mammals can be hard to see, as hunting has driven them to remote and high places. In some protected areas, you are more likely to see them.

Birds, especially doves and waterfowl, are also hunted, but a good variety can still be spotted. Alpine and glacial lakes are important waterfowl fly-way stopover points. If local hunters haven't killed or chased waterfowl off, these can be great seasonal viewing spots. The wildlife department conducts an annual valley-by-valley census in Chitral, and less regularly in the Northern Areas, maintaining records of large mammals and game birds.

The sandy-grey Himalayan lynx *(Felis lynx isabellina)* is found in the southern part of the Karakoram & Hindukush, between 2745m and 3355m altitude in summer.

Mammals

Among the more common mammals which you have a chance of viewing are: Himalayan ibex *(Capra ibex sibirica)*, golden marmot, cape hare, large-eared pika, Royale's high mountain vole, Tibetan red fox *(Vulpes vulpes montana)*, ermine, alpine weasel, and innumerable field mice. Ibex are common enough to support limited hunting. They are often seen throughout Khunjerab

The brown bear *(Ursus arctos)* usually lives above the treeline and during summer may prey on livestock grazing in the high pastures.

National Park. Golden marmots *(Marmota caudata aurea)* abound on the Deosai Plains, and other high sedge meadows close to the China border host large populations.

The shy cats, Himalayan lynx *(Felis lynx isabellina)* and leopard cat *(Felis bengalensis)*, are found in southern areas. Tiny musk deer *(Moschus moschiferus)* are here, too, but they are relentlessly hunted for their musk gland and hence rarely seen. Brown bears *(Ursus arctos)* and black bears *(Selenarctos thibetanus)* are not uncommon, but are infrequently seen. They should be considered dangerous. Brown bears are common on the Deosai Plains. Wolves *(Canis lupus pallipes)*, though common predators, are infrequently seen, as they are

The stone marten *(Martes foina)* has a uniformly dull brown coat with a white throat. These slender, graceful animals inhabit the forests or arid heights above 1525m. As well as preying on smaller animals and birds they sometimes eat honey, fruit and nuts.

shot on sight. They are especially frequent along the China border. Stone marten (*Martes foina*) are infrequently seen, as are Ladakhi urial (*Ovis orientalis*), a much hunted sheep. Blue sheep or bharal (*Pseudois nayaur*) are found only in the Ghujerab Valley and the Shimshal Pamir. They were once found along the Baltoro Glacier, but are now gone, hunted to feed expeditions.

The golden eagle *(Aquila chrysaetos)* is dark brown with a tawny neck when mature. Younger birds, with white on the wings and at the base of their tail, can sometimes be sighted well above the treeline.

Blue sheep or bharal *(Pseudois nayaur)* are now only found in the Ghujerab Valley and the Shimshal Pamir.

Birds (Avifauna)

The Lutkho, Turikho, and Yarkhun river valleys are fly ways for at least 10 species of ducks and geese migrating from Siberia. About 200,000 of these wetland birds migrate through Chitral from September to April. Waterfowl are under severe hunting pressure and the most significant lakes, such as Karamabar Lake, deserve recognition and protection under the international Ramsar waterfowl habitat convention.

Falcons are often trapped in northern Chitral and sold in Peshawar to falconers. Wealthy falconers from Arab oil states then use the falcons to hunt the Houbara bustard, a severely endangered bird of Pakistan's southern desert.

Among the many birds observable in northern Pakistan are both migratory and resident birds. They include: grebes and waterfowl (teal, mallards, pintails); raptors (sparrowhawks, march harriers, golden eagles, lammergeier (bearded vultures), black vultures, Griffon vultures, kestrels, falcons including Peregrine); partridges (snow partridges, snow cocks or ram chukor, rock partridges or chukor); herons, shorebirds, and gulls (grey herons, black winged stilts, plovers, sandpipers); pigeons (hill pigeons, snow pigeons, doves); nocturnal birds (eagle owls, night jars); cuckoos, kingfishers, rollers, and hoopoe; larks; swallows (swifts, martins); and pipits and wagtails. Much hunted thrushes include redstarts, wheatears, and blue and whistling thrushes. Others common birds are: warblers (accentors, sparrows, buntings); rosefinches and mountain finches; crows, magpies

The bearded vulture or lammergeier *(Gypaetus barbatus)*. Mature birds have a wing span of up to three metres and a brownish-golden head. This bird frequents altitudes over 1220m and scavenges near mountain villages.

(including yellow and red-billed chough) and the all black croaking ravens; monal pheasants; and many songbirds (dippers, wrens, tits, shrikes, orioles, and starlings).

POPULATION & PEOPLE

The Karakoram and Hindukush are home to a kaleidoscope of people. Far from being barriers, the high passes have always served as conduits for peoples, religions, goods, and ideas. The people who brought Vedic thought to India passed through here. Buddha's teaching spread following the high routes to China, Tibet, and beyond. The Great Silk Route trade that linked Imperial China with Rome made rich those who ventured through these mountains. Like a high water mark from a receding tide, traces of these passages remain in the high mountain valleys, often retained in the way of life of the mountain people. Cultural borrowing over millennia has led to a sharing of words and customs between many of the peoples, yet each group has retained its own unique identity.

Balti-pa

The Balti people are the westernmost extension of Tibetan language culture, speaking a Tibetan language also called Balti. Their land, known as Baltistan, lies along the Shyok and Indus rivers. Their upstream neighbours are the Buddhist Ladakhis, and their downstream neighbours are the Shina speakers of Gilgit. Balti-pa follow Shia Islam, and have been Muslims for more than five centuries. Their Tibetan cultural roots are evident in their language, clothing, food, yak husbandry, and folklore. Balti villages are densely packed clusters of interconnected houses, surrounded by intensively cultivated irrigated terraces. They make a striking contrast to the huge vertical mountains and arid glacial valleys of Baltistan. Balti men have long worked as porters, cooks, and guides for mountaineering and trekking parties going into the heart of the high Karakoram.

Burusho

The Burusho are the Burushashki-speaking people. Their language is unrelated to any other language spoken today, and their origin is shrouded in legend. Most of them live in Nagyr and Hunza. Burusho also live in the Yasin Valley. The terms Nagyrkutz and Hunzakutz (people of Nagyr/Hunza) refer not only to Burusho people, but also to the non-Burushashki-speaking people living in Nagyr and Hunza. Notable among the minority groups are the Bericho, who speak Dumaki and are the musicians and blacksmiths for the Burusho. Most Burusho in Hunza and Yasin are Ismaili Muslims and Burusho in Nagyr are Shia Muslims.

Hereditary rulers called *Tham* or *Mir* ruled the two separate states of Nagyr and Hunza. The origins of their rule are legendary, but carbon dating at Altit Fort indicates almost 1000 years have passed since its timbers were cut. By 1974, the Mirs were pensioned off by the Pakistan government, and their rule was ended.

The Burusho are renowned for their skill at agriculture and in constructing irrigation systems. Although western literature has portrayed the Burusho as exceptionally healthy and long-lived, this is just a romantic fantasy. Burusho men often work as guides for treks, and are friendly and open-minded.

Gujars

Gujar people are widespread throughout South Asia and have migrated into the mountains of northern Pakistan. They now live in southern Chitral and in Ghizar district of the Northern Areas. The name Gujar indicates their close link with cow herding (*gu* meaning cow). These people have taken the opportunity to tend animals and grow crops in marginal areas, and so have found a niche among the Kho, Shins, and Yeshkuns. They are exclusively Sunni Muslims, and marry within their own group. In Chitral they speak Khowar, and in Ghizar they speak Khowar and/or Shina.

Kalasha

The Kalasha are the only remaining non-

Muslims in northern Pakistan. About 3000 Kalasha live in three valleys in southern Chitral: Birir, Bumboret, and Rumbur. The Kalasha once controlled a much greater area, ruling the Chitral Valley as far north as Reshun, but were defeated by the Kho ruler around the 16th century. The entire Hindukush was once populated by people with similar beliefs, but the people in the Afghanistan Hindukush were converted to Islam in the 1890s. The Kalasha are the only people who still practice the old ways.

The Kalasha people are the only non-Muslims living in northern Pakistan. They are farmers and herders.

The Kalasha are farmers and herders. The two principles of their religion are the 'pure' and the 'impure'. Altars for the gods, the mountains, and their goats are examples of the pure; whereas the valley floor and the *bashali* or women's birthing and menstrual house are examples of the impure. For the Kalasha, these two principles meet at the *jestak han*, the house of *jestak*, the female deity of hearth and home. Kalasha believe in one god, the creator Dezau. Their other *dewa* (gods) function like messengers between Dezau and the Kalasha. Kalashamun is the Kalasha language.

Kho

The Kho, whose language is Khowar, make up about 80% of the population of 220,000 in Chitral, and also predominate in the upper Ghizar district of the Northern Areas and the upper Ushu Valley of Swat. The regions of Turikho and Mulkho are regarded as the original homeland of Kho people. Most Kho are Sunni Muslims, but many of the Kho in upper Chitral are Ismailis. Kho society is made up of three classes: an aristocracy, a gentry, and landless labourers. The ruler of Chitral, until the state was absorbed into Pakistan in 1970, was the *Mehtar*, a descendant of Tamerlane and Babur the Moghul emperor. The Kho are regarded as highly cultured people, and Khowar poetry and song is greatly esteemed.

Shina-Speaking People

The approximately 300,000 Shina-speaking people of the Northern Areas live in the lower Ishkoman Valley, lower Hunza Valley, Gilgit, Astor, and the Indus Valley from Haramosh to Jalkot and Palas, including Chilas, Darel, and Tangir. Some Shina speakers have settled in Baltistan, where they are called Brok-pā, and their language Brokskat. Although most Shina-speaking people are Sunni Muslims, those west of Gilgit are usually Ismaili Muslims, and those in Gilgit and east of Gilgit are usually Shia Muslims. Shina-speaking people should not be confused with Shins, who are a separate group of Shina-speaking people. In the Gilgit and Hunza valleys, as well as in Darel and Tangir, there are four communities: Shins, Yeshkuns, Kamins, and Doms. The Yeshkun are probably the original inhabitants, but the Shins have higher status. Kamins are labourers, and Doms are blacksmiths and musicians. Some scholars think the Yeshkun are Burusho who long ago adopted the Shina language from conquerors who came from the south.

Wakhi

Wakhi people live in the uppermost areas of the Yarkhun, Ishkoman, and Hunza valleys. Upriver from Hunza, their region is called Gojal. They traditionally depend on livestock husbandry, including yaks, as their villages are at the upper limit of cultivation.

Unlike for other people in Pakistan, among the Wakhi the livestock are the women's responsibility. Men generally do not go to the high pastures, but stay in the village to tend the crops.

Many Wakhi people live over the border in Afghanistan's Wakhan, in the Tajikistan Pamir, and in Xinjiang province of China. The Wakhi have apparently been living in the Wakhan and the Pamir for over 2500 years. Their language is Wakhi and they are Ismaili Muslims. Wakhi men are renowned for their endurance and often work as guides and high-altitude porters.

The Myth of Dards
No people in northern Pakistan today refer to themselves as Dards, and the term is unknown in any local languages. Although we find rock inscriptions from the 4th or 5th century referring to a great king of the Dards, and the Kashmiri Chronicle of Kings mentions Darad rulers of the 9th and 10th centuries, the idea that there is today an area populated by Dard people that is called Dardistan is essentially a colonialist construction. Even the linguistic classification of a Dardic language group is dubious.

Linguists now regard Dardic as a geographic rather than a linguistic expression. Dardistan is a problematic inheritance from colonial times that only obscures the identity of and the relationship between the people who live in northern Pakistan.

RELIGION
Islam
Islam is the state religion and 97% of Pakistanis are Muslim. Islam became the dominant religion around the 13th century. Islam translates loosely from Arabic as 'the peace that comes from total surrender to God'. God's will is articulated in the Koran. In addition to the creeds set out there, Muslims express their surrender in the form of daily prayers, alms-giving, fasting, proselytism, and pilgrimage to Mecca. In its fullest sense, Islam is an entire way of life, with guidelines for doing nearly everything. Among prohibitions honoured by the devout

are those against eating pork and drinking alcohol. In Islam, the privacy of the home is respected and both men and women are to observe a modest decorum outside the home.

In 612 AD Mohammad, a wealthy Arab merchant of Mecca, began preaching a new religion, Islam, based on direct revelations from God (to Mohammad) through the angel Gabriel and including the revelations of preceding prophets of Judaism and Christianity. The revelations to Mohammad were eventually compiled into Islam's holy book, the Koran. In 622 AD Mohammad and his followers fled to Medina (the Islamic calendar counts its year from this *hijrah* (flight)). There he established a religiously organised society that quickly spread throughout Arabia. The new and militant faith meshed nicely with a latent Arab nationalism, and within a century the empire reached from Spain to Central Asia.

Succession disputes after Mohammad's death soon split the community. When the fourth caliph (ruler), the Prophet's son-in-law Ali, was assassinated in 661 AD, his followers and descendants became the leaders of the Shia (or Shi'ite) branch. Others accepted as caliph the governor of Syria, a brother-in-law of Mohammad, and this line has become the modern-day orthodox Sunni (or Sunnite) branch. In 680 AD a chance for reconciliation was lost when Ali's surviving son Hussain and most of his male relatives were killed at Karbala in Iraq by Sunni partisans. Today over 90% of Muslims worldwide are Sunni.

Among Shia doctrines is that of the *imam* or infallible leader who continues to unfold the true meaning of the Koran and provides guidance in daily affairs. Most Shias recognise an hereditary line of 12 imams ending in the 9th century. These Shias are known as Ithna Ashariyas.

The Shia tradition predominates in Nagyr, Haramosh, and Baltistan. The Nur Bakhshiya sect of the Shia tradition has a number of followers in Baltistan, particularly in the Shigar and Hushe valleys.

An 8th-century split among Shias as to which son of the sixth imam should succeed him gave rise to the Ismaili branch. For Ismaili Shias the line of imams continues to the present. The present leader is Prince Karim Aga Khan, who is considered to be the 49th imam. The 11th-century Persian poet and philosopher, Nasir Khusro, brought Ismaili teachings to the Hindukush.

Other Religions
Christians, Hindus, Parsis (Zoroastrians), and Kalasha are officially recognised minority religions in Pakistan. They have elected representatives in the National Assembly.

LANGUAGE
Urdu is the lingua franca of the Karakoram and Hindukush and the single best language for a trekker to know. Almost all men know Urdu. Women mostly speak only their mother tongue, although with the spread of education, more women are learning Urdu. Besides Urdu there are many local languages. The main ones are Balti, Burushashki, Kalasha, Khowar, Shina and Wakhi.

English is taught in schools, but is only used for communication by the educated elite. Nevertheless, many people have a smattering of English words or phrases.

Pronunciation
All seven languages mentioned above have long and short vowels. Long vowels are differentiated from short vowels by a macron (a horizontal bar) over the vowel. Vowels are sometimes nasalised. The symbol ñ following a vowel indicates that it is nasalised.

a	as in 'above'
i	as in 'bit'
u	as in 'put'
ā	as in 'father'
ī	as in 'meet'
ū	as in 'pool'
ē	as in 'safe'
ā	as in 'go'
ai	as in 'bait'
au	as in 'law'

The following consonant sounds are particular to Wakhi:

x	pronounced as 'kh'
zh	as in 'genre'

These languages, except Balti, also distinguish between aspirated and unaspirated consonants. Aspirated consonants are pronounced with a puff of air. If you hold your hand up to your mouth and say 'tea' you will feel a puff of air. This is because the 't' in 'tea' is aspirated but if you say 'stop' you won't feel any air escaping. This is because the 't' in 'stop' in unaspirated. Aspirated consonants are indicated by the letter 'h' after the consonant.

URDU
Basics

Thank you.	*shukriā*
Special thanks.	*mehrbānī*
Yes/No.	*hāñahīñ*
Maybe.	*shayad*
Excuse me.	*māf kījiye*
Just a minute.	*ek minut*
May I?	*maiñ karūñ?*
It's all right/No problem.	*thīk hai/koī bāt nahīñ*
Sir/Madam	*jenāb/begum*
Where is the toilet?	*paikhānā kidhar?*

Greetings
Peace be with you
  asalām aleikum
and with you too
  wa aleikum salām
Goodbye.
  khudā hāfiz
See you again.
  phir mileñge
Good night.
  shab bakhair

Language Difficulties
I understand.
  samajh gayā
I don't understand.
  nahīñ samjhā
Do you speak English?
  āpko English ātī hai?
Please write it down.
  likh dījiye

Small Talk

How are you?
kyā hāl hai?
Fine/OK.
thīk hai
Where are you from?
āp kahāṅ ke haiṅ?
I'm from ...
maiṅ ... kā hūṅ
I'm ... years old.
merī ūmar ... sāl hai
What's your name?
āpkā nām kyā hai?
My name is ...
merā nām ... hai
Do you like ...?
... pasand hai?
I like ... very much.
mujhe ... bahut pasand hai
I don't like ...
mujhe ... pasand nahīṅ

Getting Around

I want to go to ...
maiṅ ... jānā chāhatā hūṅ
What time does the bus
leave/arrive?
bus kitne baje ravāna/
pahūṅchtī hai?
Where does the bus leave
from?
bus kahāṅse ravana hai?
How long does the trip take?
kitne ghante lagte haiṅ?

Trekking

Will you come with me?
mere sāth chaleṅge?
How many days will it take?
kitne din lageṅge?
How many stages?
kitne parāo
What will it cost?
kitnā paisā lagegā?
How is the trail?
rāstā kaisā hai?
Pick up the load.
sāmān ūthāo
Check the weight.
vazan dekho

Let's go.
chelo
Take a rest.
dam karo
Stop here.
yahāṅ roko

baggage/gear	*sāmān*
cooking pot	*bartan/degchī*
foam sleeping pad	*shīt*
kerosene	*mittīkātel*
matches	*machiz*
rope	*rassī*
stove	*istov*
tarpaulin	*plastik*

Along the Way

avalanche danger	*baraf girne kā khatrā*
bridge	*pūl*
valley/stream	*nālā*
cliff	*chatān*
crevasse	*crevas*
forest	*jungal*
garbage	*kucherā*
map	*nakshā*
mountain	*pahār*
pass	*tap*
path/trail	*rāstā*
river	*daryā*
summit	*choti/sār*
tree	*darakht*
yak	*khushgāo*

Weather

cloud	*bādal*
cold	*thandā*
rain	*bārish*
snow	*baraf*
sun	*sūraj*
wind	*hawā*

Directions

Where is ...?
... kahāṅ hai?
Is it (near/far)?
(nazdīk/dūr) hai?
Please show me (on the map).
dikhā dījiye

(Go) straight ahead.
   sidhā
(Turn) left.
   bayāñ
(Turn) right.
   dayāñ

east	*mashriq*
west	*maghrib*
north	*shumāl*
south	*janūb*

Around Town

Where is the/a ...?	*... kahāñ hai?*
city centre	*markaz*
hospital	*hospitāl*
market	*bāzār*
mosque	*masjid*
police	*thānā*
post office	*dāk khānā*
telephone centre	*pī sī o (PCO)*

I want to make a telephone call.
   maiñ telephone karnā chāhatā hūñ
I'd like to change some
   money...
   maiñ change karnā chāhatā hūñ

Accommodation

Is a room available?
   kamrā milēgā?
How much is it per night/
   per person?
   fī rāt ādmī kitnā?
Do you have hot water?
   āpke pās garam pānī hai?
Can I see the room?
   maiñ kamreko dekhūñ?

Food

Do you have (food)?
   āpke pās (khānā) hai?
I'm a vegetarian.
   maiñ sabzī khor hūñ

bread	*rotī*
bread (unleavened)	*chapātī*
bread (fried)	*parāthā*
butter	*makkhan*
coffee	*kāfī*

egg	*andā*
food	*khānā*
fruit	*phal*
meat	*gosht*
milk	*dūdh*
oil (cooking)	*tel*
potato	*ālū*
rice	*chāwal*
salt	*namak*
sugar	*chīnī*
tea	*chāī*
tea (green)	*sabz chāī*
tea (with milk)	*dūdh-chāī*
vegetable	*sabzī*
water	*pānī*
water (boiled)	*ublā hūā pānī*

Shopping

How much is it?
   kitnā paisā?
It's too expensive.
   bahut maheñgā
Can I look at it?
   maiñ dekhūñ?

big/bigger	*barā/isse barā*
small/smaller	*chotā/isse chotā*
more/less	*zyādā/kam*
cheap/cheaper	*sastā/isse sastā*

Health/Emergencies

Help!
   madad karo
Go away!
   chele jāo
Call a doctor/the police.
   dāktar/polīs bulāo
I'm allergic to penicillin.
   penicillin band hai
I'm diabetic.
   shakar kī bimārī hai

Times & Dates

What time is it?	*kitne baje?*
It's ... o'clock.	*... baje*
When?	*kab?*
today	*āj*
tonight	*āj rātko*
tomorrow/yesterday	*kal*

Monday	*pir*
Tuesday	*mangal*
Wednesday	*budh*
Thursday	*jūmarāt*
Friday	*jūmā*
Saturday	*haftā*
Sunday	*itwār*

Numbers

Words for numbers are somewhat regular. To add ½ to a number (except one or two which have special forms) precede it with *sarhe* (eg, 3½ is *sarhe tīn*). This is the common form used with prices and clock times.

1	*ek*
1½	*derh*
2	*do*
2½	*dhāi*
3	*tīn*
4	*chār*
5	*pānch*
6	*chhe*
7	*sāt*
8	*āth*
9	*nau*
10	*das*
20	*bīs*
25	*pachīs*
30	*tīs*
35	*pantīs*
40	*chalīs*
45	*pantalīs*
50	*pachās*
60	*sāth*
70	*sattar*
80	*assī*
90	*nabbe*
100	*sau*
1000	*hazar*

BALTI

Balti is a Tibetan language spoken in Baltistan. It is the spoken version of classical literary Tibetan. It is closely related to Ladakhi which is spoken in adjacent Indian territory. Balti ascribes gender to animate beings only. The suffix *po* indicates male; *mo* indicates female.

Basics

Welcome.	*yāng shok*
What's up?	*chī khabar?*
How are you?	*yāng chī hālyo?*
Good.	*lyākhmo*
Where are you from?	*kyāng gār paīn?*
I'm from ...	*... paīn*
What is your name?	*yari ming tākpo chīin?*
My name is ...	*nge ming tākpo ... yin*
His name is ...	*khwe ming tākpo ... yin*
How many?	*tsam?*
Where?	*gār?*

big/little	*chhogo/tsūntse*
good/bad	*lyakhmo/changmen*
heavy	*lcho*
hot/ cold	*tsho/drakhmo*
long/short	*rīngmo/chat*
near/far	*nyīmor/thagrīng*
right/left	*trang/khyun*

Trekking

How is the road?
   lāmpo chīnā yod?
It's good.
   lyākhmo dū
It's not good.
   lyākhmo med
Where does this trail go?
   di lampo gār wīn?
This trail goes to ...
   di lampo ... wīn
How far is ...?
   ... tsātse tāring yod?

Along the Way

boulder	*urdwā*
fire	*me*
flower	*mendoq*
glacier	*gang*
grass	*spāng*
ibex	*skin*
ice	*gāng*
moon	*zod*
mountain	*brak*
pass	*la*
path	*lam*

rain	*charphā*
river	*gyāmtso*
rope	*thaqpa*
snow	*khā*
spring	*chhūmik*
sun	*ngimā*
valley	*lungmā*
water	*chhū*
wind	*hlung*

Food

apricot	*chūlī*
bread (thick)	*khurbā*
butter	*mār*
buttermilk	*darbā*
chicken	*byango*
egg	*byapjun*
flour (barley)	*nas fe*
flour (wholewheat)	*baq fe*
food	*zāchas*
meat	*shā*
milk	*ongā*
rice	*blas*
salt	*paiyu*
tea	*chā*
tea (salted)	*payū chā*

Times & Dates

When?	*nām?*
dawn	*sharkā*
morning	*gyukhpa*
midday	*trobar*
early afternoon	*pishin*
sunset	*phītro*
moonrise	*lzod shār*
night	*tshan*
today	*dirīng*
tomorrow	*haske*
yesterday	*gunde*
day after tomorrow	*snang lā*
day before yesterday	*kharchak lā*

Numbers

1	*chīk*
2	*ngīs*
3	*khsūm*
4	*bjī*
5	*gā*
6	*trūk*
7	*bdūn*

8	*bgyet*
9	*rgū*
10	*phchū*
20	*ngī shū*
30	*khsūm chū*
40	*ngīshū ngīs*
50	*ngīshū ngīs na phchū*
60	*ngīshū khsūm*
70	*ngīshū khsūm na phchū*
80	*ngishū bjī*
90	*ngīshū bjī na phchū*
100	*bgya*

BURUSHASHKI

Burushaski is the language of the Burusho of Hunza, Nagyr, and Yasin. The Yasin dialect differs slightly, and neighbouring Khowar-speakers call it Werchikwor. Burushashki has four classifications of nouns: masculine and feminine (human) and animate and inanimate (nonhuman).

Basics

How are you?	*besan hāl bilā?*
	be mei bā?
I'm good.	*shūā bā*
What's your name?	*gwik besan bilā?*
Where are you going?	*ām nichen?*
I'm going to ...	*je ... nichā bā*
How?	*be?*
How much?	*bearūm?*
When?	*beshal?*
Where?	*āmūlo?*

here/there	*khole/ele*
big/small	*ūyūm/jot*
cold/hot	*chhāgūrūm/gārūrūm*
good/bad	*shūā/gūneqīsh*
left-side/right-side	*gaypā/doypā*
long/short	*gosānūm/chhat*
many or very	*būt*
near/far	*āsīr/māthan*
old/new	*men/thosh*

Trekking

Is this the road to ...?	
... *niyas gan bī?*	

Let's go.
  gūtshār chen

Along the Way

animal	*haiwān*
bird	*balas*
bridge	*brosh*
cloud	*quronch*
day/night	*gunts/thap*
fire	*pfū*
firewood	*gashil*
flower	*āsqūr*
glacier	*haguts*
horse	*hagur*
house	*hā*
ice	*gamū*
lake	*phari*
moon	*hālants*
morning/evening	*tshordīmo/shām*
mountain	*chhish*
pass	*haghost*
trail/path	*gan*
rain	*hāralt*
rope	*gashk*
shepherds' huts	*harai*
snow	*geh*
stone	*dan*
stream	*bar*
sun	*sā*
tree	*tom*
tent	*gut*
valley	*bar*
wind	*tish*
yesterday	*sabūr*
tomorrow	*jhī māle*

Food

apricot	*jū*
apricot (dried)	*batering*
bread	*shapīk*
bread (thick wheat)	*phitī*
butter	*maltāsh*
buttermilk	*diltār*
cheese (white)	*burūs*
cream	*irān*
egg	*fīngān*
flour (wholewheat)	*diram*
meat	*chap*
milk	*māmū*
mulberry	*biranch*
rice	*bras*
salt	*bāyū*
soup	*daudho*
walnut	*balring*
water	*tshil*
yoghurt	*dūmānū māmū*

Numbers

1	*han*
2	*ālta*
3	*ūsko*
4	*wālto*
5	*tshūndo*
6	*mishīndo*
7	*thalo*
8	*altāmbo*
9	*hūncho*
10	*tūrūmo*
11	*tūrmāhan*
12	*tūrmāālta*
20	*āltar*
100	*thā*

KALASHA

Kalashamun, as Kalasha speakers call their language, is an Indic language, related to Khowar. It is spoken in the Kalash valleys, in Jinjeret Kuh and the Urtsun valleys.

Basics

Hello.	*ishpāda*
Are you well?	*tabiyet prūsht?*
Good/OK/Yes.	*prūsht*
Very good.	*bo prūsht*
No.	*ne*
No problem.	*ne mishkil*
Where is ...?	*kawa ...?*
Where are you going?	*kawa pariz?*
I'm going to ...	*... ah parim*
I want ...	*ah ... khushan*
When?	*kāya?*
big/small	*gonā/chūtyak*
good/bad	*prūsht/shūm*
hot/cold	*tāpālā/osh*
long/short	*dri-ga/betsak*
near/far	*tadakā/desha*
right/left	*drach/kewī*
wet/dry	*grīlā/shūshtā*

Along the Way

day/night	*bās/rāt*
flower	*gambūrī*
goat	*pāi*
hail	*badwash*
lightning	*indochik*
moon	*mastrūk*
path/trail	*pon*
rain	*pīlīwe*
sun	*sūrī*
tree	*mūt*
water	*uk*
wind	*sīra*
yesterday	*dosh*
today	*onjā*
tomorrow	*chopa*

Food

bread	*aū*
food	*aū*
meat	*mos*
milk	*chīr*
salt	*loñ*
tea (milky)	*chīr chai*
walnuts	*birmō*
water	*ūkh*
wine	*dā*

KHOWAR

Khowar, the language of the Kho, is the chief language in Chitral district. Most side valleys have their own dialects and educated Chitralis also speak Urdu and Persian. Pushtu is becoming more common in southern Chitral. The Chitralis of Turikho are considered to speak the purest Khowar, and it is the mother tongue for many in the upper Swat, Ghizar, and Yasin valleys. Khowar is an Indic language with significant Iranian influence.

Basics

Yes.	*di*
No.	*no*
I don't understand.	*hosh no koman*
What's your name?	*ta kīāgh nām?*
My name is ...	*ma nām ...*
How are you?	*tū kichā āsūs?*
Are you fine?	*jām āsūsā?*
Fine, thanks.	*bo jām, mehrbānī*

How?	*kicha?*
What?	*kīāgh*
When?	*kia wat?*
Where?	*kura?*

Trekking

Where are you going?	*tū kurī besān?*
I'm going to ...	*āwā ... oten bīmān.*
We're going to ...	*ispā ... oten bīsīān.*
Where does this trail go?	*heyā pon kuī birān?*
This trail goes to ...	*heyā pon ... ote birān*
Is ... available?	*... leñ boyā?*
Let's go.	*bisī*

Along the Way

clothes	*chellai*
cloud	*kot*
fire	*angār*
flower	*gambūrī*
glacier/ice	*yoz*
goat	*pāī*
hemp	*bong*
horse	*istor*
house	*dūr*
moon	*mas*
mountain	*zom*
pass	*ān*
rain	*boshīk*
river	*sīn*
spring	*utz*
stone	*bort*
stream	*gol*
sun	*yor*
trail	*pon*
tree (cedar)	*rogh*
valley	*gol*
water	*ūgh*
wind	*gān*

Food

apricot	*palogh*
bread	*shāpīk*
butter	*māskā*

buttermilk	*shātū*
cheese	*shapināk*
egg	*ayūkūn*
flour (wholewheat)	*peshīrū*
meat	*phūshūr*
milk	*chīr*
mulberry	*marāch*
rice	*grinj/pakhti*
salt	*trup*

Numbers

1	*ī*
2	*jū*
3	*troī*
4	*chor*
5	*ponch*
6	*chhoī*
7	*sot*
8	*usht*
9	*nīu*
10	*jush*
11	*jush ī*
12	*johjū*
20	*bishir*
30	*bishir jush*
40	*jū bishir*
50	*jū bishir jush*
60	*troī bishir*
100	*ī shor*

SHINA

Shina is widely spoken in Gilgit and Diamir and as far north as lower Hunza, and also in the Ishkoman Valley, lower Ghizar district, and around Haramosh. Several dialects exist, notably Gilgiti, Kohistani, and Astori, with Gilgiti as the main one. Shina is an Indic language.

Basics

How are you?	*jhek hāl haiñ?*
I'm going.	*māh bojhimer*
What?	*jhek?*
Where?	*kon?*
When?	*kāre?*
How many?	*kachāk?*
Which?	*kok?*
good/bad	*mishto/khacho*
hot/cold	*tāto/shīdalo*

near/far	*kachī/dūr*
right/left	*dashīno/khabū*
yesterday	*bālāh*
today	*āsh*
tomorrow	*lūshtākī*

Along the Way

cow	*go*
day/night	*dez/rātī*
fire	*āgār*
firewood	*jhūk*
flower	*phūnar*
glacier	*gomukh*
goat	*āī*
house	*got*
morning/evening	*chalbūjī/shām*
pass	*gali*
rain	*āzho*
rope	*bālī*
stone	*bath*
stream/valley	*gah*
sun/moon	*sūrī/yūn*
trail	*pon*
tree	*tom*
wind	*oñshī*

Food

egg	*hane*
meat	*mos*
milk	*dūth*
rice	*brīūñ*
salt	*pājhū*
water	*weī*

Numbers

1	*ek*
2	*dū*
3	*che*
4	*chār*
5	*posh*
6	*shā*
7	*sat*
8	*ānsh*
9	*nāū*
10	*dāī*
11	*akāī*
12	*bāī*
20	*bī*
100	*shal*

WAKHI

The Wakhi language, or Xikwor, as the people who speak it call it, belongs to the Pamir group of Iranian languages, all of which belong to the greater Indo-European language family. Wakhi is related to Persian and is spoken wherever Wakhi people live.

Basics

How are you?	*chiz hol he/ tut sīyeta?*
I'm fine.	*vidurt em*
I'm well.	*wuzem siyet*
Where are you going?	*kūmeret takh?*
What is your name?	*tī nunge chīst?*
My name is ...	*jhu nunge ...*
What is her (his) name?	*hemā nunge chīst?*
Her/his name is ...	*hema nunge ...*
What's that?	*yāoī chīz?*
Sit down.	*nezdita*
Go!	*rech!*
Where is ... available?	*... esh kūmer goten?*
I want ...	*mārey ... dirkor*
How?	*tse sokht?*
How much (many)?	*tsūmar?*
What?	*chīz?*
When?	*tsogdar?*
Where?	*kūmar?*
bad/good	*shak/baf*
big/small	*lup/zaqlāī*
cold/hot	*sūr/thin*
difficult/easy	*zur/ausān*
dry/wet	*wesk/hashch*
light/heavy	*ranjhkh/orong*
long/short	*daroz/kūth*
right/left	*rost/chap*

Along the Way

bridge	*skord*
clothes	*lokpār*
cloud	*wītīsh*
day/night	*ror/naght*
day after tomorrow	*tort*
fire	*rakhnīgh*
firewood	*ghoz*
flower	*spregh*
glacier/ice	*yāz*

house	*xun*
ibex	*yuksh*
moon	*zhūmak*
mountain	*koh*
morning/evening	*sahār/purz*
pass	*uween*
rain	*mor*
rope	*shīven*
stone	*gar*
stream/valley	*jerab*
sun	*yīr*
trail/path	*vadekh*
wind	*dumā*
yesterday	*yezī*
today	*wuthkh*
tomorrow	*pīgā*

Food

bread	*xich*
butter	*rūgan*
cheese (dried)	*qurūt*
egg	*tukhmūrg*
flour (wholewheat)	*yumj*
food	*shāpik*
fruit	*mewā*
meat	*gusht*
milk	*zharzh*
rice	*grinj*
salt	*namik*
vegetable	*sauzi/xazk*
water	*yuphkh*

Numbers

1	*yīū*
2	*būī*
3	*throī*
4	*sabur*
5	*pānz*
6	*shāth*
7	*hub*
8	*hāth*
9	*naō*
10	*thas*
11	*thas yīū*
12	*thas boī*
20	*wīst*
100	*yīsad*

Facts for the Trekker

General Information

PLANNING
When to Go

The Karakoram and Hindukush have one trekking season, from late April to late October. From late April to mid-June, much snow remains on passes and on north-facing slopes. This is a good season for treks that do not cross passes, or that cross passes under 3000m. The peak season is from mid-June to mid-September, when the alpine meadows are in bloom. In midsummer, lower elevation river valleys are hot and dry, narrow canyon walls reflect the intense midday heat, and the rivers are swollen from glacial melt. This is the best time for traversing glaciers and crossing passes over 4000m. By mid-August, the snow cap has melted, crevasses are exposed and remaining snow becomes soft. From mid-September to late October, as snow fall begins to accumulate, passes over 4000m close. These cool, crisp days and blue skies make for fine trekking at lower elevations. As glacial melt ceases, the rivers recede and become clear again.

During major election campaigns, political expression sometimes takes violent forms. You need to be cautious while traveling through cities and large towns, but once you reach the trekking areas, you are delightfully away from such distractions.

What Kind of Trek?

Trekking in the Karakoram and Hindukush takes you through wilderness of truly breathtaking scale. The glaciers are the longest outside the polar regions and the mountains typically rise over 6000m. In the Karakoram alone, 19 peaks are over 7500m. It is a good idea to trek with a partner, and if you have not done this kind of trekking before, you should go with someone who has. Trekkers here need to be self-sufficient. Unlike in other popular Himalayan trekking destinations, you will not find tea houses offering food nor small trail-side hotels providing a night's shelter. You need to bring your shelter, bedding, cooking and eating utensils, fuel, and food.

Treks typically begin from the last village at the head of a valley, go up through summer pastures, over a high pass, and down the other side to the highest village. After you leave the last village, you will not find supplies until you come down into villages in the next valley.

In a few areas, trekkers can be tempted to make short walks to pastures, living off the generosity of shepherds there and sleeping in shepherds' huts. You will be less of an imposition on local hospitality, and have a safer and more comfortable experience, if you are supplied and equipped to deal with the conditions you will encounter while trekking. You can follow either of two basic approaches: arrange your trek yourself; or hire someone to arrange it for you.

Self-Arranged Trekking Arranging your trek yourself offers the greatest flexibility, and is the least expensive way to go. On the other hand, it requires more time and initiative; and ability to communicate with shopkeepers, drivers, and/or porters. You may be inclined to carry everything yourself, since backpacking is the typical way one goes into the mountains of North America or Europe. Backpacking is the most physically and mentally exacting way to trek, but also offers you the freedom to come and go as you please.

You can reduce the sheer physical effort, but still run your own show by hiring a porter to carry the bulk of your gear and food. Whether you decide to hire a porter or to heft your load yourself, you need a few days to shop, pack, arrange transport to the trail head, and/or hire a porter.

Backpacking Because backpacking is the least expensive way to trek and the most physically challenging, it typically appeals to younger, more intrepid trekkers. They usually have the requisite stamina and above-average physical conditioning to carry a full load up and down narrow trails and handle the camp chores: cooking, cleaning, hauling water, setting up, and making camp. It is best undertaken by someone who is patient, friendly and has an outgoing personality. Basic language skills are essential (see Language in the Facts about the Region chapter).

This style calls for a high degree of self-sufficiency. You must shoulder all of your own equipment and food and be self-reliant in adverse conditions. You should not expect to find shelter or places to buy food and supplies along the way.

Many trekking routes are sparsely populated, so risk is involved if you become lost or injured. Trails can be hard to find or follow, or sometimes nonexistent. You need good trail sense and good maps.

Unless you have experience with glacial travel, avoid backpacking on a route that crosses or traverses glaciers. Be prudent and don't go alone. Find another like-minded traveller or two to share the work and for mutual support. More crucially, a minor injury, a twisted ankle or a fall down a hillside can become life-threatening if you are alone.

The length of your itinerary is limited by your physical ability to carry food and fuel. For most people that is about seven, and at most, 10 days. This rules out backpacking for the longer open-zone routes and all restricted-zone treks (see Permits & Formalities in this chapter). You also have to arrange your own local transport to and from trail heads.

Of course, if you can do all this, backpacking can be the most rewarding way of going. It offers you the greatest freedom to have a flexible itinerary and walk at your own pace and the most open potential for discovery and interaction with local people and their culture.

Trekking with Porters Hiring a few porters can free you from carrying heavy loads and from the tedium of some camp chores. For comfort's sake, it makes sense to allow at least one porter per person for trips up to 10 days. You need to know porter wages, stages, load sizes, and be able to adequately discuss all this with whomever you hire. Basic language skills are essential. If you don't want to prepare your own meals, or if you have a large enough trekking party to make cooking a full-time job, you may want your porter to do some cooking, or to hire a separate cook. Be sure he knows how to cook the food and operate the stove you have brought. When you hire someone, you become responsible for their wellbeing and you must ensure they have sufficient food, clothing, equipment, and shelter (see Guides & Porters later in this chapter). You need a few days to arrange the trek. Any porter you hire can help you with purchasing supplies and arranging any local transport to the trail head.

Trekking with savvy porters can offer the best of both worlds; you carry less and enjoy the trail more, have more time to do as you like, and still keep expenses low enough not to break the bank. Moreover, trekking with a knowledgeable porter can open a world of experience not possible on your own.

Pre-Arranged Trekking This type of trekking relieves you of the responsibility of shopping, arranging transport, and hiring and supervising a trek crew. Contacting a trekking company in Pakistan or a tour operator abroad makes sense if you have limited time, or would rather pay an experienced person to organise your trek. Anyone who intends to trek in a restricted zone must go through a government-approved trekking company (see Permits & Formalities later in this chapter).

Trekking Companies in Pakistan Trekking companies provide a range of services depending on your inclination and budget. They can suggest routes suitable for the time of year, length of time you want to trek, and physical abilities of your trekking party. This enables you to choose your fellow trekkers and create a flexible itinerary that you can change along the way. Some companies offer fixed group departures of certain treks (eg, a trek to Fairy Meadows may go every Saturday). This style is less expensive than booking through a tour operator abroad. The trekking company arranges for an experienced trek crew (ie, a guide, cook, kitchen and camp helpers, and porters) and provides food and equipment. Ask for a list of personal equipment (eg, sleeping bags, sleeping pads, and tents) and other camping equipment (eg, dining tent, tables, chairs, toilet tent, kitchen kit, stoves, dishes and utensils, washbasins) they can provide.

A trekking company is necessary to arrange all restricted-zone treks. They can submit applications, fees, and the insurance policy necessary for permits (see Permits & Formalities in this chapter). They can also book hotels and arrange any local transport to towns or trail heads. Some companies will look after only the trekking arrangements, freeing you to handle your own hotels and transport. Trekking companies quote a fixed price inclusive of all services you request and you pay them one lump sum.

Working with a trekking company increases the likelihood of your trekking with reliable guides, crews, and porters. Guides can be the key to a successful trek. Often their experience and abilities vary widely, so ask what experience the guide has and if the guide has done the route before. Ask for references for any guide they recommend. It is worthwhile shopping around and getting quotes from three or four companies. Be specific about the services you want before you start spending money. (See Information Sources in this chapter for a list of reliable companies.)

You can contact trekking companies by mail or fax before you arrive in Pakistan to begin making plans. To plan a trek in peak season (July to September), contact trekking companies about six months in advance. Otherwise their best guides and crews may not be available. This process can be time consuming and expensive if you request

quotes for several itineraries and levels of services. It is more practical if you know where you want to trek and what services you want the trekking company to provide. When you contact trekking companies after you arrive in Pakistan, it usually takes about a week to compare companies and select one, inquire about the quality of services, decide what services you want, agree on costs, and complete the trek arrangements.

Tour Operators Abroad Tour operators in many countries market treks, guided climbs, and mountaineering expeditions. This is the most expensive way to go. If you lack the inclination or time to plan and organise your own trek, you can maximise your time since all the 'work' of organising a trek is done for you. You just show up ready to trek.

Most tour operators advertise a few popular itineraries where you join a group of like-minded trekkers – a great option for single women who prefer not to travel alone, and for those interested in meeting and travelling with people with similar interests. You follow a fixed itinerary – everything is taken care of from your arrival until you fly home.

Some tour operators customise treks for private parties. This is convenient for those who want to travel with friends, but do not wish to join a larger group, or for those interested in a route not advertised by a tour operator. Private parties can have their trek arranged before they arrive in Pakistan without having to correspond with trekking companies in Pakistan or shop around for a trekking company on arrival in Pakistan. All tour operators work with trekking companies in Pakistan to plan and outfit each trek. Therefore, the quality of services provided by the trekking company is crucial to the success of your trek.

Many tour operators provide comprehensive travel services and can book your international flights and hotels. They can answer pre-trek questions and are aware of the difficulties of the region through which you plan to trek. They can help you select a trek that is compatible with your interests and physical abilities. A single-tour price usually includes hotels and transport in Pakistan, the services of a tour leader, local guide, trek crew, porters, cook, food, equipment, permits, and fees.

Although group trekking itineraries are normally planned carefully, they are essentially fixed. You are committed to staying with the group and following the set itinerary. Even though itineraries should allow a few extra days for proper acclimatisation or in case of inclement weather, minimal flexibility exists even in case of illness. However, trekking with a group provides a support network in case of illness, accident, or injury. Many groups have a trip physician and resources for an evacuation if necessary. However, large trekking parties insulate trekkers more from local culture.

Before you book with a tour operator, ask how long they have been in business and have operated treks in the region. Ask about the tour leader's qualifications and degree of familiarity with the country, local languages, and culture, and if the tour leader has done this route before. Request references of previous clients who have done the same trek or trekked in the region or who have travelled previously with that company or tour leader. Avoid any company reluctant to give you references. (See Tour Operators Abroad in the Getting There & Away chapter for a list a reputable companies.)

Maps

Maps may not be the territory, but a good two-dimensional representation of the terrain is an indispensable tool. Knowing how to read maps and being familiar with the information they provide helps you in both planning and doing a trek. Don't even try to trek on your own without a map. For most areas, the best available maps are at a scale of 1:250,000.

Trekking Maps We list most trekking maps by publisher, but list specialised maps of the Baltoro and Batura glaciers separately.

Swiss Foundation for Alpine Research Their 1:250,000 two-sheet orographical *Karakoram* sketch maps are accurate and up-to-date. *Sheet 1* covers: the east side of Ishkoman Valley; Bagrot and Haramosh valleys; Naltar; Nagyr, Hunza and Gojal; Basha, Tormik and Stak valleys; Biafo and Hispar glaciers; and the Baltoro Glacier to Urdukas. *Sheet 2* covers the Baltoro Glacier east of Urdukas, and the Hushe and Shyok valleys. This series does not cover west of the Ishkoman and Karambar rivers, or south of the Gilgit and Indus rivers.

US Army Map Service (AMS) The US AMS 1:250,000 topographic map *Series U502 India and Pakistan* is the only series that covers all trekking areas. Last revised in 1962, these maps show most villages, but not the KKH or other recently built roads. Each map has a 'reliability diagram' which shows its degree of accuracy. The series includes:

NI 43-1 Churrai – Swat and passes to upper Ghizar River valley; Shishi & Golen valleys

NI 43-2 Gilgit – Indus River; Babusar Pass; Nanga Parbat

NI 43-3 Mundik – Chogo Lungma Glacier; Biafo Glacier; Baltoro Glacier to Concordia; Hushe Valley; Deosai Plains

NI 43-4 Chulung – Upper Baltoro Glacier from Concordia to K2 & the Gasherbrums; Kondus, Bilafond and Siachen glaciers

NI 43-6 Srinagar – Kaghan Valley, Azad Jammu & Kashmir; the Galis around Murree

NI 43-7 Kargil – Southern Deosai Plains

NJ 43-13 Mastuj – Turikho; Rich Gol; Laspur; Yarkhun; Yasin; upper Ghizar River valleys

NJ 43-14 Baltit – Ishkoman; Naltar; Nagyr and Hunza; Batura Glacier; Chapursan Valley

NJ 43-15 Shimshal – Hispar Glacier; Shimshal & Ghujerab valleys; Khunjerab Pass

In 1942, the US AMS published a separate *Afghanistan – NW Frontier Province* series at 1:253,440 (one inch to four miles). These maps are quite accurate, though out of date. You will now find them only at university libraries. Two maps cover western Chitral:

I 42-F Chitral – Chitral; Drosh; Kalash valleys (west of Churrai sheet)

J 42-X Zebak – Lutkho; Tirich Mir (west of Mastuj sheet)

Leomann Maps Leomann publishes a 1:200,000 four-sheet set of *Karakoram Trekking and Mountaineering Maps*. They appear to be based on the US AMS Series U502 maps and contain the same inaccuracies. They are: *Sheet 1: Gilgit, Hunza, Rakaposhi, Batura*; *Sheet 2: Skardu, Hispar, Biafo*; *Sheet 3: K2, Baltoro, Gasherbrum, Masherbrum, Saltoro*; and *Sheet 4: Siachen, Rimo, Saser*. Vague and useless trek descriptions are on the back of these maps.

The British Survey of India In 1930 the British Survey of India published a 1:63,360 (ie, one inch to one mile) *Afghanistan – NW Frontier Province* series. Though long out of print and very hard-to-find, these maps have extremely accurate topographic detail. You may find photocopies in university libraries. The US Library of Congress sells B&W copies. The series includes sheets:

38 M/9 – Chitral Gol (west of Chaghbini & Merin), Chimirsan An & Rumbur Valley
38 M/10 – Jinjeret Kuh, Birir & Bumboret valleys
38 M/13 – Roghili Gol & Golen Gol west of Izghor, Jughor Gol
38 M/14 – Roghili Gol & Jughor Gol, Drosh & Shishi Gol
42 D/4 – upper Golen Gol west of Jeshtanan camp
42 D/8 – Phargam Gol & Phargam An
43 A/1 – upper Madaglasht & Shishi valleys, Dok Gol & Dok An

Deutscher Alpenverein (DAV) DAV produced two 1:50,000 topographic maps: *Minapin* shows the north slopes of Rakaposhi; and *Nanga Parbat – Gruppe* shows the entire Nanga Parbat massif. These maps have 50m contour intervals and are the best and only readily available maps of these famous peaks. DAV also has a 1:100,000 map *Hunza-Karakorum* of the Hunza River valley.

US Defense Mapping Agency (DMA) US DMA has two series for pilots: 1:1,000,000 *Operational Navigation Chart (ONC)*; and 1:500,000 *Tactical Pilotage Chart (TPC)*. The scale is too large for routefinding, but the maps are excellent for trek planning –

showing land forms, but not all roads and villages. The ONC series includes:

ONC G-6 – Chitral, Swat, Yasin & Ishkoman valleys
ONC G-7 – Hunza, Gojal & Baltistan

The TPC series has unreliable place names and locations, but up-to-date landsat-derived topographic data. It includes:

TPC G-6B – Karambar & Yasin valleys, upper Gilgit River & northern Chitral
TPC G-6C – Southern Chitral & Swat Valley
TPC G-7A – Hunza Valley, Batura Glacier, Khunjerab Pass, Xinjiang & Kashgar
TPC G-7D – Baltistan, Biafo and Hispar glaciers, Gilgit & Nanga Parbat

Baltoro Glacier Yama To Kei Koku Sha published an accurate 1:100,000 sheet with 100m contour intervals called *The Baltoro Glacier* from the 1977 Japan-Pakistan K2 Expedition, which is now out of print. The beautifully coloured 1:100,000 *Ghiacciaio Baltoro* map of the Baltoro Glacier published by the Italian dai tipi dell' Instituto Geografico Militare (IGM) in 1969, and reprinted in 1977, is based on Italian 1929 and 1954 K2 expeditions. *The Eight-Thousand-Metre Peaks of the Karakoram* is a 1:50,000 orographical sketch map of the upper Baltoro, Abruzzi, and Godwin-Austen glaciers. None details the region south of the Baltoro Glacier.

Batura Glacier The Institute of Glaciology, Cryopedology & Desert Research, Academia Sinica, Lanchow, China, published a 1:60,000 *The Map of the Batura Glacier* in 1978. It is excellent, but hard to find. You can try writing to them direct. Occasionally Ghulam Muhammad at the Passu Inn in Passu has copies for sale, as does the Chinese embassy in Islamabad (reportedly for US$50). Jerzy Wala's *Batura Mustagh* 1:100,000 orographical sketch map of Batura Wall has text in English and Polish.

Country Maps Pakistan is on Bartholomew & Sons' and Nelles Verlag's 1:4,000,000 *Indian Subcontinent* maps. Bartholomew's

1:3,000,000 *Tibet & the Mountains of Central Asia* also shows the Karakoram and Himalayan ranges. Nelles Verlag has a 1:1,500,000 map of Pakistan, although it is full of misspellings and is of little use in the Northern Areas.

The Survey of Pakistan produced a 1:2,000,000 road map of Pakistan and coloured topographic maps of the whole country at 1:1,000,000 and 1:500,000. Some Survey of Pakistan offices have refused to sell maps to foreigners, and shops abroad report difficulty in getting these maps. However, you may find them in book shops in Pakistan.

Ordering Maps No matter which trekking maps you select, have them with you when you arrive in Pakistan. You cannot count on finding any trekking maps inside Pakistan. Good mail-order sources include:

Chessler Books, PO Box 339, 26030 Highway 74, Kittredge, CO 80457, USA (☎ (303) 670 9727 or (800) 654 8502; fax (303) 670 9727)

Cordee, 3A De Montfort St, Leicester, LE1 7HD, UK (☎ (0116) 254 3579; fax (0116) 247 1176)

Deutscher Alpenverein (DAV), Ingolstaedter Strasse 62 L, 80939 Munich, Germany (☎ (089) 311 5306)

Geo Buch Verlag, Rosenthal 6, D-8000 Munich 2, Germany

Italian dai tipi dell' Instituto Geografico Militare (IGM), Italy

ILH GeoCenter, Schockenriedstrasse 40A, Postfach 80 08 30, D-7000 Stuttgart 80, Germany

Libreria Alpina, via C Coroned-Berti 4, 40137 Bologna, Zona 3705, Italy

Maplink, 25 East Mason St, Santa Barbara, CA 93101, USA (☎ (805) 965 4402; fax (805) 962 0884)

National Oceanic & Atmospheric Administration (NOAA), Distribution Division, 9015 Junction Dr, Annapolis Junction, MD 20701, USA (☎ (301) 436 6990); stocks ONC and TPC maps

Edward Stanford Ltd, 12-14 Long Acre, Covent Garden, London WC2E 9LP, UK (☎ (0171) 836 1321; fax (0171) 836 0189)

Swiss Foundation for Alpine Research, Binzstrasse 23, 8045 Zürich, Switzerland (☎ (01) 461 01 47; fax (01) 287 13 68)

US Library of Congress, Geography & Map Division, 101 Independence Ave, Washington, DC 20540, USA

What to Bring

You cannot count on finding anything either for sale or for rent in Pakistan, so bring all of your essential clothing and equipment with you. When you are backpacking or hiring your own guide, trek crew, or porters, you need to bring from home most of the equipment we list. When you arrange your trek through a Pakistani trekking company or tour operator abroad, ask what equipment they provide and what you should bring.

A large, sturdy duffel bag made of cordura nylon with strong coil zippers is the best way to pack your gear for travel. If you are backpacking, you can store any extra belongings in the duffel bag at a reliable hotel. When you hire a porter, the duffel makes a secure bag for the porter to carry. Most duffels are not waterproof, so pack your gear in waterproof stuff sacks or in large, sturdy plastic bags inside the duffel. Dry bags are excellent for sleeping bags and other gear that must stay dry. Plastic sheets to cover the outside of duffel bags on the trail during inclement weather usually tear and become useless for protecting the contents from rain or wet snow.

Clothing Clothing that reveals any body parts other than the face, hands and feet or that reveals the shape of the body is deeply offensive to Muslims. Shorts, halter tops, and lycra are particularly offensive. In cities, conservative Western dress is common. Loose, non-revealing long-sleeved shirts and full-length pants are the most appropriate clothing choice. The *shalwar kameez* (local baggy pants and long shirt) are very comfortable. Both men's and women's versions are available. Ready-made shalwar kameez make fine trekking clothes and can be bought in any bazaar for Rs 350 and up. You can also have one made (you need about six metres of cloth). Get light-coloured 100% cotton, not synthetic blends. Wear long underwear tops and/or bottoms under them for warmth as you go up in elevation.

Rain can fall at any time in the mountains, and you need to bring some rain gear such as a waterproof parka or poncho. At night, you

CHECKLIST

CLOTHES

- [ ] loose-fitting long pants (2)
- [ ] long-sleeve shirt; wool or pile (1)
- [ ] long-sleeve shirt; cotton (1-2)
- [ ] underwear (2-3 sets)
- [ ] long underwear (tops and bottoms; V-neck zip tops are best; 2 sets: one light-weight and one medium-weight)
- [ ] liner socks (2-3 pairs)
- [ ] wool or pile socks (2-3 pairs)

Outerwear

- [ ] shell – wind and water resistant
- [ ] pile jacket
- [ ] down jacket with hood (medium-weight)
- [ ] liner gloves
- [ ] wool gloves or mittens (mittens are warmer than gloves)
- [ ] wool or pile hat (40 to 75% of body heat is lost through the head)
- [ ] sun hat or visor

Optional Items*

- [ ] umbrella
- [ ] down booties
- [ ] poncho
- [ ] balaclava
- [ ] fingerless gloves for cooking
- [ ] liner gloves and Goretex over-mitts

Footwear

- [ ] hiking boots
- [ ] sandals with ankle straps (eg, TEVA) or tennis shoes
- [ ] gaiters

PERSONAL ITEMS

- [ ] water bottles (2-3 one-litre)
- [ ] flashlight (torch) or head lamp and battery cells
- [ ] pocket knife
- [ ] plastic bags
- [ ] sunglasses that protect from UV and infra-red radiation and are shatterproof
- [ ] maps

Toiletries

- [ ] toothbrush and toothpaste, dental floss
- [ ] waterproof sunscreen (SPF 30 or more) that provides UVA & UVB protection
- [ ] lip salve
- [ ] moisturiser
- [ ] first aid kit (see the Health, Safety & First Aid chapter)
- [ ] water-purifying kit
- [ ] toilet paper and butane lighter
- [ ] bath and laundry soap
- [ ] hand towel
- [ ] shampoo
- [ ] repair kit (needle, thread, tape, glue)

Optional Items*

- [ ] watch
- [ ] camera, film
- [ ] compass
- [ ] altimeter
- [ ] binoculars
- [ ] journal
- [ ] plastic bags
- [ ] solar battery recharger and rechargeable cells
- [ ] short-wave radio

* This list equips you well with extras – reduce them if weight is a concern.

need a warm jacket, and a wind-proof shell. A waterproof, breathable one with a hood is best. Some consider an umbrella essential for shelter from showers and shade from the hot midsummer sun. Umbrellas available in Pakistani bazaars are cheap, but not up to the rigours of a long trek. A sturdy bamboo-handled umbrella is better.

Layering allows you to dress for change-able weather. A wicking layer passes moisture away from the skin. Capilene, wool, and silk underwear keep an adequate temperature and maintain a dry layer next to your skin. Cotton underwear is not recommended, When it gets wet (with sweat) it is cold and takes a long time to dry. Next comes an insulating layer of pile, wool, down, or thinsulate. These fabrics provide further warmth and dry quickly. The outer or protective shell layer shields you from sun, rain, wind, or snow. Jackets should include a hood. Hats for both sun and warmth are needed. Avoid bulky clothes, and select fabrics and products that compress and are easy to clean.

Boots are a trekker's most important gear. Break them in thoroughly before going trekking. Wear them on your flight to Pakistan, as it is very difficult to replace boots if lost. Buy really sturdy, all-leather boots, with scree collars and a stiff sole. Light-weight, cordura boots will last for one trek – maybe! Bringing a tube of silicon shoe repair 'goo' is good insurance. If you plan on trekking on a glacier, be sure your boots are water-proof, and don't forget gaiters, which are essential for walking across snowfields. If you will be using crampons, be sure your boots can accommodate them. Of course while trekking along river valleys on hot summer days, your feet can cook in hot heavy boots.

Some people, for whom extra weight is not a problem, may carry an additional light-weight pair of highly breathable boots for such conditions. Others will stop and cool their feet in streams, and switch to a pair of sneakers on arriving at camp. Sneakers are also good when you have to ford a river. Nowadays, sturdy river sandals are popular for this as well. Sneakers also are the best footwear for dusty bazaars and down-country cities. A pair of shower sandals, readily and inexpensively available in Pakistan, or your fancy river sandals, make it nicer when you find yourself showering in a grungy hotel or bath house, and are a nice option for bus rides in hot weather.

You can usually find toilet paper, candles, matches, non-alkaline battery cells, laundry soap, toothbrushes and toothpaste, razor blades, shampoo and aspirin in a good bazaar. In Islamabad stores, particularly those in Jinnah market, you can find just about everything including imported shampoos, cosmetics, and alkaline battery cells.

Equipment The equipment you need to bring is grouped into camping, mountaineering, and kitchen. When you hire a trek crew, you need to provide their equipment too (see Guides & Porters in this chapter).

Camping Equipment Bring this necessary camping equipment from home: sleeping tent with rain fly and waterproof ground sheet; rugged backpack with waterproof cover; sleeping sheet, bag and pad; and waterproof stuff sacks. A light, warm synthetic fill sleeping bag is the best all-round choice. If you can afford a down bag, get one with a waterproof, breathable shell. A heavy down bag will probably be too hot for all but the coldest sleepers. You can get a cotton sleeping sheet made in Pakistan. A Therm-A-Rest self-inflating foam mattress is less bulky, more comfortable, and better insulating than an ensolite sleeping pad. These qualities make them preferable for long treks over rocky and snowy terrain. The Therm-A-Rest'r chair kit converts a sleeping pad into a very comfortable camp chair, which is a nice luxury for longer treks when you get tired of squatting on rocks.

Mountaineering Equipment We mention in the route descriptions when mountaineering equipment is required. For those routes, each trekker needs: glacier goggles; one aluminium locking carabiner; a climbing (seat) harness or tubular webbing to make a swami belt; an ascender/prussik; and ski pole(s) or walking stick(s) for crossing crevasse fields or scree slopes. Each trekking party needs: one ice axe with aluminium shaft; rope(s) for glacier travel, a 45 metre nine-mm rope for every three persons (including each member of your trek crew); two belay anchors (pickets, slings, and carabiners); and at least one pair of crampons (hinged with adjustable widths).

Kitchen Equipment When cooking for

yourself, you need a personal kitchen that includes a stove with wind screen, spare parts and cleaning wires; fuel container(s); funnel and fuel filter; two cooking pots (eg, 1.5 and 2-litre) with lids and gripper (or hot pads), nesting stainless steel pots are compact and easy to clean; waterproof matches and container, or butane lighter; plate, mug (eg large, insulated ones with lids), and eating utensils (minimum of one spoon per person); dish soap, wash cloth/dish towel; and mesh bag (to hold gear).

Optional items for the kitchen are: plastic expedition barrel; kerosene lantern (Petromax with padded carrying box and extra mantles); candles; pressure cooker; ladle; plastic washbasin(s); knife, vegetable peeler and cutting board; tea strainer; griddle, rolling pin and board (for preparing chapattis), and aluminium pan to knead bread; and a tea kettle.

Expedition barrels ensure your food and gear is not damaged along the trail, keep contents clean and dry, deter theft, and pack easily into a comfortable porter load. They are readily available in the Skardu bazaar for Rs 300 to Rs 400 and are less easily found in Gilgit. Check that the barrel is in good condition, its opening is wide enough for your gear to pass through easily, and that it seals properly.

Stoves The choice of stoves depends upon the stove's durability and fuel efficiency, who will be cooking, and who will be carrying the stove and fuel. When you cook for yourself and carry your own stove and fuel, bring a stove and fuel containers from home. The MSR X-GK (II) stove, a multi-fuel lightweight wonder, is the best stove we know of because it is compact, rugged, and burns wells at high altitude. Cooks and porters find them too delicate and complicated to use. (Many trekkers we met found that the MSR WhisperLite Internationale stoves did not burn efficiently on locally available fuels.) Butane gas stoves are lightweight and also easy to use, but fuel problems make them less preferable. However, cooks and porters have no trouble cooking with them. We

always put our stove in a stuffsack and carry it ourselves instead of putting it into porter loads where there is a greater chance of it being damaged.

When you hire a cook or have porters to carry your gear, you can buy locally made kerosene stoves, which are readily available in Chitral, Gilgit, and Skardu for about Rs 225. With their large blue steel frame and fuel tank, they are heavy and make awkward loads. However, locals know how to use and repair them, and you can usually sell them back for half of what you paid when your trek is over. Russian-made brass stoves, surplus from the Afghan war, are also available in Gilgit and Chitral for Rs 180. Though more compact, they do not burn as hot.

Chapattis, flat rounds of unleaven bread, are cooked on a dry griddle. They are a staple food of the region.

Fuel Kerosene is the fuel of choice, though Pakistani kerosene burns sootily. It is inexpensive and widely available in bazaars, at petrol pumps, and even in small amounts in many villages. Bring a filter or strain it through a cloth, especially if resupplying in a village. White gas (white spirit) is not available, and denatured alcohol is available only in Rawalpindi and Islamabad. Butane cartridges (eg, Gaz, EPI Gas) are sporadically available in Skardu and less reliably so in Gilgit for about Rs 150 for a 250 cc canister. These cartridges are not allowed in checked or carry-on baggage on any flights, so you will not be able to bring your own supply. Because you cannot rely on buying the cartridges in Pakistan, and because they create disposal problems, using a butane stove is a poor choice. Some trekkers report petrol burns hot and clean in MSR stoves, but is explosive on ignition.

Bring MSR or equivalent fuel bottles if you need fuel for only a few days; they are easier to carry and do not leak. We bring ordinary fuel bottles as storage vessels and one MSR bottle as a pressurised vessel. We carry any pressurised fuel bottle ourselves so it does not get damaged in a porter load. Plastic containers to transport larger quantities of kerosene are readily available in Gilgit and Skardu bazaars. Container sizes and costs vary: Rs 50 five-litre, Rs 75 10-litre, and Rs 100 25-litre. The screw-on lids usually leak, so carry some extra plastic to cover the opening and reduce spillage.

When you share fuel with porters, monitor its usage to ensure it is not used too hastily. Fuel will be used for cooking, heating, and starting fires (eg, to burn garbage). In colder conditions, porters can easily burn three to four litres per night to keep warm. Supplying your porters with a windproof shelter and sleeping pads can be less expensive than paying a porter to carry extra kerosene. Ask your crew how much kerosene they think they will use, and bring a little extra.

Food
Very few trekkers find it necessary to import food to Pakistan. Those who do, usually bring 'goodies' or supplementary items unavailable in Pakistan. This may include energy bars, freeze-dried prepackaged meals, dried soup and sauce mixes, and pow-

dered drink or electrolyte mixes. (See Trekking Information – Trek Food below for details of food available in Pakistan.)

TOURIST OFFICES
Local Tourist Offices
The Government of Pakistan runs Pakistan Tourism Development Corporation (PTDC) and provincial governments run smaller tourist offices in Azad Jammu & Kashmir, the Northern Areas, the Northwest Frontier Province (NWFP), and in the Punjab.

PTDC PTDC is the promotional arm of the Tourism Division of the Ministry of Sports & Tourism. It runs motels, maintains tourist information centres that offer brochures and advice, holds priority seats for tourists on Northern Areas flights, and books vehicles for hire. A subsidiary, Pakistan Tours Ltd (PTL), books domestic flights, jeeps, hotels, and tours. Its offices are:

PTDC Head Office, PO Box 1465, Islamabad 44000; F-7/4, St 61, House 2 (☎ (051) 811001-4); fax 824173; telex 54356 PTDC PK)
PTDC Motels Booking Office, F-7 Markaz (southeast side of Jinnah market), Bhitai Rd, Block 4-B, Islamabad (☎ 218232, 812957, and 819384; fax 218233; telex 54356 PTDC PK); open from 9 am to 1 pm and 2 to 4 pm and closed Friday; but open seven days per week from 1 June to 14 August.
PTL Head Office, Flashman's Hotel, Rm 24, The Mall, Rawalpindi (☎ (051) 581480-5 and 563038; fax 565449; telex 5620 FH PK) and Metropole Hotel, Rm 266, Club Rd, Karachi (☎ 511776; telex 23823 PTDC PK)

PTDC Tourist Information Centres include:

Chitral
  PTDC Chitral Motel, Naya bazaar (☎ 2683)
Gilgit
  19 JSR Plaza, near PIA office (c/o Sargin Travel Service ☎ 3939) and PTDC Motel, Chinar Inn, Babar Rd (☎ 2562)
Islamabad
  F-7/2, 13-T/U College Rd, Rm 6 (☎ 816932; fax 824173; telex 54356 PTDC PK) and at international airport arrival lounge c/o United Bank counter (☎ 591535)
Kalam
  PTDC Motel (☎ 14), May to October only

Karachi
Shafi Chambers, Club Rd (☎ 568 1293), and at international airport arrival lounge
Lahore
Faletti's Hotel, Egerton Rd, Rm 3 (☎ 630 6528, 636 3946-55), and at international airport arrival lounge
Peshawar
Dean's Hotel, Islamia Rd (☎ 279781-3, ext 33)
Rawalpindi
Flashman's Hotel, The Mall, Rm 59 (☎ 517073; fax 565449, telex 5620 FH PK)
Saidu Sharif
Swat Serena Hotel (☎ and fax 5007)
Skardu
PTDC K2 Motel (☎ 2946)
Sost
Pakistan-China border check post, open 1 May to 15 November
Wagah
PTDC Reception Unit on Pakistan-India border

Provincial Tourist Offices Less useful are these provincial tourist offices, including:

Azad Jammu & Kashmir Tourism Department (☎ (058) 3090), Lower Chattar in Muzaffarabad, has reliable information on areas open for foreigners, transport, and accommodation.
Northern Areas Tourism Development Corporation is so new it had no office at the time of writing, but it will be in Gilgit.
Sarhad Tourism Development Corporation, established in 1993, has its main office for NWFP in Peshawar.
Tourism Development Corporation of Punjab (TDCP) (☎ information 636 0553 and 636 9687), 4-A Lawrence Rd, Lahore, and (☎ tours 757 6826-8; fax 758 9097), 195-B Shadman-II, Lahore. For tourist coach services reservations and inquiries call ☎ 636 0553.

Tourist Offices Abroad

PTDC maintains these offices abroad:

Canada – c/o Bestway Tours & Safaris, 2678 W Broadway, Ste 202, Vancouver, BC, V6K 2G3 (☎ (604) 732 4686; fax (604) 732 9744)
Denmark – c/o PTDC Vester, Farimagsgade 3, 1606 Copenhagen V (☎ (01) 331 2118 and 333 94455; fax 339 39799)
The Netherlands – c/o Khan Travels, Albert Cuypstraat 44, 1072 CV Amsterdam (☎ (020) 662 5255 and 675 1887; fax (020) 675 1612)
Norway – c/o Crown Travels Group, Gronlands Torg, Postpoks 9148, Gronlands, 0133 Oslo (☎ (22) 17 79 10; fax (22) 17 47 86)

VISAS & DOCUMENTS
Passport
Your most important travel document is a passport. If it is about to expire, renew it before you travel because this may not be easy to do overseas. Pakistan requires your passport be valid for at least six months after your visit. Carry extra photocopies of your passport separate from your passport. Having a photocopy makes it easier to replace a lost or stolen passport. Officials and airlines (eg, PIA international departures from Pakistan) can request photocopies of your passport.

Visas
A visa is a stamp in your passport issued by a foreign government that permits you to enter and/or travel in a country for a specified period of time. In Pakistan, there is a variety of visa types, including tourist and transit visas (also called a Landing Permit). At the time of writing, travellers arriving in Pakistan without a visa could get a 15-day Landing Permit for no charge. However, policies on this change, so it is best to get your visa before you arrive and avoid having to extend it in Pakistan. A tourist visa is usually valid for a single-entry, three-month stay from the date you enter Pakistan, and enables you to enter up to six months from the date of issue. Six-month, multiple-entry visas are also possible. Reportedly some consular offices (eg, Hong Kong and Beijing) only issue one-month, single-entry visas valid for three months from the date of issue.

You can apply for a visa at any embassy or consulate of Pakistan. Besides submitting the completed visa application, fee, your passport and passport-size photos, you may be required to produce an onward/return ticket. (This request may be deflected by saying you are leaving Pakistan over the Khunjerab Pass to China.) Visa requirements and fees change, so check with any embassy or consulate of Pakistan, visa service, or reputable travel agency before travelling.

Foreigners' Registration
Your visa is just permission to enter Pakistan.

When you arrive you need to get permission to stay, and after that permission to leave! This keeps many civil servants employed.

Embark/Disembark Card On arrival, complete an Embark/Disembark Card (Form A) and Personal Declaration of Origin & Health (Schedule 1 – Amended) and immigration puts an entry stamp in your passport. When you stay for 30 days or less, no other formalities apply. Immigration then puts an exit stamp in your passport on departure.

Certificate of Registration & Residential Permit However, when you stay more than 30 days, you become a 'resident', and before the 30 days have passed you need to register at a Foreigners' Registration Office (FRO) in the district where you stay. Bring two passport-size photos. Complete a Certificate of Registration (Form B) in duplicate and they issue you a Residential Permit. One copy of Form B and the Residential Permit are stapled and returned to you; you must carry these with you. There is no fee.

Whenever you are absent from the district in which you are registered for more than seven days, you must transfer your registration by reporting to the FRO in the new district within 24 hours of your arrival. Show your Form B and Residential Permit, inform the authorities of your local address (ie, your hotel) and get these papers stamped. For instance, if you register with the FRO in Gilgit and then go to Skardu for two weeks' trekking, you would need to go to the FRO in Skardu to report your arrival and change your registered address before the trek.

Travel Permit When you want to leave Pakistan, you must go to the FRO in the city in which you are registered and surrender your Form B and Residential Permit. Then complete and submit a Travel Permit form. There is no fee. An official will sign and return the Travel Permit, valid for seven days, during which time you must leave Pakistan. You then give your Travel Permit to immigration on departure.

Some officials may tell you to just give the

Form B and Residential Permit directly to immigration on departure. Don't believe any of it; this will just be an excuse for later 'regulations' and 'fees' you cannot verify.

FRO Locations The FROs in Islamabad and Rawalpindi are open from 9 am to 1 pm and 2 to 5 pm Saturday to Thursday and are closed on Friday.

FRO Islamabad If you stay at a guesthouse or hotel in Islamabad, register at the Islamabad FRO at Ayub market (F-8 Markaz), near the *kucheri* (civil courts) and the Senior Superintendent of Police's (SSP's) office. The door's sign reads 'Incharge Security and Foreigners' Registration Branch'. You can get inexpensive instant passport-sized photos at several nearby photo shops. The No 111 van (which has a green band) runs up the Islamabad Hwy past Zero Point to Ayub market.

FRO Rawalpindi If you stay at a hotel in Rawalpindi, register at the Rawalpindi FRO at the kucheri beside the SSP's office. Catch an airport Suzuki on Adamjee Rd and get off just past Kucheri Chowk. The No 21 van from Saddar also goes by the FRO.

FRO Northern Areas Offices are in each of the five districts: Diamir, Ghanche, Ghizar, Gilgit, and Skardu. Chilas is the administrative centre for Diamir. Khapalu is the head of Ghanche district. The FRO for Ghizar is in Gakuch. In Gilgit, the FRO is at Khomer Chowk police post. The FRO in Khapalu is in the SP's office. In Skardu, go to the SP's office, beyond the K2 Motel.

FRO NWFP Offices are in Chitral, Peshawar, and Saidu Sharif. In Chitral, the FRO is in the SP's office (☎ 2553). The FRO in Peshawar is on Police Rd (☎ 75149) on Sahibzada Gul Rd (ask for Police Chowk No 2). The FRO in Saidu Sharif is at the SP's, in the same compound as the DC's office near the playing field.

Visa Extensions & Replacement

Islamabad is the only place to extend your visa or Landing Permit, or deal with an expired visa or lost papers. If you are somewhere else and time is running out on your visa, police can give you a letter of authorisation that gives you a few extra days to get to Islamabad or to the border.

Firstly, try to get a letter from your embassy, or the Tourism Division of the Ministry of Sports & Tourism in Islamabad (F-7/2) asking that your stay be extended or your papers replaced. If you need an extension, the letter needs to specify how long you want to stay. Secondly, go to the Ministry of Interior's Regional Passports Office (☎ 810837) on Khayaban-e-Suhrawardy in Aabpara. A narrow entry way with a sign that reads 'Office of the Assistant Director – Immigration & Passport' leads upstairs to the Visa Office, which is on the 1st floor above the National Bank. With your letter(s), fee (if applicable) and photocopies of the front pages of your passport, you get a form saying your visa has been granted, extended or replaced. The Visa Office accepts applications from 9 am to 1 pm. Fees vary with length of extension requested and nationality. You can then pay them direct or pay the bank downstairs, which gives a voucher for the Visa Office. Thirdly, go to the FRO with two passport-size photos and the Visa Office's form and they will give you a Form B and Residential Permit.

For lost papers you might have to detour to the Ministry of the Interior (☎ 821213), R Block of the Secretariat, where you can also go for extending expired visas.

Re-Entry Visas

If you want to depart from and then return to Pakistan and do not already have a multiple-entry Pakistan visa, you can get a re-entry visa stamped into your passport. First go to the FRO to get your Form B and Residential Permit. Then go to the Visa Section office of the Directorate of Immigration & Passports with your Form B and Residential Permit, one photocopy of the front pages of your passport, two passport-sized photos, and your fee (if applicable). Allow at least a whole day for the paper chase.

Travellers who go to China also report leaving their Form B and Residential Permit with officials in Sost, then collecting them on return from China. This avoids getting a Travel Permit and then another Form B and Residential Permit.

Other Permits & Registration

Police jurisdictions in border areas and other sensitive spots have additional registration and permit regulations. Foreigners must register with FRO when in Chitral district and get a Temporary Registration Certificate.

Travel Insurance

It is worth taking out travel insurance. Coverage can include medical care, emergency evacuation, personal property, and trip interruption. Consider insuring yourself for the worst possible scenario – an accident requiring evacuation, hospitalisation, and possibly a flight home. For an extended trip, insurance may seem very expensive, but if you cannot afford the insurance premiums, you probably cannot afford a medical emergency overseas either. Personal property insurance covers loss or theft of your belongings. Remember to report any incident to the nearest police and obtain a police report which you may need to file a claim. If you have prepaid for any travel arrangements, trip interruption or cancellation insurance covers any unreimbursed expenses if you cannot complete your trip due to illness, an accident, or the illness of death of family members.

Before you purchase travel insurance, check any existing policy you may own to see what it covers overseas. Some policies do not pay claims if you engage in certain 'dangerous' activities; verify that trekking is a covered activity.

Travel insurance is available from private companies; you can also ask any travel agency or tour operator abroad for recommendations. The international student travel policies handled by STA Travel and other student travel organisations are good value.

They frequently include major medical and emergency evacuation coverage in the cost of the student travel ID card. (Also see Insurance and Rescue & Evacuation in the Health, Safety & First Aid chapter.)

International Certificates of Vaccination

Record all immunisations on an International Certificates of Vaccination, available from your physician or health department, and carry this yellow booklet with you to show proof of immunisation.

EMBASSIES
Pakistan Embassies Abroad

A partial list follows:

Afghanistan
    Shahr-e-No, Kabul (☎ 21374); Consulate, Kheyabun-e Herat, Kandahar (☎ 2452)
Australia & New Zealand
    59 Franklin St, PO Box 198, Manuka, Canberra, ACT 2603 (☎ (06) 295 0021/22); Consulate, 500 George St, 11th floor, Sydney, NSW 2000 (☎ (02) 9267 7250)
China
    1 Dongzhimenwai Dajie, Sanlitun Compound, Beijing (☎ (01) 532-2504, 532-2581, 532-2695).
European Union
    Permanent Mission of Pakistan, 25 Ave Delleur 57, Boitsfort 1170, Brussels, Belgium (☎ 733 97 83)
France
    116 Ave des Champs d'Elysee, 75008 Paris (☎ (44) 21 82 83)
Germany
    Rheinallee 24, 53173 Bonn-Bad Godesberg (☎ (02) 28 35 20 04)
India
    High Commission of Pakistan, 2/50-G Shantipath, Chanakyapuri-21, New Delhi (☎ (11) 60 0601 and 60 0603-5)
Iran
    Khayaban-e Dr Fatemi, 1 Khayaban-e Ahmad Eitmadzadeh, Jamshedabad Shomali, Tehran (☎ 934 332-3). Pakistan also has consulates at Zahedan and Mashad.
Italy
    via Della Camilluccia 682, 00135 Rome (☎ 329 6660)
Japan
    2-14-9 Motoazabu, Minato-Ku, Tokyo 104 (☎ 3451 4261-4)
Spain
    Av PIO XII-II, 28016 Madrid (☎ 345 9138)

UK
    35 Lowndes Square, London SW1X 9JN (☎ (0171) 235 2044); Consulate, Fraternal House, 45 Cheapside, Bradford BD1 4HP (☎ (0274) 721921). There are vice-consulates in Birmingham, Glasgow and Manchester.
USA
    2315 Massachusetts Ave NW, Washington, DC 20008 (☎ (202) 939-6200). Consulates are at 12 East 65th St, New York, NY 10021 (☎ (212) 879-5800; fax (212) 517-6987) and 10850 Wilshire Blvd, Los Angeles, CA 90024 (☎ (310) 441-5114).

Foreign Embassies in Pakistan

Trekkers should check with their high commission or embassy's consular section in Pakistan to see what services are available for citizens visiting Pakistan. Some embassies may offer emergency medical treatment or financial assistance if you run out of money. Most embassies also offer emergency evacuation (see Rescue & Evacuation in the Health, Safety & First Aid chapter).

Should someone at home need to reach you in an emergency, most governments' foreign offices maintain 24-hour operators who can contact your embassy in Pakistan (eg, the British Foreign Office (☎ (0171) 270 3000), the US State Department (☎ (202) 647-5225 and (202) 647-4000 outside business hours), and the Australian Department of Foreign Affairs & Trade (☎ (06) 261 3331)).

Most embassies are in the Diplomatic Enclave (G-5) at the east end of Islamabad. You can only get foreign visas from embassies in Islamabad, not from consulates in other cities. You may need a letter of request from your embassy.

From Aabpara, vans to Quaid-e-Azam University pass the US, Chinese, Russian Federation, and Australian embassies. The No 3 van to Bari Imam (Nurpur Shahan) passes near the Iranian, Indian, Japanese, and British embassies. A partial list follows:

Afghanistan – G-6/4, St 83, House 14 (☎ 822566)
Australia – G-5 (☎ 214902-6)
Canada – G-5 (☎ 211101)
China – G-5 (☎ 211114)
France – G-5 (☎ 213981-3)
Germany – G-5 (☎ 212412)

India – G-5 (☎ 814371-5 ext 257)
Iran – G-5/1, St 2 (☎ 212694-5)
Italy – F-6/3, 54 Khayaban-e-Margalla (☎ 210791)
Japan – G-5/4 (☎ 218063)
Nepal – G-6/4, St 84, House 11 (☎ 212754)
New Zealand – Go to the British High Commission.
Russian Federation – (eg, for Kazakstan, Tajikistan, Turkmenistan, and Uzbekistan); G-5/4 (☎ 214603-4)
Spain – G-5/1, St 6 (☎ 211070-1, 211179, 211088)
UK – G-5 (☎ 822131-5)
USA – G-5 (☎ 826161-79)

General visa information for neighbouring countries follows.

Afghanistan At the time of writing, tourist visas for Afghanistan were not being issued.

China A one-month, single-entry visa is valid for entry for 90 days from the date of issue. The visa office is open from 8.30 am to noon, except Friday and major Chinese holidays. Fees are Rs 1000 US, Rs 1575 New Zealand, Rs 600 Australia, Rs 1600 UK, and Rs 1550 Canada. Bring two passport-size photos. It usually takes four days to process an application. Because many Pakistanis travel to China expect long queues.

India A three-month single-entry visa can be obtained from the visa office at the back of the Indian High Commission. It is open from 9.30 to 11 am, and is closed on Friday. British, Australian, and other nationals may need a letter from their embassy. Americans must pay for a telex to the Indian embassy or consulate nearest their home and then wait for their reply stating no objection exists to their being issued an Indian visa. This process can take up to two weeks and longer when Pakistan-India tension is high. The fee is Rs 625 and you need two passport-size photos.

Iran Transit visas are valid for two weeks and tourist visas for one month, both visas can be extended in Iran. Non-Pakistanis can apply only at the embassy in Islamabad and the consulate in Karachi. Israeli citizens and white South Africans are not normally granted visas. When applying, wearing conservative dress and appearing that way in the three required passport-sized photos is important. If possible, bring a letter of invitation (approved by the Ministry of Foreign Affairs in Tehran) from sponsors in Iran and one from your own embassy. The process can take anywhere from two weeks to three months. Fees vary according to nationality and visa type.

CUSTOMS
Arrival
The Green Channel is for those with no goods to declare. The Red Channel is for those with goods to declare. Pakistan prohibits the import of alcohol and of firearms. No other significant import restrictions are enforced. If you exchange other currencies for a large sum of Pakistani rupees before you enter Pakistan, keep them out of sight.

Departure
Baggage inspection on departure is usually cursory for foreigners. Customs officials may ask for sales receipts and bank encashment certificates for major purchases. Put battery cells into your checked baggage, as airport security may confiscate them from carry-on baggage. Officials are sharp-eyed about pen guns and other disguised firearms. Penalties are stiff and foreigners have been arrested. Drug smuggling is punishable by death.

Export Permits
An export permit is necessary to post out any purchase with a declared value over Rs 500 and to carry out carpets. Obtaining an export permit on your own can be tedious. PTDC, shopkeepers, or your hotel staff may help. Bring the purchase receipt, encashment certificates at least for the value of the purchase, an explanatory letter to the Controller (Import & Export), and photocopies of these documents and of the front pages of your passport to the local export office.

You cannot export antiquities; if in doubt, ask a museum curator or shopkeeper who deals in them.

MONEY
Costs
The rates and wages were valid at the time of publication, expect an annual inflation rate of about 10%.

Cities & Towns By staying in lower-end hotels, eating local-style and using public transport, you can budget less than US$15 per person per day, though much depends on how widely you travel. This includes daily per person accommodation (double rooms) costing from US$5 to US$7, and from US$5 to US$8 each for food. When you stay in mid-range hotels, budget from US$20 to US$25 per person per day.

Trekking Costs while trekking vary significantly with the style of trekking you choose (see What Kind of Trek? earlier in this chapter). Backpacking averages as little as US$10 to US$15 per person per day when you carry your own pack or hire one porter, buy food locally, provide your own equipment, and use local transport to trail heads. When you hire a special jeep, guide, cook, trek crew, and/or porters on your own, total costs increase surprisingly. You then need to budget from US$25 to US$50 per person per day, which is often more expensive than staying in hotels and eating in restaurants.

Guides alone cost from US$10 to US$20 per day, including their expenses and food. Self-arranged restricted-zone treks cost up to US$50 per person per day. Budget from US$7 to US$10 per porter per stage, and not per day (see Guides & Porters – Wages in this chapter).

Trekking companies in Pakistan charge from US$35 to US$100 per person per day, depending upon the services you request. These can include the cost of a guide, cook, trek crew, porters, food, equipment, transport to/from the trail head, hotels, and permit fees and insurance premiums, if applicable. When you book a trek with a tour operator abroad, costs range from US$100 to US$175 per person per day, including all services in Pakistan and a tour leader.

Central Excise Duty A 10% Central Excise Duty (CED) is charged for some goods and services. Many non-top-end places do not charge it, and at others a discreet request for it to be omitted may pay off. When you need a proper receipt, CED must be included.

Carrying Money
Travellers' cheques, in US dollars, are the safest and easiest way to bring money to Pakistan. The redesigned US$100 bills introduced in 1996 will probably cause all old bills to be rejected. At present US$100 bills prior to 1991 are not accepted. Credit cards are not widely accepted for purchases except at top-end hotels and shops. Travel agencies usually charge a percentage fee to charge airline tickets to credit cards. Some banks arrange cash advances from credit cards, which can take a day to process and some may charge a fee for an international telex to verify the credit card number. Banks may suggest that you arrange a telex or telegraphic transfer of funds from your home bank, which can take a week or more. It is safer and simpler to have someone post a bank draft by express registered, insured mail to you at a reliable address in Pakistan.

Trekking Always carry your money yourself; do not let a guide, trek crew, or porter do so. This makes you responsible for your own money and keeps everyone else travelling with you honest. Whenever possible, keep money out of sight and in a secure place. The top pocket of a backpack is not a good place; a backpack with an interior zippered pocket is best. Put all money in a resealable plastic bag or other waterproof pouch.

Carry small notes ranging from Rs 1 to Rs 100 while trekking. On longer treks, carry 100-note bundles of five, 10, 20, and even 100-rupee notes to avoid overpaying because of lack of correct change. Guides, porters and villagers usually do not have any change for larger denomination bank notes.

It is helpful to count out the wages for anyone you have hired the night before you release them and pay their wages. Get your money out and count it in the privacy of your tent. We always carry a small note pad and make a receipt by writing the individual's name and amount of wages on a sheet of paper. Then we fold the receipt and money in half. The next day it is easy to pull this out discretely and give the correct wage to each individual.

Currency

The unit of money is the *rupee* (Rs), divided into 100 *paisa*. Paper notes come in denominations down to Rs 1; Rs 1 and 50 paisa (and a few 25 and 10 paisa) coins are used. Try to avoid change in very worn or ripped notes as merchants often refuse to accept them.

Currency Exchange

US dollars, either cash or travellers' cheques, are by far the easiest currency to exchange or cash, followed by British pounds sterling. Some banks exchange other foreign currencies in cash only. Exchange rates are higher in cities than in towns in the Northern Areas or NWFP. The approximate cash exchange rates in late 1995 follow:

A$1	=	Rs 29.74
C$1	=	Rs 27.70
DM1	=	Rs 24.70
FF1	=	Rs 6.76
NZ$1	=	Rs 23.55
Rs Ind 1	=	Rs 1.00
US$1	=	Rs 39.08
UK£1	=	Rs 58.35
Y100	=	Rs 0.345

Changing Money

You can change money at major domestic banks including Habib and National banks; foreign banks including ANZ Grindlays, Bank of America, Citibank; and American Express; top-end hotels in cities; and banks at international airports. The many licensed money changers in cities are generally quicker than banks and give a better rate. Ask for an encashment certificate whenever you change money. You may need it to reconvert unspent rupees, purchase airline tickets, or get export permits. Some shopkeepers buy

US dollars cash at slightly elevated rates, though it is not strictly legal and you get no encashment certificate.

The Bank of America (☎ 828801), near American Express in Islamabad's Blue Area, arranges cash advances from major credit cards. American Express is in Islamabad's Blue Area in Ali Plaza (☎ 272425) and in Rawalpindi on Murree Rd, Saddar bazaar (☎ 582864). Card holders can get rupees for no fee or travellers' cheques for a 1% fee from their personal cheques. They are open from 9 am to 1 pm and 2.15 to 4.45 pm Sunday to Thursday, and 9 am to 12.45 pm on Saturday.

Unspent rupees can be reconverted by certain branch banks, including those at customs and immigration posts, and at international airports. We have never had trouble converting unspent rupees (up to the total value of the encashment certificates) at the airport.

Black Market

The Pakistan rupee is freely convertible, which means Pakistanis can buy as many dollars in foreign currency as they want at the bank. It also means the black market is no longer prevalent, since no difference exists between the official and the current market rate.

Tipping

Cities & Towns Tipping (around 10%) is expected in top-end hotels and restaurants. Airport porters charge Rs 15 per trip to carry baggage. Taxi drivers do not expect tips, but it is OK to leave them loose change. Staff in guesthouses and mid-range hotels do not ask for tips, but it is appropriate to leave Rs 10 to Rs 20 per day.

Trekking When you pay guides, cooks, trek crew, and/or porters fair wages, tipping is not necessary. Tipping is a way to acknowledge and reward performance above and beyond the call of duty. You may choose to give gifts (see Baksheesh below). If you choose to give cash, a tip of 10% or roughly one day's wage per person per week is adequate. When you book a trek with a tour operator, your tour leader gives you appropriate guidelines for tipping all staff at the end of the trek. It's easiest for all trekkers to pool their tip money and have the tour leader give it out equitably to the trek crew.

Baksheesh Giving *baksheesh*, a Persian word meaning bestowing a blessing, has become a way of life in Pakistan and throughout South Asia. You might best think of it as another form of tipping. It greases the wheels, and if you can afford to distribute small bits of largess as you pass through, it eases your way. It does not take much – Rs 5 or Rs 10 for any small service rendered in the private sector. Government employees should not accept baksheesh, but always enjoy a tea or a dinner invitation. Resist the temptation to see those who ask for baksheesh as beggars. It is part of the Islamic code that better-off people give part of their income to the less well off. At the end of a trek, porters may ask for baksheesh. You can give them money, but often, what they really have their eye on is some trek gear or any items that are unavailable in Pakistan, which make truly well-appreciated baksheesh for the hard working porter.

Bargaining

Hotels and restaurants have fixed rates. However, hotels in particular frequently offer discounts if you ask for them. Generally, if the management knows you from a previous stay, they are more amenable to giving you a discount. In the bazaar, shopping without bargaining is like giving your money away. Bargaining is a knack most travellers develop quickly. Shops with fixed prices tell you so. Some basic necessities, like wheat flour, milk powder, sugar, tea, and kerosene, are also sold at fixed prices. Fares for bus tickets and airfares are fixed. Private vehicle hires and costs for trekking are negotiable. It is usually advantageous to negotiate in rupees instead of foreign currency. Remember that politeness always works best, especially if you are negotiating over the cost of services you will receive.

POST & COMMUNICATIONS

Postal Rates

Postal rates in Pakistan are only Rs 1. International rates from Pakistan are roughly the same as rates to Pakistan.

Sending Mail

International service is fast for letters and parcels from cities, but longer from remote places. To eliminate the risk of stamp theft, have letters franked in front of you. Send important letters via registered mail. Have outgoing parcels sewn into cloth bags which a tailor in the bazaar can do quickly. These need a customs declaration and postal inspection, so leave them open and finish the job yourself.

Receiving Mail

International mail service is fairly dependable when the address is well known. Parcels are less likely to arrive. The Islamabad GPO is at the north end of Melody market. The Rawalpindi GPO is on Kashmir Rd; poste restante is at the rear. American Express card and travellers' cheque holders can have letters (but not registered ones or parcels) held for up to one month at their offices. Receiving mail via poste restante in Chitral, Gilgit, or Skardu is less reliable. It these towns, it is better to arrange for a trekking company or shopkeeper to receive mail for you.

Telephone & Fax

You can place domestic and international telephone calls and send faxes from telephone exchanges, public call offices (PCOs), and hotels. Exchanges are usually open 24 hours a day. A minimum three-minute international call costs about Rs 150 to Rs 230; a person-to-person call costs about 15% more. A one-page fax costs the same as a three-minute call. Hotels usually charge higher rates.

Most large towns now have direct dialling, so you can receive international calls almost anywhere in Pakistan. To place an international call, you book the call with the international operator or dial direct from a telephone with International Direct Dialling (IDD) service. Gilgit and Skardu are linked to the international gateway in Islamabad through a satellite relay. You can receive international calls and faxes in Gilgit or Skardu, but you cannot place direct calls out.

You have to book calls through an international operator in Islamabad. The best way to send a fax from the Northern Areas is to prearrange with a trekking company, hotel, or one of the many private business centres in Islamabad to act as a relay. You can send them a fax, and they can send it again via IDD from Islamabad. Placing and receiving international calls and faxes in Chitral is significantly easier because it is linked to the international gateway in Peshawar by a series of microwave relay towers, referred to locally as 'boosters'. Along the KKH north of Gilgit, telephone calls are made through an operator at a switchboard where just reaching Gilgit is difficult.

Here is a partial list of dialling codes.

Chitral 0533
Gilgit 0572
Islamabad 051
Karachi 021
Lahore 042
Peshawar 0521
Rawalpindi 051
Saidu Sharif/Mingora 0536
Skardu 0575

Telex & Telegraph
You can send domestic and international telegrams and telexes from most telephone exchanges, hotels and guesthouses in the cities. The cheapest quick message is a telegram, with overseas rates of Rs 2 to Rs 3 per word. Telexes cost about Rs 30 per minute. For overseas calls, faxes, telexes, and cables, go to the central telegraph office, open 24 hours a day, in Rawalpindi (☎ 580276) on Kashmir Rd south of The Mall or in Islamabad (☎ 821579) on Ataturk Ave.

BOOKS
Most books are published in different editions by different publishers in different

countries. As a result, a book might be a hardcover rarity in one country while it's readily available in paperback in another. Fortunately, bookshops and libraries search by title or author, so your local bookshop or library is best placed to advise you on the availability of the following recommendations.

Learning about the area through which you plan to trek is one of the most useful preparations, so we offer an extensive list of informative titles about the Karakoram and Hindukush. If you cannot find these books at home, Pakistan is a gold mine of inexpensive reprints of travel classics.

Lonely Planet
Other excellent Lonely Planet guidebooks to the region are: *Pakistan – travel survival kit*; and *Karakoram Highway – travel survival kit*. Lonely Planet's *Hindu/Urdu phrasebook* is a good guide for grammar, pronunciation, and useful phrases.

Guidebooks
An Ecotourist's Guide to Khunjerab National Park by Daniel T Blumstein, a wildlife biologist who studied the golden marmot in Khunjerab National Park, contains excellent information on the park's mammals, birds, and flora, and is available from WWF – Pakistan.

Paddling the Frontier – Guide to Pakistan's White water by Wickliffe W Walker is the first and only river guide for Pakistan.

Pakistan Handbook by Isobel Shaw, an ex-expatriate who loves Pakistan, is rich in detail and background on historical sites, but short on practical advice for the budget-minded.

Trekking Guides
Pakistan Trekking Guide by Isobel & Ben Shaw is a useful and enthusiastic guide. Drawing on years of Pakistan experience, this mother and son team were the first to offer day-by-day trekking itineraries, some of which are from their own treks, while others are compiled from friends' not-always-accurate notes.

Trekkers Guide to Hunza and *Trekkers Guide to Chitral* are by the late Haqiqat Ali, a well-respected schoolmaster, scholar, and guide from Passu. He was first to present numerous daily trekking itineraries. However, some of the routes described are mountaineering not trekking routes, which can be dangerous for novices. The descriptions themselves are sketchy, but give an idea of the possibilities.

Trekking in Pakistan and India by Hugh Swift is the best resource on trekking in the Hindukush, Karakoram and Himalaya – a sensible and affectionate book by the legendary Himalayan walker that eschews day-by-day itineraries. Hugh's *Trekking in Pakistan and India* and *Trekking in Nepal, West Tibet, and Bhutan* are condensed into one book, *Himalaya, Guide de Trekking*, and translated into French by Hugh's friends, Martine Ferrero and Jean Michel and Hélène Strobino, one of the first Western couples to visit both Shimshal and Chapursan valleys.

Travel

Between the Oxus & the Indus by Reginald Charles Francis Schomberg chronicles travels to Gilgit, Yasin, and Hunza by this acidic British officer who found the landscapes nobler than the people.

Beyond the Northwest Frontier: Hindukush & Karakoram by Maureen Lines has a special focus on the Kalash and current environmental issues.

Blank on the Map by Eric Shipton, the master of small expeditions, treats Baltistan, Shimshal (including the route between Shimshal village and the Pamir), and Hunza (hardcover).

The Call of the Snowy Hispar by FB & WH Workman recounts the remarkable Fanny and her husband's visit to Nagyr and the Hispar Glacier.

Desert, Marsh, and Mountain: The World of a Nomad by Wilfred Thesiger recounts travels to Chitral, Broghil, Ishkoman, and Swat; including crossing the Karambar An and Chilinji An (hardcover).

The Golden Peak: Travels in Northern Pakistan by Kathleen Jamie is an insightful glimpse into the life of Muslim women and travellers.

Heart of a Continent by Francis E Younghusband relates classic journeys of a British colonial officer, including crossing the Muztagh Pass.

In the Ice World of Himalaya by FB & WH Workman is about one of the first treks up the Biafo to Snow Lake, which Shipton later termed 'Fanny's Folly'.

Innermost Asia (Vol I-V) by Sir Aurel Stein, a Hungarian-English archaeologist who focused on Central Asian sites between 1900 and the 1940s, recounts travels through Swat, Darel, Ghizar, Yasin, Darkot An, Karambar An, Chilinji An, and Chapursan Valley going to and from Taskurgan, Kashgar, and the Tarim Basin.

Kafirs and Glaciers by RCF Schomberg recounts his early journeys in Chitral and the Hindukush.

Karakoram-Himalaya, Sommets de 7000 metres is by A Roch.

Karakoram: Mountains of Pakistan by Shiro Shirahata has the finest photos of the great peaks (hardcover).

The Roof of the World by M Amin has large-format colour photos of the Karakoram, Hindukush and Pamir (hardcover).

A Short Walk in the Hindukush by Eric Newby is a delightful, humorous tale of an ill-advised, ill-planned, and ill-equipped trek.

Sisters on the Bridge of Fire: Journeys in the Crucible of High Asia by Debra Denker, who has travelled solo through Baltistan, Hunza and Chitral, and shared the lives of local women.

This My Voyage is by Tom Longstaff, a turn-of-the-century renowned explorer in Gilgit and Baltistan (hardcover).

The Traveller: An American Odyssey in the Himalayas by Eric Hansen and photos by Hugh Swift has tales of the travels of the late legendary Himalayan walker, Hugh Swift.

Travels in Kashmir, Ladak, Iskardo is by Godfrey Vigne, who in 1835 was the first Westerner to visit these parts.

Two Mountains and a River by HW Tilman has accounts of travels to Rakaposhi, Gilgit, Jaglot, Bar Valley, Chalt, and crossing the Mintaka Pass en route to Tashkurgan (hardcover).

Two Summers in the Ice-Wilds of Eastern Karakoram by FB & WH Workman describes their exploration of glaciers in Baltistan, including the Kondus, Bilafond, and Siachen glaciers.

Unknown Karakoram by RCF Schomberg recounts exploration of the area north of the main Karakoram, including Shimshal.

Where the Indus is Young by Dervla Murphy is the redoubtable account of a winter in Baltistan, travelling on foot and horseback with her six-year-old daughter.

Where Three Empires Meet by EF Knight are travels of a Victorian journalist in Kashmir, Ladakh and the Northern Areas, including a thrilling, but colonial, version of the 1891 invasion of Hunza.

History

Chitral, the Story of a Minor Siege by Sir George Robertson is a classic colonial adventure by the then Political Agent for Chitral (hardcover).

The Gilgit Game: The Explorers of the Western Himalaya 1865-95 by John Keay is a very readable account of the explorers and oddballs who played in the 'Great Game', the imperial rivalry between Britain and Russia across the Pamirs, Hindukush and Karakoram in the late 1800s.

The Great Game: On Secret Service in High Asia by Peter Hopkirk is a definitive account of the Anglo-Russian rivalry in Central Asia.

High Asia by Jill Neate gives a comprehensive illustrated history of the 7000m peaks.

The Pundits by Derek Waller is an account of the heroic but unsung journeys of Indian scholars and soothsayers trained by the British to be undercover surveyors and spies across the Hindukush and Karakoram.

A Record of Buddhistic Kingdoms by Fa-Hsien is the Buddhist monk's own dry account of his 5th-century pilgrimage through Xinjiang and the Karakoram, down the Indus to Gandhara and on to India. Excellent and much livelier descriptions of this and the later journey of another pilgrim, Hsuan Tsang, are in *The Great Chinese Travelers*, edited by Jeannette Mirsky.

When Men & Mountains Meet: Explorers of the Western Himalaya 1820-1875 by John Keay has gripping and often hilarious stories of the Europeans who first penetrated the western Himalaya in the early 1800s (hardcover).

General

Bolor and Dardistan by Karl Jettmar is a learned exposition of the ancient history of Gilgit, Hunza, and Baltistan.

Breaking the Curfew by Emma Duncan is a well-researched, thoughtful look at power and politics in Pakistan.

Hunza – Lost Kingdom of the Himalayas by John Clark portrays the good as well as the bad aspects of life in Hunza when the Mir's power was total, by an American who worked there in the 1950s (hardcover).

Kalash Solstice by Jean-Yves & Vivianne Lièvre Loude is a passionate and detailed study of the religious traditions of the non-Muslim Kalasha people of Chitral (hardcover).

Language Hunting in the Karakoram by EO Lorimer is a readable, but romanticised ,account of Hunza by the wife of the British Resident and scholar.

Human Impact on Mountains edited by Nigel JR Allan & Knapp contains several informative articles on Hunza.

Tribes of the Hindoo Kush by John Biddulph is a reprint of a 19th-century classic by the first Political Agent in Gilgit.

Waiting for Allah by Christina Lamb is a bleak tale of the rise and fall of Benazir Bhutto and the country's failure to seize the chance for democracy.

Words for My Brother by John Staley discusses the culture, politics, religious traditions and recent history of pre-Karakoram-Highway Chitral, Kohistan, Gilgit and Hunza (hardcover).

Natural History

The Birds of Pakistan (Vol I & II) by TJ Roberts is a standard reference (hardcover).

Concise Flowers of the Himalaya by Oleg Polunin & Adam Stainton is an easy-to-carry field guide. The text is abbreviated and descriptions are limited to the species illustrated.

Continents in Collision by Keith Miller discusses the geology underlying the relentless grind of Nanga Parbat against Rakaposhi.

Flowers of the Himalaya by Oleg Polunin & Adam Stainton is the standard reference, with over 690 colour illustrations, 315 B&W drawings, and 1500 entries (hardcover).

The Mammals of Pakistan by TJ Roberts is the standard reference that reminds us how quickly large mammals disappear when modern roads and weapons appear (hardcover).

Stones of Silence: Journeys in the Himalaya by George B Schaller (the biologist who first photographed the snow leopard) has tedious, but gripping accounts of his research (hardcover).

Mountaineering

All 14 Eight-Thousanders by Reinhold Messner recounts his ascents (many of them solo) without oxygen. This is probably the greatest mountaineering feat of all time (hardcover).

Climbing and Exploration in the Karakoram-Himalayas by William M Conway describes the first expedition to the Baltoro (hardcover).

Elusive Summits: Four Expeditions in the Karakoram is by Victor Saunders, leading proponent of the new generation of alpine-style exploration.

The Hard Years by Joe Brown is an account of the first ascent of the Muztagh Tower (hardcover).

Himalayan Odyssey by Trevor Braham describes small expeditions in Chitral, Swat, and Kaghan.

In the Throne Room of the Mountain Gods by Galen Rowell recounts the US K2 expedition with the best history of Baltoro exploration and fine photographs (hardcover).

K2: Triumph and Tragedy by Jim Curran recounts the 1986 season, when K2 claimed 13 lives.

Karakoram and Western Himalaya by Fillipo de Filippi recounts the Duke of the Abruzzi's 1909 Baltoro Glacier expedition, with Vittoria Sella's incredible photographs. The most sought-after rare book on Himalayan exploration (hardcover).

Karakoram: The Ascent of Gasherbrum IV by Fosco Maraini is an excellent description of the Karakoram and the upper Baltoro (hardcover).

Nanga Parbat – the Killer Mountain is by Karl M Herligkoffer, who devoted much of his life to this mountain.

Nanga Parbat Pilgrimage by Hermann Buhl is an account of the 1953 solo first ascent of Nanga Parbat (hardcover).

Rakaposhi by Mike Banks is an account of the first ascent of Rakaposhi (hardcover).

Summits and Secrets by Kurt Diemberger with accounts of Broad Peak, Chogolisa, and Tirich Mir.

Thin Air by Greg Child is an award-winning account of Karakoram alpine-style climbs.

Tirich Mir: The Norwegian Himalaya Expedition by Aarne Naess et al is the story of the first ascent of Tirich Mir (hardcover).

Walk in the Sky by Nick Clinch is an account of the first ascent of Gasherbrum I.

Where Four Worlds Meet by Fosco Maraini is a well-written account of an expedition to Saraghrar in Chitral, plus the Kalash valleys (hardcover).

Health & Safety

Glacier Travel & Crevasse Rescue by Andy Sellers contains material that anyone trekking on glaciers should know.

High Altitude: Illness and Wellness is by Charles S Houston, an MD who knows his subject.

Hypothermia, Frostbite & Cold Injuries by James A Wilkerson, MD is essential if you are travelling across glaciers.

Medicine for Mountaineering by James A Wilkerson, MD is the 'bible of mountaineering medicine' for the lay person.

Medicine for the Outdoors by Paul S Auerbach, MD, gives easy-to-understand, quality advice for all back-country emergencies and ailments.

Mountain Medicine by Fred T Darvill, MD, is a pocket-size handbook now in its 13th edition.

Mountain Sickness: Prevention, Recognition, and Treatment by Peter H Hackett, MD, is an essential handbook for anyone trekking above 4000m.

Where There is No Doctor by David Werner is a very detailed reference for the lay person, covering most diseases and injuries you might encounter, and their treatment.

Bookshops

In Rawalpindi, the Book Centre (☎ 565234) at 32 Haider Rd in Saddar has maps and used books and sells Lonely Planet titles. Capri Bookshop on Haider Rd and Pak-American Commercial Ltd on Kashmir Rd (upstairs) have magazines. In Islamabad, the London Book Company (☎ 823852) has a big Pakistan section, maps, magazines and used books. In Super market are Lok Virsa Bookstore, which also sells tapes of folk music, and Mr Books (☎ 218843). Book Fair (☎ 812198) is in Jinnah market. In Peshawar, London Book Company and Saeed Book Bank are on Arbob Rd near the PIA office. In Gilgit, GM Beg Sons book shops in Jamat Khana bazaar, and the Gilgit Serena Lodge, are an obligatory stop. In Skardu, Muhammad Abbas Kazmi has some books on Balti

history and culture at his Concordia Trekking Services shop.

NEWSPAPERS & MAGAZINES

Pakistan has 13 English-language dailies. *The News* (Karachi, Lahore and Rawalpindi) is the best. The *Frontier Post* (Peshawar) is not bad either. In Gilgit, English-language newspapers available are: the *Frontier Post* at GM Beg Sons book shops; and *Dawn* and *The Friday Times* at North News Agency in Madina Super market. In Chitral, *The News* and *The Pakistan Times* are sold by a shop near the telephone exchange.

WWF – Pakistan publishes *Natura*, a quarterly magazine. A good place to learn about Pakistani current affairs is the articulate monthly *Newsline*. In down-country book shops and top-end hotels, you can buy the *International Herald Tribune*, *Time*, *Newsweek*, *Asiaweek*, the *Far Eastern Economic Review*, and the *Economist*. *Le Monde* and *Le Figaro L'Aurore* are sold at the Marriott Hotel bookstore in Islamabad.

RADIO & TV

Radio and TV are state owned. Pakistan Broadcasting Corporation's national programming is mostly in Urdu, with some English and regional language programming. Pakistan TV (PTV) has two channels, and rebroadcasts some BBC and CNN programmes. A curious fact is that somewhere, someone is sitting with their finger on a censor button. Whenever BBC or CNN show an image deemed objectionable, such as a woman's bare shoulder or a man and woman embracing, the picture distorts until the 'naughty' bit is over.

Most hotels and guesthouses now have satellite-relayed CNN and BBC news, and Star TV. You can even find these in Chitral and the Northern Areas, at restaurants and hotels sprouting the now-ubiquitous satellite dish antennas. This uncensored programming is wildly popular, especially the racy Hindi videos on Zee TV. Bring a short-wave radio and listen to BBC World Service, Voice of America, or to your country's short-wave service to keep up on world news while trekking.

PHOTOGRAPHY
Film & Equipment
Western-brand colour-print film (much, but not all, of it quite fresh) and processing are available in cities. Processing in Islamabad costs about Rs 20 a roll, plus Rs 4 to Rs 5 per print. Colour-slide film (E6 process only, eg, Fujichrome, Agfachrome, Ektachrome) costs about Rs 200 for 36 frames. Kodachrome is scarce and cannot be processed in Pakistan. B&W film is rare and of doubtful quality, and costs more to process than colour. Posting exposed film from anywhere in Pakistan is asking for trouble; it is better to carry it out with you.

Choice of equipment is a personal matter, but an SLR camera with a mid-range zoom lens (eg, 35 to 135 mm) covers a wide range of situations. A good second lens to carry might be a 24 or 28 mm for panoramas and indoor shots. A 'skylite' filter protects the lens and cuts down on high-altitude UV glare. A polarising filter darkens the sky to avoid underexposing the landscape. A soft fill-flash eliminates shadows and keeps midday photographs of people from looking like they are wearing masks.

Photography
The best light for photography is at dawn and at dusk. Pay attention to the background when photographing people. Most built-in light meters underexpose a person's face if the background is bright sky. Cloudy days offer diffuse, soft light that gives surprisingly good results. A shaft of sunlight breaking through clouds and highlighting a mountain or glacier makes a dramatic image. Bracket exposures in unusual lighting situations.

Hazards
Heat, condensation, and dust or sand present hazards to film and equipment. If you line a stuff sack with a patch cut from an aluminised-mylar 'survival blanket', film stays cooler inside through the fiercest summer day. Camera batteries get sluggish in cold weather. Keep the camera inside your jacket and some spare batteries warm in your pocket. In very cold weather, avoid ruinous moisture on film and inside of the camera by putting them in plastic bags before going indoors or exposing them to warmer temperatures, and leave them until they have warmed. Keep everything bagged up, and carry a squeeze-bulb for blowing dust from inside the camera.

Restrictions
Prohibited subjects to photograph are military installations and equipment, airports, railway stations, major bridges.

Photographing People
When photographing, respect local residents' dignity and right to privacy. You should establish a friendly rapport, ask permission, and get their name and address so you can mail photos back to them. Letting people know you will do this may overcome their reluctance to be photographed and make friends. Photographing women is considered improper. Avoid paying people for taking their photo. This commercialises and cheapens cross-cultural interactions, allowing your economic power to dominate and overwhelm any cultural or personal reluctance to be photographed.

Airport Security
One dose of airport x-rays for inspecting carry-on bags should not harm slow or medium-speed films. However, the effects of x-rays are cumulative and too many may fog your pictures. Lead 'film-safe' pouches help, but the best solution is hand inspection. Officials usually hand-inspect film if you persist. This is crucial for high speed (ISO 1000) film. Having all your film in clear film canisters (instead of black ones) and all your film canisters in one or two larger clear plastic bags makes it easier. A customs regulation says you can bring in only one camera and five rolls of film, but foreigners routinely bring much more.

TIME

Pakistan has a single time zone, which is five hours ahead of UTC (GMT). Daylight saving time is not observed in Pakistan.

ELECTRICITY

Electricity is 220V, 50-cycle AC. 'Load-shedding', a periodic cut in power, is common in May and June down-country when the weather is hot and the reservoirs are low. Once the monsoon arrives, generating capacity usually returns to normal. Still, power cuts are common occurrences at any time in all cities and towns. In the mountains, rotating power outages are common in face of high demand and low generating capacity. Only a few locations, such as Hunza Proper, Khaibar in Gojal and Yasin in the Yasin Valley, have constant hydroelectric power. Most villages in the mountains rely on over-extended small-scale hydroelectric power or small, privately owned diesel generators.

LAUNDRY

On a trek and in villages, everyone does their own laundry. Laundry detergent is readily available, although none is biodegradable. In towns and cities, a *dhobi* (washer man) does laundry; ask at your hotel for details on this service.

WOMEN TREKKERS
Attitudes to Women

Most Muslim women stay out of sight (or at least out of reach) of other men, remaining in the house, behind the veil, in special sections of buses, and in the 'family' areas of restaurants. By the same token, most Muslim men also go out of their way to avoid direct contact with women outside their family. In some places (eg, the Tribal Areas of NWFP), such contact may bring a threat to their lives. That is why a foreign woman's questions, for example, are often answered to her male companion. It is not a sign of contempt, but of respect. Most Muslim men's views of 'other' women come largely from the media. To make matters worse, popular films full of full-hipped women, guns and violence inflame the sexuality suppressed by traditional culture. Younger Pakistani men rarely miss the chance to point out to Western women how sexually frustrated all men are and are constantly asked, 'Where is your husband?'

Paradoxically, women travellers are more likely to get a look into people's private lives. Women travellers have the benefit of speaking to both local men and women. Even in the most traditional areas, local women may invite you into their home, feed you, and show you around. Public areas (eg, at airports) often have separate waiting rooms or queues. Where they do not, women are expected to go straight to the head of the queue.

Safety Precautions

Women should not be deterred from trekking by fear of Islam or Muslim culture. We frequently meet women trekking here who are having a great time. By planning your trek carefully you can minimise any risk to your personal safety and increase your chances of having a positive experience.

The best advice we can offer is not to go

Reports from Women Trekkers

Once we met two experienced female mountaineers in Baltistan, who had been there previously. Having established contacts and previous experience, they felt confident enough to make arrangements and hire locals on their own. We also met a single woman who booked her trek directly with a trekking company in Pakistan that provided a guide, cook, trek crew, porters, food and equipment. In theory, any woman should have felt confident with these arrangements. Unfortunately, in this case, the guide relentlessly harassed the woman. Each night he persisted in giving reasons why he should sleep in her tent. This is absolutely inappropriate behaviour from a guide and an example of why women trekking alone are rare. ■

alone. In all the years we have been trekking in these mountains, we have never seen a lone female trekker (ie, backpacking on her own). The obvious alternative for women is to trek with a male partner or with a small group of male and female friends. Many women prefer to trek with a group organised by a tour operator abroad, which makes planning easy and provides security and comfort on the trail. We rarely encounter female trekkers who are not part of an organised trek or who were not accompanied by male friends.

Trying to understand how Pakistanis would think about a given situation will help you evaluate appropriate behaviour. A man who is unknown to you should not sit next to you. You can ask a man to move to another seat. If travelling alone, buy the seat next to you and refuse to allow any man to sit there.

It is definitely inappropriate for anyone to touch you for any reason. It helps to position yourself so that it would be difficult for a man to get close enough to you to touch you. A Western woman shaking hands with a local man is accepted. Often, a Western woman is simply ignored in social settings, even in cities. If you are outgoing and greet a local man by extending your hand, they usually respond politely and address you directly. In our experience, this has never been received negatively. Actual physical harassment is rare, but it does happen. If someone annoys or threatens you, don't hesitate to make a scene, particularly in public.

What to Wear

Conservative dress is very important. It would be difficult to overstate the sensitivity of this matter. Dressing in a culturally appropriate fashion shows respect and increases your own comfort level. Wear loose, long-sleeved, non-revealing shirts and full-length pants. Most Western-style pants still show the outline of the body, hence are not the best choice. Even loose skirts or dresses are not a good choice, unless they are ankle-length.

The shalwar kameez is practical in a hot climate and is culturally appropriate. This is the dress of choice for cities, towns, and villages. Get ones with buttons to close the

The *shalwar kameez* (local baggy pants and long skirt) are comfortable and practical for women to wear on a trek.

neck. A shalwar kameez can also be comfortable to wear while trekking, but this largely depends on the terrain and weather. Three style features make a difference: the length of the kameez; whether or not the sides of the kameez are slit; and the size of the opening of the legs of the shalwar. Many kameez are much too long (ie, well below the knees). This length is impractical where you might have to jump or take big steps. You can also step on the tail of a long kameez when standing up and trip yourself. Look for a kameez with side slits, so the front and back panels move independently. If the sides are not slit, it decreases mobility. The size of leg openings on men's shalwar are larger than women's. Larger openings enable you to pull the shalwar up over your knees, which is helpful when you have to ford streams. The legs of some shalwar are so voluminous that they can be hazardous on the trail, so select ones which will not trip you.

On glacier traverses and high pass crossings KO chooses not to wear a kameez.

Instead, she wears a shalwar (any baggy long pants would do), long-sleeved lightweight shirt (eg, capilene), and a baggy T-shirt over that (worn loose and not tucked in). It is not too stylish, but it is comfortable and functional. Regardless KO carries a shalwar kameez on every trek to wear when travelling to and from trail heads and towns, around villages, or in pastures. Local women feel more comfortable approaching Western women who are dressed appropriately, which is a visible sign that you are interested in local people's culture.

Chitral and Skardu are *purdah* bazaars, where local women are not allowed. Chitral is quite conservative and it is prudent to pay extra attention to your dress and behaviour. You may want to have a *dupatta* or scarf to cover your hair.

TREKKING WITH CHILDREN

LP's *Travel with Children* is a must for anyone planning to trek with children. We have met many travellers in the Karakoram and Hindukush who trekked with their children and had positive experiences. Parents should know their children's needs and abilities well. Select your route carefully and choose easier routes through villages and in valleys, avoiding ones that traverse difficult glaciers or cross high passes. Hiring a guide, cook, and porters to carry gear allows parents to turn their attention to their children, and to stop and explore interesting sights along the trail together. Hire a porter to carry children under eight years old who cannot walk a full day by themselves. Older children can walk most of a day, but still may need or want to be carried part of the way. Bring your own child-carrier and a child's bicycle helmet for routes where rock-fall danger is present. Be sure to protect your children from the harsh environment. Dress them in light-weight long-sleeved shirts and pants. Apply sunblock to all exposed skin, and have your child wear a wide-brimmed hat and sunglasses. Children are always welcomed and treated with respect and their presence opens many doors.

DANGERS & ANNOYANCES

Pakistanis are amazingly hospitable, straightforward, and honest. A few pitfalls exist for the unwary, however.

Violence

In recent years a combination of corrupt and incompetent police and bureaucrats, carte blanche passage for heavily armed Afghan guerrillas and a vigorous tribal arms industry has allowed sectarian, political and criminal violence to flourish. Some areas of the country are now simply too dangerous to visit and few middle or upper-class Pakistanis live without a gun at home. Hence, you have to make sensible choices about where to go. Be aware of the following areas:

Sind & Baluchistan Long-distance rail travel is unsafe, and when possible travel by air. A cycle of vicious political terrorism exists between Sindhis and Mohajirs (post-Partition immigrants from India) in Karachi and Hyderabad. The risk here is being caught in the crossfire in certain neighbourhoods. If you transit through Karachi, be very cautious even going into town from the airport. It is safest to stay at one of the several hotels near the airport.

Northwest Frontier Province (NWFP) In the Tribal Areas (eg, Malakand and Khyber Agency), Pakistani law has no force and the authorities are almost powerless to help you. In November 1994, radical Islamic groups forcibly brought their demand for total enforcement of Shariat Law (Quranic laws and courts) to Malakand, Swat, and Dir. If you travel off the main roads in these areas you should act and look like a sympathetic traveller in the Islamic world. Even wearing your watch on your left wrist is considered anti-Islamic by some factions! Men may be expected to have a full beard, but no moustache. Women should wear a *burqa* (the tent-like garment that covers the body from head to toe) in public.

It is easier to wander into trouble in Swat Kohistan or Indus Kohistan. Trekkers are advised to stay out of Darel, Tangir, and

Kandia valleys, where they may be unwelcome intruders. It is possible to visit the valleys in Kohistan, on the east side of the Indus River, but only accompanied by a local. Some night-time highway robbery happens in Hazara and Indus Kohistan, and on vehicles that travel the KKH after dark. Vehicles going between Mansehra and Shatial are commonly collected by police into escorted convoys.

Even celebrations can be dangerous. Pashtuns fire their weapons into the air on happy occasions, and the bullets have to fall somewhere. Peshawar residents instinctively move indoors when they hear a Pashtun wedding!

Northern Areas The Northern Areas is one of the safer parts of Pakistan. Sectarian and political (factional) conflicts occasionally arise. Tense times are the holy days at the end of Ramadan, the Prophet's birthday, the month of Muharram, and during political elections.

Drugs

Penalties for possession of drugs are stiff. Drug traffickers can receive the death penalty. Be wary of absolutely anyone who approaches you with drugs for sale. Some dealers, especially in Lahore and Peshawar, are in cahoots with the police, and will set you up in exchange for a cut of the fine or bribe. When you travel in the Pakhtun tribal areas or in Chitral's Yarkhun Valley, police may search you for hashish upon leaving.

Personal Safety & Theft

To people on marginal incomes the dollars and expensive baggage of foreigners can be hard to resist. But using common sense prevents most theft. Do not leave valuables in hotel rooms, and keep your money and passport on your person or in your line of sight always.

Looking After Valuables on a Trek While trekking, theft is almost unheard of. Still, do not leave your gear outside your tent at night, particularly your boots. As a rule, keep your valuables (ie, passport and money) in the backpack you carry and do not flash large wads of cash. When trekking with a guide or porters, ideally put your gear in a duffel bag and lock it.

Dogs In some villages in Baltistan, Chitral (including Broghil and the Kalash valleys) and Yasin, dogs are kept to reduce livestock depredation. These dogs are territorial so take extra caution when approaching or entering walled compounds. If approached by a growling dog, pick up and throw or pretend to throw a rock and they usually go away. A walking stick can come in useful too. Dogs are not kept in Hunza and Gojal.

BUSINESS HOURS

Friday is the Islamic day of rest. Most businesses are closed, though street sellers may be out. Shops are generally open from 9 or 10 am to at least 8 pm daily, except Friday. Banks are open 9 am to 1 pm Sunday to Thursday, and 9 to 11.30 am or noon Saturday. Post offices are usually open from 9 am to 2 pm Saturday to Wednesday, and on Thursday mornings. Government offices operate Sunday to Thursday, 8 am to at least 2.30 pm with closing times varying between offices. Private businesses are typically open 9 am to 1 pm and 2 to 5 pm, except on Friday and sometimes Thursday afternoons.

PUBLIC HOLIDAYS & HOLY DAYS
Public Holidays

Banks, businesses, and government offices are closed on these secular holidays except where noted:

- 23 March – Pakistan Day, celebrating the 1940 demand by the All-India Muslim League for an independent Muslim state (or, some say, the proclamation of the Pakistan republic in 1956)
- 1 May – International Labour Day
- 1 July – bank holiday only
- 14 August – Independence Day, the anniversary of the birth of Pakistan in 1947
- 6 September – Defence of Pakistan Day, commemorating the India-Pakistan War of 1965
- 11 September – *Urs*, the death anniversary of Mohammed Ali Jinnah, founder of Pakistan

9 November – Iqbal Day, honouring the poet Alama Mohammed Iqbal, who in 1930 first proposed a Muslim Pakistan

25 December – Birthday of Mohammed Ali Jinnah

31 December – bank holiday only

Holy Days

Many Islamic holy days are national holidays in Pakistan. The Islamic calendar is lunar, each month beginning with the new moon's first appearance. Religious officials have formal authority to declare the beginning of each lunar month, based on sightings of the moon's first crescent. Future holidays can be estimated, but are in doubt by a day or two until the start of that month. Holy days normally run from sunset until the next sunset. Sunni and Shia officials occasionally disagree by a day or more about when the first crescent appeared, and therefore about the start of holy days. Especially at major ones like the end of Ramadan and the Prophet's birthday, this can lead to sectarian tension, even violence. Dates listed below are approximate. Those marked with an asterisk (*) are also public holidays.

22 January to 22 February (1996), 12 January to 12 February (1997), 2 January to 2 February (1998), December 23 (1998) to January 23 (1999): *Ramadan* (pronounced 'Ramazan') is the month of total sunrise-to-sunset fasting (smoking is also forbidden), called *roza*. Children, pregnant women, the ill and infirm, non-Muslims, and Muslims who travel far from home are exempt from fasting though they are expected to not eat, drink, or smoke in front of those who are fasting. Most food shops and restaurants (except in tourist hotels and bus and train stations) are closed during daylight hours. The devout take meals in the evening and just before sunrise (in fact many Pakistanis eat more in this month than in any other). The voices of muezzins calling from nearby mosques signal the end of each day's fasting. Little gets done, tempers are short, and Pakistanis, with stomachs grumbling, are cranky and not much fun to be around. Rural people, despite loopholes for travellers and labourers, seem particularly strict about the fasting. The best places for non-Muslims to find food and drink are tourist hotels, railway restaurants and bus stations, and sometimes Chinese restaurants. Travellers can eat and smoke on trains, but not on buses. Even a non-fasting foreigner may be under stress, so pay attention to your nutrition.

Carry a water bottle and snacks, but be compassionate about eating or smoking around those who are not. If you are on trek, cook, eat, and camp in a discreet location away from villages.

22 February (1996), 11 February (1997), 31 January (1998), 20 January (1999)*: *Eid-ul-Fitr (Chhoti Eid* or Small Eid) is two or three days of celebrations marking the end of Ramadan when the new moon is sighted. This is the most joyous holiday in the Islamic world. Families visit, give gifts, enjoy banquets, get bonuses at work, and make donations to the poor.

30 April (1996), 19 April (1997), 8 April (1998), 28 March (1999)*: *Eid-ul-Azha (Bari Eid* or *Qurban)*, the Feast of Sacrifice, commemorates Abraham's promise to sacrifice his son. Those who can afford it sacrifice a goat or cow, sharing the meat with relatives and with the poor. Businesses and shops are usually closed for several days. This is also the season for *hajj* (pilgrimage to Mecca).

28 & 29 May (1996), 17 & 18 May (1997), 6 & 7 May (1998), 26 & 27 April (1999)*: *Ashura*, the 9th and 10th day of the month of Muharram, commemorates the martyrdom of Imam Hussain, grandson of the Prophet. Shias begin 40 days of mourning the death of Hussain at Karbala, Iraq. On the 10th day in trance-like processions, sometimes led by a riderless white horse, men and boys pound their chests and chant the names of those killed at Karbala. Some practise *zuljinnah*, flagellating themselves with blade-tipped chains. It is an awesome and bloody spectacle. Sunnis also mourn Hussain's death in a less dramatic way. In the Northern Areas especially, Sunni-Shia tension may be high at this time. It is advisable not to travel on the 10th day.

8 July (1996), 27 June (1997), 16 June (1998), 5 June (1999): *Chhelum* is 40 days after *Ashura*, with similar but smaller processions.

11 July: *Takht Nashin Sal Gira* is celebrated by the worldwide Ismaili community to commemorate the day the Aga Khan assumed the Imamate. A spectacular fire fall from the slopes above Hunza takes place in the evening. Most Ismaili villages also have festive celebrations.

29 July (1996), 18 July (1997), 7 July (1998), 27 June (1999)*: *Eid-Milad-ul-Nabi* celebrates the Prophet's birthday.

23 October: *Hunza Didar Sal Gira* commemorates the Aga Khan's visit to Hunza.

11 November: *Passu Didar Sal Gira* commemorates the Aga Khan's visit to Passu.

13 December: *Birthday Sal Gira* celebrates the Aga Khan's birthday, which is observed by Ismaili communities in the Northern Areas and Chitral.

Major Islamic religious observances that

may affect trekking include Ramadan, Eid-ul-Fitr, Eid-ul-Azha, and Muharram. Guides and porters may prefer to be with their families during these occasions.

Popular Cultural Festivals

21 March – *Nauroz* (New Days) is a Persian-origin spring festival popular in the north. Polo matches may be held in Gilgit. In smaller villages, people visit one another and sometimes enjoy listening to music and dancing. Celebrations may last several days.

4 to 8 July – The Shandur Pass (3800m) is a 20-km-long plateau with two lakes and two polo grounds. Teams from Chitral and Gilgit compete in an annual polo tournament that is a 'Woodstock of the Hindukush' with dynamite polo, folk dancing, and merry making. Dates may vary annually depending upon the attendance by VIP guests.

1 November – Northern Areas Independence Day or *Jashan-i-Gilgit* (Gilgit Festival) commemorates the 1947 uprising against the Maharajah of Kashmir with a week-long polo tournament.

See Kalash Valleys in the Chitral chapter for descriptions of Kalash festivals.

ACTIVITIES
You can easily combine cycling, rafting or kayaking, ski touring, fishing, and other adventure-related activities with treks in the Karakoram or Hindukush.

Cycling
The Karakoram Highway could almost have been invented for cyclists. It is a spectacular, but demanding trip from Islamabad to the Khunjerab Pass. While rarely level, it is paved in most places, at most times. Quite a few cyclists go up to the pass and back, and some ride to/from China, though most are urged to stow their bikes on the bus over the top. Others fly to Gilgit and ride up to the Khunjerab Pass. For more about the KKH, see LP's *Karakoram Highway, the high road to China – travel survival kit.*

Cyclists also ride the mostly unpaved jeep road from Gilgit to Chitral over the Shandur Pass. A harder ride than the KKH, cyclists tackling this need good brakes, front suspension, and a dust mask. Food and lodging are harder to find on this ride so cycles tend to be more heavily loaded. The road from Gilgit to Skardu, along the Indus River, is paved and has small hotels in the few oasis towns along the way. Cyclists have also ridden mountain bikes across the Deosai Plains in about five days. Pakistan has no restrictions on bringing a bike in for your own use, though you might be expected to note it on your visa application. Several tour operators abroad run cycling trips (see the Getting There & Away chapter), and Himalaya Nature Tours in Gilgit rents mountain bikes.

Rafting & Kayaking
Several NWFP and Northern Areas rivers are open for white-water rafting and kayaking. Runable rivers usually lie well below 3000m and are principally fed by snowmelt and rainfall. Class II to IV rivers are run commercially, though commercial rafting is still in its infancy. Rafting and kayaking require very different river flow. From mid-June to early September the rivers are swollen to flood stage. These raging waters are not well suited for rafting. Flow volume usually peaks in mid-July. Kayaking, however, is possible even during this summer flood stage. The best rafting season is from mid-September to late November, followed closely from April to mid-June. Below are some of the rivers that are being run. Put-ins and take-outs are given; we note differences for rafts and kayaks. The number of days given is for rafts; kayaks will be quicker.

Expert kayakers may be able to negotiate Class VI sections that rafts must avoid.

Chitral

Chitral River (Chitral bridge to Mirkhani – Class II to IV with one Class V above Ayun); big water and a strong glacial river in late May and early September

Laspur River (Sor Laspur to confluence with Mastuj River – Class IV and V); well suited to kayaks

Lutkho River (Murdan bridge to Chitral River – Class III to IV); a technical run, continuous at high water with no margin for error; best for rafting at medium levels, but overall more suited to kayaks. The river is muddy in May and June, and is best run in summer or autumn.

Gilgit

The Ishkoman and Gilgit rivers, with the upper Hunza River in Gojal, offer most potential for commercial rafting trips which are possible in summer, and combine well with treks in the area.

Hunza River (Sost to Passu – Class III to IV). This is a wonderful two to three day run, with a major jeep portage around the terminal debris of the Batura Glacier. It can easily be combined with a trek around Passu. Shorter day trips from Sost are also available. From 1 July to 31 August a two day/one night trip is feasible from Sost to Khaibar.

Hunza River (Passu to Gilgit – extreme Class VI). The Hunza River is the only river to bisect the entire Karakoram. It is choked with boulders and new landslides occur annually. Below Passu is an impossible section, and above and below Ganesh are dangerous Class VI. Only expert kayakers attempt this section of water. A two day/one night Class III to IV section from Passu to Gulmit is feasible from 1 July to 31 August.

Ishkoman River (Chatorkhand to Japūka below Singal on the Gilgit River – Class III to IV); two to three days. This can be run in summer and makes a great way to end a trek from the Naltar Valley over the Pakora Pass.

Ghizar and Gilgit rivers (Hundrup to Gilgit – Class III to V with several Class VI portages); six to eight days

Gilgit River (Gilgit to Bunji on the Indus River – Class III to IV); two days. Also possible for day trips – either Class III or V.

Indus River (Dubair for kayaks and Besham for rafts to Thakot in Indus Kohistan – Class V); powerful yet forgiving, this section of the Indus is one of the great river runs of the world.

Muzaffarabad

Kunhar River (Balakot to Jammu Rd – Class II to V);

two days. Above Balakot, the river is steep and difficult. From Naran to Kaghan is Class VI never before run. From Kaghan to Balakot is Class V+, radically altered by a 1992 flood. This river is better for kayaks.

Skardu

Braldu River (Baltoro glacier to Dassu – Class II to VI); the upper section is for expert kayakers only

Upper Indus River (Class V above Skardu)

Shigar River (Dassu to Skardu – Class III)

Shyok River (Khapalu to Gol – Class III to IV)

Swat

Swat River (Bahrain to Madyan – 11 km of continuous Class V at most levels and Madyan to Saidu Sharif – 20 km of Class V+ followed by 32 km of Class III); most suited to kayaks above Madyan. One and two day rafting trips are offered below Madyan.

Walji's Adventure Pakistan offers one to eight day rafting trips and combination rafting and trekking trips. Half-day, full-day, and overnight Class II to III trips cost about US$40 per person per day and can be booked locally in Walji's Gilgit office. They offer runs from Sost on the Hunza River during midsummer, which can also be booked in Walji's Karimabad office. Longer rafting trips and rafting trips combined with trekking cost about $80 per person per day. Trips are priced to include everything from guides and equipment, cooks and food, to life jackets and wetsuits. Their river guides have several years' experience and are highly trained by veteran US river guides.

Mountain Movers on Airport Rd in Gilgit rents kayaks. A few tour operators abroad offer rafting trips. More detailed information for independent rafters or kayakers is available from Michael Speaks, PO Box 97, Denali Park, AK 99755, USA.

Ski Touring

The large glaciers of the Karakoram, such as the Batura, Biafo, and Hispar, and the Deosai Plains attract adventurous wilderness skiers. March and April are the best months for these high-altitude traverses. This activity is only for highly skilled and experienced ski mountaineers.

Fishing

Since the beginning of this century, many of Pakistan's mountain rivers and lakes have been stocked with trout. World-record trout have been taken out of the Hundrup River in the Ghizar River valley. Popular reaches are in the Gilgit River basin (Singal, Kargah Nala, and Naltar), Astor Valley, Baltistan, Kaghan Valley, Swat, and Chitral. The season is from 10 March to 9 October. Information and licences (about US$2 per day for foreigners) are available at Fisheries offices in larger towns, and sometimes from wardens on the spot.

ACCOMMODATION

In towns throughout the region, basic accommodation is available at hotels, government resthouses, and hostels. Many also allow camping for a fee. Occasionally villagers welcome you into their homes. Away from towns, trekkers will be camping.

Hotels

Hotels are basic and range from a *charpoy*, a rope bed, without privacy, security or bedding to two and three-star hotels with a restaurant and private rooms with attached bathrooms. Most hotels do not have hot running water, but provide a bucket of hot water on request.

Government Resthouses

Most resthouses are run by the NWFP Communication & Works Department (C&W), the Northern Areas Public Works Department (NAPWD), or Forestry Districts. A booking (just a chit from a regional office to show the chowkidar) is usually necessary, but you can always drop by and take your chances.

Hostels

The Pakistan Youth Hostels Association (PYHA) (☎ 824866), Garden Rd (G-6/4), Islamabad, runs several hostels with gender-segregated dorms, and gardens where you can pitch a tent. IYHA lists many guesthouses throughout northern Pakistan as available to hostellers.

Bath Houses

Cities and towns, including Chitral, Gilgit, and Skardu, have *hammams* (bath houses). These male-only establishments are usually attached to a barber shop and identifiable by the rows of towels hanging outside. If your hotel does not have hot running water, the hammam is a good place to wash – a bucket of hot water costs a few rupees. Women should ask the hotelkeeper to provide a bucket of hot water in their hotel room.

FOOD

Pakistan has two main cuisines: the north Indian assortment of spicy and oily curries and the Central Asian oven-baked tandoori. Meat is the basic theme of Pakistani meals. Tuesday and Wednesday are 'meatless' days throughout the country when mutton and beef are not supposed to be sold or served in public places. Restaurants mostly serve chicken and fish then. Travel in Pakistan is taxing on vegetarians who can eat chapattis, yoghurt, lentils, rice, vegetables, eggs, dried fruit, and nuts. Muslims avoid handling or eating food with the left hand.

Most varieties of bread are made from unleavened wheat flour. No eatery in the land is without *chapattis*, flat rounds cooked on a dry griddle, which are used for grabbing, spooning or soaking up all the bits and juices. *Paratha* is flat and fried. It is commonly eaten for breakfast and sometimes has a vegetable filling. *Nan*, or tandoori *roti*, is a soft round or oblong baked bread with thick edges, wonderful when it is hot out of the tandoori oven. If you ask in Chitral, Hunza, Nagyr, or Gojal you can find several varieties of fine, dense whole-wheat bread, which makes good trail food. *Double roti* is Western-style sliced bread, made from processed flour.

Meat generically is called *gosht*. Mutton is *chota gosht* and beef is *bara gosht*. Chicken is called *murgi* and is not considered *gosht*. Pork is taboo for all Muslims. Among popular ways to cook meat and chicken are *tandoori* (marinated and baked), *tikka* (spiced and barbecued), and *karai* (braised with vegetables). *Qorma* is a braised meat curry in gravy. *Qofta* are lamb meatballs (or sometimes vegetable versions). *Qeema* is minced mutton or beef in a sauce. *Seekh kebabs* are minced mutton pieces barbecued on a skewer and *shami kebabs* are 'pancakes' of minced mutton and lentils.

Common vegetables *(sabzi)* are spinach, potatoes, cabbage, okra, and peas. The universal vegetarian dish is *dal* (lentils). Rice can be ordered steamed, or fried with vegetables or meat *biryani*. *Dahi* (plain yoghurt) or *raita* (curd with cumin and vegetable bits) is also served. Salad consists of sliced cucumber, tomato, and onion. Fresh fruit varies from mangoes, pomegranates, papayas, bananas and melons down-country to apricots, peaches, plums, apples, cherries, mulberries and grapes in the mountains. Nuts include peanuts, walnuts, almonds, pistachios and pecans. Apricot kernels are popular in the mountains.

Among common desserts are *kheer*, a milk and rice custard, and *kulfi*, an ice cream. Food shops dispense a variety of local and imported biscuits. Some sweet shops produce the deep-fried orange 'pretzels' called *jalebi*, which are made of flour and lots of sugar. Most common is *barfi*, which is made from dried milk solids.

Most hotels can produce a Western breakfast of fried or boiled eggs, toast and jam, sometimes porridge (oatmeal) or cornflakes, and tea or coffee. Better restaurants in down-country cities may also offer Afghan, Chinese or Middle Eastern dishes.

DRINKS
Nonalcoholic Drinks
Pakistanis drink a lot of tea. *Dudh-chai* (milky tea) is usually equal parts water, leaves, sugar and milk brought to a raging boil. In the mountains, tea is sometimes served salted. Chinese-style green tea is called *sabz-chai*. Except for at the top-end hotels, only instant coffee is available. *Lassi*, made from yoghurt and crushed ice and sometimes a pinch of salt, is popular and very refreshing. 'Freshlime' is a miraculous thirst quencher of crushed ice, salt, sugar, soda water and the juice of fresh limes.

Alcohol
Because Pakistan is an Islamic country, it is illegal for Muslims to drink alcohol. Non-Muslims are allowed to purchase alcohol if they obtain a liquor permit. A liquor permit is available for a nominal fee from some five-star hotels in major cities allowing you to drink in your room. When you stay in one city for a while, you can get a liquor permit for Rs 25 per month from city Excise & Tax offices entitling you to buy a monthly quota of alcohol. They also tell you where to buy it. Some offices may ask for a letter from PTDC. You need to bring your passport, photocopies of the front page of it and your Pakistani visa and entry stamp, and sign a form saying you are a non-Muslim. Bringing alcohol into Pakistan without prior permission is against the law. If you choose to do so and officials find any liquor, it may be confiscated and returned to you upon departure from Pakistan. Typically no penalties or fines apply.

Alcohol is legally produced at two places in Pakistan, the Murree Brewery in Rawalpindi and the Quetta Brewery in Quetta, which produce beer and several kinds of vodka, gin, rum, and whisky. Imported alcohol is unavailable. Liquor is not available in the NWFP or Northern Areas. In Hunza and Punial, some people still brew *mel*, a coarse grape wine, and a powerful mulberry brandy called *arak*. Local wine may also be found in Chitral.

THINGS TO BUY
The best big bazaars are in Peshawar (Old City), Lahore (Anarkali), Rawalpindi (Raja) and Karachi (Empress market). Outside Peshawar is the Karkhand smugglers' bazaar with over 4000 shops, where everything is available at 15 to 50% less than elsewhere in Pakistan. Islamabad's Juma bazaar comes to life on Friday as a huge handicraft market. The tourist shops have expensive carpets, brasswork, jewellery, Kashmiri shawls, carvings and antiques. Be careful of private dealers in gemstones and in artefacts such as coins; those who know say many are fake.

The hand-loomed wool cloth *(patoo)*, out of which the distinctive men's hats worn in the Northern Areas and Chitral are made, can be tailored into a warm jacket or vest.

Trekking Information

APPROACH TO TREKKING

All treks described in this guidebook can be undertaken by any physically fit person who is experienced in mountain walking. Trekking in the Karakoram and Hindukush is more aptly characterised as cross-country trekking rather than as trail hiking. As a trekking route wends up and over a pass, the trail often becomes faint and hard to find. Occasionally, crossing a pass may involve a scramble over loose scree and rock. For most trekkers, attempting such crossings without a local guide would be an ill-advised risk. When travelling over a glacier, you need to have prior experience with glacier travel, rope technique, and crevasse rescue (see Glacier Travel later in this chapter). Although these basic alpine techniques are necessary on many treks, you do not need to be a climber to trek through the Karakoram and Hindukush. Many qualified, trained guides can safely see you across difficult sections. They can demonstrate and let you practice any technique necessary. Except for a few treks through heavily glaciated regions, such as the Biafo and Hispar glaciers and the Gondogoro La, you are usually only on such terrain for one day at a time. The rest of the treks are along visible trails, through meadows and pastures.

Trekking is a physically and mentally taxing way of travelling. Day after day, one walks for hours, often going up and down several thousand metres every day. In order not to turn the trek into a gruelling endurance contest, you need to cultivate an easy-going attitude. During the first few days, when you are just getting used to life on trek, you should not try to push yourself. Plan short walking days when starting. In the Karakoram and Hindukush, where the scale is enormous, getting there first is not the most important thing. Pace yourself and stop for rests whenever you need them. Do not endanger yourself or others by pushing yourself too far. The climate is arid, so drink plenty of water, and, when you reach camp, eat well. Being physically and mentally prepared for an extended period of mountain travel means being prepared to take care of yourself. You should not rely on others to get you out of trouble. In these mountains, it is not possible to radio for a helicopter once you are trekking (see Rescue & Evacuation in the Health, Safety & First Aid chapter).

While trekking, promote mountain safety by following a few basic rules: don't trek alone; don't hike too high too fast; be law-abiding, do not trek in restricted areas without a permit; do not go higher than the 6000m limit set by the authorities; and register your name with your embassy or consulate before your trek.

Whatever type of trekking you choose, always follow the basic policy of taking only pictures and leaving only footprints. Leave your camp cleaner than you found it. Much of the Karakoram and Hindukush is still 'clean', unpolluted wilderness; make sure it is like this for those who come after you.

Make your trek an enjoyable experience. Take time to look at the mountains and sit amid the flowers. If your itinerary is leisurely, you can have opportunities to explore an interesting side valley or to spend a little more time in summer pastures. Take time to get to know your companions, whether fellow compatriots or local residents.

PERMITS & FORMALITIES
Regulations

The Tourism Division of the Government of Pakistan's Ministry of Sports & Tourism regulates trekking. The Tourism Division considers any walking below 6000m as trekking and above 6000m as mountaineering, each of which has its own regulations. They publish *Trekking Rules and Regulations* and *Mountaineering Rules and Regulations*, brochures available at the following offices.

Deputy Chief of Operations, Tourism Division (☎ 820856 and 827015), F-7/2, 13-T/U Commercial Area, Rm 8, Islamabad, at the south-west end of Jinnah market – open Sunday to Thursday from 9 am to 1 pm and 2 to 5 pm.

PTDC Tourist Information Centres in Islamabad (☎ 816932) are in F-7/2 adjacent to the Tourism Division and in Rawalpindi (☎ 517073) at the Flashman's Hotel – open Saturday to Thursday from 8 am to 2.30 pm and 3.15 to 3.45 pm.

Request an accompanying information sheet listing the maximum porter wages by region (see Guides & Porters – Wages in this chapter).

The *Trekking Rules and Regulations* details the permit process and fees, the duties of the licensed mountain guide and porters, insurance requirements, and equipment and rations you must provide them. Rules about payment of porters' wages and transport, the import and export of equipment, foreign exchange, and photography are described. There are guidelines for providing medical treatment and for dealing with accidents.

The appendices include a 'List of the Treks Approved by the Government'. Each approved trek on this list has a serial number, lists place names along the approved route, and is classified into a zone. These treks are called 'specified treks' despite the zone in which they lie. Any trek not on this list is called an 'unspecified trek'. Unless you suspect an 'unspecified trek' is in a restricted or closed zone, you can usually assume it is in an open zone and go there. However, the Tourism Division considers applications for unspecified treks, and notifies you if permission is granted or not within 15 days upon receipt of a completed application and a map detailing your proposed route. If permission is granted, a liaison officer usually accompanies the party. The list of approved treks changes; a new trek may appear, an old trek may disappear, or the zone in which a trek is classified may change. At the time of writing, the *Trekking Rules and Regulations* were being updated by the Tourism Division, so check the status of any trek with the Tourism Division before planning your trek. Climbing expeditions must consult the *Mountaineering Rules and Regulations* for guidelines about permits and fees for peaks over 6000m.

Zones

The Tourism Division has designated three zones for trekking: open, restricted, and closed. Know what type of zone you are trekking through to avoid any conflict with local authorities.

Open Zones Foreigners are allowed to trek anywhere in open zones up to 6000m without a permit or guide. Since the arrangements and route are up to you, these are the least expensive zones in which to trek.

Restricted Zones Foreigners are allowed to trek in restricted zones up to 6000m, but are required to pay a fee and obtain a permit, hire a licensed mountain guide, insure the guide and each porter, attend mandatory briefing and debriefing meetings at the Tourism Division in Islamabad, and register at check posts along these routes.

In order to complete the permit application you need to know the serial number of the trek, the start date and length of the trek, the name of your licensed mountain guide and his government registration number, and the number of porters you will engage. You must obtain a personal accident insurance policy for the guide and porters (see Guides & Porters). You must also deposit a fee of US$20 per (each non-Pakistani) person per trek directly into the Tourism Division's account at the National Bank of Pakistan. Then you submit the bank receipt for the same along with the insurance policy, and six copies of your completed application form with one passport-sized photo per person per trek to the Tourism Division.

The Tourism Division can help you in this process. However, it is easiest to work with a government-approved trekking company. They can provide a licensed mountain guide, collect the insurance premium and prepare the policy, collect and deposit the permit fee, and submit a letter of request to the Tourism Division along with the application. Permits for a specified trek in a restricted zone are, in theory, issued within 24 hours of receipt of the completed application.

The trekking party then contacts the Tourism Division, which sets meeting dates and times for the briefing before and the debriefing after a trek. Supposedly, meetings can be scheduled within 24 hours excluding Fridays and holidays. Every member of the trekking party and the licensed mountain guide are required to attend both of these meetings.

Trekking in a restricted zone is significantly more expensive than in an open zone and requires considerable planning. When arranging yourself, allow four to six days in Islamabad upon arrival to complete the tedious formalities. You can reduce this time if you hire a trekking company to make some of these arrangements in advance of your arrival in Pakistan. When you book a trek through a tour operator abroad, they handle these formalities, but you are still required to attend briefing and debriefing meetings.

Closed Zones Foreigners are prohibited in closed zones. In theory, closed zones include areas within 48 km of the Afghan border and within 16 km of the Line of Control with Indian-held Kashmir. It may be possible to get a permit for a closed zone with high-level connections, but even so you could be turned back by local authorities.

INFORMATION SOURCES

You can contact trekking companies in Pakistan and tourist offices in Pakistan and abroad (see General Information – Tourist Offices) as you plan your trek.

Trekking Companies

Trekking companies can arrange a trek ahead of or upon your arrival in Pakistan. Most trekking companies have more than one office: an office in Islamabad or Rawalpindi and branches offices in Chitral, Gilgit, Karimabad, and/or Skardu. To contact a trekking company with multiple offices, send letters, faxes, or telexes to offices in Islamabad or Rawalpindi. Most arrangements can be made once you arrive in Pakistan at any office. An alphabetised list of reputable companies by city follows: street addresses follow mailing addresses if they are different. (Also see Tour Operators Abroad in the Getting There & Away chapter.)

Islamabad & Rawalpindi

Adventure Tours Pakistan, PO Box 1780, Islamabad; G-9/1, St 53, House 551 (☎ 252759, 260820-1; fax 252145; telex 54484 TOURS PK). Owned by the first Pakistani summiteer of K2, Ashraf Aman, it specialises in expeditions and budget treks to Baltistan, Chapursan, Broghil, and Chitral.

Adventure Travel, S Malik, PO Box 2062, Islamabad; 15 Wali Centre, 86 South Blue Area (☎ 272490; fax 214580; telex 54539; internet:snmalik@adventure.sdnpk.undp.org)

Baltistan Tours, PO Box 1285, Islamabad (☎ 270338; fax 278620; telex 5811 NAIBA PK). Owner Mohammad Iqbal is from Khapalu and has over 10 years' experience guiding and outfitting treks in the Baltoro region and Hushe Valley.

Concordia Tours & Trekking Services, Haji Ahmad Khan, 35 Chughtai Plaza, 1st Mezzanine, West Blue Area, Islamabad (☎ 223849; fax 823351)

Expedition Pakistan, 16 Saeed Plaza, Blue Area, Islamabad (☎ 811457; fax 811457; telex 5537 PT PK)

Himalaya Nature Tours Pakistan, Asif Khan, F-7/1, St 45, House 5, Islamabad (☎ 811478; fax 811478); specialises in the Northern Areas

Himalaya Treks & Tours (Pvt) Ltd, Mohammad Ali Changazi, PO Box 918, Rawalpindi; 112 Rahim Plaza, Murree Rd (☎ 563014 and 515371; fax 563014). Changazi has over 15 years' trekking experience and specialises in his native Baltistan.

Hindukush Trails, Maqsood ul Mulk, F-6/1, St 28, House 37, Islamabad (☎ 821576 and 277067; fax 275031 and 217067; telex 54650 TRAIL PK); the only choice for an experienced, quality-conscious trekking company for Chitral-based treks.

Indus Guides, 7-E Egerton Rd, Lahore (☎ 304190-96; fax 872529; telex 44344 DEENS PK)

Karakorum Explorers, Mubarak Hussain, PO Box 2994, Islamabad; I-10/1, St 90, House 1295 (☎ 441258; fax 442127; telex 5811 CSCIB PK and 5945 CSCIB PK)

Karakurum Treks & Tours NA (Pvt) Ltd, PO Box 2803, Islamabad; F-7/2, St 19, 1 Baltoro House (☎ 829120; fax 271996; telex 54480 MIRZA PK). Started in 1979 by the late Nasir Abbas Mirza and now run by his son, Anchan Ali Mirza, specialises in Baltistan.

Mountain Movers, Musarat Wali Khan, PO Box 985, Rawalpindi (☎ 470519; fax 470518; telex 5948 and 5949 at 982)

Mountain Travels Pakistan, Ghulam Abbas, PO Box 2014, Islamabad; F-7/2, St 22, House 1-A (☎ 264213; fax 260469)

Nazir Sabir Expeditions, PO Box 1442, Islamabad; G-9/1, St 52, House 487 (☎ 252580 and 252553; fax 250293; telex 54627 K2 PK). Owner Nazir Sabir was the first Pakistani mountaineer to summit four 8000m peaks. They specialise in treks and expeditions throughout Hunza, Baltistan, and Nagyr.

Sitara Travel Consultants (Pvt) Ltd, Sitara House, 232 Khadim Hussain Rd; PO Box 63, Rawalpindi (☎ 564750-1, and 566272; fax 584958; telex 5751 STARA PK). One of the largest travel agencies in Pakistan, they specialise in treks to Baltistan, Hunza, and Nanga Parbat.

Trans Asian Tours, PO Box 2914, Islamabad (☎ 859367; fax 822313). This small company is owned and run by an experienced mountain guide, Ashraf Khan, from Ghulkin and outfits treks throughout Hunza, Gojal, and Baltistan.

Trans-Pakistan Adventure Services (Pvt) Ltd, PO Box 2103, Islamabad; Muzaffar Chambers, Plot 82, Apt 8, 2nd floor, Blue Area (☎ 274796; fax 213426; telex 5811 NAIBA PK and 5945 CTO IB PK)

Walji's Adventure Pakistan, Iqbal Walji, PO Box 1088, Islamabad; Walji's Building, 10 Khayaban-e-Suhrawardy (☎ 820908 and 270745-8; fax 270753; telex 5769 WALJI PK). This is the oldest travel agency in Pakistan with over 30 years' experience. Their staff includes some of the most experienced mountain and rafting guides in Pakistan.

Chitral

Hindukush Trails, Mountain Inn, Chitral (☎ 2112)

Gilgit

Adventure Center Pakistan (Pvt) Ltd, PO Box 516, Gilgit; Colonel Hassan market (☎ 2409; fax 3695; Internet: ikram@acp-glt.sdnpk.undp.org). Ikram Beg, son of the late GM Beg, runs this small company that specialises in treks around Gilgit and in Hunza.

Adventure Tours Pakistan, Airport Rd, Gilgit (☎ 2663)

Adventure Travel, PO Box 597, Gilgit; 3 Wali House, Khomer, Jutial, Gilgit

Concordia Tours & Trekking Services, NLI Chowk, Gilgit (☎ 3739)

Himalaya Nature Tours Pakistan, Chinar Bagh Link Rd, Gilgit (☎ 2946)

Karakurum Treks & Tours NA (Pvt) Ltd, Airport Rd, Gilgit (☎ 2753)

Mountain Movers, PO Box 534, Gilgit; Airport Rd (☎ 2967; fax 2525)

Pamir Tours, Zia Ullah Beg, PO Box 545, Gilgit; JSR Plaza (☎ 3939; fax 2475)

Nazir Sabir Expeditions, Gilgit (☎ 2562 and 2650; fax 2525)

Sitara Travel Consultants, Airport Rd, Gilgit

Trans Asian Tours, Chinar Bagh Link Rd, Gilgit (☎ 3419)

Trans-Pakistan Adventure Services (Pvt) Ltd, PO Box 525, Gilgit; Chinar Bagh Link Rd

Walji's Adventure Pakistan, PO Box 515, Gilgit; Airport Rd (☎ 2665; fax 2665)

Hunza Proper

Concordia Expeditions Pakistan, Karimabad (☎ (47) 010)

Karakorum Explorers, Ganesh (☎ (47) 073)

Nazir Sabir Expeditions, Aliabad (☎ (45) 048)

Walji's Adventure Pakistan, Karimabad (☎ (47) 045)

Skardu

Baltistan Tours, PO Box 604, Skardu; Satellite Town (☎ 2626; fax 2108)

Concordia Trekking Services, Syed Abbas Kazmi, PO Box 626, Skardu (☎ 3440)

Concordia Tours & Trekking Services, Naya bazaar, Skardu (☎ 2947)

Himalaya Treks & Tours (Pvt) Ltd, College Rd, Skardu (☎ 2528)

Karakurum Treks & Tours, Link Rd, Satellite Town, Skardu (☎ 2856)

Mountain Travels Pakistan, PO Box 621, Skardu; Satellite Town (☎ 2750)

Nazir Sabir Expeditions, Airport Rd, Skardu (☎ 3346)

Siachen Travels & Tours, Rozi Ali and Ghulam Ali, PO Box 622, Skardu (☎ 2649 and 2844); Rozi Ali of Hushe was Reinhold Messner's cook

Walji's Adventure Pakistan, College Rd, Skardu (☎ 3468)

Other Sources of Information

The Alpine Club of Pakistan (☎ (051) 562887), 509 Kashmir Rd, Rawalpindi, operates a Mountaineering Centre in Naltar, where they train and certify mountain guides.

Adventure Foundation of Pakistan (☎ (05921) 5526), No 1 Gulistan Colony, College Rd, Abbottabad, founded by retired Brigadier Jan Nadir Khan, promotes special-skills training and Outward-bound-style adventures for young Pakistanis. Though not a trekking company, it can arrange small-group mountaineering, trekking, white-water rafting, winter skiing and even hot-air ballooning trips for student groups and anyone able to contact them several months in advance. They also train mountain guides.

District Forestry Officer (DFO) – Wildlife, Chitral (☎ 2101) is in charge of Chitral Gol National Park, and all wildlife sanctuaries and game reserves in Chitral. Its office can give you names of game watchers who reside in or close to protected areas and are willing to work as guides.

TREKKING ROUTES

The trekking chapters contain over 65 detailed route descriptions and over 55 other routes. It is impossible to describe every trek through these mountains and we do not attempt to do so. Nor do we include every detail along the way or provide self-guiding route descriptions. You always need to rely on local knowledge and have basic routefinding ability. We do not describe routes on jeep roads unless a high probability exists that you will have to walk over that section of road. Most trekkers will select one of the routes described here. Your choice will depend upon the season, length of time you want to trek, and the route's difficulty.

We do not describe any routes in closed zones (at the time of writing). Nor do we include routes in the notoriously dangerous valleys of Indus Kohistan. Some trekkers may go to these and other valleys, but most would be ill-advised to attempt to do so.

Level of Difficulty

We offer a general relative grading of the treks based on our subjective impressions. This is simply a general guide to help you pick suitable treks. Please read the route descriptions carefully before setting out. We specify any significant difficulties and objective dangers. We mention when a route crosses scree or talus slopes, glaciated passes or traverses any glaciers or crevasse fields, and if any mountaineering experience and equipment is needed. For routes over glaciated passes, we give the angle of snow slopes

and point out any danger of avalanche, crevasses, or cornices. Being both mentally and physically prepared for the trail conditions best enables you to enjoy the beauty, isolation, and sheer immensity of the Karakoram and Hindukush. A trek done fast can seem harder than one done slowly, and adverse weather can make relatively easy routes difficult.

No recognised standard scale of grading for trekking exists as it does for climbing. A further difficulty of grading treks which cross glaciers or glaciated passes is that conditions change during each season and from year to year. Hence, no standard grading for such treks is possible. In the US, the Yosemite Decimal System (YDS), devised by the Sierra Club and based on the German Welzenbach system, gives four classes below the level at which technical climbing with ropes and belays begin. These correspond to the first four grades of the Australian system, and to grades I to minus III (ie, -III) of the Union Internationale des Associations d'Alpinisme (UIAA) system. Whenever a trek involves difficulties greater than YDS, UIAA, or Australian Class I, we describe the nature of the difficult section and give a class rating.

Times & Distances

We give the number of days or a range of days to cover each route. Optional side trips are also described in numbers of days. It is best to think in terms of days and not hours. Most trekking days involve six to eight hours of walking; some days will be longer, some shorter. The days we describe are realistic for most trekkers and allow for varying paces, photography, rest and lunch stops, and enjoying the scenery along the way. A fit trekker or one with limited time may do a trek more quickly than someone who walks more leisurely or takes a day hike.

Walking times, when given, are based on our 'moderate' pace. However, since everyone walks at their own pace, these times may not reflect your actual walking time. We chose to provide walking times for a few reasons. Clear water is rarely abundant on most routes and it is important to know how long it might take you to reach your next water source. The only camp sites on glacier traverses can be several hours apart, so it helps to know approximate times to avoid having an unplanned or undesirable camp site. You infrequently meet local people on many routes and when you meet them, they happily may tell you how long it takes to

TREKKING STANDARDS

Section Name	Trek Name	When to Trek	Days	Grading
Chitral				
Kalash valleys	Birir to Bumboret	mid-Apr to mid-Oct	1	B
Kalash valleys	Bumboret to Rumbur	mid-Apr to mid-Oct	2	B
Kalash valleys	Rumbur to Chimirsan An & Chitral Gol	July to Sept	2	B
Chitral Gol National Park	Chaghbini to Kasavir	Apr to Oct	2	A
Chitral Gol National Park	Chaghbini to Gokhshal & Chimirsan An	July to Sept	2	B
Shishi & Golen valleys	Shishi Valley & Lohigal An	July to mid-Sept	3	B+
Shishi & Golen valleys	Golen Gol & Phargam An	mid-July to mid-Sept	4	C+
Shishi & Golen valleys	Roghili Gol	mid-June to Sept	1-3	B
Lutkho Valley	Agram Gol & Besti Gol	July to mid-Sept	3-4	C+
Lutkho Valley	Owir An	mid-June to mid-Sept	2-3	B
Turikho Valley	Zani An	late Apr to Oct	1	B
Turikho Valley	Tirich Mir Base Camp	mid-June to mid-Sept	6	B+
Turikho Valley	Shah Jinali An	mid-June to mid-Sept	4	B+
Turikho Valley	Khot An	mid-June to mid-Sept	2-3	B
Turikho Valley	Hindu Raj Crest	July to early Sept	3-5	D
Upper Yarkhun Valley	Sholkuch to Broghil & Karambar An	July to Sept	7	B
Upper Yarkhun Valley	Darkot An	June to Sept	2-3	D
Laspur Valley & Bashqar Gol	Kachakani An	July to Sept	6	D
Ghizar				
Upper Ghizar River Valley	Chumarkhan Pass	July to Sept	2	B
Upper Ghizar River Valley	Dadarelli An	July to Sept	6	D
Upper Ghizar River Valley	Zagaro An	July to Aug	3-6	D
Yasin Valley	Thui An	July to mid-Sept	5-6	C
Yasin Valley	Naz Bar An	July to Aug	3-4	D
Yasin Valley	Punji Pass	July to Sept	4	C
Ishkoman Valley	Karambar Valley, lakes & Pass	June to Sept	5	C
Ishkoman Valley	Asumbar Haghost	July to Sept	4	B
Gilgit, Diamir & Kaghan Valley				
Bagrot & Haramosh valleys	Diran Base Camp	mid-June to Sept	4	B+
Bagrot & Haramosh valleys	Rakhan Gali	mid-June to mid-Sept	3-4	C
Bagrot & Haramosh valleys	Kutwal Lake	mid-June to Sept	6	A+
Nanga Parbat	Fairy Meadows	May to mid-Oct	3-6	A+
Nanga Parbat	Rupal Valley	June to Oct	5	B
Nanga Parbat	Around Nanga Parbat via Mazeno La	mid-June to Sept	8-12	E
Kaghan Valley to Indus River	Lake Saiful Mulk	mid-June to Sept	1-2	A
Kaghan Valley to Indus River	Babusar Pass	mid-June to Sept	4-6	A
Hunza River Valley				
Naltar & Pakora valleys	Pakora Pass	July to Sept	5	B+
Naltar & Pakora valleys	Daintar Pass	July to Sept	4-5	B+
Nagyr	Bar Valley	mid-June to Oct	3-8	B
Nagyr	Minapin Glacier	July to Sept	5	B
Nagyr	Barpu Glacier	mid-June to Oct	6	B+
Nagyr	Rush Phari	mid-June to Sept	3	B+

reach somewhere; however, their walking times are likely to be two or three times faster than you or we would walk.

Approximate distances are given in km on some routes. While it is easy to judge dis-tances from maps, it is almost impossible to determine how far you actually walk taking into account elevation gain and loss, twists and turns on trails, or manoeuvring through crevasse fields on a glacier. Most people

TREKKING STANDARDS

Section Name	Trek Name	When to Trek	Days	Grading
Hunza River Valley (continued)				
Hunza	Hassanabad Nala – Muchutshil Glacier	June to Oct	4-6	C
Hunza	Hassanabad Nala – Shishpar Glacier	June to Oct	4-6	C
Hunza	Ultar Nala	May to Oct	1-3	A+
Gojal	Yunz Valley	Apr to Oct	1	A
Gojal	Adbegar	Apr to Oct	2	A+
Gojal	Patundas & Borit Sar	May to Oct	3	C
Gojal	Batura Glacier	May to Oct	5-10	B+
Gojal	Werthum Nala to Lupgar Valley	mid-July to Sept	2-5	D
Gojal	Passu to Shimshal Village	Apr to Oct	2-3	B+
Gojal	Shimshal Pamir	late May to early Oct	8	C+
Gojal	Boesam Pass, Ghujerab Valley & Chapchingol Pass	June to Sept	7	D
Gojal	Boiber Valley	mid-June to Sept	3	B
Gojal	Lupgar Pir Pass & Valley	June to late Sept	6	C+
Gojal	Chilinji An	June to Sept	6	D+
Baltistan				
Basha, Tormik & Stak valleys	Chogo Lungma Glacier	late June to early Sept	5	C
Basha, Tormik & Stak valleys	Laila Base Camp & Haramosh La	late June to early Sept	10	E
Deosai Mountains & Plains	Burji La	mid-June to mid-Oct	3	B+
Biafo, Hispar & Baltoro glaciers	Biafo-Hispar Traverse	June to Sept	12	E
Biafo, Hispar & Baltoro glaciers	Askole to Concordia	June to Sept	15	D
Biafo, Hispar & Baltoro glaciers	Concordia to Hushe via Gondogoro La	late June to Aug	5	E+
Shyok & Hushe valleys	Thalle La & Tusserpo La	mid-June to mid-Sept	3-4	B
Shyok & Hushe valleys	Masherbrum Base Camp	June to Sept	5-6	B
Shyok & Hushe valleys	Gondogoro Valley	July to Sept	9	C
Shyok & Hushe valleys	Hushe to Concordia via Gondogoro La	late June to Aug	8	E+
Shyok & Hushe valleys	K7 Base Camp	July to Sept	5	B

Grade A Trekking on trails below 3500m possibly with moderate elevation changes, usually for two to three days, no glacier or pass crossings

Grade B Trekking on trails usually for no more than one week, significant elevation change usually crossing a pass under 4500m, short (a day or less) or optional glacier crossings (non-technical)

Grade C Trekking mostly on trails often for more than a week, some routefinding necessary, pass crossings with significant elevation change usually under 5000m or longer glacier crossings (non-technical)

Grade D Trekking over rugged terrain, a longer and more committed route where routefinding is required, with glaciated or difficult pass crossings usually under 5000m, usually involving several days of glacier travel, technical skills recommended for safety

Grade E Trekking for several days on rugged terrain over 4500m, serious commitment is required, crossing a glaciated pass over 5000m, extended glacial travel, technical skills needed for safety and to complete the route

+ indicates a trek with features more challenging compared with other treks in the same category

walk from two to three km per hour in the mountains, or about 10 to 15 km per day.

Maps

The maps in this guidebook are intended for planning purposes only. They should never be used by themselves to guide you on any trek and are no substitute for detailed maps brought from home. These maps show some orographic features, but not topographic features. See General Information – Maps earlier in this chapter for a list of available trekking maps. We recommend maps under Information – Maps in each section of the trekking chapters.

Altitude Measurements

The elevations we provide are composites, based on our readings using an altimeter and the Trimble Scout hand-held Global Positioning System (GPS) device. Existing published map altitudes not infrequently were estimated by early British explorers, and therefore tend to be inaccurate. We cannot claim that the elevations we provide are absolutely precise, but feel they represent elevations more accurately than existing maps. Altimeter readings vary with atmospheric pressure and temperature, and we have adjusted these readings accordingly. GPS readings also have a built-in degradation of precision, which we have allowed for by taking averaged readings. However, GPS technology is only accurate to within 100m. The best use of these elevations is to determine elevation gain or loss over a stretch of trail, not to determine whether you have cracked the 5000m mark.

Change

Change is coming quickly to the Karakoram and Hindukush, particularly in the infrastructure and the amount and variety of goods available in villages. Most villages are now reached via a jeep road. In some valleys, such as the Yarkhun and Rich in Chitral, the roads seems to lengthen a bit each year. In a few years, the existing trail heads may be changed. Eventually, all villages, even remote Shimshal, will be reachable by jeep.

Electricity comes with roads, as the hydroelectric generation capacity of the area is developed, as well as increased opportunity for work outside the village. As men leave villages for employment, the labour available for maintaining large herds in the high pastures inevitably declines. Pastures may even get greener as the grazing pressure decreases.

Place Names & Terminology

Some place names given in this guidebook, especially for places other than cities, towns, and villages, differ from those given on the available trekking maps. We detail these in the Map Notes section for each trek. Errors in place names on some maps occurred for a few reasons: some early explorers' guides were not native speakers of the language in the area where they went; mistakes were made in transliterating place names from local languages to English; and some names were made up.

We have paid particular attention to the accurate recording of both the place names and their meanings in that particular local language. Because the many languages of northern Pakistan have sounds unknown in English or other languages, attempts to render local names in English inevitably fall short. Because place names also provide information about the significance of a location for the people, we think it is important to include that as well (eg, *yarzeen* means the place where juniper grows). Distortions through inaccurate renditions corrupt such meanings and are resented by the local populations. For example, two place names on the Baltoro Glacier are Muztagh Pass and Muztagh Tower; *muztagh* means ice place. On some recent Pakistani maps, Muztagh has been inaccurately replaced by Mushtaq, an Arabic word and common male name. We want to avoid the dilution and loss of local values through such chauvinistic distortions of place names. Because so many languages are spoken, many terms exist for trail features such as 'pass', 'valley' or 'stream'. For example, pass is *la* in Balti, *haghost* in Burushashki, *an* in Khowar, *gali* in Shina, and *uween* in Wakhi. We give place names in local terminology, and avoid the redundancy of adding the English term. Thus we prefer the 'Burji La' rather than 'Burji La Pass'.

We use 'trail' when we mean a visible path you can follow and 'route' when cross-country walking is required.

GUIDES & PORTERS

When you hire a guide and/or porters, you need to understand the details outlined in the Tourism Division's *Trekking Rules and Regulations* (see Permits & Formalities). Guides and porters are savvy and surprisingly well informed about these. Familiarise yourself with this information before you hire anyone. When your trek is being handled by a trekking company or a tour operator abroad, they arrange for a guide and porters. Guides and porters are always men; women do not do this type of work for social and cultural reasons. The majority of trekkers hire at least one local person to help them navigate through the rugged Karakoram and Hindukush.

Guides

Guides usually speak English, may know other non-Pakistani languages, and are familiar with the needs of Westerners. Most are employed by trekking companies, some run their own trekking companies, and others work as freelance guides. The Tourism Division licences guides and assigns a registration number to each guide, thus entitling them to work as mountain guides. The fact that the Tourism Division has cleared a guide for handling trekking parties does not mean that a guide has any specific training. Ask any prospective guide if he is licensed and if he has completed any training courses. A licensed mountain guide is required for restricted-zone treks (see Permits & Formalities in this chapter). All worthwhile guides can show you letters of recommendation from past trekkers.

A competent guide is well informed, good-natured, knows the route, and knows where to locate water and where to camp. A guide should also know the use of ropes, crampons, and ice axe, glacial travel, and crevasse rescue. A guide also hires and supervises porters, buys provisions, and arranges transportation. Guides usually have their own cook and they work together as a team. Guides should make your trek easier and more enjoyable – that is why you are paying them. Guides carry only small loads, generally do not help with cooking, and expect you to equip them fully. It is reasonable to insist that your guide carries all of his own personal gear. Unless you are hiring enough porters to justify having a guide to manage them, a guide is a luxury for open-zone treks. A guide who also cooks, if you can find one, charges a little more because you are asking him to do more work. Otherwise, hiring a cook who also carries a porter load is a good alternative. You can pay a cook either by the day or by the stage. Wages for cooks are about Rs 300 per day plus food rations or Rs 50 per stage in addition to the normal per stage low-altitude porter wages (see Wages below). Guides are less useful for small groups (ie, four people or less) in open zones. Porters who know the route can and will show you the way (even across glaciers), locate camp sites, get water, and sometimes will cook chapattis and make tea. Guides are indispensable for some long open-zone treks (eg, Biafo-Hispar glaciers), particularly when it comes to routefinding or recruiting reliable porters.

Freelance licensed guides earn from Rs 300 to Rs 500 per day (not per stage; see Stages below) for every day they accompany you, including trekking days, rest days, transportation days, and hotel days. For restricted-zone treks, your guide is required by Tourism Division regulations to meet you in Islamabad for your briefing at the Tourism Division and be with you until you return to Islamabad and complete your debriefing. You are responsible for his daily wage plus expenses, including food and lodging, during this time. When hiring a freelance licensed guide, try to find one who is associated with (and somewhat accountable to) an established trekking company. The guide is then less likely to create problems and may have more incentive to do a good job. When you book through a trekking company or a tour operator abroad, your guide's wage will be included in the total price you negotiate.

Porters

A low-altitude porter works with trekking parties below 6000m and a high-altitude porter works with mountaineering expeditions over 6000m. Porters are not licensed by the government. Porters carry heavy loads, cook their own food, often have excellent route knowledge and experience, but speak limited English. Often porters travel only in familiar areas, close to where they live. Porters are indispensable on glacier crossings where the route can change from day to day and in remote areas where finding water can be a problem. For open-zone treks that do not require a licensed guide, it makes sense to hire a porter. When you trek in a restricted zone, you must hire porters in addition to a guide.

In late August and September, villagers are busy with the harvest and cannot get away. At this time finding a few porters is usually not a problem, but if you need a lot of porters or if an expedition is in the area, it can be tough. Along some trekking routes that pass through different valleys, you are expected to hire new porters in each valley and release your porters if they are from a different area. Before you hire any porters, you should know if you need to change porters along your route.

Porter Loads The government sets a load limit of 25 kg for elevations under 5000m and 20 kg between 5000 to 6000m per low-altitude porter. This does not include the porter's own gear and food. Porters prefer to tie loads onto a metal-frame carrier with shoulder straps, if they have one, and carry them on their backs. Otherwise, they use rope to fashion shoulder straps. The one to two kg carrier's weight is usually not included in the government load limit. Buy a hand-held scale to weigh porter loads daily. A double-spring scale is more accurate than

a single-spring scale. Porters are accustomed to using these scales and usually sort out the loads themselves. This is a very easy and inexpensive way to ensure fairness and resolve disputes. Scales are available in Rawalpindi, Islamabad's Aabpara market, Chitral, Gilgit, and Skardu for Rs 100 to Rs 125. Trekking companies and tour operators typically set their own per trekker weight limit for personal gear, which can be well below the government limits. Ask what the weight limits and charges per kg are for any overweight baggage, if any. When you cross a high pass or traverse a glacier, you will keep the pace from being too slow by lightening loads by a few kg or hiring an extra porter. The porters will reciprocate with hard work and fewer complaints. In some areas, porters may ask for a wage increase or for their loads to be lightened as altitude is gained although you may be nowhere near the 6000m limit. In the face of a unified demand, all you can do is bargain hard, and consider whatever extra you agree to pay as their baksheesh.

A villager/porter from Haringol resting below the Zagar Pass on the Zagar Pass trek.

Porter Welfare When you have more than 25 porters, the government requires you to hire a head porter (called a porter *sirdar)* to manage the other porters. When you have fewer than 25, then you either do it yourself, have your guide do it, or have the porters select one of them to manage the others.

As their employer, you are responsible for your porters' wellbeing while trekking. Make sure they are adequately equipped because their lives can depend on it. This includes providing them with shelter, stoves and fuel, warm clothing including hats, gloves, socks, jackets, and shoes, and when camping on snow or ice, sleeping pads, and heavy blankets or sleeping bags. When you trek above 4000m or across snow, make sure they have sunglasses.

You will be expected to dole out medicine for headaches, clean and bandage cuts, and organise any more serious medical help if its need arises. Insuring your porters against accidents is an inexpensive, responsible step to take. Pay your porters fair wages too and they in turn, will look after you. Your porters will help you across hard sections, carry you if you are injured, and invite you into their homes. If you keep in mind that you are all in it together, the neocolonial hierarchy of *sahib* and servant will fade and everyone will enjoy the trek more.

Trek Crew's Kitchen & Equipment

Kitchen When you hire a trek crew, you need to supply them with a kitchen besides your own. Their basic kitchen includes: stove with spare parts and cleaning wires; plastic container(s) with good seal to transport kerosene; funnel to pour kerosene; matches or butane lighter; large cooking pot; tea kettle; *tawa* (an iron griddle for cooking chapattis); rolling pin; large flat pan to mix and knead dough; and one plate, mug, and spoon per person.

Equipment Essential equipment to ensure their warmth and shelter and protection from snowblindness are: shelter (tarp or tent – several men can share); sleeping bag and/or blankets; sleeping pad per person; and sunglasses or glacial goggles per person. Ask each crew member if they have any of these items; many have their own blankets or sleeping bag, and sleeping pad. The extent to which you supply your crew with adequate shelter is a personal choice, but ask yourself if you would be warm enough sleeping in the shelter you intend to provide. The cost of providing this equipment is usually less than the cost of paying porter wages to carry the amount of kerosene a trek crew would use trying to stay warm on cold nights at higher elevations.

Additional considerations exist when you hire a guide. We provide a tent for the guide separate from the shelter for porters. If we expect a guide to break trail through fresh snow or over a difficult pass, we provide him with gaiters, snow pants, and glacial goggles (instead of sunglasses). If a guide or porters do not have their own equipment, you can either purchase or lend them gear. When you lend gear, distribute it only on the day(s) when it is needed and collect it immediately afterwards.

Hiring & Managing Guides & Porters

The key to hiring both guides and porters is knowing who to hire and how much to pay. Guides and porters from the valley or region through which you are trekking will know the route, where to camp and locate water, and have friends along the way. Upon arrival in the last village in a valley or at the trail head, ask if anyone is available. Avoid hiring anyone along the trail. Instead hire in the presence of others so at least one person witnesses who goes off with you. This increases the likelihood of hiring a reliable person and deters thieves and trouble-makers.

Ask for recommendations from trekking companies, hotels, and shopkeepers in towns. Experienced porters often have a *chit,* or letter of recommendation, from any foreigner they have previously worked for. Ask to see these to ascertain a prospective porter's range of skills and experience. If you are pleased with any guides or porters, take the time to write them a letter of recommendation. In some towns, a porter 'union' exists. This is a system by which the names of local men available for work are listed (usually in a public place) and whoever is next on the list goes with you.

Be thorough when hiring: make your requirements clear, set any limitations, and agree on wages, stages, loads, food, and clothing. Count and weight your loads and check your gear daily. Have each porter sign a contract (an example is in the *Trekking Rules and Regulations*). The contract may not be legally binding, but serves its own purpose. If possible, also collect each porter's *shenakti* or identity card. A photocopy may work, but the original is better. Keep these with you until the end of your journey; they are the cheapest insurance against disputes and strikes en route.

Keep a list of anyone you hire. Note their name, village, and place and date of hire. When you release someone, refer to this list as you calculate wages. Do not pay wages in advance or on a daily basis; pay wages when you release someone. Make a receipt noting their name, village, and date and amount you paid and ask them to sign it or give a thumb print. This can resolve disputes that may arise after the fact about payment of fair wages, but be prepared for haggling anyway.

Stages

The distance covered on most treks is divided into *parāo* or stages. A stage is loosely defined as a traditional day's walk for the locals who live in an area. The government, trying to avoid abuses and unify disparate systems of payment, initially established the stage scheme for mountaineering expeditions in restricted zones. Then locals working in open zones also began to demand wages on the stage basis, though it is rarely clear to outsiders what a stage really is. Stage lengths vary widely and may be as short as a one-hour walk or as long as a full day. They often depend upon the difficulty of the terrain over which you travel. The stage system is pervasive throughout the Northern Areas. Thankfully, the stage system is not used in the Chitral district of NWFP. Wages

in Chitral (except in the Tirich Valley) are paid on a daily basis and assume a daily wage is earned after six or seven hours of walking.

Because the length of stages varies, you walk multiple stages on some days. Walking only one stage per day is too slow a pace for most trekkers; an average of two stages per day is common. Occasionally it might be necessary to walk three or more stages in one day (eg, crossing a high pass and descending to a suitable camp site).

The number of stages on many routes is not fixed and can vary according to whom you ask and can change from year to year. Recognised halting places exist on most routes and many of these constitute stages. On heavily trekked routes, such as the Baltoro Glacier, stages are fixed and non-negotiable. However, on some routes as new place names are recognised, locals attempt to define new stages. For example, over a five-year period the number of stages on the Biafo Glacier increased by 40%, substantially increasing the cost of hiring porters. As jeep roads are pushed further up some valleys, the traditional trail heads change, thus altering the beginning stages.

Ask the headman of the village nearest your trail head how many stages your route will cover. Often he can confirm what guides or porters may have told you. When you bring porters to the headman, everyone can hear and agree upon what he says. Be sure everyone agrees on where the stages start and stop and on the total number of stages for your trek. Write down these details so you can refer to them when paying wages later. Think in terms of the number of stages and not of the number of days on a trek since wage negotiation is usually based on stages. The cost difference between a per-stage basis and a daily basis can be dramatic. Some 'amateur' guides are demanding per-stage wages, which is ridiculous since they carry almost no load.

The Tourism Division has no authoritative list of stages for treks and the stage system is widely abused. We give the accepted number and length of stages in the route descriptions, which represent our interpretations after speaking with numerous guides, porters, village leaders, and trekking companies. This may help you to avoid being ripped off or being inadvertently embroiled in wage disputes or strikes.

Stage inflation is a problem in Pakistan. If a stage means a normal day's walk, why should you pay two or three stages for an easy day of trekking? Locals do not yet understand that stage inflation discourages trekkers, leading to a decrease in the number of trekkers and hence a decrease in overall earnings for villagers. We advise you use this guidebook as a source to counter any stage inflation.

Wages

Wages in Pakistan are high among developing countries, and guides' and porters' wages are three to four times higher than those in the Nepal or the Indian Himalaya. In theory, porter wages are left to market forces, but the government sets and publishes maximum wages for high-altitude and low-altitude porters. Unfortunately, this maximum wage has become the going wage with few exceptions. These maximum wages are reviewed annually. Actual wages are often fixed locally (by the Deputy Commissioner (DC) for each district) and are independent of the maximum wages set by the government. The government does not set maximum wages for guides or cooks.

Porter wages are set for each of five regions: Baltistan, Chitral, Diamir, Ghizar, and Gilgit. Wages vary by region and loosely correlate with the region's standard of living. The total porters' wages are separated into four categories: stage, *wāpāsi* (return), food rations, and clothing and equipment allowance. Wages are also earned for rest days and for halts due to bad weather. The system is complex and often confusing, but it helps to try to understand it to reduce disagreements and avoid porter strikes.

Stage The maximum per stage low-altitude porter's wage for each region is: Rs 120 Baltistan, Rs 160 Chitral, Rs 120 Diamir, Rs 160 Ghizar, and Rs 160 Gilgit.

Wāpāsi (Return) Wāpāsi equals half of the wage for one stage and is paid in addition to the per stage porter wage. Wāpāsi is intended to cover a porter's expenses to walk with only his personal belongings and not a load back to the point where he was hired. For example, if a porter has to walk several stages to return to his village, where he was hired, it is fair to compensate him for his time to get there and for the cost of food he eats en route.

Sometimes wāpāsi is not paid. When you hire a porter for a trek that starts and ends at the same place, do not pay wāpāsi, since the porter has incurred no out-of-pocket expenses or extra time to get back to where he was hired. When a trek ends in a different place than where it started, but ends at a road head where public transport is available, it does not make sense to pay wāpāsi since your porter is not walking back. Instead pay your porter's fare on public transport back to where he was hired plus a fair amount for his food and/or lodging en route. When you and your porters travel together to/from trail heads, you are expected to cover the costs of their transport and do not pay wāpāsi. Some porters may demand wāpāsi even when it may not seem logical to pay it. Use your best bargaining skills to negotiate an acceptable compromise before starting your trek, or look for other porters.

Food Rations The government sets the maximum porter food rations at Rs 60 per day. However, this rate is accepted as a per stage ration and not a per day ration. When you insist on paying food rations per day instead of per stage, you may find yourself walking only one stage per day whether you want to or not.

Instead of paying food rations, you can provide food for your porters. An itemised list of daily food rations, including the minimum quantity per item, is set by the government and detailed in the *Trekking Rules and Regulations*. When you arrange your own trek, providing food may seem less expensive than paying food rations. But it is not easy to organise. Most porters do not want to eat the food listed, so you must negotiate what food they want. Typically, porters eat bread with salt tea, occasional meat, and like to smoke cigarettes. Figuring out what and how much to buy and buying and packing it takes time.

On the trail, you must distribute food to porters every few days. Otherwise, they may eat all the food quickly and five days into a 15-day trek you may learn that food is running out. An unexpected shortage of food may also happen when porters provide their own food. Check porters' food when they bring their own to make sure there is enough to last the length of the trek. Somehow, porters may expect to eat your 'extra' food, which usually does not exist. When you pay porters food rations and they provide their own food, their food is typically not weighed as part of the maximum porter load set by the government. Hence, it can be cheaper to pay food rations than to buy food and then pay the wage for more porters to carry the porters' food on longer treks. You must sort out what kind of food, who buys it and who cooks before hiring someone.

Clothing & Equipment Allowance Most porters expect to be paid a flat rate of Rs 200 per porter per trek as a clothing and equipment allowance. This unwritten expectation is not detailed in the *Trekking Rules and Regulations*, which gives a list of clothing and equipment you are required to provide for porters. It can be more expensive and is time consuming to provide every item on the list, so being let off the hook for Rs 200 is not such a bad deal. It is unlikely that porters will buy new gear with Rs 200, but the money helps to cover the wear-and-tear on their clothes and shoes. Some porters are willing to negotiate. If you are going on an easier, shorter trek (eg, less than one week long), you could bargain to pay a lower sum, say Rs 100 per porter. If you are doing multiple treks back-to-back with the same porters, a single clothing and equipment allowance will cover all treks. Any payment for this allowance in no way minimises your responsibility to ensure that each of your porters is properly equipped for the conditions on your trek. Ask to see porters' gear before the trek to ensure it is suitable.

Rest Days & Bad Weather Porters expect further compensation either in time off or in additional wages for rest days and for halts due to bad weather. Discuss and agree upon this before starting your trek.

Rest Days Porters expect one day off for every seven days worked. Again, 'day' is typically interpreted by porters as 'stage', much to their advantage. It is not difficult to walk seven stages in four or five days, so you should agree not to stop for a day each seven stages unless you do so for rest or acclimatisation. A distinction is made between a rest day that is taken and a rest day that is earned, but not taken. The pay for a rest day is half of the wage for one stage. If the rest day is taken, you also pay full rations, but you do not pay wāpāsi. If your porters agree not to take a rest day they have earned, you pay the half-stage wage, but you do not pay wāpāsi or food rations. When day hikes or side trips do not require shifting camp and your porters stay put, pay your porters for a 'rest day'.

Bad Weather If a trekking party halts due to bad weather, government regulations require you to pay your porters one full-stage wage per day. However, porters often accept a rest day (ie, a half-stage) wage for such halt days. Full rations are expected, but wāpāsi is not.

Insurance
The government requires you to insure the guide and porters on restricted-zone treks. No insurance requirements apply to open-zone treks. The coverage limits set by the government are: Rs 100,000 per person for guides and liaison officers; and Rs 50,000 per person for low-altitude porters. The premium for this personal accident policy is inexpensive and varies depending on the length of your trek (ie, the insured period). For example, for a four-week trek, the premium for Rs 100,000 coverage is about

Rs 110 per person and for Rs 50,000 coverage is about Rs 50 per person; about 8% taxes are added to the base premiums.

When you make you own arrangements, you must purchase the insurance policy before you submit an application to the Tourism Division for a restricted-zone permit. It is easiest to hire a trekking company to help you purchase the insurance.

TREK FOOD

To trek long distances over rugged terrain, you need to eat between 3000 and 4500 calories per day. When trekking on your own, planning your food needs is vital to the success of your trek. Going with a trekking company or a tour operator abroad eliminates the hassle of diet planning. You can either buy food in Pakistan or import food from your home country. Most trekkers can easily purchase everything they need in Pakistan. However, once you set off into the mountains you cannot expect to purchase much, if anything, from local residents.

On shorter treks, consider eating the same food as your porters (ie, rice, chapattis, vegetables, tea, sugar and powdered milk). You may wish to add items from local markets. Here are a few of our meal tips: oatmeal is vastly improved by stewing local dried apricots and raisins with it. Mixing powdered chocolate and Ovaltine with powdered milk makes a good, hot energy drink. Macaroni and canned tuna is the easiest and fastest-cooking dinner. Adding the contents of sauce packets brought from home varies the taste and keeps it interesting. For long-distance travel in uninhabited country or at high elevations, lightweight freeze-dried food (not available in Pakistan) reduces the weight of food and fuel and can, therefore, extend your range. Pack your food into plastic storage bags, waterproof stuff sacks, or cloth bags that can easily be stitched in any bazaar.

Imported Food

In the speciality stores in Islamabad, a wide variety of imported food is available. Many of these same items can be found by scouring the bazaars of Chitral, Peshawar, Saidu

Staples & Local Food
Basic staples and other foods are readily available in the bazaars of Chitral, Gilgit, Skardu and even Karimabad and Passu.

- rice (cooks OK with a lid up to 4500m, but takes a long time)
- whole-wheat flour
- lentils (you need a pressure cooker to cook them)
- tea (loose leaves and tea bags)
- instant coffee (Nescafe)
- milk powder (both full-cream and 2% milk fat)
- powdered drink mixes (Ovaltine, Milo)
- sugar
- cooking oil (sunflower, corn, and canola/rape seed)
- jams (Hunza apricot and cherry jam is delicious) and honey
- noodles, macaroni, and spaghetti (gets mushy easily)
- biscuits (crackers and cookies)
- dried fruits (apricots, mulberries, raisins)
- nuts (walnuts, almonds, peanuts, pistachios, cashews)
- fresh vegetables in season (potatoes, cabbage, carrots, beets, tomatoes, onions, garlic, and ginger)
- fresh fruits in season (apricots, apples, peaches, plums, mulberries, lemons, limes, mangos, and bananas)
- whole-wheat bread
- oatmeal, porridge, cornflakes
- custard, pudding, jelly
- bouillon cubes (chicken or beef)
- spices
- salt
- dried onions
- eggs

Sharif, Gilgit, and Skardu. Sometimes items left by expeditions can be purchased in Gilgit, Skardu, and Chitral. Butter, parmesan cheese, soya sauce, and mustard are usually not found outside Islamabad and Rawalpindi. When you fly into Chitral, Gilgit, Saidu Sharif, or Skardu, remember a 20 kg total weight limit per person applies on domestic PIA flights. This prevents most trekkers from buying too much food downcountry. However, when you travel by road,

Tinned Food
- tuna in brine or oil (chunks are better than flakes)
- sardines, mackerel, or salmon
- cheddar cheese
- tomato sauce and paste
- butter
- meat (corned beef, chicken, Spam)
- vegetables (peas, beans, and baked beans)
- fruits and fruit cocktail

Packaged Food
- parmesan cheese
- soya sauce
- mustard
- peanut butter
- cocoa mix/drinking chocolate
- hard candy
- soft cheeses
- pasta
- instant coffee (Taster's Choice, decaf)
- varieties of tea leaves and bags
- oatmeal/cream of wheat/porridge
- powdered fruit drinks (Tang)
- soup mixes

it is easier, more reliable, and less expensive to purchase food in Islamabad or Rawalpindi. If you want to stock up before heading for the mountains, try shopping in Islamabad's Jinnah market (F-7/2) or Covered market (G-6/4), in Rawalpindi's Saddar bazaar, or Peshawar's Saddar bazaar.

These imported tinned and packaged foods can serve as supplements to staple grain-based meals and local food:

TREKKING EQUIPMENT SHOPS
A very limited selection of basic equipment, typically used expedition gear, is for sale or rent in Chitral, Gilgit, Hushe, Passu, and Skardu. Generally available are ensolite sleeping pads (Rs 200 to Rs 450), plastic expedition barrels (Rs 300 to Rs 400), rope, carabiners, ice screws, crampons, ice axes, tarpaulins, clothing for porters, and basic cooking equipment (eg, aluminium cooking pots with flat lids, aluminium tea kettles, steel spoons and plates, and enamelled tin

mugs). Used boots can be found, but any selection is meagre. Backpacks, sleeping bags, down jackets, and gaiters are much harder to find. Buying and then reselling an item (eg, stove or ensolite pads) after your trek usually works out cheaper than renting it. Ask if any expeditions are around or check with trekking companies.

Equipment
- **Chitral** Check with Hindukush Trails at the Mountain Inn. Shops in Shahi and Naya bazaar sell stoves, shoes, barrels, fuel containers, and kitchen equipment.
- **Gilgit** Dad Ali Shah, who runs Hunza Handicrafts, next to the Park Hotel, sells used equipment. Dad Ali was the first in Gilgit to offer advice and assistance to trekkers, before there were trekking companies, and enjoys sharing stories. Ali Ahmed at Mountaineering Equipment on Airport Rd has used boots, ice axes, ropes, sleeping pads, used jackets and sleeping bags, and occasionally EPI gas cylinders.
- **Hushe** The K2 Shop has gear for rent or sale including tents, sleeping bags, jackets, boots, and crampons.
- **Passu** Abdul Rashid, proprietor of the Passu general store, stocks gear for rent including sleeping bags, sleeping pads, stoves, tents, and some other mountaineering equipment.
- **Skardu** Most mountaineering expeditions stage themselves out of the K2 Motel in Skardu, so ask there if anything is for sale. Skardu has the best selection of used boots and mountaineering equipment. Look in the old bazaar, which is off Hussaini Chowk just past the aqueduct. This is also where to find tarpaulins, barrels, and porters' clothing.

ON THE TREK
Daily Routine
Porters arise at first light, make tea, and have it along with the bread they baked the previous night. Then they are ready to go. If you want to get into this routine, fine. If not, be sure your porters know when you plan to

Yaks are sometimes used to carry trek loads. This one is at Shuijerab on the Shimshal Pamir trek.

wake up and when you plan to start walking. Generally you should start walking early, when the day is still cool. Porters usually want to stop around 11 am for mid-morning tea and bread, when you can take your midday meal. This may seem early, but porters who consume just bread and tea need to stop more frequently for food. When you are with a group, your kitchen will serve lunch at the time you choose. Stops are often dictated by where water is available, rather than by the clock or by your stomach. Carrying some food, such as dried apricots or biscuits, can help you through any long stretches. Most trekkers and porters like to stop for the day in mid-afternoon, whenever a nice camp is reached, rather than grind on into the late afternoon.

Check Posts

Formal check posts are a rarity while trekking in Pakistan. If you are trekking in an open zone, you should not encounter any. In restricted zones, though, plain-clothes and uniformed Border Police, Khunjerab Security Force (KSF) police, the army at any military outpost, or forestry personnel will ask to see your permit. Carry at least six photocopies of your permit to give to such authorities. Your guide also has to meet any of these officials. Often, these guardians of the frontier are bored, and look upon your arrival as an opportunity to talk and relieve the tedium of a remote post. If you take up any invitation for tea, you earn goodwill not only for yourself and your trekking party, but also for any future parties. This helps to alleviate any anxiety about trekkers and encourages the policy of opening such areas to trekkers.

Objective Dangers

The sheerness of the Karakoram and Hindukush, the extensive glaciation, and lack of vegetation produce objective dangers on the trail. Recognition of these conditions and a sensible approach to them reduce any chance of accident or injury. These conditions are rock fall on unstable scree slopes, river crossings, and crevasses on glaciers. Pakistanis euphemistically term these conditions 'adventure'. They add excitement to trekking, but to keep your 'adventure' from turning into a nightmare, it is important to be aware of your immediate surroundings and use proper techniques to reduce your exposure to objective dangers. If you have no experience with such conditions or are at all uncertain of your ability to deal with these conditions, hire a competent guide.

Scree Slopes Walking on scree is a skill that gets easier with practice. You will probably encounter scree along most trekking routes. The scale of some scree slopes is impressive; some can be 1500m high and more than one km wide and may take a half-hour to cross. Before stepping onto any scree slope, look up carefully for any rock fall. Rocks fall any time, but be especially cautious if it is windy or rainy. Winds typically come up in the afternoon, so plan to cross scree slopes in the morning, if possible. Be aware if a scree slope is above you, even if you are not walking directly on one. If any rock is falling, stop. Do not proceed until all rock fall has stopped. Check with any local person, your guide, or porter(s) before proceeding. Stop and look for any trail across the entire scree slope. The scree will be more stable where footprints are visible. On scree and on narrow trails, often a left-right order to footsteps exists. Take footsteps in the correct sequence; don't cross your legs or you are likely to trip yourself.

If you are inexperienced walking on scree slopes, get out on one to see what it feels like. Take one or two steps to see how far, or if, you slide down as you walk. It is similar to walking on a sand dune. Make sure you are comfortable with this feeling before setting off to cross a longer scree slope. You should be able to stand on the scree slope and to take a step up or down and feel some sense of stability. If you are hesitant, ask someone to take your hand. If they walk in front of you and support you, it is quite easy to hang on and to follow in their foot steps. Once you start traversing a scree slope, keep moving steadily and as quickly as possible. Don't panic if you slip.

Local people usually use a walking stick on scree slopes. Hold the stick with both hands in front of you, keeping the long end of the stick on the uphill side of the slope. Lean into the uphill side if you feel yourself slipping. When descending a scree slope, use the stick like a rudder. Hold the stick to one side and lean back gently onto it for support and 'ski' down. This is an amazingly effective technique that enables you to descend quickly. Ascending scree is slow and tedious. When ascending or descending scree, be careful not to kick rocks loose that may fall on or in the path of others. If rocks are sliding and falling, increase the distance between you and others for safety.

Talus Piles of large boulders, called talus, are common, especially on glaciers. Talus is usually unstable and always tiring and tedious to cross. A few techniques can make it easier. Test your foothold before placing your weight on it. Give the rock a little push;

if it feels solid you can step on it, and if not, try another rock. Look several steps ahead to where you want to go. Pick out your route and figure out a sequence of three or four footsteps, rather than stopping on every rock to figure out your next step. You can use angled rocks for intermediate steps. You may not be able to stop and stand on such rocks, but you can step on them as you move to a flatter rock, thereby keeping your forward momentum.

River Crossings Always ask for current conditions. Footbridges often wash away in high water and may not be present where they once used to be, or may be missing essential parts. You should be prepared to ford a stream or river if necessary.

Footbridges Footbridges are infrequent or nonexistent on most trekking routes. Footbridges may be constructed of any combination of logs, planks, rocks, or dirt and usually do not have any hand hold. Many bridges are poorly maintained and were constructed solely for one-time use to bring skittish livestock over a river when going to or from summer pastures. Take deliberate steps and watch for loose planks or rocks or for gaping holes in the bridge material. Even a short fall into a raging river can be fatal.

Cables & Pulleys When resources are not available to construct a proper bridge, a cable may be strung across the width of the river. A small metal or wooden basket, in varying degrees of repair, may be suspended from the cable. A rope hangs beneath the cable and is used to pull the basket across the river. If the setup looks dubious, back it up by securing a short piece of two-cm-wide nylon tubular webbing or rope to the cable with a locking steel carabiner. Do not use an aluminium carabiner on a steel cable since the friction will destroy it. Secure the other end of the webbing or rope to the passenger with a carabiner secured to either a harness or equivalent. Secure backpacks and other loads to the basket and/or cable with a carabiner or rope. The rope used to pull the basket may be frayed, too short, or nonexistent. Carry extra rope or tubular webbing in case an on-the-spot repair job is needed. When no basket is present, the local style of crossing is to grab the cable with both hands, and swing one leg up over the cable. A short rope is tied around the waist and secured to a steel shackle or wire loop around the cable for safety. Then the person pulls hand over hand across the length of the cable. Do not try this; instead rig a seat with a rope or a harness.

Fording Rivers More often than not, you will be getting your feet wet when fording rivers. Find the widest spot where water is more shallow and flows more slowly to ford. Always choose braided sections of the river instead of a single channel. Water that is more than knee-deep may be too dangerous to cross. The deeper the water is, the more swiftly the current flows, and the greater likelihood that rocks or boulders are being carried downstream. Even small rocks can knock you off your feet or break an ankle or leg. Before fording, listen carefully for any rocks that may be rolling down the river. Do not cross if you hear anything; wait for a safer time. River levels rise and fall dramatically. Water levels are lowest in the morning and on cloudy or overcast days and are highest in the afternoon and on sunny days. If the water is too high in the afternoon, wait until the next morning to cross.

Do not ford a river alone; cross with one or more partners, preferably with locals. When crossing with one other person, position the stronger person upstream. When crossing with two or more other people, position the stronger persons on either side of the person(s) in the middle. Avoid holding hands since this grip is not adequate to support someone if they lose their balance. Try interlocking one another's forearms or upper arms or slipping your whole arm through the shoulder straps of your partners' backpacks. Use a walking stick for greater stability and to probe the water before each step to find out the water's depth. Allow someone else to carry your backpack across the river if you are hesitant.

Take your boots off; tie the shoelaces from each boot together and put them around your neck. Do not carry your boots in your hands. If you lose your balance while crossing, you cannot afford to risk losing your boots. Sandals with ankle straps or old tennis shoes protect your feet from rocks. Socks can help if the water is icy or if the crossing is very wide. Wear loose-fitting pants that you can pull up over your knees. When you know a crossing will be icy, deep, or wide, or that you will have multiple crossings on a given day, wear long underwear bottoms for insulation.

Ford a river on a diagonal from upstream to downstream, crossing with the current. Do not cross perpendicular to or against the current. When the water level is knee-to-crotch deep and you must cross, use a rope for safety. Secure the rope across the river on a diagonal from upstream to downstream. When the current is swift, clip onto the rope with a locking carabiner and use a walking stick or partner(s) for balance. Often local men will take you piggyback-style across rivers. Feel comfortable accepting these offers; these men are very strong and capable.

Glacier Travel Most trekking in Pakistan involves some walking next to glaciers, and possibly walking on them. Glaciers descend to as low as 2500m. At elevations below 4000m, the surface of a glacier is mostly covered by rock, called moraine. This moraine rubble varies in size from gravel to large boulders, and, when densely piled, makes for tedious and difficult walking. Moraine along the margins of glaciers, called lateral moraine, is typically dense and jumbled, since a glacier's margins are more broken than its mid-sections. The moraine in the middle of a glacier is called medial moraine, and as one gets higher on the glacier, usually offers the easiest walking. Above 4000m, medial moraine typically ends and the ice is either covered by snow or lies exposed. At even higher elevations, the snow cover is permanent. Crevasses are found at any elevation, and are most dangerous when hidden by snow cover. The ablation valleys alongside glaciers are often the easiest routes up and down the lower sections of most glaciers, and also offer grassy camp sites and clear water. Herders typically graze livestock in meadows above these ablation valleys.

Never go onto a glacier alone. When you plan to walk on a glacier, hire a local person to show you the best route, both on the glacier and to the exit and entry routes to camps in ablation valleys. When you go onto the upper, snow-covered section of a glacier where crevasses lie hidden, you must go with at least two other people, use a rope and probe for hidden crevasses. Routes across such terrain are only for those experienced in glacier travel, glacier camping, crevasse rescue, and routefinding on glaciers. Glacier camping requires carefully probing for crevasses in the camp area, and using wands to mark the boundary of the safe, crevasse-free area. Crevasse rescue requires use of rope, ascenders or prussiks, crampons and ice axe: essential gear for any trekking party crossing crevasse fields. If you do not have this technical experience, you can travel safely across such terrain but only in the company of a trained and properly equipped guide.

Ropes & Knots Learn to tie your own knots before you actually need to. Local people very rarely know how to tie secure knots. The basic knots are: figure eight, water knot or ringbend (to use with tubular or flat webbing); bowline or double figure eight (to clip onto the rope); and a double Fisherman's knot (to secure two dissimilar rope lengths). These knots are also useful when crossing rivers.

Ecotourism

'Ecotourism' means being environmentally, economically and culturally responsible while travelling. Ecotrekking means applying these values while trekking. Ask yourself what you can do to lessen the impact trekking

has on the environment and local culture. Taking care of yourself and taking responsibility for your actions is a basic obligation of all trekkers. The point is not to become part of the problem.

Voluntary codes of conduct for tourists, tour operators, and host communities have been developed in many parts of the world. In Pakistan, the government, NGOs, and trekking companies are working to develop guidelines, but such information is not yet readily available and little has been done to implement ecotrekking principles. Hence, much depends upon you as an individual adopting an activist approach. The first step is to learn about the culture and environment before you come to Pakistan. The books we list will give you some starters (see Books earlier in this chapter). If you book a trek with a tour operator abroad, ask for information about their practices, any guidelines they may have, and appropriate reading material. Contact grass-roots organisations and NGOs working in Pakistan for more specific information about ecotourism and the environment. Make trekking a positive experience for you, your friends, and for local people, by sharing what you learn with others and teaching by example.

Everybody is glad to see more trekkers coming to Pakistan. What everyone is not glad to see are the piles of garbage at camp sites, the trees cut down, the toilet paper strewn along trails, the heaps of plastic bottles behind hotels, villagers angry with trekkers for wearing indiscreet clothing, and trekkers arguing with guides and porters over wages. Trekkers, local people, and trekking companies need to be aware of these problems and learn how to deal with them.

MINIMUM IMPACT GUIDELINES
Perhaps the most important single action you can take is to reduce the size of your trekking party, which minimises your overall impact. Other actions fall into three areas: environmental, economic, and cultural considerations. Following these guidelines will help sustain the Karakoram and Hindukush and its people.

Environmental Considerations

Whenever and wherever you find people working to conserve the natural environment, encourage them and compliment their efforts. Beyond this, make an effort to keep your trek from increasing pollution, erosion, deforestation, and loss of wildlife. Avoid overvisited trekking areas by selecting a less known trekking destination and travelling off-peak season when possible.

Pollution You can control pollution by managing waste disposal and avoiding water contamination. Waste disposal systems do not exist along trekking routes, so everyone in a trekking party shares this responsibility, including the trekkers, the guide, trek crew, porters and any trekking company and/or tour operator abroad. Act responsibly yourself and supervise anyone you hire to ensure no one in your party pollutes.

Waste Disposal Three types of waste are produced on a trek: organic, burnable; and non-burnable. Organic waste (eg, food scraps) is best disposed of by feeding it to domestic animals or allowing it to decompose underground. Ask the local people if it is OK to feed scraps to the animals. When no domestic animals are around, bury organic waste. Over 4000m high, organic waste takes decades to decay and should be carried to lower elevations for disposal. Rather than throwing away burnables, such as paper or wood products, collect and burn them. Cigarette butts should not be discarded along the trail. Be mindful of when and where you burn rubbish. Organise a camp routine to collect and burn rubbish, preferably where a fire scar already exists.

Tins, bottles, aluminium foil, and plastics are examples of non-burnable waste. Do not bury non-burnable waste because it does not decompose and animals may dig it up and scatter it. Tins and bottles can be given to locals along the trail if they want them, but do not leave them if no one is there to take them. Aluminium foil, foil-lined packages, and plastics do not burn properly and when burned release toxic ozone-depleting gases.

Carry non-burnable waste out and dispose of it properly in the nearest city. No formal recycling facilities exist, but bottles, aluminium, and plastic are informally recycled in cities. Take used battery cells to your home country for proper recycling or disposal. If you find an existing waste pit at a camp site, ideally carry its contents out. When this isn't possible, partially cover the hole with large flat stones or wood to keep the rubbish from being scattered by weather or animals. Carry a container to collect and transport your non-burnable waste. Carrying out non-burnable waste does not increase porterage costs; the added weight is minimal and only requires a separate porter load with a large party. Pick up others' rubbish when you see it along the trail and encourage everyone with you to do the same. None of this is difficult or time consuming, but it makes a great difference.

Minimise the waste you produce by avoiding non-biodegradable, non-burnable packaging. Purchase food for a trek that has minimal packaging and where you have a choice, avoid plastic, cellophane and foil-packaged foods. Buy in bulk and transport items like flour, rice, lentils, sugar, and salt in reusable cloth bags or stuff sacks. You can further minimise waste on the trek by removing packaging from dry and powdered foods and repacking them into sturdy reusable containers. Do not buy or drink beverages in unrecycleable plastic containers or tin cans, but in reusable glass bottles instead.

Women may need tampons or sanitary napkins on the trek. Bring these from home, but avoid tampons with plastic applicators in favour of cardboard ones, which can be disposed of more easily. Tampons and sanitary napkins are generally difficult to burn and do not readily decompose. Although it may seem inconvenient or unpleasant, plan to carry these out (bring a few sturdy plastic bags for this) for disposal in a city.

Water Contamination Water contamination occurs when human waste and other contaminants enter open water sources. Human-waste contamination spreads hepatitis, typhoid and intestinal parasites such as giardia, amoebas, and round worms, posing a health risk for residents, trekkers, and wild-life alike.

Trekkers can avoid contaminating water sources by taking care when washing or bathing and when going to the toilet. Do not put soaps, even biodegradable soaps, or toothpaste in open water sources. Wash yourself, your dishes, and your clothes in a basin and discard soapy water at least 50m from open water sources. A light-weight collapsible plastic basin works well.

Find a discreet location at least 50m from any open water source to relieve yourself. Use toilet paper sparingly and burn it using matches or a butane lighter. Pull the paper apart; a wad does not burn. Carrying a small bag to collect toilet paper to burn later in camp also works.

How to best deal with human faeces will depend on where you are. Below the treeline, bury it with other organic matter where soil microbes and worms will decompose it. You may want to carry a light-weight trowel for this. Above the treeline, organic matter decomposes slowly as frosts are frequent and microbes and worms are few. In remote, uninhabited areas, spread faeces out thinly on rocks to dry it in the sun. The sun's UV rays kill some bacteria and micro-organisms. On a glacier using a crevasse is actually environmentally sound. The glacier's crushing motion kills some bacteria and the waste will be dispersed and diluted over the many years it will take it to emerge into the river below.

At camp sites, use any existing toilet facility or pit. When a pit is dirty, clean it. Create a toilet site only when none exists, and ensure it is at least 50m from any open water source and half a metre deep. Ask locals if they have any concerns about the spot you have selected. Make sure it is not where others may want to sleep or cook. When you are with a trekking company that carries a portable toilet tent, ensure they follow these guidelines. Do not put toilet paper or rubbish in a toilet pit or crevasse; burn it. Have some dirt available to sprinkle in the pit after each use; this helps faeces to decompose and reduces odours. Encourage your guide, trek crew, or porters to use the same toilet site. When leaving the camp site, cover the pit with dirt at least three to four cm above ground level allowing for decomposition and settling.

Other Pollution Graffiti on rocks is a permanent form of environmental pollution. Discourage your trek crew from writing their names or drawing on rocks. Remember that many people find smoking offensive. The Aga Khan encourages Ismaili Muslims not to smoke, so please respect the wishes of others. Minimise noise and don't make any unnecessary noise. Ask your trek crew to do the same. It is astounding how noisy a crowded camp site along the Baltoro Glacier can be at 4.30 am!

Erosion The extreme steepness of the land in the Karakoram and Hindukush means erosion is a constant natural process. Arable land is a scarce and valuable resource and plants that help hold the soil together on steep slopes are few. When trekking, keep this in mind and trek gently; do not damage or collect plants or flowers; stay on trails where they exist; and do not cut switchbacks.

Use established camp sites and places for cooking, sleeping, and toilet. Although this concentrates the environmental impact, it minimises the overall disturbance. If there is no established camp site, select a level site at least 50m from open water sources and the trail, where you do not need to clear away vegetation. Avoid camping in fragile meadows where you will damage the grass and other plants. Do not cut trees, limbs, or brush to make camp improvements. Do not make trenches around tents because loosening the soil leaves it prone to wind and rain erosion. Before leaving a camp site, naturalise the area, and replace rocks, wood, or anything else you moved and repair anything you've damaged.

Deforestation Trees grow slowly in these arid mountains making wood a scarce and highly valued local resource for timber and fuel. Some old cedar and juniper trees in some valleys are several thousand years old. Most trekkers agree it would be a crime to cut such slow-growing and ancient trees, and villagers have moved to ban cutting in such areas. Remember that any wood belongs to that area's inhabitants and you, as a visitor, have no right to deplete their scarce resources. Refrain from using what are essentially non-renewable natural resources. Therefore, cook on a kerosene stove and not on wood fires. When trekking with a guide, trek crew, or porters, provide stoves and fuel or cooked food for everyone in your party. Consider preparing the same food for everyone simultaneously to conserve fuel.

Bathe with warm water only when the water is heated without wood (eg, by solar heat) or on fuel-saving stoves. Instead of requesting boiled drinking water, carry your own water bottles and purify water yourself.

Bring adequate warm clothes so you do not depend on campfires for warmth. When trekking with a guide, trek crew, or porters, outfit everyone properly so they do not depend on fires for warmth. And in hot, dry places, don't throw cigarettes and matches where they might cause fires.

Wildlife Conservation Unauthorised hunting of and trade in endangered species is illegal – do not condone or engage in it. Please do not eat wild game, harass, or feed wildlife. Villagers are just beginning to realise that tourists will come to view wildlife, and so are working to prevent poaching. Encourage these first steps at local wildlife conservation.

Economic Considerations

In Pakistan tourism is the ninth largest source of foreign currency. Tourism provides economic incentives to promote conservation of wild lands, generates income for park management, and brings needed income to rural populations. You can help reduce tourism's overall impact by patronising tour operators abroad, trekking companies in Pakistan, airlines, and hotels that make a commitment to environmentally responsible tourism.

When local people receive economic benefits from tourism, they are more likely to respond positively and work with tourists and trekkers to protect and manage their natural resource base. Giving business to locally owned and operated trekking companies and hotels and buying local products keeps tourist revenue in the local economy. When you bring freeze-dried food from home, or buy imported food in big city shops, you are not contributing to the local economy. An excellent way to make a positive contribution is to hire a porter. Often when you enter a new valley you are expected to hire new porters from that valley and release any porters from a different area. Instead of viewing this as an inconvenience, realise that the local people through whose area you are walking will now benefit directly from your being there.

Purchase locally grown grains and vegetables in market towns like Chitral, Gilgit, and Skardu whenever possible and plan to be self-sufficient while trekking. Living off the land may allow you to travel light, but it imposes a burden on local resources. Villagers grow just enough food for themselves, so do not expect to be able to buy grains and vegetables from them. Where villagers do have a seasonal surplus of fruits, nuts, and dairy products, buying these helps put needed cash into the local economy. Inform yourself about current wages and prices so you can bargain for and pay a fair price for food, lodging, and other services. Avoid giving inappropriate tips. Paying too much contributes to inflation by forcing wages and prices up, while paying too little denies a fair return.

Cultural Considerations

Don't ask people to behave in ways or accept values contrary to their own traditions. Tell people what you like about their culture. Be respectful while visiting religious places.

Show respect for local values by dressing conservatively. Tight-fitting or revealing dress offends and embarrasses people throughout the Karakoram and Hindukush, who are usually too polite to say anything to foreigners. Being on vacation is not an excuse for inappropriate behaviour! Once, in a village apricot orchard crowded with dozens of boys and girls, a male trekker standing outside his tent stripped down to his underpants in order to change his trousers. His thoughtless behaviour offended everyone present. Avoid public displays of affection. Holding hands, hugging, and kissing are considered private acts, not to be openly and shamelessly displayed. However, public hand-holding between men is common as an expression of friendship and rarely has any sexual overtones.

'Holiday romances' with local men harm the image of Western women. Most local men are married and either see the relationship as a ticket to the West or as validation of the misconception that most Western women are sexually available. Nude bathing is also considered vulgar and shameless. Wash your body in your tent, using a wash cloth and a basin of water. Washing hair, face, hands, and feet outside is fine as Islam emphasises personal cleanliness.

Discourage begging and do not give anything to beggars. It is a superficial and negative interaction. If you want to make a contribution, approach an appropriate person, such as a school headmaster, a community leader, or a representative of a local service organisation, and ask how you can best make a donation. Whatever your status in your own country, most people in Pakistan will perceive you as rich, leading to an idealised image of life in the West. Please make an effort to present a more balanced picture of life in the West by showing how earnings are linked to the cost of living.

The cultures of the Karakoram and Hindukush are now subject to a barrage of new influences that will inevitably change them. In the face of this change, encourage and acknowledge local cultural pride.

INFORMATION SOURCES

Communities in the Karakoram and Hindukush are realising that their environ-

ment constitutes perhaps their greatest asset, and are taking steps to conserve and manage it. Trekkers can help by supporting grass-roots organisations that work to preserve the environment and address problems created by tourism. Some are:

Karakoram Foundation (☎ 252580, 252553 and 853672; fax 250293), PO Box 2262, Islamabad, exists to raise environmental awareness, construct clean water supply systems, offer student scholarships, operate health camps, and train guides in responsible tourism.

Karakoram Society for Natural and Environmental Rehabilitation (KASONER) (☎ 3787), PO Box 551, Al-Kamal House, Gilgit, promotes awareness and education to combat environmental problems before they become irreversible. KASONER has held anti-pollution marches through the Gilgit bazaar, surveyed the town's water supply, and led protest action at the annual Shandur polo tournament.

Khunjerab Student Welfare Federation (KSWF), PO Sost, Village Morkhun, Gojal, Hunza District, Gilgit, formed by student activists in 1990, promotes education and 'green' work because of ecological degradation along the KKH. They launched a campaign to ban the use of plastic bags and stop the burning of plastic. Litter containers have been placed in areas where villagers gather, particularly in Sost. They also train guides in ecologically responsible trekking.

Globe Chasers Tourist Club, 21-A Bazaar Area, Gujranwala Cantt, Punjab, promotes conservation of the environment and natural resources through ongoing educational programmes and participation in outdoor sports. They can arrange treks for student groups. Their most ambitious project, which began in 1992, is an annual environmental clean-up of lake Saiful Muluk in the Kaghan Valley. Their representatives include: Aftab Rana (☎ 757 6826-8) c/o TDCP, Lahore; Tayyab Nisar Mir (☎ 816932) c/o PTDC Information Centre, Islamabad; and Ikram Beg (☎ 2409) c/o GM Beg Sons, Gilgit.

Green Earth Organisation (GEO), a Lahore-based NGO, launched clean-up campaigns in the Rupal Valley and helped villagers plant willow saplings. They plan to establish rubbish dumps and pit toilets at Tarashing, Herligkoffer base camp, Latobah, and Mazeno base camp and organise annual waste removal. They also plan to nominate villagers as 'Green Guardians' to ensure trekkers and mountaineers dispose of waste properly.

Health, Safety & First Aid

Staying healthy while trekking depends on your predeparture preparations, daily health care while trekking, and response to any medical problem or emergency that arises. With adequate preparation, information and some basic sensible practices you can minimise any chance of disease or injury.

Predeparture Preparation

PHYSICAL EXAMINATION & PRESCRIPTIONS

Make sure you do not have any physical problems before you start travelling. Have your physician check any nagging problem and discuss any prescriptions you may be taking. If you require a particular medication bring an adequate supply, as it may not be available locally. Also take the prescription, preferably written with the generic rather than the brand name so it is easier to refill. Having a legible prescription with you shows you legally use the medication. Over-the-counter drugs from one country are often illegal in another without the prescription. If you wear eye glasses, carry a spare pair and your prescription with you. Visit your dentist to make sure your teeth are OK. Air trapped in cavities or cracked fillings may expand at high altitude and cause tooth trauma.

PHYSICAL CONDITIONING

Several months before your trek, begin an aerobic conditioning programme. Being in good shape makes any trek easier and more enjoyable. Typically fit trekkers are less bothered by minor illness. However, being fit does not reduce the potential for altitude problems (see AMS below).

INSURANCE

For trekkers, major medical and emergency evacuation coverage is strongly recommended. Some policies pay only for a medical emergency overseas and not for non-emergency care. You may prefer a policy that pays doctors or hospitals direct rather than your paying on the spot and filing a claim later. If you will claim later, ensure you keep all documentation. Some policies require you to call (reversing the charges) them at a centre in your home country to authorise treatment or to assess your situation. Others may require you to get a second opinion before receiving any medical care. Check if the policy covers helicopter evacuation, ambulances and medi-vac, including an emergency flight home.

IMMUNISATIONS & PROPHYLAXIS
Immunisations

Immunisations protect against diseases you may encounter along the way. A distinction exists between immunisations recommended for travel and those required by law. Currently yellow fever is the only vaccine subject to international health regulations. Immunisation as an entry requirement is usually only enforced when you are coming from an infected area, and is not required for travel in South Asia. No immunisations are required by law for entry into Pakistan, but the following are recommended.

Cholera Outbreaks of cholera are not uncommon in Pakistan, but risk of infection for trekkers is low. The vaccine gives minimal protection for six months.

Diptheria & Tetanus Boosters are highly recommended every 10 years.

Hepatitis This is a preventable, but common illness. Protection can be conveyed in two ways: either with the ready-made antibody gamma globulin; or with a new vaccine called Havrix. Gamma globulin may interfere with the development of immunity, and should be given one to two weeks after administration of your last vaccine. It should be given as close as possible to departure as it is most effective in the first few weeks after administration, tapering off gradually depending upon the dosage given (eg, two cc for three months or five cc for six months). Havrix is given in two doses, an initial dose and a booster six to 12 months later. For most people immunity is obtained after 15 days. Havrix is only effective against Hepatitis A and reportedly conveys immunity for 10 years. Hepatitis B immunisation is not recommended for trekkers.

Rabies An immunisation for pre-exposure to rabies is available, but is only recommended for individuals in a high-risk category (eg, if you intend to explore caves where bat bites could be dangerous, to work with animals, or to travel for an extended period).

Typhoid Immunisation is available either as an injection, which protects for three years, or orally, which protects for five years. Though neither confers total immunity, it is recommended.

At the time of writing, cholera and typhoid immunisations are required for travellers entering China at Tashkurgan. Officials at the Health check post in Afiyatabad (just beyond Sost), administer single-dose immunisations for Rs 50 each to anyone who does not have proof of immunisation. Avoid being immunised there since sanitary conditions and use of disposable syringes cannot be guaranteed.

Most travellers from Western countries will have been immunised against various diseases during childhood. Your physician may still recommend booster shots against measles or polio, diseases still prevalent in South Asia. Plan to get your immunisations at least six weeks before travel.

Malaria Prophylaxis

Vivax and falciparum are two types of malaria parasites spread by mosquitoes.

Both occur in Pakistan and northern India, though they are not prevalent in northern Pakistan. Vivax is more common, but is not severe and is never fatal. Falciparum is a serious, cerebral malaria and can be fatal when untreated. These parasites may lay dormant in the liver, so symptoms may not appear until long after you leave an infected area. Vivax parasites are sensitive to Chloroquine and Falciparum parasites are resistant to many drugs.

For malaria prophylaxis that protects you from both types of malaria choose from any one of these methods: 300 mg Chloroquine weekly plus 200 mg daily proguanil (Paludrine); 250 mg mefloquine (Lariam) weekly; or 100 mg doxycycline (Vibramycin, Doryx) daily. If you buy your Chloroquine tablets in Pakistan, however, they will probably be 250 mg Chloroquine phosphate tablets, containing 150 mg of Chloroquine. Take two of these each week.

With each method, begin the week or day you arrive in a risk area, and continue for four weeks after you leave. Discuss the best malaria prophylaxis and potential treatment for you with your physician. Factors to consider are the area you will visit, the risk of exposure to malaria-carrying mosquitoes, your current medical condition, and your age and pregnancy status. It is also important to discuss the possible side effects, so you can weigh the level of risk versus benefit ratio. Prophylaxis does not prevent you from being infected, but kills the parasites during a stage in their development.

FIRST AID KIT

A first aid kit is essential in remote regions and contains the following.

Dressings & Supplies

Bring an assortment of sterile and non-sterile bandages for dressing wounds. Sterile adhesive bandages and waterproof butterfly closures are used for minor cuts, abrasions, puncture wounds and to hold wound edges together. Flexible rolled gauze that stretches secures dressings or sterile non-adherent dressings. Include fingertip/knuckle band-aids, a high-compression elastic bandage with velcro closure, a triangular bandage, and an oval eye pad. Absorbent, nonstick (nonsterile) pads cushion and protect larger wounds. Absorbent, nonstick sterile pads are used with bleeding or draining wounds. Bring eight-ply sterile pads to cleanse open wounds and dress minor wounds. Waterproof tape, safety pins, and bandage scissors may help to secure dressings.

Other useful supplies are: an ammonia inhalant (for faintness, dizziness); blister treatment (adhesive pads such as moleskin and molefoam); cotton swabs; eye drops for washing out dust; Q-tips, latex surgical gloves; matches; a 'space' blanket; thermometer; tweezers; and your water-purification treatment. A knee or ankle brace is useful too. Bring disposable needles and syringes, in case you need injections. Ask your physician for a note explaining why they have been dispensed to you.

Medications

In Pakistan, medications are generally available over the counter at a much lower cost than in the West. However, some medications, especially the more costly antibiotics, may be of substandard quality, past the expiry date, or stored improperly. Bogus drugs are common and it is possible drugs that are no longer recommended, or have been banned in the West, are still being sold. Ideally antibiotics should be administered only under medical supervision and should never be taken indiscriminately. Take only the recommended dose at the prescribed intervals and continue using the antibiotic for the prescribed period, even if the symptoms are gone. Stop immediately if there are any serious reactions and do not self-administer an antibiotic if you are unsure that you have the correct one.

The generic names for recommended medications are listed below with common brand names in parentheses followed by their suggested use.

Altitude Acetazolamide 250 mg (Diamox) can be taken before ascent to prevent mild AMS (Acute Mountain Sickness) symptoms. It also helps relieve symptoms of mild AMS such as headache and nausea and can help you sleep at altitude. Recent studies indicate that half a pill is just as effective with fewer side effects. Dexamethasone (Decadron and Oradexon), a steroid drug thought to reduce brain swelling, is useful for HACE. However, it should never to taken to prevent the onset of AMS. Nifedipine (Procardia and Adalat) lowers pulmonary artery pressure and is useful for HAPE. It too should never be taken as a prophylaxis.

Analgesics Aspirin, ibuprofen (Brufen, Advil, Motrin), acetaminophen 500 mg (Tylenol, Paracetamol, Atasol), and acetaminophen with 15 mg codeine (Tylenol with codeine, Beserol) reduce pain and fever. Please bring enough to treat minor aches and pains of any porters or trek crew you may hire or local people who will ask. Because local people may be allergic to aspirin or ibuprofen, acetaminophen (Paracetamol) is the best choice for locals.

Antibiotics These may include ampicillin; cephalexin 250 mg (Keflex, Sporidex); ciprofloxacin 500 mg; erythromycin 250 mg; metronidazole 250 mg (Flagyl); norfloxacin (Noroxin); tinidazole 250 mg (Fasigyn); and trimethoprim sulphamethoxazole 250 mg (Bactrim, Septra DS). If you are allergic to commonly prescribed antibiotics, such as penicillin or sulfa drugs, carry this information with you at all times.

Antidiarrhoeal Take Kaolin preparation, or sodium bismuth preparation (Pepto-Bismol) for loose bowels.

Antifungal A powder or cream (Tiniderm, Tinactin, and Tineafax) with 1% Tolnaftate is an effective treatment for fungal infections.

Antihistamines Diphenhydramine 25 mg (Benadryl, Vistaril) eases the itch from insect bites and stings, helps prevent motion sickness, and relieves symptoms from allergic reactions.

Antihelminthic Mebendazole 10 mg (Vermox, Wormin) gets rid of worms.

Antiinflammatory Ibuprofen (Advil, Motrin, Brufen) eases aches, pain, and swelling.

Antimotility Diphenoxylate (Lomotil, Phenatol), loperamide (Imodium A-D). Do not take them if blood or pus is present in the stool. Use as a last resort to keep from dehydrating. Take Pepto-Bismol or an antibiotic before you use these.

Antimotion Dimenhydrinate (Dramamine) is also a mild sedative and has antihistaminic qualities.

Antinausea Metoclopramide 25 mg (Maxolon) and prochlorperazine (Compazine) are given as suppositories, tablets or as intramuscular injections to reduce nausea.

Antiseptic Povidone and iodine (Betadine), which come as impregnated swabs, liquid, or ointment, disinfect wounds.

Antispasmodic/Antacids Mylanta, Maalox, Gelusil, Pepto-Bismol soothe upset stomachs.

Constipation Bisacodyl (Dulcolax) is a laxative that relieves symptoms.

Decongestant Psuedophedrine (Sudafed) dries running noses. Psuedophedrine with triploidine (Actifed) can cause drowsiness. Slow release decongestants (eg, Ornade, Histade) help with upper respiratory infections.

Oral Rehydration Salts (ORS) ORS and powdered electrolyte mixes can be added to drinking water to replace essential salts lost through diarrhoea or sweating.

Skin Applications Calamine lotion, hydrocortisone cream, and Campho Phenique ease inflammation or irritation from sunburn, bites, or stings. A liniment is helpful for sore joints or muscles. Bring high-SPF sunscreen and lip salve. Insect repellent is also useful. Bring a small tube of antibiotic ointment (eg, bacitracin, neosporin, polysporin, or mycolog) to prevent infection of minor wounds.

Staying Healthy

Being careful about what you eat and drink is the best way to stay healthy.

WATER PURIFICATION

Water is often contaminated with bacteria, cysts, and viruses. When you do not know for certain that the water is uncontaminated, it is necessary to purify drinking water. Find the cleanest water available to purify. When water has much sediment or silt, let it stand in another container until the sediment has settled to the container's bottom. If the only available water is brown or muddy, allow it to filter through sand or fine cloth into another container, if possible. Collect the clearer water towards the top of the container to use. Boiling, treating chemically, and filtering are practical ways to purify water.

Boiling

The best way of purifying water is to bring it to a rolling boil for at least one minute, which kills all intestinal-disease-causing organisms. As altitude increases, water boils at a lower temperature, but these temperatures are still adequate for disinfection.

Chemical Treatment

When used correctly, iodine is a very effective chemical treatment to purify water. It is available in three forms: tablets, tincture, and crystals. Iodine products are lightweight and easy to use, although their effectiveness depends on concentration, exposure time, temperature, pH, and turbidity of the water. After treating water with any form of iodine, treated water should be left to stand for at least 20 minutes before drinking. If the water is particularly cold, let it warm up in the sun before treating it. Otherwise, allow treated water to stand longer.

Iodine in tablet form is marketed under various brand names (eg, Potable Aqua). Tablets are easy to carry and use and dissolve quickly. However, if the tablets get wet, they become ineffective. Tincture of iodine is a liquid form typically sold in a glass bottle (eg, Lugol's solution, Povidone, or Betadine). The recommended dosage is two to three drops per litre of water.

Iodine crystals are also sold in glass bottles. Prepare a saturated iodine solution by filling the bottle with water. After this solution stands for one hour, it is ready to use. Remember to protect glass bottles from breaking.

Add flavoured drinking powder, rehydration mixtures, or herbal tea bags to disguise the taste of iodine-treated water after the water is disinfected. Vitamin C binds with any excess iodine and improves the taste.

Chlorine tablets, sold under various brand names (eg, Puritabs, Steritabs), do not kill all pathogens (eg, giardia and amoebic cysts) and are not recommended.

Filtration

Filtration works by straining out chemicals, microorganisms, and suspended solids. The size of the pores in a water filter determine its effectiveness. All filters remove giardia, some remove smaller bacteria, but none remove viruses. To kill viruses, chemical disinfection or boiling is necessary. Only filters that combine filtration with disinfection produce water safe to drink.

FOOD & DRINK PREPARATION

Follow the old adage 'cook it, boil it, peel it, or forget it'. Locally available dried fruit is safe to eat only when it is sulphured to kill fly larvae. Unfortunately, sulphured fruit is not as tasty as the unsulphured variety. Soaking dried fruit overnight in iodised water or boiling it are effective solutions. Treat milk with suspicion, as it is often unpasteurised, and can transmit tuberculosis and brucellosis. Milk must be boiled and stored hygienically. Yoghurt is safe to eat, if flies have not been landing on it. Take care with lassi since water may have been added. All bottled water produced in Pakistan has been found to be contaminated and is not safe to drink. Imported brands are advised when available.

Buy bottled water in containers with a serrated seal; not pop or screw tops and corks. Busy restaurants where food is being cooked and eaten quickly are best. Avoid food that has been left to cool or has been reheated. When trekking with a cook and kitchen crew, make sure they have a bar of soap and wash their hands before preparing or serving food. Make sure dishes and utensils are washed properly with soap and not just rinsed off. Avoid drinking from cups or eating from plates that are not thoroughly dried.

Nutrition

If your food is poor or limited in quantity or availability, if you are travelling hard and fast and therefore missing meals, or if you simply lose your appetite, you can soon start to lose weight and place your health at risk. You cannot trek if you do not eat enough. You need extra calories, especially carbohydrates (ie, grains, bread, and potatoes). Dairy products, eggs, beans, lentils, and nuts are all good sources of protein. Make sure your diet is well balanced. If your intake of vitamin-rich foods (eg, fruit) is insufficient, consider taking vitamin supplements. Make sure you drink enough and do not wait until you feel thirsty to drink. Always carry water when you trek or take long road journeys.

PERSONAL HYGIENE

It helps to adjust some personal hygiene habits. Always wash your hands with soap before you eat. Brush your teeth with purified water. When trekking, change your sweaty clothes, including your socks, immediately when you get into camp. Wear shoes at all times and wear rubber sandals when you bathe. Avoid insect bites by covering bare skin when insects are around, by screening windows or bedding, or by using insect repellents.

Common Medical Problems

Wherever possible seek qualified medical help before treating any illness or injury. Although we give advice and treatments in this section, it is intended only for reference in an emergency.

CLIMATIC FACTORS

Dehydration, sunburn, fungal infections, heat exhaustion, and heat stroke occur with exposure to heat and sun. When trekking and camping at high altitudes be prepared for cold, wet or windy conditions even if you are just out for a few days. Snow blindness, hypothermia, and frostbite occur with exposure to cold and snow.

Dehydration

Dehydration can occur in cold as well as hot conditions and as a result of diarrhoea and vomiting. The body expends fluids in saliva, urine, and sweat that need to be replenished. Urine is normally pale yellow. Darkening urine and decreased urination are signs of dehydration. Drink more fluid and avoid diuretics, such as caffeine.

Sunburn

At high altitude you can get sunburnt quickly, even on hazy, cloudy, or overcast days and even when it snows. Use a high-quality sunscreen and lip moisturiser with a

Sun Protection Factor (SPF) of 15 or above and reapply throughout the day. Cover areas which do not normally see sun (eg, under your nose and chin). Wear protective clothing for your face, ears, and neck. A wide-brimmed hat, scarf, bandanna, or an umbrella offer added protection. Use zinc oxide or another cream or physical barrier for your nose when travelling on snow for extended periods.

Fungal Infections

To prevent fungal infections wear loose, comfortable clothing, avoid artificial fibres, wash frequently and dry carefully. If you get an infection, wash the infected area daily with a disinfectant or medicated soap and water, and rinse and dry thoroughly. Apply a topical antifungal treatment. Try to expose the infected area to air or sunlight as much as possible. Wash all socks and underwear in hot water and change them often.

Heat Exhaustion

Overexposure to heat and sun, dehydration, or deficiency of salts can cause heat exhaustion. Symptoms include faintness, a weak and rapid pulse, shallow breathing, cold or clammy skin, and profuse perspiration. Lie a victim down in a cool, shaded area. Elevate their feet and massage their legs towards the heart. Give them a drink of cool salty water (ie, ½ teaspoon of salt in a glass of water) or a sweet drink. Allow them to rest and do not let them sit up too soon.

Heat Stroke

Heat stroke is the onset of a high fever caused by sun exposure when the body's heat-regulating mechanism breaks down. Heat stroke is a life-threatening condition and must be treated as an emergency. The symptoms are extremely high body temperature (39 to 41°C), rapid pulse, profusion followed by a cessation of sweating, and then dry, red, hot skin. Severe, throbbing headaches and lack of coordination may also occur, and a victim may be confused or aggressive. Eventually a victim will convulse and become unconscious. Hospitalisation is essential.

Meanwhile it is imperative to lower the body temperature. Get the victim out of the sun, cool in water, sponge briskly with a cool cloth, or wrap in cold clothes or a wet sheet or towel and then fan continually. Do not give stimulating beverages (eg, coffee, tea, or soda).

Snowblindness

Exposure to UV light can burn the cornea of the eye in as little as two hours. At 5000m there is 75% more UV penetration than at sea level. Any time you walk on snow or go above 3500m your eyes need protection that filters a minimum of 90% UV-A and UV-B radiation. Extend precautions on cloudy days as well. Buy sunglasses for anyone you hire; do not give them money to buy glasses for themselves. If you do not have sunglasses for someone you hire, insist on wrapping a cloth around their head and face, leaving the smallest slit possible for them to see. Snowblindness is extremely painful. If it occurs, patch the eye(s) and apply a cold compress and give analgesics for pain. It can take two days or longer for symptoms to subside. Ophthalmic ointment or drops may soothe the eye(s) and prevent possible infection.

Hypothermia

Hypothermia occurs when the body loses heat faster than it produces it, lowering the core body temperature. Even when the air temperature is above freezing, the combination of wind, wet clothing, fatigue, and hunger, can lead to hypothermia. Dress in insulating layers and wear a hat, as much heat is lost through the head. On the trail, carry food containing simple sugars to generate heat quickly and keep water intake high.

The symptoms of hypothermia are shivering, loss of coordination (eg, slurred speech), and disorientation or confusion. This can be accompanied by exhaustion, numb skin (particularly toes and fingers), irrational or violent behaviour, lethargy, dizzy spells, muscle cramps and violent bursts of energy. To treat the early stages of hypothermia, first get the victim out of the elements (ie, wind, rain, or snow) and add more layers of clothing. Then prevent heat loss by replacing any wet clothes with dry, warm ones. Next have the victim drink warm liquids, avoiding alcohol, and eat high-caloric food with sugars or carbohydrates. Do not rub the victim, but place them near a fire or gently bathe with warm, not hot, water. It may be necessary to place the victim, naked, in warm sleeping bags and get in with them.

Frostbite

Frostbite occurs when extremities freeze. Signs include crystals on the skin, whitish coloured or waxy skin accompanied by itching, numbness, and pain. If blisters develop, do not break them. Warm affected areas, by covering with warm clothing or a sleeping bag, or by immersing in warm, not hot, water. When skin becomes flushed, stop warming, elevate, and expect pain and swelling. Exercise area if possible. Apply dressings only if victim must be moved. When fingers or toes are affected, separate the digits with sterile pads.

ACUTE MOUNTAIN SICKNESS (AMS)

AMS occurs from a failure of the body to adapt to higher elevations resulting in a build up of inter-cellular fluid, which accumulates in the lungs and/or in the brain. Fluid build up in the lungs is called high altitude pulmonary edema (HAPE). Fluid build up in the brain is called high altitude cerebral edema (HACE). HACE and HAPE are both progressive, life-threatening conditions, which may occur simultaneously. Ignoring progressive symptoms may lead to unconsciousness and death within hours.

Prevention & Symptoms

AMS can be prevented easily and should never be fatal. Although AMS generally occurs and is more severe at higher elevations, it has occurred as low as 1800m. The key to preventing AMS is to ascend slowly so acclimatisation can take place. When trekking over 3000m, limit your daily ascent to 300m. Exercise caution when flying to Chitral, Gilgit, or Skardu. Do not drive to high-elevation villages or trail heads on the same day you fly into these towns. Spend at least one night in Chitral or Gilgit and two nights in Skardu. Keep your fluid intake high and avoid diuretics, such as caffeine and alcohol. Since the body takes in less oxygen while sleeping, do not take sedatives to help you sleep, which lower your breathing rate and decrease oxygen levels in your blood.

Guides and porters in Pakistan, where no educational material about AMS is available, are inadequately trained in recognition and treatment of AMS. Trekkers need to understand and recognise the symptoms of AMS, be aware of its risks, and know how to respond to symptoms when present. Be alert for symptoms in yourself and those in your trekking party.

AMS progresses slowly but steadily over 24 to 48 hours. Early signs of AMS are headache, persistent yawning, hyperventilation, shortness of breath, loss of appetite, poor sleep, and waking up at night gasping for breath (ie, Cheyne-Stokes breathing). It is not uncommon to experience these symptoms when ascending. They indicate you have reached your limit of acclimatisation and that you should stop and rest in order to acclimatise further.

When you continue to ascend, symptoms will steadily worsen. As the fluid accumulates in the lungs, the person with HAPE becomes progressively more breathless, at first while walking and eventually even at rest. Breathlessness is accompanied by a cough, dry at first, and a discernible rattling or gurgling in the lungs, which progresses to production of pink, frothy sputum, then bloody. Death from drowning results. As fluid collects in the brain, a person with HACE experiences headache, loss of appetite, nausea, and becomes lethargic and tired. As the severity increases, disorientation and loss of coordination develop. A trekker with HACE has difficulty lacing boots, putting on crampons, or tying knots. With increasing lethargy comes a desire to lie down, followed by coma. Without immediate descent, death is inevitable.

Studies conducted by the Himalayan

Rescue Association of Nepal at health posts en route to Mt Everest base camp found that 80% of fatalities from AMS occurred in groups, even though only 40% of trekkers were in groups. The reason for this is that fixed trekking itineraries put pressure on trekkers and tour leaders to continue ascending even when AMS symptoms appear. Trekkers will often hide their early symptoms and inexperienced tour leaders hesitate to split the group and trek crew – mistakes which can have fatal consequences.

Treatment

Treatment of AMS is simple. When you experience any symptoms, especially headache and/or breathlessness, stop and rest until they go away. Symptoms may be confused with a cold or an upset stomach, or being out of shape. Do not ascend when you have any symptoms. If the symptoms do not go away, or get worse, descend immediately to the last elevation where you were symptom-free regardless of the time of day. A person suffering from AMS may not think clearly and may have to be forced to descend. Even if the diagnosis of AMS is uncertain, descend when you suspect AMS. You can always reascend later. AMS should never be fatal in trekkers, as a prompt descent always relieves symptoms.

Prophylaxis is not recommended to prevent AMS. It is safer to rely on planned, slow ascent. However, acetazolamide (Diamox), dexamethasone, and nifedipine have proven effective for AMS and trekkers should include them in a first aid kit (see First Aid Kit above).

Portable Hyperbaric Chamber The Gamow Bag, a portable hyperbaric chamber, has been shown to be an effective device to treat altitude-related illness by simulating descent to lower elevations. It is used when the victim is unable to walk or be moved to lower elevations. The bag costs over US$2000, so suppliers in some countries offer weekly and monthly rental rates. None are available in Pakistan.

INFECTIOUS DISEASES
Diarrhoea

Diarrhoea that results from ingesting toxins produced by bacteria growing on food is called food poisoning. However, most diarrhoea results from infection caused by consuming faecally contaminated food or water. Diarrhoea leaves you miserable, interrupts travel plans, can jeopardise the success of your trek, and is likely to be the most common illness among travellers in the Karakoram and Hindukush. In other mountain areas of South Asia, bacterial diarrhoea has been found to cause 85% of travellers' diarrhoea. Giardiasis, often thought to be the most common, is responsible for only 12% and amoebiasis accounts for only 1%. The good news is that almost all travellers' diarrhoea can be effectively treated with antibiotics. Dehydration is the main danger with any diarrhoea. Severe dehydration almost always results from diarrhoea plus vomiting, not from diarrhoea alone.

Fluid replacement remains the mainstay of management. Taking frequent sips of liquid is the best approach. Diphenoxylate hydrochloride (Lomotil) or loperamide (Immodium) can be used to bring symptomatic relief from diarrhoea, although neither treats the problem. Because they keep the pathogens from passing through your gut, only use these if absolutely necessary (eg, if you must travel). Infectious diarrhoea can be treated with antibiotics. Although a stool test is necessary to accurately identify which pathogen is causing diarrhoea, the nature of the onset of symptoms has been found to be a useful diagnostic as to the cause of diarrhoea.

Bacterial Diarrhoea Although bacterial diarrhoea is self-limiting and will usually go away within one week, there is no reason to avoid treatment. Bacterial diarrhoea is characterised by its sudden onset, and is often accompanied by vomiting, fever, and blood in the stool. You will probably be able to recall just what time of day your diarrhoea began, and the symptoms will be uncomfortable from the start. It can be treated with either of two related antibiotics: Norfloxacin (400 mg) twice daily for five days; or Ciprofloxacin (500 mg) twice daily for three days.

Giardiasis The parasites responsible for giardiasis reside in the upper intestine, and move from host to host as nonactive cysts that exit the body with faeces. The cysts survive in streams and dust. They can be killed by boiling water or by purifying it with iodine. This infection is characterised by a slow onset, and a grumbly, gassy gut. Symptoms occur one to two weeks after ingesting the parasite. The symptoms may disappear for a few days and then return. This often goes on for several weeks before travellers decide to seek treatment.

The common treatment is tinidazole (Fasigyn) in a two-gram dose for two days. In the US, metronidazole (Flagyl) is used in a 250 mg dose three times daily for seven days. Both drugs produce mild nausea, fatigue, and a metallic taste in the mouth and cannot be taken with alcohol.

Amoebiasis Amoebiasis is caused by a single species of amoebas, *entamoeba histolytica*. Symptoms usually appear gradually, often over several weeks, with cramping and infrequent vomiting. The diarrhoea may come and go every few days, even alternating with constipation. It is not a self-limiting disease; it will persist until treated and can recur and cause long-term health problems. The treatment is a two-gram dose of tinidazole daily for three days followed by 500 mg of diloxanide furoate (Furamide) three times daily for 10 days to prevent reinfection from amoebic cysts. In the USA, treatment is 250 mg of metronidazole three times daily for 10 days.

Cholera
The bacteria responsible for cholera are found in faecally contaminated water. The disease is characterised by a sudden onset of acute diarrhoea with 'rice-water' stools, vomiting, muscular cramps, and extreme weakness. You need immediate medical help. Treat for dehydration, which can be

extreme, and if there is an appreciable delay in getting to a hospital then begin taking 250 mg tetracycline four times daily. Ampicillin is an alternate drug. Remember that while antibiotics might kill the bacteria, it is the toxin produced by the bacteria which causes the massive fluid loss. Fluid replacement is by far the most important aspect of treatment.

Enteric Fever
Enteric (or typhoid) fever is a dangerous intestinal infection that travels the faecal-oral route. In the early stages, a victim may feel like they have a bad cold or flu on the way. Early symptoms are headache, sore throat, and a fever which rises a little each day until it is around 40°C or more. The victim's pulse is often slow compared with the degree of fever present and gets slower as the fever rises – unlike a normal fever where the pulse increases. There may also be vomiting, diarrhoea or constipation. Typically in the second week the high fever and slow pulse continue and a few pink spots may appear on the body; trembling, delirium, weakness, muscle aches, bone-rattling chills, weight loss and dehydration are other symptoms. If there are no further complications, the fever and other symptoms will slowly go away during the third week. However you must seek medical help before this because pneumonia (acute infection of the lungs) or peritonitis (perforated bowel) are common complications, and because typhoid is very infectious. Treat the fever by keeping the victim cool and watch for dehydration. Recommended treatment is a one-gram daily dose of ciprofloxacin for 14 days. Chloramphenicol is an alternate drug that has been the mainstay of treatment for many years. In many countries it is still the recommended antibiotic but there are fewer side effects with Ampicillin. The adult dosage is 500 mg four times a day.

Hepatitis
Hepatitis is a virus that attacks and damages the liver. Five types of Hepatitis called types A, B, C, D, and E are known. Types A and E

are common throughout Pakistan. The incubation period is two weeks to two months. You are contagious before the onset of symptoms and for some time afterwards. Hepatitis A is spread by faecally contaminated food or water. People who have previously contracted the virus have a natural virus-specific immunity. Initial symptoms may include fever, chills, headache, fatigue, feelings of weakness, aches and pains. This is followed by loss of appetite, nausea, vomiting, abdominal pain, dark urine, light coloured faeces, jaundiced skin, and yellowing of the whites of the eyes. Once the jaundice appears, the person is no longer infectious.

Hepatitis B, or serum hepatitis, is spread through contact with infected blood, blood products or bodily fluids (eg, through sexual contact, the use of unsterilised needles, and blood transfusions). The symptoms of type B are similar to type A but are more severe.

Hepatitis Non-A Non-B is a blanket term formerly used for several different strains of hepatitis, which have now been identified as types C, D, and E. Hepatitis C is similar to type B but is less common. Hepatitis D (the 'delta particle') is also similar to type B and always occurs in concert with it; its occurrence is currently limited to IV drug users. Hepatitis E, however, is similar to type A and is spread in the same manner. Isolated cases of Type E in pregnant women in Pakistan have been fatal.

Anyone suspected of having hepatitis should seek medical advice and confirm the diagnosis with a simple blood test. Tests to detect hepatitis strains are only available at a few medical facilities in major cities. In Pakistan, tests only differentiate types A, B, and E. There is not much you can do apart from rest, drink lots of fluids, eat lightly and avoid fatty foods and alcohol. You must forego alcohol for at least one year afterward to allow the liver to recover.

Rabies

Rabies is caused by a bite or scratch from an infected animal. Dogs are noted carriers as are bats, monkeys, wolves, foxes, and cats. Any bite, scratch or even a lick from a warm-blooded, furry animal should be cleaned immediately with soap and water, and then with an alcohol disinfectant and antibiotic ointment. If any possibility exists that the animal is rabid, seek medical help immediately because rabies is 100% lethal. Treatment for rabies is a series of injections administered over a few weeks. Treatment can be difficult to get and is expensive, but be conservative in your judgment. Even if the animal is not rabid, all bites should be treated seriously as they may become infected or may result in tetanus.

Tetanus

This potentially fatal infection occurs throughout the world. It is difficult to treat but is preventable with immunisation. Tetanus occurs when a wound becomes infected by a bacteria that lives in faeces, so clean all cuts, punctures, or animal bites. Tetanus is also known as lockjaw, and the first symptom may be discomfort in swallowing, or stiffening of the jaw and neck; this is followed by painful convulsions of the jaw and whole body, typically leading to death.

Upper Respiratory Tract Infection

Upper respiratory ailments such as a cold, sore throat, sinusitis, and bronchitis are common trekking ailments. Treat a cold with decongestants (psuedoephrine) and aspirin or acetaminophen. If it progresses to sinusitis, treat with an antibiotic. Sore throats can be soothed by moistening the throat with a lozenge or hard candy. This is particularly helpful when making long ascents and crossing passes. Bronchitis is characterised by a yellow-green sputum with fever and needs to be treated with antibiotics. Be cautious at higher elevations; bronchitis can predispose you to AMS. Accompanying cough or complaint of chest pain may be indicative of HAPE.

Tuberculosis (TB)

TB is widespread, but is not generally a serious risk to travellers. TB is commonly spread by coughing or by consuming unpasteurised dairy products from infected animals. TB is prevalent in high-altitude villages where people live closely with cows, yaks, sheep, and goats. Avoid staying in homes in such villages where anyone has a persistent cough. Get a TB skin test after you return home.

Sexually Transmitted Diseases

Sexual contact with an infected sexual partner or carrier spreads these diseases. While abstinence is the only 100% preventive, practicing safe sex and using condoms reduces exposure and can be effective. Common sexually transmitted diseases include gonorrhoea, syphilis, chlamydia, trichomonas, herpes, hepatitis B, and yeast infections. Effective antibiotic treatment is available for most sexually transmitted diseases.

HIV/AIDS

The Human Immunodeficiency Virus (HIV) is a virus that attacks the cells in the body that help protect a person against infections. A person infected with this virus may be asymptomatic; may have symptoms; or may have Acquired Immune Deficiency Syndrome (AIDS), a life-threatening illness for which no cure exists. It is impossible to know if an otherwise healthy-looking person is infected with HIV or has AIDS without a blood test.

Any exposure to blood, blood products, or bodily fluids may put an individual at risk of transmission. HIV/AIDS can also be spread by transfusions with infected blood. Pakistan only began screening blood at some hospitals in 1994; blood is still not screened at most facilities. HIV/AIDS can also be spread by use of dirty needles. Immunisations, acupuncture, tattooing, and body piercing can potentially be as dangerous as IV drug use if the equipment is not sterilised. If you need an injection, ask to see the syringe unwrapped in front of you, or better still, take a needle and syringe pack with you.

The best preventive measure is to minimise exposure to the HIV virus by abstaining from any sexual contact; avoiding sexual contact with persons known or suspected of being HIV positive or IV drug users; avoiding sexual contact with multiple partners or with those who have had multiple partners; practicing safe sex and using a condom every time you have any sexual contact; abstaining from IV drug use or from sharing needles if you do use IV drugs; ensuring that your health care provider uses disposable needles and syringes if an injection is unavoidable; and only agreeing to a blood transfusion when medically mandatory and only if you can be assured the blood supply has been screened for HIV. Fear of HIV infection should never preclude treatment for serious medical conditions.

INSECT BORNE DISEASES

Dengue Fever is a sudden onset of fever, frontal headache, backache, and severe joint and muscle pain followed by a rash that starts on the trunk of the body and spreads to the limbs and face. No prophylaxis nor effective antibiotic treatment are available for this mosquito-spread virus. After a few days, fever subsides and recovery begins. Serious complications are not common and the disease goes away after a week. October is the main season for dengue fever, so take added precaution during this time to avoid mosquito bites. Dengue fever is common in the Delhi-Agra-Jaipur area, and presumably in Pakistan's Punjab.

Malaria

Primary prevention is mosquito avoidance. The Anopheles mosquitoes that transmit malaria bite from dusk to dawn. During this period travellers are advised to wear light coloured clothing; wear long pants and long-sleeved shirts; use mosquito repellents containing the compound DEET on exposed areas of skin and on clothing; avoid highly scented perfumes or aftershave; and use a mosquito net. Symptoms include headaches, fever, chills and sweating that may subside and recur. Headaches, abdominal pains, and a vague feeling of ill health may be present. Without treatment malaria can develop more serious, potentially fatal effects. Malaria is treatable and can be diagnosed by a simple blood test, so seek medical help immediately when symptoms occur.

Typhus

Typhus is spread by ticks, mites, and lice. It begins like a bad cold, followed by a fever, chills, headache, muscle pains, and a body rash. There is often a large painful sore at the site of the bite and nearby lymph nodes are swollen and painful. Lice are common where people live closely with sheep and goats. Always check your body and clothing carefully for ticks after walking through a tick-infested area. Ticks are rare, but not unknown in the Karakoram and Hindukush. A strong insect repellent (with DEET) can help.

OTHER CONCERNS
Blisters

As soon as you feel a hot spot on your foot, put tape or an adhesive foam pad on it. If a blister develops, do not pop it. Pad it, wait for it to burst, and keep the new skin clean. Blisters turn into calluses eventually.

Trekker's or Sahib's Knee

Swelling of the knee from pounding descents can be incapacitating. If prone to this, take anti-inflammatory drugs before you start walking. A brace may also help. Minimise the pounding by taking small steps with slightly bent knees, and carry less weight.

Bedbugs, Lice, Fleas & Scabies

These pests are a major nuisance. If encountered, shake your bedding well and expose it to sunlight. Avoid sleeping in local homes or shepherd's huts, many of which harbour these pests. Sleep in your tent rather than accepting invitations to share local shelter.

Bedbugs found in bedding and bed frames are relatively large and leave itchy bites. Bedbugs come out when it is dark or when body heat is present. They can be difficult to spot as they disappear quickly when exposed to light.

Lice cause itching and discomfort and can cause typhus. Lice make themselves at home in your hair (head lice), the seams of your clothing (body lice) or in your pubic hair (crabs). You can see lice and may notice a small welt after they bite. You catch lice through direct contact with infected people, animals or bedding, or by sharing combs, clothing, and the like. Powder, cream, lotion, or shampoo treatment of 1% lindane (eg, Kwell, Gamene, Gammexane) will kill the lice and the many eggs or nits they lay. Other effective treatments are 1% permethrin (eg, Nix) and pyretrins with piperonyl butoxide (ie, Rid, XXX). These are toxic, so wash your hands thoroughly after using and avoid applying to your face or to any broken skin. Washing infected clothing in very hot water may help, but it does not always get rid of lice.

Fleas are tiny jumping insects whose bites itch for some time. Look closely in the seams of your sleeping sheet and bag and try to catch any fleas. You can also use a commercial pet flea collar. Put the open flea collar in your sleeping bag before you pack your sleeping bag into its stuff sack. During the day, this kills any fleas that may have jumped in. Then at night, take the flea collar out of your sleeping bag before you go to sleep.

Scabies is caused by a tiny mite that burrows under the skin causing intense itching. The mites are too small to see. Use the same treatment as for lice.

Worms

These parasites enter the intestines, consume the food and its nutrients, and lay eggs that hatch and multiply. They can be present on unwashed vegetables or in undercooked meat and you can pick them up through your skin by walking bare foot. Infestations may not show up for some time, and although they are generally not serious, if left untreated can lead to severe health problems. Symptoms include upper abdominal pain, feelings of fatigue or hunger even when eating regularly, reduced quantity in or irregular bowel movements, and spotting spaghetti-like strands in your faeces. A stool test is necessary to pinpoint the problem and is not a bad idea when you return home. Treatment is 100 mg of mebendazole twice daily for three days. Mebendazole is very safe, with few side effects.

WOUNDS & TRAUMA

Cleanse a small wound with an iodine solution and apply an antibiotic ointment. Bandage and keep the bandage on for cleanliness. For larger wounds with gaping skin, irrigate the wound with disinfected water to wash out any debris and with an iodine solution to kill any bacteria. Tape the wound shut and bandage it. For serious facial wounds, open fractures, and penetrating wounds, no treatment you can administer while trekking is effective. Administer antibiotics (eg, 250 mg penicillin or erythromycin four times a day for five days), and evacuate the victim as quickly as possible. Treat for shock, and use pressure to control bleeding. For extensive trauma when bones or tendons are visible, treat the victim for shock, use pressure to control bleeding, administer antibiotics, and evacuate.

Women's Health

GYNAECOLOGICAL CONCERNS

Women often find that their menstrual cycles become irregular or even cease while they travel. This is not uncommon when travelling or engaging in strenuous activities, like trekking. Remember that a missed period in these circumstances does not necessarily suggest pregnancy. You can seek advice and get a pregnancy test at family planning clinics in some cities and towns.

Poor diet, lowered resistance due to the use of antibiotics for minor illness, and even taking contraceptive pills, can lead to vaginal infections particularly in hot climates. Keeping the genital area clean and wearing loose-fitting pants and cotton underwear helps prevent infections.

PREGNANCY

If you think you might be or know you are pregnant and you go trekking, you may require extra time for acclimatisation and should stay below 5000m. It may be prudent to limit your trekking to a week or two keeping in mind the distance you are from transportation and medical care should complications arise. Miscarriage is not uncommon and most miscarriages occur during the first three months of pregnancy, so this is the most risky time to travel as far as your own health is concerned. The last three months of pregnancy should also be spent within reasonable distance of good medical care.

Pregnant women generally should avoid all unnecessary medication, but inoculations and malaria prophylaxis should still be taken where possible – consult your doctor.

Rescue & Evacuation

Choosing to trek in remote regions where medical facilities are limited has inherent risks and uncertainties. The environment is inhospitable and the weather unpredictable, which can be potentially dangerous. To help make your trek a safe one, plan to be self-sufficient. Obtain the best available trekking maps, recognising that some regions are not fully or accurately mapped. Be prepared for changeable and severe weather by ensuring your clothing and equipment are adequate. Choose a trek that is within your range of physical ability. And always seek local advice on trails, routes, equipment, and climate extremes before heading out. Adverse weather increases the risks of trekking. Be aware of the objective dangers of your route and pay attention on the trail. Despite objective dangers, studies in the Nepal Himalaya show less than 1% chance of serious injury or death exists when trekking. However, sometimes rescue and evacuation becomes necessary. When this happens, assess your situation and don't panic. Rescue doesn't always imply someone else coming to 'rescue' you. On the long, isolated Karakoram glaciers where crevasse danger is real, you may have to rescue yourself or a fellow trekker. Carry the proper equipment and know what to do.

Evacuation can mean shortening a trek because of a minor illness or injury, or responding to a serious illness or injury that requires immediate action. For minor illness or injury, the victim may be able to walk with assistance. If the victim cannot walk, perhaps they can be carried on a porter's back or on a donkey, horse, or yak. Helicopter evacuation is to be considered only for life-threatening medical emergencies (eg, serious trauma caused by falling, rock fall, avalanche, or frostbite, a serious illness, or advanced AMS).

Helicopter Evacuation

The Tourism Division requires all mountaineering expeditions to secure prior authorisation for helicopter evacuation. This requirement does not apply to trekking parties. However, trekking parties which go on a restricted-zone trek have the option to arrange this through the Tourism Division; trekkers on open-zone treks do not.

The Tourism Division gives you a letter, addressed to the Flight Control Northern Areas (FCNA), stating that you have made prior arrangements to guarantee payment in the event a helicopter evacuation becomes necessary. In order for the Tourism Division to issue this letter, they must have either: a letter to the Tourism Division from your embassy stating they guarantee payment; a similar letter to the Tourism Division from a Pakistani trekking company; or US$4000 deposited into the Tourism Division's bank account at the National Bank of Pakistan. The Tourism Division returns these funds after your trek if no evacuation is necessary. Trekking parties typically arrange for this through a Pakistani trekking company.

FCNA has offices in Gilgit and Skardu but no office in Chitral. Before your trek, give a copy of the letter from the Tourism Division to the nearest FCNA office. In Chitral, leave this letter with the DC.

If a life-threatening illness or injury occurs on trek, you can send someone down to the nearest FCNA or DC's office to request a helicopter. With your authorisation letter on file, they can then dispatch a Pakistani army helicopter. If you have not taken the above steps to guarantee payment, a helicopter cannot be dispatched until you can come up with an authorisation letter or the money. These arrangements do not guarantee a helicopter evacuation.

Helicopter evacuations are difficult and usually take more than 48 hours to arrange because of the remoteness of most trekking areas, poor communication systems, and variable mountain weather. Generally helicopters cannot land or take off above 5500m, so you cannot expect a rescue above that elevation.

Studies in the Nepal Himalaya shows that severely ill or injured trekkers are likely to die before a helicopter arrives. If alternatives exist to evacuate the victim, use them. However, for those who are rescued by helicopter, the survival rate is almost 100%. No statistics are available for Pakistan.

Here are some key points from Nepal's experience. Helicopter evacuation may fail to save a life because of lack of details. Assess the need for a physician to accompany the helicopter and communicate this clearly with whoever is sent to request a helicopter. Detail the victim's condition and the degree of urgency of the evacuation (eg, is the patient unconscious?).

This critical information may alter a pilot's decision to fly in marginal weather. Place names are confusing, so be explicit and stay put for two days once you send a message. Pick a spot where a helicopter can land, but do not mark the centre of the landing spot with materials or objects that can get caught in and damage the helicopter's rotors. If you see a helicopter and have not sent for one, do not wave at it. This avoids pilots having to make unnecessary landings and minimises their risk.

Getting There & Away

Flying is the most convenient way to travel to and from Pakistan. Travelling overland or by sea may be more interesting but not the most practical. Tour operators abroad that specialise in adventure travel can also handle all of your travel plans to and from Pakistan.

AIR
Airports & Airlines
Pakistan has four international airports of interest to trekkers: Islamabad, Karachi, Lahore, and Peshawar.

Islamabad Islamabad is the most convenient city in which to arrive to go trekking. However, Pakistan International Airlines (PIA), British Airways, and Saudi Arabian Airlines (Saudia) are the only carriers that operate direct flights. Customs and immigration formalities here are faintly more civilised because Islamabad is the airport most diplomats use.

In the arrival lounge are several banks that do foreign exchange, telephones, and a car rental counter. Outside are booking offices for Pakistan's domestic carriers. Courtesy vans run to the Pearl Continental in Rawalpindi and the Marriott Hotel in Islamabad.

Karachi Most international carriers are given landing rights only in Karachi. Hence, it offers travellers the most options for carriers, routes, schedules, and fares. Frequent daily connections operate to most other major cities in Pakistan. However, the law-and-order situation in Karachi has deteriorated. Travellers are advised to avoid Karachi whenever possible. If you cannot avoid flying via Karachi, try to schedule an immediate domestic connection to your final destination. If your flight schedule forces an overnight in Karachi, stay at one of the hotels near the airport to avoid going into town.

The international arrival terminal is run-down, immigration formalities are slow, and information is scarce. A hotel reservation office is inside the international arrival terminal, a train ticket reservation office is outside (in a converted railway carriage), and a left-luggage room is outside Terminal 2. If you are taking a connecting flight, change a little money so you can pay the Rs 20 domestic departure tax at check-in. The bank inside the terminal changes only cash; go outside to change travellers' cheques.

Lahore PIA, Indian Airlines, Saudia, and Thai Airways International are the only carriers that operate direct flights from Delhi, Bangkok, the Middle East, New York, Toronto, Frankfurt and Amsterdam. From Lahore, it is easy to connect by air or by road to Islamabad or Peshawar.

In the arrival lounge are banks, a post office, a telephone, fax, and telex office, PTDC and TDCP information counters, a taxi desk, and booking offices for Thai Airways and each of the domestic airlines.

Peshawar PIA and Shaheen Air International are the only international carriers using Peshawar. Both carriers operate several flights per week to/from Dubai.

Buying Tickets
Airlines can tell you about their routes, timetables, and fares. Advance-purchase, non-refundable tickets are usually the least expensive airfares that airlines offer. You should shop around several travel agencies to compare airfares. The various types of discounted tickets can save you a lot and/or increase the scope of your travel at marginal extra cost.

Some cheaper tickets must be purchased months in advance, while some bargains appear only at the last minute. Especially in London and some Asian capitals (notably Delhi and Bangkok), the lowest fares are offered by 'bucket shops'. Many of these businesses are honest and solvent, but some may take your money and disappear only to reopen elsewhere later under a new name.

Travellers are safest when using a travel agency that is a member of the International Air Transport Association (IATA) or a national association like the American Society of Travel Agents (ASTA) in the USA, the Association of British Travel Agents (ABTA) in the UK, or the Australian Federation of Travel Agents (AFTA) in Australia. These self-regulatory bodies protect you if a member travel agency accepts your money and then goes out of business. In this unlikely event, you should receive a refund.

Before you part with any money, ask the name of the carriers on all flights, the airports of departure and destination, the dates and time of the flights, the length of layovers, and about any restrictions. Ask whether all your money can be refunded if the flight is cancelled or changed to a date that is unacceptable. Travel agencies should never charge booking fees because they get commissions directly from the airlines.

If you have a preferred carrier, ask if it has a 'consolidator' authorised to sell discounted tickets on that carrier. The consolidator, or a travel agency that works with the consolidator, is likely to have the cheapest fares for that airline and to be trustworthy. Some carriers may not work with consolidators and do not sell discounted tickets to the public.

Once you purchase a ticket, contact the airline yourself to confirm that you are actually booked on the flight. To minimise your chances of being 'bumped' from a flight due to overbooking, reconfirm your reservations again directly with the airline at least 72 hours before departure and whenever you break your journey for more than 72 hours.

If you plan to buy international airline tickets in Pakistan, shop around for travel agencies. Some discount published airfares, but may not do so unless you ask. As elsewhere, airlines themselves do not always sell the cheapest tickets. Typically travel agencies in Pakistan do not offer very big discounts on international flights. When paying for tickets in rupees, travel agencies and airlines may require a bank encashment certificate (at least for the full value of the ticket) issued in the same month as the month of travel. Others accept payment by credit card (no processing fee should be charged) or in US dollars and other major currencies.

The following sections offer suggestions for where to buy tickets overseas. The sample fares listed are published base fares for tickets purchased in each country; applicable taxes are not included. None of the listed fares constitute a recommendation for any airline. Use these airfares as a guide only; they are likely to have changed by the time you read this.

When you are flexible with travel dates and times and the carrier and routing you fly, you can take advantage of the lowest available fares. If a fare decreases after you purchase your ticket, the airline can usually reissue the ticket and refund the savings to you if fare rules permit. Generally low season is 16 January to 31 May and 1 August to 30 November and high season is 1 December to 15 January and 1 June to 31 August. Fares are mostly less expensive when you travel in low season.

North America

The *New York Times*, *San Francisco Examiner*, *Los Angeles Times*, *Chicago Tribune*, and other major dailies produce weekly travel sections in which you find travel agencies' ads. STA Travel and Council Travel have offices in major cities nationwide. An authorised PIA sales agent and reliable source is Himalayan Treasures & Travel (☎ (510) 222 5307 or toll free (800) 223 1813). The *Travel Unlimited* newsletter, PO Box 1058, Allston, MA 02134, publishes details of the cheapest airfares and courier possibilities from the USA and other countries. In Canada, many travel agencies advertise in the *Toronto Globe & Mail*, *Toronto Star*, and *Vancouver Province*. Travel Cuts has offices in all major cities.

PIA has services from New York and Toronto. Published airfares to/from Karachi or Lahore are usually less than airfares to/from Islamabad. One-way/return New York-Karachi airfares cost US$800/1250,

New York-Lahore US$800/1329, and New York-Islamabad US$ 850/1375. Return San Francisco-Karachi airfares cost US$1295 and San Francisco-Lahore US$1412, and San Francisco-Islamabad US$1468. One-way/return airfares Toronto-Karachi cost C$1770/2445 and Vancouver-Karachi C$1496/2193.

UK

The Saturday *Independent* and *Daily Telegraph*, and the *Sunday Times* have good travel sections, including advertisements for scores of 'bucket shops'. Also check out the ads in the 'What's On' section of *Time Out* magazine. The Globetrotters Club (BCM Roving, London, WC1N 3XX) publishes a newsletter called *Globe* that covers obscure destinations.

The best known bargain-ticket agencies are Trailfinders (☎ (0171) 938 3939) at 42-48 Earl's Court Rd, 194 Kensington High St, London, W8 6EJ; Campus Travel (☎ (0171) 730 8111) at 52 Grosvenor Gardens, London, SW1W 0AG; and STA Travel (☎ (0171) 938 4711) at Priory House, 6 Wrights Lane, London, W8 6TA. STA's telephone numbers for Asia sales are (☎ (0171) 937 9962; fax (0171) 938 5321). All have branches all over London and the UK, and Campus Travel is also in many YHA shops. Travel Cuts (☎ (071) 255 2191) and Council Travel (☎ (071) 437 7767) also have London offices.

PIA flies London-Islamabad and London-Karachi four times per week. British Airways has a convenient twice weekly service London/Gatwick-Islamabad. Fares to/from Karachi may offer up to 19% savings and to/from Lahore a 4% savings compared with those to/from Islamabad. Return fares London-Karachi cost £1833 and London-Islamabad £2258.

Continental Europe

A reliable source of bargain tickets in Europe is NBBS Travels: (☎ 638 1738) Leidsestraat 53, 1017 NV, Amsterdam; and (☎ 624 0989) Rokin 38, Amsterdam. STA has several offices in Paris; the main one is at 49 rue Pierre Charron (☎ 43 59 23 69). Check the newsletter *Farang* (La Rue 8 à 4261 Braives, Belgium) and the magazine *Aventure du Bout du Monde* (116 rue de Javel, 75015 Paris) for ads.

PIA and many other carriers have several flights weekly to and from Amsterdam, Athens, Frankfurt, Istanbul, Paris, Rome, and Zurich to and from Islamabad, Lahore, and Karachi. Fares to Karachi may be up to 20% less expensive than those to Lahore or Islamabad. Return airfares from most of these cities cost from US$1194 to US$1328.

Central Asia

PIA schedules weekly flights between Almaty, Kazakstan and Islamabad. One-way/return airfares cost US$316/370. PIA also schedules weekly flights between Ashkabad, Turkmenistan and Karachi. One-way/return airfares cost US$355/420. One-way/return airfares between Tashkent, Uzbekistan and Islamabad cost US$240/285 and Peshawar-Tashkent cost US$250/295. PIA schedules weekly flights on both routes.

South & West Asia

India PIA and Indian Airlines fly Delhi-Karachi three times per week, Delhi-Lahore four times per week and Bombay-Karachi five times per week. PIA and Malaysian Airlines fly Delhi-Karachi. Air Lanka also flies Bombay-Karachi. Flights to/from Delhi can fill up weeks ahead, so book as far in advance as possible. One-way/return airfares cost Delhi-Lahore US$57/104, Delhi-Karachi US$90/164, and Bombay-Karachi US$72/130.

Rest of South & West Asia PIA also operates twice-weekly Dhaka-Karachi and Kathmandu-Karachi. One-way/return airfares cost US$343/625 and US$253/461. Flights to/from Colombo and Malé operate twice weekly to/from Karachi on PIA and Air Lanka. One-way/return airfares cost US$193/382. PIA and Iran Air each have weekly flights Karachi-Tehran that cost one-way/return US$228/456. PIA also flies weekly Quetta-Mashhad. PIA flies twice weekly Peshawar-Dubai and Gwadar-Muscat. PIA operates twice weekly from Lahore and Karachi to/from Kuwait City and to/from Abu Dhabi. They also serve Dubai, Riyadh, Dhahran, Jeddah, and Damascus. Kuwait Airways also flies to Lahore and Karachi. Regularly scheduled flights between Pakistan and Afghanistan are suspended indefinitely.

East & South-East Asia
China Air China (CAAC division that flies major domestic and international routes) and PIA each have twice-weekly flights between Beijing-Islamabad and Beijing-Karachi. Air France and other carriers also have weekly flights Beijing-Karachi. One-way/return airfares cost US$920/1106. Xinjiang Airlines schedules once weekly flights Islamabad-Urumchi.

Hong Kong A reliable agency for budget travel is Hong Kong Student Travel Bureau, 1021 Star House, Tsimshatsui, Kowloon, (☎ 730 3269), or 901 Wing On Central Bldg, 26 Des Voeux Rd, Central, (☎ 810 7272), plus half a dozen other branches in the territory.

Routings to/from Karachi may offer up to a 5% savings from those to/from Lahore and Islamabad. One-way/return Karachi fares cost US$583/854.

Rest of East & South-East Asia STA Travel has branches in Bangkok, Kuala Lumpur, Osaka, Singapore, and Tokyo. PIA has service to/from Bangkok, Jakarta, Kuala Lumpur, Manila, and Singapore. Fares to/from Karachi may offer up to 24% savings and to/from Lahore up to 8% savings compared with fares to/from Islamabad. Return Bangkok-Karachi fares cost US$488 and Bangkok-Lahore/Islamabad cost US$562/586. Thai Airways International flies Bangkok-Karachi four times per week and Bangkok-Lahore three times per week. PIA and Malaysian Airlines each fly twice weekly Karachi-Kuala Lumpur; one-way/return fare costs US$674/896. Singapore Airlines flies thrice weekly Singapore-Karachi. Return Tokyo-Karachi air fares cost US$1640.

Australia & New Zealand
STA Travel and Flight Centres International are major dealers in cheap airfares, each with at least 50 offices in Australia and a dozen or more in New Zealand. Airfares to and from Karachi and Lahore are usually cheaper than those to Islamabad. Return Karachi airfares cost about A$1994.

LAND
Afghanistan, China, India, and Iran have overland routes to and from Pakistan.

Afghanistan
Fifteen years of ongoing political instability means it is unsafe and almost impossible for foreigners to cross legally between Pakistan and Afghanistan by land. Typically only Pakistani and Afghani nationals and UN personnel are allowed to cross the border either at Torkham (on the Khyber Pass, on the Peshawar to Kabul highway) or at Chaman (on the road and railway line from Quetta to Kandahar). Afghan consulates in Quetta and in Peshawar may provide updates on current regulations. Any illegal crossing is a highly dangerous prospect with millions of unexploded landmines across the country, ongoing fighting, and bandits. Foreigners have been kidnapped and been killed.

China
The Karakoram Highway (KKH), which links Kashgar in Xinjiang, China, to Islamabad via the Khunjerab Pass, is the only overland route to and from China. From China, travellers ride a Chinese vehicle from Kashgar to the Pakistan customs and immigration post at Sost. From Pakistan, NATCO buses and Landcruisers leave Sost from 8 am to noon and take travellers as far as the Chinese immigration post at Tashkurgan, from where they continue to Kashgar in Chinese vehicles. The trip takes two days in either direction with an overnight stop at Tashkurgan. From June to September as many buses as necessary

operate daily; earlier or later in the year buses may not operate every day. You can also hire a special van or jeep Kashgar-Sost or Sost-Tashkurgan. By jeep, Kashgar-Sost is possible in one long day. The Khunjerab Pass is formally open from 1 May to 30 November. However, snow often keeps the pass closed longer in the spring or closes it earlier in autumn.

India
The only legal border crossing between Pakistan and India is Wagah (on the Pakistan side), east of Lahore, and Attari (on the Indian side). The border opens daily at 8.30 am and closes at 2.30 pm. However, the crossing remains hostage to Pakistan-India relations and Sikh separatist activity in the Punjab, so get current information before heading to the border. You can cross by road or rail, although it is usually much quicker and easier by road (eg, Lahore-Amritsar in 3½ hours).

No direct bus service operates between Lahore and Amritsar, but plenty of vehicles go to/from the border on both sides. Minibus No 12 costs Rs 4 and leaves the Lahore railway station all day long, taking about one hour to Jila Mor (*mor* means crossing). From Jila Mor, another van takes you the last three km to the border for Rs 2. At the border, everybody piles out for customs, immigration and health checks. Taking a taxi from Jila Mor may save you from queuing with bus or train passengers. Taxis from the Lahore railway station to the border cost Rs 150.

There are regular train services Lahore-Amritsar. Trains depart from Lahore on Monday and Thursday at 11 am, and reach Attari in one hour, from where they continue to Amritsar. Trains do not leave from the main Lahore railway station, but from Platform 1 at a nearby building called *musāfir khānā*. This unlabelled shed-like building is some 150m to the right of the entrance of the main railway station, just beyond a large pipal tree. All signs in both buildings are in Urdu, not English, so allow extra time to find your way. Economy-class seats cost Rs 10;

upper-class seats costs Rs 65. From Amritsar, trains leave about 9.30 am. Reporting time is usually 2½ hours before departure.

Iran
The only legal border crossing is at Taftan (also called Kuh-i-Taftan; Mirjavé on the Iran side) between Quetta in Pakistan and Zahedan in Iran. A weekly Quetta-Zahedan train departs from Quetta on Tuesday mornings and Zahedan on Sunday mornings. The trip takes about 28 hours, including a change of trains in Zahedan. Another train departs from Quetta on Tuesday mornings and Taftan on Wednesday afternoons, taking about 22 hours.

Several buses go daily Quetta-Taftan and cost Rs 85. Buses also go frequently to and from Zahedan, a two-hour trip costing 1000 rials plus 500 rials per bag. Check current information before you head for the border. Expect to spend at least four hours in Taftan. Take food and water whichever way you go. Anyone driving their own vehicles through the interior of Pakistani Baluchistan should travel in a convoy.

Driving Your Own Vehicle
You can bring in your own car, van, bus or motorcycle, duty-free, for up to three months. You need a *carnet de passage en douane* (ie, essentially a passport for the vehicle) plus registration papers, liability insurance, and an International Driving Permit. For more information on paperwork, insurance and the availability of petrol and spare parts, ask your automobile association before leaving home. On entry, you sign a form saying you promise not to sell the vehicle while you are in Pakistan.

Bicycle
The only route presently safe enough for cycling to or from Pakistan is the KKH, over the Khunjerab Pass to or from Xinjiang, China. You do not need a permit to take a bicycle into or out of Pakistan, but you may be expected to note it on your visa application. To bring a bicycle into China you need

an import permit, which you can theoretically get on arrival at any port of entry. Chinese customs at Tashkurgan usually admits bicycles. However, few long-distance roads in China are open to foreign cyclists and you may not be allowed to ride your bicycle to or from the border.

SEA

No scheduled international passenger services operate to or from Pakistan.

TOUR OPERATORS ABROAD

Some reliable tour operators abroad are:

North America

Above the Clouds Trekking, PO Box 398, Worcester, MA 01602 0398, USA (☎ (508) 799 4499 or (800) 233-4499; fax (508) 797-4779)

Concordia Expeditions, PO Box 4159, Buena Vista, CO 81211, USA (☎ (719) 395 9191; fax (719) 395 8258)

Explore South Asia Tours Inc, 500 Summer St, Ste 203, Stamford, CT 06901, USA (☎ (203) 961 8194 or (800) 221 6941; fax (203) 348 6489)

Geographic Expeditions, 2627 Lombard St, San Francisco, CA 94123, USA (☎ (415) 922 0448 or (800) 777 8183; fax (415) 346 5535; Internet:info@geoex.com)

Ibex Expeditions, Bruce Klepinger, 2657 W 28th Ave, Eugene, OR 94075-1461, USA (☎ (503) 345 1289 or (800) 842 8139; fax (503) 343 9002)

Mountain Madness, 4218 SW Alaska St, Ste 206, Seattle, WA 98116, USA (☎ (206) 937 8389 or (800) 328 5925; fax (206) 937 1772)

Mountain Travel-Sobek, 6420 Fairmount Ave, El Cerrito, CA 94530, USA (☎ (510) 527 8100 or (800) 227 2384; fax (510) 525 7710; Internet:mtinfo@mtsobek.com)

One World Expeditions – Karakoram Experience, PO Box 10538, Aspen, CO 81612, USA (☎ (970) 925 8368 or (800) 497 9675; fax (970) 925 6704)

Pete Owens' Asian Treks c/o Govind Shahi, Himalayan Treasures & Travel, 3596 Ponderosa Trail, Pinole, CA 94564, USA (☎ (510) 222 5307 or (800) 223 1813; fax (510) 223 5309)

Sitara Travel Consultants (Pvt) Ltd, 3526 W 41st Ave, Vancouver, BC, V6N 3E6, Canada, (☎ (604) 264 8747, from Canada (800) 387 1974, and from USA (800) 888 7216; fax (604) 264 7774; telex 0455768 VCR)

Snow Lion Expeditions, 350 S 400 East, Ste G2, Salt Lake City, UT 84111, USA (☎ (801) 355 6555 or (800) 525 TREK; fax (801) 355 6566)

Wilderness Travel, 801 Allston Way, Berkeley, CA 94710, USA (☎ (510) 548 0420 or (800) 368 2794; fax (510) 548 0347; Internet:info@wildernesstravel.com)

UK

Dragoman, Camp Green, Debenham, Suffolk IP14 6LA, UK (☎ (01728) 861133; fax (01728) 861127; telex 987009)

Exodus Expeditions, 9 Weir Rd, London SW12 0LT, UK (☎ (0181) 673 0859 or 675 5550; overland calls (0181) 675 7996; fax (0181) 673 0779)

ExplorAsia, Sloane Square House, Holbein Place, London SW1W 8N2, UK (☎ (0171) 730 7795; fax (0171) 973 0482)

Explore Worldwide Ltd, 1 Frederick St, Aldershot, Hants, Hampshire GU11 1LQ, UK (☎ (01252) 319448; fax (01252) 343170)

High Adventure, 91 Telford Ave, London SW2 4XN

Himalayan Kingdoms Ltd, 20 The Mall, Clifton, Bristol BS8 4DR (☎ (0117) 923 7163; fax (0117) 974 4993) and Himalayan Kingdoms Expeditions, 45 Mowbray St, Sheffield S3 8EN, UK (☎ (0114) 276 3322; fax (0114) 276 3344)

Karakoram Experience Ltd, 32 Lake Rd, Keswick, Cumbria CA12 5DQ, UK (☎ (017687) 73966; fax (017687) 74693)

OTT Expeditions, 62 Nettleham Rd, Sheffield, S8 8SX, UK (☎ (0114) 258 8508 and (0114) 250 1134; fax (0114) 255 1603; Internet: andy@ottexpd.demon.co.uk)

Ramblers Holidays Ltd, Box 43, Welwyn Garden, Hertfordshire AL8 6PQ, UK (☎ (01707) 331 133; fax (01707) 333 276)

Worldwide Journeys & Expeditions, 8 Comeragh Rd, London W14 9HP, UK (☎ (0171) 381 8636; fax (0171) 381 0836; telex 296 871)

Continental Europe

Allibert, route de Grenoble, 38530 Chapareillan, France (☎ (76) 45 22 26; fax (76) 45 27 28) and 14 rue de l'Asile Popincourt, 75011 Paris, France (☎ (1) 48 06 16 61; fax (1) 48 06 47 22)

Ashraf Travel, Alex Schrrama, Haarlemmerstraat 140, PO Box 468, 1000 al Amsterdam, the Netherlands (☎ (020) 6232450; fax (020) 6229028)

Aventure del Mundo (Viaggi Nel Mundo), Circonvallazione Gianicolense 41, 00152 Rome, Italy (☎ (6) 588 0661; fax (6) 580 9540)

Beek Trekking Tours, Vorderdohr 41, 5600 Wuppertal 12, Germany (☎ (202) 47 19 39; fax (202) 47 74 96)

DAV Summit Club GmbH, Am Perlacher Forst 186, D-80997 Munich 90, Germany (☎ (89) 65 10 72 0)

Hauser Exkursionen International GmbH, Marienstrasse 17, D-80331 Munich, Germany (☎ (89) 23 50 06 0; fax (89) 291 37 14)

Ikarus, PO Box 1220, Fasanenweg 1, D-6240, Königstein, Germany (☎ (06174) 29020; fax (06174) 22952)

International Mountain Climbing (IMC), Gerhart-Haputmann Strasse 28, D-69221, Dossenheim, Germany (☎ (06221) 86 39 51; fax (06221) 86 03 96)

Mini Trek, Berg Strasse 153, D-6900 Heidelberg, Germany (☎ (06221) 401443)

Nouvelles Frontiéres, 87 Boulevard de Grenelle, 75015 Paris, France (☎ (1) 41 41 58 58)

Pineapple Tours, Reiser GmbH, Währinger Strasse 135, 1180 Vienna, Austria (☎ (0222) 403 98 83 0; fax (0222) 403 98 833)

Terres d'Aventure, 6 rue Saint-Victor, 75005 Paris, France (☎ (1) 53 73 77 77; fax (1) 43 29 96 31)

Tjaereborg, Kaervej 8, DK-6731, Tjaereborg, Denmark (☎ (75) 177111; fax (75) 176006)

Trekking Y Aventura, Don Ramón de la Cruz 93, 28006 Madrid, Spain (☎ (1) 401 2208; fax (1) 401 1151) and Gran Vía 523, 08011 Barcelona, Spain (☎ (3) 454 3702; fax (3) 323 5288)

Viajes Astrolabio – Avial, Santísima Trinidad 15, 28010 Madrid, Spain (☎ (1) 447 8000 and (1) 447 9809; fax (1) 447 8380)

Viajes Sanga, Alameda 8, Bajo Centro, 28014 Madrid, Spain (☎ (1) 420 09 55; fax (1) 429 67 08)

Zig Zag, 54, rue de Dunkerque, 75009 Paris, France (☎ (1) 42 85 13 93 and (1) 42 85 13 18; fax (1) 45 26 32 85)

Asia

Alpine Tour Service Co Ltd, 5-F Shimbashi Towa Bldg, 2-13-8 Shimbashi, Minato-Ku, Tokyo 105, Japan (☎ (03) 3506 8411; fax (03) 3506 8417)

Himalaya Treks & Tours (Pvt) Ltd, Sayed Sajaad Hussain Shahji, Kyoto Shi Kita, Ku Shichiku, Kamitake Dono Cho, 42-2, Japan T603 (☎ (075) 491 3060; fax (075) 491 4200)

Independent Tours Centre (ITC), Tsukasa Bldg, 3-23-7, Nishi-Shimbashi, Minatoku, Tokyo 105, Japan (☎ (03) 3431 7497; fax (03) 3438 1280)

Saiyu Travel Co Ltd, Shinekai Bldg 5F, 2-2 Kanda Jimbocho, Chiyoda-Ku, Tokyo, Japan (☎ (03) 3237 1391; telex 2323189) and Kitagawa Bldg 5F, 6-4 Kamiyamacho, Kita-ku, Osaka, Japan (☎ (06) 367 1391; fax (06) 367 1966)

Australia

World Expeditions, 441 Kent St, 3rd floor, Sydney, NSW 2000, Australia (☎ (02) 264 3366 or toll free (008) 803 688; fax (02) 261 1974); 393 Little Bourke St, 1st floor, Melbourne, Victoria 3000, Australia (☎ (03) 9670 8400; fax (03) 9670 7474); and 145 Charlotte St, 1st floor, Brisbane, Queensland 4000, Australia (☎ (07) 236 4388; fax (07) 229 5602)

LEAVING PAKISTAN
Travel Permit
The law requires anyone who has been in Pakistan for more than 30 days to obtain a Travel Permit (see Documents in the Facts for the Trekker chapter).

Reconfirming Reservations
Reconfirm outbound international flights at least 72 hours in advance or the airline will cancel your reservations. When you reconfirm, make sure the airline puts a reconfirmation stamp directly on the ticket coupon and/or staples a hard copy of the reconfirmed reservation to your ticket. Many flights are overbooked and proof of reconfirmation may become necessary.

If you do not have an outbound reservation, make a booking before your trek. If you wait to book a seat until after your trek, you may have to wait several days to get a confirmed reservation. When you plan to fly from Chitral, Gilgit, or Skardu, allow a two to three-day buffer after your trek before an international departure.

Reporting Time
Due to security, reporting time for check-in is three hours for international flights and usually two hours for domestic flights.

Departure Tax
Departure tax is payable in rupees when you check in. Departure tax for domestic flights costs Rs 20. International departure tax costs Rs 200 for coach class, Rs 300 for business class, and Rs 400 for 1st class.

Getting Around

The easiest way to reach trekking destinations in northern Pakistan is by air from Islamabad or Peshawar. However, since flights are heavily booked and subject to delays and cancellations, most people travel by road to either Chitral, Gilgit, or Skardu. Travelling by road can be gruelling, but it is affordable and the scenery is spectacular. Most people travel to trekking areas by air or road. Few travel by train.

AIR

Four airlines now serve Pakistan's 35 domestic airports: state-owned Pakistan International Airlines (PIA), Shaheen Air International, Aero Asia, and Bhoja Airlines. The private airlines do not yet have landing rights in cities other than the major ones.

PIA Domestic Service

PIA's service includes standard domestic routes, Northern Areas routes, helicopter charters, and the Air Safari. The government subsidises the cost of some domestic flights for its nationals and charges higher fares for foreigners. Applicable taxes (usually 10 to 15%) are added to the one-way base fares for foreigners we list below. Routings and fares are subject to change without notice.

Aircraft Boeing 737 and Airbus A300 jet aircraft operate on most longer domestic sectors. Older prop-driven Fokker F27 Friendships, which seat about 40 passengers, are used on many short routes, including all flights to/from Chitral, Gilgit, and Saidu Sharif.

PIA Domestic Routes Trekking destinations in NWFP that PIA serves are Peshawar and Saidu Sharif. Flights to Peshawar operate to and from Islamabad, Karachi, Lahore, and Saidu Sharif. PIA schedules several daily flights Peshawar-Islamabad that cost Rs 255. Flights Peshawar-Karachi also operate several times daily. Flights

Peshawar-Lahore operate twice a day and cost Rs 815. PIA schedules a daily Fokker flight Peshawar-Saidu Sharif that costs Rs 460. Fokker flights to Saidu Sharif operate to and from Islamabad. PIA schedules daily flights Saidu Sharif-Islamabad that cost Rs 510.

Other PIA destinations include Islamabad, Lahore, and Karachi. Several flights operate between these cities every day. PIA offers 'night coach' fares on these sectors, which are 25% cheaper, on flights scheduled from 11.15 pm to 5.59 am. One-way/night-coach fares are: Islamabad-Karachi Rs 1860/1400; Islamabad-Lahore Rs 600/450; Karachi-Lahore Rs 1530/1150; and Karachi-Peshawar Rs 1860/1400.

PIA Northern Areas Routes PIA is the only carrier serving Gilgit and Skardu. Flights operate Islamabad-Gilgit, Islamabad-Skardu, and Skardu-Gilgit. Flights to and from Chitral also fall into what PIA calls 'Northern Area Ticketing', even though Chitral is in NWFP. When we refer to Northern Areas routes, we include flights to Chitral, Gilgit, and Skardu.

Fokker flights Islamabad-Gilgit are scheduled daily. Depending on the day of the week, one to three flights per day are scheduled. The fare is Rs 575 and the flight time is 1¼ hours.

One Boeing 737 flight is scheduled daily Islamabad-Skardu. The fare is Rs 690 and the flight time is 1½ hours. Business-class fares Islamabad-Skardu are slightly more. Once a week on Saturday, a Fokker flight operates Islamabad-Skardu for Rs 600, and continues Skardu-Gilgit for Rs 395. On Thursday the reverse direction operates Gilgit-Skardu and Skardu-Islamabad.

Fokker flights to Chitral operate from Peshawar and Saidu Sharif. Daily flights Chitral-Peshawar operate three times a day for Rs 440 and take 45 minutes. The first two daily flights originate in Peshawar and hence are more reliable than the third flight, whose aircraft comes from Islamabad. Flights Chitral-Saidu Sharif are scheduled twice a week from Thursday and Saturday for Rs 460 with connections to Islamabad. (However, Fokker flights Islamabad-Saidu Sharif-Chitral are suspended indefinitely due to lack of aircraft.)

Bookings for these flights are handled differently than bookings for other domestic PIA bookings because all Northern Areas flights operate subject to weather conditions. During the monsoon (July to September), perhaps only 30% of flights to Chitral and Gilgit and 50% to Skardu operate as scheduled. Delays up to one week are not uncommon.

Northern Areas flights can be booked and tickets purchased only at certain PIA offices. Gilgit and Skardu flights are handled only at PIA in Rawalpindi (on The Mall), Gilgit, and Skardu. At the Rawalpindi PIA office, go to the Northern Areas section, which has a separate entrance on the right side of the building towards the rear. Chitral flights are only handled at PIA in Peshawar (in Saddar bazaar). At the Peshawar PIA office, go to the PIA 'Northern Area Ticketing' office, which has a separate entrance on the left side of the building towards the rear.

Reservations You can buy an 'open' ticket for any Northern Areas route any time. Then when you make reservations for a Northern Areas flight, your reservation is either confirmed or you are put on a wait list. Having a confirmed reservation is necessary, but it does not guarantee you will actually fly on a given day. Two factors affect this: backlog and the weather. Backlog refers to any passengers whose flights were cancelled in the day(s) preceding your flight who are still waiting to fly. These passengers are given priority to fly on the next flights that operate. Regardless of whether you have a confirmed reservation, you have to wait for any backlog to clear. If it looks like you'll have to wait around for several days, it would be best to travel by road. However, if there is no backlog and inclement weather cancels your

flight, you know you will go on the next flight.

PTDC Information Centres have two priority seats every day on Northern Areas flights, which must be reserved in advance. In Rawalpindi, go to their office in the Flashman's Hotel. Go to the reception desks at the Chinar Inn in Gilgit or at the K2 Motel in Skardu. In Peshawar, go to their office at Dean's. If priority seats are available, PTDC writes your name(s) down and advises you to come back by 10 am on the day before the flight. Buy your 'open' ticket from PIA before this time. PTDC then gives you a letter for PIA assigning you a priority seat. You then take the PTDC letter and your ticket to PIA by 12.30 pm that same day for reconfirmation. This little known system is convenient and beats standing around in crowds at PIA offices.

Only the smaller Fokker F27s can land on Gilgit's short runway. Therefore, the capacity to handle more passengers cannot increase until the runway is lengthened. The prospect for this may be years away. Meanwhile, another strategy exists for reaching Gilgit if you want to avoid the long journey up the KKH. It is easier to get a confirmed seat and fly on a Boeing 737, which seats up to 120 passengers, to Skardu. Boeing 737 flights to Skardu have a higher ceiling and operate a greater percentage of the time. Then you can take inexpensive local transport from Skardu to Gilgit.

Reconfirmation The day before your Northern Areas flight, you must go to the PIA office to drop off your ticket (usually before 12.30 pm). Then later that same afternoon (typically after 1 or 2 pm), you pick up your ticket. If your ticket is confirmed, PIA puts the next day's flight information in your ticket. If you are not confirmed, your ticket is returned to you unchanged.

Flight Operation Call PIA Flight Inquiry before reporting to the airport. The final determination to operate any flight is not made until shortly before the scheduled flight departure time. Reporting time for check-in is one hour before the scheduled flight time, but check-in can be delayed and may not begin until PIA feels there is a good chance the flight can operate. Particularly in hot weather, Fokker F27s cannot get enough lift (eg, to climb out of the Gilgit Valley) when they are full to capacity. Hence, PIA may not fill every seat with passengers when a flight has a lot of cargo or may fill every seat with passengers and offload cargo. A strict 20 kg total weight limit for baggage applies.

Cancellation Northern Areas flights can be cancelled at any stage of the process. This can be before you report to the airport, after you have checked in and gone through security, and even after you have boarded the aircraft. The most extreme case is after the flight has taken off. You can be 30 minutes into an hour-long flight, sipping milky tea, when the pilot announces that the aircraft is turning back! If your flight is cancelled and there are later flights scheduled that same day, you are given priority for the next flight. If there are no later flights scheduled that day, you must go back to the PIA office to reconfirm your seat for the next day. You can either try again for a flight the next day or ask for a refund and travel by road.

PIA Helicopter Charters PIA charters Russian-made MI-8 MTV helicopters to any destination, including Chitral, Gilgit, Kalam, and Skardu. These 20-seat helicopters can lift four tonnes total with a 4000m ceiling. Each flight itinerary must be approved by the Civil Aviation Authority (CAA). PIA needs at least two weeks' advance notice in order to obtain route clearance from CAA. For security reasons, an army officer is on board each charter flight. The cost is US$2000 per hour, with a three-hour minimum charge. A US$1000 overnight fee applies with a six-hour minimum charge for any flights requiring an overnight stay. Contact PIA's Manager of Helicopter Services in Islamabad (☎ 815041 ext 225) or the PIA Information Officer (☎ 815041 ext 227-8).

PIA Air Safari PIA's Air Safari is a spectacular one-hour mountain flight from Islamabad. For Rs 6225 you can book one of the 46 window seats on this Boeing 737 flight and enjoy views of the highest peaks of the Karakoram. Flights are scheduled from Islamabad once weekly on Saturday and are subject to weather.

Buying PIA Tickets Domestic tickets may be more expensive when purchased overseas. It is usually best to wait and purchase domestic PIA tickets in Pakistan, although it can be difficult to get reservations on short notice. Some travel agencies are General Sales Agents (GSA) for PIA. PIA extends up to a 12% discount to their GSAs, some of whom may pass a portion of that discount on to you. Not all travel agencies are totally scrupulous (eg, they may knowingly overbook), so buy tickets only from PIA or IATA-licensed travel agencies. Northern Areas flights are not discounted.

PIA Booking Offices PIA booking offices are open daily 9 am to 1 pm and 2 to 5 pm. Useful PIA booking offices follow:

Chitral
    Atalig Bazaar (☎ 2863 and 2963)
Gilgit
    Airport Rd (☎ 3389-90), airport traffic control (ATC) (☎ 3947)
Islamabad
    PIA Building 49 Blue Area at 7th Ave, reservations (☎ 816051-8, 825091-4, 815041-284); Flight Information (☎ 591071); Flight Inquiry (☎ 114 and 567011)
Karachi
    Sidco Centre Stretchen Rd (☎ 568 9631-50), Pearl Continental Hotel (☎ 568 5021), Civic Centre KDA Complex (☎ 493 9397), Hotel Midway (☎ 487 3081), Flight Inquiry (☎ 114 and 457 2221), airport (☎ 457 2011)
Lahore
    PIA Building, Egerton Rd (☎ 630 6411, 300 5218 and 300 5522); Main Blvd, Aurig Complex (☎ 871279, 871289); Flight Inquiry (☎ 114 and 637 7245)
Peshawar
    33 The Mall (☎ 273081-9, 279162-4, Northern Areas flights only (☎ 273081 ext 230)

Rawalpindi
  5 The Mall, Reservations (☎ 568071-8); Nazir Plaza, Satellite Town (☎ 426760 and 426782); Flight Inquiry (☎ 114 and 567011)
Saidu Sharif
  Faizabad Rd (☎ 4624 and 4049)
Skardu
  Naya Bazaar (☎ 2491 and 3325), airport (☎ 2492)

Shaheen Air International

Shaheen Air International operates daily Airbus A300 and Boeing 737 flights Karachi-Islamabad and four times weekly Karachi-Lahore. Other sectors are: Lahore-Islamabad, Lahore-Peshawar, Karachi-Peshawar, and Islamabad-Peshawar.

Aero Asia

Aero Asia operates Karachi-Islamabad (four times a day), Lahore (six times a day), and Peshawar (once a day). Night coach fares are available from Islamabad and Lahore to Karachi.

Bhoja Airlines

Bhoja operates twice daily Boeing 737 flights Karachi-Lahore.

Travel Agencies

The following are reputable travel agencies:

American Express Travel Service, 1-E Ali Plaza, Blue Area, Islamabad (☎ 212425-32); Karachi (☎ 263 0260-9); 112 Rafi Mansion, The Mall, Lahore (☎ 627 9230-6); and Rahim Plaza, Murree Rd, Rawalpindi (☎ 582864, 565766 and 566001-5)

Shakil Express, I&T Centre, Khayaban-e-Suhrawardy, Islamabad (☎ 815691-4 and 828512-4); Pearl Continental Hotel, Karachi (☎ 568 4461 and 568 4962); and Haider Rd, Saddar Bazaar, Rawalpindi (☎ 580153-4 and 562194)

Rohtas Travel Consultants, 60-A/5 Khan Chambers, Canning Rd, Saddar Bazaar, Rawalpindi (☎ 563224, 566434 and 566469) and 2 Kashmir Plaza, Blue Area, Islamabad (☎ 213976 and 818971)

Travel Walji's (Pvt) Ltd, 10 Khayaban-e-Suhrawardy, Aabpara, Islamabad (☎ 270745-8; fax 270753); 13 Services Mess, Karachi (☎ 516698 and 526295; fax 522563); 23 Empress Rd, Ali Complex, Lahore (☎ 631 6031); and 12 Saddar Rd, Rm 14, Doctor's Plaza, Peshawar (☎ 274130)

ROAD

Except for flights to and from Gilgit and Skardu, all transport in the Northern Areas is by road. Likewise, except for flights to and from Chitral, Peshawar, and Saidu Sharif, all transport in NWFP is also by road. Public transport is inexpensive and readily available, but always crowded. Travelling by road is not necessarily comfortable and many journeys are lengthy.

Types of Transport

The transport you take depends on the road head for your trek and your budget. Here is what is available.

Bus Buses are usually the cheapest, but slowest transport. They usually run on fixed schedules.

Coaster 21-seat Toyota Coasters run regional and long-distance routes. They are faster, more comfortable, slightly more expensive, and usually operate from different stands than buses. Coasters usually have air-con, although drivers rarely use it between Abbottabad and Gilgit.

Van/Wagon Fifteen-seat Toyota Hi-Ace vans and old 15-seat Ford wagons are common on regional routes. Some may be available for private hire.

Suzuki The most common short-haul transport is the converted Suzuki light-duty truck, which seats eight to 10 passengers on two rows of benches. Suzukis usually have a conductor, though in towns (eg, Gilgit) they do not. Here you stomp on the floor or tap on the cab window to signal when you want to get out. Avoid Suzukis on longer trips since they do not have much power and are slow.

Pick-up Truck Datsun and Toyota pick-up trucks are common. Some 4WD pick-ups go to remote villages.

Jeep/Landcruiser Where mountain roads permit nothing else, 4WD jeeps and landcruisers serve remote villages. Jeeps are referred to as either VIP, cargo, passenger, or special jeeps. The driver of a VIP jeep typically allows a maximum of four passengers plus their baggage. In Hunza, many jeeps for hire are VIP jeeps. Cargo and passenger jeeps are more common in Baltistan and Chitral. Operating on loose schedules, these jeeps depart when they are full. Passenger jeeps may load as many as 20 people, all standing, into the vehicle. Cargo jeeps tend to be loaded well beyond capacity. Seating on top of the cargo, or perhaps standing, is first-come, first-serve. In more remote areas you usually travel by cargo jeep to the trail head. Be prepared for a dusty, rough ride, and don't plan to reach your destination at any particular time. When you hire a jeep privately it is known as a 'special' jeep.

Car/Taxi Cars are increasingly available. Avis Rent-a-Car has offices in Islamabad, Karachi, Lahore, and Gilgit. Car rentals usually include a driver. Of course, taxis are found in down-country cities. Yellow cabs are also found in Gilgit and Skardu, and can be hired for longer journeys. Taxi drivers down-country sometimes refuse to use their meter. If so, the older black and yellow taxis and larger yellow taxis cost Rs 6 per km. The newer, small yellow metered taxis cost Rs 5 per km.

Options

Public & Private Transport Government Transport Service (GTS) and Northern Areas Transport Company (NATCO) are government-run transport companies. GTS runs intercity buses down-country. NATCO operates vehicles on the KKH and throughout the Northern Areas. Many other privately-run transport companies exist. We describe the routes these companies operate below. For treks that start or end close to main roads, you can rely on scheduled transport, which is cheap and generally dependable. For more remote road heads, you can take passenger or cargo jeeps or hire your own vehicle.

Hiring Your Own Transport Hiring your own vehicle and driver, called a 'special', is expensive, but allows you to choose your departure time and determine rest stops, photography breaks and overnight stays. You can also arrange to be picked up at the end of your trek. Payment is by day or by distance, or a combination of both. The longer you want it, the more leverage you have in negotiating a price. A special hire can be a good value if you can share costs with others. Before you reach an agreement make sure the driver knows the road you intend to travel and where your final destination is, and inspect the vehicle.

If you require a drop-off in a remote area, prepare to pay for the return journey as well, as the jeep may have to return empty. If people are waiting for a ride at the trail head when you are dropped off, be sure to negotiate with them directly. After all, you paid for the jeep. It is cheaper to arrange a special hire directly with the vehicle's owner then through a travel agency, trekking company, or hotel. In some towns (eg, Skardu), it is best to negotiate directly with jeep contractors who control most special hires. Typical rates for private jeep hires are about Rs 8 per km plus Rs 200 per overnight, or fixed totals for common destinations. Some towns have special stands with for-hire Suzukis or jeeps, and you can often hire one right off the street.

Hitching Hitch-hiking is possible and generally safe for men. Hitch-hiking for unaccompanied women is definitely risky and is not recommended. Hitch-hiking strikes Pakistanis as odd. Bus fares are so cheap, no one understands why you might want to bump along in a slow, dirty, crowded truck cab when you could be travelling more quickly in a comfortable seat on a bus. However, you can signal drivers by holding your hand in front of you parallel to the ground and making a downward patting motion. If drivers have space they usually stop, but may ask for a fare. Some drivers have been known to offer lifts and then, on arrival, demand payment. It is easier to get rides if you wait at check posts, where vehicles stop. Along the KKH between Gilgit and Sost, drivers usually pick up riders. Hitch-hiking on the KKH in Kohistan carries more risk.

Segregation of Women

Women and families are seated separately from men in all types of transport. Women are usually placed in the front seats or towards the front of vehicles. If you are not assigned one of these seats, ask to move. In vans, coasters, and buses, it is preferable for a woman to sit next to the window while her male travelling companion sits in the aisle seat. On passenger and cargo jeeps, women are likely to be seated up the front. Women should not pay extra for the privilege of sitting in the front seat.

It is acceptable for a woman to ask to sit in the front seat of Suzukis that run up and down the Gilgit and Skardu bazaars. If the front seat is already occupied by a man, ask him to move into the back. If a woman is travelling with a man, it is preferable that he also sits in the front seat between the woman and the driver. Some Suzuki drivers may not stop to give a woman a ride; try again someone always does. If a woman travels alone, she should avoid inviting trouble by not sitting in the back of a crowded Suzuki. It is OK to ride in the back of a Suzuki when a woman has a companion, but it can become uncomfortable if it fills with other male passengers.

Regional Road Routes

Five regional routes link the cities and towns from which you can obtain local transport to the trail heads for most treks. These are: the Grand Trunk (GT) Road and down-country roads; the Karakoram Highway (KKH) between Islamabad and the Khunjerab Pass via Gilgit; the Gilgit-Skardu road; the Gilgit-Chitral road over the Shandur Pass; and the Peshawar-Chitral route via Dir over the Lowari Pass.

Grand Trunk (GT) Road & Down-country Roads The Grand Trunk (GT) Road, which once linked Kabul to Calcutta, was built by the Moghuls and now serves as Pakistan's main east-west artery. Frequent transport

runs along this corridor between Peshawar and Rawalpindi or Lahore. Numerous companies offer inexpensive, reasonably comfortable fast 'flying coach' service between these cities. Flying coaches range from Toyota Hi-Ace vans and larger Toyota Coasters to large Mercedes and Hino buses. The large buses are the safest and most comfortable. Most do not take reservations and sell tickets only for the same day. Some coasters along the GT Road have air-con.

Lahore-Rawalpindi In Lahore, many flying coach companies operate across Iqbal Rd from the railway station along Nicholson Rd before its intersection with McLeod Rd. The Modern Hotel, Asia Hotel and Clifton Hotel are landmarks. Some of the companies are Flying Coach, New Flying Coach, National Flying Coach, Shaheenways Flying Coach, Khasif Flying Coach, Continental Flying Coach, RoadRunners Flying Coach, Skyways, and Road Liner. Road Liner operates large Hino buses. The fare is Rs 80, and it takes five or six hours. Most arrive near Committee Chowk. TDCP (Tourism Development Corporation of Punjab) operates large Hino buses from the TDCP Information Centre (☎ (042) 636 0553 and 636 9687), 4 Lawrence Rd near Plaza Chowk, at 9 am and 2 pm. The fare is Rs 85. Inter City Transport Systems (a Pakistan government-affiliated project) (☎ (042) 636 7213-15) also operates Hino buses from Falettis Hotel at 1, 9 and 11 am; 1, 4 and 11 pm, and midnight for Rs 85.

Rawalpindi-Lahore In Rawalpindi, most flying coaches leave from Committee Chowk, behind the cinema halls. Some of these are New Flying Coach (☎ 70136 and 74501), Kohistan Luxury Coach (☎ 72409), New Khan Road Runners (☎ 72229), and Super National Flying Coach (☎ 71341). The fare is Rs 80. Skyways (☎ 844765) operates Mercedes buses from Faizabad Chowk (the intersection of Murree Rd and the Islamabad Hwy). They take reservations one day in advance and are reported to be good. Flying Coach (with Mercedes buses)

(☎ 70050 and 72950) leaves from near the Shangrila Hotel on Murree Rd at Liaquat Chowk. Intercity Transport Systems (☎ 553375) leaves from behind the Shangrila Hotel near Liaquat Chowk. GTS goes hourly from Pir Wadhai for Rs 45, and from the station on Adamjee Rd in Saddar bazaar. TDCP (☎ 564824) runs deluxe aircon coaches from the corner of Kashmir Rd and 44 The Mall, which cost Rs 85.

Islamabad-Lahore From Islamabad's F-8 Markaz (Ayub market), opposite the OGDC office, City Linkers (☎ 260137, 253369 and 254254) operates Mercedes buses and coasters. They leave at 1.30 and 8.30 am; 4, 5.30 and 11.30 pm. The fare is Rs 90. Air-con buses also go from G-9/1. You can buy tickets one day in advance.

Lahore-Peshawar-Lahore Most of the above flying coach operators in Lahore also make the nine-hour trip to Peshawar. From Peshawar, buses and coasters depart further east along the GT Road just west of the bridge across the river to Sikandar Town. One-way fares are Rs 120.

Islamabad/Rawalpindi-Peshawar Daily air-con coasters go regularly from Islamabad's G-9/1 (Karachi Company) near the petrol pump for Rs 40. From Rawalpindi, New Flying Coach buses and coaches go hourly from Committee Chowk via the Shangrila Hotel at Liaquat Chowk for Rs 45. Most other operators also go from Committee Chowk. GTS and private buses go all day from Pir Wadhai for about Rs 25.

Peshawar-Islamabad/Rawalpindi Coasters to Islamabad depart regularly from GT Road across the street from the petrol station in front of Bala Hisar fort. Buses and coasters to Rawalpindi depart nearby all along GT Road.

Rawalpindi-Mansehra via Abbottabad Coasters depart from Haider Rd near Siroj Cinema in Saddar bazaar for Rs 30, taking three hours. GTS and private buses go from Pir Wadhai all day for Rs 25.

Rawalpindi-Saidu Sharif-Rawalpindi Regular services depart throughout the day. Quick Service (☎ 423608) operates coasters for Rs 70 and vans for Rs 50 from Faizabad Chowk. Ordinary buses leave for Mardan and Mingora from outside the Pir Wadhai bus station. Afridi Flying Coach (AFC) departs regularly from the main bus stand in Mingora to Rawalpindi (and to Peshawar); look for their AFC stickers.

Karakoram Highway (KKH): Islamabad to Khunjerab Pass Travel on the KKH is anything but predictable. Landslides, mudslides, rock falls, and even avalanches can sever it for hours, days or weeks at a time. Maintenance workers are busy full time keeping the road open. Nevertheless, it is an awesome and beautiful road journey. The KKH actually begins at the Thakot bridge over the Indus River below Besham, about six hours north of Islamabad. From here, it follows the Indus River north through Kohistan and Chilas, passing beneath the Nanga Parbat massif, to Gilgit. From Gilgit, the KKH follows the Hunza River to the Khunjerab Pass, Pakistan's border with China.

Rawalpindi-Gilgit Depending on the vehicle and the road conditions, this trip takes 16 to 20 hours. Hameed Travels Service (☎ 73387) has vans and coasters that depart from the Mashriq Hotel on City-Saddar (Jinnah) Rd, south of Fowara Chowk, at 3 pm for Rs 250. Sargin Travel Service (☎ 74130) has coasters that depart from the Modern Hotel opposite the Novelty Cinema in Kashmiri bazaar (south-west of Fowara Chowk) at 3 and 6 pm for Rs 250. Hunza Coach Service (HCS) (☎ 472705 and 471849) has vans and coasters from the Anarkali Hotel in Pir Wadhai at noon and 4 pm. It costs Rs 250. Mashabrum Tours (☎ 863595) has daily buses that depart from Pir Wadhai at 1.30, 6 and 9 pm and cost Rs 181. The 'office' is a person sitting in a chair at the east end of the yard. NATCO

(☎ 860283 and 861028) buses depart from Pir Wadhai daily at 4 and 9 am; 1, 5, 8 and 11 pm. Departures at 9 am and 5 pm are on 'deluxe' buses and cost Rs 220. Other departures are on regular buses and cost Rs 180. You can buy tickets from the window at the bus stand. A 50% student discount is available on all but the deluxe service (with a maximum of four discount tickets per departure). NATCO and Mashabrum Tours buses normally cannot be booked in advance. A special hire costs Rs 6500 to Rs 9000.

Gilgit-Rawalpindi The trip may take a couple of hours less in this direction. Hameed Travels Service (☎ 3181 and 3026) departs from Skyways Hotel at 3 and 5 pm. It costs Rs 250. Sargin Travel Service (☎ 3939 and 2959) is at JSR Plaza for Rs 250. Hunza Coach Service (HCS) (☎ 3553) has coasters that depart at noon and 4 pm for Rs 250. They are just past the second petrol pump on Airport Rd. NATCO (☎ 3381) near NLI Chowk has buses that depart at 4 and 11 am that cost Rs 180. A coaster departs at 7 am and costs Rs 250. Their deluxe buses depart at 2, 5 and 8 pm and cost Rs 220. Mashabrum Tours at Cinema bazaar has buses that depart at 1 and 4 pm. A deluxe bus departs at 7 pm. The regular bus costs Rs 180 and the deluxe Rs 220. Their coasters depart at 2 pm and 4 pm and cost Rs 280.

Gilgit-Sost-Gilgit It takes from five to seven hours to travel between Gilgit and Sost. A NATCO bus departs from Gilgit near NLI Chowk at 8 am and costs Rs 70. Their deluxe bus departs from Sost at 5 am. Hunza Coach Service (HCS) (☎ 3553) on Airport Rd has wagons that cost Rs 80 and coasters that cost Rs 100. They depart from Gilgit at 8 am and 2 pm. HCS usually departs from Sost at 7 am. Neelum Transports (☎ 2856) is in Taj Super market (between the two petrol pumps). Their 18-seat vans cost Rs 100 and depart at 7 and 10 am, noon, 2 and 4 pm or more typically when full. You can get off along the way at Aliabad or Ganesh for Rs 50, Gulmit for Rs 60, and Passu for Rs 70. Sargin Travel Service (☎ 3939 and 2959) at JSR Plaza does

not operate regularly, but departs from Gilgit about 8 am and costs Rs 100.

Sost-Khunjerab Pass You can leave your passport with Pakistan immigration officials in Sost and take a day trip to the Khunjerab Pass. Special jeeps cost Rs 600 to Rs 800.

Gilgit-Skardu Road The 230 km trip Gilgit-Skardu takes six to eight hours. South of Gilgit and north of the juncture of the Gilgit and Indus rivers, the road leaves the KKH and crosses a bridge over the Gilgit River. Beyond the bridge is a beautiful panorama of the Nanga Parbat massif and a brief view of Rakaposhi's south face.

Gilgit-Skardu-Gilgit Mashabrum Tours in Cinema bazaar has a van that departs from Gilgit at 6 am, a bus at 7 am, and coasters at 10 am and 1.30 pm. From Skardu, Mashabrum Tours (☎ 2616 and 2634) has a bus that departs at 5 am and coasters that depart at 7 and 10 am, and 2 pm. Their vans cost Rs 81, the buses and coasters Rs 115. NATCO has a bus that departs from Gilgit at 5.30 am and costs Rs 81. NATCO departs from Skardu at 6 am.

Rawalpindi-Skardu-Rawalpindi NATCO and Mashabrum Tours buses cost Rs 260. NATCO departs from Rawalpindi at 11 am. Mashabrum Tours has a regular bus that departs from Rawalpindi at noon and a coaster that departs at 4 pm. Both NATCO and Mashabrum Tours (☎ 2616 and 2634) buses depart from Skardu at 4 pm This 760 km 24 hour ride is only for hard-core fans of long-haul road trips.

Gilgit-Chitral & the Shandur Pass The largely unpaved road between Gilgit and Chitral crosses the Shandur Pass (3800m), which is usually open from 1 June to 15 November. Access to the pass can be blocked longer on either side by avalanches. No regular transport operates between Gilgit and Chitral. It takes two long days with an overnight stop, usually in Gupis or Phunder. The trip takes about five hours Gilgit-Gupis,

2½ hours Gupis-Phunder, five hours Phunder-Mastuj, and six hours Mastuj-Chitral. The best overnight camp sites are in Phunder and about five km beyond Mastuj in Sunoghor.

NATCO buses from Gilgit go as far as Gupis and cost Rs 50. From Gupis, passenger and cargo jeeps go as far as Teru and Barsat. It is usually difficult to catch a ride over the Shandur Pass from here to Chitral. From Gilgit, a special jeep to Chitral costs Rs 5000 to Rs 7000. From Chitral, regular passenger jeeps go daily to Mastuj for Rs 45. Beyond Mastuj to Sor Laspur, passenger and cargo jeeps operate sporadically.

Peshawar-Chitral & the Lowari Pass The road between Peshawar and Chitral crosses the Lowari Pass (3118m), which is usually open from 15 May to 15 November. However, snow may keep the pass closed longer in the spring or close it earlier in autumn. The road is subject to blockage by avalanche until June.

Direct one-day coaster service to Chitral leaves from three locations in Peshawar: Chitrali bazaar off Qissa Khawani bazaar; Namak Mandi at the Spogmey Hotel; and south of Outer Circular Rd on Kohat Rd. Buses and coasters that leave from the GTS bus stand on GT Road (east of the canal) go only to Dir and Swat. The trip takes about six hours and costs Rs 50. From Dir, jeeps and coasters to Chitral cost Rs 80 to Rs 120. If you are lucky, you can get on a vehicle from Dir to Chitral the same day you reach Dir. Otherwise, there is an overnight stay in sometimes xenophobic Dir. The trip is faster in jeeps and smaller vehicles. A special hire costs Rs 2000 per day plus a 50% drop fee. It takes about six to seven hours Peshawar-Dir and five to six hours Dir-Chitral.

From Chitral, Peshawar vehicles leave from Naya bazaar. Shaheen Station/Depot, near PTDC, has vans that depart at 6 and 10 am and cost Rs 200. Herkala Rasha Flying Coach, next to Al-Farooq Hotel also goes regularly. At the time of writing only Shaheen goes direct to Peshawar; with other flying coaches you must transfer in Dir.

From Dir, you can also easily get transport to Swat.

TRAIN

Train service does not exist in northern Pakistan. We mention it here for those who may want to travel by train to and from Islamabad or Peshawar. Train travel is no longer safe and generally is not recommended.

Types of Train Service

Trains are express, mail, or passenger, in the order of increasing frequency of stops. Express trains operate several times daily between major cities. Classes are air-con 1st (soft seats, closed compartment), 1st (soft seats, open compartment), economy (soft seats, no compartment), and 2nd (hard seats, no compartments). Long distance routes also offer sleepers in air-con 1st and in 1st. Major railway stations typically have retiring rooms and showers. Sample journeys in a 1st-class sleeper from Karachi are: Lahore (express train 20 hours, Rs 375), Peshawar (32 hours, Rs 475), and Rawalpindi (28 hours, Rs 445). A 'rail car' shuttle operates Rawalpindi-Peshawar (four hours, 2nd class Rs 30). Trains also operate Rawalpindi-Lahore (six hours, Rs 55).

Concessions

If you have a student ID card you pay half-fare and 25% discount is available to non-student foreign tourists for tickets in all classes except air-con 1st. To receive discounts, go to a local PTDC office and ask for a letter for the Divisional Superintendent of Railways (at the station), who then gives you a form to show at the ticket window with your passport.

Booking Offices

Pakistan Railways' booking offices are open from 9 am to 1 pm and 2 to 5 pm, except 9 am to 2.30 pm Friday.

GETTING TO THE TREKKING AREAS

Most trekkers going to Gilgit or Skardu pass through Islamabad or Rawalpindi and nearly everyone who heads to Chitral goes to

Peshawar. Basic information about these cities follows. Trekkers who spend time in Lahore or Karachi usually do so only to connect with international flights or to transit to another country (see LP's *Pakistan – travel survival kit*).

Margalla Hills

If you are stuck in Islamabad waiting for flights or permits, you can go hiking in the Margalla Hills north of town. The many trails and rest houses here are described in the Capital Development Authority's (CDA) map-brochure, *Trekking in the Margalla Hills*, available from CDA's public relations office (☎ 828301) on Khayaban-e-Suhrawardy west of Aabpara. *Hiking Around Islamabad*, a handy guide for short hikes in the Margalla Hills, is available at most book stores. ∎

ISLAMABAD

Islamabad is a more convenient city in which to stay if you need to deal with the Tourism Division for a restricted area permit, visit an embassy, or extend or replace visas or passports. The city is spread out with much open, green space, making it quieter than Rawalpindi's bazaars. The city is laid out in sectors across a grid, with each sector having its own residences, shops and parks. Sectors are built around a *markaz* (commercial centre) and are designated by a letter and number (eg, F-7).

Each sector is further divided into quarters that are numbered clockwise (eg, F-7/1 is in the south-west corner, F-7/2 is in the north-west, etc). The coordinates have names (eg, F is Shalimar, G is Ramna, so F-7 is Shalimar-7), but sectors are more commonly called by their market names. The main ones are Aabpara (south-west G-6), Melody or Civic Centre (G-6), Sitara (G-7), Super (F-6), Jinnah or Jinnah Super (F-7), Ayub (F-8), and Karachi Company (G-9). Blue Area is a commercial belt between F and G sectors. Federal government offices are on the east

side of the city. Most foreign embassies are in the Diplomatic Enclave (G-5).

The police emergency numbers are ☎ 15 and 823333 for Islamabad and ☎ 828265 for Aabpara. For medical services Shifa International (☎ 25260) is a small, private facility, and reportedly the best in Islamabad. Ali Medical Center (F-7) is the next best facility.

Places to Stay – bottom end

The *Tourist Camp Site* is near Aabpara. A tent platform or space in a concrete 'bungalow' (no beds) costs Rs 15. It costs Rs 10 per tent and Rs 5 to sleep on the ground. Locked storage is available and the maximum stay is two weeks. On Garden Rd (G-6/4) the *Pakistan Youth Hostel* (☎ 826899) has dozens of four-bed rooms, a communal toilet and cold shower, but no cooking facilities and no camping. Beds cost Rs 35 for IYHA card holders, and Rs 25 if you also have a student card. The maximum stay is three days when it is crowded.

Shehrazad Hotel (☎ 822295) in F-6 markaz has doubles with hot shower that cost Rs 200. Sitara market (G-7) is a quiet location with four cheap hotels. *Sitara Hotel* (☎ 215208 and 819953), G-7/2, has singles/doubles for Rs 100/150. *Al-Habib Hotel* (☎ 217333 and 810753), which has two properties there, and *Al-Hujrat* (☎ 218373) cost about the same. *Blue Star Motel* (☎ 282866 and 852810), G-8/4, 1 I&T Centre has doubles for Rs 200, but is inconveniently located near Zero Point.

Places to Stay – middle

Capital Inn (☎ 251493 and 256146-7), G-8 markaz, has singles for Rs 250 to Rs 400 and doubles for Rs 325 to Rs 500. *Pak Tures Motel* (☎ 824503), near Rawal dam, has singles/doubles for Rs 320/385.

Places to Stay – top end

The best values are the numerous guest-houses on the cities' quieter residential streets. Each of the several dozen guest-houses has from four to 10 air-con rooms and offers meals.

Several recommendations follow with

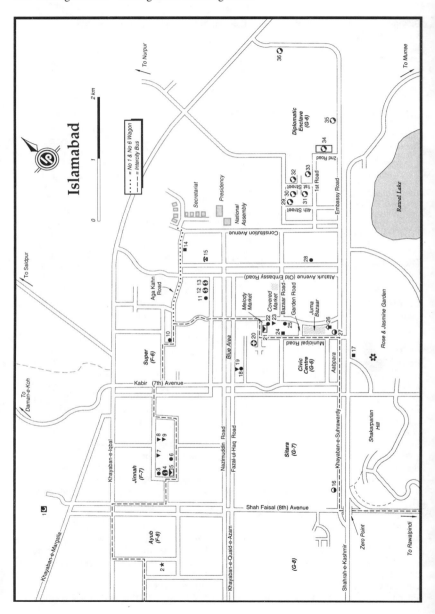

Islamabad

| = No 1 & No 6 Wagon |
| = Intercity Bus |

PLACES TO STAY		OTHER		18	PIA
14	Marriott Hotel	1	Shah Faisal Mosque	20	Capital Hospital
17	Tourist Campsite	2	Police & Foreigners'	21	General Post Office
24	Holiday Inn Islamabad		Registration Office	22	Pakistan Railways
	Hotel		(FRO)		Booking Office
26	Pakistan Youth Hostel	3	Tourism Division	25	British Council Library
		4	PTDC Tourist Information	27	GTS Bus Stand
PLACES TO EAT			Centre	28	US Consular Office
7	Kabul Restaurant &	5	Post Office	29	German Embassy
	Afghan Bakery	6	PTDC Motels Booking	30	French Embassy
8	Kim-Mun Chinese		Office	31	Indian High Commission
	Restaurant	10	Lok Virsa Book Store	32	Iranian Embassy
9	Pappasalli's Italian	11	American Centre	33	British High Commission
	Restaurant	12	Bank of America	34	US Embassy
19	Omar Khayyam Iranian	13	American Express	35	Chinese Embassy
	Restaurant	15	Central Telegraph Office	36	Australian High
23	French Bakery	16	Bus Stop		Commission

costs, when available, for singles/doubles: *Accommodators II* (☎ 817320), F-7/1, St 36, House 9, Rs 900/1000; *Best Accommodators* (☎ 818547), F-7/4, St 54, House 6, Rs 800/900; *Continental House* F-8/4, Nazim-ud-Din Rd, House 94; *Decent Accommodators* (☎ 815275), F-7/2, St 15, House 2, Rs 800/1000; *Host Inn Guest House* (☎ 856621), F-8 markaz, Kaghan Rd; *Lodgings Guest House* (☎ 826146; fax 220523), F-7/2, 41-A College Rd, Rs 600/700; *Shelton House* (☎ 856956 and 856428; fax 262049), F-8/3, House 11, Kaghan Rd, Rs 800/900; *Su Casa House* (☎ 825578), F-7/2, St 20, House 3; and *VIP Accommodators* (☎ 815144, 815146; fax 214924), F-6/1, St 30, House 18.

The *Dreamland Hotel* (☎ 858102; fax 252915), G-9/4, St 54, House 2; *Dreamland Motel* (☎ 814381-5; fax 815886), Club Rd, and *Shawnze International* (☎ 211771-4, 823703; fax 823519), F-6 markaz, have singles/doubles that cost about Rs 770/990. *Adventure Inn Hotel & Restaurant* (☎ 212536-7; fax 212540), PO Box 1807, Murree Link Rd near Shakarparian Hill costs Rs 800/1000.

Places to Stay – over the top end

The top hotels are *Holiday Inn Islamabad Hotel* (☎ 827311; fax 820763), G-6 in Civic Centre, and the *Marriott Hotel* (☎ 826121-35; fax 820648), F-5/1, Aga Khan Rd.

Places to Eat

Aabpara and Melody markets have cheap kebab stands and cafes. The *French Bakery* (☎ 821086) on Garden Rd in Melody market has pies, brownies, banana bread, and pizza. *Omar Khayyam* (☎ 812847), an Iranian restaurant in Blue Area, is very good.

Nearby is an *Usmania Restaurant. The Village Restaurant* (☎ 815629) on Fazal-e-Haq Rd in Blue Area (back side) has a pleasant, rustic atmosphere. Super and Jinnah markets are full of fast-food cafes. Jinnah market also has some excellent restaurants, including the popular *Kabul Restaurant* and the *Afghan Bakery* at the west end and *Pappasalli's Italian Restaurant*, and *Shifung* and *Kim-Mun* Chinese restaurants at the east end; all are along College Rd. The *Marriott Hotel* has all-you-can-eat lunch and dinner buffets and *Dynasty*, a good Chinese restaurant.

RAWALPINDI

Rawalpindi is 15 km south of Islamabad. The axes are Murree Rd and The Mall. Cheaper hotels are in Saddar and Raja bazaars and along Murree Rd at Liaquat Chowk and Committee Chowk. The railway station is in Saddar bazaar, Pir Wadhai bus stand is northwest of town, and the airport is to the north-east. South of Saddar bazaar, the Cantonment has top-end hotels. At Raja, the biggest bazaar, six-way Fowara Chowk has 'spoke' roads to Saddar, Pir Wadhai and Murree Rd.

The police emergency numbers for Rawalpindi are ☎ 15, 562222, and 563333. Hospitals include Rawalpindi General (☎ 847761) on Murree Rd at Ashgar Mall Rd, and Cantonment General (☎ 562254) on Saddar Rd in Saddar bazaar.

Places to Stay – bottom end
Pir Wadhai Hotels here are sleazy and not fond of foreigners, but try the *Al-Medina*.

Raja Bazaar Behind the tonga stand at Fowara Chowk, the *Hotel Al-Falah* (☎ 553206) has hot water and singles/doubles for about Rs 60/100. The *Hotel Evergreen* has similar rates. *Al-Rauf* (☎ 556293-5) costs Rs 85/135.

Saddar Bazaar Several hotels have noisy singles/doubles for about Rs 50/80. The *Venus Hotel* (☎ 566501) is the best; others are the *Lalazar* and *Shah Taj* on Adamjee Rd, the old wing of the *Kamran Hotel* on

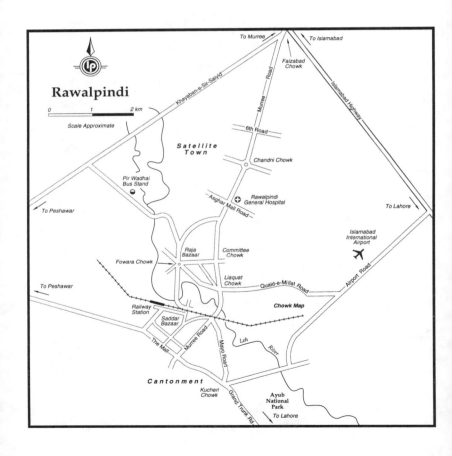

Kashmir Rd and the *Bolan Hotel* (☎ 563416) on Railway Rd.

Places to Stay – middle
Committee Chowk The *Mushtaq Hotel & Restaurant* (☎ 553998) on Murree Rd has doubles/triples/quads with toilet and hot water that cost Rs 250/300/350. Doubles at the *Al-Farooq Hotel* (☎ 556200-2) and *Queens Hotel & Restaurant* (☎ 73240) cost about Rs 160. *Rawal Hotel* (☎ 556241-5) on Hotel Square, Murree Rd, has deluxe singles/doubles that cost Rs 450/550.

Liaquat Chowk *City Hotel* (☎ 552532), 12 College Rd, has dorms/doubles/triples for Rs 50/150/175 and morning hot water. On Murree Rd, *Faisal Hotel* (☎ 73210) and *Al-Hayat Hotel* (☎ 557660) doubles cost about Rs 100; at the *Citizen Hotel & Restaurant* (☎ 554074) doubles cost Rs 150. The *Park Hotel* (☎ 70594) and *National City Hotel* (☎ 555236) cost from Rs 250.

Raja Bazaar Half a km south of Fowara Chowk is the *Mashriq Hotel* (☎ 556161), where hot-water doubles/triples cost Rs 160/200. On Liaquat Rd, the *Palace Hotel* (☎ 70672) has doubles for Rs 120. Opposite it *Seven Brothers Hotel* (☎ 551112) costs slightly more. *Avanti* (☎ 566905) is also good.

Saddar Bazaar On Kashmir Rd the *New Kamran Hotel* (☎ 582040) has doubles/triples with hot shower for Rs 130/150. Opposite is the slightly more expensive *Khyaban Hotel*. Nearby, at the *Marhaba Hotel* (☎ 566021), doubles cost Rs 300. At the *Kashmir Inn* (☎ 514017 and 514099), B55/5 Bank Rd, singles/doubles cost Rs 100/160. Deluxe rooms cost Rs 210. The *Paradise Inn* (☎ 568594-5; fax 567048), 109 Adamjee Rd, has comfortable singles/doubles for Rs 275/325, or Rs 450/550 with air-con.

The Hotel Holiday (☎ 568068-70), on Iftikhar Khan Rd behind the State Bank of Pakistan, has single/doubles for Rs 400/450. Also on the Mall is *Kashmirwalas*, where run-down rooms cost Rs 575. *Comfort Inn* (☎ 516161-5; fax 568228), 189/3 Kashmir Rd, has clean, air-con rooms with TV for Rs 500/650.

Places to Stay – top end
Hotel Al-Baddar (☎ 502380-4; fax 502330), on Murree Rd near the Rawal Hotel in Committee Chowk, has air-con singles/doubles for Rs 700/800. PTDC's *Flashman's Hotel* (☎ 581480-1) on The Mall has seen better days and costs Rs 975/1375. Nearby *Hotel Shalimar* (☎ 562901; fax 566061) costs Rs 800/1000.

The *Pearl Continental* (☎ 566011) on The Mall is the only five-star hotel.

Places to Eat
Committee Chowk Travellers give *Hotel Mushtaq* good marks for food. *Usmania Restaurant* isn't cheap but the Pakistani dishes are varied and good. Almost as good is the *Larosh Restaurant* next door. *Tabaq Restaurant* serves good grilled dishes.

Raja Bazaar The restaurant upstairs at the *Lodhi Hotel* on Liaquat Rd has cheap dishes. The Palace and Seven Brothers hotels also have so-so *restaurants*.

Saddar Bazaar A recommended cheap place with good Pakistani dishes is *Data Restaurant* in an alley off Haider Rd. Other decent places are *Cafe Khurshid* north of Hathi Chowk and *Kamran Cafe* on Bank Rd. *Jehangir* is a popular outdoor kabob and tandoori restaurant opposite Comfort Inn on Kashmir Rd. Fast-food places with hot sandwiches, chips, and the like are everywhere.

Getting Around
To/From the Airport There is no direct public transport to Islamabad. You can take a Suzuki to Rawalpindi's Raja bazaar and change at Liaquat Chowk to an Islamabad-bound vehicle. A taxi costs about Rs 120 to Rs 150 to/from Islamabad.

From Rawalpindi, Suzukis to the airport cost Rs 3 and go from Adamjee Rd in Saddar bazaar and from Fowara Chowk in Raja bazaar. To catch one from the airport, turn right outside the gate. Those to Raja bazaar are near a petrol station about 100m up; those to Saddar bazaar are 100m further at a fork on the right. A taxi costs about Rs 60 to/from Rawalpindi. If your Northern Areas flight is cancelled, you can usually get a free ride on PIA's bus to the PIA office on The Mall.

Rawalpindi-Islamabad Bedford buses link Saddar bazaar (ie, Haider Rd) and Murree Rd markets to Aabpara and Islamabad markets in one tedious line. Saddar bazaar to Super market costs just Rs 4, but takes at least one hour. Buses also go from the railway station to Islamabad.

Ford wagons and Toyota Hi-Ace vans have numbered routes, are much quicker and the same price. They leave from Haider Rd in Saddar bazaar and run up Murree Rd past Liaquat Chowk, Committee Chowk, Faizabad Chowk, up the Islamabad Highway to Zero Point and Aabpara. The No 1 then goes to the GPO, Super market and the Secretariat. The No 3 leaves from the old GTS bus stand near Bara bazaar in Raja bazaar and goes to Zero Point, Aabpara, and contin-

ues past the Japanese Embassy and British High Commission. The No 6 goes to the PIA office. The No 21, which has a green stripe along its body, goes from Kucheri Chowk past the airport, up the Islamabad Highway to Zero Point, Aabpara, and the Secretariat. The No 105 runs from Aabpara via Sitara market and Zero Point to Karachi Company (G-9/1). The No 111, which also has a green stripe, leaves from Riwat on the GT Road, and goes via Faizabad Chowk past Zero Point to Ayub market and the FRO.

PESHAWAR
The Bala Hisar Fort is a landmark on the GT Road. The old city is south and east of it. The cantonment is west of the railway line and includes Saddar bazaar. University Town is four km west of the cantonment off Jamrud Rd, as is the airport. Police emergency numbers are ☎ 15, 212222, 213222, 213333. Taxis rarely use meters and the fare rate tends to be more than Rs per km.

Places to stay – bottom end
Saddar has the most of these. *Tourists Inn* (☎ 275632) has singles/doubles that cost Rs

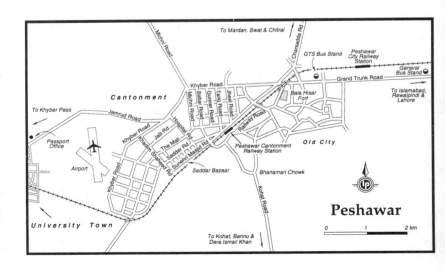

40/50. At *Sheri* (☎ 278449) singles/doubles cost Rs 40/60, *Shehzad* (☎ 275741) Rs 50/75, *New Golden* Rs 60/80 and *Sindbad* (☎ 275020) Rs 60/100. On Sunehri Masjid Rd are *Five Star* (☎ 276950) where singles/doubles cost Rs 50/70, and *Paradise* (☎ 273654) where they cost Rs 60/100. *City* (☎ 214162), S Circular Rd, has singles/ doubles that cost Rs 33/60. *Spogmey* (☎ 213255) in Namak Mandi costs Rs 50/80. On GT Road, *Three Star* (☎ 215408) costs Rs 50/100 and *Al-Mansoor* (☎ 213106) costs Rs 85/199.

Places to Stay – middle
Galaxy (☎ 212172), Khyber Rd, has singles/ doubles that cost Rs 385/595. In Saddar bazaar is *Khanis* (☎ 277512), where rooms cost Rs 100 to Rs 700. *Amin* (☎ 218215), GT Road, costs Rs 350/450. *VIP House*

(☎ 42378 and 842806; fax 843392), Bara Rd, University Town, is also good.

Places to stay – top end
Shelton Guest House (☎ 45255 and 40772; fax 42383), Old Jamrud Rd, House 15-B, University Town, is quiet and a better value than hotels near Saddar. Singles/doubles cost Rs 800/900. *Greens* (☎ 273604), Saddar Rd, costs Rs 770/1100 and *Dean's* (☎ 279781), Islamia Rd, costs Rs 1512/1815. *Pearl Continental Hotel* (☎ 276360-9; fax 276465), Khyber Rd, has singles/doubles for Rs 4307/4799.

INTERNAL CUSTOMS CHECKS
Police (Frontier Constabulary) check posts are along many roads in the Northern Areas and NWFP and along the KKH. Foreigners must sign a register, but are rarely searched.

Chitral

The view of Chitral from the Lowari Pass is that of a wild, alpine country with narrow fissure-like valleys, a reef of refuge for ancient tribes.

Linguist Georg Morgenstierne wrote the above on his 1929 visit. Chitral is still remote and isolated. Its only road links with the rest of Pakistan are two unpaved jeep roads, one over the Lowari Pass from the south and the other over the Shandur Pass from the east. Both are closed by snow for half the year. Tucked into the north-west corner of Pakistan, Chitral is separated from Afghanistan to the west and north by the Kafiristan and Hindukush ranges, from the Northern Areas to the east by the Shandur range, and from Dir and Swat districts to the south by the Hindu Raj range. The snow-capped peaks of these ranges tower over Chitral's valleys; and from vantage points throughout the district, Tirich Mir, the highest peak of the Hindukush range, is visible. The 14850 sq km district is drained by the Chitral River, which begins at the confluence of the Lutkho and Mastuj rivers, and flows into Afghanistan where it becomes the Kunar River. The entire district is divided administratively into two subdivisions: Mastuj, and Chitral. Each subdivision is then further divided into administrative zones, or tehsils. In Chitral's 516 villages live about 225,000 people, almost all of whom speak Khowar as their mother tongue. Most are farmers and herders, and all are famous for their hospitality. Perhaps because of its isolation, Chitral remains a trekker's delight.

REGIONAL HISTORY

Chitral has been populated for well over 3000 years. Under the Achaemenian empire of Persia in the 5th and 4th centuries BC, the Zoroastrian religion was widespread. Later, under the Kushan empire, Buddhism took root and spread. Chitral's location south of the passes linking China to the west made it an important state along the great Silk Route.

Highlights – Chitral
The heart of the high Hindukush – the southern valleys are heavily forested, northern valleys are open and arid. Home of the hospitable Kho culture and minority Kalasha. Isolated, less frequently visited

By the 6th century AD, the Han dynasty of China had extended its control to Chitral. In the 8th century, the Tibetans displaced the Chinese, but in the 9th century, Arab armies defeated the Buddhist ruler of Chitral. In the 11th century, the Kalasha moved into southern Chitral, ruling the area as far as the present-day town of Reshun. Upper Chitral was ruled by Kho kings whose power extended to Gilgit. In the 14th century, Shah Rais invaded from neighbouring Badakshan, defeated the Kalasha, and ruled all Chitral and Gilgit. Islam spread under his rule. The Rais dynasty continued until the 16th century, when it was displaced by the Katur dynasty, descendants of Timur, the Mongol emperor.

At its greatest extent, Chitral encompassed Kafiristan in Afghanistan and Gilgit. Two Katur brothers, Muhtaram Shah and Kushwaqt, divided the state, with southern Chitral, Mulkho and Turikho going to the former and Mastuj, Yarkhun, Yasin, Ghizar and Ishkoman going to the Kushwaqt family. The Katur ruler of Chitral became the dominant power, known by the title of Mehtar. This arrangement continued into the 19th century, when the British, anxious about Russian advances towards the borders of their Indian empire, learned that Mehtar Aman ul Mulk had approached the Maharaja of Kashmir about a possible treaty to counteract Afghan pressure on Chitral. They advised the Maharaja to accept and suggested the basis of an alliance to him. This culminated in the Kashmir-Chitral treaty of 1879. Aman ul Mulk received an annual subsidy of Rs 8000 and protection from Afghan aggression. Kashmir received his allegiance and a tribute of horses, hawks, and hounds. Britain then set about establishing a direct alliance with Chitral, and demarcating the boundary with Afghanistan. Aman ul Mulk's brother, Sher Afzal, opposed to the British and Kashmir alliances, fled across the border to Afghanistan. In 1892, Aman died, and a bloody succession fight ensued.

Aman's second son, Afzal, seized the throne and Nizam, the eldest, fled to Gilgit. Aman's brother Sher Afzal returned from Afghanistan and murdered his nephew Afzal. Nizam returned from Gilgit and drove Sher Afzal out of Chitral, but was then murdered by his own younger brother Amir ul Mulk, who was allied with the Afghan ruler of Dir state, Umra Khan. Umra Khan was a strong anti-British advocate, and the exiled Sher Afzal joined forces with him to throw the British out of Chitral. A small British force under the command of George Robertson occupied the Mehtar's fort in Chitral where they were besieged by the Chitral partisans. The British held out there for 46 days until relief arrived from Gilgit over the Shandur Pass and from Peshawar over the Lowari Pass. The Siege of Chitral, as it became known, captured the British imagination as a heroic exploit on the wild Afghan frontier. George Robertson was knighted, Sher Afzal and Amir ul Mulk were imprisoned and eventually died in south India, and Umra Khan fled to Afghanistan.

The British placed Shuja ul Mulk, the 14-year-old son of Aman ul Mulk, on the throne, but only gave him Chitral, Mulkho, and Turikho to rule. Mastuj, Yasin and Ghizar were separated from Chitral and ruled by British-appointed governors. In 1914, Mastuj was reincorporated into Chitral and the state's present borders were settled. Chitral trade shifted from a Central Asian focus to an Indian orientation under British influence. One third of all exports were opium, and one third of all tax revenues came from hashish. Shuja was granted the title of His Highness in 1919 with a personal salute of 11 guns and a substantial subsidy. Shuja ruled until 1936, his son Nasir until 1943, and Nasir's brother Muzaffar until 1949. These Mehtars abolished oppressive taxes, opened free schools, and brought Chitral into Pakistan in 1947. Saifur Rehman, Muzaffar's son, died in a plane crash on Lowari Pass in 1954 and his son Saif ul Mulk Nasir, then five years old, became Mehtar. In 1969 Chitral was administratively merged with the rest of Pakistan, bringing an end to the centuries of princely rule. The large family of princes remains influential and active in Chitral affairs.

CHITRAL TOWN

Chitral town, the former capital of the princely state of Chitral, is the administrative seat for Chitral district of NWFP. The town is along the bank of the Chitral River (1518m). Chitral has been a trade centre for as long as anyone remembers. As recently as 1929, caravans from Badakshan in Afghanistan carrying rugs and Russian porcelain passed through Chitral on their way to Peshawar. Today the cross-border trade has largely halted, although the occasional mule-load of lapis lazuli from the Badakshan mines still makes its way through Chitral to

CHITRAL

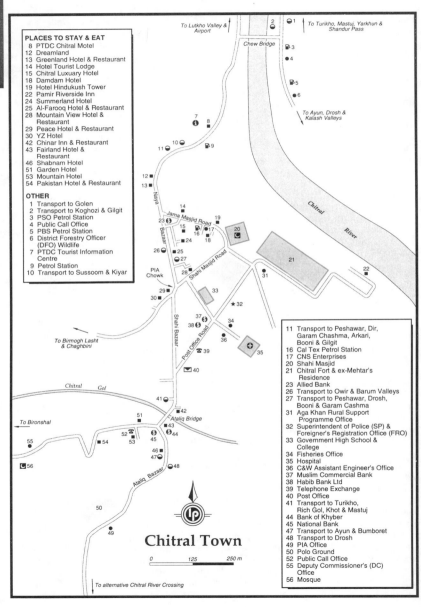

PLACES TO STAY & EAT
- 8 PTDC Chitral Motel
- 12 Dreamland
- 13 Greenland Hotel & Restaurant
- 14 Hotel Tourist Lodge
- 15 Chitral Luxury Hotel
- 18 Damdam Hotel
- 19 Hotel Hindukush Tower
- 22 Pamir Riverside Inn
- 24 Summerland Hotel
- 25 Al-Farooq Hotel & Restaurant
- 28 Mountain View Hotel & Restaurant
- 29 Peace Hotel & Restaurant
- 30 YZ Hotel
- 42 Chinar Inn & Restaurant
- 43 Fairland Hotel & Restaurant
- 46 Shabnam Hotel
- 51 Garden Hotel
- 53 Mountain Hotel
- 54 Pakistan Hotel & Restaurant

OTHER
- 1 Transport to Golen
- 2 Transport to Koghozi & Gilgit
- 3 PSO Petrol Station
- 4 Public Call Office
- 5 PBS Petrol Station
- 6 District Forestry Officer (DFO) Wildlife
- 7 PTDC Tourist Information Centre
- 9 Petrol Station
- 10 Transport to Sussoom & Kiyar

- 11 Transport to Peshawar, Dir, Garam Chashma, Arkari, Booni & Gilgit
- 16 Cal Tex Petrol Station
- 17 CNS Enterprises
- 20 Shahi Masjid
- 21 Chitral Fort & ex-Mehtar's Residence
- 23 Allied Bank
- 26 Transport to Owir & Barum Valleys
- 27 Transport to Peshawar, Drosh, Booni & Garam Cashma
- 31 Aga Khan Rural Support Programme Office
- 32 Superintendent of Police (SP) & Foreigner's Registration Office (FRO)
- 33 Government High School & College
- 34 Fisheries Office
- 35 Hospital
- 36 C&W Assistant Engineer's Office
- 37 Muslim Commercial Bank
- 38 Habib Bank Ltd
- 39 Telephone Exchange
- 40 Post Office
- 41 Transport to Turikho, Rich Gol, Khot & Mastuj
- 44 Bank of Khyber
- 45 National Bank
- 47 Transport to Ayun & Bumboret
- 48 Transport to Drosh
- 49 PIA Office
- 50 Polo Ground
- 52 Public Call Office
- 55 Deputy Commissioner's (DC) Office
- 56 Mosque

Chitral Town

0   125   250 m

the Peshawar market. The town is the principal market centre for the entire district. There is an airport, a bustling bazaar, and hotels.

Regulations
All foreigners must register at the Chitral FRO and receive a Temporary Registration Certificate regardless of length of stay.

Police
In Chitral district, emergency numbers in towns are: Ayun (☎ 7), Booni (☎ 24), Chitral (☎ 2913), Chitral SP's office (☎ 2553), Drosh (☎ 207), Garam Chashma (☎ 11), Mastuj (☎ 6), and Mastuj DSP's office (☎ 45).

Segregation of Women
Chitral town has a purdah bazaar and local women do not go into the bazaar. Female development workers also do not walk in the bazaar. On rare occasions, you may see a young girl or an elderly woman. Foreign women can walk in the bazaar, but it is preferable to be accompanied by a man and to dress appropriately. When travelling alone, ask someone from your hotel or a jeep driver to accompany you. Chitralis are gracious hosts and will gladly help you.

Places to Stay & Eat
No hot running water or geysers exist except at top-end hotels. Hot water is available in buckets on request. Most hotels need advance warning to prepare food. Almost invisible sand flies plague Chitral in late summer, when fleas are also common in hotels.

Places to Stay & Eat – bottom end These hotels all have charpoys; no beds. *YZ Hotel* (☎ 2690) above PIA Chowk costs Rs 50 per person; doubles with toilet cost Rs 100. The old rooms with no toilet at *Chinar Inn & Restaurant*, near the bridge in Shahi bazaar, cost Rs 40. *Pakistan Hotel & Restaurant* in Ataliq bazaar, above the Mountain Inn, has rooms for Rs 50 with two or three charpoys and a toilet. Also in Ataliq bazaar is the

Garden Hotel where three charpoys per room cost Rs 60 and camping costs Rs 30 per tent. The Kalash-owned *Shabnam Hotel* costs Rs 40 per room for four charpoys. Off the Jama Masjid road, *Chitral Luxury Hotel & Restaurant* has doubles/triples for Rs 90/110 and *Damdam Hotel & Restaurant* is the worst of the lot with charpoys for Rs 20.

Places to Stay & Eat – middle Hotels in this category have beds instead of charpoys. *Peace Hotel* just above PIA Chowk has doubles for Rs 120 with toilet. *Chinar Inn & Restaurant* has three doubles with attached bathroom (new in 1995). A good bet for Rs 150, it is quieter than most places, and is off the main road in Shahi bazaar near the bridge. *Fairland Hotel & Restaurant* in Ataliq bazaar has singles/doubles for Rs 100/150 and a cool, dark restaurant downstairs along the river. In Naya bazaar, two hotels off the main road are quieter. *Mountain View Hotel & Restaurant* (☎ 2559) boasts it is 'cheaper than the others' and *Summerland Hotel* (☎ 2337) has doubles/triples for Rs 100/150 with attached toilet and sinks. *Al-Farooq Hotel & Restaurant* has doubles for Rs 200 to Rs 250. *Hotel Hindukush Tower* (☎ 2888), next to Shahi Masjid, has ground-floor singles/doubles for Rs 120/150 and 1st-floor ones for Rs 200/300 with attached bathroom. The popular *Dreamland* has doubles with attached bathrooms around a cool, shady courtyard for Rs 200. *Greenland Hotel & Restaurant* is under construction behind Dreamland. *Hotel Tourist Lodge* (☎ 2452) with a secure, quiet compound and restaurant with TV is the best of the lot. Their doubles/triples cost Rs 250/300.

Places to Stay & Eat – top end The *Mountain Inn* (☎ 2370, 2800, and 2112; fax 2668) in Ataliq bazaar has friendly, helpful staff and a relaxing sheltered garden tended by its owner Haider Ali Shah. Their singles/doubles/suites cost Rs 600/750/900. Deluxe rooms cost Rs 900/1000/1250. Fixed meals are breakfast/lunch/dinner for Rs 70/150/175. *PTDC Chitral Motel* (☎ 2683) is in

Naya bazaar. Singles/doubles cost Rs 700/ 800. *Pamir Riverside Inn* (☎ 2525) is in a peaceful location along the river beyond the fort. These cottages were the former guest cottages of the Mehtar of Chitral. Singles/ doubles cost Rs 800/900 and deluxe rooms cost Rs 950/1050. In the summer it is cooler along the river than in town. *Hindu Kush Heights* is the newest hotel, built with traditional architecture on a rocky ridge in Dalamutz, 10 minutes north of the airport.

Getting Around

Outside the airport gate passenger jeeps and Suzukis to town cost Rs 5 per person plus Rs 5 per bag. A special jeep to or from the airport costs Rs 40. The bazaar is small and everyone walks.

GETTING THERE & AWAY

Treks throughout Chitral district usually begin or end in Chitral town (see the Getting Around chapter for more information). PIA schedules three daily flights Peshawar-Chitral and the fare costs Rs 440. Two unpaved roads link Chitral to the rest of Pakistan: one to Peshawar, the other to Gilgit. From Peshawar, the road goes to Dir and over the Lowari Pass to Chitral. From Gilgit, a road goes over the Shandur Pass to Mastuj and on to Chitral town.

Kalash Valleys

The Kalasha people are the only non-Muslim group left in the Hindukush. Their religion may represent a branch of the old Vedic religion that entered the Indian subcontinent via these mountains several thousand years ago, and until 100 years ago, was widespread throughout the Hindukush. Only about 3000 Kalasha practise their pre-Islamic religion.

Birir, Bumboret, and Rumbur are the common Khowar names for three valleys inhabited by the remaining Kalasha. In Kalashamun, the language of the Kalasha, Birir is Biriyoo, Rumbur is Roghmo, and Bumboret is Bumboret. These valleys lie south and west of Chitral town, and west of the Chitral River.

Kalasha are subsistence farmers who herd goats in mountain pastures. Their fields, while irrigated, are not terraced. Villages are located just above fields, at the base of rocky hills. The flat-roofed houses are tightly clustered. The two realms of the Kalasha, the pure and the impure, meet in the *jestak han*, the house in a Kalasha village of the female deity of hearth and home. The skylight opening in the ceiling of the jestak han is the place where a mythological iron pillar connects heaven and the underworld. The doorway of the jestak han is flanked by wooden carved rams' heads. The doorway is always on the impure downhill, valley side. The purest part of the jestak han is opposite the doorway, inside, below the mountain above. Here are the statues of gods and sacred juniper branches. Carved wooden figures of men, standing or mounted on a horse, are called Gandao, and honour ancestors. These are now scarce, most having been removed by collectors and museums.

Since the construction of jeep roads into the Kalash valleys, tourists have flocked to see the last survivors of an ancient culture. Unfortunately, some tourists who visit the Kalash valleys, particularly Pakistani men, leer and gawk at the unveiled Kalasha women. Tourism is being promoted with little regard to the sensibilities of the Kalasha, and most of the income generated from tourism never reaches them. In addition, Muslim and Christian missionaries are working to convert young Kalasha. The Kalasha want roads, bridges and hospitals, but they do not want interference in their culture or religion. They want to be asked before development projects are brought to the valleys and for those projects to work through Kalasha village organisations.

When you visit the Kalash valleys, be sensitive to their condition and try to ensure that at least some financial benefit goes to the Kalasha. You can find English-speaking Kalasha men who are happy to tell you more about their culture. Trekking from valley to valley offers you the opportunity not only to travel with the Kalasha, but to get to know, respect, and appreciate them and their land more fully.

INFORMATION
Maps
The British Survey of India 1930 edition *Afghanistan – NW Frontier Province* 1:63,360 sheet *38 M/9* covers the Rumbur Valley and sheet *38 M/10* covers Bumboret and Birir valleys. The US AMS 1942 edition *Afghanistan – NW Frontier Province* 1:253,400 *Chitral (I-42F)* sheet shows all three Kalash valleys. The more recent 1:50,000 Survey of Pakistan maps are classified and hence unavailable.

Regulations
A Tourism Division permit and a licensed mountain guide are not necessary, although the Kalash valleys are in a restricted zone. The Tourism Division's zone classification is superseded by three Chitral district requirements. Firstly, all foreigners must register at the Chitral FRO and receive a Temporary Registration Certificate. Secondly, anyone visiting the Kalash valleys for more than seven days must request permission from the Deputy Commissioner (DC) in Chitral. (However, staying an extra day or two seems to go unnoticed.) Finally, all foreigners register with and pay a 'toll tax' to the Border Police in the Kalash valleys.

The Border Police (District Chitral) maintain two check posts for the three valleys. Border Police are stationed in Guru in Birir (and usually find you) and at the Border Police check post at the junction of the Bumboret and Rumbur rivers. Carry your Temporary Registration Certificate since you need to know its serial number. Then fill out a 'toll tax' form and pay a one-time Rs 50 per person 'toll tax', which is valid for all valleys. Keep your receipt if you plan to visit more than one valley.

Kalasha Festivals
Kalasha celebrate their festivals with reunions, feasts, ceremonies, singing and dancing. It is an excellent time to visit the Kalash valleys. Inquire locally for exact dates. The main festivals are:

mid-May
: *Chilimjust* or *Joshi* is dedicated to spring and to future harvests. Festivities are held in each of the three valleys on consecutive days.

mid-July
: *Utchal* celebrates the wheat and barley harvests. It includes evening dancing every few days in successive villages in all valleys.

late September
: *Phool* is celebrated only in Birir to mark the walnut and grape harvest and the end of wine making. Its origins concern the return of shepherds from high pastures.

mid-December
: *Chaumos* is a solstice festival with feasting and evening dancing, closed to Muslims. Foreigners are expected to participate and possibly offer a goat (Rs 1500 or more) for sacrifice!

Accommodation & Supplies
No hotels have hot running water or geysers. Hot water is available in buckets on request. Hotels do not have attached bathrooms except in Bumboret as noted below. Most hotels prepare basic meals for Rs 20 to Rs 30 per person.

Ayun The home of Prince Khush Ahmed ul Mulk, on the true left bank of Ayun Gol, on cliffs overlooking the river, offers camping in a very large peaceful and private orchard, with interesting gardens of indigenous herbs and exotic flowers. Ask at the Mountain Inn in Chitral for details.

Birir Valley Birir's two hotels are in Guru. *Paradise Hotel* rooms cost Rs 50 to Rs 100. At *Mehran Hotel*, just up the road from the school, rooms cost Rs 80 to Rs 100. Rooms are upstairs; each hotel has a shop with expensive basic supplies downstairs. Book the *C&W Rest House*, in a walled compound, with the Assistant Engineer in Chitral or Drosh.

Bumboret Valley Hotels are in four villages: Anish, Brun, Batrik, and Krakal. Shops with basic supplies are in each village. Most hotel

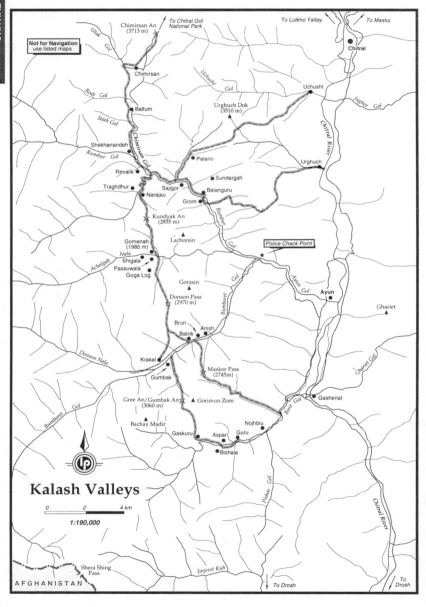

Not for Navigation
use listed maps

Uluk Gol

Chimirsan An
(3713 m)

To Chitral Gol
National Park

To Lutkho Valley

To Mastui

Chitral

Chimirsan

Uchusht Gol

Uchusht

Rodi Gol

Baltum

Urghuch Dok
(3510 m)

Jalah Gol

Shekhanandeh

Rumbur Gol

Palario

Urghuch

Revalik

Sajigor

Sundargah

Balanguru

Traghdhur

Narajau

Grom

Chitral River

Jughor Gol

Chimirsan Gol

Kundyak An
(2855 m)

Lachorsin

Gomenah
(1980 m)

Nala

Shigala

Passuwala

Goga Log

Acholgoh

Gorasin

Donson Pass
(2970 m)

Rumbur Gol

Police Check Point

Ayun Gol

Ayun

Ghariet

Brun

Batrik

Anish

Bumboret Gol

Krakal

Maskor Pass
(2745m)

Ghariet Gol

Gumbak

Gree An/Gumbak An
(3060 m)

Gorimun Zom

Birir Gol

Gasheriat

Bachay Madir

Gaskuru

Aspar

Guru

Nojhbiu

Bumboret Gol

Bishala

Kalash Valleys

0   2   4 km

1:190,000

Poihko Gol

Chitral River

Shera Shing
Pass

Jinjeret Kuh

To Drosh

To Drosh

AFGHANISTAN

owners are willing to negotiate rates, especially if your stay is not during festival time.

Anish *Valley Inn – Jinnah Kalash Hotel & Restaurant* has two and three-bed rooms with attached bathrooms upstairs for Rs 250 per room. Downstairs are four-bed rooms with no toilet that cost Rs 150 per room, Rs 60 for one person, or Rs 100 for two people. Off the jeep road, it is quieter and there are flat, grassy areas for camping. *Benazir Hotel & Restaurant* on the jeep road has a walled compound with a garden and space for camping. Three rooms (new in 1996) have attached bathroom for Rs 100 to Rs 150. A controversial PTDC motel is under construction across the road.

Brun Along the jeep road's north side are four hotels. *Foreigner's Tourist Inn* does not have an English sign, but is the walled compound below the mosque. Doubles/triples with attached bathrooms cost Rs 200/300. You can also camp in the garden. Just beyond the jeep road to Brun village are the Kalasha-owned *Hotel Kalash Hilton Inn* and *Taj Mahal Hotel & Restaurant* with charpoys for Rs 20 per person or Rs 50 for a four-bed room. The *Frontier Hotel & Restaurant* has charpoys on the porch for Rs 15, doubles for Rs 50 and Rs 60, and triples for Rs 80. In Brun, up a short, steep jeep road with good valley views, are two hotels. *Kalash Guest House* has a large, flat lawn for camping and the *Kalash View Hotel* is in a traditional Kalasha house in the village centre.

Batrik *Peace Hotel* has doubles with charpoys and attached toilet for Rs 50. Doubles with beds, toilet and running water cost Rs 200. Their 'deluxe' doubles cost Rs 400 and are on the top floor with carpeting, electricity, and attached shower.

Krakal The *Lahore Motel & Camping Place* is a fixed camping ground with canvas tents erected on crowded wooden platforms with beds, electricity, and showers for Rs 100 per person. Three Kalasha-owned hotels are along the jeep road. *Hotel Jahangir* has

doubles for Rs 50. *Alexandra* dorm/doubles cost Rs 35/120. You can camp inside their compound or on a large grassy terrace across the road for Rs 25 per tent. The *Kalash Hotel* has a dorm for Rs 50 and a large lawn and garden with room for camping. *Mateen Hotel* is above the jeep road in the Kalasha village of Krakal.

Rumbur Valley Rumbur's three hotels are in Grom near the end of the jeep road. First is the *Exlant Hotel & Restaurant*, which is easily recognisable by its inviting shaded garden across the road. Singles/doubles with charpoys cost Rs 50/100. Next are the *Kalash Hiltan Hotel* and *Green Kalash Hotel*. Shops are nearby.

GETTING THERE & AWAY
Kalash Valleys
Cargo jeeps run regularly only to Bumboret Valley for Rs 20 and leave from near the Shabnam Hotel in Chitral's Ataliq bazaar. Tarichmir Trail (☎ 2762 and 2768) in Chitral town arranges jeeps to Bumboret; their Peshawar office is at the Hotel Shahzad (☎ 27574). Special jeeps to any valley cost Rs 500 to Rs 600 and take $1\frac{1}{2}$ to two hours.

For Birir Valley, catch any vehicle heading south from Chitral to Drosh and get off near Ghariet Gol at Gasheriat where a bridge to Birir crosses the Chitral River. Then try to catch a local jeep going up the Birir Valley or walk for about two to three hours to Guru. For Rumbur Valley, take any cargo jeep going to Bumboret and get off at the Border Police check post. Either walk eight km to Grom, or wait for a local jeep going up the valley. Cargo jeeps Chitral-Ayun cost Rs 7 and Rs 10 Ayun-Bumboret. Special jeeps to Birir or Rumbur from Ayun cost Rs 200 to Rs 250.

Jinjeret Valley
The best way to reach the Jinjeret Valley is from Drosh. You can arrange a special hire from Chitral, or take a public van to Drosh and then hire a special jeep to the end of the road in the Jinjeret Valley for about Rs 200. More pleasant is taking a jeep Drosh-Jinjeret

village (at the mouth of the Jinjeret Valley), and then walking three hours up the valley to Jinjeret Kuh.

GUIDES & PORTERS

Kalasha prefer that trekkers hire a local guide or porter(s). It is useful to have someone show you the trails, which are steep and not always obvious. Ask for recommendations at a hotel or school. Wages are a reasonable Rs 100 to Rs 125 per day.

Extra concern for personal safety is warranted because many 'outsiders' come and go through all the Kalash valleys and unregulated passes into Afghanistan lie at the head of these valleys. Do not hire anyone along the trail. Instead hire in a village in the presence of others, so at least one responsible person witnesses who goes off with you. This ensures your hiring a reliable person rather than troublemakers or thieves. When you trek between valleys, hire a person from the valley in which you start. When you reach the next valley, they can introduce you to a responsible person whom they know (ie, a relative, friend, or hotel owner) in that valley. They can also suggest secure camp sites, preferably inside a compound.

You may see signboards in some Chitral hotels from the Kalash Environmental Protection Society (KEPS) stating Kalasha have uniformed guides who have permits (ie, licences) and that all tourists must take a guide over the passes. At the time of writing, there were no uniformed Kalasha guides or such requirements being enforced, but this may change.

BIRIR TO BUMBORET

(1 day; mid-April to mid-October)
Two routes cross the scenic ridge between Birir and Bumboret valleys. Below we describe the seven-km-long route from Guru in Birir to Gumbak in Bumboret over a pass called Gree An (3060m) by Birir villagers and Gumbak An by villagers from Bumboret. The route is steep on both sides of the pass and two km longer on the Birir side. It lies to the west, or up valley, from Gorimun Zom.

An alternative and slightly longer route is over the Maskor Pass (2745m), which begins in Brun, Bumboret. Cross the bridge over the Bumboret River in front of the Frontier Hotel and ascend to the pass, which lies east or down valley from Gorimun Zom. The descent is via Gandal village to Nojhbiu, below Guru, in Birir.

Map Notes

The US AMS *Afghanistan – NW Frontier Province Chitral (I-42F) sheet names only* Aspar and Bishala villages in Birir and does not name any of the villages in Bumboret. It shows only the route over the Maskor Pass, not the more frequently used route over the Gree/Gumbak An. The British sheet *38 M/10* calls the pass Ghumbak Gri.

Route Description

Day 1: Guru to Gumbak (5 to 7 hours) From Guru (1740m), walk up the Birir Gol 20 minutes to Bishala and cross the river. A *bashali*, or women's birthing and menstruation house, is on the true left bank just below the bridge. Continue up the true left bank for 10 minutes to Gaskuru. Turn north up a side valley, and go through the village 15 minutes to where the trail splits. Two trails lead from this point towards the pass. Straight ahead up a rocky slope with a few trees is a much steeper, but shorter, shepherds' trail. Instead take the trail to the right, entering a narrow black-walled gorge or *tang* whose high rock walls provide morning shade. Most of the way to the pass is dry, so get water from the irrigation canal before heading up the canyon.

Follow the relentlessly steep, rocky trail 1½ to 2¼ hours. Gradually the canyon opens up as the trail passes scattered oak, holly, pine, cedar, and the occasional juniper. Water may be found halfway up, but is not always reliable. The steepness lessens as you reach an open grazing area with a lot of dead wood on the ground. The steeper shepherds' trail meets the trail up the gorge here. (If descending to Birir from the pass, the shepherds' trail is clearly visible traversing the hillside. The trail down into the gorge is less distinct, but bears east (left).) The pass is first visible from the head of this grazing area. Turn north-east (right) and continue to the pass in 45 minutes to one hour up switchbacks of loose, steep rock through chilgoza pine. The pass (3060m) has superb views north to Tirich Mir and Noshaq; Istor-o-nal hides behind Tirich Mir.

The descent is to Gumbak, a Muslim village in Bumboret. Descend through forest along the true right side of a gully (snow-filled early in the season and dry later on). Where the first side nala joins from the east the trail crosses and then shortly recrosses the gully. A second side nala further down offers water. Reach Gumbak (2130m) in 1½ to two hours. The pass is easily visible from the Bumboret Valley. It lies at the east of the forested low point on the ridge, where the trees meet the rock of Gorimun Zom. The darker peak west of the pass is Bachay Madir.

BUMBORET TO RUMBUR

(2 days; mid-April to October)
A scenic, forested route connects Bumboret to the upper Rumbur Valley by crossing the Donson Pass, the intervening Acholgah Valley, and the Kundyak An. This 14 km trek is best done from south to north because Bumboret villagers from Anish and Batrik live in the Acholgah Valley and know the way. People from Rumbur rarely travel this route and may not know the way.

Map Notes

The US AMS *Afghanistan – NW Frontier Province Chitral (I-42F)* sheet shows only the western alternative crossing of Kundyak An. It shows the higher trail into the upper Rumbur Valley that leads to Shekhanandeh, and does not show the riverside trail. It names Shekhanandeh as Bashgaliandeh. It does not name any settlements in the Acholgah Valley or along the river in Rumbur. The British *38 M/9* sheet shows both passes. It incorrectly shows a trail along the true right bank of the stream coming from the Kundyak An. It does not name the Kalasha village of Ravelik. Balanguru is

positioned incorrectly and is mislabelled Kalashan Deh.

Route Description
Day 1: Batrik or Krakal to Acholgah Valley
(3½ to 4½ hours) Trails from both Batrik and Krakal join in the forest about two hours from either trail head. From Batrik (2040m), ascend the gully behind the village on a steep, but solid and well-defined trail. Pass through forest of massive cedars and occasional chilgoza pine. Aggressive logging by forestry contractors is evident. From Krakal, walk from the Mateen Hotel on the more gentle and wide donkey trail that traverses east and north to join the path up from Batrik at 2700m.

Proceed up gentle switchbacks on the wide trail 45 minutes to one hour to Donson Pass (2970m), 2.5 km from Batrik. Donson Pass is crowned by stunning cedars which must be at least 1000 years old. A rocky pyramid called Gorasin lies to the east and a forested ridge lies to the west. Goats and cows graze on the grassy slopes to the north. The Acholgah Valley is visible below while the Rumbur Valley is hidden behind the Kundyak An ridge. Tirich Mir and Noshaq are prominent to the north.

Descend north through grassy flower-filled meadows at first and then go steeply down a spur 30 minutes, following a trail. The trunks of some cedars in this forest are three metres in diameter. Just west of the spur is a small gully. Cross the gully to its true left side. In five to 10 minutes pass through forest to a wooden shelter called Owzurie (2460m). Continue down 45 minutes, crossing a side stream and traversing high above the Donson Nala on a good trail. Pass below Gogalog, a shepherd's hut above the trail, to an obvious viewpoint and westward bend in the trail (2220m).

Below, Donson Nala joins the Acholgah near a hot spring. Ghariet peak dominates the view down valley to the east. Looking south up the Donson Nala, the entire valley is forested and the route back to the pass is visible with Gorasin peak rising east of the pass. Continuing north, just around the bend of the trail, are two enormous cedars. From here, either drop down to the fields below or continue 15 minutes on the trail to the settlement of Shigala. Camp anywhere in the three settlements of Passuwala, Shigala, or across the river in Gomenah (1980m), 3.5 km below the pass. Several log and stone bridges cross the Acholgah. The villages are inhabited year-round by Kalasha men from Anish and Batrik villages who tend their livestock. A few Kalasha women come in July and August to tend the fields.

A jeep road connects the Acholgah Valley to the lower Rumbur Valley about three km above the Border Police check post. The road is open only in low water and is usually impassable from May to July. To the east of Gomenah rises Lachorsin peak. In Kalashamun, it is called *pushak* or snow leopard hill because of the snow leopard that is known to come down and raid the villages' livestock. A mineral-water spring is a two hour walk west up the Acholgah Nala.

Day 2: Acholgah Valley to Rumbur (5 to 6 hours) Once across the Acholgah, walk north 30 minutes up the jeep road to its end, passing through an impressive cedar forest (2460m). Extensive logging and milling by forestry contractors is apparent. Ascend either the slope to the west or the barren hillside, both of which cross the Kundyak An a short distance apart. Climb up the barren hillside, also called Kundyak, 15 to 30 minutes on goat paths to a small wooden shelter (2670m). You may notice notches cut into trees to encourage bees to build hives so Kalasha can collect honey.

Continue up a 10m-wide logging scar one to 1½ hours. Eventually this strip narrows and becomes a gully with dead wood lying around. The trail then disappears and the heavily forested route to the pass heads up and to the right of the gully. In May and June, the forest floor offers *qutsi* or morel mushrooms and later, wild strawberries. The Kundyak An (2855m) is forested and is not visible from below. Views to the north from the pass are obscured by trees. However, the sweeping views south towards the Donson

Pass are excellent. This 1.25 km ascent is through an old-growth forest with trees from 300 to 1000 years old.

No obvious trail exists north of the Kundyak An until you reach the first settlements below in 1¼ to 1½ hours. A local companion who knows the way down is essential, as the overgrown trail appears and disappears. The route stays to the right, bearing north to north-east, and traverses high for about an hour before descending steeply to a Kalasha house and a barley field at Narajau (2225m), two km below the pass. Traghdhur, a Muslim and Gujar settlement, is across the valley. The Kalasha village of Ravelik lies high above the junction of this side nala and the Rumbur River. The fields of Shekhanandeh are to the distant north. Shekhanandeh, where Kati-speaking people of the Bashgali tribe live, used to be called Bashgaliandeh. *Shekh* is a term used for converts to Islam.

It is a short descent to the bridge over the side nala below Narajau. Cross to the true left bank on the first of eight bridges (the number changes depending on the water level). Steep cliffs flank the true right bank and the stream enters a gorge. After 30 minutes and several river crossings reach the Rumbur River (2070m). From the junction there are views west towards the Gangalwat Pass into Afghanistan.

Cross the Rumbur River on a sturdy plank bridge. Follow a good trail along its true left bank 30 minutes to the first shepherds' huts and fields where a side stream comes in from the north. A trail up this valley crosses the ridge to Uchusht in the main Chitral River valley. In 15 minutes the trail crosses another side nala as the river bends south. East up this valley lies the Kalasha settlement of Sundargah.

Across the Rumbur River from this bend, in the midst of an oak grove, is the Sajigor shrine beneath a giant oak tree. Only males can visit this sacred place where men gather for festival rituals and young virgin boys offer goats as sacrifice. Elaborately carved wooden pillars stand behind the altar and the Sajigor tree.

The main trail above the true left bank continues 15 minutes to where a bridge crosses over to Sajigor. Follow the main trail 15 minutes more to Balanguru (1860m), 4.75 km from Narajau. Across the suspension bridge below Balanguru is Grom and the jeep road down valley.

RUMBUR TO CHIMIRSAN AN & CHITRAL GOL

(2 days; July to September)
This is the first of three treks towards Chitral town from Rumbur, the northernmost of the Kalash valleys. The trek goes up Chimirsan Gol past homes of Kati-speaking Bashgali settlers, and crosses the Chimirsan An into Chitral Gol National Park. (See Other Routes below for the descriptions of two other walks from Rumbur towards Chitral town.)

Guides & Porters

Hire a guide or porters in Balanguru. Balanguru shepherds use the Chimirsan pastures. You may also be able to hire someone in Shekhanandeh.

Route Description

Day 1: Grom to Chimirsan Huts (5½ to 6½ hours) From the end of the jeep road, cross the bridge into Balanguru. Continue along the trail one to 1½ hours to Shekhanandeh, between the confluence of the Rumbur and Chimirsan rivers. The trail ascends the ridge behind Shekhanandeh, staying well above Chimirsan Gol. After 1½ hours, it climbs a spur through corn fields to Nuristani-style homes above the north bank of the Jājok Gol. Contouring through forest, pass the start of an irrigation canal and reach Baltum hut (2762m) on the south bank of the Rodi Gol in another hour. Cross the Rodi Gol and ascend steadily, crossing small side streams, passing through 500-year-old cedar forests to reach Utak Gol, 1½ to two hours from Rodi Gol. Across Utak Gol and up an old lateral moraine 30 minutes are the Chimirsan huts. These huts are used by shepherds from Rumbur and Uchusht.

A difficult and closed-zone route over the Utak An (4654m) to Garam Chashma in the Lutkho Valley follows the Utak Gol.

Day 2: Chimirsan Huts into Chitral Gol National Park (7 to 8 hours) Cross the Chimirsan stream at the north end of the level plain. The pass is obvious. Ascend the middle of three ridges coming from the east side of the pass, contouring around and up the bowl at the head of the valley. Reach the Chimirsan An (3713m) in 1½ to two hours, where the view of Tirich Mir (7706m) is spectacular. Descend along the eastern side of Dooni Gol. Head for an obvious isolated stand of large cedars, passing about 100 metres below them. The trail is faint with occasional cairns, and some stone shelters. Descend steadily and reach a spring with willows about 1½ to two hours from the pass.

Descend to a permanent snowfield in the stream bed, cross Dooni Gol via this snowfield and continue along the true left (west) bank of Dooni Gol, through trees one hour to a ridge above the Dundini Gol. Descend to Dundini Gol, and a wooden bridge, then contour up one hour towards the prominent ridge dividing Dundini Gol and Gokhshal Gol. The route is almost invisible, and a local guide is essential. Join a main trail about 15 minutes below the ridge top. From the ridge top, Gokhshal hut is visible below. Descend to the hut in one hour. (See Chitral Gol National Park in this chapter for route descriptions through the park towards Chitral town.)

OTHER ROUTES
Rumbur to Urghuch

This one day walk goes from the Rumbur Valley to Urghuch village in the main Chitral River valley 6.5 km south of Chitral town. Head east up the side valley just south of Balanguru. Follow the true right bank for 0.5 km and then cross to the true left bank. About 0.75 km beyond the crossing, as the trail enters the higher forest, turn south, then contour east up towards the ridge. Cross the ridge south of Sunwat (3066m). The route heads north-east and 0.5 km below the ridge

CHITRAL

lies an abandoned rest house of the ex-Mehtar of Chitral. From here, the trail descends north 1.5 km to a spring (2272m) and the main Urghuch Valley. Follow it 2.5 km east to Urghuch village. Find a local jeep in Urghuch, walk to Chitral or Ayun, or cross the footbridge over the Chitral River and wait along the main Drosh-Chitral road for a ride.

Rumbur to Uchusht

Another route from Rumbur Valley towards Chitral goes to Uchusht, just 1.5 km south of Chitral town, in two days. Take a local guide from Balanguru since the trail is seldom used and can be tricky. From Balanguru, walk up the main Rumbur Valley west about 30 minutes. Head north-east up the true left (east) bank of the second side valley above Balanguru, beyond the Sundargah Valley. Some 1.5 km up the side valley, cross a side stream to reach the shepherd's hut at Palario. Then work steeply east about two km to the top of a forested ridge that separates Rumbur from Urghuch. From the ridge top, turn north and contour the upper Urghuch Valley. You can camp in this upper basin where water is available. Water is not found on the ridge top – only views. Ascend to the ridge between Urghuch Gol and Uchusht Gol, 0.75 km south and east of the high point, Urghuch Dok (3510m). Follow the ridge east into forest (3025m) then descend north-east past shepherds' huts. Follow the true left bank of a small stream, then the spur north of this stream down to Uchusht village.

Jinjeret Kuh

Jinjeret Kuh, a western side valley of the Chitral River, just south of the Birir Valley, is inhabited by now-converted Kalasha, who became Muslims in this century. They still speak Kalashamun, and live in Kalasha-style homes. Several interesting old forts or *kot*, still stand in the valley, near the last village, a three hour walk from Jinjeret. These old Kalasha-style forts are not found elsewhere and are the subject of current research. Jinjeret Kuh is scenic, the people are friendly and welcome foreign tourists. A visit to the

Jinjeret Valley makes an excellent day trip from Chitral town or an overnight trip from Drosh.

Chitral Gol National Park

Chitral Gol was declared a permanent wildlife sanctuary in 1979 and a national park in 1984. This beautiful, easily accessible, but rarely visited sanctuary is Chitral's best kept secret. It has lovely old-growth cedar and pine forests, and is home to several hundred magnificent markhor. A mating pair of snow leopards and their two cubs (born in 1995) are known to reside in the park and move between Kasavir, Dooni Gol and Gokhshal as the snow level changes. World-famous wildlife biologist George Schaller spotted his first snow leopard here. Other mammals are black bear, urial, wolf, ibex, marmot, and weasel. The park is rich in bird life such as falcon, hawk, eagle, lammergeier, monal pheasant, snow cock and many smaller species.

The wolf *(Canis lupus)* usually has a sandy coloured coat with black stipple. In colder conditions, the coat will often be blacker. A wolf lives up to 15 years and can be nomadic, adapting to seasonal changes.

Hunting is prohibited. Hunters especially covet the long and sinuously twisted horns of the male markhor. The national park conducts an annual wildlife census, regulates livestock grazing, the chopping of fuel wood and timber and the gathering of qutsi in May

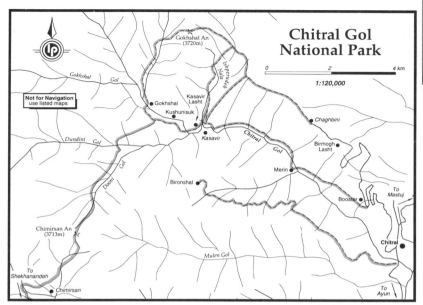

Chitral Gol
National Park

Gokhshal An
(3720m)

Gokhshal   Gol

Ishpernduk Nala

Not for Navigation
use listed maps

Kasavir
Lasht

● Gokhshal

Kushunisuk

Chaghbini ●

Dundini   Gol

Kasavir

Chitral

Gol

Birmogh
Lasht

Dooni

Gol

Merin ●

Bironshal ●

To
Mastuj

Booster ●

Chimirsan An
(3713m)

Chitral ●

Mulen Gol

To
Shekhanandeh

● Chimirsan

To
Ayun

0   2   4 km

1:120,000

and June and chilgoza pine nuts in September and October. The markhor enjoy the qutsi, which sell fresh for Rs 200 per kg and dried for over Rs 3200 per kg in Chitral's bazaars!

Unfortunately, Chitral Gol has been the subject of law suits since 1975. The ex-Mehtar of Chitral maintains the entire watershed area, almost 8,000 hectares, is his personal property. The government maintains that only his bungalows and cultivated land (about 80 hectares), are his personal property. It would be a loss to all if this litigation resulted in an end to the protection of this special wildlife habitat.

Chitral Gol National Park is to the immediate west of Chitral town. The Chitral River flows under the bridge between Ataliq and Shahi bazaars. The park makes for great spring trekking although the passes only open in July. Until August, high water in Chitral River makes the section between Merin and Kasavir impassable. Ask locally

about conditions. In the spring, markhor are readily viewed from Kasavir. A good three day summertime walk is from Chaghbini to Gokhshal and via Kasavir to Merin and Chitral. An excellent, more ambitious walk is from Chaghbini to Gokhshal then over the Chimirsan An into the upper Rumbur Valley.

INFORMATION
Maps
The British Survey of India 1930 edition *Afghanistan – NW Frontier Province* 1,63,360 *38 M/9* sheet covers the area west of Chaghbini and Merin and the *38 M/13* sheet covers the area east of Chaghbini and Merin, including Chitral town. The US AMS 1942 edition *Afghanistan – NW Frontier Province* 1:253,440 *Chitral (I-42F)* sheet is also useful.

Regulations
Foreigners are allowed to trek anywhere in this open zone. Neither a permit from the

CHITRAL

Tourism Division nor a licensed mountain guide is required.

Accommodation & Supplies

The District Forestry Officer (DFO) – Wildlife, Chitral operates two-room rest houses they call *Inspection & Watchers' Houses* at Merin, Gokhshal, and Chaghbini. The one at Merin is sometimes referred to as the *Merin Special Hut*. Rooms have a single bed and attached toilets. At Chaghbini water must be carried from a spring 30 minutes away or snow must be melted. If your walk starts from Chaghbini, bring full water bottles with you. Contact the DFO – Wildlife's office in Chitral town (☎ 2101) to book a room; no rate is set. You can also camp at the rest houses. Bring your own food; the game watchers are happy to cook it for you. A PTDC motel is under construction below Birmogh Lasht.

GETTING THERE & AWAY

Cargo jeeps do not go to the microwave relay tower (locally called the 'booster') or to Birmogh Lasht and Chaghbini. Special jeeps cost Rs 500 to Rs 600 to Chaghbini and take one hour. From Chitral, a paved road goes west from PIA Chowk. Then take the first jeep road up to the left (the paved road continues to the governor's cottage). The jeep road forks to the left to the booster and to the right into Chitral Gol National Park (a park sign is posted there). Birmogh Lasht (2580m), the abandoned summer residence of the ex-Mehtar of Chitral, is 15 km and 45 minutes above Chitral town. Chaghbini is three km and 15 minutes further up the ridge. The views from Birmogh Lasht and Chaghbini are spectacular – an almost 360° mountain panorama! Tirich Mir is to the north, Buni Zom to the north-east, and Ghariet peak is the sheer rock summit to the south-east.

You can walk from town to the booster or Chaghbini, which usually adds one day to your trek. Follow the more direct, but steeper, route up the ridge to avoid the lengthy switchbacks on the jeep road. The walk up to the booster takes about two hours

and the steep descent one to 1½ hours. Uphill to Chaghbini takes 3½ to five hours and downhill, two to 3½ hours. The route is dry and hot.

GUIDES & PORTERS

The DFO – Wildlife is in charge of Chitral Gol National Park. The office is across the Chitral River from town (☎ 2101). The DFO can arrange for a game watcher to work as a guide. Since game watchers are salaried employees, a daily wage is not expected. However, it is appropriate to compensate them for the extra work. Game watchers buy and carry all their own food from Chitral town, and appreciate it when you bring extra food (eg, rice, dal, flour, bread, eggs, tea, sugar, or milk powder) for them.

CHAGHBINI TO KASAVIR

(2 days; April to October)
A visit to Kasavir, one of the ex-Mehtar's hunting lodges, is a beautiful walk into the heart of the park. From Chaghbini, you plunge 880m over 3.5 km into this sanctuary. In early spring, snow leopards have been photographed here. In spring and early summer, markhor are readily visible on the cliffs above Kasavir.

Before mid-July, you have to return to Chaghbini from Kasavir. From August on, the water level in the Chitral River is low enough to permit returning along the river to the booster via Merin. Or, you can make your way from Kasavir to Gokhshal and the Dooni Gol, and cross the Chimirsan An to Rumbur.

Map Notes

The British *38 M/13* sheet shows neither the jeep road beyond Birmogh Lasht nor the booster. Sheet *38 M/9* does not show the game watcher's trail down the lateral ridge to Kasavir. The *Chitral (I-42F)* sheet does not show any trail. It calls Ishperudeh Zom (4156m) Sowarmapur Tak.

Route Description

Day 1: Chaghbini to Kasavir (3½ to 4 hours) Chaghbini means 'place where there is always shade' for the space beneath a huge cedar tree (whose top was lopped off by a lightning strike) below the Inspection & Watchers' House. Traverse west from the rest house (2925m) along a level trail on the south-facing side of the ridge through conifer forest. Where the trail makes an obvious bend to the north, you can choose between two routes to Kasavir. A steep route drops dramatically down a lateral ridge to Kasavir in about two hours, but you need a game watcher to show the way. Or, you can follow the longer, but more gradual trail down the Ishperudeh Nala. Ishperudeh means 'white place', referring to the light-coloured cliffs above. Both routes are shaded by cedar and chilgoza pine forests with scattered oak, holly and juniper as you descend. From the bend, continue to traverse north passing a spring in 15 minutes and meeting the Ishperudeh Nala in another 15 minutes. Cross the nala and descend along its banks.

If you come down the game watcher's route, you pass through abandoned apple and walnut orchards and cross two old irrigation canals above the left bank of the Chitral River as you near Kasavir. Cross the Ishperudeh Nala and head upstream a short distance to find a suitable place to ford the Chitral River. Kasavir (2195m) is the now dilapidated hunting bungalow of the ex-Mehtar of Chitral, Saif ul Mulk Nasir, on the opposite side of the river.

A few minutes' climb above Kasavir is a distinctive rock outcrop called Mroi Lodini which means 'the markhor viewing place'. From Chaghbini, Mroi Lodini is visible deep in the gorge below. Climb onto Mroi Lodini and look west across the river to the grassy plateau and the rocky cliffs above. At dusk, markhor can usually be spotted with binoculars. *Mroi* refers to markhor in general whereas *shahrah* refers to adult males and *majher* refers to females and young.

Day 2: Kasavir to Chaghbini (6 to 7 hours) The climb from Kasavir is steep and hot, so start early to minimise the time you climb in direct sunlight. The trail up the Ishperudeh Nala is more gradual, easier to follow, and

the best choice. Unless you book a special jeep, walk down to Chitral town from Chaghbini. At Birmogh Lasht (2580m), 30 to 45 minutes below Chaghbini, you may get lucky and find a jeep that has brought tourists up and is willing to take you down if there is room.

CHAGHBINI TO GOKHSHAL & CHIMIRSAN AN

(2 days; July to September)
This walk begins with stunning views from Chaghbini and crosses over the Ishperudeh ridge to Gokhshal. From Gokhshal, you can either traverse the upper Dooni Gol and cross Chimirsan An into upper Rumbur Valley, one of the Kalash valleys, or return via Kasavir to Chaghbini or to Merin, the booster, and Chitral.

Map Notes
The British *38 M/9* sheet does not show the trail between Gokhshal and Dooni Gol. It indicates a route up Chitral Gol from Kasavir via Krui Dheri to Dooni Gol, which has been destroyed by landslides. It names the pass between Gokhshal and Awireth Gol to the north as Gokhshal An, but game watchers call that pass Chikan. They call the pass over the Ishperudeh ridge Gokhshal An. The *Chitral (I-42F)* sheet does not show the route over the Ishperudeh ridge to Gokhshal.

Route Description
Day 1: Chaghbini to Gokhshal (5 to 6½ hours) Do not take the ridge-top trail, which leads to a 3rd-class traverse across a rock face before joining the easier trail described here. From Chaghbini, follow the trail along the south side of the ridge through open forest at the head of the Ishperudeh stream, passing a spring. Then angle up a grassy slope towards the rocky Ishperudeh ridge. The pass, the lowest point, is a small notch to the south (left) of a larger, but higher saddle. Follow a stock trail (used by cows) up, passing the junction with the 3rd-class route from the right about two hours from Chaghbini. Reach the top, the Gokhshal An (3720m) in another 45 minutes to one hour,

with sweeping views from the Lowari Pass to Buni Zom.

Carefully descend over steep, loose gravel switchbacks to reach the gentler vegetated slopes 30 minutes below. After 10 to 15 minutes, pass a tiny spring then cross two small clear streams and follow the trail above the true right bank of the second stream. Fifteen minutes further along, cross another small stream and follow down its true right bank rather than going ahead into cedar forest. Reach the valley floor in 30 minutes, and follow the trail down the bank (the true left is best) of the Gokhshal Gol to reach the tin-roofed game-watcher's hut in another 30 minutes. Nearby are walnut trees and a spring near the willows. The hut sits in an amazing amphitheatre-like rocky gorge with a pine-forested boulder area nearby. Unfortunately, cows of herders whose huts are nearby graze around the hut, so all grass is gone and dung piles lie under the trees. An enclosed camp site is needed here for trekkers, as is an appropriate toilet.

Day 2: Gokhshal to Chimirsan (7 to 8 hours) Cross the stream, heading west southwest and ascend the easternmost (first) of three forested spurs from the ridge separating the Gokhshal Gol and Dūndini Gol. A former bridle trail, now faint, works southeast, contouring up one hour to the top of the ridge (3049m) due south of the Gokhshal hut visible below. Descend 10 minutes, then leave the trail and follow a very faint watcher's cross-country route to the west and south (right). The main trail into Dooni Gol has been wiped out by a slide. Contour 45 minutes to Dūndini Gol (2772m), locally called Chhato ūsh ('water from the lake'), and a good water and rest spot. Cross a log bridge and climb steeply 20 minutes to a forested ridge. Contour south south-west into Dooni Gol and meet the stream in about 30 minutes. Cross a snow bridge, which is present even late in the season, and climb a grassy hill on the opposite bank 30 minutes to a small spring amid willows. Follow the remains of the old trail steeply up switchbacks well above the true right bank of the main stream, passing some stone shelters next to boulders. A few small cairns mark the trail. Pass beneath a prominent stand of five or six large cedars. Ascend a gully south of these trees a short distance and emerge onto a grassy ridge with scrub junipers. Tirich Mir comes into view prominently. Follow livestock trails, switchbacking up the grassy, flowered slopes another hour to the Chimirsan An (3713m), the southern boundary of the Chitral Gol watershed. Tirich Mir is impressive and Buni Zom is visible in the distance. To the west above the many feeder streams of the Dooni Gol is the summer habitat of the markhor herds.

From Chimirsan An, descend and contour the east (left) side of the bowl below the pass. Aim for the northern end of a level plain with shepherds' huts visible below on the true right (west) side of the stream. Follow the middle spur that leads to this point. Cross the stream and reach the level area one to 1½ hours from the pass. Just 15 minutes ahead, behind the low spur at the south end of the plain are the huts of Chimirsan, along either side of the stream coming from the Utak An. Urghuch and Rumbur people, both Kalasha and Muslim, herd goats here. Camp on the slightly sloping grassy area with abundant clear water. From here follow the trail to Shekhanandeh and on to Balanguru. (See the Kalash Valleys section for further description.)

Alternative Day 2: Gokhshal via Kasavir to Merin or Chaghbini (6 to 7 hours) From the Gokhshal hut, head south-east and ascend the ridge in 30 to 45 minutes, then follow the ridge 15 minutes to reach Kushunisuk, a ridge trail overlooking the gorge. The trail is exposed and narrow. Descend to the grassy Kasavir Lasht (plain) and then down to the Chitral River. Cross the river to Kasavir two to three hours from Gokhshal.

Depending on the time of year and water level, you have two options. First, you can ascend via the Ishperudeh Nala to Chaghbini. You may want to spend a night and ascend to Chaghbini the following morning.

From August on, if the water level in the Chitral River is low, you can follow the river route to Merin and the booster described below. To reach Dooni Gol from Kasavir, you must go via Gokhshal.

OTHER ROUTES
The Booster to Merin

Merin consists of several bungalows occupied by the ex-Mehtar's servants south of and above Chitral Gol. Female and young markhor live year-round on the cliffs north of Chitral Gol and can be seen from Merin. Merin is best visited from April to October. However, in December male markhor come to the booster and mate with the females. The aggressive displays and competition between males are an unforgettable sight. You can visit Merin on a day hike from Chitral town or camp in Merin and make this an easy two day trip. From the booster, descend 45 minutes to a bridge over the Chitral River and then ascend 15 minutes to the houses at Merin (1981m). The climb up the northern hillside back to the booster takes 1½ hours. Mohammad Deen, the ex-Mehtar's huntsman, lives in Merin and can show you where the markhor are. Bring binoculars. At Merin, figs, apples, pears, apricots, and grapes grow near the crumbling ex-Mehtar's bungalow. A former British officers' bungalow, with fine woodwork, is also dilapidated.

The British *38 M/13* sheet does not, of course, show the booster. It does show the trail to Merin and the jeep road. The booster is very near where the trail meets the jeep road.

Merin to Kasavir

An overnight trip to Kasavir is worthwhile to watch the markhor herds at dawn and dusk. However, you could easily visit Kasavir and return to Merin the same day. The trail fords the Chitral River many times and is passable only when the water is low and clear, usually from August to October. Follow the route upstream about three hours, fording the river as many as 10 times. It takes

about two hours to retrace your steps downstream to Merin.

Chitral to Bironshal

The ex-Mehtar of Chitral has a bungalow in Bironshal (3068m), which sits in lovely mixed forest and grassland. It is in ruins and is no longer used and the trail is not in good repair. Bironshal is best visited from April to October. The 10 km route to Bironshal begins from the paved road past the DC's office in Chitral town. It takes about six to eight hours to ascend about 1600m to Bironshal. This is too far for a day hike, so plan on spending two days. Return via the same route in about four to six hours. Or, if you have a local guide, you could return to Chitral town via Merin and the booster.

No trail exists beyond Bironshal, except a seldom-used, difficult game-watchers' track to Kasavir. Shepherds take goats from Merin up to Bironshal over a faint track. Reaching Dooni Gol from Bironshal is very difficult. The cross-country route with 2nd and 3rd-class sections is in bad shape and is not recommended.

Shishi & Golen Valleys

These two large valleys lie east of Chitral town and the Chitral River. They are the principal watersheds for the chain of peaks including Buni Zom (6550m) and Ghuchhar Sar (6250m). The long Shishi Valley joins the Chitral River valley just north of Drosh, and about 40 km south of Chitral. The last village in the Shishi Valley, Madaglasht, is a community of Persian-speaking Ismailis who migrated here in the 19th century from northern Afghanistan, to make guns for the Mehtar of Chitral. The upper Shishi Valley beyond Madaglasht has forested slopes, green pastures, streams, and friendly shepherds. It connects to the Golen Valley via three passes: the Roghili An, the Dok An, and the Lohigal An.

The Golen Gol refers broadly to the main Golen Valley and its four side valleys. *Golen*

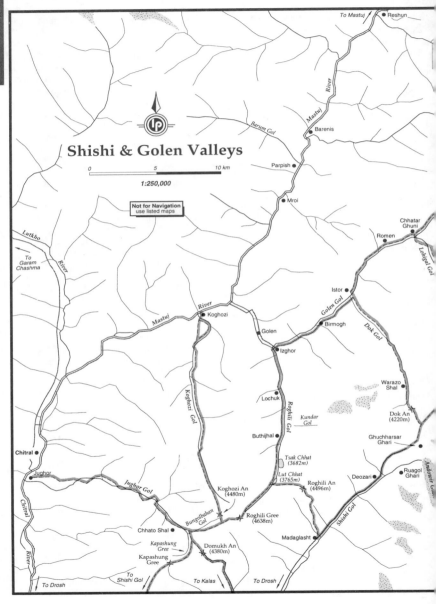

Shishi & Golen Valleys

0   5   10 km

1:250,000

Not for Navigation
use listed maps

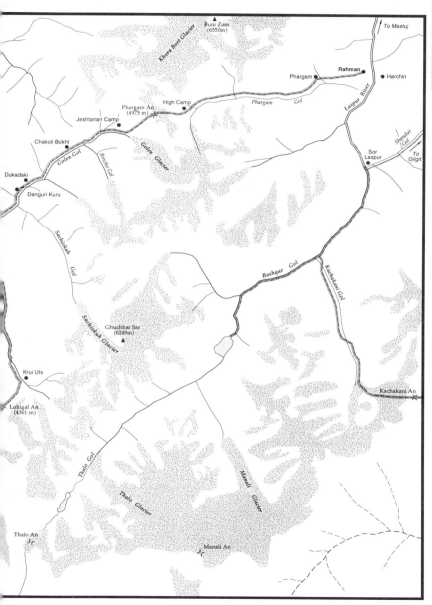

means 'many valleys' in Khowar. The entire Golen Gol has been declared a game reserve by the government. The area is home to a variety of wildlife including bears, ibex, and snow leopards, as well as many species of trees and flowers. The Golen Valley via the Phargam An provides the most direct route to the Laspur Valley at the western base of the Shandur Pass. This route was used regularly in summer before construction of the main Chitral-Gilgit jeep road. It passes between Buni Zom and Ghuchhar Sar.

The most popular treks in this area are the Shishi Valley to Lohigal Gol via the Lohigal An, and the Golen Valley to the Laspur Valley via the Phargam An. These two routes can be combined into one long, strenuous trek. A shorter loop itinerary starting from Istor in the Golen Valley ascends the Lohigal Gol, crosses the Lohigal An and the Dok An, and descends the Dok Gol back to Istor.

INFORMATION
Maps

The British Survey of India 1930 edition *Afghanistan – NW Frontier Province* 1:63,360 sheets include *38 M/13*, *38 M/14*, *43 A/1*, *42 D/4*, and *42 D/8*. Sheet *38 M/13* shows the Roghili Gol and the Golen Gol west of Izghor. Sheet *38 M/14* shows the Jughor Gol and Roghili Gol. Sheet *43 A/1* shows the upper Madaglasht and the upper Shishi valleys, the Golen Valley west of Chhatar Ghuni, Dok Gol, Dok An, Lohigal Gol and Lohigal An. Sheet *42 D/4* shows the upper Golen Gol west of Jeshtanan and sheet *42 D/8* shows the Phargam Gol and Phargam An.

The US AMS *India and Pakistan Series U502* 1:250,000 *Churrai (NI 43-1)* sheet shows the Golen Gol between Izghor and Chhatar Ghuni and the Shishi Valley east of Madaglasht, including the Dok Gol, Dok An, Lohigal Gol and Lohigal An, and the lower Roghili Gol. The *Mastuj (NJ 43-13)* sheet shows the upper Golen Gol, the Phargam An and the Phargam Gol. The only equivalent scale map showing the area west of Izghor and Madaglasht, including the upper Roghili Gol and Chitral town, is the US AMS 1942 edition *Afghanistan – NW Frontier Province* 1:253,400 *Chitral (I-42F)* sheet.

Regulations

Foreigners are allowed to trek anywhere in this open zone. Neither a permit from the Tourism Division nor a licensed mountain guide is required.

Accommodation & Supplies

Drosh Near Mirkhani village, half an hour south of Drosh, is *Nagar*, the house of Prince Sirajuddin, across the river from the road. It costs Rs 50 per tent to camp in a very large private, peaceful orchard, with a kitchen building and toilets.

Mastuj If you cross the Phargam An and return to Mastuj, you can sleep and eat at the small *Tourist Lodge* and *Restaurant*. Larger trekking parties can camp outside Mastuj at a spring amid willow trees, which is visible as you ride into Mastuj from Harchin.

GETTING THERE & AWAY
Golen Gol

Cargo jeeps to Izghor go daily except Friday, cost Rs 30 and take 1½ hours. They usually leave Golen Gol in the early morning and depart from Chitral in the late morning. The staging area is a small tea shop, the Kohinoor Hotel, across Chew Bridge, just north of Chitral town on the east side of the road. The proprietor, Hakim Khan, who also runs the adjacent store, can help you get the right jeep. You can also take cargo jeeps to Koghozi in 45 minutes for Rs 15 and walk to Izghor. Special jeeps cost Rs 500 to Rs 600 (ie, Rs 300 Chitral-Koghozi and Rs 200 to Rs 300 Koghozi-Izghor).

Just north of Koghozi, 18 km from Chitral, the Golen Gol jeep road leaves the main Chitral-Mastuj road. This narrow road traverses steep cliffs above the Golen stream. Golen (1890m) is the first village in the valley, where the houses are built of the ever-present speckled granite. The next village is Izghor (2225m), where an enormous spring pours forth at the base of the cliff just north of town. Near where the jeep road crosses the stream from the spring is an open, grassy area for a camp site. Izghor is where jeeps usually stop in order to return to Chitral the same day. Between Golen and Izghor, the fragrant yellow-blossomed *beshoo* or laburnum blanket the valley walls in the early season. Jeeps sometimes continue up to Birmogh and Istor, but you can only rely on reaching as far as Izghor by jeep.

Harchin

You can most likely flag down a cargo jeep to take you 20 km from Harchin to Mastuj for about Rs 20. You may have to wait overnight, but you can easily catch a jeep from Mastuj back to Chitral for about Rs 45, or go up the Yarkhun Valley.

Madaglasht

Regular cargo jeeps ply Drosh-Madaglasht. Vans also run regularly Chitral-Drosh and cost Rs 20 and leave from Chitral's Ataliq bazaar. Special jeeps Drosh-Madaglasht cost Rs 800 to Rs 1000 and those Chitral-Madaglasht cost Rs 3000.

GUIDES & PORTERS

Porter wages are Rs 160 per day. Wāpāsi and food rations are paid.

SHISHI VALLEY & LOHIGAL AN

(3 days; July to mid-September)
The Lohigal An is a non-glaciated pass at the head of the Shishi Valley that leads northeast to the Lohigal Gol, a southern side valley of the main Golen Valley. It is also the easternmost of three passes which connect the Shishi and Golen valleys; the other two passes are the Dok An and Roghili An. The Dok An route branches north off the Lohigal An route on the south-west side of the Lohigal An. The route from Madaglasht over the Lohigal An into the Lohigal Gol is not difficult and is the most popular route linking Shishi and Golen. The pass is usually approached from Madaglasht because of the more gradual ascent; the descent into the Lohigal Gol is steep.

Guides & Porters

Hire porters in Madaglasht. When you cross the Phargam An, you need someone familiar with that tricky route. Madaglasht men typically know only the Lohigal An. Hence, you either have to bring someone with you, or detour down Golen Gol to Istor. You cannot count on hiring someone at Chakoli Bokht, the highest summer hut of the Golen people. The other summer settlements in Golen Gol are used by Gujars, who are not familiar with the Phargam An.

Map Notes

The Dok An and the Lohigal An are very close to each other, and the placement of their names on the U502 *Churrai (NI 43-1)* sheet is misleading. At first glance, it can appear that the Dok An is mislabelled as the Lohigal An and the Lohigal An as the Dok An. Shepherds on the Madaglasht side of the pass refer to the Lohigal An as the Ghuchhar Sar An.

Route Description
Day 1: Madaglasht to Ghuchharsar Ghari
(4 to 6 hours) Follow the true right (north) bank of the river north-west from Madaglasht. Pass through fields and pastures two to three hours or about 10 km to Deozari. Beyond Deozari about 0.5 km, another trail branches east up a side stream coming from the Andowir Glacier. Some maps show a route to a pass (ie, Andowir An) at the head of the glacier that leads to the upper Panjkora Valley in Dir just south of the Thalo An. However, the route is over crevassed glaciers, rarely used, and neither feasible nor advisable for trekkers. The main trail to the Lohigal An continues another hour or 1.5 km from this junction through trees to Ruagol Ghari. From this Gujar shepherds' summer settlement, follow the trail up, steeply at times, one to two hours to the huts at Ghuchharsar Ghari (3505m). Several good camp sites are nearby.

Day 2: Ghuchharsar Ghari to Krui Uts
(4½ to 6 hours) Follow the true right (north) bank of the stream up. In about one hour, the

route to the Dok An heads north, climbing quickly to that pass. The trail to the Lohigal An (4361m) continues north-east and reaches it in another hour with a fine view of Ghuchhar Sar (6249m). Descend into the upper Lohigal Gol through flower-filled meadows 6.5 km or about two to three hours to the summer huts of Krui Uts (3581m). (*Krui* means 'red' and *uts* means 'spring'.)

Day 3: Krui Uts to Chhatar Ghuni (Jungal)
(4 to 5 hours) From Krui Uts, the main Lohigal Gol stream flows north. Follow its true left (west) bank a short way, then cross to the opposite bank. Continue down valley through several summer settlements to where the Lohigal Gol joins the main Golen Valley (3150m). You can camp anywhere in this broad valley with springs and meadows.

From Chhatar Ghuni, you can easily descend the Golen Gol to Istor in three to four hours. Below Istor, you can reach Birmogh in 45 minutes and Izghor in another 45 minutes, from where you can catch cargo jeeps. You can also walk on the jeep road from Izghor to the main Chitral-Gilgit road in three to four hours. Or, from Chhatar Ghuni you can go east and cross the Phargam An reaching Rahmān and Harchin in the Laspur Valley in 2½ days (see Golen Gol & Phargam An).

GOLEN GOL & PHARGAM AN
(4 days; mid-July to mid-September)
This trek goes through the lovely and infrequently visited Golen Gol and over the Phargam An (4975m) to the village of Phargam and the Laspur Valley. It crosses a shoulder of the Buni Zom massif, and offers glimpses of this peak, as well as a 'short-cut' between Chitral and Sor Laspur at the base of the Shandur Pass along the Gilgit-Chitral road. Crossing the Phargam An involves several hours of 2nd-class scrambling up huge talus on a not-obvious route. Until mid-August, expect to find a fair amount of snow on the pass.

Guides & Porters
A guide or knowledgeable porter is defi-

nitely recommended for this route. One trekker, a 'jungly' veteran of long solo journeys throughout the Himalaya and Karakoram, spent several days looking for the Phargam An before finally making it over. Hire someone in Istor. The trek involves two nights at high camps above the treeline on either side of the pass, so ensure any locals going with you are adequately equipped.

Map Notes
On the U502 *Churrai (NI 43-1)* sheet Izghor is spelled Uzghor and Istor is spelled Ustur.

Route Description
Day 1: Izghor to Chhatar Ghuni (Jungal)
(5½ hours) A steep eight km walk 2½ hours on the jeep road brings you to Istor (2700m), the last village in the Golen Gol. Istor means 'horse' in Khowar. Across the Golen stream from Istor is a spring and a grassy, shaded camp site. The Dok Gol leads south from Istor to the Dok An, which connects with the upper Madaglasht Valley (see Dok Gol & Dok An below). The trail up Golen Gol narrows and continues 4.75 km to Romen, a level place with huts, fields, and clear springs. Another 2.5 km beyond is a broad, grassy plain with big, clear streams, a few huts, and some fields. This is called Chhatar Ghuni (3000m) on maps, but Jungal by locals. The Lohigal Gol heads south from Jungal to the Lohigal An and Madaglasht in the Shishi Valley.

Day 2: Chhatar Ghuni (Jungal) to Jeshtanan Camp (5 hours) After an easy five km beyond Jungal, you will reach the Gujar huts of Danguri Kuru (3150m). From here, a side valley, the Sachiokuh Gol, leads south over a pass and then east via the Bashqar Gol to Sor Laspur village at the base of the Shandur Pass. The U502 *Churrai (NI 43-1)* sheet inaccurately depicts this unnamed pass. The pass is higher (about 5070m) and completely glaciated. It involves a steep glaciated ascent and descent with serious crevasses, and is not feasible for trekkers.

About one km beyond the Danguri Kuru huts are the Gujar huts of Dukadaki. The U502 *Mastuj (NJ 43-13)* sheet shows a route north from Dukadaki over a 4633m pass to Reshun village in the Mastuj River valley. Neither locals in Golen nor those in Reshun are familiar with this steep route, which seems to be no longer used. Some five km beyond Dukadaki, in a stony barren area, are the huts of Chakoli Bokht (3600m), where the Golen Gol villagers tend their sheep and goats. Springs flow from the base of the cliff here, and a bit of grass is surrounded by talus-covered hills.

Beyond the last grass at Chakoli Bokht, cross the talus fields and two side streams from the north, and head for the cliffs at the base of the Golen Glacier. Reach the three small stone shelters against the cliff known as Jeshtanan camp (4050m) about six km from Chakoli Bokht. Good, clear water is near this picturesque though sometimes windy camp. Locals tell that at this place *jeshtan* spirits are sometimes seen. They are small beings, the size of children, and wear only a small, pointed hat the colour of juniper wood. Among the Kalasha of Chitral, the cognate term *jestak* refers to the family goddess.

Day 3: Jeshtanan Camp to Upper Phargam Valley (8 to 10 hours) Ascend the moraine along the true right (north) bank of the stream from the Golen Glacier. Some sparse grass grows on the moraine, but it is mostly talus and the route is steep. About 1½ to two hours from camp, at the top of the moraine and talus ascent, where it levels off with a black moraine ahead and a grassy hillock on the right, turn left 40° and head up an unlikely seeming talus slope. Ascend these huge 2nd-class granite blocks one to 1½ hours to a lovely grassy area where wildflowers bloom in profusion and snow cocks abound. From here, ascend more gradual talus towards the pass. You may find the remains of an old trail, built for a past Mehtar of Chitral to ride his horse over! On the final steep climb to the pass, the old trail is obliterated until close to the top, where water and the trail are again encountered. It takes from 4½ to six hours to reach the Phargam An (4975m). On a cairn at the top is a metal plaque commemorating an Austrian mountaineering casualty, Georg Kronberger, who 'sleeps forever in the glacier'.

A small snow cornice is usually on the north side of the pass, but after that, the descent is across rocky talus, where the old trail is occasionally encountered, until you reach a grassy, flower-strewn ibex-habitat area. No doubt snow leopards are also about, though they are rarely seen. You can camp here (and reach Harchin in a long day by starting early the following morning).

Just beyond this spot is a rocky hill. Leave it on your left and head right and down a scree slope. Below you can see the old trail and clear streams. Flowers and low willows abound here, and the stream is cool and clear on a hot day, inviting you to wash the dust out of your hair under a waterfall. Descend into the upper Phargam Valley with its steep, jagged cliffs. On your left to the north, a spectacular waterfall booms off the Khora Bort Glacier from Buni Zom peak. On summer days, the river from this huge waterfall can be crossed only in the morning. In the afternoon, large boulders roll down the river bed, and to ford it is impossible. Camp before the river in the grassy area among the clear streams (3900m) three to four hours from the pass. Enjoy the sunset on the cliffs and mountains of this lovely upper valley after your crossing of the steep and rocky Phargam An.

Day 4: Upper Phargam Valley to Harchin (6 to 8 hours) In the morning, the river is no longer muddy brown, but a cool milky white, and is easily forded. Descending, cross another glacial side stream and pick up the trail down valley, passing awesome hanging glaciers on either side of the Phargam Valley. Above Phargam village is a small spring, and a jeep road leads from Phargam to Rahmān. Crossing the Laspur River over a bridge, reach Harchin village (3000m) and the Gilgit-Chitral road after 20 km.

ROGHILI GOL

(1 to 3 days; mid-June to September)
South from Izghor in the main Golen Valley
is the Roghili Gol named for its cedar forests
(*rogh* means 'cedar' in Khowar) with two
turquoise lakes and wildlife, including ibex
and snow leopard. The lower lake is Tsak
Chhat and the upper one is Lut Chhat. You
can walk up the valley for one or two days
and return via the same route. Longer walks
are also possible beyond the upper basin of
Roghili Gol. By July when the snow has
melted, you can cross the Roghili An to
Madaglasht in the Shishi Valley or cross the
more difficult Roghili Gree to the Bungolbahan Gol. From Bungolbahan Gol, you
can ascend and cross the very difficult
Koghozi An to Koghozi village, the Domukh
An to Kalas in the Shishi Valley, or descend
the Jughor Gol to Jughor.

Map Notes

On the British *38 M/13* and *38 M/14* sheets,
Tsak Chhat is labelled More Chhat and Lut
Chhat is called Tore Chhat. Locals call these
lakes *tsak* (little) and *lut* (big); *chhat* means
'lake'. They are also called locally *turi*
(upper) and *muli* (lower).

Route Description

Day 1: Izghor to Lochuk (2 hours) If you
take a jeep to Izghor (2225m) in the morning,
you can walk up to Lochuk in the late afternoon shade. Follow the true left bank of the
Roghili stream up a good, but steep, trail
through a rich cedar forest. The clear stream
subsides by July when the melt slows. In
1¾ hours reach the huts at Molassi, where
chir (pine) trees with long needles and long,
thin cones mix with the cedars. Cross an
alluvial fan and a stream over two logs and
in 15 minutes reach the pleasant flat, grassy
forested area and huts called Lochuk
(2640m). The views down valley and north-
west to Tirich Mir are good. Uncontrolled
cutting of trees in these magnificent, but
finite, forests for timber, fuel wood, and
clearing of fields is evident. Some Izghor
villagers are starting to realise that if felling

of the forest continues at its present rate, no
forest will be left for their children.

Day 2: Lochuk to Buthijhal (1½ hours)
Continue up the trail through chir forest,
passing a few occasional huts. In 15 minutes,
reach the treeline. Kundar Gol is the side nala
to the east, which is home to ibex herds.
Overgrazing by livestock is apparent. As the
trail ends, keep walking along the true right
bank of the stream up the rocky route.
Willows line the stream, but many have been
nibbled away by goats. It takes one to 1½
hours to reach Buthijhal (3030m). *Buthi*
means 'birch' in Khowar, and the large birch
trees are visible west of the stream. Buthijhal
is also a grazing area with a few rudimentary
huts. Irrigation canals run along each side of
the valley and may be mistaken for trails.
Stop here for acclimatisation.

Day 3: Buthijhal to Lut Chhat (3 hours)
Pass one more small cultivated area in 15
minutes with its few rudimentary huts at the
base of a cliff, right in the path of possible
rock fall and avalanche. Ascend rocky rubble
one hour to a few scattered birch trees
(3240m) on a rise. From here, continue up
valley as it turns to the south-west and
narrows. Pass through the narrow defile
called *tang* and 1½ to two hours from
Buthijhal reach the first of two aqua-green
lakes, Tsak Chhat (3682m). The trail continues up the true left (west) bank of the stream
1.25 km to the second lake, Lut Chhat
(3765m).

Day 4: Lut Chhat to Izghor (4 to 6 hours)
You can easily return from the lakes to Izghor
in one day. Otherwise you can explore the
upper Roghili basin or cross a pass. Continue
along the north and west shores of Lut Chhat.
Beyond the lake 0.5 km, cross the stream to
its southern bank. Here two routes branch
off: one to the Roghili An and the other to
the Roghili Gree. The route to the Roghili An
(4496m) heads south-east and crosses a steep
ridge to Madaglasht in the Shishi Valley. Or,
you can walk west up the upper basin following the south bank of the stream to its head,

and then ascend steeply over scree to the Roghili Gree (4638m) to descend west into the Bungolbahan Gol and the upper Jughor Valley (see Jughor Valley & Passes to Shishi & Roghili Valleys below).

OTHER ROUTES
Jughor Valley & Passes to Shishi & Roghili Valleys

The village of Jughor, at the mouth of the Jughor Gol, is just south of and across the river from Chitral town. The steep, rocky passes at the head of the Jughor Gol are not free of snow until July. They are best crossed before late September. Walks in the valleys can be done from May to October. Take a local who knows the way since map references are poor and routes are not obvious. Plan to visit Jughor the day before you start walking in order to arrange this.

From Jughor, walk up valley to a hut called Chhato Shal (3048m). At Chhato Shal, the trail crosses to the true left bank. Go 0.75 km further to a junction (3161m) of two trails. One leads east up the Bungolbahan Gol and the other leads south up the Kapashung Gol. The Kapashung Gol route splits further up valley. At this split, the route to the south-east crosses the Domukh An (4380m) to Kalas in the Shishi Valley. The route to the south follows the true right bank of the Kapashung Gol three km, along the highest branch, to Kapashung Gree (4318m), which also leads into the Shishi Valley.

The route east up the Bungolbahan Gol stays on the true left (south) bank and offers two options. Firstly, from the 3161m trail junction, you can proceed up valley three km and cross the river. A very steep 500m climb north brings you to the difficult Koghozi An (about 4480m) from where you descend steeply into the Koghozi Valley to Koghozi village on the Chitral-Mastuj road. This is a difficult cross-country 3rd-class route and is not recommended.

Secondly, you can ascend 0.5 km further north-east along the true left bank of the Bungolbahan Gol to Roghili Gree (4638m). It is then a steep 850m scree descent into the

basin of the upper Roghili Gol. The basin in the upper Roghili Gol is labelled Angarbah on the *Chitral (I-42F)* sheet, but locals do not recognise this name. Eight km further is the lake called Lut Chhat (3764m).

Once in this upper valley, two routes are possible from the trail junction 0.5 km above Lut Chhat. You can either walk north down the Roghili Gol to Izghor in Golen Gol or cross the steep Roghili An (4496m) to the south-east and descend to Madaglasht in the Shishi Valley. To head down Roghili Gol, cross the stream feeding Lut Chhat and contour along its north bank (see Roghili Gol above). To cross the Roghili An to Madaglasht, head south-east at the trail junction above Lut Chhat. The route to the pass is steep.

The routes over all of these passes are infrequently used, if exploring them, be sure to hire a local shepherd who knows the way.

Dok Gol & Dok An

The Dok An links the upper Shishi Valley to the Dok Gol, which runs west to Istor, the last village in the Golen Gol. It offers clear streams, flower-filled meadows, and enormous sheer cliffs typical of the Golen area. Istor villagers graze flocks in its upper pastures. Their summer settlement is called Warazo Shal. This area of the upper Dok Gol is one day from Istor. From here it is a one day walk over the Dok An, which is usually open from mid-June to September, to the Shishi Valley. Or, once over the Dok An you can turn north-east into the upper Shishi Valley, cross the Lohigal An and descend into the Lohigal Gol, returning to Istor.

Lutkho Valley

Lutkho is a tehsil of the Chitral subdivision of Chitral District. Geographically, it covers the drainage basin of the Lutkho River and its main tributary, the Arkari Gol. The Lutkho River flows from the Afghan border, where several passes cross the Hindukush range, which is relatively low here. The

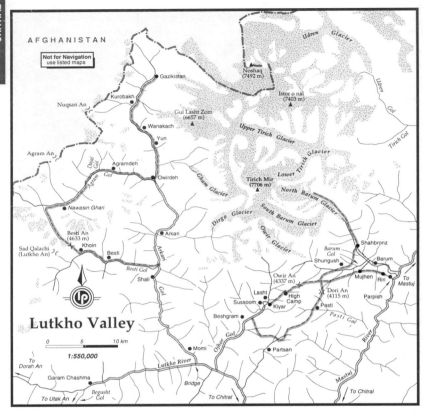

lowest and most used of these passes is the Dorah An. During the 1980s, it served as an important supply-line for the Afghan *mujahideen*, who ferried arms and material from the Garam Chashma staging area in Lutkho, using mules imported from China via the KKH.

Today during July and August 4WD vehicles traverse the Dorah An between Zebak in Afghanistan and Garam Chashma in Chitral. A tantalising sign at the Flying Coach booking office in Chitral bazaar gives Badakshan as a destination. (A special hire to Zebak costs Rs 12,000 and to Faizabad Rs 15,000.) But, the Lutkho Valley beyond Garam Chashma is closed to foreigners. Foreigners can visit the interesting Begusht Valley, which leads south from Garam Chashma. The Utak An, at the head of a branch of the Begusht Gol, leads to the Rumbur Valley, and is closed to foreigners.

The only trekking areas for foreigners are the Arkari Gol and the Ojhor Gol. These valleys drain the south and western flanks of Tirich Mir (7706m) and Gul Lasht Zom (6657m). Several infrequently used glaciated passes lead from the upper Arkari Valley over the Hindukush to Afghanistan. These passes are, of course, closed to foreigners. The Agram and Besti valleys are linked by the Besti An and offer a loop trek. The glaciated Gazikistan region of the upper Arkari Valley offers mountaineering challenges. By far the most frequently trekked area is Ojhor. An easy pass, the Owir An, crosses from Ojhor to the Owir Valley, on the eastern side of Tirich Mir.

INFORMATION
Maps

The Lutkho, Arkari, Ojhor, and upper Owir valleys are shown on the US AMS 1942 edition *Afghanistan – NW Frontier Province* 1:253,400 *Zebak (J-42X)* sheet. The Begusht Valley is shown on the *Chitral (I 42-F)* sheet. The lower Owir Valley is shown on the US AMS *India and Pakistan Series U502* 1:250,000 *Mastuj (NJ 43-13)* sheet.

Regulations

The Ojhor and Owir valleys are in an open zone. Neither a permit from the Tourism Division nor a licensed mountain guide is required. The Lutkho Valley beyond Garam Chashma is in a closed zone. The Begusht Valley beyond Begusht village is closed. The Ustui An and Utak An are also closed to foreigners. The Arkari Valley, including Gazikistan, Agram Gol, Besti Gol, Sad Qalachi (Lutkho) An, Besti An, and Begusht Gol are unspecified by the Tourism Division. Seek permission from the DC in Chitral or from the Tourism Division to trek in these areas. At the time of writing, no permit was required. The Border Police in these valleys will stop you if you attempt to approach any of the passes leading to Afghanistan.

Accommodation & Supplies

Garam Chashma The *Hotel Innjigaan*, east of the bazaar, has dorms/doubles for Rs 45/200 and a hot spring. Across the road is the *Muslim Khuzar Hotel* where doubles with no toilet cost Rs 50. A small *C&W Rest House* can be booked through the Assistant Engineer in Chitral town.

GETTING THERE & AWAY
Arkari Valley

Cargo jeeps to Owirdeh, the end of the jeep road in the Arkari Valley, cost Rs 100 and take about six hours. Special jeeps cost Rs 1400. Cargo jeeps to Besti cost Rs 70. Cargo jeeps leave from the Garam Chashma sarai across from the large chestnut trees in Chitral's Naya bazaar between PTDC and the Dreamland Hotel.

Garam Chashma

Cargo jeeps cost Rs 20 and take 2½ hours. Special jeeps cost Rs 300 to Rs 400. All jeeps leave from the Garam Chashma sarai.

Ojhor Valley

Cargo jeeps cost Rs 30 to Sussoom or Kiyar. Special jeeps to Sussoom cost Rs 500 and Rs 600 to Kiyar. VIP jeeps cost double these amounts. Cargo jeeps leave from the petrol pump across from PTDC in Chitral and take two hours to cover the 30 km to Sussoom. The first 20 km up the paved Garam Chashma road to the bridge at Shoghor takes 45 minutes. The steep climb up a narrow jeep road 10 km to Sussoom and Kiyar takes 1¼ hours.

Owir & Barum Valleys

Cargo jeeps to Mujhen, the main village in the Owir Valley, cost Rs 100. Special jeeps cost Rs 2000. Cargo jeeps leave from the Owir sarai across the street from the Al-Farooq Hotel in Naya bazaar. The proprietor of a small tea shop in the corner of the sarai can help you get on a jeep. Cargo jeeps to Shahbronz, the last village in the Barum Valley, also cost Rs 100 and leave from the same Owir sarai. Cargo jeeps to Riri, at the mouth of the Owir Valley, cost Rs 60 and go from the same place.

Jeeps to Riri and jeeps to Mujhen and Shahbronz use different bridges over the Mastuj River. The road from the Parpish bridge goes only as far as Riri. Beyond Riri, a foot trail links it to the upper Owir jeep road. The jeep road to upper Owir and Barum crosses the Mastuj River about three km north of the older Parpish bridge.

CHITRAL

GUIDES & PORTERS

No guide is required for trekking in open zones. However, if you are venturing into the Arkari Valley, a knowledgeable local guide is indispensable. Porters can be hired in any of the trail-head villages. Daily wages vary from valley to valley, but the maximum is Rs 160 per day, plus wāpāsi. Porters bring their own food and gear.

AGRAM GOL & BESTI GOL

(3 to 4 days; July to mid-September)
Agram Gol and Besti Gol valley are western tributaries of the main Arkari Valley, north of the Lutkho River valley. Agram-Besti is a wildlife sanctuary, which borders Afghanistan. Trekkers should be cautious in the Agram Gol, as the Agram An is an uncontrolled pass leading to Afghanistan. The Besti An links the two valleys. A second pass, the Sad Qalachi (Lutkho) An links the Agram Valley with the upper Lutkho Valley. Because of the steepness of the south side of the Besti An, the trek is best begun from Owirdeh and Agram Gol.

Guides & Porters

No one should trek in the Agram Gol without a knowledgeable local guide. Ask at the Mountain Inn in Chitral for a reference.

Map Notes

Some confusion exists about the two passes at the head of the south end of Agram Gol. One heads south and west into the Siruik Valley and on to the main Lutkho Valley, the other heads south and east into the Besti Gol. The *Zebak (J 42-X)* sheet names the first pass the Sad Qalachi An. However, the British Survey of India 1930 edition *Afghanistan – NW Frontier Province* 1:63,360 *37 P/SE* sheet and the editors of the *Himalayan Journal* call this same pass the Lutkho An.

The second pass, which leads to Besti Gol, is named on the *Zebak (J 42-X)* as the Lutkho An. However, the British *37 P/SE* sheet as well as the editors of the *Himalayan Journal* call this pass the Sad Qalachi! We prefer to call the pass leading to the upper Lutkho Valley the Lutkho An and the pass leading to

Besti Gol the Besti An, a name given by George Cockerill who travelled here in 1894. Sad Qalachi, then, is an alternative name for what we call the Lutkho An.

Route Description

Day 1: Owirdeh to Nawasin Ghari (8 to 9 hours) From Owirdeh village, with Gul Lasht Zom (6657m) prominent to the northeast, the trail leads up the true right (south) bank five km, then crosses a bridge. Four km above the bridge, reach Agramdeh village in a broad grassy area. Three km beyond, the valley widens and offers dramatic views of limestone crags above glaciers, with scree slopes descending to the grassy valley floor. Cross the Dajal Gol coming from the north, and 6.5 km from Agramdeh reach the junction (3220m) of the trail coming from the Agram An. Cross to the true right (south) bank of the main river and beyond a grove of old willows, reach the shepherds' huts of Nawasin Ghari (3447m) after another eight km.

Day 2: Nawasin Ghari to Khoin (6 to 7 hours) Continue up the true right bank of the Agram Gol as it curves south. Eight km from Nawasin Ghari, the routes to the Sad Qalachi (Lutkho) An and the Besti An divide. Take the left (east) fork of the stream, alongside a glacier, and ascend about 600m to the Besti An (4633m). Descend about 1200m to Khoin village in the upper Besti Gol in 2.5 km.

Day 3: Khoin to Arkari Gol Jeep Road (5 to 6 hours) Follow the trail down the Besti Gol 6.5 km to Besti village, then 9.5 km more to the junction with the main Arkari Gol and the jeep road to Chitral. Cargo jeeps occasionally come up Besti Gol as far as Besti village.

OWIR AN

(2 to 3 days; mid-June to mid-September)
This short, easy, and popular 13 km trek offers close up views of the southern flanks of the Tirich Mir massif. It can be done in either direction. In addition, you can add a

Top Left: Crossing the Dumordo River en route to the Baltoro Glacier by basket
Middle Left: Wildflowers at Urdukas, the last camp site along the Baltoro Glacier
Bottom Left: A yak relaxes after carrying trekkers' gear at Japerwask, Shimshal.
Right: Trekkers ascending the Gondogoro La (5940m) near Concordia.

JOHN MOCK

JOHN MOCK

LINDSAY BROWN

JOHN MOCK

JOHN MOCK

Top Left: A sign saying that Chitral Gol National Park was once the Mehtar's reserve.
Top Middle: The snow leopard, an endangered species, lives in the Chitral region.
Top Right: Apricot blossoms near Birmogh Lasht, Chitral
Bottom: View of K2 (8611m) from the Gondogoro La on the Baltoro Glacier

four-day side trip up the Barum Glacier to the base camp for the 1950 Norwegian first ascent of Tirich Mir. The Owir Valley can also be reached via the Dori An (4115m) from Pasti village in Pasti Gol. Pasti Gol is the summer home of the Tooshi Gol markhor herd. The owner of the Garden Hotel in Chitral town is from Pasti and can help you make arrangements to visit Pasti.

Guides & Porters

A guide is not necessary as the trail over the Owir An is not hard to find. Hire porters in the Ojhor Valley from either Lasht or Kiyar villages. Ojhor porters charge Rs 200 for two days over the Owir An to the first village in Owir, plus Rs 100 wāpāsi. If you continue up the North Barum Glacier to the Tirich Mir base camp, you must hire Owir porters for this section from Shahbronz. Owir porters charge Rs 200 per day plus wāpāsi.

Map Notes

The *Zebak (J-42X)* sheet accurately depicts the route, but does not show Lasht village in Ojhor. In Owir, it does not show the large settlement of Mujhen, along the true right bank of the Owir River across from Shungush village. The U502 *Mastuj (NJ 43-13)* sheet labels Riri village as Reri.

Route Description

Day 1: Shahguch to Kiyar High Camp (2 to 2½ hours) Sussoom (2896m) and Kiyar are separated by the Ojhor River, along whose true right bank is the village of Lasht. Shahguch, a large, well-watered grassy area, lies just upstream from the jeep bridge over the river. Camp in Shahguch (3000m), before ascending further. From Shahguch, follow the jeep road 15 minutes to Kiyar. From the polo field, head left and follow a trail up through fields. Keep the obvious dry rocky spur with a small cairn on it to your left and head for the highest trees and fields. On your right, but further away, are three vertical rock outcrops, and a waterfall up valley from them. Reach the last fields and houses and continue on a trail to the saddle

crossing the dry rocky spur on your left, one hour from Kiyar.

This vantage point has a superb view of Tirich Mir and the upper Ojhor Valley. From the saddle, contour gently up the eastern side of the Ojhor Valley 45 minutes to one hour, crossing several small clear streams, to a sheltered level grassy area (3500m), large enough for many tents. Those wishing to save the pass crossing for the next day can camp here, as can those coming from the Owir side.

Day 2: Kiyar High Camp to Owir High Camp (4 to 4½ hours) The trail reaches a ridge in 15 minutes and turns east to head up the southern side of the valley leading towards the pass. Contour around for 30 minutes to the snow pack at the junction of two small streams. The ascent to the Owir An is up the north (left) side of the rocky bluffs above. From the snowfield, ascend to the gully on the left of the rocky outcrop, with a small stream in it, in 30 minutes. From here, it is a steep one to 1½ hour climb to the pass itself. A small black outcrop lies just left of the pass (4337m). In heavy snow years, or early in the season, a snowfield lies on both sides of the pass. In light snow years or later in the season, it is often snow-free. From the pass, the Buni Zom massif dominates the view with the Shandur range stretching to the distant horizon. The fields of Shungush are visible below.

Descend along the small stream, crossing another small side stream from the left. The trail descends a ridge, well above the true left side of the main stream. One hour from the pass, you reach a level area with some grass and a few tent sites where two streams meet.

If ascending from the Owir Valley, follow the ridge trail up steeply. The pass is not visible until you reach the top of the ridge, above the true left bank of the stream below. As the trail and the stream near each other, a small hill is visible ahead with a prominent squared-off rock outcrop to its south (left). The Owir An lies just to the north of this hill.

If crossing from the Ojhor Valley and going to Tirich Mir base camp, follow the trail along the true left bank of the main stream from the level area. About 30 minutes ahead, reach the grassy area called Gologari, and camp. The next day, continue four hours to Shahbronz, where you change porters. Shukushal, the base camp, is five hours up the Barum Valley.

If going to Mujhen, cross the main stream to its true right bank, on a trail. Head across rolling hills and grassland 45 minutes to another stream and a large grassy area. A large camp site is near a small pool at the base of a rock outcrop.

Day 3: Owir High Camp to Mujhen (2 to 2½ hours) Cross the stream to its eastern side and follow along an abandoned irrigation channel. The trail contours around several ridges, and, as you leave the camp, you can see the square-topped rock outcrop and small hill that mark the Owir An. The view up the Owir Valley to Tirich Mir is impressive. Contour to a ridge overlooking fields and houses, then descend to the upper Mujhen settlement, one hour from camp. Follow the large trail through the village one hour.

You can make prior arrangements for a jeep to meet you in Mujhen. You can also find cargo jeeps in Mujhen. Otherwise, it is a full day's slog down the eight km jeep road through Mujhen, across barren land to Riri, down to the bridge over the Mastuj River at Parpish and the Chitral road.

OTHER ROUTES
Begusht Gol
The large valley south of Garam Chashma is the Begusht Gol, with a jeep road going to Begusht, an Ismaili village. At the head of Begusht Gol is the Shui Pass (4578m) to Afghanistan. Begusht is in an unspecified zone and the DC in Chitral can authorise visits. Several passes cross the ridge east of Begusht Gol into the upper Rumbur Valley. The Ustui An (4650m) is closed to foreigners as is the Utak An (4647m). Both require crossing snowfields. Eight km up the Begusht Gol at the village of Turi Beshgar, the Mohur Gol flows in from the south and east.

About 25 km up the Mohur Gol is the village of Putrik. At Putrik, two streams join. The one from the east leads to the Utak An. Below Utak An on the east is a lake, Dundīni Chhat in the upper Chitral Gol watershed, which is the summer-grazing area for Chitral Gol's markhor. The route from the pass leads south-east to the Chimirsan huts (see Kalash Valleys and Chitral Gol National Park in this chapter).

Sad Qalachi (Lutkho) An
This difficult pass links the upper Agram Valley with the Siruik Valley, a northern tributary of the main Lutkho Valley. The approach from the Agram Valley is very steep and long. The approach from Siruik Valley is perhaps more difficult, involving what seems to be 3rd-class rock. Sad Qalachi means 'seven lengths of outstretched arms' as the final 15 to 20m on the Lutkho side require traversing a narrow ledge along a 75m cliff. Take a local guide and a rope.

Gazikistan
Gazikistan means 'grassy place', and is a pleasant camp site between the lower and upper Gazikistan glaciers, which descend from Gul Lasht Zom (6657m). It makes a good base camp for climbs on the surrounding peaks. The jeep road up the Arkari Valley goes to Owirdeh, at the mouth of the Agram Gol. From Owirdeh to Gazikistan is a two day walk. Camp at Yun, a summer village 6.5 km from Owirdeh, or at Kurobakh, 14.5 km from Owirdeh, at the mouth of the Nuqsan Valley. Gazikistan lies 6.5 km beyond Kurobakh. A local guide is strongly recommended.

Turikho Valley

Mulkho, Tirich, Turikho, and Rich are valleys that collectively refer to the area drained by the Turikho River and its tributaries. Mulkho refers to the area on the south and eastern side of the ridge extending north-east from Tirich Mir. The Zani An crosses this ridge and on its opposite side lies the Tirich Valley. The Tirich Valley drains the large glaciers that descend from Tirich Mir (7706m), Noshaq (7492m), Istor-o-nal (7403m), and Saraghrar (7349m). Turikho refers to the area along the east side of the Turikho River, including the Khot Valley, as well as the area along the west side of the river north of the Tirich Gol and south of the Uzhnu Valley. The Rich Valley refers to the upper Turikho River area, north of the Uzhnu Valley. Mulkho tehsil includes Mulkho and Tirich. Turikho tehsil includes Turikho, Rich, Khot, Ziwor, and Uzhnu valleys.

Mulkho and Turikho are regarded as the homeland of the Kho people whose language, Khowar, is the language of Chitral. *Muli* means 'lower' and *turi* means 'upper'; hence Mulkho is the lower Kho region and Turikho, the upper Kho region. The Khowar spoken in Turikho is regarded as the purest.

The extensive glaciation at the head of the Tirich, Turikho, and Rich valleys prevents crossing the Hindukush range. Most of the side valleys are uninhabited, including the Udren and Rosh, which branch north off the Tirich Valley, and the Ziwor and Uzhnu valleys in Turikho. You can walk up these long side valleys and along the glaciers lying in their upper reaches and encounter no one but the occasional shepherd or hunter.

Several valleys leading east from Turikho are populated. Melph, Khot, and Chakosh descend from the ridge separating Turikho from the larger Yarkhun Valley. This ridge can be crossed via the Khot An at the head of the Khot Valley and via the Nizhdaru An at the head of the Chakosh Gol. A cross-country route runs along the crest of this ridge north to Yashkist village in upper Yarkhun. At the northern end of the Rich Gol is the side valley of Shah Jinali. A popular restricted-zone route up this valley crosses the Shah Jinali An to Yashkist.

INFORMATION
Maps
The US AMS *India and Pakistan Series U502* 1:250,000 *Mastuj (NJ 43-13)* sheet is the only readily available map for most of

upper Chitral. It does not cover the area west of 72° (ie, the Tirich glaciers and Tirich Mir, Noshaq, and Istor-o-nal peaks), which are on the US AMS 1942 edition *Afghanistan – NW Frontier Province* 1:253,400 *Zebak (J-42X)* sheet.

Regulations
A permit from the Tourism Division and a licensed mountain guide are required to trek in the restricted zones of the Tirich Valley and Rich Gol (ie, Ziwor and Uzhnu valleys, and over the Shah Jinali An). However, there is no police check post in the Tirich Valley. The rest of the area, including Zani An, Khot An, Hindu Raj Crest, and Nizhdaru An, is in an open zone, where no permit or guide is required.

Accommodation & Supplies
Along the main Chitral-Mastuj road below the turn-off to Mulkho and Turikho, cargo jeeps stop in Mroi for either tea or lunch. They also stop in Koragh at the clean, friendly, but spartan *Kohistan Inn* where rooms are available. At Zindrauli, above the west bank of the Turikho River and the bridge to Warkup, are several basic shops and a tea house. On the eastern bank, before Warkup, is the roadside *Drivers Hotel* offering basic meals and charpoys.

GETTING THERE & AWAY
All jeeps for the Mulkho, Tirich, Turikho, and Rich valleys depart from and arrive at Shahi bazaar in Chitral town. Go there in the afternoon when jeeps arrive, locate the drivers of jeeps coming from where you want to go, and arrange to travel with them the next day.

If you cannot find a jeep going to your final destination, you can take a more frequent cargo jeep going to Booni or Mastuj as far as Koragh. If you are coming from Mastuj, you can also get off at Koragh. All jeeps going to and from Mulkho and Turikho stop in Koragh. You can wait there for another cargo jeep to your destination. You may have to wait until the next day.

CHITRAL

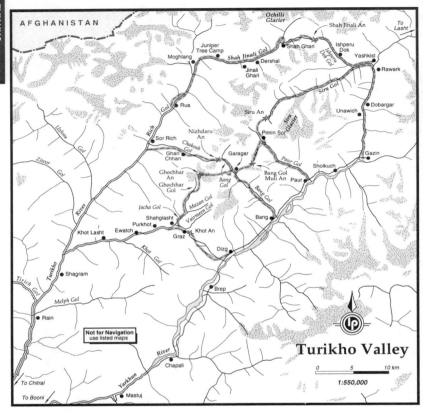

Turikho Valley

0   5   10 km

1:550,000

Not for Navigation
use listed maps

Mulkho

Warijun is the main village in Mulkho along the jeep road. A link road before Warijun leads to Uthool and one just beyond leads to Zani village. The Uthool link road is the most direct route to Uthool and the trail head for the Zani An.

The jeep road continues above Uthool to the Zani An and even a few km beyond it. An irrigation canal has been under construction since 1992 to bring water to drier Mulkho Valley from a lake on top of the ridge. The road was built specifically to get an air compressor up to the construction site. It is not regularly maintained beyond Uthool, so you can only rely on taking a jeep as far as Uthool. Drivers may take you further if you pay extra, but rock fall higher up can block the road. Ask in Uthool about road conditions.

Cargo jeeps Chitral-Mulkho cost Rs 50. Any cargo jeep going on to Tirich can drop you in Warijun. From there, you can either wait for a local jeep to Uthool, hire a special jeep Warijun-Uthool, or walk several hours to Uthool, some 675m above Warijun. Cargo jeeps Chitral-Uthool cost Rs 60, and take five hours. However, they are infrequent since there are only three jeeps in the village. Special jeeps Chitral-Uthool cost Rs 1200.

Khot Lasht – Khot Valley
Cargo jeeps cost Rs 150; special jeeps cost Rs 3000 and take about six hours. North of the village of Rain across from the mouth of the Tirich Gol is a Buddhist stupa with an inscription carved on a large boulder next to the road. As the road to Khot climbs from Turikho, you pass a large boulder with ibex graffiti and a three-tiered Buddhist stupa design on it. The jeep track continues to Shahglasht (3780m), where there is a weather station. However, the bridge before Ewatch village was out of commission at the time of writing, so jeeps cannot go further. Regardless, stopping at Khot Lasht (3048m) is recommended for acclimatisation and to hire porters.

Rua – Rich Gol
Cargo jeeps go regularly up the Rich Gol to Sor Rich and beyond to Rua, the last village in the valley. This trip takes all day. The jeep road is not dependent on water levels and usually jeeps make it all the way to Rua. Cargo jeeps cost Rs 120 to Rs 150; special jeeps cost Rs 2500 to Rs 5000.

Shagrom – Tirich Valley
Cargo jeeps cost Rs 120; special jeeps cost Rs 2500 to Rs 3000. Jeeps from Chitral take about 14 hours, but jeeps down do it in about nine hours (usually leaving Shagrom at 4 am). Jeeps do not go on Friday and run only every three or four days. You can also take any cargo jeep going to Turikho and get off at Warkup, cross the bridge to Zindrauli and wait for a local jeep going up the Tirich Valley, or walk. It is quicker, less expensive and more fun to walk over Zani An from Uthool to Shagrom (see the Mulkho & Tirich Valley map).

Sholkuch – Yarkhun Valley
A few cargo jeeps run between Sholkuch and Mastuj (see the Turikho Valley map). As you go south down the Yarkhun Valley, passing

through Paur, Bang, and Dizg, more cargo jeeps become available.

GUIDES & PORTERS
Porters' wages range from Rs 140 to Rs 160 per day plus food rations. For all treks in this area, it is easier to pay a porter an additional Rs 20 to Rs 30 per day for food than for you to buy food and give it to the porters. Wāpāsi is paid. No clothing and equipment allowance is paid. However, you need to provide food and proper clothing and equipment for glacier travel and pass crossing. A stage system operates in the Tirich Valley (see Tirich Mir Base Camp below for details).

ZANI AN
(1 day; late April to October)
The Zani An (3840m) links Uthool in Mulkho to Shagrom in the Tirich Valley (see the Mulkho & Tirich Valley map). Tirich villagers still cross the pass, because the 12 km path is the quickest access to the Tirich Valley. The jeep road is a pleasant, wide trail that eases the 1200m climb from Uthool to the pass and the views are magnificent. Istoro-nal is splendid, as is Saraghrar. To the east, the Buni Zom massif soars over the Mastuj and Turikho rivers. Crossing the Zani An from Mulkho to Tirich has advantages. Transport to Mulkho is significantly cheaper and takes less than half the time of transport to the Tirich Valley. Because of the jeep road, the ascent from Mulkho is much easier even though it requires 300m more ascent than crossing in the opposite direction. This is the best way to enter the upper Tirich Valley. Until June snow remains on the Zani An, especially on its north side.

Even though this is a one day walk, proper acclimatisation is necessary. Most trekkers experience difficulties if they go by jeep to Uthool (2640m) and begin walking the same day. Spend one night in Uthool (larger trekking parties may like camping in the large meadows across from the school below the village) and cross the pass the following morning. The pass crossing is short and easy by local standards, but Uthool villagers have plenty of stories about foreigners who quickly developed altitude problems. Uthool is a scenic village with sweeping views over Mulkho and Booni. Friendly villagers may show you to a lovely camp site in the village amid an open grassy area beneath walnut trees with a gushing spring nearby.

Guides & Porters
The route is fairly obvious, so a guide is not necessary. Uthool is the best place to find porters to take you to Shagrom for Rs 300 to Rs 400. Porters usually spend the night in Shagrom and recross the pass the next day, so their pay includes wāpāsi and rations. If you trek in the Tirich Valley, you must hire a guide and porters from Tirich (eg, usually in Shagrom). Let your needs be known when you arrive in Uthool where the helpful school teacher speaks some English.

Map Notes
The villagers in Uthool call the Zani An the Tirich An. However, it is called Zani An by the villagers in the Tirich Valley. The U502 *Mastuj (NJ 43-13)* sheet shows the route, but not the jeep road. It spells Uthool as Uthul, Warijun as Warinjun, and Shagrom as Shagram. (Three villages have similar names, which are often confused and are misprinted on maps. Shagrom is at the head of the Tirich Valley, Shagram is the main village in Turikho, and Shogram is along the true right bank of the Mastuj River opposite Reshun.)

Route Description
Day 1: Uthool to Shagrom (5½ to 6 hours) Follow the jeep road from Uthool to the Zani An. You climb quickly, ascending 300m in the first hour. Water is available at the last green area near a few willow trees after about two hours. Later in the season when snow in the gullies above has melted, water is unavailable higher. Continue another hour to

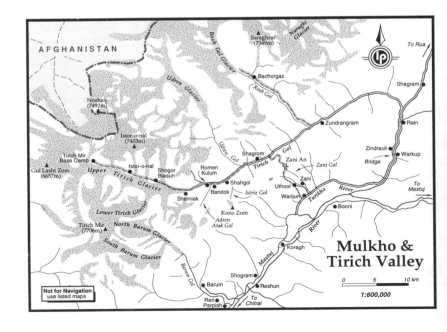

Mulkho & Tirich Valley

0   5   10 km

1:600,000

Not for Navigation use listed maps

the pass (3840m), 7.5 km from Uthool. From the top, follow a clear trail down. Several large cairns mark the trail as you descend into the narrow Tirich Valley. Shagrom is visible up valley, 4.5 km from the pass. Descend through fields and past houses to a bridge over the Tirich River two to 2½ hours from the pass. Cross the bridge and stop to rest your knees after this long descent. You can head downstream along the jeep road for five to 10 minutes and camp under poplar trees along the river or walk upstream into the village to camp.

TIRICH MIR BASE CAMP
(6 days; mid-June to mid-September)
The Tirich Valley is a long, westward branch off the main Turikho Valley. It leads to the base of the highest Hindukush peaks: Noshaq, Istor-o-nal, and Tirich Mir. The road to Tirich passes through Zindrauli where a bridge to Warkup and Turikho crosses the Turikho River. The jeep road goes to Shagrom, the last village in the Tirich Valley. The most popular trekking route up the Tirich Valley to Babu camp (ie, Tirich Mir base camp) traverses the Lower Tirich Glacier, so experience in glacial travel is helpful. The best close-up views of Tirich Mir are from Shoghor Biasun, a two day walk from Shagrom.

The Rosh Gol and Udren Gol are two side valleys that offer good hiking. The route up the Rosh Gol begins in Zundrangram, the main village in the Tirich Valley on the jeep road. Cross the Tirich River and walk up the Rosh Gol two or three days for close-up views of Saraghrar. The route up the Udren Gol just beyond Shagrom leads to Istor-o-nal base camp.

Guides & Porters
Because numerous mountaineering expeditions visit the Tirich Valley every year, the stage system is in place, unlike in the rest of Chitral district. The stages, however, correspond to a reasonable day's walk. From Shagrom, porters ask for Rs 600 to Shoghor Biasun and Rs 1200 to Babu camp to carry loads up and return without a load. They ask

Rs 800 and Rs 1600 to carry loads both directions. Expeditions usually pay the above wages plus provide rations, clothing, and gear, so don't be surprised if the porters ask you to do the same. Porters for expeditions usually carry 25 kg loads. If your loads are not that heavy, negotiate a compromise. No huts or shelters for porters exist on this route, so provide them with shelter. Porters expect further compensation if you plan rest days or have to halt because of weather.

What happens in the Tirich Valley is an example of expeditions and trekkers using the same areas. The main activity of an expedition takes place beyond the base camp. Expeditions need to transport large loads to base camp, and equip porters for conditions beyond. The result is that it generally becomes more expensive for trekkers to walk to base camp.

The birch and willow grove at Sherniak, the last available wood source on this route, is extensively abused. Villagers graze livestock as far as Sherniak and hunt in the upper valley, but climbers and trekkers share responsibility for the deforestation at Sherniak. Porters chop wood here and carry it higher to cook and stay warm. Provide kerosene and stoves for your porters and ensure they have adequate clothing and bedding.

Although the stage beginning and end is referred to as Shagrom, it is understood to mean the large, shaded area along the river about 30 minutes below the village where large parties camp.

8 stages: Shagrom to Sherniak, Sherniak to Shoghor Biasun, Shoghor Biasun to Istor-o-nal, and Istor-o-nal to Babu camp, and four stages return

Map Notes
The U502 *Mastuj (NJ 43-13)* sheet mislabels the Udren Gol as the Atrak Gol. Locals are quite definite that the map mistakenly names this major side valley. The map does not show a trail beyond Bandok. The *Zebak (J 42-X)* sheet labels Sherniak as Shekhniyak. It does not show the route over the glacier to the three upper camp sites.

Route Description

Day 1: Shagrom to Sherniak (3½ to 5 hours) Follow the trail out of Shagrom (2760m) through willow groves. Beyond them lie several shallow ponds. Shagrom villagers built these ponds to attract migratory ducks, which land on them in spring and autumn. Then Shagrom men sneak up behind the rock walls of the ponds, poke shotguns through small holes in the walls and fire away. Beyond these ponds is a wooden bridge to the true right bank of the Tirich River, one hour from town. After another 15 minutes of flat walking on a good trail through dry, rocky terrain is the confluence of the Tirich Valley and the Udren Gol (2880m). Gradually ascend the main valley 30 minutes to some springs. Water also flows here from cultivated moraine terraces above. Cross a gully, usually choked with snow till July, and after 30 minutes come to the fields and summer huts of Shahgol (3150m). Prominently ahead is the rocky peak called Kono Zom.

Follow the good trail for 15 minutes, ascending slightly to more huts at Bandok. Beyond Bandok, a narrow valley called Adren Atak heads south (left). Locals say a difficult pass at its head leads to Owir. Cross the Adren Atak stream to the last huts of Romen Kulum in 15 minutes. When the Tirich River is swollen by glacial melt, the trail climbs the scree slope 50m above the true right bank and contours high to reach Sherniak in one hour. Before July follow the Tirich River, crossing and recrossing the river over snow bridges to Sherniak (3540m), 12.5 km from Shagrom.

Days 2 & 3: Sherniak to Shoghor Biasun

(5 to 6 hours) A small trail, made by years of expeditions, goes through willow stands, under a rock perched over two large boulders, and climbs the terminal-moraine ridge of the glacier one hour from Sherniak. From here, follow the true right bank of the main glacial stream. Head towards the north side of the glacier near its mouth. Beyond the mouth, ascend onto moraine-covered glacier and move up the glacier, working towards the north margin. A large water channel can be difficult to cross in midsummer. The ice slope on its up-glacier side is steep and slippery, and using a rope here is warranted.

Ascend the ice slope and reach more level moraine-covered terrain. The route continues up the north margin of the glacier, past a prominent lateral-moraine ridge from a north side stream. In the centre of the glacier, across from this side stream, are white seracs. Stay close to the north margin. Shoghor Biasun (4038m) is just beyond and west of the large moraine hill. Leave the glacier and descend into camp. Shoghor Biasun means 'sandy base'. You get the best views of Tirich Mir south up the Lower Tirich Glacier from Shoghor Biasun; it is obscured by the time you reach Babu camp. You usually need to spend the next day here acclimatising.

Day 4: Shoghor Biasun to Babu Camp (6

to 8 hours) The route to Babu camp stays in an ablation valley and does not go out on the glacier. Follow the crest of an old lateral moraine ridge to Istor-o-nal (4267m) camp. Have lunch and continue another three to four hours to Babu camp (4724m), named after Babu Mohammad, a veteran trekking guide. He is a vast resource and when not out with groups is at the Mountain Inn in Chitral. You may want to spend an extra day or two to explore the area.

Days 5 & 6: Babu Camp to Shagrom

Retrace your steps down valley, spending a night in Sherniak en route.

SHAH JINALI AN

(4 days; mid-June to mid-September)

This popular and relatively easy pass parallels the Afghan border less than eight km from the Wakhan corridor (see the Turikho Valley map). The Shah Jinali An connects Rich Gol with upper Yarkhun. It is often included as part of a west-to-east trek crossing the Karambar An, or an east-to-west trek crossing the Thui An.

Map Notes

The U502 *Mastuj (NJ 43-13)* sheet terms Jinali Ghari as Shah Jinali.

Route Description

Day 1: Rua to Juniper Tree Camp (4 to 5 hours) Go by jeep to Rua, the last village in the Rich Gol. The trail starts along the true right (west) bank. Walk one hour, then cross a bridge to the true left (east) bank. Continue one to 1½ hours up the stony valley to Moghlang, where four rivers meet. A shepherd's hut is on the true right bank. Head up the true left (south) bank of Shah Jinali Gol, crossing small side streams. Enter a gorge and after 30 minutes, cross the river over a natural bridge of boulders to the true right (north) bank. The trail is narrow and at times loose along scree slopes well above the river. After one to 1½ hours, the gorge opens into a marble valley, and on the trail is a juniper tree with many sticks placed on it. RCF Schomberg mentioned this as a shrine to the valley spirits, revered by shepherds. A hut is below, along the stream and waterfall, and a small camp site.

Day 2: Juniper Tree Camp to Shah Ghari (6 to 7 hours) Two hours beyond camp, enter a wooded area where cold water comes out of a cliff with scree at its base. Another 1½ hours further on is (sometimes) a bridge to the true left (south) bank to Jinali Ghari. There may be a bridge one hour beyond that leads to Dershal (3350m) on the true left bank. Both are possible camp sites if you go further the first day or if you manage to take a jeep beyond Sor Rich to Rua. You can also camp on the true right bank opposite Jinali Ghari.

If there are no bridges, continue up valley traversing scree slopes and cross by a snow bridge, just above where the small stream coming from Shah Jinali An meets the main river coming from the Shah Jinali and Ochilli glaciers. Across the small stream coming from the pass, on its true left bank, is an old Gujar camp (3600m) with several huts and a sheep pen, called Shah Ghari. If crossing the main river at Jinali Ghari and Dershal, con-tinue up the trail along the true left bank, crossing many small tributaries along the way. From Derhsal to Shah Ghari is 2½ to three hours.

Day 3: Shah Ghari to Ishperu Dok (4 to 5 hours) Follow the true left bank of the stream up one to 1½ hours. Then cross the small stream and follow it to a spring, its source. This is a fine camp site with sweeping views. The pass itself is not far beyond. The level Shah Jinali An means 'king's pologround' in Khowar. From the pass, descend 1½ hours to Ishperu Dok, a summer village with 20 houses, where the Yarkhun Valley people of Shost, Yakhdan, and Yashkist bring their livestock. Above Ishperu Dok is the prominent white mountain that gives its name to the place.

Day 4: Ishperu Dok to Yashkist (3 to 4 hours) Descend a clear trail, steeply at times, crossing the river over bridges to Yashkist. Camp in the polo field below. A lake occasionally forms here, which can be good for a dip. From Yashkist, head up valley to Lasht, where a bridge crosses the Yarkhun River to the main Yarkhun trail (see Upper Yarkhun Valley in this chapter).

KHOT AN

(2 to 3 days; mid-June to mid-September)
The Khot An is a nonglaciated pass that links the Khot Valley in Turikho to Dizg village in the Yarkhun Valley (see the Turikho Valley map). This easy pass is regularly used by villagers of upper Khot to reach Dizg, with which they have close relations. Although the trail is quite gentle on the Khot side, the eight km descent to the Yarkhun Valley is long and tedious. Hence, the trek should be done from west to east. Its a way to reach the Yarkhun Valley if you are already in Turikho. Villagers go from upper Khot to Dizg in one long day, but trekkers can enjoy the pretty upper Khot yak pastures if they take two days to cover the 16 km.

Guides & Porters

Porters are found in any of the villages of

upper Khot. It is easiest to hire porters in Khot Lasht, the largest village, with a high school and several stores. Wages are fixed at Rs 300 plus Rs 150 wāpāsi from Khot to Dizg, for a either a one or two day trek.

Map Notes

The U502 *Mastuj (NJ 43-13)* sheet accurately depicts the route over the Khot An. It does not give proper names for the last two villages of upper Khot, Ewatch, and Purkhot; Shahglasht is termed Shah Lasht.

Route Description
Day 1: Khot Lasht to Shahglasht or Graz

(3½ to 5 hours) Follow the jeep road for one to 1½ hours to the bridge over the Khot Gol above Ewatch village (3180m). About 45 minutes up the jeep road, you are across the river from Purkhot, the last 'year-round' village in the valley. It is inhabited by Ismaili Muslims, who have close relations with Dizg villagers in Yarkhun. The last houses, used in summer only, are another 30 minutes up the road. Continue climbing another 45 minutes, through rolling hills, then enter the level Shahglasht area, reaching a solar-powered weather station (3780m) in another 15 minutes.

Here, several streams join to form the main Khot River. Above and south-east of the weather station are the huts of Pushet. Across the river to the north-west are the huts of Jinali Shah, and upstream from them are the huts of Tarwatin. The stream coming from the north is the Jacha Gol. A trail leads up it to the Ghochhar Gol and a high pass connecting to the Bang Gol (see Hindu Raj Crest below). Across from Tarwatin huts on the true left bank of the Jacha Gol are the huts of Jharogh. You can camp at Shahglasht, in the grassy meadows, and visit the herders' huts. Khot porters appreciate being able to stay in these huts.

Day 2: Shahglasht or Graz to Dizg (5 to 7 hours) Follow the trail up the true left bank of the Vairmeen Gol passing between two large rocky hills. As the Vairmeen stream bears to the north (left), continue straight,

reaching a level grassy area called Graz, 1¼ hours from Shahglasht. This is a good high camp alternative to Shahglasht when your porters are equipped to spend the night at 3600m.

Beyond Graz 30 minutes is another grassy area called Trushko Chat (3900m). This is the last reliable water until over the Khot An, and the last possible camp site. Bear south south-east, passing below the base of the large rock face. Reach a knoll in 15 minutes and turn south-east towards the Khot An, which is first visible from the small knoll. Reach the pass 30 minutes from the knoll. Yaks graze on the Khot An (4230m) in the summer. Ahead and east are the peaks above Thui. Behind to the west are the high Hindukush peaks, including infrequently seen Akher Chhīsh (7019m) at the head of the Uzhnu Gol. Descend south south-east across scree 30 minutes to a small, cold spring. This is the only water until Dizg. Contour around the south slopes of the valley, with fine views of the Shandur range peaks and the Yarkhun Valley below. After one to 1½ hours, reach a ridge directly above Yarkhun, and turn north-east heading down the ridge top. After passing a solitary juniper tree, switchback down the east face of the ridge one hour on a steep, loose gravel trail. Then descend a steep gully between fantastic eroded loess towers on loose gravel another hour to the Yarkhun Valley floor. Follow a trail across the alluvial fan for 30 minutes to the jeep road into Dizg, and another 15 minutes to the shops. Shopkeepers of this pleasant Ismaili village can offer trekkers grassy areas for camping. Plenty of water is available.

HINDU RAJ CREST

(3 days Khot to Bang, 4 days Khot to Paur, or 5 days Khot to Yashkist; July to early September)

An alternative cross-country route for leaving the pleasant upper Khot Valley is to trek north, over the Ghochhar An (4724m) to the Bang Gol. The descent of the Bang Gol is less steep than the descent from the Khot An. Locals from Khot and from Bang say this is not a difficult route. There are no relations between Khot and Bang; hence, it is rarely used by locals. The pass is significantly higher than the Khot An (4230m) and is undoubtedly much harder. From upper Bang Gol, one joins the Nizhdaru An route (see Other Routes below). Additionally, one can continue north and east via the difficult Bang Gol Muli An (4648m) to upper Paur Gol, and then down to Paur village. Or, more interestingly, one can head north-east over the Siru An (4572m) into the upper Siru Gol and continue 14.5 km to Yashkist at the confluence of the Ishperu Dok Gol and the Yarkhun River.

Guides & Porters
Since Khot villagers do not use this route, it can be difficult to find a local guide or porter who has crossed the pass between Khot and Bang. Khot herders know the way to the pass, but not to Bang. Bang men know the way to both the pass to Khot and the pass to Paur, but not beyond. Paur men know the route to the Siru Gol. Anyone attempting this route must be experienced in Hindukush trekking, accomplished at routefinding, completely self-reliant, and able to communicate with local herders in high pastures. Herders leave the pastures by early September, though the passes remain snow-free until mid-to late September.

Map Notes
The U502 *Mastuj (NJ 43-13)* sheet indicates the route. Shahglasht is called Shah Lasht on this map and other summer herders' huts are not shown. Jacha Gol is not named.

Route Description
Day 1: Khot Lasht to Shahglasht (3½ to 4 hours) See the Khot An trek above.

Day 2: Shahglasht to Garagar (7 to 9 hours) Leave the trail to the Khot An and continue to the huts of Jharogh, on the true left bank of the Jacha Gol. Cross the Jacha Gol to its true right bank and continue up. The Jacha Gol and the Ghochhar Gol meet just beyond. Continue along the true right

(west) bank of the Ghochhar Gol 1.5 km to the confluence with the Mazan Gol. Follow the Ghochhar Gol, and after passing beneath several small permanent snowfields, cross the stream to its true left bank and ascend to the pass. This high pass appears to involve a steep scree ascent. The descent from the pass is over a small glacier. Continue to Garagar, a shepherds' settlement in the upper Bang Gol. The Nizhdaru An route joins here.

Day 3: Garagar to Pimin Sor (5 to 8 hours) Paur villagers describe the route as bad. It heads north-east to the Bang Gol Muli An (4763m). The descent to Pimin Sor apparently involves traversing a small glacier, so using a rope is advisable. From Pimin Sor, Paur is eight km down Paur Gol.

Day 4: Pimin Sor to Upper Siru Valley (5 to 7 hours) From Pimin Sor, a herders' settlement in the upper Paur Gol, head north, then north-east to the Siru An (4572m). Paur villagers describe this route as good, and the upper Siru Gol as pleasant. Over the pass, descend to a camp beyond the Siru Glacier.

Day 5: Upper Siru Valley to Yashkist (5 to 7 hours) Continue down the herders' trail along the true right (south) bank to the confluence of the Siru Gol and Ishperu Dok Gol. Here is a bridge over the Ishperu Dok Gol and the trail to Ishperu Dok and the Shah Jinali An (see route description above). Descend along the southern bank of the Ishperu Dok Gol to Yashkist village.

OTHER ROUTES
Uzhnu & Ziwor Valleys
Uzhnu and Ziwor are uninhabited valleys that branch west from the main Turikho River. Uzhnu is the northernmost of these parallel valleys. The long Ziwor Gol used to be inhabited, but people abandoned it when the glacier at its head advanced. It has since receded, but has not been resettled. Ziwor Gol provides the best views of Saraghrar (7349m). A five to seven day route leaves the jeep road in Turikho from Uzhnu village and heads up the Uzhnu Valley, south across the

Chikor Pass and then east down the Ziwor Valley returning to the main Turikho Valley. The pass should be open from mid-July to mid-September. This is an unspecified route, which falls within a restricted zone.

Nizhdaru An

The high Nizhdaru An (5087m) is an infrequently crossed pass that links Sor Rich in the Rich Gol to Bang in the Yarkhun Valley. This 25 km walk takes two to three days and is best done from July to August. From Sor Rich (2785m) walk up the true left (south) bank of the Chakosh Gol five km to the shepherds' huts of Ghari Chhan. Continue another eight km and camp below the base of a small glacier coming from the pass. The next day, ascend the glacier steeply to the Nizhdaru An. A rope, an ice axe, and crampons are recommended. Descend steeply over scree on the west side to the meadows of Garagar (4023m). Camp here or continue to Bang in a long day. From Garagar, you can also head to Khot over the Ghochhar An, or to Pimin Sor over the Bang Gol Muli An (see Hindu Raj Crest above).

Upper Yarkhun Valley

The Karambar and Darkot passes link the upper Yarkhun with the Gilgit River region. The glaciated Darkot An leads south to the Yasin Valley, and the grassy Karambar An leads east to the Karambar Valley, which joins the Ishkoman Valley below Imit. The western approach from Yarkhun to both passes goes through the Broghil area, populated by Wakhi people. The Wakhi in Broghil have large herds of yaks, sheep, and goats and also horses and camels. These areas have opened to foreigners only recently since the end of the Russian occupation of Afghanistan. The Broghil Pass itself leads to Afghanistan and is closed to foreigners.

An important Central Asian trade route ran through the Yarkhun Valley, over the easy Broghil Pass to Kashgar and Yarkand. As recently as 1930, over 1000 horse loads crossed the Broghil each summer. From Central Asia, three-quarters of all trade through Chitral was in hashish or *charas*. When the Chinese border closed in 1950, increased cannabis cultivation in Yarkhun filled the gap. After Pakistan made charas illegal in the late 1970s, production declined, but continues as a cottage industry. Almost all Yarkhun people are Ismaili Muslims, friendly folk who enjoy song and poetry.

Treks in the upper Yarkhun Valley and Broghil are easily combined with other trekking routes. Instead of riding in a jeep up the Yarkhun Valley, you can trek over the Shah Janali An from Rich Gol and join the Yarkhun Valley at Lasht (see Turikho Valley in this chapter) or cross the Thui An from Yasin and join the Yarkhun Valley at Gazin (see Yasin Valley in the Upper Ghizar River Valley section). You can also reach Broghil from the east by trekking up the Karambar Valley from Ishkoman (see Ishkoman Valley in the Upper Ghizar River Valley chapter) or by crossing the Chilinji An (see Gojal in the Hunza River Valley chapter) from Chapursan.

INFORMATION
Maps

The US AMS *India and Pakistan Series U502* 1:250,000 *Mastuj (NJ 43-13)* and *Baltit (NJ 43-14)* sheets accurately portray the routes, passes, and most place names. However, physical features, especially those not in the main river valleys, are inaccurate.

Regulations

These routes are in a restricted zone, requiring you to get a permit from the Tourism Division and a licensed mountain guide. The Broghil Pass (3600m) and other passes into Afghanistan are strictly off-limits to foreigners. Foreigners must register at the Chitral Scouts posts in Lasht and Ishkarwaz.

Accommodation & Supplies

Mastuj has a National Bank and hotels with charpoys for Rs 20. Chapali has a few stores, but no hotels. Chonj, about four km south of Chapali, has a large well-stocked bazaar and

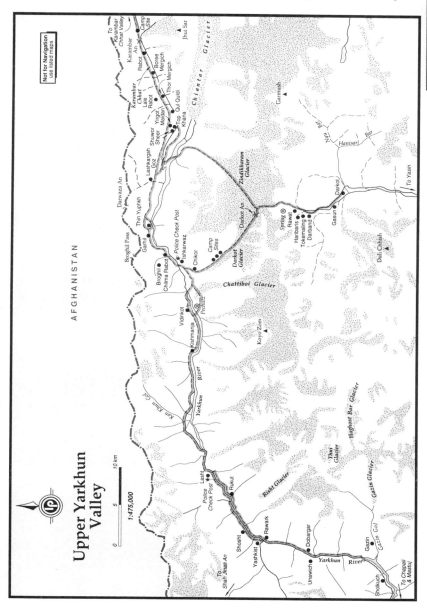

Not for Navigation
use listed maps

Upper Yarkhun
Valley

0   5   10 km

1:475,000

AFGHANISTAN

at the *Khyber Hotel* charpoys cost Rs 15. Sholkuch and Lasht have a few shops with basic supplies. Chikor has several small stores where you may find basic supplies such as rice, flour, salt, milk powder, tea, sugar, cigarettes, and kerosene. Men from Chikor bring the goods they sell over the Darkot An from Darkot village where shops are regularly supplied by jeeps from Gilgit.

GETTING THERE & AWAY
Sholkuch – Yarkhun Valley
Passenger jeeps go Chitral-Mastuj for Rs 40. From Mastuj, cargo jeeps go up the Yarkhun Valley as far as Sholkuch, just beyond Paur, and cost Rs 100. Special hires Chitral-Mastuj cost about Rs 2000 and Mastuj-Sholkuch cost about Rs 1200. Cargo jeeps to Sholkuch are few, so you may have to settle for one to Bang or Paur. Paur is a one hour walk from Sholkuch. In low water, jeeps go beyond Sholkuch to Lasht.

Darkot – Yasin Valley
Darkot village, at the head of the Yasin Valley, is the trail head for treks over the Darkot An. Cargo jeeps go Darkot-Gilgit for Rs 110 to Rs 125 per person, including 20 kg of baggage. Darkot villagers can help you get a ride. Special hires from Darkot to Gilgit cost Rs 2500 to Rs 3000. You may have to wait a day or two for a ride. Jeeps to Darkot leave sporadically from Gilgit's Jamat Khana bazaar; go to Qurban Garments and ask for Suleiman Baig.

NATCO buses go Gilgit-Gupis for Rs 50, and to Noh in Yasin for Rs 60. NATCO plans to extend bus services to Yasin village for Rs 70. From Gupis or Yasin, you can reach Darkot by cargo jeeps or special hire, which cost about Rs 1500. It takes two to three days to walk from Yasin village north along the jeep road to Darkot village.

GUIDES & PORTERS
When you hire Chitrali porters, they work on a per day basis. Porters from Darkot and Imit usually also work on a per day basis. The maximum low-altitude porter's wage is Rs 160 per day, plus wāpāsi. They may ask for a food allowance. If you have brought porters from Hunza over the Chilinji An, they expect to be paid on a per stage basis and to also be paid wāpāsi, food rations, and a Rs 200 clothing and equipment allowance.

A guide is required and is needed for routefinding across the Darkot and Zindikharam glaciers and across the Chattiboi Glacier when you approach Broghil from the Karambar Valley.

When you come from Chitral, porters, most likely from Lasht in the upper Yarkhun Valley, go with you to the road head. When you come from the Chapursan or Karambar valleys, or from Darkot, you may be asked to hire local Chitrali porters when you reach Lasht.

SHOLKUCH TO BROGHIL & KARAMBAR AN
(7 days; June to September)
The Karambar An marks the boundary between Chitral and the Northern Areas, linking the Yarkhun Valley on the west with the Karambar and Ishkoman valleys on the east. The trek to the Yarkhun River headwaters passes through the picturesque Broghil area, dotted with green meadows and small lakes, and populated by yakherding Wakhi people. The Karambar An (4320m) is, apart from the Deosai Plains, the largest alpine meadow in Pakistan. At the crest of these well-watered grasslands are several large blue lakes. Over 1000 years ago, Chinese pilgrims travelling south in search of Buddhist teachings wrote of a 'wild onion' pass. This may have been the Karambar An, where wild onions abound. It is one of the most beautiful places in the Karakoram and Hindukush.

We describe the route from west to east, but you can also walk east to west. The trek is typically combined with the Karambar Valley trek, making a loop, or as part of a longer traverse across Pakistan's northernmost valleys by combining it with the Shah Jinali An and/or the Chilinji An trek.

Map Notes
The U502 *Mastuj (NJ 43-13)* sheet shows the

Yarkhun Valley, the Broghil Pass area, and the Darkot An and is highly reliable. The *Baltit (NJ 43-14)* sheet is the only readily available map showing the upper Broghil area and the Karambar An. It does not show the Karambar lakes and slightly alters place names. It labels Shuwor Sheer as Shuwar Shur, Qul Quldi as Qiu Quldi, Boree Mergich as Margach, and Rabot as Ribat. It does not show Tōp Khāna. It calls the river flowing west from the Karambar An the Ribat Bar. Locals disagree with this name and call it Karambar Chhat, which means 'the valley of Karambar lake'.

Route Description

Day 1: Sholkuch to Dobargar (5½ to 6½ hours) Jeeps can go beyond Sholkuch to a point across from Gazin Gol where a shaky footbridge crosses the Yarkhun River. It is a one hour walk to the bridge from Sholkuch. Trails go up both sides of the Yarkhun, but the main trail is on the true left (east) side. Continue up the main trail five hours to a good camp site by clear springs, just before Dobargar and across the Yarkhun from scenic Unawich village.

Day 2: Dobargar to Lasht (6 to 7 hours) Continue up valley, fording side streams as needed. Climb 250m to scenic Rawark, a good lunch spot or camp site with a spring, across from Yashkist and the Ishperu Dok Gol. One hour above Rawark, you may find a footbridge over the Yarkhun to Shosht. Cross if possible, otherwise continue up the true left bank, crossing two side streams (with possible fords) to Rukut village. Ford the side stream here, cross a short ridge and come to the solid bridge over the Yarkhun River at Lasht. Chitral Scouts check permits here. Camp on a grassy plain with clear streams.

Day 3: Lasht to Kishmanja (5½ to 6½ hours) Leave the Chitrali village of Lasht and walk up the true right bank of the Yarkhun as it bends east. Across the valley, large glaciers descend from unclimbed summits. Ford the Kan Khun stream.

Beyond Kan Khun, stay in the river bed in low water. In high water, July and August, scramble up and down cliffs and come to Kishmanja, a Wakhi settlement.

Day 4: Kishmanja to Chikor (5 to 6 hours) Continue on the good trail to Vidinkot with fine views across the valley of Koyo Zom (6872m), which Broghil villagers call Ghaliyat. Across from Vidinkot are the hot springs of Pechutz. Just beyond the foot of the enormous Chattiboi Glacier (not to be confused with a glacier of the same name in the Karambar Valley), which protrudes into the Yarkhun, cross a footbridge to the south bank and ascend the hill ahead. The trail forks; the right fork goes to Chikor; and the left fork goes straight to Ishkarwaz. A Rs 20 per tent fee is charged to camp overnight in the large meadows at Chikor. The trail to the Darkot An heads south-east from Chikor (see Darkot An below).

Day 5: Chikor to Garhil (3 to 4 hours) From the Wakhi village of Chikor *(chikor* means 'willow') (3570m), the trail goes over a ridge 45 minutes to Ishkarwaz where you register at the Chitral Scouts post. Descend to the bridge over the river, which flows through a deep gorge. Climb gently for 30 to 45 minutes to Chilma Rabot (3570m), a south-facing village, spread out amid open, terraced fields with the Broghil stream passing through the middle of the village. Ask the Chitral Scouts at Ishkarwaz for permission to visit the Broghil Pass for the day. You can rent horses in Chilma Rabot or Garhil.

Continue through grasslands above the true right bank, as the river runs through a gorge with two watchtowers perched high above the opposite bank, one hour to picturesque Garhil *(gar* means 'rock'; *hil*, 'a sheep pen'), a settlement with a spring by big rocks north of the trail. From Garhil, the Darwaza Pass crosses into Afghanistan's Wakhan Corridor and is closed to foreigners, although Wakhi riders regularly cross the pass during the summer.

Day 6: Garhil to Shuwor Sheer (4 to 5 hours) Ascend past scattered huts to a small lake amid luxuriant grass, and continue along the ridge, well above the Yarkhun. The Chiantar Glacier and a striking solitary peak at its head dominate the view. You can descend to Thin Yuphkh *(thin* means 'hot'; *yuphkh*, 'water') (3690m) where a hot spring flows into a small lake, which is also warm, or you can follow the trail down the ridge past a cairn to a stream, where the trail from Thin Yuphkh rejoins. (In low water, you can proceed from Garhil to Thin Yuphkh up the main river valley, but in high water this route should be avoided because of the seven or eight difficult fordings.) Several small lakes lie 30 minutes further.

Shortly after reach Lashkargah Goz (3660m) where 22 Wakhi households are spread out along the hillside. Below the village is a broad grassy plain, a perfect place for an army to camp and graze its horses. The name *lashkar* means 'army'; *gah*, 'a place'; and *goz*, 'grass'. The Wakhi in Broghil are sadly much habituated to opium. On their plentiful grasslands, they produce surplus livestock. With the money they earn from selling it, some buy opium to while away the cold winter months.

Continue through Lashkargah Goz village and along the base of the hills on the north of this broad, green valley to some mill houses and a stream. Head up a narrow canyon passing a large spring. The small canyon opens onto a peat bog (3480m) and you ascend past springs to reach Shuwor Sheer, two to 2½ hours from Lashkargah Goz.

Three summer villages are here: Shuwor Sheer (3690m), the largest; Yirgot Maidan *(yirgot* means 'vulture'), higher on the eastern hillside; and Tōp Khāna *(tōp* means 'cannon'; *khāna*, a house), a 10-minute walk from Shuwor Sheer. A level, grassy camp site by a clear stream lies between Shuwor Sheer and Tōp Khāna.

Tōp Khāna, at the base of a rocky hill, is named for the crumbling hilltop fort, which once commanded the trail to the Karambar An and the upper Yarkhun Valley. The Wakhi

people here speak Khowar as their second language with a smattering of Urdu and Persian. Local dairy products are abundant. From Shuwor Sheer, you look across the broad valley to the Zindikharam Glacier (see Other Routes below).

Day 7: Shuwor Sheer to Karambar An & Lakes (4 to 5 hours) The beautiful lakes lie 10 km up the gentle Karambar Chhat Valley. Clear water is abundant from streams and springs along the trail. In one hour reach Qul Quldi, a Wakhi settlement with a Turkish name, situated above the river on a rock outcrop.

Shortly after pass the huts of Lale Rabot, perched on the hillside high above the trail and cross a clear stream just beyond. The huts of Thor Mergich (3990m) are hidden from view south of (below) the trail along a clear stream one hour from Qul Quldi. Boree Mergich lies beyond another stream one hour from Thor Mergich. Rabot, two crumbling huts, lies beyond another stream one hour from Boree Mergich. This entire valley is considered *mergich* by the Wakhi, a term that means 'a pure, clean place where female fairy spirits dwell'.

About 45 minutes beyond Rabot a large cairn marks the Karambar An (4320m). The western, smaller lake with an island in it lies 15 minutes further and is connected to the much larger lake by a stream. Continue along the stream another 15 minutes to a large boulder with a cairn. Here are several stone shelters for porters and excellent camp sites.

The enormous blue Karambar Lake lies another 15 minutes east. It takes 1¼ hours to walk along its northern shore. If you have the time, enjoy at least one extra day at this remarkable spot.

Above the lake's southern shore is Jhui Sar *(jhui* means 'lake'; *sar*, 'a peak'), a snowy peak with a glacier that falls into the lake itself. From here you can descend the Karambar Valley (see Ishkoman Valley in the Ghizar chapter), return to Chikor and cross the Darkot An (see below), or retrace your steps down the Yarkhun Valley.

DARKOT AN
(2 to 3 days; June to September)

The Darkot An (4650m) is a glaciated pass linking Chikor in Broghil with Darkot in the Yasin Valley to the south (see the Upper Yarkhun Valley map). A well-known PTDC poster shows a yak caravan crossing the pass. The broad and level pass is not difficult, but it has some crevasses. Crampons are not necessary, but a rope is.

The pass is best crossed from north to south, because it is easier to descend 1800m from the pass to Darkot village. The 25-km-long route can be crossed in two or three days. To do it in two days, start from Chikor and camp either at the base camp or on the pass, where you must be careful of crevasses. In three days, camp the first night either at the base camp or on the pass and the next night in Rawat, continuing on to Darkot the following day. A Chinese Army led by a Korean general crossed the Darkot An in 747 AD and conquered Gilgit, then ruled by Tibetans. A Tibetan inscription commemorating the offering of a stupa is on the south side of the pass.

Guides & Porters ·
The Darkot Glacier presents moderate route-finding problems to avoid crevasses. A licensed guide is required. Hire porters at your road head (ie, Chapursan, Imit, or Darkot) or if coming from Yarkhun, hire new porters in Lasht or at Chikor. Chikor men know the route. Most porters consider it three stages from Chikor to Darkot village.

Route Description
Day 1: Chikor to Darkot An Base Camp
(2½ to 3 hours) Snow on the Darkot An softens by mid-morning and makes walking an effort. Cross the pass early (ie, by 9 am). To do this, either walk further up valley and camp beside the glacier or leave Chikor before dawn.

Thirty minutes from Chikor is an excellent spring at the edge of the fields. The first possible camp site lies 1½ hours further where a side valley opens into the main ablation valley along the eastern margin of the Darkot Glacier. Water is well above camp, flowing over scree. A better camp site is half an hour further up the trail, at the upper limit of the scrub willow, six km from Chikor. In a small ablation valley at the mouth of a side valley is space for three or four tents (4140m). Clear water flows from the side valley over rocks above the camp. Directly across the glacier is a distinctive black rock outcrop separating two major ice falls coming down from a prominent snowy peak.

Day 2: Darkot An Base Camp to Rawat
(5½ to 6 hours) The 6.5 km, 500m ascent to the pass takes 2½ to 3 hours. Continue up the lateral moraine, cross a ravine to a few tent platforms on the rocky moraine (a more exposed and less desirable camp site), and in 30 to 45 minutes, reach a cairn. Descend onto the glacier itself and walk 45 minutes up the left side of the smooth, white Darkot Glacier. Head for a rock outcrop at the eastern head of the glacier. Rope up and ascend a steep 30° section just west of this rock outcrop 45 minutes. Traverse right and up, passing below and to the right of a broken section to reach the level upper pass area. Do not go up the lower-angled, but more heavily crevassed middle and western part of the glacier. Cross the top of the pass, probing for crevasses, in about 30 minutes.

The 6.5 km descent drops 1800m. Descend on the west side of the pass, and contour back east passing below a crevasse bowl. Then head to the west margin of the glacier and descend quickly to the end of the ice, 45 minutes from the top of the pass. The slope steepens here and may be icy, requiring step cutting, but crampons are not really necessary.

Descend over rock to the level area below the mouth of the glacier in 15 minutes. Cross the outflow stream to its true left bank and pass a small stone shelter. This is the base camp for those crossing the pass from south to north.

The trail becomes clear and traverses left, out of the main glacier stream valley, and over a small ridge that ends in a dark brown pinnacle, crowned by a large square cairn. In 30 minutes reach a camp site with room for a few tents and a stone circle for porters. However, water must be carried from the main glacial stream.

Five minutes below this camp site is a boulder next to the trail on which is carved a stupa and a Tibetan inscription dating from the 8th or 9th century when Tibetans ruled Gilgit, or Bru-shal as the Tibetans called it. The inscription, translated by AH Francke and published by Aurel Stein, names a person Lirnidor, with the clan or family name of Me-or, as the donor of the stupa.

The trail descends steeply 1½ hours. Chikor men carry goods from Darkot up this trail on donkeys. Continue east, crossing several streams, one of which tumbles over the cliff in a nice waterfall. Below, on the valley floor at the base of the cliff, you can see the trail to the hot spring. The trail from the pass does not go by the hot spring. The trail to the hot spring branches north off the main trail just outside Rawat. The hot spring here is said to be good for aching joints and bones and to cure infertility in women. Descend to the huts at Rawat (3100m), a lovely summer herding settlement.

Six or seven large streams come down all around this secluded valley and three or four glaciers perch above. To the west, the rough broken tongue of a small glacier hangs down the cliff, almost licking the valley floor. This well-watered green valley bowl has a sanctuary-like quality to it. The people are Burusho, and speak the Yasin dialect of Burushashki. The women wear tall stitched hats, which are three times the height of Hunza women's hats. Unlike other Burusho settlements, here the women tend the herds, a division of labour usually found among their Wakhi neighbours to the north.

Day 3: Rawat to Darkot Village (2 to 2½ hours) From Rawat, continue 15 minutes to a bridge (2970m) to the true right bank of the main stream. Pass by the permanent settlements of Haribaris and Tokemaling west of the trail. Climb a short but steep 100 metres to the top of Darband (*dar* means 'door';

band, 'closed'), an ancient moraine ridge that almost blocks the main river. Two trails cross Darband: a shorter, but steeper footpath and a more gradual path for animals. Descend steeply 15 minutes and cross the river via a sturdy, wooden bridge, obscured from view descending from Darband.

Follow a jeep road 45 minutes to the west end of Darkot village (2760m). It takes 30 minutes to walk along the jeep road west to east along the northern side of town. Darkot is green and lush with some 300 households, all speaking Yasin Burushashki. The big mountain called Dhuli Chhīsh (frowning mountain) is usually shrouded in clouds. Beneath Dhuli Chhīsh is a rock called Lamokor and the village of Gasun, along the true right bank of the river. In Darkot, expect to pay a Rs 20 per tent camping fee.

OTHER ROUTES
Zindikharam Glacier

The Zindikharam Glacier connects Shuwor Sheer in upper Broghil to Darkot village in Yasin. Locals report this glacier is heavily crevassed, but can be crossed in two to three days between June and September. Locals prefer to cross the easier and shorter Darkot An. If you are coming from Broghil, hire a knowledgeable local to show you the route over this glacier. If coming from Darkot, hire porters there. Aurel Stein believed the Chinese army crossed this glacier, rather than the Darkot. But Stein himself found the Zindikharam route closed by bergschrunds and opted to cross the easier Darkot An.

Laspur Valley & Bashqar Gol

The Laspur River and its tributaries drain the eastern flank of the Hindu Raj range and the Buni Zom spur (see the Shisi & Golen Valleys map earlier in this chapter). The Bashqar and Shandur rivers join at Sor Laspur village to form the Laspur River, which flows north to Mastuj and joins the

Yarkhun River at Mastuj to form the Mastuj River. The Chitral-Gilgit road follows the Laspur River between Mastuj and Sor Laspur, then turns north-east up the Shandur Gol, entering the Northern Areas at the Shandur Pass. The Laspur Valley is part of the Mastuj tehsil.

Several passes cross the rugged mountains around Sor Laspur. The Phargam An (see Shishi & Golen Valleys in this chapter) trail head is at Rahmān village on the true left (west) bank of the Laspur River. Up the Bashqar Gol is the Thalo An to the Panjkora Valley in Dir, and the Manali and Kachakani passes to the upper Swat Valley. These passes are difficult and lead to areas where people are armed, may not welcome trekkers, and should be considered dangerous (see Dangers & Annoyances in Facts about the Region). The Kachakani An is the only pass crossed by trekkers. The scenic upper Bashqar Gol has several glacial lakes, and according to the Chitral Wildlife Division, the largest population of snow leopards in Chitral.

INFORMATION
Maps
The US AMS *India and Pakistan Series U502* 1:250,000 *Mastuj (NJ 43-13)* sheet shows the Laspur Valley and the start of the Bashqar Gol. The *Churrai (NI 43-1)* sheet shows the Bashqar Gol, the Kachakani An and the upper Swat and Panjkora valleys, although the Swat and Panjkora areas have poor reliability, and show no topographic features.

Regulations
Foreigners can trek anywhere in this open zone. Neither a permit from the Tourism Division nor a licensed mountain guide is required. However, no one should trek in Swat without a reliable guide. Register with the police on arrival in Kalam. The Fisheries office in Kalam issues fishing licences.

Accommodation & Supplies
In Kalam, the *PTDC Motel* (☎ 14) is open from 1 May to 31 October; singles/doubles cost Rs 700/800 and its huts cost Rs 950. Many inexpensive hotels line the road. Basic supplies are available in the bazaar. In Matiltan, the Forestry rest house can be booked with the NWFP Forestry department in Peshawar or with the Conservator of Forests in Saidu Sharif. In Sor Laspur, there are a few basic shops (get supplies in Mastuj or in Chitral) and a Government rest house.

GETTING THERE & AWAY
Swat Valley
Regular transport runs all day from the General Bus Stand in Mingora to Kalam. The trip costs Rs 30 and takes about 2½ hours. The road is paved up the Ushu Valley to Matiltan village and jeeps can go as far as Mahodand lake. Matiltan is 16 km above Kalam and minibuses generally run there.

Laspur Valley
Sor Laspur is west of the Shandur Pass on the Chitral-Gilgit road, so can be reached from either Chitral or Gilgit. However, no regular transport goes over the Shandur Pass from Gilgit or to Sor Laspur from Chitral. You can find passenger jeeps Chitral-Mastuj and perhaps some Mastuj-Sor Laspur. A special hire to and from Chitral costs Rs 3000; from Gilgit Rs 5000 to Rs 7000.

GUIDES & PORTERS
Porter wages are a maximum of Rs 160 per day. Wāpāsi and food rations are paid.

KACHAKANI AN
(6 days; July to September)
The scenic Kachakani An crosses a glacier and high pass (see the Upper Ghizar River Valley map). The upper Ushu Valley in Swat has lush pastures, forested hillsides, turquoise lakes and trout-filled streams. It also has a heavily armed populace. Those who travel without a local guide and an armed escort have been robbed or worse. This trek is usually done from south to north (a more gradual ascent). Never attempt it alone – an armed escort is necessary.

CHITRAL

Guides & Porters
A guide is indispensable for this trek. Be sure your local guide has ties with a trekking company or the government and is thus reliable and responsible. Porters from Laspur are more reliable than those from Swat.

Route Description
Day 1: Matiltan to Machiangaas (6 to 7 hours) From Matiltan, walk up the road, or continue by jeep to Mahodand Lake. You can also camp just before the lake, which is famous for its trout, at the Machiangaas pastures.

Day 2: Machiangaas to Shonz (7 to 8 hours) Continue up valley, through Diwagar where the Dadarelli An route joins (see Upper Ghizar River Valley in the Ghizar chapter) and on to Shonz, a Gujar summer camp at the foot of Bashkaro An. Beware of theft; post guards at night if locals are present.

Day 3: Shonz to Bokhtshal (6 to 7 hours) Continue past a series of small lakes with trout to Bokhtshal, a summer pasture.

Day 4: Bokhtshal to Konzaotz (8 to 9 hours) Start early and climb to the pass (4766m), which is snowy near the top. Descend over the glacier, then onto the lateral moraine along its true right margin. Beware of rock fall, especially in the afternoon and later in the season.

Days 5 & 6: Konzaotz to Sor Laspur Follow the Kachakani Gol to the junction with the Bashqar Gol. Camp along the Bashqar Gol and the next day walk to Sor Laspur.

OTHER ROUTES
Thalo Gol & Manali Gol
Above the Bashqar Gol lake towers Ghuchhar Sar (6249m) and beyond the glacial lake the valley divides. The Thalo Gol heads south-west and the Manali Gol heads south south-east. These upper valleys offer interesting trekking and climbing possibilities. Thalo Gol, a long, rocky valley, has numerous hanging glaciers. The moraine of the Thalo Glacier descends to the valley floor and it is tedious going up this valley. Another glacial lake lies beyond the Thalo Glacier. Do not attempt to cross the Thalo An without an armed escort, and in the company of influential friends from Dir. The way up the shorter Manali Gol leads over the large Manali Glacier, and on to an upper cirque bowl. This area is for mountaineers only. The Manali An leads into the upper Gabral River valley of a lawless region of Swat.

Ghizar

Ghizar is the westernmost district of the Northern Areas. It comprises the area drained by the upper Ghizar and Gilgit rivers, which flow west to east, and their many northern and southern tributaries. The valleys of two major northern tributaries, the Yasin and Ishkoman, have large populated areas and offer many fine treks. The third and westernmost of the northern tributaries, the Bahushtaro Gol, has few settlements, but some good trekking and mountaineering. The southern tributaries are largely unpopulated and lead via high passes to the valleys of Indus Kohistan and Swat. The Ghizar River's headwaters descend from Shandur Pass on the Chitral boundary and the Chitral-Gilgit road follows it all the way to Gilgit. The Ghizar and the Gilgit are actually the same river, with the Gilgit River starting from the junction of the Ghizar and Yasin rivers. Apart from the villages in Yasin and Ishkoman, most settlements are in the main Ghizar-Gilgit River valley. The people of Ghizar expect that the ongoing improvement of the Gilgit-Chitral road will eventually bring increased growth and income to the area.

Trekkers should note the following about Khowar place names. In Khowar, the letter 'o' at the end of a word means something similar to the English 'of'. For example, Bahushtaro Gol means 'the valley of the Bahushtar'. The valley itself is actually named Bahushtar. Zagaro An means 'the pass of Zagar', but the pass itself is named Zagar.

REGIONAL HISTORY

All the northern valleys of present day Ghizar appear to have once been occupied by Burusho people. Today, they reside only in the Yasin Valley. Migrations of Shina speakers from the south and Khowar speakers from the west probably displaced the Burusho, but Burushashki place names in the

Highlights – Ghizar
Numerous rivers flow from rugged Hindu Raj peaks. Best trout fishing and rafting area. Infrequently visited, isolated valleys with traditional villages of the Kho and Burusho culture

Bahushtaro Gol and Ishkoman Valley indicate these valleys were once part of a greater Burusho region. Chinese travellers of the 5th to 8th centuries, who passed through the Yasin and Ishkoman valleys on their way to visit renowned Buddhist monasteries in Darel and Swat, knew the region as Bru-zha, indicating a Burusho identity for the population. From the 11th century on, Kho rulers in Chitral controlled Ghizar. The Kushwaqt family, a branch of Chitral's Katur dynasty, won control of upper Chitral and Ghizar, ruling from Yasin. The lower region of Ghizar, known as Punial, became a bone of contention between Gilgit and Chitral, and by the 19th century, Punial had become a separate state with its own Raja.

During this time refugees from blood feuds in Indus Kohistan migrated north into Ghizar and Punial. Although about half of the present population of Ghizar and Punial are descendants of these refugees, almost all people speak Khowar. In the Yasin Valley, Burushashki is the mother tongue, and in Ishkoman, both Shina and Khowar are widely spoken. After the settlement of Chitral's boundary in 1918, Ghizar became part of the Gilgit administration. Ghizar, which has long had its own identity, was made a separate district of the Northern Areas in 1975, but under General Zia, it was merged with Gilgit. In 1989 Ghizar once again became a district.

GAKUCH
Gakuch is the administrative centre of Ghizar district and is in Punial. Now linked by road with Gilgit and the rest of Pakistan, it is fast becoming an important regional centre. It is on the south bank of the Gilgit River along the Gilgit-Chitral road about 80 km west of Gilgit. The Ishkoman River from the north meets the Gilgit River here.

Places to Stay & Eat
In Gakuch is an *NAPWD Rest House*, the *Shandur Tourist House*, the *Welcome Hotel*, the *Tajikistan Inn*, the *International Hotel* (no English sign) with charpoys for Rs 10 and one private room, and the *Pathan Hotel*, a popular roadside dining spot. Further east in Singal is the *Singal Rest House* and the AKHS hospital.

GUPIS
Gupis, a regional market town, is also along the Gilgit-Chitral road about 30 km west of Gakuch. The Yasin River flows in from the north and meets the Ghizar River here to form the Gilgit River.

Places to Stay & Eat
The *Gulistan Hotel* is about five minutes from the Chinese bridge over the river and has food and tea. The *NAPWD Rest House*,

in a large walled compound along the road, is a popular camp site. The *Snow Leopard Inn* in Raja bazaar has meals and charpoys. Nearby the *Sarhad Hotel* also has cheap charpoys.

GETTING THERE & AWAY
Trail heads throughout Ghizar district are reachable only by road from Gilgit. The Gilgit-Chitral road runs through the district following the Gilgit and Ghizar rivers. NATCO buses go (from their Punial Rd booking office) Gilgit-Gakuch for Rs 40 and Rs 50 Gilgit-Gupis, from where you can then find cargo jeeps up the Ishkoman and Yasin valleys. Cargo jeeps also go direct to most trail heads from Punial Rd in Gilgit (see individual route descriptions) as well as to Gakuch and Gupis.

Upper Ghizar River Valley

The scenic Ghizar River valley lies west of the Yasin Valley and continues to the Shandur Pass. The clear blue Ghizar River is a highly regarded kayak run, and its sparkling southern tributaries are renowned trout streams. Near Pingal, west of Gupis, the river forms a large blue lake, as it does at Phundar. The largely uninhabited Bahushtaro Gol joins the Ghizar at Chashi, just east of Phundar. Many under-6000m peaks up this side valley have recently begun attracting mountaineering attention. The southern tributaries of the Ghizar lead to Indus Kohistan, a dangerous area that cannot presently be visited. However, the Hundrup and Khokush valleys, the westernmost of these tributaries, lead to Swat and are occasionally trekked.

INFORMATION
Maps
The US AMS *India and Pakistan Series U502* 1:250,000 *Mastuj (NJ 43-13)* sheet shows the Chumarkhan Pass, Zagaro An, and the Khokush and lower Hundrup valleys.

The *Churrai (NI 43-1)* sheet shows the Dadarelli An, Bashkaro An, and the upper Hundrup Valley.

Regulations
Foreigners are allowed to trek anywhere in this open zone. Neither a permit from the tourism Division nor a licensed mountain guide is required.

Accommodation & Supplies
Ghizar Valley Basic supplies are available in Phundar and Teru. Phundar has a few shops with bulk supplies only (eg, dal, sugar, salt, tea, cooking oil, candles and kerosene). Phundar and Teru have *NAPWD Rest Houses* with comfortable rooms and a kitchen, but you must bring your own food. Also in Phundar is *Tourest Hotel No 1*. In Teru charpoys cost Rs 30 at the *Sarhad Hotel*. Nothing is available in Chashi or Barsat.

Swat Valley In Kalam, the *PTDC Motel* (☎ 14) is open from 1 May to 31 October; singles/doubles cost Rs 700/800 and huts cost Rs 950. Many inexpensive hotels are in the bazaar where basic supplies are available.

Yarkhun Valley Chapali has a few stores, but no hotels. Chonj, about four km south of Chapali, has a large well-stocked bazaar and at the *Khyber Hotel* charpoys cost Rs 15.

GETTING THERE & AWAY
Ghizar River Valley
Chashi, Hundrup, and Barsat are trail heads along the Chitral-Gilgit road west of Gupis and east of the Shandur Pass. They are most easily reached from Gilgit. Chashi is three hours from Gupis. Phundar is half an hour beyond Chashi. Hundrup is one hour beyond Phundar before Teru. Barsat is beyond Teru where the Chumarkhan Gol joins the Ghizar River. Cargo jeeps go to these villages from Gilgit, leaving from Punial Rd. For cargo jeeps to Phundar, see shopkeeper Havaldar Adinasha. NATCO buses go as far as Gupis. From Gupis look for a cargo or passenger jeep. Special hires probably cost Rs 2500.

Swat Valley
Regular transport runs all day from the general bus stand in Mingora to Kalam. The trip costs Rs 30 and takes about 2½ hours. The road is paved up the Ushu Valley 16 km to Matiltan village, but jeeps can reach Mahodand Lake. Vehicles regularly run Matiltan-Kalam.

Yarkhun Valley
In the morning, cargo jeeps from Mastuj go up the Yarkhun Valley to Brep, Dizg, Bang, Paur, and Sholkuch for Rs 50 to Rs 100. From Chapali, jeeps to Mastuj leave in the morning. At other times of day, flag down any jeep heading south. To go up valley, flag down any jeep heading north. Cargo jeeps also go regularly Mastuj-Chitral for Rs 40 and occasionally Mastuj-Sor Laspur.

GUIDES & PORTERS
Porters' wages are Rs 160 per day plus wāpāsi and food rations. Provide proper gear to any porters who cross a pass.

The Ushu Valley in Swat is a dangerous area where locals are heavily armed and may be hostile. Trekkers should always have a reliable guide and an armed escort.

CHUMARKHAN PASS
(2 days; July to September)
The Chumarkhan Pass (4328m) links Barsat along the Gilgit-Chitral road with Chapali in Chitral's Yarkhun Valley to the north. It offers quick access to Yarkhun and an alternative to travelling the road between the upper Ghizar Valley and Mastuj. Cargo jeeps infrequently cross the Shandur Pass between Barsat and Mastuj and special jeeps are expensive. When faced with the necessity of walking, it is shorter and more pleasant to walk over the gentle Chumarkhan Pass than walking on the road over the Shandur Pass. The pass is usually crossed from south to north because the descent into Zagaro Gol is steep. Chumarkhan, which means 'iron fort', is a rolling plain where livestock graze in summer. The route is also open in June and October, but shepherds are not in the pastures then.

GHIZAR

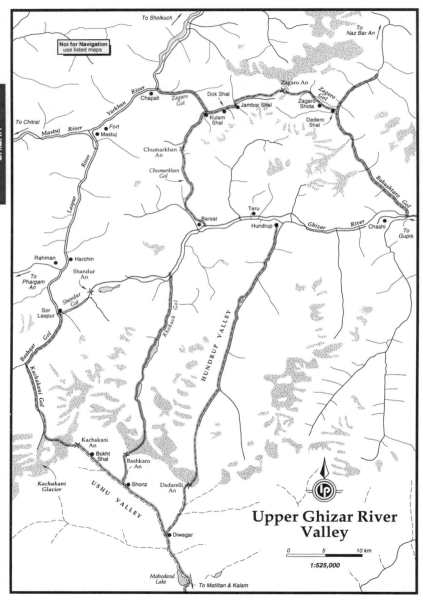

To Sholkuch
To Naz Bar An
Not for Navigation
use listed maps
Yarkhun River
Chapali
Zagaro Gol
Dok Shal
Zagaro An
Zagaro Gol
Jambor Shal
Zagaro Shota
Kulam Shal
Dedero Shal
To Chitral
Mastuj River
Fort
Mastuj
Chumarkhan An
Chumarkhan Gol
Bahushtaro Gol
Laspur River
Barsat
Teru
Hundrup
Ghizar River
Chashi
To Gupis
Rahman
Harchin
Shandur An
Shandur Gol
Sor Laspur
Bashqar Gol
Khotush Gol
HUNDRUP VALLEY
Kachakani Gol
To Phargam An
Kachakani An
Bokht Shal
Bashkaro An
Kachakani Glacier
USHU VALLEY
Shonz
Dadarelli An
Diwagar

Upper Ghizar River Valley

0   5   10 km
1:525,000

Mahodand Lake
To Matiltan & Kalam

Guides & Porters

The many trails in the Chumarkhan Valley south of the pass can be confusing, so hire a local to show the way if you are uncertain.

Route Description

Day 1: Barsat to Upper Chumarkhan Valley (3 to 4 hours) Barsat (3353m) lies along the north bank of the upper Ghizar. Nearby at the junction of the Chumarkhan and Ghizar rivers are the tents of the Chumarkhan police check post on the Gilgit-Chitral road. From the check post, follow the Chumarkhan up river, keeping on its true left (east) side. Several large tributaries and many livestock trails can make the way to the pass confusing. Stay in the middle of the broad valley with the main stream to the west (left). Camp anywhere in the upper meadows.

Day 2: Upper Chumarkhan Valley to Chapali (5 hours) Continue to the broad, rolling pass. Herders here may offer fresh yoghurt. The descent into Chitral is steep, through meadows along the true right (east) side of the Chumarkhan stream. The scattered, mostly deserted settlement of Kulam Shal (3429m) lies to your right as you descend into the Zagaro Gol. The path soon meets the trail coming from the Zagaro An (see Zagaro An below) and in 15 minutes, crosses to the true right bank of Zagaro Gol over a log bridge, just above the confluence of the birch-lined Chumarkhan Gol and Zagaro Gol.

Follow the large, well-used trail one hour to the first houses. The trail widens here to jeep width. Continue another hour to the footbridge over the river and the start of Chapali village (2550m) and its jeep road. Follow the road 30 minutes past the water supply house through the village to the main Yarkhun Valley jeep road. At this intersection is a sign reading 'Water Supply Scheme Chapari' and a store on the opposite side of the road. The shopkeeper lets trekkers camp in the field behind the store.

DADARELLI AN

(6 days; July to September)

The infrequently crossed Dadarelli An (5030m) links the Hundrup Valley, a southern tributary of the Ghizar River, with the Ushu Valley in Swat. The scenic Hundrup Valley is a recently declared national park, and the clear river and lake are famous for trout (see Ecology in the Facts about the Region chapter). Although Hundrup villagers speak Khowar, most are immigrants from the Darel Valley in Indus Kohistan. The Dadarelli An appears to be glaciated, so bring a rope and ice axe. A challenging loop trek can be made by combining this trek with the Kachakani An (see Laspur Valley & Bashqar Gol in the Chitral chapter).

Guides & Porters

Hire porters in Hundrup. A reliable local guide is essential, especially in Swat where an armed escort is necessary.

Map Notes

The U502 *Churrai (NI 43-1)* sheet is unreliable for areas south of the pass, in the Ushu Valley, with no features or place names shown.

Route Description

Day 1: Hundrup Village to Hundrup Lake (4 to 5 hours) Jeeps cross a bridge over the Ghizar River to Hundrup village, on the west bank of the Hundrup River. Follow the trail 13 km to Hundrup lake. The world-record brown trout was taken out of these waters. Camp at the southern end of this tree-lined lake.

Day 2: Hundrup Lake to Upper Hundrup Valley (5 to 6 hours) Continue up the pleasant valley 14 km to where the valley divides (3593m), and take the south fork (ie, main branch). The branch to the south-east goes to high passes leading into the Kandia Valley of Indus Kohistan. Camp a few km past the divide.

Day 3: Upper Hundrup Valley to Dadarelli Base Camp (4 hours) Continue up the open, barren valley, passing several lakes, and camp near the upper lake.

Day 4: Dadarelli Base Camp to Dadarelli High Camp (7 to 8 hours) Because of rockfall danger on the southern side of the pass, start early. Ascend over a glacier to the pass, then descend steep scree and detour around a large snowfield. Several hours from the pass, reach meadows and camp.

Day 5: Dadarelli High Camp to Machiangaas (5 to 6 hours) Descend the shepherds' trail along the Dadarelli stream, past summer huts to Diwagar, a settlement at the junction of the Dadarelli and Kachakani valleys. Continue down the main Ushu Valley to Mahodand Lake and the jeep road to Kalam. Camp at Machiangaas below the lake.

Day 6: Machiangaas to Matiltan (5 to 6 hours) You can prearrange transport to meet you in Machiangaas. Otherwise, walk to Matiltan and find transport to Kalam.

ZAGARO AN
(3 to 6 days; July to August)
The 26 km route over the Zagaro An connects the Bahushtaro Gol with the Chumarkhan Gol and Chapali village in Chitral's Yarkhun Valley (see the Yarkhun Valley to Yasin Valley map). The pass itself marks the boundary of the Northern Areas with the NWFP. The Zagaro An (4920m) is a difficult 2nd-class pass. Although unglaciated, it has a permanent snow cornice on its western side. It is unused by locals and only infrequently crossed by trekkers. It is not recommended for novice trekkers or organised trekking parties. Adventurous trekkers who relish a challenging, little-used route through high and hard country may wish to attempt it.

This trek is usually done from east to west in conjunction with the equally difficult Naz Bar An (see Naz Bar An in the Yasin Valley section of this chapter), by which it takes three days to reach Dedero Shal in the Bahushtaro Gol. Alternatively, you can walk from Chashi on the Gilgit-Chitral road north up the Bahushtaro Gol to Dedero Shal in one day. We begin the route description from Dedero Shal.

Guides & Porters
A local guide is essential! Naz Bar men do not know the route, so even if you have a Naz Bar porter, hire a local herder to show the way. You may need to send a message to Haringol Shal (or Donjo Shal) to find someone, as Dedero Shal is inhabited by a single small family. In 1995, it cost Rs 300 to hire someone to go to the top of the pass.

2½ stages: half a stage Dedero Shal to Zagar Shota, Zagar Shota to Jambor Shal, Jambor Shal to Chapali

Map Notes
The U502 *Mastuj (NJ 43-13)* sheet indicates the general route, but the scale is so big that it is not much help in finding the route over the pass, particularly on the west side.

Route Description
Day 1: Dedero Shal to Zagar Shota (1½ to 2 hours) Climb the steep hill behind Deder huts (3300m) on a trail. Contour high above the true right (south) bank of the Zagaro Gol, continuously working up the slopes on stock trails. Reach a hut by the stream after 45 minutes, and continue up valley. The valley opens up and 1½ to two hours from Dedero Shal, reach Zagar Shota (3800m), a small round hut and a stock pen by the stream. Camp here to enable reaching the camp site in upper Zagaro Gol on the western side the next day.

Day 2: Zagar Shota to Jambor Shal (7 to 9 hours) Leave the stream after 15 minutes, and climb steeply to the shoulder of the grassy ridge ahead. Go around the shoulder of the ridge, to the right of a rock outcrop, following a faint trail. Behind the ridge is a valley with grassy slopes, one hour from camp. Continue up valley to a small bowl, marked by a cairn, where wild onions abound. Turn right, up grassy slopes, and 45 minutes after rounding the ridge see the

Zagaro An, the obvious low point with a scree slope beneath it.

Continue up a series of hillocks with grass, herbs, and flowers amid rocks, switchbacking steadily. In 30 minutes, reach the highest vegetation at the base of an old terminal moraine (4410m). Work right around the northern base of the moraine, on easy scree below talus slopes for another 20 minutes. Follow the base of this moraine as it turns back west and south. Reach a small snowfield, and head along its western edge 20 minutes to a yellow scree slope coming from the base of a yellowish rock outcrop. Traverse right across the scree to reach the rock rib on the south (left) side of another scree slope coming from the pass itself.

Ascend this 2nd-class rock rib to avoid rock-fall danger on either side. When the rock rib becomes too steep to continue, exit right and climb the 45 to 50° scree slope coming from the pass. Keep close to the rock rib, the occasional protrusions of which provide solid footing. This is 2nd-class scree, and a pole or walking stick is essential for balance. Near the top, the angle lessens and the scree becomes more stable. It takes 1½ to two hours to ascend the pass. From the top of the Zagaro An, Tirich Mir dominates the western view. There is no cairn and a small cornice lies on the western side.

Descend left down scree one hour to a level basin and the first water, looking straight at Buni Zom's dramatic summit. Looking back, the pass is the low point with the jagged snow cornice in it, between two dry hills; the one to the north rounded and the one to the south more rocky. Continuing down the stream for 30 minutes, the valley opens into a large bowl with some grass and flowers. An emergency high camp could be made here.

Keep to the south (left) of the stream, and cross pleasant, rolling hills of ungrazed grass and flowers 30 minutes. As they end, traverse left over and around the western edge of an awkward slate talus slope 30 minutes. Then descend a short scree slope 20 minutes to the level grassy area along the stream and to the north (right) of the enormous moraine

mass that fills the entire valley. Follow the stream all the way past the moraine mass to the alluvial fan below. If the stream has too much water to make this possible, continue on the talus of the moraine mass, working down its tedious slope to the alluvial fan below, and then cross the stream from the pass.

On this more level area (4110m) find a trail along the true right bank of the main stream, which flows on the south (left) side of the valley. One hour down valley, reach a goat pen and grassy area. Camp here. Across the stream, on its true left (south) bank is the well-built hut, goat pen, and small spring of Jambor Shal (3780m).

Day 3: Jambor Shal to Chapali (4 to 5 hours) Cross the stream via a bridge and follow the stock trail above the true left bank of Zagaro Gol. Reach Dok Shal (3600m), with many abandoned huts and a clear stream in 45 minutes. Alternatively, you could stay on the true right bank of the Zagaro Gol and continue past abandoned huts and once irrigated fields to cross a bridge at a level area before Dok Shal. A lone herder's hut is in use at Dok Shal, perched on a small spur. Continue 30 minutes on the main trail to more abandoned settlements at Kulam Shal (3429m). Meet the main trail from Chumarkhan Pass after another 30 minutes. Continue down the good trail, and reach Chapali (2550m) and the main Yarkhun Valley jeep road in 2½ hours (see Day 2 of the Chumarkhan Pass trek above for more information).

OTHER ROUTES
Bashkaro An

The Bashkaro An (4924m) is a difficult and rarely crossed pass that links the upper Ghizar with the Ushu Valley. West of Barsat, the Gilgit-Chitral road runs south, past peat bogs. Leave the road where it turns west to the Shandur Pass and the Khokush Gol meets the Ghizar River. The trek begins here and heads south up the Khokush Gol, which has many large lakes and good fishing. Continue up valley, along the western shores and camp

GHIZAR

beyond the last lake. The ascent to the Bashkaro An appears to be several km over a glacier. Local shepherds in the Khokush Gol may be able to guide you to the pass. Bring a rope and ice axe. South of the pass, descend into the Kachakani Valley, to a shepherds' camp at Shonz (see Laspur Valley & Bashqar Gol in the Chitral chapter).

Yasin Valley

The Yasin Valley is the westernmost major tributary of the Gilgit River and offers many fine treks. It can be approached from the north over the restricted Darkot An from Broghil, from the east over the Punji Pass and Asumbar Haghost from Ishkoman Valley, and from the west over the Thui An from Yarkhun and the Naz Bar An from the Bahushtaro Gol. From the south, it is linked by a jeep road to Gilgit. Yasin inhabitants are friendly and easy going. Most speak Burushashki, though men also speak Khowar and Urdu. Almost 95% of the people are Ismaili Muslims. Villages are carefully cultivated, and in the summer, fresh fruit is abundant. Remote Yasin Valley is not frequently visited by foreigners. Its attractive villages, friendly inhabitants, and many fine trekking routes should lead to an increasing interest in this splendid area.

INFORMATION
Maps
The US AMS *India and Pakistan Series U502* 1:250,000 *Mastuj (NJ 43-13)* sheet shows the Yasin Valley, including the Thui An and Naz Bar An. The *Baltit (NJ 43-14)* sheet shows the region east of the Yasin Valley, including the Punji and Atar passes.

Regulations
Foreigners are allowed to trek anywhere in this open zone. Neither a permit from the tourism Division nor a licensed mountain guide is required.

Accommodation & Supplies
Road-head villages have a few stores with basic supplies. However, you cannot rely on finding all the food you may want for your trek. It is best to buy supplies in Gilgit or Chitral.

Ghizar River Valley Chashi has no services. In Phundar, the *NAPWD Rest House* is east of the bazaar high above Phundar Lake. You can book it in Gilgit or take your chances and drop in. Bring your own food and the chowkidar will cook it for you.

Yasin Valley Taus and Yasin villages have large bazaars with the basics, but less variety than in Gilgit's bazaars. Darkot has a few stores, but the stores south of Darkot in Umalsit are better. Yasin also has a *NAPWD Rest House*.

Yarkhun Valley Villages along the main road have basic supplies. The only hotel is in Chonj, four km south of Chapali, which also has a remarkably well-stocked bazaar.

GETTING THERE & AWAY
Cargo jeeps leave from Gilgit's Punial Rd to most road heads in Ghizar, Yasin, and Ishkoman. NATCO buses leave from the Punial Rd booking office in Gilgit and go to Gupis for Rs 50, and to Noh in Yasin for Rs 60. NATCO plans to extend bus service to Yasin village for Rs 70.

Ghizar River Valley
Chashi, on the main Gilgit-Chitral road near Phundar, is the southern road head for the Bahushtaro Gol and treks over the Naz Bar An and the Zagaro An (see Upper Ghizar River Valley in this chapter). Cargo jeeps ply daily between Gilgit and Chashi.

Ishkoman Valley
Ghotulti This is the eastern road head for treks over the Punji and Atar passes. Passenger jeeps Ghotulti-Gilgit cost Rs 70. Although they are infrequent, it is better to wait for one in Ghotulti rather than walk down to Ishkoman village. All jeeps start

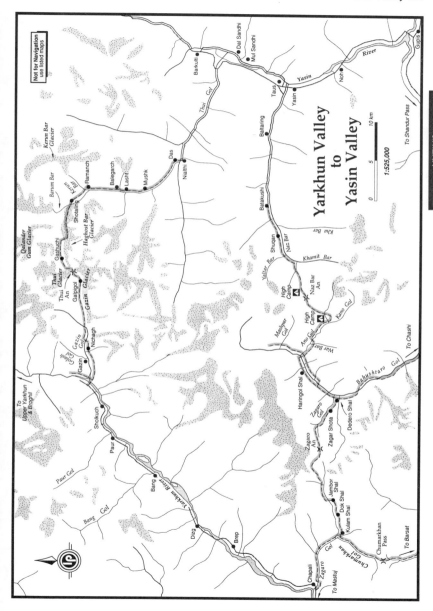

from and go to Ghotulti passing Ishkoman on the way.

Yarkhun Valley
Sholkuch This is the western road head for treks over the Thui An. Passenger jeeps go Chitral-Mastuj for Rs 40. From Mastuj, cargo jeeps go up the Yarkhun Valley as far as Sholkuch and cost Rs 100. Since cargo jeeps to Sholkuch are few, you may have to settle for a jeep to Paur, a one hour walk below Sholkuch. Special hires Chitral-Mastuj cost about Rs 2000 and Rs 1200 Mastuj-Sholkuch.

Yasin Valley
Batakushi Batakushi is the eastern road head for treks over the Naz Bar An. The Naz Bar branches south-west off the Yasin Valley from Yasin village. Most jeeps only go up the Naz Bar as far as Baltaring. A special hire Nialthi-Baltaring costs Rs 1000.

Dal Sandhi Dal Sandhi is the western road head for treks over the Asumbar Haghost. Cargo jeeps Dal Sandhi-Gilgit cost Rs 100. A special hire to Gilgit can be difficult to arrange, but a special hire to Gakuch costs about Rs 1800.

To travel between Dal Sandhi and Darkot when combining the Asumbar Haghost and Punji Pass treks, either walk the 25 km along the road in two days or look for a jeep. Jeeps come infrequently to Dal Sandhi, so to find a jeep walk to either Taus or Barkulti. Taus is the closest, a few km to the south. Barkulti is seven km to the north, a two hour walk. Passenger jeeps Barkulti-Darkot cost Rs 30 and take two hours. A special hire costs Rs 600 Barkulti-Darkot, Rs 800 Dal Sandhi-Darkot, and Rs 1000 Yasin-Darkot.

Darkot Darkot, at the head of the valley, is the western road head for treks over the Punji and Atar passes and the southern road head for treks over the Darkot An. Cargo jeeps Darkot-Gilgit cost Rs 110 to Rs 125, and take about nine hours. Darkot villagers can help you get a ride. A special hire Darkot-Gilgit costs Rs 2500 to Rs 3000. You may have to

wait a day or two for a jeep. Jeeps to Darkot leave sporadically from Gilgit's Jamat Khana bazaar; go to Qurban Garments and ask for Suleiman Baig.

From Gupis or Yasin, you can reach Darkot by cargo jeeps or by special hire, which costs about Rs 1500. It takes two to three days to walk from Yasin village north along the road to Darkot.

Nialthi Nialthi is the eastern road head for treks over the Thui An. The Thui Valley branches west off the Yasin Valley above Taus. Cargo jeeps Gilgit-Nialthi cost Rs 100. Cargo jeeps from Noh or Yasin village, if you can get on, cost Rs 30. Special jeeps Yasin-Nialthi cost Rs 800 to Rs 1000 and Gupis-Nialthi cost Rs 1200 to Rs 1500.

Yasin Village At the time of writing, NATCO plans to run buses to Yasin village for Rs 70 when a remaining bridge is completed.

GUIDES & PORTERS
The stage system is not fully instituted in this area. You can pay wages on either the stage system or on a daily basis. The maximum low-altitude porter's wage is Rs 160 per stage or Rs 160 per day plus wāpāsi and food rations. They do not ask to be paid the clothing and equipment allowance.

THUI AN
(5 to 6 days; July to mid-September)
The Thui An (4500m) crosses the Shandur range, a branch of the Hindu Raj range, between the Yasin Valley and Chitral's Yarkhun Valley (see the Yarkhun Valley to Yasin Valley map). The trek offers dramatic close-up views of 6000m-plus peaks, lovely alpine meadows, and the opportunity to meet the Burushashki-speaking people of the beautiful Thui Valley, as well as the Khowar-speakers of the Gazin Valley. The hardest part of the trek is traversing the Haghost Bar Glacier. Otherwise, there is a clear trail all the way.

The Thui An is a deservedly popular trek, and is the most frequently trekked route between the Gilgit region and Chitral. The trek can be done in either direction, and is often combined with the Shah Jinali An (see Turikho Valley in the Chitral chapter) and/or the Asumbar Haghost (see route description below). We describe the route from east to west (ie, Yasin to Yarkhun).

Guides & Porters

You need a local guide to show the way over the Haghost Bar Glacier. You can hire someone in Nialthi village in the Thui Valley, or in Gazin or Nichagh villages in the Gazin Valley.

5½ to 6 stages: Nialthi to Lasht, Lasht to Shotaling, Shotaling to Gashuchi, Gashuchi to Galpigol, Galpigol to Nichagh; from Nichagh it is half a stage to Sholkuch or one stage to Paur

Map Notes

The U502 *Mastuj (NJ 43-13)* sheet does not name Galpigol west of the pass or Gashuchi east of it. It shows a route along the north margin of the Haghost Bar Glacier, but the route actually goes up the middle. It shows the Gazin Glacier and the Thui Glacier, both west of the pass, as joined. They are separate, with a large alluvial fan between them.

Route Description

Day 1: Nialthi to Shotaling (5½ to 6½ hours) At Ali Murad Shah's store in Nialthi (2790m), the government road ends and the narrower community-constructed road continues. Spend a night in Nialthi; Mohammad Ali Shah, Ali Murad's father, makes his orchard available to trekkers. From Nialthi descend to the footbridge over the Thui River and climb 20 minutes to the village of Das, along the true left (north) bank. Continue up the good trail one to 1½ hours to the village of Mushk, with its tall poplars and clear stream. It is another one to 1½ hours to the summer village of Lasht. Just 15 minutes beyond Lasht, around the alluvial fan and across a small, clear stream, is Balegarch. Balegarch is a fine lunch spot, or a nice camp site.

Continue 1½ hours up the wide valley,

with granite cliffs on either side over which flow waterfalls, through birch and willow stands to the well-made huts of Ramanch. Beyond Ramanch 15 minutes is the bridge over the Kerun Bar (3078m) and another hour is Shotaling (3185m) *(taling* means 'birch' in Burushashki). Here are the last birch trees along small grassy plots watered by a small, but very clear spring.

Day 2: Shotaling to Gashuchi (4 to 5 hours) This is the most strenuous day of the trek. Follow the true left (east) bank of the river a short distance to where the ice of the Haghost Bar Glacier bridges the river. Cross this permanent ice bridge and climb steeply, but briefly, up the moraine-covered ice to the more level glacier. (An alternative to this route is to continue up valley and ford the Barum Bar. In summer, this river has too much water and is not possible to ford.) Once on the glacier, follow the stable, fairly even seam between the broken north margin and the heavily crevassed white ice along its south margin, which flows from a massive ice fall down a high snowy peak. Continue up the brown medial moraine, finding occasional cairns. Move up the glacier, keeping in the level, uncrevassed mid-section. As you climb towards the junction of the Qalander Gum Glacier, leave the medial moraine to the north and work onto the smooth central ice section, lightly covered with small rocks. Follow this up and around to a knoll of brown rock-covered glacier opposite the Qalander Gum Glacier. From here, the grassy Gashuchi area and the pass are visible ahead.

Leave the brown moraine knoll and cross the smooth white ice towards the grassy area. Follow the edge of the white-ice glacier and the brown moraine on the north margin, detouring around a few small crevasses, until opposite the grassy hill. Cross the moraine band in 15 minutes. Climb a trail up the verdant hillside, past a large cairn on a rock, and contour through profuse wild onions, willows and flowers, over many small streams, to reach Gashuchi in another hour. Gashuchi (4170m) is on a level alluvial plain, near a large boulder on the hillside with a rock shelter next to it. *Gashuchi* means 'wild onion' in Burushashki, but is called Kachili by Gazin men.

Day 3: Rest Day in Gashuchi Enjoy a rest day here, strolling the alpine meadows where ibex are occasionally spotted, surrounded by dramatic, snowy peaks in a splendid alpine amphitheatre.

Day 4: Gashuchi to Galpigol (3 to 4 hours) Crossing the Thui An is not difficult. The trail is clear and not overly steep. Continue around to the western slopes of the grassy hill, then cross the stream via a solid snow-field to the grassy area on its western bank. Walk up to a small cairn that marks the point where the trail leaves the grass and begins to traverse west south-west over scree to the pass. It takes about 1½ to two hours of steady walking to reach the Thui An (4500m).

Descend a trail, keeping to the north (right) to avoid rock-fall danger along the south side of the gully that runs west from the pass. Reach a solid snowfield at the base of the pass in about 30 minutes. Cross the snowfield to rocks on its opposite side. Turn south and descend a trail over the rocky moraine towards the level alluvial area ahead. Do not go too far west; be sure to keep to the true left (east) side of the stream issuing from the Thui Glacier. Continue south, towards the northern lateral moraine ridge of the Gazin Glacier (4200m). Once you reach it, bear west along the trail that parallels this moraine ridge for 20 minutes to Galpigol, the small grassy level area between the moraine ridge and the Thui Glacier stream. Just over the first moraine ridge is an enormous boulder with rock shelters all around it for porters. There is no wood here, so be sure your porters have fuel.

Day 5: Galpigol to Nichagh (4 to 5 hours) Follow the trail along the side of the Gazin Glacier lateral moraine, next to the stream from the Thui Glacier. After 15 minutes, the Thui Glacier stream turns and flows into the Gazin Glacier, blocking the path. Descend to

the Gazin Glacier and detour 30 minutes around this obstacle, then climb back to the northern lateral moraine. Continue down the moraine ridge trail another 30 minutes to a small ablation valley. Follow the ablation valley 45 minutes over a small stream to a large alluvial fan and another clear stream, which makes a good lunch spot. The entire area from here to the Golash Gol below is called Golash.

Leave the wide alluvial fan of the side stream, and enter the more narrow ablation valley north of the Gazin Glacier. Thirty minutes from the stream, the trail begins to descend. The Yarkhun Valley and the jeep road on its west bank are visible far below. In 30 minutes more, reach a small hut at the end of the ablation valley with a small trickle of water. Contour the hillside, descending to the alluvial plain of Golash dotted with birch, willow, and a few juniper.

Reach the clear Golash Gol (3450m) after 30 minutes, and cross it over a small bridge. The first summer huts are 15 to 20 minutes from here. Below them 30 minutes are the few houses of Shunup, where the trail crosses a bridge to the true left (south) bank of the Gazin River. Continue down the trail for 30 minutes to the village of Nichagh (3139m) where the traditional camp is in an orchard.

Day 6: Nichagh to Sholkuch or Paur (2½ to 4 hours) From Nichagh, walk 1½ to two hours down valley to the shaky foot-bridge over the Yarkhun River to the jeep road on its west bank. Walk one hour to Sholkuch or another hour on to Paur for transport. If heading up the Yarkhun, cross a bridge over the Gazin River and take the main trail up the east bank of the Yarkhun River.

NAZ BAR AN

(3 to 4 days; July to August)
This route leads west from the Naz Bar, a tributary of the Yasin Valley, to the Bahushtaro Gol, a tributary flowing south into the large Ghizar River at Chashi (see the Yarkhun Valley to Yasin Valley map). The

JOHN MOCK

JOHN MOCK

JOHN MOCK

JOHN MOCK

Top: View of Shost village in the Yarkhun Valley
Left: An old Kalasha man joins in the Chilimjust festivities in Brun village.
Middle Right: A typical sign urging villagers to refrain from hunting snow leopards, Chitral.
Bottom Right: Kalasha women dancing at the Chilimjust festival in Batrik village.

JOHN MOCK

JOHN MOCK

JOHN MOCK

JOHN MOCK

Top: A typical thatched bridge of leaves and branches over the Asumbar Nala
Middle Left: On snow-free passes locals often use donkeys to transport trekkers' gear.
Middle Right: Wooden shepherds' huts at Babusar in the Baru Gah
Bottom: In autumn Wakhi people bring their livestock down from the high pastures.

route is infrequently trekked, and is not used by local people. The steep Naz Bar An (4980m) has a brief 2nd-class section at its top. The pass is not glaciated, but has a permanent cornice on its eastern side. It also receives strong winds. It is not for novice trekkers, or for organised trekking parties. Rather it is a challenging alternative route west from the Yasin Valley, through rarely visited country.

Mountaineers heading for the under-6000m peaks of Kano Gol and Mashpar Gol in the upper Bahushtaro Gol may choose the Naz Bar An approach as a means of acclimatisation. Trekkers usually cross the Naz Bar An in conjunction with the Zagaro An, an equally difficult high pass on the border of Chitral (see Zagaro An in the Upper Ghizar River Valley section in this chapter). The Naz Bar An and Zagaro An are probably the most difficult nonglaciated trekking passes in northern Pakistan. They are best crossed in August, when snow has melted from the slopes and the rock-fall danger is lower.

Guides & Porters

A local guide is essential as the route to the pass is not straightforward. Herders in the upper Naz Bar village of Batakushi know the route to and over the Naz Bar An.

4 stages: Batakushi to high camp, high camp to Ano Gol huts, Ano Gol huts to Dedero Shal, Dedero Shal to Chashi

Map Notes

The U502 *Mastuj (NJ 43-13)* sheet indicates the general route over the pass, but does not show sufficient detail to enable trekkers to actually find their way to the pass. On the map, the pass appears fairly level, but the large scale of the map is the cause of this deceptive aberration.

Route Description

Day 1: Batakushi to High Camp (5 to 6 hours) The jeep road up the Naz Bar ends at Batakushi. However, drivers often stop at Baltaring (2682m), where the last stores are

and the electric line ends. It is a 2½ to three hour walk from Baltaring to Batakushi. (If you walk from Yasin village, it takes a full day to reach Batakushi.) If you are not already acclimatised, you should not drive directly to Batakushi (3400m), but should start walking from a lower elevation.

The Naz Bar An is visible from Batakushi. It is the lowest snowy saddle between the peaks ahead to the west. From Batakushi, follow a trail up the true left (north) bank of the Naz Bar. Many sheep and goats graze the grassy slopes above the wide valley. One hour beyond Batakushi, the Kha Bar enters from the south. Shuqan (3505m), the last Burushashki-speaking summer settlement, is 45 minutes further. This level grassy area with springs and willows makes a good camp site, from where the huts of upper Ano Gol could be reached in one long day.

From Shuqan, it is 30 minutes to the alluvial plain where the Yaltar Bar meets the Naz Bar (3690m). Cross the Yaltar Bar stream and head west. Across the alluvial plain is a small grassy area where the valley and trail turn south. The trail ascends a talus slope, climbing above the true left (west) bank of the Khamit Bar as the stream is now called. In 45 minutes from the Yaltar Bar crossing, reach the confluence of the Khamit Bar (3810m) with a stream coming from the west. Turn west and head up the true left (north) bank of this stream. Ahead is a rocky bluff. Two streams descend either side of this bluff and join to form this western tributary of the Khamit Bar. Take the north (right) fork of this stream past the rocky bluff. As the stream rises to the level of the top of the rocky bluff, cross it and climb the grassy slope to the top of the bluff. Continue angling south-west up a trail along the red streak that leads to the top of a grassy north-south ridge well above the small rocky bluff. It takes one hour to make this climb or 1½ hours from the confluence with the Khamit Bar. From the top of this alpine ridge, the mountains above the pass are visible, but the pass itself is not.

Head west, contouring down to meet the stream below. These extensive alpine grasslands are high summer pastures, and along the stream you can make a high camp. Forty-five minutes from the ridge top is a large boulder with a cairn on top with a stone shelter next to it, which is the highest possible camp site (about 4450m).

Day 2: High Camp to Ano Gol Huts (5 to 6 hours)

Head along the true left (east) bank of the stream. Where two streams join to form this stream, take the right fork, heading around the base of and behind the last grassy hill, where horses and cows graze in summer. This hill rises into a ridge. Curve around and behind (west of) this ridge, entering a valley with a black moraine ridge in its centre. To the south and west is a small glacier and snowfield. Ahead is the steep scree ascent topped by a snow cornice that is the Naz Bar An. It is the southernmost scree chute, reddish in colour, on the pass ridge. Continue along the black moraine ridge towards the pass. From the high camp, it takes 1½ to two hours to reach the end of this moraine ridge and the base of the pass.

Cross the top of the snowfield, working as high up on the snow as possible. Then ascend the 45° to 50° scree slope to the pass in 45 minutes to one hour. At the top, scramble over a 2nd-class rock outcrop on the north edge of the pass to get around the cornice lying in the pass itself. On top of the Naz Bar An (4980m) is a small cairn, not visible from below. The views all around are stunning.

Descend straight down reddish scree on the western side, moving onto the easier snowfield to the left as the angle eases. Reach the level area at the base of the pass in 20 minutes, and follow a faint trail. After 10 minutes, descend to white granite talus amid sparse grass and flowers. As the valley turns south south-west, follow a trail, with occasional cairns, 30 minutes to the junction with a black moraine-filled valley coming from the east.

Turn west (right) and continue along a rocky moraine ridge down the valley for another hour. Keep to the grassier south-east side to avoid a steep descent over scree. At the base of this grassy hill, amid scrub

willow by a stream side, is a boulder with a cairn on it with a small rock shelter next to it. This is the first possible camp, two to 2½ hours below the pass. A further 10 minutes down the stream side is another more open area. Another 30 minutes down a grassy hillside, the stream called Naz Bar by local herders opens into a large alluvial river bed and joins the larger stream coming from Kano Gol. The junction of these two streams marks the start of the Ano Gol. Ano Gol simply means 'the valley *(gol)* coming from a pass' *(an)*. Local herders say it is possible to reach Pingal village in Ghizar District over a high pass at the head of the Kano Gol, where several under-6000m peaks have attracted mountaineers in recent years. Cross the Naz Bar and follow a now-clear trail along the true right (north) bank of the Ano Gol. Ten minutes beyond the crossing of the Naz Bar are the first shepherds' huts and a good level camp site.

Day 3: Ano Gol Huts to Dedero Shal (3½ to 4 hours)

It is one hour down the Ano Gol to the confluence with the War Bar, which enters from the south. Cross the Ano Gol over a bridge to the thriving summer huts on the true left bank of both the War Bar and Ano Gol. The trail down valley stays high above the Ano Gol. A trail on the true right (north) bank is a longer way down, but is the trail to take if heading up to the Mashpar Gol for climbing peaks there. Thirty minutes down the true left bank you are high above the junction of the Ano Gol and Mashpar Gol (about 3566m). Turn left and continue high above the true left bank of the Bahushtaro Gol (formed at the junction of the above two). In 30 minutes, you are opposite Haringol Shal settlement (3420m) and the grassy plain called Rushkot. Parties going up the true right (west) side of the Bahushtaro Gol camp in Rushkot.

Another hour down the trail brings you to a bridge over the Bahushtaro Gol. Descend, cross it, and continue down the level alluvial river bed. In 30 minutes reach the huts of Deder (3300m), also called Dedero Shal, at the mouth of the clear Zagaro Gol.

Day 4: Dedero Shal to Chashi The herders in the Bahushtaro Gol are Khowar-speaking Ismaili Muslims from Chashi village. They are very friendly, hospitable, and helpful to travellers. Women wear the embroidered pill-box hats. From Dedero Shal, Chashi on the Gilgit-Chitral road is a one day walk. Alternatively, continue up the Zagaro Gol to Chitral (see Zagaro An in the Upper Ghizar River Valley section of this chapter).

PUNJI PASS

(4 days; July to September)
The 40-km-long trek over the Punji Pass (4680m) links Darkot at the head of the Yasin Valley to Ghotulti and Ishkoman villages in the Ishkoman Valley (see the Yasin Valley to Ishkoman Valley map). The pass is usually crossed west to east from Darkot to Ghotulti. The pass is named after a distinctive cairn about 2.25 km west of and 350m below the pass. *Punji* is the Burushashki word for cairn and it marks the highest possible camp site on the west side of the pass. This pass is also called Ishkoman Haghost by Darkot villagers. It is also occasionally called the Ishkoman Pass (as is the Asumbar Haghost to the south).

Guides & Porters

Porters occasionally use donkeys to carry loads on this trek. However, porters must unload the donkeys to cross the pass itself, which takes time. Stages are not really fixed, although some trekking parties pay by stages. Darkot porters seem happy to work on a daily basis. Porters do not ask for food rations. If you cannot find porters in Darkot village, walk up to Gartens and the surrounding villages and ask there.

Map Notes

The U502 *Baltit (NJ 43-14)* sheet calls the pass Ishkuman Aghost. What appears as a second pass is confusingly marked Panji Pass. However, Ishkoman Haghost and Punji Pass are the same – there is only one pass. The *Mastuj (NJ 43-13)* sheet shows Darkot, Gartens, and Gamelti, but incorrectly places Gamelti on the south side of the river. It is on the north side of the river east of Gartens and west of the Alam Bar. The Nyu Bar is labelled as Neo Bar and the Hanisar Bar as Anesar Bar.

Route Description

Day 1: Darkot to Boimoshani (5 to 6 hours)
Climb the obvious trail that snakes its dusty way up the hillside east from Darkot village (2760m). In about 1½ hours reach Gartens (2880m) and then Gamelti (3139m). From Gamelti, cross the Alam Bar. Walk along the willow-lined path through Sawarey village and in 15 minutes reach the sturdy bridge over the Gasho Gol. Locals say a difficult, seldom used two day route goes up the Gasho Gol and over a 5700m pass via the Chiantar Glacier to Shuwor Sheer in Broghil.

Continue through a cultivated area called Mardain for 45 minutes. Pass the last trees and reach the junction of the Nyu Bar *(nyu* means 'big') from the north-east and the Hanisar Bar from the south. Locals refer to Nyu Bar as Tshili Harang, which is the name of the main summer settlement upriver. Up the Nyu Bar, beyond Tshili Harang, lies the Atar Pass (see Other Routes below). Pyramid-shaped Garmush peak (6243m) rises above the head of the Nyu Bar; the snowy peak with the distinctive glacier to the left of Garmush peak is unnamed. Further west is the wide, flat, snowy pass between the Gasho Gol and Broghil.

Cross a bridge (3270m) to the true left bank of the Nyu Bar just above its juncture with the Hanisar Bar. A short way ahead the trail divides. The left branch follows the true left bank of the Nyu Bar to Mamutshil. Continue on the other (right) branch up the steep spur between the two rivers 150m to the fields and huts of Gawat Kutu. Like their northern Wakhi neighbours, Burusho women here tend livestock in summer settlements while men tend the fields around permanent villages. They wear tall pillbox hats, with their hair in multiple braids on the sides of their head. Relatives and friends, including KO, are greeted in traditional fashion by kissing the top of one another's hands. From Gawat Kutu (3450m), traverse high above the Hanisar Bar on a level trail to the small settlement of Hanisar Bar. Hapey, a large cultivated area with several huts, lies across a bridge above the true left bank.

Marmots *(Marmota caudata aurea)*, which live in large colonies, inhabit the mountains to the north of the valley of Kashmir and as far as Gilgit and the mountains of Central Asia. They have mainly orange or even reddish coats with black backs.

Beyond, both sides of the valley are barren scree slopes. The narrow, rocky trail stays on the true right bank and ascends gradually one hour. Around a bend to the south-east grass appears and the pass is visible. Continue along the river bank 30 minutes to Boimoshani where marmots give a whistling alarm call and dive into their burrows when approached. Boimoshani (3960m) is a small camp site amid willows near a spring. The name Boimoshani means 'Boi's vegetable garden'. Larger trekking parties camp in the grassy areas along the river. Porters need shelter as there are no huts here and nights get cold. Across the river valley from Boimoshani are two reddish mineral springs. Locals say these waters cure upset stomachs and headaches. Access to the other side of the river is usually via snow bridges.

The 1200m elevation gain from Darkot to Boimoshani should be done over two days by those not previously acclimatised. Ascend from Darkot to Sawarey or Mardain (camp sites for large trekking parties are

limited) the first day, and then to Boimoshani the next day.

Day 2: Boimoshani to Holojut (5 hours)
Follow the trail gradually up through thyme and wildflowers for 45 minutes to a deep ravine. Cross the stream in the ravine, which is usually icy in the morning, and climb 15 minutes to the highest possible camp site where a one-metre-high cairn (4250m), or punji, stands. Cows graze the grassy well-watered slopes. Porters need adequate gear to camp here. Marmots here provide food for snow leopards. The views down valley are superb, especially the peaks and dramatic ice falls south of the Darkot Pass above Rawat village. South of Punji Pass rises the distinctive snow pyramid of Punji peak (about 5800m).

Continue up a faint trail, then work south (right) over moraine rubble towards the small cirque glacier flowing from the pass, reaching its margin in about one hour (4410m). Cross onto the glacier on the lower angle (20 to 30°) south (right) side, rather than lower down to the left, where the angle is steeper (40°). The north (far left) side of the glacier is exposed to rock fall from the cliffs above. Contour towards the two cairns visible on the pass. The upper glacier is not crevassed, so a rope is optional. Crampons are not needed on the gentle slope. Reach Punji Pass (4680m) in about 45 minutes, which has sweeping views of the peaks above Darkot and the Thui An.

Descend over shale and small snowfields, following a faint trail along the true right (south) bank of the stream. As the stream descends, follow the trail south south-east along the rocky ridge above the stream for 45 minutes. At the end of the ridge, turn sharply back west (right) to avoid a deep ravine ahead. Descend steep switchbacks and a short scree slope on a trail to a flower-filled bowl below. Cross the meadow in 15 minutes to its western end and a clear stream, which tumbles down into a waterfall below the trail. Cross the stream and descend 125m on switchbacks along its true right bank to a smaller meadow. Recross the stream and pass left of many boulders, one of which is topped by a cairn.

Descend towards the alluvial plain below, traversing grassy slopes along the north (left) side of the valley for 15 minutes to a cascading waterfall, which is the stream originating at the pass. Cross the stream and descend 15 minutes across scree to the valley floor. Walk along the river bed 15 minutes to Holojut (3870m). Surrounded by peaks and hanging glaciers, this grassy expanse is a superb camp site with a large bubbling spring of deliciously cold water!

Punji Pass is not visible from Holojut. However, the eastern approach to the pass is marked by two prominent rock towers and a large light-coloured cliff just north (right) of the pass. The taller or southern (left) tower has a distinctive finger on it. The pass is at the base of these and is obscured by the black rock rib. Holojut is a Burushashki word *(jut* means 'grassy land').

Day 3: Holojut to Handis (5½ hours) Descend steeply 15 minutes. Across the river, three dramatic ice falls meet. Traverse through scrub juniper and tall-stemmed weeds with berries called *laka*. After 15 minutes, turn east, with the glaciers and a glacial lake below. Continue 30 minutes to a clear stream and a birch grove. Continue well above the river 15 minutes to Talas, a cluster of 'wigwam'-style conical-roofed huts built of juniper branches. This is the highest of the many summer settlements of Shina-speaking people from Ishkoman village.

Continue 15 minutes through birch to the river, here called the Baru Gah, where the trail divides. A bridge leads to the true right bank and on to Babusar (3480m), a settlement below a clear pond fed by a spring. The level grassy area along the pond makes a comfortable camp site, but leaves a long walk to Ghotulti the next day. Alternatively, stay on the true left side of the Baru Gah, bypass Babusar and cross another bridge downstream at Dorutsar settlement.

Babusar sits along a side stream. Young girls here coyly extracted a 'bridge toll' from JM and KO to cross a bridge over this stream.

The main trail stays on the true right bank of the Baru Gah two hours to Galtir, passing through pleasant juniper and birch groves. The bridge over the Baru Gah from Dorutsar is 15 minutes below Babusar. A bridge to Dajapuk *(daj* means 'a dry place'; *japul*, birch bark) is 30 minutes below the Dorutsar bridge. The wigwams here perch on a steep, dry hillside with no room for camp sites. Springs are on either side of the bridge on the true right bank.

Cross several side streams, then continue on through a chir pine forest as the trail climbs gently and traverses high above the river. Pass the huts of Sheramut below. Then pass below four one-metre-high cairns and through a mature juniper forest with a small spring. Above and out of view is the settlement of Barbalah. Descend to the river. Galtir (3280m) is a summer settlement with huts on both sides of the river. Cross a bridge to the true left bank. No water is available from Galtir to Handis, so fill water bottles in Galtir. A clear side stream on the north bank offers water, with a camp site nearby.

From Galtir, the trail climbs and stays high above the true left bank through juniper and sage-covered hillsides to Kai. Across the Baru Gah is the once-cultivated settlement of Phaiz. From Kai, continue high above the true left bank 45 minutes, then pass through boulders and juniper from where Handis (2930m), the first cultivated land in the valley, is a short 15 minutes ahead. Trails are along both sides of the Baru Gah from Handis to Ghotulti. If continuing to Ghotulti the same day, cross a bridge over the Baru Gah above Handis and follow the trail along its true right bank two hours to Ghotulti to meet the road just south of the jeep bridge. Otherwise cross the bridge over the Mathantir Gah, which leads to the Atar lake and pass (see Other Routes below). Walk through Handis village about 15 minutes to good camp sites in flat, grassy, shaded areas near a large, clear stream.

Day 4: Handis to Ghotulti (2½ hours) Continue above the true left bank, passing through cultivated fields, then high above

GHIZAR

the river 1¼ hours. The river becomes a gorge below. Just above the Chiantir Gah and Ghotulti is a large circle of stones covered in sage and enclosed by a square stone wall. This is a shrine to a saint who once visited the area. The saint's legend is remarkably similar to that of Baba Ghundi, whose shrine is in the Chapursan Valley (see Gojal in the Hunza River Valley chapter). Descend steeply 30 minutes to Ghotulti. Camp in the enclosed orchard of Maiun Jan, son of Hussain Ali. The Chiantir Gah, which leads north-east towards the Chiantar Glacier, joins the Baru Gah below the village to become the Ishkoman River. In Burushashki, *chian* means 'near'; *tir*, 'a valley'. A jeep bridge crosses the Baru Gah just below Ghotulti village.

OTHER ROUTES
Atar Lake & Pass
Atar, a less well-known, but very scenic pass between the Yasin and Ishkoman valleys, is usually open from July to September. Atar is also the name of a large lake, which flows into the Mathantir Gah (in Burushashki, *mathan* means 'far; *tir*, valley'). Colonel RCF Schomberg explored this route in 1933 and village elders in Ghotulti still remember him. The route shown on the U502 *Baltit (NJ 43-14)* sheet is based on Colonel Schomberg's notes. Atar is a longer, but seemingly easier route between Ishkoman and Darkot than the Punji Pass. A local guide is essential.

Some villagers from Darkot and Ghotulti know the route. It may be preferable to trek from east to west since many villagers go up to Atar Lake from Ghotulti and few people from Darkot cross the Atar Pass to the lake. Donkeys can cross the Atar Pass. Plan on three to five days for the trek.

From Darkot, head east past Mardain. Cross to the true left bank of the Nyu Bar and follow it to Mamutshil with its few trees, huts, and animal pens. Tshili Harang is the main summer settlement and Chordes is a high pasture above the true right bank of the Nyu Bar. Recross the Nyu Bar to Tshili

Harang and continue up the eastern arm of the valley, here called the Jut Bar.

The Jut Bar divides, with the Bhorik Bar continuing south. The route to the pass turns east and heads up the Atar Bar. Schomberg found a small glacier beneath the pass, which became steep near the top. The glacier is not difficult, but could be avoided by keeping to the north side. Schomberg was met by Ishkoman men on top of the pass and so had to change porters there. He describes the view towards Ishkoman as 'an immense amphitheatre surrounded by a circle of snowy peaks and hanging glaciers'. The descent is steep to Atar Lake, a greenish glacial lake about four km long. The path skirts its southern shore with a fine camp at its eastern end. Follow the Mathantir Gah to Handis and the confluence of the Baru Gah. From Handis trails on both sides of the Baru Gah lead to the road head at Ghotulti.

Ishkoman Valley

The Ishkoman River joins the Gilgit River at Gakuch. Just below Imit, the Karambar River joins the Ishkoman River. The name Ishkoman comes from the Burushashki word for green, *shiqam*. Most villagers in the valley are Ismaili Muslims, whose native language is Shina. Many so-called Gujars, who are actually migrants from Indus Kohistan, have moved into the Ishkoman Valley. Imit and Bar Jangal are predominantly Wakhi villages. Khowar is also widely spoken in Ishkoman, which was once part of greater Chitral. Not so long ago, the Ishkoman Valley had its own Raja, who ruled from Chatorkhand, the main village. His descendants still live there. Pir Sayed Karam Ali Shah, currently head of the elected Northern Areas Council, and a venerated spiritual leader of Ismaili Muslims in northern Pakistan, also lives in Chatorkhand.

INFORMATION
Maps
The US AMS *India and Pakistan Series*

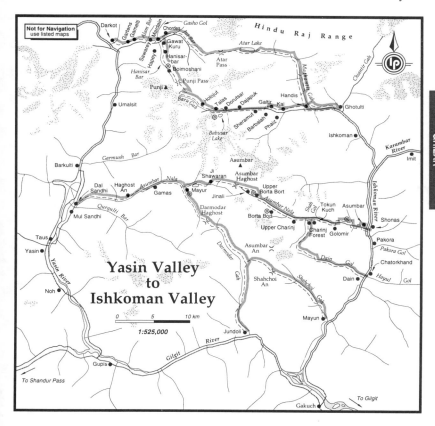

Not for Navigation use listed maps

GHIZAR

Yasin Valley to Ishkoman Valley

0   5   10 km

1:525,000

U502 1:250,000 *Baltit (NJ 43-14)* sheet is the only readily available map that shows the Ishkoman, Karambar, and Asumbar valleys. The *Mastuj (NJ 43-13)* sheet shows the valley west of the Asumbar Haghost from Gamas to Dal Sandhi in the Yasin Valley.

Regulations

The Ishkoman and Asumbar valleys are in an open zone where neither a permit from the Tourism Division nor a licensed mountain guide is necessary. However, the Karambar Valley above Imit is in a restricted zone and a permit and guide are required. Foreigners

must register with police at check posts in Chatorkhand and Imit.

Accommodation & Supplies

Basic supplies are available in Chatorkhand, Pakora, and Imit villages. Chatorkhand and Imit have *NAPWD Rest Houses*, which can be booked in Gilgit.

GETTING THERE & AWAY

Cargo jeeps to the Ishkoman Valley leave from Punial Rd in Gilgit; see Naushat, a Pathan shopkeeper. Cargo jeeps are also available in Gakuch, the district headquarters.

Ishkoman Valley

Asumbar village is the eastern trail head for the Asumbar Haghost trek. Cargo jeeps Asumbar-Gilgit cost Rs 60. When you combine the Pakora Pass and Asumbar Haghost treks, you can walk between Pakora and Asumbar villages on the jeep road in about one hour. From Pakora, head north to the bridge over the Ishkoman River and cross to its true right bank. The trail head is at the jeep bridge over the Asumbar Nala along its true right bank.

Karambar Valley

The road goes as far as Bort, but in summer, high water usually blocks the road at Bilhanz, below Bad Swat. Cargo jeeps Gilgit-Bilhanz cost Rs 100. Cargo jeeps also go regularly to Imit from Gilgit and Chatorkhand; from Imit you can arrange a special hire as close to Bort as road conditions permit.

Yasin Valley

Dal Sandhi Dal Sandhi is the western trail head for the Asumbar Haghost. Cargo jeeps Dal Sandhi-Gilgit cost Rs 100. A special hire to Gilgit can be difficult to arrange, but a special hire Dal Sandhi-Gakuch costs about Rs 1800. If combining the Asumbar Haghost trek with either the Darkot An or Punji Pass, a special hire Dal Sandhi-Darkot costs Rs 800. Otherwise, it takes two days to walk.

Yasin Village From their Punial Rd booking office in Gilgit, NATCO buses go Gilgit-Gupis and continue up the Yasin Valley to Noh. Gilgit-Gupis costs Rs 50, and Gilgit-Noh costs Rs 60. NATCO plans to extend bus service to Yasin village for Rs 70. From Gupis, you can also reach Yasin or Dal Sandhi by cargo jeep or special hire.

GUIDES & PORTERS

The stage system is not fully instituted in this area. You can pay wages on either the stage system or a daily basis. The maximum low-altitude porter's wage is Rs 160 per stage or Rs 160 per day plus wāpāsi and food rations. They do not ask to be paid the clothing and equipment allowance.

KARAMBAR VALLEY, LAKES & PASS

(5 days; June to September)

The Karambar River joins the Ishkoman River south of Imit and marks the dividing line between the Hindu Raj range to the west and the Karakoram range to the east. The valley was apparently used as a Buddhist pilgrimage route from the Wakhan Corridor to Gilgit. The government of Pakistan now proposes building a highway to Tajikistan up the valley and over the Khodarg Werth Pass. This rugged valley leads to some of the largest alpine meadows in Pakistan. These are pastures for Gujars in the Karambar Valley and Wakhi in Broghil. The Karambar An (4230m) rolls through the crest of these well-watered grasslands with several, large blue lakes where migrating waterfowl stop. It is one of the most scenic places in all the Karakoram and Hindukush.

We describe the trek from east to west, but you can also walk from west to east. This trek is often done in conjunction with a trek over the Shah Jinali An in western Chitral (see Turikho Valley in the Chitral chapter). It can also be combined with a trek south from Broghil over the Darkot An to Yasin (see Upper Yarkhun Valley in the Chitral chapter). The Karambar Valley is also linked by the Chilinji An to the Chapursan Valley (see Gojal in the Hunza River Valley chapter).

Guides & Porters

The trek crosses two glaciers, the Karambar and the Chattiboi, both of which are tricky and require routefinding, so hiring a local guide is essential. The Chattiboi Glacier is more difficult to negotiate. Few porters from Imit, Bad Swat, Bilhanz, Bort, or Chapursan will have crossed the Chattiboi Glacier, so find a local shepherd from Sokhter Rabot to lead you across this glacier. The route changes from year to year, so porters who have crossed the Chattiboi in previous years may still have difficulty.

Map Notes
The U502 *Baltit (NJ 43-14)* sheet shows incorrect trails across the Chattiboi Glacier and along the true right bank of the river from the Chattiboi Glacier to Shuyinj. It also does not show the sizeable Karambar lakes. Bort is labelled Bhurt, and Maturamdas as Mahtram Dan.

Route Description
Day 1: Bilhanz to Bort (4 hours) When the road to Bort is blocked by high water, walk along it, fording side streams as needed.

Day 2: Bort to Maturamdas (4 to 5 hours) Above Bort, the trail stays along the true left bank of the Karambar River. Cross the Karambar Glacier which descends from the east, pushing its way into the river valley. This glacier stopped John Biddulph, a late 19th-century British officer, from proceeding up the valley and can present a serious obstacle.

Day 3: Maturamdas to Sokhter Rabot (5 to 6 hours) Beyond Maturamdas, the Chilinji Glacier also makes its way into the valley. Traverse the glacier above a small lake that has formed near its western end. Descend to Chilinj, a Gujar settlement. At Chilinj (3450m), the trail from the Chilinji An and Chapursan meets the Karambar Valley (see Gojal in the Hunza River Valley chapter). From Chilinj cross to the true right (west) bank of the Karambar River via a metal box suspended from a steel cable. The valley here is grassy and forested with steep cliffs above the river. Forty-five minutes beyond the cable crossing, ascend briefly and ford the stream coming from a large unnamed glacier. After 15 minutes across moraine rubble, the trail descends to a broad alluvial plain and the huts of Sokhter Rabot *(rabot* means 'a dwelling place').

This broad alluvial plain was apparently formed when the large unnamed glacier advanced and dammed the Karambar River.

Across the valley is a reddish scree slope below the narrow mouth of a valley at the head of which Wakhi shepherds say is a pass to the Agh Glacier in Chapursan above Biatar. Fifteen minutes further up the trail is a clear stream. After another 30 minutes are more huts, also called Sokhter Rabot (3420m), with willows and a grassy meadow for camping.

Day 4: Sokhter Rabot to Shuyinj (5 to 6 hours) Continue up the grassy plain. A route from the Wakhan over the Khodarg Werth or Khora Bort Pass (Wakhi and Khowar words respectively for millstone) enters from the north. This was the route crossed by Qirghiz nomads fleeing the Russian invasion of the Wakhan in the early 1980s. Reach the lateral moraine of the Chattiboi Glacier (3510m) in 1¼ hours. This glacier fills the entire valley, and the Karambar River runs underneath it. Follow the black medial moraine up the middle of the glacier until it is easy to move right onto the white ice. Follow the white ice parallel to the black medial moraine until even with the main ice fall to the south (left). As crevasses become more frequent, work towards the north (right) and the polished granite cliffs until just next to them. Parallel these cliffs 10 to 15 minutes, then leave the ice and climb up the true left (north) bank of the Karambar River to a trail marked by cairns. (An old trail, which is more difficult and less preferable, exits the glacier to the true right (south) bank of the river and continues up river to a cable crossing below Shuyinj.)

A few huts are nestled against the grassy hillside above the trail. Continue up valley one hour to the base of a hill, passing many clear streams on the way. Ascend for 15 minutes to a large cairn. Continue 30 minutes to the two huts of Shuyinj. A much better camp site is 20 minutes beyond these huts. Cross the stone bridge over the Shuyinj *(shu* means 'black'; *yinj,* 'a narrow gorge') stream, and ascend a short distance to a large grassy meadow near two other huts, a rushing stream, and marmot burrows.

GHIZAR

Day 5: Shuyinj to Karambar Lake (4 hours)
Above Shuyinj, the Karambar River is clear.
Continue through grasslands 1¼ hours to the
base of a large old moraine hill that runs
north-south. A few huts are visible at its base,
across the river to the south. Keep to the true
left bank of the river and wind around the hill
and up 30 minutes into the immense grasslands of the pass area. Clear streams abound
and wild onions grow in profusion along
their banks. Ram chukor and big golden
marmots are on every south-facing hillside.
The marmots' piercing alarm calls whistle

you into the beautiful, gently rolling pass. An
hour further on lies the enormous blue
Karambar Lake (4260m). It takes 1¼ hours
to walk along its northern shore, and another
15 minutes further is a large boulder with a
cairn at its western end. Here are several
stone shelters for porters and excellent camp
sites. If you have the time, enjoy at least one
extra day at this remarkable spot. Above the
lake's southern shore is Jhui Sar (*jhui* means
'lake'; *sar*, 'a peak'), a snowy peak with a
glacier that falls into the lake itself.
   From the Karambar lakes continue west to

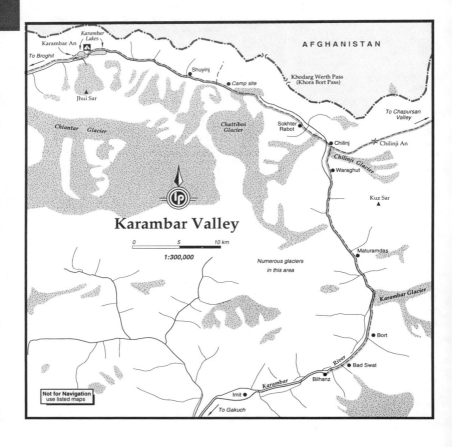

Broghil and then either cross the Darkot An to Yasin or continue down the Yarkhun Valley to Chitral (see Upper Yarkhun Valley in the Chitral chapter).

ASUMBAR HAGHOST

(4 days; July to September)

The Asumbar Haghost is a nonglaciated east-west pass that links the Ishkoman Valley to the Yasin Valley. The pass is occasionally called the Ishkoman Pass. (This is not to be confused with the Punji Pass, which is also sometimes referred to as the Ishkoman Pass.) The 45-km-long route over the Asumbar Haghost begins in Asumbar village (2190m) in the Ishkoman Valley, climbs steadily to the nonglaciated pass (4560m) and descends to Dal Sandhi (2700m) in the Yasin Valley. The Asumbar Haghost is one of the most gentle and easiest passes to cross anywhere in the Karakoram and Hindukush, and the trek is one of the most linguistically diverse. Along the trail you can hear Shina, Khowar, Wakhi and Burushashki spoken, not to mention Urdu. This trek is usually combined with at least one other trek. The Pakora Pass is often done before the Asumbar Haghost, or it can be followed by either the Punji Pass or Thui An treks.

Guides & Porters

The route is fairly obvious so a local guide is not necessary. Porters use donkeys to carry their loads. The rate is about Rs 400 per donkey for 50 kg (ie, equal to two 25 kg porter loads). The rate for a fully loaded donkey should be equal to two porters' wages. If you have less than 50 kg, try negotiating a lower price. Wages can be paid on either the stage system or on a daily system. The stages are not universally fixed, but four stages seem appropriate. Trekkers who agreed to three stages had problems. The total distance is difficult for trekkers, porters, and donkeys to walk comfortably in three stages (ie, three days).

When you combine the Asumbar Haghost trek with the Punji Pass, hire porters for both passes from either Pakora or Asumbar villages. That way, the porters end up in Ghotulti in the Ishkoman Valley just one stage away from their homes, minimising the wāpāsi.

Map Notes

On the U502 *Mastuj (NJ 43-13)* the village labelled Chucho Aho Tik is called Haghost An by villagers. The *Baltit (NJ 43-14)* sheet does not show any summer settlements east of the pass.

Route Description

Day 1: Asumbar Village to (Lower) Charinj Forest (4 to 6 hours) Climb steadily up the true right (south) bank of the Asumbar Nala passing fields and in one hour reach the first of four bridges. Cross to the true left bank and in 15 minutes cross the second bridge, an enormous boulder, back to the true right bank. Climb steeply 45 minutes passing corn fields to a silty stream from the south. A Gujar's house with a large willow sits across the stream. Continue 15 minutes and cross the third bridge to the true left bank. Springs along the trail here provide the only clear water until Charinj. Ahead is a dark rock pile, about 100m high, known as Shah Dheri (black rocks). Continue along the now-forested stream around Shah Dheri in about 30 minutes.

Back down valley are good views of the Pakora Gol. Reach the fourth bridge in another 15 minutes and get the first views up valley towards the Asumbar Haghost. The first possible camp site, Golomir, is 15 minutes further in an open, grassy, but rocky and shadeless field. In 30 minutes pass above Tokun Kuch, an inviting forest along both banks of the river with flat, grassy areas for camping. Tokun Kuch means 'the place where grass grew up to the bottom of the horse's saddle blanket' *(tokun* is a saddle blanket). However, the only water is silty water from the river. Continue high above the true right bank for 15 minutes to a beautiful chir pine forest called Charinj. This is a great camp site with lots of flat, grassy fields, and a series of clear streams running through the forest. Gujars have conical huts here, but in midsummer, they are usually vacant. This camp site is also called Lower Charinj (3180m) and Zokhinewar by the Wakhi speakers who live further up valley. The lower Asumbar Valley can be very hot and dry in summer; carry a lot of water and enjoy the shady places along the river.

Day 2: Charinj Forest to (Upper) Borta Bort (3¾ to 4 hours) Continue through the dense stand of pine trees 15 minutes to the first of five side streams that flow in from the south. Ford this large stream and climb 30 minutes past a few huts high above the river to Upper Charinj. Continue past juniper and tall birch and pass above the treeline to reach Wakhikandeh, a year-round Wakhi settlement with three households. Just past the houses, cross the second side stream over a good bridge. This large side valley leads to Daīn Gol and/or Asumbar An (see Other Routes below). A few Gujar huts are across this stream. Reach a third stream and more Gujar settlements in 30 minutes. The trail begins a steady climb, contouring up the rocky hillside past scrub juniper, to emerge after an hour in a grassy pasture. This is Borta Bort, an area which gets its name from the huge obvious boulder visible up valley. The pass is visible far ahead.

Four houses, also called Borta Bort, lie 15 minutes ahead, and are inhabited by one Ismaili household from Shonas and three Gujar households from Asumbar in the Ishkoman Valley. Women here also wear tall pillbox-style hats.

Continue, passing several large scree slopes and more huts on the opposite side of the river, and in 30 minutes come to a large alluvial fan and the fourth stream. A possible camp lies across this side stream, but a better camp site is 30 minutes ahead. Cross over a grassy knoll, with huts below its western side (beware of dogs here), and cross a silty glacial side stream via a bridge. Climb through grassy flower-filled meadows along clear streams from springs. Camp here below the large boulders (3990m) and enjoy spectacular views to the east. The Hayal Pass, Shani (5887m) and Twin Peaks (5798m and

5700m), and distant Rakaposhi (7788m) are visible.

Day 3: (Upper) Borta Bort to Mayur (5½ hours) The trail continues through the boulder field for 45 minutes to a broad grassland locally called jinali or pologround, a possible, though less desirable high camp. Porters prefer staying near Borta Bort where they can get shelter in homes.

Ahead are two low points (ie, passes) with a hill between. The route goes over the northern low point. The southern one is steep on the western side, passes close to an ice fall, and cannot be crossed by donkeys. Cross Jinali, fording a silty side stream, and follow the northern (right) fork of the river past springs 45 minutes to the base of the hill leading to the pass.

Ascend over grass one hour to the gentle flower-carpeted pass (4560m). The hill south of this pass does not offer any substantially different view from the pass itself. Rakaposhi and Diran (7257m) peaks to the east and the peaks of the high Hindukush to the west are visible.

Snow patches lie just below and west of the pass. Descend one hour following a clear willow-lined stream to grassy meadows. Continue north (right) on a trail, skirting willows. Cross the clear side stream from Asumbar peak to the north, above its junction with the milky main stream, and continue past small springs to the huts of Ji Shawaran (*shawaran* is Shina for pologround), two hours from the pass. The pass is visible from here.

Cross a bridge over the river to its true left (south) bank, and head down. Cross a low rise with two cairns on it to a large unnamed pond, visible from the pass, 45 minutes from Ji Shawaran. The slightly green water is deep enough for a swim and is a possible camp site.

A better camp site is 45 minutes further on through extensive juniper to the huts of Mayur (3630m). Springs abound below the huts along the clear river from the south. Up this river are routes leading to the Qurqulti Bar and over the Darmodar Haghost to

Jundoli village in the Ghizar River valley (see Other Routes below).

Day 4: Mayur to Dal Sandhi ($5\frac{1}{2}$ to 6 hours)
From Mayur, the main trail follows the true left bank of the Asumbar River, although another trail goes along its true right bank through three areas cultivated by Burusho people from Sandhi. In one hour, reach Gamas, a huge cultivated area bisected by a large side stream, high above the south bank of the main river. Below Gamas, cross a bridge to the true right bank where the trail stays to Dal Sandhi. After 30 minutes reach the start of a settlement called Haghost An. Haghost An used to be called Chucho Ano Tok. In Khowar, *chucho* means 'dry place' and *ano*, 'the top of'. When villagers irrigated this land and brought the area under cultivation, they changed the name to Haghost An.

However, the Burusho refer to it as Bay Haghost. At the west end of this cultivated area, descend steeply to tall willows along the river, then more gradually down the valley on a good trail. Pass Bericho Batan, where low-status Bericho people used to live, and ford a clear side stream. Descend the broad valley to Dal Sandhi, $2\frac{1}{2}$ hours from Haghost An. Damage from a massive 1995 flood is evident. Camp in a lovely orchard in Dal Sandhi. If continuing to the Thui An, cross the Yasin River at Barkulti, two hours from Dal Sandhi.

OTHER ROUTES
Shahchoi Gah
The Shahchoi Gah is a valley branching north-west from the Ishkoman Valley at Mayun, below Chatorkhand. The Shahchoi An (about 4500m) at its head leads into the Darmodar Gah.

Daīn Gol
This valley also branches north-west from the Ishkoman Valley across from Chatorkhand. At the head of this valley are two infrequently used passes. One is the Asumbar An, which heads west over a high saddle (about 4800m) to Darmodar Gah. The route to the other pass turns north, crossing a ridge (4500m) to descend steeply into the Asumbar Valley.

Daīn villagers prefer walking the jeep road to Asumbar village and then up the Asumbar Valley rather than crossing this steep pass. It is a good one day walk from Daīn to the summer settlements in the Asumbar Valley, and one day from Daīn to the Darmodar Gah.

Darmodar Gah
The Darmodar Gah is a north-south valley, which enters the Gilgit River at Jundoli village, about 10 km upstream from its junction with the Ishkoman River. Two passes at its head lead to the Yasin Valley. The Darmodar Haghost (about 4495m) crosses to Mayur west of the Asumbar Haghost (see above). It takes two to three days to walk Jundoli to Mayur. The other pass, about the same elevation, heads west into the Qurqulti Bar and joins the Yasin Valley above Sandhi village. This route is used by Gujars from Ghizar, who ride horses to the medicinal springs above Barkulti in the Yasin Valley. It takes about three days to walk from Jundoli to Sandhi.

GHIZAR

Gilgit, Diamir & Kaghan Valley

Gilgit and Diamir are two districts of the Northern Areas. The Gilgit district also includes the Hunza River valley, but that area is treated as a separate chapter (see the Hunza River Valley chapter). Diamir district centres on Nanga Parbat (8125m), the ninth highest peak in the world and the western end of the Himalayan range. The local name for Nanga Parbat is Diamir. The Astor Valley, which skirts the north-east flanks of Nanga Parbat and joins the Indus River at Jaglot, is in Diamir district. Diamir's administrative centre is Chilas, one of the hottest places in Pakistan, on the Indus River.

The Kaghan Valley, actually in NWFP, is just south of and linked to Diamir district by a jeep road over the Babusar Pass. Gilgit town, a booming administrative and market centre, sits at the intersection of the main north-south and east-west routes of northern Pakistan.

REGIONAL HISTORY

Most of what is known about the prehistory and early history of the Gilgit and Chilas region comes from rock art. These carvings and inscriptions on polished boulders are found along the Indus and Gilgit rivers, especially at the mouths of side valleys. The earliest rock art was probably made by late stone age hunters, who incised totemistic ibex and markhor figures as part of hunting rituals. Rock carvings and inscriptions indicate an extensive network of travel and communication through the region.

Between Gandhara, Kashmir and Central Asia, merchants and monks travelled the Silk Route paths through the mountains. Monastic as well as trading centres were established near Chilas. Shatial, across from the mouth of the important Darel Valley, and Thalpan, on the north bank of the Indus River across from the route to the Babusar Pass, were two such sites. Near Gilgit, at Naupur, a small village at the mouth of the Kargah Valley, was the site of another Buddhist monastery

Highlights – Nagyr Parbat
Nagyr Parbat, a huge massif, is the western end of the Himalayan range. Receives more rainfall and has more forests. Main valleys for trekking and climbing are western Raikhot and south-eastern Rupal

with a well-known standing Buddha figure carved on the hillside. The location of these sites, at the entrances to important side valleys or where a route would have to cross the Indus River, shows that travel was not along the deep gorges of the Indus River, but rather over passes joining smaller side valleys.

From the 5th to 8th century, Buddhism flourished along these routes, and Gilgit and Chilas were important centres. No doubt the wealth from Silk Route trade helped support the cultural and artistic achievements of the region. Gilgit's kings belonged to the Patola

Shahi dynasty, and the region was known to the Chinese as 'Little Balur'. In the 8th century, Tibetan armies succeeded in conquering the Gilgit region, and the Gilgit king married a Tibetan princess.

As Arab armies pushed east along the Silk Route, China and Tibet lost influence in Gilgit. With no external power to unify the area, small independent kingdoms arose. These independent, unruly wine drinkers of Gilgit and Chilas continually harassed the neighbouring Kashmiri kings. In Gilgit, the Trakhan dynasty, probably of Turkic origin, more or less continuously ruled from the 12th to the 19th century.

In the 17th century, the Gilgit Raja called upon the Raja of Skardu for aid against Chitral, which held Yasin and threatened Gilgit. In 1841, again pressed by the Chitrali rulers of Yasin, the Gilgit Raja called for help from the Sikh armies holding Kashmir. The arrival of Dogra troops brought an end to Trakhan rule and set off a 35 year struggle with Kashmir. Time and time again the Sikh armies captured Gilgit, only to be driven off by local tribesmen. The massacre of an entire regiment under General Bhup Singh in 1852 by rolling rocks down on them is known to every Gilgit schoolchild.

Britain, nervous about Russian designs on the area, sought through Kashmir to control the independent states, and sent a Political Agent to Gilgit in 1877. Chilas rebelled in 1892 and Chitral in 1895, but finally the British held the frontier. In 1935 Britain actually leased back the entire Gilgit Agency from Kashmir and raised a local militia, the Gilgit Scouts.

In anticipation of independence from Britain, set for 14 August 1947, Kashmir sent General Ghansara Singh to Gilgit as its new governor. On 1 August, the British Political Agent handed over the entire Gilgit Agency to him. However, two British officers, one at Chilas and one at Gilgit, stayed on to command the Gilgit Scouts. As independence came and went, Kashmir's Maharaja Hari Singh hesitated to join India or Pakistan. Finally on 26 October, he acceded to India. The people of Gilgit had little love for Kashmir after over 100 years of Kashmiri rule, and they had even less desire to become part of India. On the news of Kashmir joining India, Gilgit rose to claim its independence. The Gilgit Scouts, led by Mohammad Babar Khan, arrested Ghansara Singh and the following day, 2 November, Gilgit joined Pakistan. Remarkably, members of the ruling families and the two British officers kept bloodshed to a minimum. Joining Pakistan closed the old Kashmir-Gilgit route via Astor, and the Babusar Pass became the route down country. The much disliked Kashmiri shopkeepers and officials left Gilgit, and their positions were filled by local men. Gilgit now celebrates 1 November as Independence Day with music, dancing, and a polo tournament.

GILGIT

Gilgit town is along the Gilgit River, 10 km west of the KKH. Another road leads into Gilgit from Dainyor along the KKH via bridges over the Hunza and Gilgit rivers, saving 10 km for those coming from the Hunza River valley. The airport is east of the bazaar. Jutial is primarily a military cantonment, east of the airport.

Information

To book *NAPWD Rest Houses* in the region, and in Hunza, Nagyr and Gojal, see the Administrative Officer, office of the NAPWD Chief Engineer (☎ 3375), on Bank Rd opposite the National Bank.

British Cemetery

On lower Bank Rd is an overgrown graveyard, surrounded by barbed wire. Among those buried there is George Hayward, a British explorer, murdered in Darkot in 1870 by Mir Wali, ruler of Yasin. Ask for the key in the shop of Sarwar the tailor across the street.

Places to Stay & Eat

Places to Stay & Eat – bottom end The *Madina Hotel & Guest House*, by the NLI barracks, remains popular. Rooms cost Rs 80 to Rs 150 and camping in the garden costs

GILGIT, DIAMIR & KAGHAN VALLEY

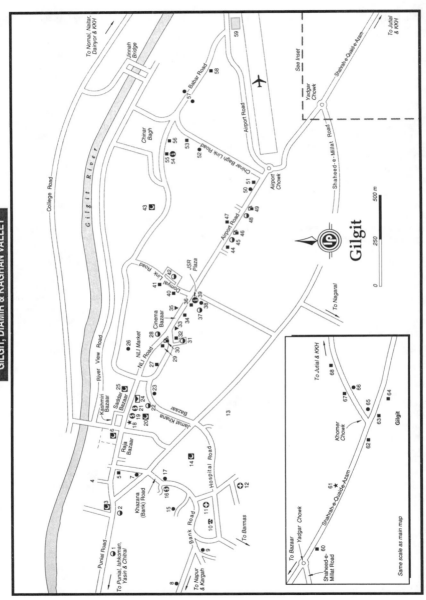

Gilgit

PLACES TO STAY				26	Gohar Aman's Tower
5	NAPWD Rest House		Gakuch, Gupis &	28	NATCO Transport to
27	Kashgar Inn		Yasin Valley		Rawalpindi, Sost &
29	Madina Hotel & Guest	2	Transport to Punial,		Skardu
	House		Ishkoman & Yasin	30	Petrol Station
32	Indus Hotel		Valleys	31	Mashabrum Tours
34	Skyways Hotel	3	Imamia Mosque		Transport to
36	JSR Hotel	4	Pologround		Rawalpindi & Skardu
40	Alflah Hotel	6	Jama Masjid	37	Transport to Rawalpindi
41	Mir's Lodge	7	British Cemetery	38	PIA
44	Vershigoom Inn	8	Fisheries Office	39	PTDC Tourist
47	Karakorum Inn	9	Deputy		Information Centre
51	Park Hotel		Commissioner's	42	General Bus Stand
53	Chinese Lodge Hotel &		(DC) Office	43	Mosque
	Restaurant	10	Telephone Exchange	45	Transport to
55	PTDC Chinar Inn	11	District Hospital		Rawalpindi & Sost
56	Hunza Inn	12	Women's Hospital	46	Petrol Station
58	Hunza Tourist House	13	Old Pologround	48	Transport to Sost
60	Golden Peak Inn	14	Mosque	49	Petrol Station
62	North Inn	15	Library	50	Hunza Handicrafts
63	Kinbridge Hotel	16	National Bank	52	Laundry
64	Gilgit Serena Hotel	17	NAPWD Office	54	PTDC Tourist Informa-
67	Tourist Hamlet	18	Police		tion Centre
68	Tourist Cottage	19	Allied Bank	57	Aga Khan Rural
		20	Jamat Khana		Support Programme
PLACES TO EAT		21	Habib Bank	59	Airport Terminal
33	Madina Cafe	22	Transport to Hunza &	61	Police Headquarters
35	Pathan Hotel		Gojal	65	Foreigners' Registra-
		23	GM Beg Sons Book		tion Office
OTHER			Shop	66	Aga Khan Maternity
1	NATCO Transport to	24	Post Office		Home
		25	Moti Mosque		

Rs 15. Near Chinar Bagh, the *Hunza Inn* (☎ 2814) has cold-shower doubles for Rs 100, deluxe rooms for Rs 300, and a garden. At the *Park Hotel*, dorms (with morning hot water) cost Rs 50. *Chinese Lodge Hotel* on Chinar Bagh Link Rd has dorms/doubles for Rs 35/120. *Tourist Cottage* (☎ 2376) on Shahrah-e-Quaid-e-Azam Rd has dorms and a garden. Singles/doubles cost about Rs 55/80. *Golden Peak Inn* (☎ 3538) on Shahrah-e-Quaid-e-Azam Rd, east of Yadgar Chowk, also has dorms and a garden. Doubles/triples cost Rs 150/200. The *New Lahore Hotel* (☎ 3327) on lower Hospital Rd has doubles/triples for about Rs 100/120 and quads with shared toilet for Rs 125. In noisy Cinema bazaar, the *Kashgar Inn* has doubles for Rs 60 to Rs 80 and rooms at the *Indus Hotel* cost about Rs 70. Rooms at the *Karakorum Inn* and *Vershigoom Inn* on Airport Rd are dismal.

Places to Stay & Eat – middle Doubles at

Skyways Hotel & Restaurent (☎ 2742) and *JSR Hotel* (☎ 3971), Cinema bazaar, cost Rs 150, but JSR's have shared toilet and shower. JSR's carpeted doubles/triples/quads with shower cost Rs 250/300/350. A clean, comfortable *NAPWD Rest House* is on the corner of Bank and Punial roads. Doubles in the *Alflah Hotel* by the general bus stand cost Rs 150. The *Park Hotel* (☎ 2379 and 3379) on Airport Rd has doubles with hot shower from Rs 300.

The *North Inn* (☎ 2887) on Shahrah-e-Quaid-e-Azam Rd has doubles with 24-hour hot showers that cost Rs 300, some without for Rs 200. Nearby *Gateway Hotel* has singles/doubles that cost Rs 800/1000. The friendly *Hunza Tourist House* (☎ 3788, 2338) on Babar Rd, close to the airport and with a garden, has singles/doubles for Rs 350/470. *Tourist Hamlet* (☎ 2934 and 2754) near Khomer Chowk has TV, hot running water, a large garden for camping, and a swimming pool is planned. Basic singles/

doubles cost Rs 280/350, and standard ones cost Rs 375/500.

Places to Stay & Eat – top end At PTDC's *Chinar Inn* (☎ 2562) singles/doubles cost Rs 600/750. *Mir's Lodge* (☎ 2875) on Domyal Link Rd costs Rs 500/650; suites cost Rs 775/900. *Tourist Hamlet* has deluxe doubles that cost Rs 800. The *Gilgit Serena Hotel* (☎ 2330-1; fax 2525) in Jutial has deluxe singles/doubles for Rs 1700/2150. Its all-you-can-eat buffets are a tasty value. The Gilgit Serena Hotel runs a free shuttle to and from the bazaar.

Getting Around

To/From the Airport Suzukis to Airport Chowk (the roundabout at the end of the runway) cost Rs 2. The terminal is a few minutes' walk from here. A special hire costs Rs 20 to Rs 30 between the bazaar and the terminal.

Suzukis Suzuki central is by the post office. Most Suzukis go through the bazaar to Jutial. Some turn at Chinar Bagh Link Rd, and cross the Gilgit and Hunza rivers to Dainyor. Most can be flagged down anywhere, though they do not run regularly after dark. Ask the driver if it's Jutial or Dainyor bound. Suzukis cost Rs 2 to Airport Chowk or to the intersection of Chinar Bagh Link and Babar roads. Anywhere beyond is Rs 3. Suzukis also run west from Punial Rd.

GETTING THERE & AWAY

Treks throughout Gilgit district usually begin or end in Gilgit town, although the Kaghan Valley and Chilas can be visited without first going to Gilgit. The general bus stand is on Domyal Link Rd off JSR Plaza, though much regional transport tends to start where people from outlying towns have shops. (See Getting Around for more information.)

PIA schedules one to three daily flights Islamabad-Gilgit depending on the day of the week and once weekly flights Skardu-Gilgit. The fares cost Rs 575 and Rs 395 respectively.

The KKH links Gilgit to Islamabad. From Islamabad, the road goes through Abbottabad and Mansehra and meets the Indus River at the Thakot bridge. From Mansehra the road to the Kaghan Valley turns north. The KKH actually begins at the Thakot bridge below Besham and follows the Indus River valley through Chilas in Indus Kohistan to Gilgit. Trekkers can get off at the Raikhot bridge, an hour east of Chilas, for treks on the north side of Nanga Parbat.

Bagrot & Haramosh Valleys

Fifteen km down river from Gilgit, a broad alluvial fan on the north bank of the Gilgit River marks the Bagrot Valley. Its narrow, lower reaches are desolate, but above Sinakkar the valley is broad and densely cultivated. The isolated Bagrot Valley where pre-Islamic traditions are still remembered has drawn the interest of foreign scholars. East of the Bagrot Valley, the Haramosh Valley branches north from the Indus Valley. Villagers in both valleys are Shia Muslims who speak Shina. The Bagrot and Haramosh valleys are seldom on trekkers' itineraries. Yet treks in these valleys are readily accessible by road, with mostly easy trails and superb views. From the Bagrot Valley, the stunning south faces of Rakaposhi (7788m) and Diran (7257m) peaks, as well as the lovely twin summits of Bilchar Dobani (6134m) are visible. Phuparash (6574m), Malubiting (7458m), Laila (6986m), and Haramosh (7409m) peaks can be seen from the Haramosh Valley.

INFORMATION
Maps

The Swiss Foundation for Alpine Research 1:250,000 orographical sketch map *Karakoram (Sheet 1)* shows the Bagrot and Haramosh valleys. The US AMS *India and Pakistan Series U502* 1:250,000 *Baltit (NJ 43-14)* sheet shows Diran base camp and the

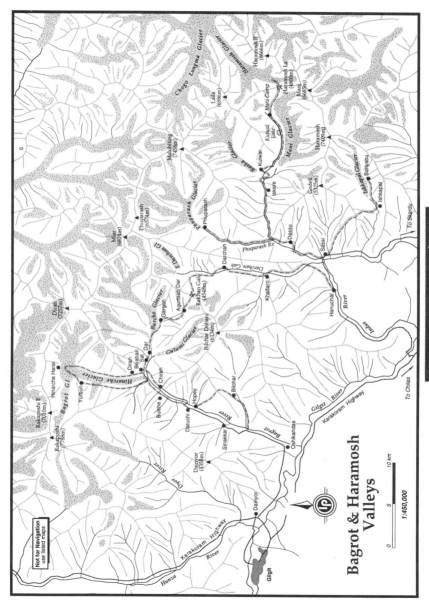

Bagrot & Haramosh Valleys

Not for Navigation
use listed maps

0   5   10 km

1:450,000

Gilgit (NI 43-2) sheet shows Kutwal Lake and the lower Bagrot Valley. Both of these maps are necessary for the Rakhan Gali trek. Leomann's 1:200,000 *Karakoram Trekking and Mountaineering* maps *Sheet 1: (Gilgit, Hunza, Rakaposhi, Batura)* also shows the area.

Regulations
Foreigners are allowed to trek anywhere in this open zone. Neither a permit from the Tourism Division nor a licensed mountain guide is required.

Accommodation & Supplies
The *Bagrote Sarai* (☎ 37 Oshikandas) in Chirah village has a restaurant, rooms, and grassy camp sites and welcomes all visitors. In Sassi, on the Gilgit-Skardu road, is a restaurant at the petrol pump.

GETTING THERE & AWAY
Chirah – Bagrot Valley
Cargo jeeps cost Rs 20 and depart from Garhi Bagh in Gilgit, around midday, and return early the next morning. Special jeeps charge Rs 600 to drop you in Bagrot and Rs 900 return. Do not take the bus to Jalalabad, which has no connections up the Bagrot Valley. On the improved jeep road, it only takes about 1¼ hours to Sinakkar, 1½ hours to Datuchi, and two hours to reach Chirah.

Dainyor
Suzukis go regularly from the Gilgit bazaar via the suspension bridge over the Hunza River and tunnel.

Hanuchal & Sassi
Hanuchal and Sassi are along the Gilgit-Skardu road about 1½ hours from Gilgit; Hanuchal is west of Sassi. Daily NATCO and Mashabrum Tours buses travelling between Gilgit and Skardu pass through them. Most vehicles stop at Sassi for fuel. A daily wagon costs Rs 30 and goes to Sassi in mid-afternoon from Garhi Bagh in Gilgit, and comes back from Sassi around 7 am the next day.

GUIDES & PORTERS
The maximum low-altitude porter's wage is Rs 160 per stage plus wāpāsi and food rations. Local guides can be found in Chirah and in Datuchi villages in the Bagrot Valley, many have worked as scholars' assistants and are happy to share their knowledge of local lore.

DIRAN BASE CAMP
(4 days; mid-June to September)
Hinarche Harai is the local name for Diran base camp. Two routes lead to Hinarche Harai from the head of the Bagrot Valley. The main trail follows the east margin of the Hinarche Glacier from Chirah and crosses the upper Hinarche Glacier to the base camp.

The other route begins in Bulche, follows the west margin of the Hinarche Glacier to Yurbun, a seasonal village in a grassy ablation valley, and then crosses the Bagrot Glacier. Because this route is longer, more heavily crevassed and requires roping up, it is less frequently used. The six hour walk to Yurbun, however, is pleasant through forest and cultivated areas.

Guides & Porters
A local guide can show you the way across the glacier safely to base camp.

Map Notes
Place names along the Hinarche Glacier are not shown on any maps. Hinarche Harai is mistakenly shown as being in the middle of the upper Hinarche Glacier.

Route Description
Day 1: Chirah to Biyabari (2 hours) From Chirah, follow the trail along the true left bank of the Bagrot River, past the confluence with the Hinarche Glacier stream. Cross the Burche Glacier stream on a good bridge to its true right (north) bank. Biyabari, a grassy area with chir pine trees, is just beneath Diran village along the east margin of the Hinarche Glacier.

Day 2: Biyabari to Hinarche Hari (10 to 12 hours) Several slides along the east margin of the Hinarche Glacier make this a long walk. At the end of the long ablation valley, cross the upper Hinarche Glacier in one to two hours to Hinarche Harai, a summer settlement with livestock and huts.

Days 3 & 4 Retrace the route back to the road head at Chirah.

RAKHAN GALI
(3 to 4 days; mid-June to mid-September)
Rakhan Gali (4548m) is a pass that connects the Bagrot and Haramosh valleys. It is seldom used because locals prefer to travel by road. The east side is extremely steep.

Guides & Porters
Since the Rakhan Gali is the boundary of Bagrot territory, larger trekking parties need to switch porters there. Bagrot porters carry from Chirah to Rakhan Gali and Haramosh porters carry from Rakhan Gali to the Gilgit-Skardu road. This can be accomplished by sending a message in advance to Khaltaro village. Smaller parties with only a few porters may not need to do so.

Map Notes
The summer settlements on either side of the Rakhan Gali are not shown on the Swiss map.

Route Description
Day 1: Chirah to Gargoh (4 to 5 hours) From Chirah, a trail climbs the east side of the valley above the Hinarche Glacier, then drops to the silty stream coming from the Burche Glacier. Cross this stream on a good bridge and ascend through Sat village, whose fields and forests hug the north side of the Burche Valley. Continue to Dar, a summer settlement, two to three hours from Chirah. From Dar, descend to the Burche Glacier. The trail moves onto the glacier and in about 1.5 km it divides. One branch head east to the Rakhan Gali and the other heads north off the glacier. The north branch follows a clear stream through a pretty valley bustling with logging activity. Beyond this valley are summer pastures and glaciers at

the base of Miar peaks (6824m). From these pastures, it is also possible to do a day hike or to camp on the ridge that rises to the north. Continue south along the east branch of the trail about two hours over the moraine-covered Burche glacier to Gargoh. These shepherds' huts are along the south margin of the Burche Glacier, in a level area with trees and plentiful water.

Day 2: Gargoh to Agurtsab Dar (2 to 3 hours) Continue south and east up the Gargoh Valley two to three hours to Agurtsab Dar, a good high camp with water from a clear stream. This high pasture has no shepherds' huts.

Day 3: Agurtsab Dar to Ber or Darchan (5 to 6 hours) Agurtsab Dar to the top of Rakhan Gali takes three hours, following the stream up to the pass. The last grass ends 1½ hours above Agurtsab Dar after which the route ascends over tedious scree and rock. Expect to find some snow in the saddle. From the pass, descend very steeply two to three hours to Ber, a high pasture used by Darchan herders. Darchan summer settlement is one to 1½ hours further down this charming sylvan valley.

Day 4: Ber or Darchan to Hanuchal (6 to 7 hours) Continue down the Darchan Gah on a trail to Khaltaro, the main village, three hours from Ber. The main trail continues three to four hours to Hanuchal on the KKH.

KUTWAL LAKE
(6 days; mid-June to September)
Kutwal Lake (3260m) nestles along the north margin of the Mani Glacier, surrounded by green meadows and pine and birch forest, with good views of Mani (6685m) and Haramosh. The trek to Kutwal Lake is easy and often done after the Rakhan Gali (see above). Above Kutwal Lake, the trail continues towards the Haramosh La (4800m), a technical pass, to the Chogo Lungma Glacier. The Haramosh La is usually crossed from east to west, from the

Chogo Lungma Glacier (see Basha, Tormik & Stak Valleys in the Baltistan chapter).

Guides & Porters

8 stages: Sassi to Dassu, Dassu to Iskere, Iskere to Kutwal village, Kutwal village to Kutwal Lake, and return via the same route

Map Notes

The village marked as Dache on maps is also referred to as Dassu.

Route Description

Day 1: Sassi to Dassu From Sassi, head down river one or two km where the jeep road to Dassu turns north off the main Gilgit-Skardu road by the bridge over the Phuparash River. Follow the jeep road along the Phuparash River to Dassu village, on the bluffs above the east side of the river.

Day 2: Dassu to Iskere The trail stays on the true left bank to Iskere. Climb steeply then continue to Iskere (2500m). Dassu villagers live here from May to December grazing livestock and cutting timber. About one km above Iskere is a good camp site near the mouth of the Mani Glacier with views up the Baska Glacier, and of Malubiting, Laila, and Haramosh peaks.

Day 3: Iskere to Kutwal Village From Iskere, cross the river over a bridge to Gure, a south-facing summer pasture. Continue east crossing the Baska Glacier outflow to Kutwal summer village.

Day 4: Kutwal Village to Kutwal Lake Walk along the north margin of the Mani Glacier to Kutwal Lake.

Days 5 & 6: Kutwal Lake to Sassi Retrace your steps down valley to Sassi.

OTHER ROUTES
Sinakkar to Dainyor

This three day route links Sinakkar village in the Bagrot Valley to Dainyor village on the KKH. The route should be mostly snow-free between mid-June and mid-September,

though it is best to go when shepherds are in the pastures from late June to late August. Hire Sinakkar villagers who work as local guides-cum-porters to show the way since the route is not shown on any map. On the first day, go from Sinakkar to Walo, the summer pasture for Sinakkar's herders in four to five hours.

The next day cross the 4000m ridge with views of Nanga Parbat and descend to Munugah, the summer pasture for Dainyor villagers in about five or six hours. The next day, descend to Dainyor in four or five hours. Dainyor, a mostly Ismaili Muslim village, has some interesting historical items. Overlooking the Hunza River is a shrine to a 14th-century Shia preacher, Sultan Alib. A rock with 8th-century Sanskrit inscriptions is on the property of Rafid Ullah, who shows it for a few rupees.

Hopey to Bilchar

This day hike begins in Hopey village, in the Bagrot Valley, and heads south-east over a 3100m ridge to Bilchar village (2300m) in the Bilchar Gah. Trekkers meet local herders and have fine views of Bilchar Dobani (6134m). It takes three to four hours to reach Taisot and another hour to descend to Bilchar.

Ishkapal Glacier

The approach to Haramosh base camp starts from Sassi village, crosses the Chonga ridge (3300m), then descends to Ishkapal village (2740m). From Ishkapal, it is a short walk up the south margin of the Ishkapal Glacier to Bariyabu (3600m), beneath the south-west face of Haramosh.

Phuparash Glacier

Attractive Phuparash (6574m) peak is visible from the start of this trek. From Sassi, head up valley to Dassu. Beyond Dassu cross the river and follow the true left (east) bank of the Phuparash River to Phuparash pastures. It is usually done in two days. Miar, the Phuparash peaks, and Malubiting (7200m) form a very imposing, steep corniced wall above the glacier.

Nanga Parbat

Nanga Parbat (8125m), the westernmost peak of the Great Himalayan range, is one of five 8000m peaks in Pakistan. This 20-km-long series of peaks and ridges forms a huge massif. Its solitary white appearance, visible from the south for at least 100 km, prompted the name Nanga Parbat, which means 'the Naked Mountain'. It is also known as the 'Killer Mountain' because of the difficulties of reaching the summit. The first ascent was an almost miraculous solo ascent without oxygen in 1953 by the German Hermann Buhl. Its sheer south face, called the Rupal face, rises over 5000m from the valley floor to the summit and offers trekkers breathtaking close-up views. The north or Raikhot face plunges over 7000m from the summit to the Indus River, forming one of the world's deepest gorges.

The Rupal Valley, on the south side of Nanga Parbat, is accessed via the Astor Valley, which leaves the KKH at Jaglot 60 km south of Gilgit. Short, easy routes lead east to the Deosai Plains (see Deosai Mountains & Plains in the Baltistan chapter).

The north side of the mountain is accessed from the Raikhot Gah and the well-known Fairy Meadows. Many short treks and climbs are possible here. A longer route around the mountain is best done clockwise, beginning from the Rupal Valley.

INFORMATION
Maps
The US AMS *India and Pakistan Series U502* 1:250,000 *Gilgit (NI 43-2)* sheet shows the entire Nanga Parbat massif, the Astor and Rupal valleys, the Mazeno La, and Raikhot Gah. The excellent Deutscher Alpenverein (DAV) 1:50,000 *Nanga Parbat – Gruppe* map does not show the region west of the Mazeno La or the Diamir, Bunar, Gunar, and Patro valleys (ie, the region west of the Jalipur peaks).

Regulations
Foreigners are allowed to trek anywhere in this open zone. Neither a permit from the Tourism Division nor a licensed mountain guide is required.

Accommodation & Supplies
Some food is available in Astor and Raikhot, but plan to bring everything from Gilgit.

Astor Valley Astor village is along both banks of the Rama Gah. The bazaar is on the north side; the road continues on the south side. The *Dreamland Tourist Inn* at the top of the bazaar has dorms for Rs 50 and a garden for camping; doubles with shared toilet cost Rs 200. Other hotels are cheaper; the *Rama* and the *Tourist Cottage* have doubles with toilet for about Rs 70, and basic restaurants. The *NAPWD Rest House* in Astor and in Rama can be booked with the Executive Engineer in Astor or in Gilgit.

Fairy Meadows The *Raikhot Sarai* has two and four-person tents, toilet facilities, a semi-permanent kitchen and a dining area. Staff arrange day-long hikes and treks and can provide everything. Rates range up to Rs 600 per day per person. Reservations should be made at least two weeks in advance at (☎ (051) 216117; fax (051) 216116), F-7/2, Street 15, Centre-One, Islamabad.

Tarashing The *Nanga Parbat Tourist Cottage* costs about Rs 50 per bed. It has a kitchen and you can camp in the garden.

GETTING THERE & AWAY
Astor Valley
At Jaglot the road to Astor leaves the KKH and crosses a bridge over the Indus River and heads 40 km south-east up the narrow Astor Valley. Vehicles go all day from Gilgit's general bus stand to Jaglot for about Rs 20,

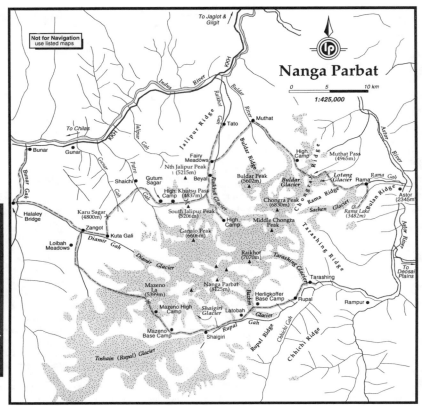

from where passenger jeeps go regularly to Astor. Occasionally vehicles go direct Gilgit-Astor and cost about Rs 50. Special hires Gilgit-Astor cost Rs 1600. Astor is about six hours from Gilgit.

Chilas
Vehicles go regularly from Gilgit's general bus stand and cost Rs 50.

Tarashing – Rupal Valley
A special hire is the easiest way to reach Tarashing from Gilgit. Passenger jeeps go occasionally Astor-Tarashing.

Raikhot Bridge on KKH
About 80 km south of Gilgit or 50 km east of Chilas on the KKH, the Raikhot bridge spans the Indus River. A special jeep Gilgit-Raikhot bridge costs about Rs 1500. From the bridge you can then hire a local special jeep to Tato (see below).

Tato – Raikhot Gah
From the Raikhot bridge, a special jeep for the 15 km to Tato costs Rs 700 and takes 1½ hours. These rates are fixed and are usually not negotiable. Do not hire a special jeep Gilgit-Tato, which costs Rs 2100, unless

the driver is from Tato. 'Outside' jeeps are not allowed beyond the Raikhot bridge to Tato unless you pay an additional Rs 700 to the local jeep drivers' union at the Raikhot bridge. When you hike in, the climb from the Raikhot bridge to Tato (2600m) takes about four hours. It is usually extremely hot and dry, so start before dawn.

GUIDES & PORTERS

The maximum low-altitude porter's wage is Rs 120 per stage plus wāpāsi. Porters do not ask for the clothing and equipment allowance. Porters expect large parties to buy a goat at Shaigiri in the Rupal Valley.

FAIRY MEADOWS

(3 to 6 days; May to mid-October)
Fairy Meadows (3200m), amid pine forests in the Raikhot Gah on the north side of Nanga Parbat, has spectacular views of Nanga Parbat's north face and the Raikhot Glacier and ice fall. The Raikhot Gah flows north and joins the Indus River at the Raikhot bridge. The walk to the meadows is very easy. Beyond the meadows are day hikes, short treks, and mountaineering peaks. It is also the end of one version of the Around Nanga Parbat trek over the Mazeno La (see below).

Guides & Porters

Regardless of whether your porters walk or ride in a jeep between the Raikhot bridge and Tato, you pay all porters for the one stage from the Raikhot bridge to Tato in both directions. This hardly seems fair, but it is the fixed position of the local porters' union.

6 stages: Raikhot to Tato, Tato to Fairy Meadows, Fairy Meadows to Beyal and return via the same route

Side trip to Nanga Parbat Base Camp 4 stages: Beyal to Nanga Parbat base camp, Nanga Parbat base camp to Camp 1, and return via the same route

Map Notes

Beyal is not on any maps. On the DAV map, Nanga Parbat (north) base camp is marked

Hauptlager (high camp) and Fairy Meadows as Marchen Wiese.

Route Description

Day 1: Tato to Fairy Meadows (2 to 3 hours) The jeep road presently ends near Tato and is under construction to Fairy Meadows. It is a gentle walk up the Raikhot Gah to Fairy Meadows (3306m), overlooking the Raikhot Glacier to the south.

Day 2: Fairy Meadows to Beyal (1 to 2 hours) This short stage is an easy stroll through meadows and pine forest to Beyal (about 3500m), typically a less crowded camp site.

Day 3: Beyal to Tato (2 to 4 hours) Retrace your steps down valley to the road head at Tato.

Side Trip: Beyal to Nanga Parbat (North) Base Camp & Camp 1

It takes two to three days to visit Nanga Parbat (north) base camp for impressive views of its north face and of Raikhot Peak (7070m). From Beyal, continue south along the west margin of the forested valley, crossing the snout of the Ganalo Glacier. Follow the trail to flower-filled meadows, beyond which is the Drexel Monument to German climbers killed on Nanga Parbat and the base camp (3967m), about four hours from Beyal beneath Raikhot and Ganalo (6606m) peaks. A large spring flows from under a boulder here. From base camp, the more adventurous trekkers can continue two hours to Camp 1 for more big vistas. The route ascends steeply 500m over snow-free moraine. At Camp 1 you are right under Silberzacken (7597m), Raikhot and Chongra (6830m) peaks. The next day, retrace your steps down valley to Beyal in four to six hours.

Side Trip: Beyal to Climb South Jalipur Peak

South Jalipur Peak (5206m) is west of the Raikhot Gah and south of the Khutsu (Jalipur) Pass (4837m). From Beyal, it takes two days for this trip. Continue up the west margin of the Raikhot Glacier and head east, ascending to the pass and placing a high camp on its west side. The next day, make the day-long technical ascent of South Jalipur Peak and descend to Beyal to camp.

Side Trip: Beyal to Climb Buldar Peak

Buldar Peak (5602m) is east of the Raikhot Glacier across from Beyal. The technical ascent of Buldar Peak takes two days from Beyal. Cross the Raikhot Glacier and place a high camp below the ridge. The next day, the ascent is via Buldar cleft, then up the ridge line to the summit, returning to camp in Beyal.

Side Trip: Fairy Meadows to Gunar on KKH

From Fairy Meadows, it is possible to return to the KKH at Gunar in three days. Head north-west and cross the Jalipur ridge (4062m). On the first day, camp in Baizer in the Jalipur Valley and the next day in Khustu.

RUPAL VALLEY

(5 days; June to October)

This short and relatively easy trek brings you directly beneath the awesome south face of Nanga Parbat, known as the Rupal face. The Rupal Valley, though popular, is less visited than Fairy Meadows. A very narrow jeep road goes up the Rupal Valley from the Astor Valley.

Guides & Porters

6 stages: Tarashing to Herligkoffer base camp, Herligkoffer base camp to Latobah, Latobah to Shaigiri, and return via the same route

Map Notes

The Tarashing Glacier is called Chhungphar on the U502 *Gilgit (NI 43-2)* sheet.

Route Description

Day 1: Tarashing to Herligkoffer Base Camp (5 hours) From Tarashing, climb the lateral moraine of the Tarashing Glacier, near the northern edge of the village, and cross the glacier on a clear trail. Continue up the gentle valley through Rupal village.

Rising gradually through the lush fields of Rupal, the trail follows the north side of the valley to Herligkoffer base camp (3656m), a beautiful, though much used meadow along the east margin of the Bazhin Glacier. In 1982, JM met Dr Herligkoffer here leading a Nanga Parbat South Pillar expedition. A large spring bubbles up here and a huge boulder marks the kitchen site for trekking parties. An optional hike up this ablation valley takes several hours to a point on the moraine ridge directly above the Bazhin Glacier and across from the huge ice fall coming from the summit.

Day 2: Herligkoffer Base Camp to Latobah (2 hours) Cross the Bazhin Glacier over a trail in about 1½ hours to reach Latobah, the broad, level meadows frequented by Rupal herders. Latobah is also known as Tupp Meadows.

Day 3: Latobah to Shaigiri (4 hours) The trail stays to the north of the Rupal Gah, skirting a terminal moraine with a silty lake on top. Continue through a series of alluvial fans and then skirt the terminal moraine of the Shaigiri Glacier. Just beyond is Shaigiri (3655m), a summer settlement marked by a white boulder *(shaigiri* means 'white rock' in Shina) with more awesome views of the south face.

Days 4 & 5: Return to Tarashing Retrace your steps down valley to Tarashing. Unless you prearrange transport to meet you or find a jeep in Tarashing, you have to walk towards Astor to find transport.

AROUND NANGA PARBAT VIA MAZENO LA

(8 to 12 days; mid-June to September)

The trek commonly called 'Around Nanga Parbat' does not actually go all the way 'around' Nanga Parbat. Instead it goes halfway around Nanga Parbat, beginning on the south side of Nanga Parbat from Tarashing in the Rupal Valley. The route heads west up the Rupal Valley, and turns north to cross the Mazeno La to Zangot. From Zangot two routes exist. A shorter two day trek descends the Diamir and Bunar valleys to Bunar on the KKH. A more strenuous route heads northeast from Zangot, crossing two more passes to Fairy Meadows in the Raikhot Gah.

The Mazeno La is known for its technical difficulties and rock-fall danger, primarily on the north side of the pass. Experienced guides say most trekkers do not succeed in crossing the Mazeno La. Hence, this should be attempted only by experienced trekkers with basic mountaineering skills. Bring at least 300m of rope and crevasse rescue gear along with proper equipment for your guide, trek crew, and porters. Some guides feel too much snow is on the route in June and July and that the ideal time to trek is early August to the third week of September. Be sure you are properly acclimatised before attempting to cross the Mazeno La (5399m). Spend a few more days in the upper Rupal Valley if necessary.

Guides & Porters
A guide and porters are strongly recommended. An experienced Shina-speaking guide from Chilas who can manage the complex porter situations and who knows the less obvious routes over the passes is best. An armed local escort for the Diamir, Bunar, and Gunar valleys is recommended. It is necessary to change porters as you pass through different valleys. The first group of porters, usually hired in Tarashing, goes as far as the Mazeno La. Here these porters are replaced by ones from Bunar. To coordinate this change of porters, you must make arrangements with the shopkeeper in Bunar before your trek begins, telling him how many porters you need on the Mazeno La on what date. He then arranges for porters to meet you. The Bunar porters either take you to the KKH or to Shaichī when you continue to Fairy Meadows from Zangot. Then in Shaichī, Gunar porters replace the Bunar ones. These complex logistics are mandatory for large trekking parties. Otherwise, locals may not allow the party to proceed. However, a few trekkers can usually get by

without changing porters. Regardless, trekkers must be prepared to change porters and be prepared for the financial consequences. Each group of porters is paid wāpāsi, making this an expensive route!

Tarashing to Zangot and Bunar on KKH 11 stages: Tarashing to Herligkoffer base camp, Herligkoffer base camp to Latobah, Latobah to Shaigiri, Shaigiri to Mazeno La base camp, Mazeno La base camp to Mazeno high camp, Mazeno high camp to the top of Mazeno La, Mazeno La to upper Loibah, upper Loibah to Loibah meadows, Loibah meadows to Zangot, Zangot to Halaley bridge, Halaley bridge to Bunar Das

Alternative route – Tarashing to Zangot & Fairy Meadows 18 stages: 9 stages Tarashing to Zangot as above plus 9 stages: Zangot to Kutagali, Kutagali to Karu Sagar, Karu Sagar to Shaichī, Shaichī to Gutum Sagar, Gutum Sagar to Jalipur base camp, Jalipur base camp to Beyal, Beyal to Fairy Meadows, Fairy Meadows to Tato, Tato to Raikhot bridge

Map Notes
The pass, Karu Sagar, is shown on the U502 *Gilgit (NI 43-2)* sheet as Kachal Gali and Kutagali as Kachal. The pass between North and South Jalipur peaks is not named on maps, but on the DAV map it is marked as 4837m. Locally, this pass is called the Khutsu Pass.

Route Description
Days 1 & 2: Tarashing to Shaigiri Camp at either Herligkoffer base camp or Latobah en route to Shaigiri (see Rupal Valley above).

Day 3: Shaigiri to Mazeno Base Camp (3 to 5 hours) Beyond Shaigiri, the trail follows the north margin of the Toshain (Rupal) Glacier, crossing several streams before reaching Mazeno base camp, below the southern terminus of the Mazeno Glacier.

Day 4: Mazeno Base Camp to Mazeno High Camp (4 to 6 hours) The route turns sharply north and climbs steeply towards the Mazeno La (5399m). The high camp (4700m) is along the east margin of the glacier.

Day 5: Mazeno High Camp to Upper Loibah Meadows (6 to 8 hours) Ascend along the north-east margin of the Mazeno Glacier, crossing it higher up, and reach the pass in about three hours. The descent is very steep and technical for about 300m to the upper Loibah Glacier. Continue down the glacier to the upper Loibah meadows (4200m).

Day 6: Upper Loibah Meadows to Zangot (5 to 6 hours) Descend the valley passing through Loibah meadows to Zangot.

Day 7: Zangot to Halaley Bridge (3 to 4 hours) Descend north-west down the Diamir Gah to its junction with the Bunar Gah and camp near the Halaley bridge.

Day 8: Halaley Bridge to Bunar (3 to 4 hours) Descend the Bunar Gah to Bunar on the KKH. From Bunar transport is available east to Chilas or up the KKH to Gilgit.

Alternative Route: Zangot to Fairy Meadows
Instead of heading down the Diamir and Bunar valleys to the KKH in two days, you can continue in six days from Zangot to reach Fairy Meadows in the Raikhot Gah.

Day 7: Zangot to Kutagali (3 to 4 hours) Climb along the stream to the summer settlement at Kutagali (about 3000m). From Kutagali, an optional hike several hours up valley to the Diamir Glacier offers closer views of Nanga Parbat's west face.

Day 8: Kutagali to Shaichī (5 to 6 hours) Climb steadily to the Karu Sagar Pass (about 4800m) and descend to Shaichī (*shaich* means 'field' in Shina) and the Patro Valley.

Day 9: Shaichī to Gutum Sagar (5 to 6 hours) Head up the Patro Valley through forest, crossing side streams for a few hours to the summer pastures of Gunar villagers. Ganalo Peak (6606m) dominates the views. Continue up valley to the pastures of Gutum Sagar (3500m).

Day 10: Gutum Sagar to Jalipur High Camp (4 to 6 hours) Ascend along a stream through the meadows of the bowl below the Jalipur peaks and make a high camp (about 4400m). It is possible to climb the technical South Jalipur Peak (5206m) in one day from this high camp.

Day 11: Jalipur High Camp to Beyal (6 to 8 hours) Climb steeply east towards the east-west Khutsu Pass (4837m), between North Jalipur Peak (5215m) and South Jalipur Peak. Climb a steep talus slope for one to two hours, emerging near a snowfield. The Nanga Parbat massif is visible from the pass. The descent is also steep on loose talus for about one hour to meadows that lead past willows and forest to the Raikhot Gah. Follow the west margin of the Raikhot Glacier to Beyal, reaching Beyal about four hours from the pass. A side trip to Nanga Parbat (north) base camp and Camp 1 is possible (See Fairy Meadows – Side Trip to Nanga Parbat Base Camp above).

Day 12: Beyal to Tato (2 to 4 hours) Enjoy the easy walk to Fairy Meadows and on to Tato.

OTHER ROUTES
Rama Lake
Rama Lake (3482m) lies along the south margin of the Sachen Glacier above Rama about six km west of Astor (2345m) in the Astor Valley. A jeep road goes to Rama, 1200m above Astor, so unless you want to walk, hire a special jeep for about Rs 500 or Rs 600 to the lake. A two or three day visit to the lake (shown as Sango Sar See on the DAV map) and the surrounding area takes you through flower-filled meadows and pine, fir, cedar and juniper forests with spectacular views of the Chongra peaks (over 6400m).

Fairy Meadows to Astor
After successfully crossing the Mazeno La from the Rupal Valley and continuing on to Fairy Meadows (see Around Nanga Parbat via Mazeno La above), a circumambulation

of Nanga Parbat can be completed by continuing clockwise from Fairy Meadows to the Astor Valley. This route is more technically difficult than the Mazeno La and should only be considered by experienced trekkers with mountaineering skills in the company of an experienced local guide who knows the route.

From Fairy Meadows in the Raikhot Gah, head north-east over a ridge (3362m) and descend to a stream, then cross the Buldar River to Muthat village (3000m). From Muthat, follow the south-east margin of the Buldar Glacier to about 4000m. Then ascend the difficult route up a crevassed glacier to the Muthat Pass (4965m). Descend steeply to the Lotang Glacier, following its north margin to a point where you can cross to its south side. A ridge separates the Lotang Glacier from the Sachen Glacier above Rama and Astor in the Astor Valley to the east. The route over the ridge is not obvious.

Kaghan Valley to Indus River

The 160-km-long Kaghan Valley is renowned for its alpine lakes nestled among 4000m and 5000m peaks. At the head of the valley is the Babusar Pass, over which runs a jeep road to Chilas on the Indus River. The mountains here are part of the Greater Himalaya range. Most trekkers only glimpse Kaghan's vast meadows and sparkling lakes from the air while flying to or from Gilgit. Every year a few trekkers walk this road as an alternative to the long road trip on the KKH. The alpine plateau of Babusar and Lulusar amply rewards those who do.

The Kaghan Valley is formed by the Kunhar River, but the valley takes its name from Kaghan village. The Kunhar is regarded as perhaps Pakistan's finest trout stream. Along its steep lower sections are dense pine forests where logging is an important activity with timbers floated down the river to mills below. Kaghan is in the Hazara District of the NWFP. The local language is Hindko, similar to Punjabi, with Pushtu and Urdu also widely spoken. The upland meadows attract Gujars, nomadic herders who bring their flocks each spring in a colourful migration.

INFORMATION
Maps
The US AMS *India and Pakistan Series U502* 1:250,000 *Gilgit (NI 43-2)* sheet shows the Indus River valley, the Babusar Pass, and Dudibach and Lulusar lakes. The *Srinagar (NI 43-6)* sheet shows the Kaghan Valley up to Burawai and the Saral lakes.

Regulations
Foreigners are allowed to trek anywhere in this open zone. Neither a permit from the Tourism Division nor a licensed mountain guide is required. Fishing permits are available in Naran at the Fisheries Office off the main road, on the road to Saiful Mulk.

Foreigners are not allowed to enter the Neelum Valley in Azad Jammu & Kashmir, east of the Kaghan Valley, without a permit from the Azad Jammu & Kashmir Home Department in Muzaffarabad.

Accommodation & Supplies
Diamir District Rest houses can be booked with the NAPWD Executive Engineer (☎ 515) on Ranoi Rd in Chilas.

Babusar Village Babusar has a primitive *NAPWD Rest House* and a few shops.

Chilas Most hotels are along the KKH. The town and old bazaar are three km above on a plateau. In the old bazaar the *Deluxe Hotel* (☎ 208), the *Hamalaya* (☎ 209) next door and the *Khanjrab* (☎ 290, no English sign) at the top of Hospital Rd, have charpoys for about Rs 50. A *NAPWD Rest House* is west of the bazaar. The *Kashmir Inn* (☎ 315) is on the KKH with doubles/triples with toilet and cold shower for Rs 100/150. Nearby, the *New Shimla Hotel* (☎ 212) costs Rs 120/180. Also on the KKH, singles/doubles at the *Chilas Inn* (☎ 211) cost Rs 525/600, and Rs

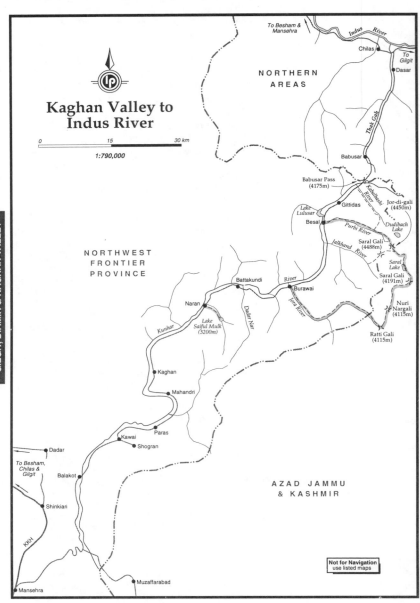

GILGIT, DIAMIR & KAGHAN VALLEY

450/600 at the *Panorama Hotel Chilas*. Across the KKH is the *Shangri-La Midway House Hotel*, which can be booked in Rawalpindi (☎ (051) 538657-8 and 73006) and Peshawar (☎ (0521) 272085 and 276035), where singles/doubles cost from Rs 960/1160.

Kaghan Valley Most rest houses in Kaghan are booked well in advance. Pakistan Youth Hostels tend to be full and run-down. The DFO in Balakot can book some Forestry rest houses as can the Kaghan Valley Project Director in Abbottabad (☎ (05921) 2893). Most are booked through the NWFP Forestry Ministry in Peshawar (☎ (0521) 217025). The C&W rest houses are booked through the NWFP Construction & Works Ministry in Peshawar (☎ (0521) 70455). Balakot, Shogran, Kaghan, Naran, and Burawai are all in the Kaghan Valley.

Balakot Balakot is of little interest except for information and transportation. The *PTDC Motel* (☎ (05987) 208) at the south end of town has doubles for Rs 450 and a tourist information centre. Staff there can arrange jeeps and recommend guides. The police, post office, telephone exchange and hospital are nearby. The *Mashriq Hotel* has barren doubles for Rs 50. The *Pakistan Youth Hostel*, near the hospital, costs Rs 25 per bed. *Kuh-i-Noor* and *Taj Mahal* have doubles for Rs 100. At the *Balakot Hotel* doubles cost Rs 150. The *Park Hotel* doubles cost Rs 250.

Shogran Lovely Shogran, 24 km north of Balakot and 10 km off the main road east from Kawai, has two *Forestry Rest Houses*: one booked through Abbottabad, the other through Peshawar.

Kaghan This dreary place has some cheap hotels and a *Forestry Rest House*, which can been booked through Peshawar. The *Lalazar Hotel* has doubles from Rs 400. The *Vershigoom Hotel* is a bit cheaper.

Naran Naran is the jumping-off point for trips up valley. In the summer it is jam

packed with domestic tourists. Singles/doubles at the *PTDC Motel* (☎ 2) cost Rs 800/900; cottages cost from Rs 1100. The *Sarhad*, *Zam Zam*, *Pakistan*, *Shalimar*, *Madina*, and *Frontier* cost Rs 200 and up when busy. Two *C&W Rest Houses* can be booked in Peshawar. There are two *Forestry Rest Houses*; the old one is booked in Abbottabad, and the new one in Peshawar. The *Lalazar*, *Naran*, and *New Park* hotels have doubles from Rs 400.

Burawai Burawai has several shops and a *C&W Rest House*.

GETTING THERE & AWAY
Babusar Village
NATCO pickup trucks ply the 39-km-long road Babusar-Chilas for Rs 30.

Chilas
Vehicles Gilgit-Chilas cost about Rs 40 and leave from Gilgit's general bus stand every few hours. Get off any Islamabad/Rawalpindi-Gilgit vehicle at the police check post on the KKH and catch a ride three km to town.

Kaghan Valley
From Islamabad, it is a one or an easy two-day drive. If making the trip in two days, try spending the first night in scenic Shogran, and the next day drive to Naran or beyond. At Mansehra, the road to the Kaghan Valley leaves the KKH and heads north-east. The road follows the Kunhar River through Balakot, the main town in the valley, to Kaghan and Naran. Buses and wagons go all morning to the Kaghan Valley from the bus stands along Abbottabad Rd in Mansehra. Fares cost Rs 15 Mansehra-Balakot, and Rs 25 Balakot-Naran by bus or Rs 45 by wagon. Buses and wagons go to Kaghan and Naran all day from Balakot. From Naran, passenger jeeps go up valley during the summer to Battakundi, Burawai and Besal. Naran-Burawai costs Rs 50. Special hires Naran-Burawai cost Rs 600, and Rs 3000 Naran-Chilas.

GUIDES & PORTERS

The maximum low-altitude porter's wage is Rs 120 per stage plus wāpāsi and food rations. Make sure any guide or porter is reliable by hiring through PTDC, on trustworthy recommendations, and in the presence of others.

LAKE SAIFUL MULK

(1 to 2 days; mid-June to September)
Most visitors to Kaghan make the day hike from Naran to Lake Saiful Mulk (3200m). The lake lies amid flowered meadows, surrounded by glacier-clad peaks. Above its far shore rises Malika Parbat (5290m), the Queen of the Mountains, which is Kaghan's highest peak. Legend has it that fairies would gather at the lake to dance on moonlit nights. A young prince caught a glimpse of them and fell in love with the fairy princess. The illicit love between the fairy and the mortal human ended tragically, and the lake is named for the prince, Saif ul Mulk. This fairy realm has lately become spoiled by human visitors, who thoughtlessly leave rubbish along the lake shore. A small rest house and several tea stalls mark the spot.

Route Description

From Naran, follow the 10-km-long jeep road up through forest three hours to the lake. Walk an hour around the lake to camp in the meadows below Saiful Mulk Glacier. It is possible to cross the ridge (about 4191m) at the south-west end of the valley and descend steeply into the upper Manūr Valley, which joins the Kunhar Valley at Mahandri, 37 km south of Naran.

BABUSAR PASS

(4 to 6 days; mid-June to September)
The Babusar Pass (4175m) links Kaghan with Chilas on the Indus River to the north. Once the only road linking Gilgit with downcountry Pakistan, it is now an infrequently used jeep track. The grassy plateau area around the pass has many clear lakes, where herders graze their flocks in the summer. The area would make for fine early spring skiing before the herders arrive.

It is 91 km on the jeep road from Naran to Babusar, and the road is usually walked in four days. Trekkers planning to walk over the Babusar Pass will enjoy leaving the boring jeep road and visiting the high lakes south of the pass and east of the jeep road. A two-day side trip to Dudibach Lake from Besal is the easiest option. However, an enjoyable loop leaving the jeep road at Burawai and rejoining it at Besal or Gittidas crosses four easy passes, and adds three days to the walk. We describe this trek below.

Trekkers must be careful not to wander east into the Neelum Valley of Azad Jammu & Kashmir, which is the Pakistan-India ceasefire zone. It is strictly off limits and is a militarised zone. Additionally, villagers in upper Chilas are usually armed and have been hostile to foreigners. Trekkers should be cautious and travel with a trustworthy local guide. An armed escort in upper Chilas is not needed at the time of writing, but the situation should be checked before starting out.

Route Description

Day 1: Burawai to Upper Jora Valley (6 to 8 hours) Burawai is 13 km beyond Battakundi and 26 km up the jeep road from Naran. Follow the good trail south-east up the Jora Valley, passing the stone huts of Jora, and camp in the meadows up valley.

Day 2: Upper Jora Valley to Nuri Nar Camp (4 to 5 hours) At the head of the Jora Valley is Ratti Gali, a 4115m pass leading south-east into the upper Dhorian Valley. The pass marks the boundary between the NWFP and Azad Jammu & Kashmir. Follow the stream down from the pass. At its junction with another stream, turn north and follow up the stream about five km to Nuri Nar Gali, another gentle pass (4115m) leading north to the upper Nuri Valley. Camp in meadows along the stream.

Day 3: Nuri Nar Camp to Saral Lake (5 to 6 hours) Follow the stream down to the main valley, which flows east and down to the Neelum River. A trail leads north-west over

Trekkers camp near the shepherds' huts at Biatar in the Chapursan Valley, the last grassy camp site below the Chilinji An.

Top: Crystal clear Karambar Lake extends over three km through alpine meadows on the crest of Karambar An.

Bottom: South of the Darkot An is an 8-9th century Tibetan inscription commemorating the meritous donation of a stupa.

a pass to Jalkhand River and back to the Kunhar River. Instead, follow the north-east fork as it bends around to the east past a small lake and then north over Saral Gali (4191m) into the upper Saral Valley. Camp near Saral Lake.

Day 4: Saral Lake to Dudibach (4 to 5 hours) From Saral Lake, walk a short way down the stream, then turn west and follow a stream up two km. Here the trail splits. Going west leads shortly to Saral-di-Gali (4488m), a pass to Jalkhand Valley and on to the Kunhar Valley. Going north leads to Jor-di-Gali (4450m) and Dudibach Lake (3962m). As you cross the pass, you re-enter NWFP. Descend to Dudibach and camp near the lake.

Day 5: Dudibach to Lulusar Lake (6 to 7 hours) From Dudibach Lake, descend the Purbi Valley west to Besal in the Kunhar Valley, then head two km up the Kunhar to Lulusar Lake and camp.

Another option is to walk four km down the Purbi Valley west of Dudibach, then head north across a ridge into Kabalbashi Valley. Camp in the upper valley and the next day continue down valley to Gittidas in the Kunhar Valley and over the Babusar Pass. Gittidas, although south of the Babusar Pass, is a Chilasi summer settlement; do not camp near Gittidas.

Day 6: Lulusar Lake to Babusar Village (6 to 8 hours) This is a long day along the road through Gittidas and over the flat Babusar pass to Babusar village. Stay at the NAPWD Rest House, and continue to Chilas the next day.

GILGIT, DIAMIR & KAGHAN VALLEY

Hunza River Valley

The Hunza River, the only river to cut through the Karakoram range, starts from the junction of the Kilik and Khunjerab rivers, and joins the Gilgit River just east of Gilgit. Along its banks are the three areas of Gojal, Hunza, and Nagyr, although 'Hunza' is commonly and inaccurately used to refer to the entire valley.

Before 1972, the valley was divided into the two princely states of Hunza and Nagyr. Hunza included all areas on the north bank of the river, except for Chalt, and all of Gojal. Nagyr included all areas on the south bank plus Chalt, Chaprot, and Bar on the north bank. The valley has three different languages: Shina, spoken in the Shinaki area of Lower Hunza and Lower Nagyr; Burushashki, spoken in Upper Hunza and Upper Nagyr; and Wakhi, spoken in Gojal.

In all of Gojal and almost all of Hunza, people practise Ismaili Islam. In Nagyr, and notably Ganesh village in Hunza, Shia Islam is practised. Old shamanic traditions once common throughout the Karakoram and Hindukush still linger, as do traces of Hinduism and Buddhism. It was through the shamans that humans could contact the fairies, who lived in the pure realm above.

The reputed longevity and extraordinary health of Hunza and Nagyr people is just fiction, originating from the romantic impressions of early 20th-century visitors who found in Hunza the Shangri-la of their dreams. The valley's friendly people and its breathtaking landscape have always impressed visitors.

Above the carefully tended fields of Hunza and Nagyr soars 7788m-high Rakaposhi. Gojal's villages lie in the heart of the Karakoram, where glaciers come right to the edge of the KKH. Although the Hunza River valley is changing rapidly because of the impact of the highway, it remains incomparable and is the main destination of all visitors to the Karakoram and Hindukush.

Highlights – Hunza Valley
The Hunza is the only river to transect the Karakoram. Burusho live in Hunza and Nagyr. Further north, Gogal is home to Wakhi people. The Karakoram Highway provides ready access to the once remote region which is now frequently visited. Remote side valleys in Gogal still have few visitors.

REGIONAL HISTORY

The history of Hunza and Nagyr is largely the history of the rulers, the descendants of Girkis and Moglot. The story begins with the Trakhan dynasty of Gilgit, which also ruled Hunza and Nagyr. The Ra, or king of Gilgit, gave Hunza to his son Girkis, and Nagyr to his son Moglot. The rival brothers fought each other, and Moglot killed Girkis, leaving only Girkis' daughter as heir to the Hunza throne. Alarmed, the Wazir (Prime Minister) of Hunza went in search of a suitable prince. When asked where the young lad he brought back had come from, the Wazir replied 'from *ayesh* (the sky)', and therefore the Hunza dynasty became known as 'Ayesho', or 'skyborn'.

The Nagyr dynasty continued through the sons of Moglot, and the descendants of both dynasties have houses in the old capitals, Baltit and Nagyr, today. The rulers of Hunza and Nagyr were called Tham, or Mir. Through their close affinity with the fairies, whose realm was the sky and the mountains, Thams controlled the weather and ensured agricultural fertility. Ultar peak, which towers above the old Baltit castle, was where the fairy queen lived in a crystal palace.

For most of their history, the tiny kingdoms of Hunza and Nagyr confronted each other across the Hunza River, carrying on the sibling rivalry of Girkis and Moglot through raids and intrigue. In its early days Hunza had only three villages: Altit, Baltit, and Ganesh. The Altit fort is at least 1000 years old. Although Hunza and Nagyr were always linked with Gilgit, by the middle of the 18th century Hunza had moved to forge ties with China, which had annexed Turkestan (now Xinjiang). In 1790 Silum III became Tham in Hunza, and Hunza changed irrevocably.

Silum had spent his youth near the Afghan Pamir, where Ismaili Islam was prevalent. Under his rule, Altit and Baltit adopted Ismaili Islam. Ganesh, however, like neighbouring Nagyr, retained Shia Islam. Silum also brought new canal building techniques, and by constructing new water channels, established the villages of Haiderabad and Aliabad. Hunza expanded in size and strength, and Silum pushed north into Gojal, driving out the Qirghiz nomads and securing the routes to Turkestan. Hunza gained access to the rich trade route between Kashmir and Yarkand, and began raiding caravans. The loot from these raids enriched the Tham, who continued to placate the Chinese governor with annual gifts of gold dust.

As the British empire expanded northwest in the 19th century, independent Hunza became a thorn in its side. A free-booting state that intrigued with Russia and China

and plundered the caravan trade grew intolerable. Hunza, however, was ready to play off one side against the other. Hunza asked China for guns and bullets to fight Kashmir, yet sent a present of gold dust to Kashmir as a sign of loyalty. Britain moved forward in 1877 to control Gilgit and the north-west frontier, yet Hunza continued to send gifts of gold to China and hold talks with Russian emissaries. Finally, in 1891, British and Kashmiri troops forcibly brought Hunza and Nagyr into the colonial fold. The Mir of Nagyr kept his throne, but his son was jailed. The Mir of Hunza fled to Xinjiang, and his stepbrother was installed on the throne.

As part of the colonial empire, Hunza and Nagyr became less involved in Central Asia and more involved with Gilgit and Kashmir. When the British empire ended, Hunza and Nagyr aided in the revolt against the Maharaja of Kashmir and joined Pakistan. The first motor road reached Hunza in 1957, and in 1963, with the Pakistan-China border settlement, Hunza and China gave up all mutual claims on each other's territory. By 1974, Pakistan had fully incorporated both Hunza and Nagyr states into the nation, and the 1000 years of rule by the Mirs came to a close. In 1978 the KKH was completed to Hunza, and with the opening of the Khunjerab Pass in 1986, the valley once again became a vital conduit between Central Asia and South Asia.

GILGIT

The Hunza River valley is part of Gilgit district and Gilgit is the main town in the region. Places to Stay & Eat in Gilgit are detailed in the Gilgit, Diamir & Kaghan Valley chapter.

GETTING THERE & AWAY

You can reach trail heads throughout the Hunza River valley by road from Gilgit to the south and Sost to the north. All villages, except remote Shimshal, are linked by roads to the KKH, which runs along the valley following the Hunza River between Gilgit and Sost. NATCO, Hunza Coach Service, and Neelum Transport run between Gilgit

HUNZA RIVER VALLEY

and Sost several times daily. Rates range up to Rs 100 depending on where you get off (see Getting Around for more information).

Naltar & Pakora Valleys

The green and forested Naltar Valley receives more rainfall than other areas in the Hunza Valley, and its alpine scenery is a refreshing change in the arid Karakoram. The Naltar Valley runs north-west from Nomal village, on the west bank of the Hunza River 25 km north-east of Gilgit. Naltar was a hill station for the British and has some military facilities, including a Pakistan Air Force winter survival school. The peaks above the upper valley attract climbers each year. Sentinel (5260m) is a moderately difficult alpine climb, while Shani peak (5887m) is a very serious mixed rock and snow climb. Trekkers enjoy the meadows up valley, and the Pakora Pass trek from Naltar to Pakora has become a popular walk. Shina-speaking Naltar villagers are both Sunni and Shia Muslims and some tension exists between these communities. Pakora villagers in the Ishkoman Valley are mostly Khowar-speaking Ismaili and Sunni Muslims, and welcome trekkers.

INFORMATION
Maps
The *Swiss Foundation for Alpine Research* 1:250,000 orographical sketch map *Karakoram Sheet 1* accurately shows the Naltar and Pakora valleys and their tributaries. The US AMS *India and Pakistan Series U502* 1:250,000 *Baltit (NJ 43-14)* sheet and *Sheet 1: (Gilgit, Hunza, Rakaposhi, Batura)* of Leomann's 1:200,000 *Karakoram Trekking and Mountaineering* maps depict the region less accurately.

Regulations
Foreigners are allowed to trek anywhere in this open zone. Neither a permit from the Tourism Division nor a licensed mountain guide is required.

Accommodation & Supplies
Little is available in bazaars in these towns, so bring food and supplies from Gilgit.

Chatorkhand Travellers recommend the *NAPWD Rest House* in this, the main village in the Ishkoman Valley.

Naltar Lake The *Lake View Hotel* consists of a hut where food is prepared and a large canvas tent with blankets for sleeping.

Upper Naltar (Dumian) At the *Hilltop Hotel* a room costs from Rs 200 to Rs 300, a bed in the dorm costs Rs 50, and camping costs Rs 30 per tent. *Prince Hotel* costs Rs 50 per bed. The *Pasban Hotel* is on the west side of the river near the Pakistan Air Force winter training school. Two *NAPWD Rest Houses* nearby are heavily used. Book them with the Chief Engineer in Gilgit. Doubles cost from Rs 200, or you can camp on the lawn.

Nomal Nomal has a small, run-down *NAPWD Rest House*. The *Prince Hotel* and *Aliar Hotel* are open in summer.

GETTING THERE & AWAY
From Gilgit, vehicles to Nomal and Naltar go from the general bus stand on Domyal Link Rd, near JSR Plaza just below Mir's Lodge. Those going to Punial and Ishkoman leave from Gilgit's Punial Rd.

Chatorkhand & Pakora
Cargo jeeps leave Pakora for Gilgit early in the morning. The ride takes five to six hours. To book a special jeep to Gilgit you may have to go another nine km south to Chatorkhand.

Naltar & Naltar Lake
Several cargo jeeps go daily to Lower Naltar and cost Rs 20, and Rs 30 to Upper Naltar (Dumian). Special jeeps cost Rs 800. The trip takes two hours. The jeep road continues beyond Upper Naltar to Naltar Lake. Most special hires from Gilgit to Naltar only go as far as Upper Naltar. If you can convince a jeep driver to go all the way to the lake, it costs an additional Rs 700 to Rs 800.

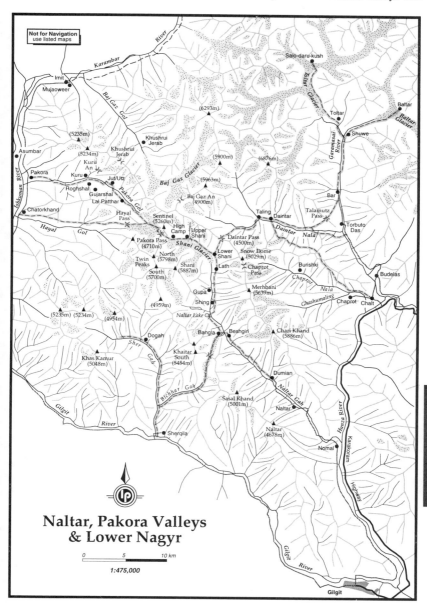

Not for Navigation
use listed maps

Naltar, Pakora Valleys
& Lower Nagyr

0   5   10 km

1:475,000

HUNZA RIVER VALLEY

Nomal

Nomal is 25 km north of Gilgit on an unpaved jeep road that follows the true right bank of the Hunza River. One NATCO bus and three private buses go daily to Nomal. The one hour trip costs Rs 10; buses depart from Gilgit mid-morning, returning the next morning. From Nomal, it takes five to six hours to walk the 16 km to Naltar. A plan to build a bridge over the Hunza River at Nomal, linking these villages to the KKH, is under consideration.

Sherqila

Sherqila is a one hour drive north-west from Gilgit on the north bank of the Gilgit River in Punial. Cargo jeeps go regularly or you can get off the daily NATCO buses to and from Gupis at the bridge to Sherqila.

GUIDES & PORTERS

The maximum low-altitude porter's wage is Rs 160 per stage, not including food rations. You can usually negotiate total wages including food rations between Rs 160 and Rs 200 per stage. Porters also expect large trekking parties to buy a sheep or goat, but smaller parties are usually excused, or at most have to buy a chicken. Wāpāsi is also paid regardless of whether porters walk back to their village or go by road. They ask for a clothing and equipment allowance, but on treks less than one week they usually settle for about Rs 120 per person.

Lower Naltar is Shia, and Upper Naltar is Sunni. Sectarian differences have led to disputes over portering between the two communities. They have 'resolved' this by agreeing that half of all porters for any party should be from Lower Naltar and half from Upper Naltar. This holds true even if you have just two porters. Unfortunately, Lower and Upper Naltar porters do not necessarily get along well on the trek, refusing to eat and sleep together and bickering over the correct trail. Any local tensions tend to be diffused in larger parties, but ask carefully if you plan to trek with just a couple of porters. Try to convince the assembly of prospective porters to select people from just one community,

and for the next small party to select porters from the other community.

PAKORA PASS

(5 days; July to September)

The Pakora Pass (4710m) links the Naltar Gah to the Pakora Gol in the Ishkoman Valley. This 47 km trek is usually done from east to west. It is easily combined with the Asumbar Haghost and then either the Punji Pass or the Thui An, making superb two-week combinations over three spectacular passes (see Ishkoman Valley and Yasin Valley in the Ghizar chapter).

Guides & Porters

Porters are usually willing to negotiate the wage per stage, but not the number of stages or wāpāsi. Porters may load gear on donkeys to Lower Shani and carry it beyond there. A donkey might carry two loads, but wages are still paid per porter per stage and not per donkey. Horses are also available for hire.

6 stages: Upper Naltar to Naltar Lake, Naltar Lake to Lower Shani, Lower Shani to Upper Shani, Upper Shani to the top of Pakora Pass, top of pass to Lal Patthar, Lal Patthar to Pakora village

Map Notes

Beshgiri is called Bichgari on the Swiss map. It does not show the trail going to Naltar lakes. In the Pakora Gol, Krui Bokht, Utz, and Kuru are not shown.

Route Description

Day 1: Upper Naltar (Dumian) to Naltar Lake (3 to 3½ hours) From Dumian (2820m), walk on the jeep road up the east side of the Naltar Valley. In 1¾ hours ford a side stream at the start of Beshgiri (in Shina, *besh* means 'red lichen'; *giri*, 'a boulder'), named for the distinctive boulders east of the trail. Pass through lush forest of cedar, chir pine, and birch. Ford another side stream in 45 minutes, marking the start of Bangla, an area named after a 'bungalow' that used to be nearby. Cross a bridge to the true right (west) bank of the Naltar Gah. Continue 45 minutes to the first lake (3270m) at the end of the jeep road.

Day 2: Naltar Lake to Lower Shani (3½ hours) Skirt the lake and in 15 minutes cross a bridge to the true left (east) bank of the Naltar Gah. Over a low rise, two more lakes up the western side valley come into view, and the river ahead braids out. Cross this broad area called Shing in 45 minutes, walking along the river bed and fording a huge side stream that tumbles down from the east. Where the river narrows, the Gujar settlement of Gupa sits on the true right (west) side of the river. Bridges above and below Gupa give access to the settlement, but the main trail stays on the true left (east) side.

After one hour, ford a major side stream from the east, which leads to the unused, glaciated Chaprot Pass between Snow Dome (5029m) and Merhbani (5639m). Beyond the stream 15 minutes, high above the river, are the huts of Lath and the first view of the terminus of the Shani Glacier. The Pakora Pass is visible from above Lath. Junipers dot the hillside and the trail becomes faint as it skirts the north-east margin of the Shani Glacier, reaching Lower Shani in one to 1½ hours. In Shina, *shani* means 'a pure place where fairies dwell'. The fairies are attracted by the scent and sight of the flowers in such meadows. A stream and grassy area marks Lower Shani (3690m), with shepherds' huts near the glacier. Beware of the shepherds' dogs. South-west across the Shani Glacier is Shani peak. Though not high by Karakoram standards, it is an impressive and technically difficult peak.

Day 3: Lower Shani to Pakora High Camp (2½ to 3½ hours) Rhubarb and juniper cover the hillside, and the trail continues past huts in 45 minutes, marking the start of Upper Shani. Go over a rise above these huts and descend immediately into the ablation valley. Cross a bridge over the river just above where the river goes under the glacier. Do not continue traversing above the true right bank, because the river is too wide and

deep to ford higher up. Walk 15 minutes along the true right side of the river bed, with the pink and orange rock of the Shani Glacier's lateral moraine to your left, to the upper end of the flat alluvial ablation valley.

This is a fine camp site in the shelter of the lateral moraine, one to 1½ hours from Lower Shani. If you are not acclimatised, camp here and at the Pakora high camp the next day. To continue to Pakora high camp, cross the small side stream and ascend the steep, grassy flower-carpeted slope where horses and yaks graze. Continue through rockier terrain to where the slope levels out. Follow the true right bank of the large, clear stream a short way to the standard high camp before the pass, one to 1½ hours from Upper Shani camp. A few stone shelters mark the site (4230m). You can also camp just before the stone shelters on either side of the stream in this very pretty area.

Day 4: Pakora High Camp to Jut/Utz (6 to 8 hours) Behind the high camp a side stream flows from the west, south of a large rock outcrop. An indistinct trail follows this stream up steep, loose rock about one hour, passing a few cairns. The east side of the pass has several small snowfields and a large crevasse-free snowfield just below the top. Cross the snowfields in 30 minutes and reach the obvious Pakora Pass (4710m).

The west side of the Pakora Pass is glaciated and crevassed lower down. Descend across snowfields, working to the north (right) onto the obvious grey moraine ridge in about 15 to 30 minutes. Follow a faint trail down the moraine ridge about 30 minutes to its end, where it abuts the main Pakora Gomukh *(gomukh* means 'glacier' in Shina). Cross the width of the icy glacier in about 30 minutes, heading towards the reddish rocks on its far west side (4230m). Once across the glacier, the route to the snowy Hayal Pass heads west (left) ascending the rock along the north margin of the Hayal Glacier (see Other Routes below). To reach Pakora, walk down the lateral moraine ridge high above the south-west margin of the Pakora Glacier, which fills the upper valley. Continue about

HUNZA RIVER VALLEY

two hours on a faint trail to Lal Patthar (3690m) (Urdu for 'red rock', also called Krui Bokht in Khowar), named for the huge reddish boulder amid a few junipers. The boulder provides shelter for porters and a few possible tent sites are nearby, but the sloping hillside and distant water makes this an undesirable camp.

Beyond Lal Patthar, cross a side stream in a steep ravine. Continue down valley one hour through beautiful, dense forest of birch, pine, and juniper on a pine-needle blanketed trail and cross a bridge (3750m) to the true right bank of the Pakora Gol. The bridge cannot be seen easily from the trail. Where the trail is level with the river continue along the river bed and walk a few minutes to the bridge. (Do not ascend the obvious trail that climbs some 50m.) Once across the river, the narrow trail follows the river and then climbs onto a forested plateau to the Gujar huts of Jut/Utz (3390m) where horses, cows, sheep, and goats graze, 1½ hours from Lal Patthar. Jut is the Burushashki name, which means 'grassy place'; Utz is the Khowar name for spring.

Day 5: Jut/Utz to Pakora (3½ to 5 hours) The descent from Jut to Pakora is over 1100m, getting progressively steeper as the canyon narrows. The Pakora Gol can be brutally hot and dry on sunny days, so get an early start and carry water. From the far end of the pasture, descend and cross the river on a good bridge. The trail is in poor condition and stays on the true left (south) bank, low along the river bed about one hour, passing beneath the Gujar settlements of Gujarshal and Roghshal high above. Kuru, a settlement above the confluences of the Kuru An Gol and the Pakora Gol, is visible across the river. A route leads up this side stream to the Kuru An (see Other Routes below).

The main trail down valley stays on the true left side of the Pakora Gol, contouring a sage-covered hillside on a wide donkey trail. It stays high above the raging river, often on exposed galleries. The river falls into a deep gorge with waterfalls tumbling down both sides. Reach a side stream and a large, soli-

tary willow in about 1½ hours. Cross a plank bridge to the true right bank in 30 minutes to reach the first cultivated fields of Pakora. In 15 minutes reach the jeep road and the centre of Pakora (2220m).

DAINTAR PASS
(4 to 5 days; July to September)
The Daintar Pass (4500m) links the upper Naltar Valley with the Daintar Nala and Chalt. It was first crossed by George Cockerill in 1893 who described the southern side as 'almost vertical'. The pass is steep on both sides, but easier to cross from south to north from the Naltar Valley. The north side is extremely steep with a snow cornice and a glacier below. Carry rope for safety descending. Trevor Braham, who spent some 30 years in the Himalaya, describes the northern descent as '230m of shattered rock at a 50° angle, ending in a wide crevasse'. The approach to beautiful Snow Dome (5029m) is along the ridge east south-east from the Daintar Pass.

Guides & Porters
Naltar porters have the right to work only up to the Daintar Pass. Porters from Daintar work from the Daintar Pass down to Chalt. You must prearrange to change porters at the pass on a specified date. These logistics and the necessity of paying wāpāsi to two groups of porters adds to the complexity and expense of the trek. Although small trekking parties may be able to avoid switching porters en route, it is difficult for large parties to do so.

6 stages: Naltar village to Naltar Lake, Naltar Lake to camp above Lower Shani, camp above Lower Shani and cross Daintar Pass to Khaniwal, Khaniwal to Tole Bari, Tole Bari to Taling, Taling to Torbuto Das

Route Description
Days 1 & 2: Upper Naltar (Dumian) to Lower Shani See Pakora Pass above for route description. The Daintar Pass is visible from Shing. If camping at Lower Shani, you also need to make a high camp before crossing the pass. The high camp can be reached

from Naltar Lake on Day 2, but for acclimatisation and enjoyment, spend at least one additional day at Shani, and explore the beautiful upper Naltar Valley.

Day 3: Lower Shani to Daintar High Camp
(1 to 2 hours) Daintar Pass is north of Lower Shani. The trail stays east (right) of the stream coming down from the ridge. The high camp is below an obvious snowfield in a level spot.

Day 4: Daintar High Camp to Tolebari (5 to 5½ hours) The ascent to the pass follows the crest of a spur from the main ridge. Near the top the angle is quite steep and a rope may be needed. It appears to be 2nd class. The cornice on top can be large. A cairn marks the top. A steep scree gully is the standard descent. Beware of rock fall, and the glacier below may be crevassed. Tolebari huts and pastures are three to 3½ hours from the pass.

Day 5: Tolebari to Torbuto Das (4 to 5 hours) Descend the Tolebari Nala to the huts of Taling in about two hours. At the Daintar huts (2743m), you can cross the river and take a trail south-east over the ridge (3657m) to Chaprot village. Further down the north side of the Daintar Nala, a trail heads north-east crossing a ridge and the Talamutz Pass to Bar village (see Bar Valley in the Nagyr section of this chapter). The trail down the Daintar Nala continues through a gorge to Torbuto Das village.

OTHER ROUTES
Hayal Pass
The Hayal Pass is a seldom-used glaciated pass that links the upper Pakora Valley to Chatorkhand in the Ishkoman Valley. The route (from east to west) begins on the west margin of the Pakora Glacier (at N 36° 20' 17.3" and E 74° 01' 00.1"), about three km west of and 450m below the top of the Pakora Pass. The route is depicted incorrectly on the U502 *Baltit (NJ 43-14)* sheet and on the Swiss map, which show it splitting off at the top of the Pakora Pass. Most trekkers who cross the Pakora Pass from east to west

descend the Pakora Valley to Pakora village and forego also crossing the Hayal Pass to Chatorkhand.

Baj Gaz Valley
The Baj Gaz Valley heads south-east from Mujaoweer village (spelled Munjawar on maps) near Imit in the Ishkoman Valley. The Baj Gaz Pass at the head of the valley, shown on all maps, is glaciated, heavily corniced, and technically difficult. It is never crossed. The only known crossing of this pass was by Francis Younghusband in about 1925. Baj Gaz means 'where there is a lot of grass'. Locals also refer to it as Bazi Gah. The trail in the Baj Gaz Gol goes only as far as a summer pasture, Khushrui Jerab (in Wakhi *khushrui* means 'beautiful'; *jerab* 'valley').

Kuru An
Another pass, the Kuru An, links Kuru in the Pakora Gol to Khushrui Jerab in the Baj Gaz Gol. Neither Kuru, a small settlement in the Pakora Gol, nor the pass are named on maps. The route is not marked on the U502 *Baltit (NJ 43-14)* sheet. Kuru is about one hour west of Jut/Utz and is reached via a bridge to the true right bank of the Pakora Gol above where the valley narrows into a gorge. (The main trail in the Pakora Gol is along the true left bank.) The route follows the side stream, the Kuru An Gol, which heads north-east behind the settlement. Locals report that hunters occasionally cross this pass, as ibex are plentiful.

Bichhar Gah to Sherqila
Across the valley from Beshgiri in the Naltar Valley, a two day route heads south-west over a glaciated pass beneath Khaitar peak (5591m) and descends the Bichhar Gah to Sherqila, an infrequently visited village in Punial on the Gilgit-Chitral road. From Sherqila, you can also walk up the Sher Gah to summer pastures at Dogah and above. The Sherqila Women's Art Group (SWAG), in the courtyard of the residence of the last Raja of Punial, is a women's cooperative that produces wood block prints on handmade paper.

Nagyr

Nagyr consists of two geographically separate administrative zones: Nagyr 1; and Nagyr 2. Nagyr 1, or Upper Nagyr, is on the south side of the Hunza River. It includes Nagyr Proper, Hispar village, Hoper, and the villages along the south bank of the Hunza River from Nilt to the Hispar River. Nagyr Proper refers to the village of Nagyr, which was the capital of the former state. The ex-Mir of Nagyr, Shaukat Ali Khan, still lives here. It has a few shops, a hospital and a police post. Hoper refers to the five villages (Hakalshal, Ratal, Buroshal, Holshal, and Gashoshal) that lie along the south-west margin of the Bualtar Glacier. Hoper is also called *tsindigram*, which means 'the five hamlets' in Burushashki, the language spoken in Upper Nagyr. Nagyr 2, or Lower Nagyr, includes Chalt, and the Chaprot and Bar valleys, all on the north side of the Hunza River. Chalt village, at the junction of the Chaprot and Bar valleys, is the central village of Lower Nagyr. The attractive and prosperous village where the ex-Mir of Nagyr maintains a house receives fewer than 100 visitors a year. Both Upper and Lower Nagyr receive heavier snow fall and have more water than neighbouring Hunza. Lower Nagyr residents speak Shina, and all Nagyr residents are Shia Muslims. Many treks in Nagyr are quite easy on good trails and offer unsurpassed views of the well-known mountains of Nagyr such as Rakaposhi (7788m), Diran (7257m), and Spantik (7027m).

INFORMATION
Maps
The best map is the 1:250,000 orographical sketch map *Karakoram Sheet 1* published by the Swiss Foundation for Alpine Research. Others are the 1:250,000 US AMS *India and Pakistan Series U502 Baltit (NJ 43-14)* sheet and Leomann Maps 1:200,000 *Karakoram Trekking and Mountaineering* map *Sheet 1: (Gilgit, Hunza, Rakaposhi, Batura Area)*.

The Deutscher Alpenverein (DAV) 1:100,000 *Hunza – Karakoram* map depicts Lower Nagyr.

Regulations
Foreigners are allowed to trek anywhere in this open zone. Neither a permit from the Tourism Division nor a licensed mountain guide is required.

According to a 1994 ruling, the ex-Mir of Nagyr retains the right to collect a Rs 30 per tent fee for anyone camping in the Barpu Valley between Tagaphari and Shuja Basa (Spantik base camp). His *chowkidar*, or watchman, Mr Haider, wanders the valley with a typewritten letter in English explaining the fee and collects rupees from trekkers.

Accommodation & Supplies
NAPWD Rest Houses in Nagyr can be booked with the Chief Engineer in Gilgit.

Chalt Chalt has a small bazaar across the bridge on the west bank of the Chaprot River. *Baltar Cottage* in the bazaar has charpoys and double rooms. Doubles at the nearby pleasant *NAPWD Rest House* cost Rs 150.

Hoper All accommodation is at the end of the jeep road. There is a two-room *NAPWD Rest House*. The *Hoper Hilton Inn*, managed by Amir Hamza, has two triples with hot running water that cost Rs 300. It costs Rs 20 per tent to camp or Rs 40 per bed to sleep in its four-bed canvas tents. You can camp at the *Hoper Inn* for Rs 10 per bed in its canvas tents or pitch your own tent. Both inns serve meals.

Minapin At *Diran Guest House* doubles cost Rs 200 with hot water. Its traditional house sleeps about six; food is good and costs about Rs 50. *Alpine Hotel* has only two rooms and lets trekkers camp. Across the road is a *NAPWD Rest House*.

Nagyr Proper There are two hotels here, the *Distaghil Sar Hotel* and an *NAPWD Rest House*.

GETTING THERE & AWAY

Wagons and passenger jeeps to Nagyr go from lower Khazana (Bank) Rd in Gilgit. Two Nagyr shopkeepers, Ibrahim who runs a cloth shop and Haji Ramzan who has a general store, can help you find the right vehicle. Latif Anwar, who owns the Golden Peak Inn in Gilgit, can also help with vehicles or in arranging porters or a guide.

Lower Nagyr

Bar Valley Cargo jeeps go to Budelas and on to Torbuto Das. A jeep road continues up the Daintar Nala valley to Daintar village and another jeep road goes up the Bar Valley to Bar village, but jeeps are infrequent. Plan on walking up valley from Torbuto Das.

Chalt Chalt-bound jeeps and vans go often in the early morning for Rs 20 and return the next morning. From a large rock outcrop on the KKH one km west of a petrol station, a jeep road crosses the river to Chalt. Any vehicle going up the KKH will let you off across from the bridge, and you can walk to Chalt.

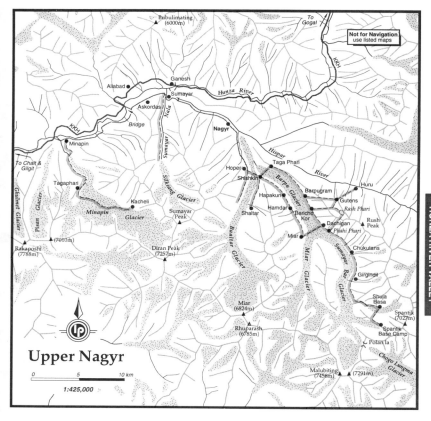

HUNZA RIVER VALLEY

Chaprot The jeep road continues beyond Chalt to Chaprot village. A few cargo jeeps ply between Gilgit and Chaprot.

Upper Nagyr

Hoper A wagon leaves Gilgit daily about 8 am. It cost Rs 50 and takes about 4½ hours. A wagon leaves Hoper daily for Gilgit about 6 am. Special jeeps from Ganesh or Karimabad to and from Hoper cost Rs 800 and take 1½ hours.

Huru & Hispar Vehicles directly to or from Huru and Hispar are infrequent. Take a vehicle to Nagyr Proper and look for a cargo jeep or hire a special jeep between Nagyr Proper and the Hispar Valley. From June to September, you can only get transport to and from Huru and should plan to walk between Huru and Hispar. Special jeeps Hunza-Huru cost Rs 1200 and Nagyr-Hispar cost Rs 1500.

Minapin Passenger jeeps from Gilgit cost Rs 35. The jeep road to Minapin village leaves the KKH at Pisan, just east of Ghulmet. From here, it takes about 45 minutes to walk to the village.

Nagyr Proper Wagons leave Gilgit throughout the day and cost Rs 45.

GUIDES & PORTERS
Lower Nagyr

The maximum low-altitude porter's wage is Rs 160 per stage plus wāpāsi. Food rations are also paid, though you can often negotiate a lower rate. Porters ask for a clothing and equipment allowance, but if your trek is less than a week negotiate this to a more reasonable Rs 100 per person.

Upper Nagyr

The maximum low-altitude porter's wage is Rs 160 per stage, plus wāpāsi and Rs 60 food rations. Guides and porters bring their own food. You are expected to pay from Rs 120 to Rs 200 clothing and equipment allowance. A rest day equal to half a stage's wage is paid after every seven stages.

BAR VALLEY

(3 to 8 days; mid-June to October)

The Bar Valley (see the Naltar, Pakora Valleys & Lower Nagyr map) runs north from Chalt village with a jeep road to the village of Torbuto Das at the junction of the Daintar Nala from the west and the Garamasai, or Tutu Uns, River, from the north. The Daintar Valley can be reached three different ways: by a jeep road from Torbuto Das, by walking over the ridge from Chaprot village, or by crossing the Daintar Pass from Naltar (see Naltar & Pakora Valleys in this chapter). Bar village is on the west bank of the Tutu Uns River, and is the road head for treks to the glaciers and meadows up the Bar Valley.

The many pastures along the Toltar and Baltar glaciers of the upper Bar Valley offer fine summer walks. The Toltar Glacier descends from Kampir Dior (7168m), and numerous 6500m peaks. The Baltar Glacier descends from the Batura Wall with most peaks over 7500m. Bar villagers graze yaks, sheep, and goats in the pastures, and Toltar is the main pasture settlement. Between March and May is reportedly the best time for ibex viewing, July and August for visiting the upper pastures.

Guides & Porters

Porters can be hired in any village. The former hunters, now turned game keepers, are the best local guides for ibex viewing.

Baltar Glacier 4 stages: Torbuto Das to Shuwe, Shuwe to Baltar, and return via the same route

Toltar Glacier 10 stages: Torbuto Das to Bitale Tok, Bitale Tok to Kukuay, Kukuay to Baru-daru-kush, Baru-daru-kush to Dudio-daru-kush, Dudio-daru-kush to Saio-daru- kush, and return via the same route

Map Notes

The Swiss map shows the road crossing the river between Budelas and Torbuto Das, but it stays on the east bank. Most place names and locations along the Toltar and Baltar glaciers are inaccurately shown on the Swiss map. The U502 *Baltit (NJ 43-14)* sheet is square. Kukuay pastures along the west side of the Toltar Glacier, and Saio-daru-kush pastures, on the hillside above the junction of the east and north Toltar glaciers, are not shown.

Route Description – Toltar Glacier

Day 1: Torbuto Das to Bitale Tok Follow the jeep road to Bar village (2200m) and continue up the west bank of the river to Bitale Tok. If you start from Bar, Toltar can be reached the same day.

Day 2: Bitale Tok to Toltar Cross the river issuing from the Toltar Glacier to Toltar summer settlement (2900m). Above Toltar are the yak pastures of Fagurgutum (3400m), a good day hike.

Day 3: Toltar to Baru-daru-kush Continue along the east side of the Toltar Glacier, passing through Kukuay summer settlement to Baru-daru-kush pastures.

Day 4: Baru-daru-kush to Dudio-daru-kush Beyond Baru-daru-kush, cross the Toltar Glacier to the north side and Dudio-daru-kush.

Day 5: Dudio-daru-kush to Saio-daru-kush Continue along the north margin of the main glacier, and make the difficult crossing of the north Toltar Glacier to the Saio-daru-kush pastures (over 4000m). The peak above (6771m) has the same name as the pastures, but is called Seiri Porkush on the Swiss map.

Days 6 to 8: Saio-daru-kush to Torbuto Das Retrace your steps down valley.

Route Description – Baltar Glacier

Day 1: Torbuto Das to Shuwe Follow the jeep road to Bar village (2200m). Above Bar, cross the main river and follow the trail up its east side to Shuwe, a summer-pasture area with huts.

Day 2: Shuwe to Baltar Continue up the true left bank of the river issuing from the Baltar Glacier as it bends east. Cross the

---

Ibex Conservation

In October 1990, the people of the Bar Valley swore to protect their wildlife and in particular to refrain from hunting ibex. As part of a WWF-sponsored programme, hunters are now employed as game keepers, and earn Rs 400 per month. The government issues up to five licences annually for hunting of 'trophy' male ibexes, five years of age or older, in the Bar Valley. Hunting takes place in December, when snows bring the males to lower snow-free areas. A fee of US$3000 for foreigners or Rs 20,000 for Pakistanis is charged. Seventy-five per cent of the fee goes to the Bar Valley people, and 25% is retained by the Wildlife Department for publicising the programme and replicating it in other areas of northern Pakistan. The villagers derive economic benefit from wildlife conservation, giving them a stake in the animal's survival. The ibex population had increased to over 1000 in 1994, and visitors can see these mountain monarchs more easily. Villagers have established observation points. The Bar Valley also supports a good snow leopard population. ■

---

wildly inaccurate. The Swiss map names the large northern arm of the Baltar Glacier as the Toltar Glacier, but the glacier identified on the map as Kukuar is called Toltar by local people. Baltar pastures are shown on the west side of the northern arm of the Baltar Glacier, but Baltar is actually on the east side where the Swiss map has an unnamed black moraine-covered Baltar Glacier to the large south and west facing pastures of Baltar, on the north side of the Baltar Glacier and the east side of its large northern arm.

Day 3: Baltar to Torbuto Das Retrace your steps down valley.

MINAPIN GLACIER
(5 days; July to September)
Minapin village sits above the true left (south) bank of the Hunza River at the base of the Minapin Glacier (see the Upper Nagyr map). Rakaposhi and Diran peaks tower above the head of the glacier. Rakaposhi base camp is a two day walk, and Diran base camp one day further.

Guides & Porters
4 stages: Minapin to Hapakun, Hapakun to Tagaphari and return via same route

2 stages: Tagaphari to Diran base camp and return via same route

Route Description
Day 1: Minapin to Hapakun (3 to 4 hours) The main trail starts behind the rest house and climbs to a bridge over the Minapin River to its true left (west) bank. Continue steeply about one hour to the first huts. The huts of Hapakun lie another hour up valley.

Day 2: Hapakun to Tagaphari (2 to 3 hours) From Hapakun, ascend a trail through forest with excellent views of Diran as you rise above the Minapin Glacier. The meadows and shepherd's hut at Tagaphari are in an ablation valley overlooking the glacier's upper ice fields, some 1500m above Minapin village. This is also a base camp for Rakaposhi. Walk up the 4000m ridge for excellent views of the Batura peaks, and Shishpar and Ultar peaks above Hunza.

Day 3: Day Hike to Diran Base Camp (6 hours) It takes about three hours to cross the broad glacier and reach Diran base camp near Kacheli. If you go on a day hike, your porters can have a rest day. This is a less

expensive option than camping at Kacheli and paying porters for the two additional stages. However, take a local guide who knows the way and a rope for safety.

Days 4 & 5: Tagaphari to Minapin Return via the same route camping in Hapakun en route.

BARPU GLACIER
(6 days; mid-June to October)
The Sumayar Bar and Miar glaciers, which flow from Malubiting (7458m) and Phuparash peaks respectively, join to form the Barpu Glacier (see the Upper Nagyr map). The river issuing from the mouth of the Barpu Glacier flows north-west into the Bualtar Glacier opposite Hoper. Access to the Barpu Glacier is either from Hoper then across the Bualtar Glacier, or from Huru in the Hispar Valley across a 4000m high ridge that separates Huru from the Barpu Glacier. The trails in the ablation valleys along both sides of the Barpu Glacier offer easy, scenic walks through flower-filled meadows. Side trips to Rush Phari (see below) and to Spantik Base Camp (see Other Routes below) are easily combined with the Barpu Glacier trek.

Guides & Porters
The route involves five glacier crossings – twice across the Bualtar Glacier, and once across the Barpu, Sumayar Bar and Miar glaciers. A guide or knowledgeable porter is essential for all crossings, especially the constantly shifting Bualtar Glacier where the route changes daily.

9 stages: Hoper to Lower Shishkin, Lower Shishkin to Barpugram, Barpugram to Phahi Phari, Phahi Phari to Girgindil, Girgindil to Sumayar Bar, Sumayar Bar to Miar, Miar to Hamdar, Hamdar to Upper Shishkin, Upper Shishkin to Hoper

Map Notes
The Bualtar and Barpu glaciers do not join one another as depicted on the Swiss map. Bericho Kor is misplaced; it is due west of

Rush Phari along the south-east margin of the Barpu Glacier.

Route Description

Day 1: Hoper to Bericho Kor (4 to 5 hours) Once you leave Hoper, there is no reliable water until Bericho Kor. Carry water and start early to avoid the midday heat. From Hoper (2790m), descend steeply to the edge of the Bualtar Glacier. The crossing is a relatively short distance, but the constantly moving Bualtar Glacier is icy and broken, and has no fixed route. It can take anywhere from 30 minutes to three hours to cross it.

At Lower Shishkin on the opposite side of the glacier, the trail divides. The higher trail heads south-east to Upper Shishkin along the south-west margin of the Barpu Glacier. Take the lower trail east to an obvious notch and the first views of the Barpu Glacier. The Barpu is more stable than the Bualtar, but just as bleak. Cross it on a consolidated trail in about 45 minutes to the ablation valley on its south-east margin with views of Diran to the west, Spantik to the south, and Ultar peak and Bubulimating to the north. Tagaphari is a dry, barren place in the long ablation valley. Fifteen years ago before the Barpu Glacier retreated, Tagaphari was well watered and green. Reach Barpugram, the first huts, about 30 minutes from the start of the ablation valley. Barpugram's water source is snow melt, unreliable after May. Two trails lead up the hillside behind Barpugram: the north-east one goes to Huru; and the south-east one leads to Gutens, an alternative route to Rush Phari (see Rush Phari below).

The ablation valley narrows and larger juniper and wild roses appear. One hour from Barpugram, reach the huts and pastures of Mulharai where tamarisk offers shade. Just beyond is the grassy camp site of Bericho Kor (3300m) where a porters' shelter hugs a boulder, 5.5 km from Tagaphari. *Bericho* are musicians, and *kor* means 'cave'. A trickle of water runs through the camp site, but its larger source is a few minutes above camp.

Day 2: Bericho Kor to Phahi Phari (1½ to 2 hours) An easy four km trail follows the ablation valley to Phahi Phari (3450m), passing Dachigan about one hour from Bericho Kor. A large boulder with ibex carvings on it sits at Dachigan. An alternative route crosses the Barpu Glacier from Dachigan to Miar in two to three hours to return along the south-west side of the glacier.

Day 3: Phahi Phari to Girgindil (3 to 4 hours) Continue up the now-forested ablation valley with flower-filled grassy meadows. In one hour pass through Chukutans with its several huts. Girgindil with its hut and beautiful meadows is two hours further. From the ridge above Girgindil are great views of Spantik. From Girgindil, you can continue up valley to Spantik Base Camp (see Other Routes below).

Day 4: Girgindil to Sumayar Bar (4 to 5 hours) Retrace your steps down valley to Chukutans and cross the Sumayar Bar Glacier in one hour to the huts of Sumayar Bar nestled near the junction of the Sumayar Bar and Miar glaciers below a forested ridge.

Day 5: Sumayar Bar to Hapakun (3½ to 4½ hours) Cross the wide white ice of the Miar Glacier to Miar settlement at the juncture of the Miar and Barpu glaciers. Follow the trail along the south-west margin of the Barpu Glacier from Miar to Hamdar, reaching Hamdar in about 1½ hours. Continue to Hapakun in one hour.

Day 6: Hapakun to Hoper *(3 to 4 hours)* From Hapakun, the trail passes through Upper Shishkin before dropping to Lower Shishkin at the edge of the Bualtar Glacier. Cross the tricky Bualtar Glacier and return to Hoper.

RUSH PHARI

(3 days; mid-June to September)
Rush Phari (4694m) is a turquoise lake on a ridge between the Hispar Valley and Barpu Glacier with incredible mountain panoramas (see the Upper Nagyr map). In a 360° sweep, almost all the giant peaks of Hunza are

visible, and remarkably, a distant K2 (8611m), Broad Peak (8047m) and Gasherbrum IV (7925m) can also be seen. The strenuous two day 1500m climb to the lake can be combined with the Barpu Glacier trek. Begin the Rush Phari trek from Bericho Kor and return to Phahi Phari. Because of the rapid ascent and the altitude at Rush Phari, do this trek only when already acclimatised. No options for alternative camp sites exist due to lack of water, so if you experience altitude problems, descend to Phahi Phari or Bericho Kor immediately.

Two other trails lead to Rush Phari. One leaves the margin of the Barpu Glacier at Barpugram (see Barpu Glacier above), climbing the hillside to Gutens, a summer settlement on the ridge. The other climbs steeply from Huru in the Hispar Valley to Gutens. From Gutens, follow the ridge and join the trail from Bericho Kor below Chidin Harai. By May water in Barpugram dries up and by June water in Gutens does, making these alternative trails dry and undesirable.

Guides & Porters

Porters need bedding and shelter for the camp at Rush Phari, which can be windy and cold. The descent from Rush Phari to Phahi Phari is not obvious, so take someone who knows the route. When you go via Gutens, hire someone to carry water. Several variations on stages follow.

2½ stages: 1½ stage Bericho Kor to Rush Phari, and one stage Rush Phari to Phahi Phari

3 stages: Bericho Kor to Rush Phari, and return via the same route

3 stages: Barpugram to Gutens, Gutens to Rush Phari, Rush Phari to Phahi Phari

4 stages: Barpugram to Gutens, Gutens to Rush Phari, and return via the same route

4 stages: Huru to Gutens, Gutens to Rush Phari, and return via the same route.

(The distance between Barpugram and Bericho Kor is half a stage. Bericho Kor to Phahi Phari is also half a stage.)

Map Notes

The trails from Bericho Kor to the ridge and from Rush Phari to Phahi Phari are not shown on the Swiss map. Bericho Kor is incorrectly positioned. Chidin Harai and Huru are not marked.

Route Description

Day 1: Bericho Kor to Chidin Harai (4½ to 5½ hours) This 1140m climb is relentlessly steep, hot and dry, with no water until Chidin Harai, so carry as much water as you can from Bericho Kor. Start early to reach the ridge top before the sun. Head east from Bericho Kor (3300m) behind two large boulders. The trail rises steadily, north (left) of the scree gully descending from the ridge. Climb 2½ to four hours through sage, thyme and scattered juniper to the ridge top, marked by a cairn (4020m). The trail from Gutens joins this trail at the cairn. The icy Miar Glacier below snowy Phuparash and Diran dominates the views west.

Continue east south-east up the grassy ridge one to 1½ hours to Chidin Harai. A faint trail exists by a rocky water channel, which may be dry. Chidin Harai (4440m) has a goat pen, a few shepherds' huts, and grassy areas for camping. Year-round water flows about five minutes above the huts. (*Chidin* means 'a rounded cast iron cooking pot', named for the shape of this *harai*, or pasture.) Chidin Harai enjoys late afternoon light and is a perfect camp from which to enjoy sunset and sunrise on the imposing Hispar Muztagh to the north-east. This wall of 7000m peaks includes: Lupgar Sar (7200m), Momhil Sar (7343m), Trivor (7728m), Mulungutti Sar (7025m), and Disteghil Sar (7885m).

Day 2: Chidin Harai to Rush Phari (1½ hours) Head up the left side of the rocky slope above the water source. Towards the top of the slope, before it makes an obvious bend to the left, cross right to avoid talus and reach a Barpu Glacier overlook one hour above Chidin Harai. Turn south-east and cross the talus. Keep to the right of the stream and to the left of the unnamed rocky peak. Cross a low rise and reach Rush Phari (4694m) in about 30 minutes. Although stone shelters are on the west shore, the less windy camp sites are along the lake's south-west shores. Enjoy the views of the Miar

Glacier, Spantik, Diran, and Phuparash. Two unclimbed 6000m-to-6200m peaks to the south are visible behind the rocky Rush Peak.

From the south side of the lake, climb the flowered slopes for one hour to a hilltop (4938m) with a cairn and several tent platforms, but no water. From here, the distant pyramid of K2 is visible to the east. However, the best views are from Rush Peak. From the cairn, follow the northern ridge, then ascend easy 2nd-class talus to the summit, also marked by a cairn. From here, K2 is dramatically larger, Broad Peak and Gasherbrum IV are visible, and Baintha Brak looms above the Hispar La (5151m). Nowhere else in the Karakoram can you get such magnificent mountain views on such a short trek.

Day 3: Rush Phari to Phahi Phari (2 to 3 hours) The descent 1250m to Phahi Phari in 4.5 km is steep. From the stone shelters and cairns along the lake, an obvious gully descends towards the Barpu Glacier. The route stays right of the gully, traversing talus then descending juniper and grassy slopes and more steeply over artemisia steppes. Views of the Sumayar Bar and Miar glaciers, and Malubiting and Phuparash peaks are awesome. Phahi Phari (3450m) has reliable water and shade.

OTHER ROUTES
Chaprot Valley
The Chaprot Valley in Lower Nagyr runs west from Chalt village, where the Chaprot River flows into the Hunza River (see the Naltar, Pakora Valleys & Lower Nagyr map). Called 'more beautiful than any other valley in the Gilgit Agency' by British officer Reginald Schomberg in the 1930s, the valley also has good views of Rakaposhi and offers easy one to two day walks from mid-June to October. Horses can be hired.

Chaprot village (about 2134m) is a one hour walk on the jeep road up the north side of the valley from Chalt (1981m). A one day walk leads north-west from Chaprot, up and over the ridge (3657m) to Daintar village

(2743m) on the Daintar Nala. The Ghashumaling Valley (called Rashumaling on the Swiss map) branches slightly south from Chaprot village. With gentle trails through mulberry, peach, apple and walnut orchards, it is a popular day hike and picnic area. Follow the trail past the high school in Chaprot to Rahbat village and continue up valley through a canyon. The Kacheli Glacier lies at the head of this side valley. Three to four hours up the Chaprot Valley from Chaprot village is Burishki (2591m), a summer settlement. The glaciated Chaprot Pass at the head of the Chaprot valley leads to the upper Naltar Valley. The west side of this pass is a steep, crevassed hanging glacier, and the glacier on the Chaprot side is larger. Locals never cross the pass.

Spantik Base Camp
Spantik soars above the head of the Barpu Glacier. Its base camp, known as Shuja Basa (the place Shuja stayed), is a two day walk from Girgindil, the last camp reached on the Barpu Glacier trek (see route description above and the Nagyr map). The entire area between Girgindil and Shuja Basa is called Malunghushi. The faint trail from Girgindil skirts the upper Sumayar Bar Glacier to the huts of Makhphona Phari in two hours, then continues three to four hours to Yakhzena, at times climbing the hillside to avoid bad sections.

Trekkers usually camp at Yakhzena. Yakhzena, with its huge boulders, means 'a place where leopards store their kill'. From Yakhzena, continue along the glacier, then ascend through meadows to Shuja Basa. The base of the dramatic golden granite north face of Spantik (7027m) can be approached from Shuja Basa. The route is best done from July to September. The six stages are: Girgindil to Makhphona Phari, Makhphona Phari to Yakhzena, Yakhzena to Shuja Bhasa, and return via the same route. Spantik is usually climbed by the relatively easy route from the Chogo Lungma Glacier (see Basha, Tormik & Stak Valleys in the Baltistan chapter).

Bualtar Glacier

Two options exist to explore the Bualtar Glacier above Hoper (see the Upper Nagyr map). First is a 12-hour day hike to the pastures along the south-west margin of the glacier. Two trails, a higher and a lower one, head to the pastures. From the ridge above the pastures are good mountain views. Second is a two day route to Shaltar, the pastures on the opposite side of the Bualtar Glacier. From Hoper, cross the Bualtar Glacier to Lower Shishkin and head up the south-east margin to the pastures and camp. Return the next day via the same route. The mountain views from Shaltar are limited to Diran peak.

Sumayar Nala & Silkiang Glacier

High above the Sumayar Valley and Silkiang Glacier are the mines of Chuman Bakhūr. Since 1989, the discovery of large aquamarine crystals up to 15 cm across and 30 cm long at this site has made Pakistan a world-famous source for these gem specimens. The two day walk to these mines combines gorgeous views with a visit to a Karakoram growth industry. The large new mosque at Askordas, built with revenue from the mines, gives an idea of the wealth of the deposits.

Above Sumayar village, the road ends beyond the hydroelectric plant. Fida Hussain of Sumayar has set up tents here for visitors to stay in. Climb steeply up the hillside, and enter the Mamubar area, the ex-Mir of Nagyr's hunting grounds. A large three metre by 20m flat rock about one hour above the tents is where the queen of Nagyr would sit to watch her husband hunt. Cross the river twice over bridges, with a clear spring below the second bridge. Ascend glacial moraine on the east side of the valley, and climb about 600m to a spring at the herders' huts of Madur Kushi and camp, 3½ to four hours from Sumayar.

The next day continue steeply about 750m in two hours. Then level off and traverse to the crystal mines at Chuman Bakhūr in another hour. The views of Diran above and the Silkiang Glacier below are breathtaking. From Chuman Bakhūr, either return to Sumayar in one day, or, for an adventurous trek, cross the ridge east (behind) the mines and continue across three high ridges to Hoper. The arduous route takes several days. Few locals know the route via Bartar and Supaltar pastures to Hoper, so be sure to go with someone who does.

Hunza

Hunza consists of the villages on the north bank of the Hunza River from Maiyun to Atabad. The Shina-speaking villages below the Hassanabad Nala are called Shinaki or Lower Hunza. The Burushashki-speaking villages above the Hassanabad Nala are called Hunza Proper or Central Hunza. Above Hunza stand the prominent rock spire of Bubulimating (6000m), and the Ultar peaks, which continue to turn back climbers. Baltit, with its old fort, was the capital of Hunza state. The fort has now been restored by the Aga Khan Foundation. Ghazanfar Ali, the ex-Mir of Hunza, resides in a modern palace in Karimabad. Karimabad, named for Prince Karim, the Aga Khan, is now the centre of Hunza tourism.

INFORMATION
Maps

The Swiss Foundation for Alpine Research 1:250,000 orographical sketch map *Karakoram Sheet 1* and the Deutscher Alpenverein (DAV) 1:100,000 *Hunza – Karakoram* map shows the area accurately. The US AMS *India and Pakistan Series U502* 1:250,000 *Baltit (NJ 43 14)* sheet and Leomann's *Karakoram Trekking and Mountaineering* map 1:200,000 *Sheet 1: (Gilgit, Hunza, Rakaposhi, Batura Area)* are less accurate.

Regulations

Foreigners are allowed to trek anywhere in this open zone. Neither a permit from the Tourism Division nor a licensed mountain guide is required.

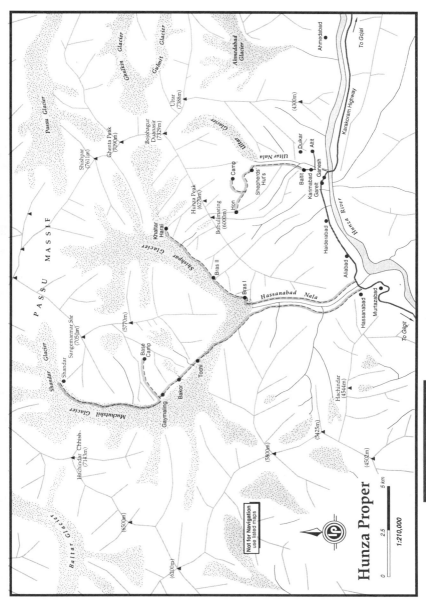

Hunza Proper

Not for Navigation
use listed maps

1:210,000

0   2.5   5 km

Accommodation & Supplies

The best variety of food and supplies is found in Aliabad and Karimabad. Almost everything available in Gilgit can be found here.

Aliabad Aliabad's bazaar is the transport hub and administrative centre with a bank, hospital, restaurants, and hotels. Vehicles travelling to and from Sost stop at the *Prince Hotel* for lunch. At the *Rakaposhi Inn* (☎ (045) 096) basic singles/doubles cost Rs 300/450 and food is OK. The *SR Hotel* on Hospital Rd costs Rs 200/250. The *Moonland Restaurant* is popular. At the *Dumani View Hotel* doubles with cold shower cost from Rs 200.

Altit Altit is a quiet village two km east of Karimabad. At *Amir Jan's Village Guest House* (☎ (47) 024), below the pologround, singles/doubles cost Rs 350/400. *Ideal View Hotel & Camping Point* is secluded and picturesque, just east of the bridge over the Ultar Nala. It costs Rs 30 per tent to camp or Rs 50 per person for a bed in one of its large canvas tents. *Kisar Inn* by the pologround remains popular; singles/doubles with attached bathrooms cost Rs 50/100 for smaller rooms and Rs 100/200 for larger ones. At *Williat Ali's Guest House* singles/doubles cost Rs 250/300.

Ganesh Adjacent to the NATCO bus stop on the KKH, *Karakoram Highway Inn* (☎ (47) 095 and 072) costs Rs 250/300.

Garelt Garelt is between Aliabad and Ganesh on the KKH. From this awkward location, you need to take a jeep to get most places. The new *Golden Peak View Hotel* looks nice. At PTDC's *Hunza Motel* (☎ (47) 069) singles/doubles cost Rs 650/750.

Karimabad – bottom end A few hotels are near the kerosene depot. You can camp at the *Garden Lodge*. The *Rainbow Hotel* has rooms that cost Rs 80/100/150. At the *Hunza Lodge* (☎ (47) 061) doubles cost Rs 120. Up the road to Baltit is the *Karim Hotel & Res-*

taurant where rooms with no toilet cost Rs 80/150; doubles cost Rs 200. The *New Mountain Refuge Inn* is popular with dorms/singles/doubles that cost Rs 30/150/200. You can camp in the garden. Charpoys at the *Hunza Inn* cost Rs 10.

Karimabad – middle At the *Hill View Hotel*, at the far end of the Haiderabad road, singles/doubles cost Rs 350/400; two rooms have good views. Nearby, the *Wajid Guest House* costs Rs 300/350. The family lives next door and is friendly. *Karim Hotel & Restaurant* rents a six-bed traditional style house for Rs 400. *New Golden Lodge* (☎ (47) 094) is a good bet. Small rooms with hot running water cost Rs 150/250; larger ones cost Rs 300/350. The *Hilltop Hotel* costs Rs 400/500. Known for its good food, the *Tourist Park Hotel* (☎ (47) 045) costs Rs 300/400. With a camping area, the *Karakurum Hotel & Restaurant* costs about Rs 250 but rates fluctuate with demand. Below is the pleasant *Mountain View Hotel* (☎ (47) 053), which costs Rs 450/600. The *Hunza View Hotel*, below the hospital near the telephone exchange on the new jeep road up from the KKH, costs Rs 400/450 and has panoramic views.

Karimabad – top end Managed by the reputable Serena Hotels, hot-water singles/doubles cost Rs 600/800 at the *Hunza Baltit Inn*. *Mountain View Hotel* has suites on its top floor with hot running water for Rs 700. Ghazanfar Ali, the ex-Mir of Hunza, rents rooms in his *Rakaposhi Palace* (☎ (47) 012) for Rs 850/950. He is also proprietor of the *Rakaposhi View Hotel*, which will be the most deluxe and expensive property when construction is complete.

Murtazabad West of Aliabad and below the Hassanabad Nala in Murtazabad is the isolated, peaceful *Eagle Nest Hotel* with three clean doubles with toilet and shower for Rs 150.

GETTING THERE & AWAY

Unlike other areas, modern Hunza does not

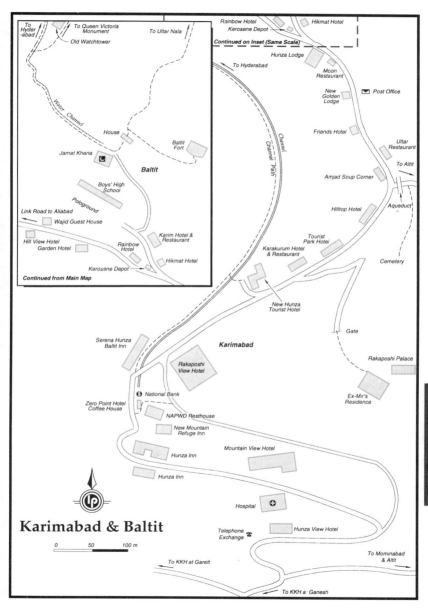

To Hyder-abad
To Queen Victoria Monument
Old Watchtower
To Ultar Nala
Rainbow Hotel
Kerosene Depot
Hikmat Hotel
Continued on Inset (Same Scale)
Hunza Lodge
To Hyderabad
Moon Restaurant
Post Office
New Golden Lodge
Water Channel
House
Baltit Fort
Friends Hotel
Ultar Restaurant
To Altit
Jamat Khana
Baltit
Channel
Channel Path
Amjad Soup Corner
Aqueduct
Boys' High School
Pologround
Hilltop Hotel
Link Road to Aliabad
Wajid Guest House
Karim Hotel & Restaurant
Tourist Park Hotel
Cemetery
Hill View Hotel
Garden Hotel
Rainbow Hotel
Karakurum Hotel & Restaurant
Hikmat Hotel
Kerosene Depot
Continued from Main Map
New Hunza Tourist Hotel
Gate
Serena Hunza Baltit Inn
Karimabad
Rakaposhi Palace
Rakaposhi View Hotel
National Bank
Zero Point Hotel Coffee House
NAPWD Resthouse
New Mountain Refuge Inn
Ex-Mir's Residence
Hunza Inn
Mountain View Hotel
Hunza Inn
Hospital
Karimabad & Baltit
Telephone Exchange
Hunza View Hotel
0   50   100 m
To KKH at Garelt
To Mominabad & Altit
To KKH a: Ganesh

HUNZA RIVER VALLEY

have cargo jeeps. Instead vans, wagons, and VIP jeeps are the norm. In Hunza Proper, Suzukis go between Ganesh and Aliabad (some also go to Murtazabad) all day and cost Rs 4.

A new paved road runs from Garelt, before Ganesh, past the hospital and telephone exchange up to Karimabad. The road continues west through Haiderabad to rejoin the KKH west of Aliabad. Karimabad and Altit are linked by an unpaved jeep road.

Gilgit

Vans and wagons for the three hour trip to Hunza leave from Gilgit's Jamat Khana bazaar daily (across the street from GM Beg Sons book shop) from 8 am to about 2 pm. The trip to Aliabad, Garelt, or Ganesh costs Rs 35 and to Karimabad costs Rs 40. If you want to go to Karimabad, ask as some vehicles do not go there. (Those that do not go to Karimabad usually go to Ganesh.) From Ganesh you can either walk the steep jeep road to Karimabad, Baltit or Altit, or hire a jeep for Rs 120. Others usually share the cost of a private jeep hire with you. From Karimabad, vehicles to Gilgit honk their horns up and down the road about 5 to 5.30 am in search of passengers.

A daily NATCO bus departs from near Gilgit's NLI Chowk for Sost about 8 am reaching Aliabad about 11 am. The daily NATCO bus also leaves Sost for Gilgit about 5 am and stops in Ganesh and Aliabad about 8 am. Vans and wagons make fewer stops, are quicker and more comfortable than NATCO buses.

Sost

No transport goes directly to or from Karimabad north on the KKH. It is best to be in Aliabad near the Prince Hotel by about 11 am to catch the daily NATCO bus or other vehicles going to Sost.

GUIDES & PORTERS

Guides and porters are not necessary for any of these treks but are sometimes recommended. Porter rates are Rs 160 per stage plus wāpāsi and food rations.

HASSANABAD NALA

(4 to 6 days; late May to early October)
The Hassanabad Nala is bridged by the KKH just above Murtazabad, and about five km below Aliabad. The river drains two glaciers: the Muchutshil coming from the north-west; and the Shishpar (also called Hassanabad) from the north-east. From the bridge, you can walk to summer pastures along either glacier. These routes take you towards the south side of the 7500m Batura wall. The Muchutshil Glacier has good views of Muchu Chhīsh (7453m) and Hacindar Chhīsh (7143m). The Shishpar Glacier offers excellent views of seldom-seen sides of Bubulimating, Ultar, and Shishpar peaks.

Guides & Porters

The routes change from year to year over both glaciers, so take a local to show the way.

Map Notes

The peak the Swiss map labels Sangemar Mar (*sangemarmar* means 'marble' in Urdu) is more correctly called Sangemarmar Sar. The Muchutshil Glacier is shown as the Muchuhar Glacier. It vaguely indicates the trail to Gaymaling, which it calls Gychalin. The U502 *Baltit (NJ 43-14)* sheet labels the glaciers Muchiohul and Hasanabad, but has no detail, rendering it useless for this trek.

Route Description – Muchutshil Glacier

Day 1: KKH to Mouth of the Glacier (2 to 3 hours) Follow the trail along the true right (west) side of the Hassanabad Nala, following the channel that feeds Hunza's hydroelectric plant. Camp in a sandy spot with a spring near the river and below the mouth of the glacier.

Day 2: Mouth of the Glacier to Gaymaling (5 to 7 hours) Climb high above the Muchutshil Glacier before dropping onto the debris-covered glacier and crossing to its north-east margin. Scramble up scree to a path on a narrow plateau, which widens as you head north-west through the pastures of Tochi and Bakor. Continue to Gaymaling (3600m), another pasture that is now unused.

From Gaymaling you can explore the lower reaches of Sangemarmar Sar (7050m) to the north-east and visit the base camp.

Day 3: Gaymaling towards Sangemarmar Sar (4 to 5 hours) Head north, climbing through scrub forest to an immense meadow with huts and a mill. With clear, flowing water and great vistas to the east and north, this tranquil spot offers a wonderful camping respite.

Days 4 to 6: Return to the KKH Retrace your steps down valley.

Route Description – Shishpar Glacier
Day 1: KKH to Bras I (3 to 4 hours) From the KKH, follow the east side of Hassanabad Nala to the mouth of the glacier on the jeep track behind the highway maintenance station. Climb the terminal moraine and continue on the glacier about 1.5 km to a steep gully off the glacier to the right. At the top of this gully and in front of the ridge rising to the east is a waterless camp site called Bras I. A short distance along the trail to the north-east, a spur drops to a pool of clear water on the glacier.

Day 2: Bras I to Khaltar Harai (4 to 5 hours) Beyond Bras I, pass another possible camp site, Bras II. Continue on moraine to Khaltar Harai (also called Dudara Harai), a summer pasture about seven km from Bras I, with fine views of the glacier and the Ultar and Passu peaks.

Days 3 & 4: Return to the KKH Retrace your steps down valley.

ULTAR NALA
(1 to 3 days; May to October)
Ultar Nala is a steep narrow slash that opens in its upper reaches into a wide pasture surrounded by a cascade of glaciers and granite. The strenuous walk to the meadows and back can be done as a long day hike, but spending a night near the huts is an unforgettable experience. There are several clear-water sources on the way up, but there is no reliable

water beyond the huts. Swirling winds off the glacier can be quite cool. Rock-fall hazard is high after prolonged rain, high winds, or a thaw. Do not go onto the heavily crevassed glacier – it is too dangerous.

Guides & Porters
Some trekkers hire a local guide for about Rs 250 per day. Though useful, it is not necessary. However, do not go alone. Trekkers have been lost and injured. A trekker who went there alone in 1994 has never been seen again and tragically is presumed dead.

Route Description
Day 1: Baltit to Ultar Meadows (3 to 4 hours) The trail begins from the north end of Baltit village, just before Baltit Fort. Follow the water channel into the mouth of the canyon. A spring is just past the channel's headworks 15 minutes from Baltit. Climb steadily on a well-used, but sometimes difficult and indistinct trail, up the steep moraine on the true right (south) side of the Ultar stream. Several level camp sites near water are below the shepherds' huts. Ask the shepherds for permission before camping. On moonlit nights, Ultar peak (7388m) is sublime. Avalanches booming off the ice fall punctuate the stillness and echo off the peaks and cliffs surrounding the meadow.

Day 2: Ultar Meadows to Hon (4 to 5 hours) The morning sun comes late in Ultar. Hon (4600m) is a viewpoint on a steep north-south ridge above Ultar. Carry water as there is none at Hon. From the huts, work up towards an obvious low point, then follow a series of ramps on the left to the top of the ridge with some exposure the last 200m. Across the ridge is a small shelter built against the rocks. Larger, level camp sites are further down. The views of Nagyr, Spantik and Rakaposhi are magnificent.

Another walk above the meadow involves less elevation gain. Head up the ridge towards Hon, but two-thirds of the way up turn north on a trail crossing a small stream from the right. About one km up is a camp site with equally stunning views where the trail ends in a sheer drop into the canyon below Bubulimating. You could also day-hike to Hon from this camp.

Day 3: Hon to Baltit (5 to 7 hours) Be careful not to follow a water channel by mistake as you descend the trail along Ultar Nala.

OTHER ROUTES
No long treks begin from Hunza Proper, but many fine day hikes and excursions are possible.

Channel Walks
Walking along the irrigation channels is an enjoyable way to see village life. The many channels distribute the silty water from Ultar Nala. Stay off the delicate side channels and do not swim in any channel. This is Hunza's drinking water. From Baltit's pologround, bear left beside the channel called Barber. The path goes down valley all the way to Haiderabad Nala, where you can walk down the stream bed to the link road. Here you reach another channel that goes all the way back to Karimabad and on around past Mominabad to behind Baltit Fort.

Queen Victoria Monument
At the top of the rock face behind Baltit is a monument to Queen Victoria which can be reached in one to two strenuous hours from Baltit. Follow the channel path above the pologround five minutes. Then cross it and climb stone steps beside the old watchtower. At the top of the village, scramble to a shallow cleft with some very large boulders. Go straight up to the base of the cliff before crossing to the monument, to avoid the water channel spilling down the face.

Altit Fort
Altit's small fort, with carved lintels and window frames, is older than Baltit's. In front is an apricot orchard, behind is a vertical 300m drop to the river. The interior rooms have an old phallic stone from the Hindu era, and records of spring sowing festivals, where the Mir magically ensured fertility by blessing the seed. The dusty jeep road linking Altit to Karimabad is a three km walk.

Duikar & Altit Peak
Duikar is a summer village 300m above Altit. A jeep road turns off the Altit link road west of Altit's pologround. From Karimabad or Altit, the ride takes about one hour. A day hike takes about five or six hours. The views of the Hunza River valley are spectacular. For a magical experience, visit Duikar on a moonlit night. Above Duikar are summer pastures and rocky peaks, including little-known Altit peak (about 5181m). You can easily spend four or five days trekking in this area, which is popular with local hunters in winter. Take someone who knows the way around these dry, rocky peaks.

Ahmedabad Glacier
The Ahmedabad Glacier is east of and parallel to the Ultar Glacier. Few foreigners visit the village and the summer pastures above. From Altit, follow the narrow jeep road above the true right bank of the Hunza River through Faizabad to Ahmedabad. From Ahmedabad, ascend to the pastures and descend to the village of Sarat, which is on the jeep road. Local shepherds can show the way. Plan on five to six days for this trek. The six stages are Ahmedabad to Gurpi, Gurpi to Teish, Teish to Godian, Godian to Baldiat, and Baldiat to Sarat.

Gojal

Gojal is the area along the upper Hunza River, from Shishkut village to the Khunjerab Pass, populated by Wakhi people, or Xik, as they call themselves (see the Passu & Batura Glaciers map). They migrated to Gojal several hundred years ago from the Wakhan corridor of Afghanistan. Their language is Wakhi, or Xikwor, and is very close to Tajik. The Wakhi view themselves as part of the larger Tajik ethnic community of Tajikistan, Afghanistan, Xinjiang in China, and Pakistan.

Among Wakhi, women do all dairy tasks (eg, milking, cheese and butter making) and much of the herding. This contrasts with Hunza where dairy tasks and herding are men's work. Although all Wakhi visit the summer pastures, men recognise it as the women's zone and do not stay long. These flower-filled grasslands with sparkling streams beneath snowy mountains are more than just a pleasant place for the Wakhi. They are places of renewal and contentment, perhaps the main source of their wellbeing.

The green and pleasant Wakhi villages of Gojal offer stunning views of towering peaks and spires, and a peaceful place to rest and contemplate. Gojal's villages, south to north along the KKH, are Shishkut, Gulmit, Ghulkin, Hussaini, Passu, Khaibar, Ghalapan, Morkhun, Jamalabad, Gircha, and Sost. The remote Chapursan and Shimshal valleys lie west and east of the KKH. Gulmit is the main village of Gojal with a post office, library, and Wakhi cultural museum.

Peaceful Passu is at the centre of trekking in Gojal. It sits between the Passu and Batura glaciers along the west bank of the Hunza River and is also the jumping off place for treks to Shimshal (see the Shimshal & Boiber Valleys map). Sost, where customs and immigration posts for the Pakistan-China border are, is somewhat of a boom town and the entry point for Chapursan Valley and the Khunjerab National Park. Most treks in Gojal go to the alpine pasture areas along or above the extensive glaciers of the region.

INFORMATION
Maps
The Swiss Foundation for Alpine Research 1:250,000 orographical sketch map *Karakoram Sheet 1* covers all of Gojal. The US AMS *India and Pakistan Series U502* 1:250,000 *Baltit (NJ 43-14)* sheet and the Leomann 1:200,000 *Karakoram Trekking and Mountaineering* maps *Sheet 1: (Gilgit, Hunza, Rakaposhi, Batura Area)* show the Batura Glacier, Chapursan and Lupgar valleys, and other areas west of the Hunza

River. The U502 *Shimshal (NJ 43-15)* sheet covers Shimshal village, the Pamir, and Ghujerab Valley. Leomann's *Sheet 2: (Skardu, Hispar, Biafo)* covers Shimshal village and the Pamir. The best map of the Batura Glacier is the 1:60,000 *The Map of the Batura Wall* published by Academia Sinica, Lanchow, China, in 1978. The 1:1,000,000 *Batura Muztagh* orographic sketch map and the Deutscher Alpenverein (DAV) 1:100,000 *Hunza – Karakoram* map are also excellent.

Regulations
All of Gojal except Chapursan is in an open zone where neither a permit from the Tourism Division nor a licensed mountain guide is required. Chapursan is in a restricted zone, where you are required to get a permit and hire a licensed guide. When you cross from the Batura Glacier over the Werthum Pass to the Lupgar Valley, the area north of the pass is also in a restricted zone.

Shimshal Foreigners are not allowed beyond Shuwerth in the Shimshal Pamir. Previously, some foreigners took advantage of Shimshali trust and crossed into Chinese territory where they were arrested. The KSF at Koksil does not normally allow trekkers to enter the Koksil Valley from the KKH. If you want to trek from Koksil to Shimshal village, you need special permission from the DC, the IG, or the AIG in Gilgit.

Chapursan According to the Tourism Division, Chapursan is in a restricted zone. Chapursan was in a closed zone for years and only within the last few years have foreigners visited here. The Khunjerab Security Force (KSF) police guard the bridge over the Khunjerab River (above Sost) into the Chapursan Valley. Trekkers with a valid permit issued by the Tourism Division have been refused entry and sent to Gilgit and/or Islamabad for 'proper' permission. Confusion still exists between the Ministry of Sports & Tourism and the Ministry of Interior, who supervise the police, whether Chapursan is in a closed or restricted zone. Until this is resolved, you should also obtain either written permission from the Ministry of Interior in Islamabad or visit the DC (☎ 2325), IG or AIG (☎ 2502), or SSP (☎ 3302) in Gilgit with your Tourism Division permit to request their cooperation. They can contact the KSF post to announce your permission to enter Chapursan.

You need to leave photocopies of your Tourism Division permit with the KSF at the Chapursan bridge and with the army at Baba Ghundi Ziarat. When crossing the Chilinji An (see the Chapursan & Lupgar Valleys map), you also need to give photocopies to the police in Imit or those in Upper Chitral.

Accommodation & Supplies
NAPWD Rest Houses can be booked with the Chief Engineer in Gilgit.

Gulmit Abdul Bari, owner of *Gulmit Tourist Cottage* (☎ (046) 19), has dorms/doubles that cost Rs 40/150. The *Village Hotel* (☎ (046) 12) near the pologround has a few doubles with shared bathrooms for equivalent rates and comfortable doubles from Rs 200. The *Evershine Hotel*, run by Sikander and Nadir, is at the north end of Gulmit on the KKH. Dorms/doubles cost Rs 30/150. A run-down *NAPWD Rest House* has doubles. The *Marco Polo Inn* (☎ (46) 107) has singles/doubles from Rs 600/700. The *Silk Route Lodge* (☎ (046) 18) and its annex, the *Horse Shoe Motel*, cost Rs 650/850. A *Village Guest House* (☎ 12), just south of the pologround, is run by Ghulam Uddin where rooms in his traditional Wakhi home cost Rs 220/330.

Ghulkin Along the KKH at the Ghulkin link road is the *Al-Rahim Hotel* where doubles cost from Rs 250. Ghulkin village, well above the KKH, has no accommodation.

Borit Lake Along the lake's south-east end is the *Borit Lake Hotel*; camping is free, beds cost Rs 25 to Rs 30.

Passu The spartan, but cheerful, *Batura Inn*, just north of the bus stop, began in 1974 as a canteen for Chinese officers overseeing KKH construction. Owner Izzatullah Baig is an excellent cook. Camping is free, dorms cost Rs 35. Private rooms with attached bathroom cost Rs 50 per person. Check out the 'rumour book' full of good (and bad) advice about the area. Staff provide hot water in buckets upon request. The *Passu Inn* (☎ 1) is adjacent to the bus stop and Passu stores and has the only telephone in town. Owner Ghulam Muhammed has dorms for Rs 50 and doubles for Rs 100. Hot-shower doubles cost Rs 350 and up.

The *Shisper View Hotel* is 0.5 km south of the centre of Passu and gets several hours more sunlight than the other hotels. The sign on the KKH says 'Sheeshper Hotel'. Owner Azim Shah offers camping for Rs 20 per person, doubles without bathroom in the building nearest the road for Rs 35 per person, and doubles in the main building with attached bathroom for Rs 50 per person. Hot water is provided in buckets upon request.

Ahmed Karim runs the well-appointed *Village Guest House Passu* in the village itself, a five minute walk from the bus stop. Patterned after a traditional Wakhi-style home, the dorm costs Rs 50 and carpeted singles/doubles with attached bathrooms cost Rs 150/300. All bathrooms have hot running water. Travellers recommend food in all hotels. All owners provide information freely. A *NAPWD Rest House* is opposite the Passu Inn.

Shimshal Valley A shop at Dūt has basic supplies, but bring everything with you. Pots, pans, plates, cups, and a stove are in the huts at Dūt and Ziarat. These are conveniences for the Shimshalis who constantly travel this trail to bring supplies to their village. Do not abuse this open hospitality; always leave these huts clean and tidy. Tourism is still new to Shimshal, but a few families make their orchards available for trekkers, and offer to cook Shimshal-style meals in their homes. The *Disteghil Cottage* was the first Shimshal home to cater to trekkers and has a pleasant orchard enclosed by stone walls. Trekkers are expected to pay a reasonable fee for food.

Sost The border check post, commonly known as Sost, has physically moved a few km north of Sost village and is called Afiyatabad. The immigration, health check post, and booking offices for transport are here. Along the KKH are over 40 stores, many selling Chinese goods. Hotels are popping up everywhere and most are overpriced. Cheap places line the KKH and are usually full of Pakistani men going to Kashgar. The *Tourist Lodge*, popular with groups, has dorms/singles/doubles from Rs 35/350/450. The *Dreamland Hotel* has dorms/doubles from Rs 25/150. At the south end are the *Mountain Refuge Hotel*, which costs from Rs 60/250 and serves family-style meals, and the *Khunjerab View Hotel*, which costs Rs 70/350. Singles/doubles cost Rs 700/800 at the *PTDC Motel*.

Chapursan Valley The only hotel is the small and unused *Irshad Peak Inn* in Sher-e-sabz, five minutes beyond Reshit. More hotels will no doubt spring up as tourism expands. Villagers generally can sell a few eggs, potatoes, or small quantities of wheat flour, sugar, milk, tea, and kerosene. Everything, except potatoes and eggs, is more expensive because it is brought up by road.

GETTING THERE & AWAY
Gojal Villages
A daily NATCO bus goes between Gilgit and Sost and another goes from Sost to Gilgit. Passengers can get on or off anywhere along the way. From the NATCO bus stand near NLI Chowk in Gilgit, the bus departs at 8 am, stopping for lunch in Aliabad about 11 am, and reaching Gulmit about 1 pm, Passu about 1.30 pm, and Sost by 3 pm. From Sost, the bus departs about 5 am, reaching Passu about 6.30 am, Gulmit about 7 am, Aliabad about 8 am, and Gilgit by noon. From Gilgit, NATCO bus fares are Rs 30 to Aliabad, Rs 40 to Gulmit, Rs 50 to Passu, and Rs 60 to Sost.

Private transport companies run vans and minibuses in both directions. In Gilgit, Hunza Coach Service (HCS) (☎ 3553) and Neelum Transports (☎ 2856), both on Airport Rd near the petrol pumps, operate vehicles regularly. These vehicles tend to be quicker and more comfortable than NATCO buses. They usually depart in the morning when full of passengers. From Gilgit, private fares are about Rs 50 to Aliabad, Rs 60 to Gulmit, Rs 70 to Passu, and from Rs 80 to Rs 100 to Sost.

Shimshal Valley
From Passu (see the Shimshal & Boiber Valleys map) you can either walk or hire a vehicle to go 12 km up the jeep road to Jurjur, and possibly beyond to Shewgarden or Dūt. Follow the KKH north out of Passu 3.5 km to where the KKH reaches the bluffs above the Hunza River and bends north. The Shimshal road turns off the KKH 0.5 km beyond the bend and crosses the Hunza River over a suspension bridge, which was completed in 1990. A foot trail leads steeply down from the bend to the bridge. Shimshal villagers, using compressors, drills and dynamite provided by the AKRSP, began this road themselves in 1985 after the government had declared it impossible. However, the government is now committed to completing the rest of the link road. As you go to Shimshal, imagine trying not only to build such a road, but also trying to keep it clear and open! The road has become a real symbol of the Shimshal people's aspiration. Special jeeps or tractors to Jurjur cost Rs 300 to Rs 600. Ask at any Passu hotel or ask any jeep or tractor driver. If you hired a porter, ask him to arrange a vehicle.

Chapursan Valley
A 70-km-long jeep road begins beyond Sost at the Chapursan bridge on the KKH and goes to Baba Ghundi Ziarat at the head of the valley (see the Chapursan & Lupgar Valleys map). Usually several jeeps or pickup trucks leave Sost every afternoon, shortly after the daily NATCO bus from Gilgit arrives. Most locals and trekkers travel the length of the valley by road. Vehicles go to each of the

three trail heads: Raminj, Yishkuk, and Baba Ghundi Ziarat.

The drive from Sost to Raminj takes one hour, to Yishkuk three hours, and to Ziarat four hours. As one of many passengers in a jeep or pickup truck, you can travel inexpensively. Passenger rates Sost-Raminj are Rs 20 to Rs 30, and Sost-Zood Khun Rs 40 to Rs 50. Special hires cost Sost-Raminj Rs 400 to Rs 600, Sost-Zood Khun Rs 800 to Rs 1000, Sost-Ziarat Rs 1200 to Rs 1500, and Zood Khun-Ziarat Rs 500 to Rs 700.

When you combine two or more treks in Chapursan, you may travel along the road between villages. Vehicles going daily up and down the valley pick up passengers for fixed rates (eg Raminj-Zood Khun costs Rs 30 per person plus Rs 10 per bag). Beyond Zood Khun, either hire a vehicle to take you to Yishkuk or walk the one stage along the jeep road in two hours. It is a one hour drive from Zood Khun to Ziarat. If you walk these 10 km, it is two stages. If you take porters in a vehicle, pay them only for stages over which they carry a load.

Koksil

Koksil, along the KKH, is the trail head for treks coming over the Chapchingol Pass from the Ghujerab Valley (see the Shimshal Pamir & Ghujerab Valley map). Unless you arrange a special vehicle to meet you, you must catch whatever type of ride you can to Sost. Daily Chinese buses are usually full and do not pick up trekkers. The NATCO Landcruisers and buses returning empty from Tashkurgan may stop. Local jeeps and tractors occasionally pass and may stop. No set fares exist, so be patient and negotiate.

GUIDES & PORTERS
Chapursan

Porters from other valleys generally are not allowed to carry loads in Chapursan. When a trekking party comes from Chitral, Chitrali porters carry loads to the trail head at Baba Ghundi Ziarat, from where they walk back to Chitral. The maximum low-altitude porter's wage per stage is Rs 160 per person. They ask for wāpāsi, food rations, and Rs 200 for the clothing and equipment allowance.

Passu & Ghulkin

When you cross either the Passu or Batura glaciers, hire a local guide and/or porter(s) to ensure safer glacier crossings. Trekkers do get lost or injured (some die) trying to cross these glaciers without a guide or porters. When unaccompanied foreigners have an accident or die, authorities hold villagers responsible. They have pressured villagers into not allowing any trekker to go onto a glacier without a local person. When you try to go on a glacier without a local, you make life more difficult for the villagers. If you try to hire someone solely for a glacier crossing, the charge may be the same as for an entire trek, so this strategy is not likely to save money.

Passu villagers have a rotational system for assigning local guides and porters. A list of all village men is kept at the Passu general store and men are sent in the order their name appears on the list. This assures that everyone gets their turn to earn money. The maximum low-altitude porter's wage per stage is a flat rate of Rs 220. Porters bring their own food and equipment. Wāpāsi, food rations, and the clothing and equipment allowance are included in the flat rate.

Shimshal

Shimshalis are amazing porters who carry heavy loads all day long over trails that would leave most trekkers dragging. They are the choice as high-altitude porters on most mountaineering expeditions. Shimshalis eager to work as porters often wait at Passu hotels, and also at the Evershine Hotel in Gulmit. Passu men also wait at Passu hotels, and they, too, are eager for work. Passu porters have rights to work as porters up to Shewgarden. Shimshalis have rights to work from Shewgarden to Shimshal. Even if you hire Passu porters to Shimshal village, beyond that point you have to hire Shimshali porters.

The maximum low-altitude porter's wage is Rs 160 per stage, plus Rs 60 per stage food rations. Wāpāsi is also paid, but they do not ask for the clothing and equipment allowance. This does not excuse you from being sure they are properly equipped for any glacier travel.

Porters may ask for higher per stage wages or for reduced weight of loads when going to the Pamir or to the Ghujerab Valley. Porters usually do not carry more than 25 kg to the Pamir, including their personal food and gear. However, these trekking routes are below 5000m and government regulations do not require you to reduce load weight. Bargain hard to reach a fair agreement about wages and weights of loads before starting.

You can also hire yaks to carry loads instead of porters above Shimshal village. These shaggy, wonderful beasts can also be ridden over steep or difficult sections. A yak carries two porter loads. You pay a standard porter wage for each yak. The yak's owner also comes along, and receives a standard porter wage, even though that load is being carried by the yak. This strategy saves money only if one person handles two or more yaks at a time.

YUNZ VALLEY

(1 day; April to October)

The Yunz Valley, which was formed by a glacier, runs south to north, parallel to and west of the main Hunza Valley, between the Passu and Batura glaciers. This is an easy day hike to stretch your legs before tackling any of the longer treks out of Passu. The Yunz Valley is dry, so carry water from Passu. Water at Passu Lake and at Yunzben is silty and undesirable. You get excellent views of both the Passu and Batura glaciers on this walk, which you will appreciate if you plan to trek up either of them. The view of Passu village and the Hunza Valley from Zard Sar, the rocky plateau east of and above the Yunz Valley, is worthwhile. The old trail to the Yunz Valley was destroyed by a landslide, and now you can only go via Passu Lake.

Guides & Porters

A guide is not necessary, but if you are uncertain about finding your way through unfamiliar terrain, do not hesitate to hire one. Do not go alone; look for a companion at any of Passu's hotels.

2 stages: Passu to Yunzben and Yunzben to Passu

Map Notes

On the Swiss map, Zard Sar is labelled as Sart. The Leomann map is not recommended and is inaccurate for this walk. Recently formed Passu Lake is not on any map.

Route Description

Day 1: Passu Village via Yunz Valley Round Trip (6 to 8 hours) From Passu village (2400m), walk 10 minutes south on the KKH (see the Passu & Batura Glaciers map). The trail starts from behind the first building, a jeep shed, on the west side of the KKH before the bridge. Pass an open, usually empty concrete water tank, following the irrigation channel through thorny scrub. The clear trail, marked by small cairns, skirts the base of a whitish rock buttress. Cross a flat, open, stony area 15 minutes from the KKH and ascend a small terminal moraine ridge to see Passu Lake, formed about 1989 when the Passu Glacier retreated.

Continue around the north shore of the lake to its far west end. Follow cairns and ascend the gravelly gullies amid dark, smooth, glacially polished rock. At times, the trail and the cairns are hard to find. As you ascend, you see the Passu Glacier's dark ice to the south (left). Do not stray too far left, and do not go onto the crevassed glacier. The trail soon becomes more obvious. As the angle begins to lessen, you see the white-toothed seracs of the Passu Glacier to the west, and the Yunz Valley to the north.

Continue up the now scree-covered trail to the top of the rock formation, 30 minutes from the lake. A clear trail angles up and to the east (right) across the face of the grey lateral moraine on the north side of the valley. Reach the base of this moraine wall in 15 minutes and go up the trail. At the top, turn west and enter an ablation valley, with a few junipers, sage brush, and wild rose bushes. Follow a trail through the ablation valley for 10 minutes. Then turn north up a gully five to 10 minutes reaching the slate-slab bench at the top and the actual start of the Yunz Valley (2775m).

After about one hour, at the upper (north) end of the valley there are two huts west of the trail. From these huts (3000m), another trail heads east and around the north end of the rock bluffs that rise above the eastern side of the Yunz Valley. On top of these bluffs is the ridge top called Zard Sar (*zard* means 'yellow'; *sar*, the top) overlooking Passu

village and the Hunza River valley. It is an additional 1½ to two hours round trip to visit Zard Sar and return to the huts.

The main Yunz Valley trail continues north. Stay right and descend briefly to a small terrace overlooking the Batura Glacier with some tumble-down huts, only one of which is used. This view point is a good place for lunch. Descend steeply over scree and loose soil about 15 minutes to the main ablation valley along the south side of the Batura Glacier. Get water on the Batura Glacier, north of the Yunzben hut. The hut is called

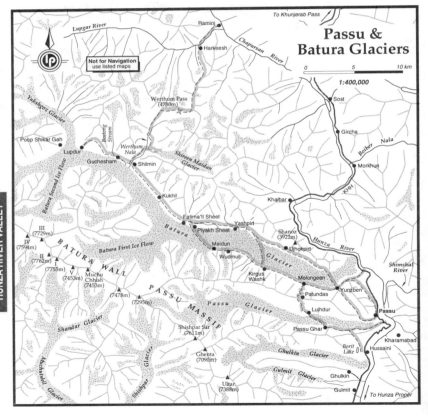

'Summer House', in memory of Summer Beg, the father of Passu guide Sanjar Beg.

From here, return as you would from the Batura Glacier trek, heading east along the well-used and dusty trail through the ablation valley and down the rocky moraine ridge (see Day 7 Batura Glacier below). It takes two to three hours to reach Passu from Yunzben via the trail crossing the plateau between the Batura Glacier and Passu.

ABDEGAR

(2 days; April to October)

Abdegar is a winter pasture area for Passu's yaks east of and about 1200m above Passu and the Hunza River. From Abdegar there are fantastic views to the west of the Passu and Batura glaciers and the peaks above them. The trek to Abdegar takes two days, camping overnight at the pastures. It can also be done as a very strenuous day hike of eight to 10 hours. Regardless, this walk should be attempted only by fit and already acclimatised trekkers, as the route is relentlessly steep and gains elevation rapidly. When you go to the ridge top above the Abdegar pastures, plan on a three-day trip, camping two nights at the pastures. For those short on time or not yet acclimatised, walking the loop from Passu via Yashbandan, crossing the Hunza River, passing through Zarabad, and recrossing the Hunza River at Hussaini is a good five to six-hour day hike.

Guides & Porters

Hiring a guide removes any uncertainty about finding your way through unfamiliar terrain. The trail is very steep, so hiring a porter to carry your gear makes this a more pleasant walk.

4 stages: Passu to Kharamabad, Kharamabad to Abdegar, and return via the same route. When you go to the ridge above Abdegar pastures it is another two stages; one up, one down.

Map Notes

The Swiss map locates Yashbandan village incorrectly; it is on the true right (west) side of the Hunza River. Hussaini village is labelled as Sesoni. Abdegar pastures are not marked and the Abdegar Glacier is labelled as Abdigar Dur Glacier. Abdegar pastures and the Abdegar Glacier are not marked on the Leomann map, but the route is. The U502 *Baltit (NJ 43-14)* sheet does not show the route or the pastures.

Route Description

Day 1: Passu to Abdegar (5 to 7 hours)
From Passu, walk south on the KKH for 10 minutes past the Shisper View Hotel to the first hairpin bend. On the east (river) side of the road is a wider section where jeeps can turn around and a footpath to the small village of Yashbandan (*yash* means 'horse'; *bandan*, 'a place to tie up something'), where the Mir of Hunza used to keep horses. Continue on the KKH about 10m to a well-used foot trail down and east into a small valley, skirting the stone walls around the fields of Yashbandan. At the far end of the stone walls, a jeep track from the KKH intersects the trail. Follow the foot trail up the other side of this small valley. Looking back and to your right, you see 'Welcome to Passu' in white letters on the hillside above the KKH.

The well-used trail dips through rocky gullies as it heads south and east towards the Hunza River. In the second small gully, a boulder just east of the trail has ibex graffiti. The high-water trail, used from June to August, stays on the hillside above the Hunza River. In April and May, and in September and October, the low-water trail descends to cross the gravelly flood plain in a more direct line to the bridge. The high-water trail takes about 30 minutes from the KKH to the bridge, while the low-water trail takes about 20 minutes. Villagers call the bridge *dūt*. It takes about 10 minutes and some 435 careful steps on narrow boards spaced 0.75m apart to cross. This would be difficult, and may not be possible, for anyone who experiences vertigo. In high winds, the bridge tilts radically and is impossible to cross. Winds can arise any time and are especially common in the afternoon and in the spring.

HUNZA RIVER VALLEY

Across the bridge and up the bank, the trail forks; the left-hand trail goes north-east to Kharamabad, and the right-hand trail goes south-east to Zarabad and on to the footbridge over the Hunza River to Hussaini. To go to Abdegar, bear north-east and follow the footpath about 45 minutes to Kharamabad. Ascend to the irrigation channel above Kharamabad and follow it north (left) and up about 30 minutes to where the channel begins in a stream coming from a waterfall. Fill water bottles here, as water above is scarce. Go up the stream a short way, until about 100m below the waterfall, and cross the stream. Ascend the steep scree slope. No single trail exists, so ascend where it seems easiest. As the angle lessens, avoid the temptation to head north (left). Continue straight up the juniper-dotted slope to the more level grassy pasture called Abdegar (3600m), three to five hours from Kharamabad. Camp here, taking water from a stream descending from the rocks at the south (right) end of this grassy area. You can also traverse the grassy areas to the last, northernmost (left) area and camp there (3700m), where water can also be found.

The views of the Ghulkin, Passu, and Batura glaciers and the peaks above them are spectacular, as though one were flying above them in a helicopter. The morning sun lights the glaciers and the peaks of the Batura Muztagh nicely. Even more perspective can be gained by ascending to the notch in the ridge above, where a rock finger points up. From the first large grassy area, head north (left) and cross the first large scree slope into a grassy area. Then cross a smaller scree slope and ascend the grassy area beyond, switchbacking up the rock above the highest extent of grass. Passu yaks do this, which seems unlikely, but is true. The elevation on the ridge is 3900m to 4100m. However, the views from the grassy pastures below are superb and most trekkers do not attempt the more rigorous climb to the ridge top.

Day 2: Abdegar to Passu (5 to 7 hours)
Return to Passu via the same route. Alterna-

tively, take the south-east trail fork at the bridge to Zarabad, and follow the trail that skirts the cliffs above the Hunza River to an equally interesting foot bridge crossing the Hunza River to Hussaini village and return to Passu along the KKH.

PATUNDAS & BORIT SAR
(3 days; May to October)
Patundas (4100m) is a dry pasture, with a cluster of huts and goat pens on the ridge top between the Passu and Batura glaciers (see the Passu & Batura Glaciers map). The views from Patundas are spectacular in all directions, and it is quite enjoyable to stroll through the alpine meadows for hours along the ridge top. The steep 1700m ascent from either Borit Lake or Passu and return is usually done in three days. Because of the rapid elevation gain, you must be already acclimatised. Do this trek after, for instance, having trekked up the Batura Glacier. Crossing the tricky Passu Glacier requires a rope for safety. Crampons are recommended, but are optional. The optional day hike to the base camp for the snowy peaks along the ridge adds a day to the trip. The walk to Passu Ghar huts requires no guide and can be done in one long day, or more leisurely as an overnight trip. Borit Sar is also a day hike.

Guides & Porters
You need a guide who knows the current route across the dangerous Passu Glacier. Since Patundas pastures are the property of Ghulkin villagers, they have exclusive portering rights. If you are staying in Passu, arrange for a guide or porters by sending a message to Ghulkin with any Ghulkin tractor or jeep driver going down the KKH. This takes at least one day. A quicker way is to go to the Al-Rahim Hotel along the KKH, just north of Gulmit. The owner can send a message for a guide and/or porters to meet you at your hotel in Passu. Alternatively, you can arrange this from the Borit Lake Hotel. Do not try to cross the Passu Glacier without a guide; trekkers have been lost and died doing that.

JOHN MOCK

JOHN MOCK

JOHN MOCK

Top: Famous Hunza apricots being dried in Garelt on woven willow racks
Left: A spectacular camp site beneath the Rupal face of Nanga Parbat (8126m)
Middle Right: Villagers in the remote Shimshal region rely heavily on their yaks.
Bottom Right: Shimshalis and trekkers cross the Ghujerab River by cable at Wariben.

JOHN MOCK

JOHN MOCK

JOHN MOCK

Top Left: A shaky bridge crosses over the Momhil River on the way to Shimshal village.
Top Right: The grassy amphitheatre of Ultar beneath glaciers and Ultar Peak (7388m)
Bottom: The shrine Baba Ghundi Ziarat (on the Chapursan trek) holds deep
significance for local people.

6 stages: Passu or Borit Lake to Passu Ghar, Passu Ghar to Lujhdur, Lujhdur to Patundas, and return via the same route

Map Notes

On the Swiss map, Lujhdur is labelled as Lazhdar and Molongeen as Mulung Hil. The trail marked on the north side of the Passu Glacier between Passu village and Lujhdur no longer exists, due to changes in the glacier. The route shown to Patundas from the Yunz Valley is exposed, tricky, and not recommended. The route to Patundas is not marked on the Leomann map.

Route Description

Day 1: Passu to Passu Ghar (3 to 4 hours)
This route begins from Passu village or Borit Lake. All trails join at a large slate platform at the base of Borit Sar.

From Passu, walk five minutes south of the Shisper View Hotel along the KKH. A triangular road sign is before the first hairpin bend in the road. Just before this sign, and just beyond where the irrigation channel on the south side of the road goes underground and the vegetation ends, leave the KKH and go up five metres to a good trail heading west. Ascend gradually along a low spur with the KKH below on both sides.

Follow the telephone lines, switchbacking 20 to 30 minutes to a saddle. Hussaini and the KKH to the south are visible. The rock above the saddle has many pockets, which provide nesting sites for crows. Just to the west of the saddle is a large boulder with ibex graffiti low on its west side. The trail to Patundas turns west, and curves around the south-west side of a ridge above the Passu Glacier, joining an abandoned irrigation channel that curves back to the edge of the Passu Glacier valley. Ascend briefly to a large slate platform at the base of Borit Sar 45 minutes to one hour from the saddle. The slate platform overlooks Passu Lake at the mouth of the Passu Glacier and the trail north up the Yunz Valley.

From Borit Lake, the trail ascends north towards the ridge above the Passu Glacier and joins the abandoned water channel before the slate platform. It takes one hour from Borit Lake to this point.

Locals take an alternative, steep, cross-country route to this point from Passu village. Consider this route only if you are accompanied by someone from Passu who knows the way. Leave the KKH at the south end of the bridge over the Passu River. Turn west (right) up the true right bank of the Passu River to the small hotel (under construction at the time of writing) overlooking the KKH and the river. Continue through scrub and thorny brush, cross a low stone wall and continue through open wasteland, heading towards the largest moraine ridge. Ascend this moraine heap and follow the crest until it is possible to traverse to the ablation valley between the moraine ridge and the cliffs to the south. Walk up the ablation valley to its end and climb easy 2nd-class shale to the abandoned water channel just west of the slate platform mentioned above. Going quickly, it takes one hour to reach this point.

An optional side trip or day hike ascends Borit Sar. Leave the trail at the slate platform and scramble up over broken slate slabs, then over open artemisia-dotted slopes, and easily on up to the high point. This is a five to six-hour round trip from Passu if you are going quickly, or an eight to 10-hour round trip if going more leisurely. The high point overlooks the Passu and Ghulkin glaciers and Borit Lake. From the slate platform to Borit Sar and back takes three to six hours.

To go to Passu Ghar, continue from the slate platform (2730m) 30 minutes along the old water channel that traverses the cliff face above the Passu Glacier to an ablation valley. From the western end of this level ablation valley, ascend steadily, climbing 240m in 30 minutes to a well-deserved rest point at the edge of the lateral moraine, overlooking the incredibly broken white seracs of the Passu Glacier to the north. Descend slightly to meet another abandoned water channel through an ablation valley. Twenty to 30 years ago, the Passu Glacier extended much further down valley, and had a higher level. Then, streams flowed in these now dry ablation valleys, which enabled people to irrigate the now arid land between Passu, Hussaini, and Borit Lake.

At the west end of this ablation valley is a level area with room for many tents. At the base of the slope is a small water source that is often cloudy with glacial silt. A better camp site with five or six small, level tent sites amid junipers is above on the east-facing hillside. Where junipers first appear along the old irrigation channel, take a well-worn path up five to 10 minutes to a clear, small, year-round stream. A good pit latrine, with a high stone wall for privacy, is on the opposite (east) side of the small stream. This camp, and the larger camp below, are the Passu Ghar camp sites (3100m).

Day 2: Passu Ghar to Patundas (3 to 6 hours) Ascend through junipers 15 minutes to the four huts and goat pen of Passu Ghar, a summer herding settlement for the Ghulkin villagers. Cross in five minutes to the top of the lateral moraine ridge of the heavily broken and crevassed Passu Glacier. Its white seracs are beautiful, but deadly. Fix a rope along narrow ice ramps above deep crevasses, from which rescue would be difficult. Cut steps on the steep, slippery ice, or wear crampons.

This dangerous section eases after the first 100m. Go directly out to the middle of the glacier, then turn west and head up the middle of the glacier. When opposite the light-coloured cliffs on the north margin of the glacier, turn north and head for the cliffs.

The difficult route across the Passu Glacier changes from year to year as the glacier shifts. It passes towering seracs and deep, wide crevasses, and the footing is treacherous. The margins of the glacier are more broken, difficult and dangerous, and steps need to be cut. The crossing takes from one to 2½ hours of moving steadily.

Lujhdur (3400m), with its five huts and goat pen, is in the ablation valley at the base of the light-coloured cliffs on the north side of the glacier, five minutes up from the edge of the ice. Lujhdur has water early in the season, but by late August, it must be carried from the glacier. Beyond Lujhdur, water is scarce, so carry all the water you need. Switchback steeply up a clear trail. Pause at the several rest benches to admire the view.

Reach the first ridge 250m above Lujhdur overlooking the Passu Glacier in 30 to 45 minutes. Continue up switchbacks for another 150m amid large, ancient juniper trees, with several more rest benches along the trail.

After 30 to 45 minutes reach the tumble-down walls of an old hut called Lujhdur Sar, where the angle lessens. From April to early June, water from snow melt makes this a possible camp site, but in summer, the water dries up.

Ascend more gradually, and work westward, through the rolling alpine meadows of Patundas. Ibex and Himalayan snow cock abound here, though the ibex are hard to spot. Local shepherds report that snow leopards frequent Patundas.

After 30 minutes of steady walking, reach the huts and pens of Patundas, situated at the northern edge of the plateau, high above the Batura Glacier. From here, you see the unclimbed Kuk Sar peaks at the northern head of the Batura Glacier.

Across the Hunza River to the east are the high peaks of the Hispar Muztagh; Disteghil Sar (7885m), Momhil Sar (7343m), Kanjut Sar (7760m), and Trivor (7728m). To the west, at the head of the Passu Glacier, is Shishpar (7611m). A slate-viewing platform overlooks the Batura Glacier just behind the huts.

Patundas has no water in the summer. A small trickle comes out of the rock on the north-facing cliff below Patundas huts. However, it is hard to find, and is the local people's water supply, so do not count on using it. Ghulkin villagers have established a NGO and plan to construct a water tank at Patundas.

An optional day hike is to the base camp for the peaks west of Patundas. Follow the ridge line until it becomes necessary to angle south-west (left) and down towards the upper Passu Glacier. Camp here where water comes from the nearby Passu Glacier.

Day 3: Patundas to Passu (1½ to 3 hours)
Return to Passu via the same route. The descent to Lujhdur takes half the time of the ascent. An alternative return route descends to Molongeen on the south margin of the Batura Glacier. Start just west (left) of the viewpoint, and descend precipitously 1200m. In the ablation valley, join the main route back to Passu (see Batura Glacier below).

BATURA GLACIER
(5 to 10 days; May to October)
The Batura Glacier is the most accessible of the giant Karakoram glaciers. From the KKH it stretches west about 56 km with more than 10 peaks over 7000m towering above. The trek is one of the finest in the Karakoram with beautiful scenery, and no major difficulties. Most of the trek is through ablation valleys along streams, with almost no steep sections. The pastures of Lupdur (3700m), the farthest point most trekkers go, are reached after four or five days, allowing ample time for acclimatisation.

Views of the six Batura peaks and the huge ice falls from them to the glacier below are among the more remarkable mountain scenes anywhere in the Karakoram. Spending time with the Passu people and their yaks in the pastures allows a glimpse into their unique way of life. Although the trek crosses the glacier twice, the crossings are less difficult than most glacier crossings. Those with less time or disinclined to undertake the glacier crossings can walk up the south margin of the Batura Glacier, through ablation valleys and pasture settlements used by Hussaini villagers, to the last huts at Maidūn and return by the same route. This is a pleasant three to four day trek, but does not give views of the Batura wall.

Guides & Porters
Trekkers do get lost trying to cross the glacier, so hiring someone is necessary. Additionally, government authorities now insist that all trekkers going onto the glacier must be accompanied by someone from Passu. Typically porters are hired for the duration of a trek and are not released along the way. Bring your own food. Although the Wakhi are generous and traditionally share food with visitors, you cannot expect to get food from people in the pastures. Porters also bring their own food, but may expect large trekking parties to buy a goat or sheep.

10 stages: The five stages Passu to Lupdur, when crossing via Yunzben, are Passu to Yunzben, Yunzben to Ujhokpirt, Ujhokpirt to Yashpirt, Yashpirt to Kukhil, and Kukhil to Lupdur. There are five stages to return via the same route. Most trekkers only camp as high as Guchesham, which is half a stage from Kukhil. Although Passu to Guchesham is only 4½ stages, porters charge five stages for this distance. Porters may ask for an extra stage if you cross the glacier other than at Yunzben, so negotiate this before starting.

Map Notes
Ujhokpirt is not marked on the Swiss map. It is beneath the peak labelled Shanoz (3922m). The Werthum stream is labelled Wartom Nala, the Yukshgoz Glacier is labelled as Yoksugoz Ice Flow, and Shireen Maidan Glacier is labelled as Shelin Maidan. The Leomann map does not mark the route across the Batura Glacier at Yunzben, nor is Ujhokpirt marked. Many of the place names along the north margin of the Batura Glacier are mislabelled. The route marked over to the Lugpar River valley is not a trekking route and in all likelihood is not possible to undertake. On the U502 *Baltit (NJ 43-14)* sheet, routes are marked accurately, but not all place names are shown. The depiction of the upper Batura Glacier is wildly inaccurate.

Route Description
The shortest, easiest, and most frequently used way across the Batura Glacier is between Yunzben and Ujhokpirt. You can also cross between Kirgus Washk and Yashpirt, and also between Maidūn and Piyakh Sheet. Both of these crossings are longer and more difficult than the crossing at Yunzben. From June to August, the south margin of the glacier presents a more shaded and cooler alternative to walking up and

back on the hot north side of the glacier, crossing both times at Yunzben.

We describe crossing the glacier from Yunzben to Ujhokpirt going up; and from Piyakh Sheet to Maidūn on the return, descending along the south side of the glacier. You could just as easily walk up the south side of the glacier to Kirgus Washk or Maidūn to cross to the north side and return along the north side to Ujhokpirt, and cross to Yunzben. Locals prefer the Yunzben crossing both coming and going.

Day 1: Passu or China Camp to Ujhokpirt (5 to 6½ hours) From Passu (2400m), a tractor or a jeep costs about Rs 100 to go 15 minutes north on the KKH to China Camp where Chinese road labourers working on the KKH stayed. This is the typical way to start the trek. (Otherwise, walk two to 2 ½ hours from Passu to Yunzben across the mesa, following the description from Yunzben to Passu in reverse. See Day 7.)

From China Camp, follow the irrigation channel upstream about 10 minutes to its head on the true right bank of the Batura Glacier river. Ascend the lateral moraine rubble of the Batura Glacier 45 minutes to one hour to the top of the moraine. Follow the trail through the dusty ablation valley 30 minutes to 'Summer House' at Yunzben (at the base of Yunz). It typically takes all morning to get from Passu to here. At Yunzben (2680m), water comes from small pools on the glacier. Yunzben is not a very desirable camp site, so plan to camp at either Ujhokpirt on the north side or at Kirgus Washk on the south side of the glacier.

It takes three to four hours from Yunzben to Ujhokpirt. Reach the south margin of the Batura Glacier in about 10 minutes. Bits of dung and small cairns faintly mark the route. Aim for the yellow rock face on the far side. It has a prominent white streak on its east (right) edge separating it from a black rock face. Cross the glacier in one to 1½ hours. Fill water bottles from its clear streams.

Near the north margin of the glacier, beneath the yellow rock face, turn west and continue up the unshaded lateral moraine

rubble two to 2½ hours to a small, cloudy lake. Pass the lake on its north side. Amid the willows and junipers beyond the lake is Ujhokpirt (2900m). A stream provides water in the summer, but by August it is dry, and water comes from the lake or the glacier. Although Passu people typically walk to Yashpirt in one day, it is too far for most trekkers.

Day 2: Ujhokpirt to Yashpirt (2½ to 3 hours) Walk through pretty ablation valleys, amid willows, wild rose, and some juniper two to 2½ hours, emerging into an open, level area where a stream descends from the northern cliffs. Cross this stream and contour gradually up the juniper-dotted hill directly ahead on a trail. The huts and pasture of Yashpirt (3100m) are 30 minutes ahead. Yashpirt *(yash* means 'horse'; *pirt,* 'a sloping meadow')* is a lovely spot. Across the Batura Glacier, the Batura First Ice Flow descends some 4000m from the Batura Wall to the glacier. Passu women here tend herds of yak, sheep, and goats, and may invite you to sample local delicacies such as fresh *qurut* (cheese), *pai* (yoghurt), or *mirik* (cream). Camp east of and away from the huts. Get water from a small stream flowing through the pasture area.

Day 3: Yashpirt to Guchesham (4½ to 5 hours) Descend west past some large junipers to the alluvial plain in the ablation valley. Follow the easy trail up the glacier (west), through a lovely series of small ablation valleys, amid abundant juniper, willow, and birch. In one hour, the terrain opens onto a huge alluvial plain called Fatima'il Sheet. The huts are at the western end of this plain, against the aeolian fluted cliff. Continue up the ablation valley and reach a good-sized stream 30 minutes from Fatima'il. This is the Werthum stream, which drains the glaciers in the Werthum Nala, and disappears under the Batura Glacier. Cross it and continue along its true right (south) bank another hour to Kukhil *(kuk* means 'spring'; *hil,* 'a sheep fold')*. A gravelly spot on the south side of the Werthum stream, 100m below Kukhil, is the best camp site. Across a wooden bridge are the huts and goat pen of Kukhil.

From Kukhil, follow the true right (south) bank 1½ to two hours to another large alluvial fan where the Werthum stream descends from the northern Werthum Nala (see Werthum Nala to Lupgar Valley below). This open area is Shilmin (3385m), named after *shil*, a flower abundant here. Cross the alluvial fan and descend to a ford of the Bostong stream. Climb up onto a level terrace, and 30 minutes from Shilmin, reach Guchesham (*gul* means 'flower' in Persian; *chesham*, 'an eye'), with its 10 huts and goat pen. The camp site is directly across the Bostong stream from Guchesham (3400m) on a flat plain at the base of a white scree slope, from which a spring emerges. The views of the Batura Wall from the moraine ridge south of Guchesham are spectacular. In the distance to the east is Disteghil Sar, the highest peak west of K2.

Day 4: Day Hike to Lupdur (6 hours) Lupdur offers great views of the Batura Second Ice Flow, the upper Batura Glacier and Kampir Dior (7143m). From Guchesham, stay on the true right (south) bank of the Bostong stream and walk up valley for 30 minutes, towards the obvious trail up the grassy slope. The trail eases after the first steep 100m. Follow the trail one hour to the Lupdur meadows (3750m to 4000m). Ibex and Himalayan snow cock frequent these slopes. The views from here are worth the whole trek. Lupdur, which means 'big meadow', is bisected by a large ravine with a small pool at its bottom. Cross this ravine, continue through more pastures for better views of the Batura Second Ice Flow, and a view up the Yukshgoz (ibex grass) Glacier. Across the Yukshgoz Glacier, on the western side, is another meadow called Poop Shikar Gah (grandfather's hunting grounds). Beyond Lupdur lie the base camps for Kampir Dior and Pamiri Sar (7016m).

Day 5: Guchesham to Piyakh Sheet (4 to 5 hours) From Guchesham to Shilmin takes 30 minutes, and from Shilmin, it is a two to

2½ hour easy walk back to Kukhil. From Kukhil, it takes 45 minutes to one hour to the Werthum stream crossing. Fatima'il is another 30 minutes further. Cross the Fatima'il Sheet, passing through a strange stand of *turugokh* trees, a kind of poplar. Where the broad alluvial fan narrows to enter the ablation valley, 30 minutes below the picturesque Fatima'il huts, is Piyakh Sheet. Camp here and get water from the Fatima'il stream, or if it is too silty, from the glacier.

Day 6: Piyakh Sheet to Kirgus Washk (4 to 5 hours) Turn south and cross moraine rubble for five minutes, then descend the lateral moraine ridge to reach the Batura Glacier in a few minutes. Crossing the glacier here is not easy. Go up and down on steep moraine rubble 45 minutes to one hour. Then reach white ice and go up and down and around crevasses 30 to 45 minutes, after which again come heaps of moraine rubble that take another 30 to 45 minutes to work through. Most of the rock is very loose and unstable, making for treacherous, constantly shifting footing. A local guide is necessary since there is no trail at all. After two to three hours, emerge on the southern margin of the glacier at the five huts of Maidūn, the highest pasture area of Hussaini villagers.

Follow a trail down the ablation valley 10 minutes to a small stream on an alluvial fan, and stop for water. Twenty minutes beyond this, reach the two huts and goat pen of Wudmull. Below Wudmull, leave the ablation valley and walk on a juniper-forested terrace well above the ablation valley. The trail grows faint as it crosses a rocky fan, which it ascends to avoid cliffs. Thirty to 45 minutes from Wudmull, a deep, narrow ravine slices through this terrace, just beyond the end of the nice juniper forest. Cross the ravine, which can be difficult in the summer when it holds a rushing stream, and descend five minutes to a small flat area at the base of a juniper-forested cliff. Cross this and descend gradually to a very big alluvial fan that has some snow pack in it. Cross this fan in 10 to 15 minutes. On its east side is a small stream. Just beyond this is Kirgus Washk *(kirgus* means 'eagle'; *washk* 'alighted'), with two huts and a goat pen. Just before Kirgus Washk, near a small hillside and close to the stream, is a good flat, grassy camp site.

Day 7: Kirgus Washk to Passu (5 to 7 hours) The trail goes along the top of the southern and lower of two parallel moraine ridges. Some 30 minutes below Kirgus Washk are two small blue lakes, suitable for a dip. Skirt the hillside beyond these lakes, staying high above the ablation valley, passing through nice stands of juniper and wild rose. Below Kirgus Washk 1½ hours is a very large, light-coloured boulder with a cairn on top and a goat pen underneath. This area, with its mixed grass and scree slopes, is called Landgarben (the base of the big rock). Thirty minutes below the large boulder is a dry lake bed, and 15 minutes beyond that are the four huts and goat pen of Molongeen, where the steep trail from Patundas joins the main trail. Just below Molongeen are two helipads, built by the Pakistan Army. The trail bends slightly north-east as it descends the ablation valley, reaching Yunzben 45 minutes to one hour from Molongeen.

Follow the dusty trail from Yunzben, and start down the moraine rubble on switchbacks. Continue down the trail and along the water channel to China Camp in one hour, and have a prearranged vehicle meet you for the 15 minute drive to Passu village, or walk the five km along the KKH in 1½ hours back to Passu. Alternatively, about 30 minutes after leaving Yunzben, take the right-hand or southerly fork in the trail as you descend the moraine. From this fork, climb the lateral moraine a few minutes to a cairn at the top and descend into the ablation valley. The trail again divides, and is marked by many cairns. Take the trail to the right, contouring across the slope 10 minutes to a rocky outcrop. Then descend amid boulders to the level plateau between the Batura Glacier valley and Passu village. Head south across this mesa through a boulder field with some goat shelters 20 minutes to the top of the scree slope, which you traverse and then descend.

Above, on the slope, in white-painted rocks are the words 'Long Live Pakistan'. This descent takes 10 to 15 minutes, and the KKH is 10 to 15 minutes ahead. As you approach the KKH you pass some ruined buildings, the remains of an old Chinese KKH labour camp. On the west side of the KKH is a rectangular sign reading AKRSP SWAP Passu Orchard. The Batura Inn is 15 minutes south along the KKH.

WERTHUM NALA TO LUPGAR VALLEY
(2 to 5 days; mid-July to September only to cross the Werthum Pass, and May to October for Werthum Nala)

The Werthum Nala is a difficult side trip from the Batura Glacier trek. This valley is popular with climbers. Several technical peaks in the 5800m to 5900m range are at the head of the Werthum Nala and also along the Shireen Maidan (sweet field) Glacier. The pastures of Shireen Maidan can be visited as a day hike from Guchesham or Shilmin. The Werthum Pass (4780m) is a difficult and infrequently crossed pass that leads north to Chapursan's Lupgar Valley. The views from the pass include Batura I (7795m) and II (7762m), Shishpar, and the Karūn Pir Pass. The pass is not technical, but before mid-July there is much snow on the pass and a cornice on its north side.

Guides & Porters
Hiring a guide and porters is recommended for the Werthum Nala and unavoidable when crossing the Werthum Pass. Only three Passu guides (Sanjar Beg, Qamar Jan, and Ali Aman) know the route over the Werthum Pass; and only one person from Raminj does. These Passu guides are training younger guides on the route over the pass.

4 stages: Shilmin to Shireen Maidan, Shireen Maidan to Werthum, and return via the same route. Stages are not fixed beyond Werthum over the Werthum Pass

Route Description
At Shilmin, half an hour below Guchesham, along the north margin of the Batura Glacier are two clear blue pools that make for nice

bathing. Camp above these pools in a level, less rocky area. From Shilmin, follow the true right (west) bank of the Werthum stream. No trail exists up the east bank. After 10 minutes, climb steeply over scree, then traverse some big slides to reach Furzeen (birch grove) after 30 minutes. This trail is narrow and more difficult than any trail along the Batura Glacier. Stroll through birch and scrub juniper 10 minutes, then descend steeply to the river, following it to the confluence of the Werthum stream and the stream from the Shireen Maidan Glacier. Ford the Werthum branch above the confluence.

On the other side is a level area, sheltered from the wind, with six stone circles for camping. Litter here indicates its frequent usage. Across Shireen Maidan pastures at the base of the big terminal moraine of the Shireen Maidan Glacier is a nice blue small pool. The return to Shilmin takes one hour. Continuing to Werthum involves difficult walking on a poor trail and requires concentration. Werthum camp, the base for climbs, is at the junction of two streams.

From Werthum camp, setting up a high camp below the pass is recommended. It takes four to five hours to reach the top of the pass. The descent goes to Bayeen Shikar Gah, a hunting place named after a local man from Chapursan, and a camp. Continue down the Bayeen Shikar Gah Nala to its juncture with the Furzeen and Lupgar valleys at Harkeesh. Continue to Raminj (see Lupgar Pir Pass & Valley below).

PASSU TO SHIMSHAL VILLAGE

(2 to 3 days; April to October, but open year-round)

The 60 km trek from Passu to Shimshal village follows the polished sandstone of the Shimshal River gorge due east from the Hunza River. Shimshal is the oldest of the Wakhi-speaking villages in Gojal. Established over 400 years ago, the 1200 residents maintain customs no longer practiced in other villages. Their large herds of yaks, sheep, and goats roam the high rolling summer grasslands of the Pamir, on the divide between South Asia and Central Asia. They also have large herds in Ghujerab and Lupgar. In the centuries prior to 1974, when the Hunza Mirs ruled Gojal, the Mir occasionally banished Hunza men to remote Shimshal. The notorious Hunza raids on the Leh-Yarkand caravan route were conducted from the Shimshal Pamir. Shimshal was closed to outsiders until 1986. Since then, only handfuls of foreigners have made the trek each year.

Shimshal's high pastures are right in the middle of the Khunjerab National Park (KNP). The KNP has been a bone of contention between Shimshal and the government since its establishment in 1975. Some Shimshalis view it as an opportunity for economic development; others view it as a vehicle through which the government could seize control of the Pamir and so threaten Shimshal's survival. The government has agreed to leave the Shimshal area out of the KNP management jurisdiction until the Shimshalis agree to accept the park.

Shimshal has a central Jamat Khana, an Aga Khan girls' school, and a government-funded boys' school. The dispenser for the Aga Khan Health Services, Farman Ullah, appreciates any donations of medicine or medical supplies, which are always scarce.

You can make short side treks to the pastures along the Lupgar or Momhil glaciers. Beyond Shimshal village, you can trek to pasture areas along the Yazghil, Khurdopin, and Virjerab glaciers. The heavily crevassed East Khurdopin Glacier leads to the difficult Khurdopin Pass and Snow Lake. You need a guide to show you the way across the Yazghil Glacier and beyond. Shimshal village is the starting point for longer treks to the Pamir and the Ghujerab Valley and Chapchingol Pass (see below).

Guides & Porters

Trekkers are more welcome in the village if accompanied by a resident. Hire someone to alert you to rock-fall danger. You pay only for stages over which loads are carried. If porters meet you at the end of the jeep road or ride in a vehicle with you from Passu to the trail head, you should not pay for these stages.

5 stages: Passu to Jurjur, Jurjur to Dūt (it is half a stage from Jurjur to Shewgarden and half a stage from Shewgarden to Dūt), Dūt to Ziarat, Ziarat to the Mulungutti Glacier, and across the Mulungutti Glacier to Shimshal. Traditionally it has always been three stages Dūt to Shimshal village, but now with the road to Dūt, porters try to charge four stages.

Map Notes
The Swiss map does not show Jurjur or the bridges over the Shimshal River before Ziarat. It shows a trail along the true right (north) bank of the Shimshal River beyond Shewgarden to a crossing at Dūt that does not exist. The existing bridge across the Shimshal River to the true left (south) bank beyond Shewgarden is not shown. The entire Shimshal settlement is larger than shown and extends further west along the river.

Leomann's sheet 2 shows the route east from Dūt. However, from Passu to Dūt is not depicted. The U502 *Baltit (NJ 43-14)* sheet does not show the route along the Shimshal River; instead it marks the unused route over the Karūn Pir Pass to Dūt.

Route Description
Day 1: Jurjur to Dūt (3 to 4 hours) Either hire a vehicle or walk from Passu (2400m) to Dūt on the jeep road. From the bridge over the swift, grey Hunza River, the jeep road follows the true right bank of the Shimshal River, contouring beneath the spires of Tupopdan peak and into the narrow Shimshal River gorge. In the late afternoon, strong winds frequently blow clouds of dust and grit down the gorge and also start rock slides. Look carefully for any sign of rock fall, and do not attempt to cross through an active rock-fall zone until it subsides.

Before the road was extended, Jurjur (2450m) was the point where vehicles

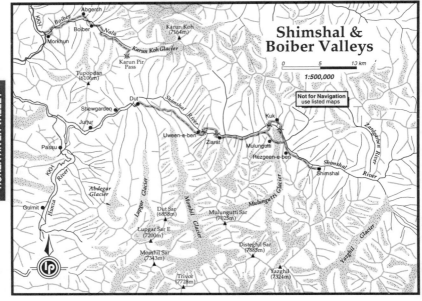

usually turned around. It is a deep cleft in the rock wall with a cooking place, and there are numerous trunks in which Shimshalis store goods for later carrying to their village.

A spring above Jurjur flows down the rock face just west of the actual cave-like camp. Fill water bottles here or in a small, clear stream just before Jurjur. Water is scarce and the sun quite hot in the gorge.

Beyond Jurjur, the road climbs above the river's true right bank. About 1.5 km beyond Jurjur, a glacial stream enters from the north. Ahead, the road rises above the river and comes to Shewgarden, the first of many large scree slopes. From the top, the descent to the river is steep. The jeep road goes beyond Shewgarden, but rock fall and high water often block the road here. The jeep bridge (under construction at the time of writing) crosses the river beyond the old footbridge.

The old trail crosses polished rock at the edge of the narrow river gorge, and 2½ to three hours' walk from Jurjur, crosses the river over a narrow, bouncy bridge made of wood planks suspended from solid steel cables.

The trail crosses a sandy stretch amid boulders, hugging the southern cliff of the gorge. After an hour, it enters an open area and reaches Dūt (2580m), where the now-abandoned trail over the Karūn Pir Pass descends to the raging river (see Boiber Valley below). An eastern hut has more open area near it, but the western one is better equipped inside.

The huts are separated by the surging dark stream that descends from the Lupgar Glacier, and clear water can usually be found in a small pool in the sand along the Lupgar stream above the huts. Otherwise, let the silty stream water settle in a large pan before using it. The huts are built in traditional Wakhi style, with a central stove and raised areas for sleeping on three sides.

The sturdy support beams will likely have bags of flour hanging from them. Shimshali men leave the flour they need for their return journey here, in order to lighten their loads. Also inside the huts are communal cooking pots, enamel tea mugs, and boards for rolling

out flat bread, which is baked on the top of the metal stove.

Day 2: Dūt to Ziarat (4 to 5½ hours) Cross the glacial Lupgar stream over a wooden bridge. It is a stiff full day's hike to the meadows along the Lupgar Glacier from here. Beyond the eastern Dūt hut, the Shimshal trail rises between dark boulders over barren ground, and descends to the small, precarious bridge built with steel cables over the Momhil River. The trail then steadily ascends cliffs above the Shimshal River's true left bank with several galleries constructed across the cliff face, which is the way all trails in Hunza used to be. The exposed trail crosses several huge scree slopes, where it is only a faint line across the ever-shifting scree.

After a 600m climb, the trail levels out high above the river, at a spot marked by cairns, before climbing briefly again through short, steep switchbacks. The trail then descends across an enormous scree slope to the sandy wastes along the Shimshal River. Rocks often come hurtling down this scree slope, and to be struck by one would be fatal. Stop and look carefully for any rock-fall activity before venturing onto the scree slope. On windy or rainy days, the likelihood of rock fall is greatly increased. The sandy area along the river bank at the base of this scree slope is called Uween-e-ben, (the place at the base of the pass). Water can often be found at the river's edge, where a spring flows from beneath rocks. When the river is at its highest, this small spring will be covered by the dark, silty torrent.

A short distance ahead, the trail crosses and then recrosses the Shimshal River over two bridges. These bridges were built in 1993 by Shimshalis using money donated by the Global Activity Group, a group of students from Nihon University in Tokyo, Japan, lead by Hideki Yamauchi and Chieko Arai, who are great friends of Shimshal. Before these bridges were built, only single steel cables spanned the river in these two locations with a small wooden box suspended from the cable. The river is crossed and recrossed here to avoid the 1000m high 'Shams' slides on the true left bank of the river. These constantly active scree slopes rain rock on the old trail along the river's edge. In addition, there is a 5th-class technical rock section that Shimshali men would traverse with huge loads! Even before the bridges were constructed, the cable crossings were preferable to the dangers of the Shams slide trail.

Just past the second bridge on the true left bank of the river, the two huts of Ziarat (2600m) sit above the river bed on a small terrace. They are in much better condition than the huts at Dūt. The largest hut has a full set of pots, white enamel mugs, many blankets hanging from beams, and hand-woven goat-hair rugs *(palōs)* covering the sleeping areas. A green wooden box sits inside the hut. It is common courtesy to leave a donation in the box for the continued maintenance of the communal hut.

In addition, you receive the blessing of the saint, Shams-e-Tabriz, whose grave site lies across the river, high on a narrow terrace, and is marked by a tiny white flag. *Ziarat* means 'saint's tomb', so this is a holy shrine and should be respected. The two huts are technically the *langar*, or kitchen, for the actual shrine. Because it is almost impossible to reach the saint's actual tomb, and it is believed to be unlucky and unwise to even attempt to do so, the area for prayer lies behind the huts and is marked by numerous coloured flags.

The area around the huts has room for only a few tents. Be very careful at night; trekkers have fallen off the terrace and broken bones. A toilet area, with privacy, is below among the rocks. Drinking water is available at the river's edge, where a small spring trickles into the river.

Day 3: Ziarat to Shimshal (8 to 9 hours) The trail goes along the river's edge, beneath 10m high cliffs. About 30 minutes from Ziarat, a stream from a side glacier enters the river. In the morning, this is a small stream, but on a hot summer afternoon, it presents a broad, brown, knee-deep obstacle.

Shimshali porters will no doubt insist upon carrying you across. A short distance beyond this stream is a willow grove at the base of a talus slope. A few tent sites can be found here, but the stream, although clear in the morning, is usually muddy in the afternoon. A short distance beyond this pleasant shady spot is a larger glacial tributary that requires caution in crossing. Follow the main Shimshal River bed, beneath the riverine terraces carved by the enormous Shimshal River floods, which are caused when the Khurdopin Glacier above Shimshal village dams the river and forms a large lake that scours the valley when it bursts. Much of Passu's soil was washed away by one such flood.

Because of a surging advance of the Mulungutti Glacier, at the time of writing a new trail bypassing the glacier was being used. Rather than ascending the sandy slope to the western ablation valley of the glacier and the Mulungutti hut, continue along the Shimshal River. This trail detours below the mouth of the glacier, crossing the Shimshal River to its northern side where the hot springs called Kuk are. Recross the river and ascend into the eastern ablation valley of the Mulungutti Glacier to join the old trail where it climbs up to the terrace above the glacier. Because conditions constantly change, the old route description follows.

About three hours after leaving Ziarat, the old trail scrambles up a loose sandy slope into the lateral moraine ablation valley of the Mulungutti Glacier. Rose bushes and willow trees form a pleasant oasis here where many birds can be observed. A small, clear stream flows near a very small and rough hut next to several fields. This makes a nice, small camping spot, and with the time saved crossing the river over the two bridges beyond Uween-e-ben, it is possible to reach this camping spot in one long day from Dūt.

Beyond the small hut, the old trail descends onto the immense, white Mulungutti Glacier (2800m). The trail across this glacier has no cairns to mark the route. The crossing is tricky, and local assistance will greatly speed the crossing, which takes one to two hours. Water is abundant on the glacier. To the south, at the head of the glacier, is Disteghil Sar, the highest peak in Hunza. Across the glacier, the climb to the terrace above is steep, narrow in places, and occasionally loose and crumbly.

From the broad, level terrace above the glacier, Shimshal village comes into view. Tiny pockets of agriculture can be seen on either side of the river, with the broad cultivated area of Shimshal proper some 10 km distant. The trail descends through a notch in the terrace wall to the river bed and the first cultivated area called Rezgeen-e-ben (2820m). It is an easy three hour walk to Shimshal village (2880m). Beyond Shimshal village, it is a long day's walk across the Yazghil Glacier uphill to the Yazghil pastures and huts (about 4500m). It is three stages from Shimshal village to the highest huts.

SHIMSHAL PAMIR

(8 days; late May to early October)

Shimshal villagers have rights to the entire Shimshal River drainage, the Ghujerab River drainage, and to the only part of Pakistan not in South Asia, the Braldu and the upper Oprang River valleys. These two rivers are actually in Central Asia. Trekkers can visit the Pamir, and cross the Shimshal Pass to Shuwerth, the main summer settlement (see the Shimshal Pamir & Ghujerab Valley map). Women and children regularly traverse the difficult and challenging trails to the Pamir. In late May, they go to the Pamir and in early October, they return to the village. The annual migration to these high grasslands and flower-strewn meadows crosses three passes (each over 4100m) to reach Shuwerth. The Shimshal area contains probably the largest population of snow leopards in all Asia, and large herds of blue sheep and ibex. It is difficult to see any of these large mammals, for they stay on the inaccessible heights. Collections of ibex and blue-sheep horns along the trail are evidence of their numbers. Ibex and blue sheep are now worth more alive than as meat in the pot.

Guides & Porters

Local assistance is indispensable ascending and descending the massive scree slopes, the Uween-e-sar and Shachmirk passes, and the difficult trails into and out of Purien-e-ben. Porters carry a maximum of 25 kg including their own gear and food on this trek.

12 stages: Shimshal village to Zardgarben, Zardgarben to Yarzeen, Yarzeen to Purien-e-ben, Purien-e-ben to Arbob Purien, Arbob Purien to Shuijerab, Shuijerab to Shuwerth, and return via the same route

Map Notes

The Swiss map does not show Zardgarben, the Uween-e-sar and Shachmirk passes, or any other place names on the trail to Shuijerab. It shows a trail along the lower Pamir-e-Tang River that is used only in winter months during low water. It is an extremely difficult trail and is definitely not advised for trekkers. Shuwerth and Shpodeen are also misspelled. The U502 *Shimshal (NJ 43-15)* sheet shows the route, but no place names along it. The Leomann map shows the route, although it erroneously shows the trail crossing the Pamir-e-Tang River. It misnames the two passes above Zardgarben.

Route Description

Day 1: Shimshal Village to Zardgarben (4 to 5 hours) Descend to the Shimshal River bed and follow it upstream to 'Michael Bridge', built in 1984 with money donated by Dr Michael Pflug of Canada. Across the bridge, turn north into the steep, narrow canyon of the Zardgarben stream. Ascend along the steam, crossing it twice. After two to 2½ hours, reach Shaushau (3360m), by a fresh spring. A sheltered flat place is five minutes beyond. From here, cross the stream again and ascend a 250m steep scree slope 45 minutes on switchbacks to a wooden portal, Tung-e-sar (3600m).

A clear stream lies 10 minutes beyond. Continue about 30 minutes to the broad, level plain of Zardgarben (3810m). This picturesque camp site has several small huts.

The yellow cliffs above Zardgarben are the source of its name, which means 'the place beneath the yellow rock'.

Day 2: Zardgarben to Purien-e-ben (10 hours) Two demanding passes are crossed en route to Purien-e-ben. This long, arduous day has 2700m of total elevation gain and loss, so start early. The only possible camp site between the two passes is Yarzeen where no more than four people could camp. Larger trekking parties must continue over the second pass.

From Zardgarben, Uween-e-sar, the first pass, is clearly visible to the east. Climb 200m in about 45 minutes to a grassy area which has the last reliable water until Yarzeen. Climb another 180m in 45 more minutes to 4110m, working north past a small seasonal water source. Ascend a final hour to reach Uween-e-sar (4420m). Views are of the Pamir peaks, three days distant, and Disteghil Sar. The trail descends a 765m scree slope to Yarzeen (the place of the juniper). The last 30 minutes is extremely steep and exposed. Take care not to knock loose rock down onto anyone below. The rushing stream at Yarzeen (3627m) makes a great lunch spot. However, years of cooking fires have eliminated almost all the junipers.

The 2½ hour steady ascent to the second pass, Shachmirk (4160m), begins immediately. The trail is clearly visible, steep, and in a few places, loose. From the top of the pass are fine views of the white Yazghil Glacier, Yukshin Garden (7530m), and Kunyang Chhīsh (7852m). It takes about 1½ hours to descend 570m over scree to the stream at Targeen (3597m). A small, four to six-person camp is possible here, though there is rock-fall danger. Purien-e-ben (3322m) is a one hour walk from Targeen, ending in a very steep 240m scree descent. This camp site is in a narrow box canyon amidst fantastic eroded loess towers.

Day 3: Purien-e-ben to Shuijerab (6 to 8 hours) Climb the steep, exposed canyon wall out of Purien-e-ben one hour to the level plain above, called Purien-e-sar (3597m).

From Purien-e-sar, the walk to Shuijerab becomes easier. The trail traverses high above the Pamir-e-Tang River crossing several tributary streams in their narrow gorges. Arbob Purien (3657m) is the nicest of these side valleys and makes a good spot for lunch. A clear spring flows near the small hut next to the rushing stream. The trail beyond passes through dry, rocky artemisia (sage brush) steppes. At the confluence of the streams from the Gunj-e-dur and Shuijerab valleys, cross a sturdy wooden bridge to the true right bank of the Shuijerab River. Follow the river 1½ to two hours to the large summer settlement of Shuijerab (black valley), with many huts on both sides of the river. Just across the bridge and beyond Shuijerab (4084m) is a grassy meadow for camping amid quiet mountain splendour.

Day 4: Shuijerab to Shuwerth (3 hours) The easy climb to the Abdullah Khan Maidan (4389m) takes one hour. These high pastures are the precincts of women and children who have a rule: one cannot enter the pastures in a sad mood. Everyone must be happy and it is best to enter the pastures singing.

Stroll two hours through flowery fields amid herds of yaks and sheep, skirting the two large lakes that lie on the watershed between South Asia and Central Asia to the Shimshal Pass (4420m). When Eric Shipton was here, he wrote:

I sat for a long time on the crest of the pass caught up in the magic of the view. Below the pass was a great blue lake. Beside this was an extensive plain. Soon, we came upon large herds of yak and sheep and heard the melodious calls of the shepherd children.

It still seems much the same. A 15 minute walk beyond the almost unnoticeable Shimshal Pass is the main summer settlement of Shuwerth. Women here are constantly busy with milking, herding, and converting the milk to qurut (cheese). Over 700 yaks and several thousand sheep and goats graze here. The most pleasant camp sites are in the level area north of the

Shimshal Pass, in view of the lakes. If you want to camp closer to Shuwerth, ask the villagers to find a suitable spot.

Day 5: Shuwerth Take at least one day to visit Shuwerth. For those equipped and motivated, an ascent of the non-technical 5900m snow peak, Mingli Sar, first climbed by Nazir Sabir in 1988, is possible. Mingli Sar is shown as Peak 6050 on the Swiss map. Shimshalis do not allow foreigners to travel beyond Shuwerth, unless they have a special Tourism Division permit for the Braldu Valley, from where a technical route crosses a high pass, the Lukpe La, to reach Snow Lake.

Day 6: Shuwerth to Purien-e-ben (6 to 9 hours) Leave the Pamir by retracing the trail to Purien-e-ben, stopping for tea at Shuijerab. From Purien-e-sar, a trail heading north offers two alternative and difficult cross-country routes. The trail goes through barren country and over talus to a shepherd's hut at Mai Dur (sheep valley). From Mai Dur, one route heads west over the Shpodeen Pass (5180m) to Shpodeen (the place of rhubarb) in the Zardgarben Valley. The other route heads north over the high glaciated Mai Dur Pass to the upper Ghujerab Valley. To reach Shpodeen, follow the valley west beyond Mai Dur to the Shpodeen Pass. Shpodeen, on the true right bank of the Zardgarben stream, is visible below. A snow-field covers the east side of the pass. However, the west side of the pass is dry and the descent is over extreme, steep scree. Locals do not use either of these passes as they are too difficult for livestock. These alternative routes should only be attempted by fit, experienced, well-equipped trekkers and only with a knowledgeable local guide.

Day 7: Purien-e-ben to Zardgarben (7 to 9 hours) Recrossing the Shachmirk and Uween-e-sar passes to Zardgarben is the normal route used by Shimshalis. On the other side of the Pamir-e-Tang River is the striking Chat Pirt massif. Blue sheep live on the grassy slopes of this peak, which can be

reached only via faint, difficult hunters' paths. These paths cross the impossible-seeming eroded loess tower areas by scrambling up 5th-class rock chutes and chimneys. This route is too dangerous even for most Shimshalis and should not be attempted by trekkers. Below Purien-e-ben, along the river, is a hot spring. Unfortunately, it too is difficult to reach. Shimshalis hope one day to build a good trail along the Pamir-e-Tang River and so eliminate the need to cross the arduous Shachmirk and Uween-e-sar passes. From Zardgarben, the trail to the Boesam and Chapchingol passes heads north (see below).

Day 8: Zardgarben to Shimshal Village (2 to 3 hours) Retrace the path down to Shimshal.

BOESAM PASS, GHUJERAB VALLEY & CHAPCHINGOL PASS
(7 days; June to September)
This walk begins in Shimshal village, crosses two high passes through the remote Ghujerab mountains, and ends in Koksil on the KKH below the Khunjerab Pass (see the Shimshal Pamir & Ghujerab Valley map). Crossing the higher of the two passes, the glaciated Chapchingol, involves fording a deep, swift torrent several times, a 2nd-class ascent over scree and loose rock, and a descent over a crevassed glacier. It is a spectacularly beautiful and challenging walk, and the nicest of the treks from Shimshal. A rope and climbing gear are necessary for the river crossings and for descending the glacier on the north side of the Chapchingol Pass. Bring at least 150m of rope for the Chapchingol Glacier. Because the KSF at Koksil does not permit foreigners to enter the Koksil Valley, this trek is usually done from south to north, finishing at Koksil.

Guides & Porters
A local guide and/or porters are indispensable for the river crossings and the Chapchingol Pass. Be sure all porters have sunglasses. The multiple times we have done this trek, it was only nine stages Shimshal to

Koksil. Shimshalis are now asking 12 stages for this trek (see below). Japerwask to Avduji was only two stages, whereas it is now four. Chapchingol base camp to Koksil Valley was only one stage and now it is two. Discuss this before starting.

12 stages: Shimshal to Zardgarben, Zardgarben to Japerwask, Japerwask to Boesam Pass, Boesam Pass to Perchodwask, Perchodwask to Mandikshlak, Mandikshlak to Avduji, Avduji to Wariben, Wariben to Targeen, Targeen to Chapchingol base camp, Chapchingol base camp to Chapchingol Pass, Chapchingol Pass to Koksil Valley, and Koksil Valley to Koksil on the KKH.

Map Notes

The Swiss map shows a trail along the Ghujerab River below Spesyngo leading to the Khunjerab River and the KKH. This trail is only possible in winter when the river is extremely low. Shpodeen is incorrectly labelled Shekhdalga. No other place names are shown in the Zardgarben or Boesam valleys. The route descending the Boesam Pass is shown incorrectly on the true right or east side of the river. The actual route is on the true left or west side. In the Ghujerab Valley, Mandikshlak is labelled Mandi Kushlag, and Avduji is labelled Hapdija. Wariben is not shown. No place names are shown in the Chapchingol Valley. The route shown up the Chapchingol does not indicate the several river crossings necessary. The U502 *Shimshal (NJ 43-15)* sheet has the same inaccuracies as the Swiss map.

Route Description

Day 1: Shimshal to Zardgarben (4 to 5 hours) See Shimshal Pamir for the route description. Stop in Zardgarben for acclimatisation; do not continue to Japerwask unless previously acclimatised.

Day 2: Zardgarben to Japerwask (4 hours) Head north up the valley, passing through the Shpodeen (the place where *shpod* (rhubarb) grows) meadows to the high pastures of Japerwask (the place where 'Jafer' got tired) (4328m). The rock cliffs and moraine fields

provide a spectacular backdrop to this flower-strewn spot and are home to ibex.

Day 3: Japerwask to Perchodwask (5 to 6 hours) It is a two hour climb to the Boesam Pass (4725m). On the north side, below the pass, lies a beautiful cirque lake. After skirting the north-west side of this cirque, cross moraine rubble 1½ hours through spectacular glacial mountain scenery beneath great snowy peaks. Once off the rubble, follow the stream down two hours. Two streams join in the meadow beside the hut at Perchodwask, 'the place where the young girl got tired', (4160m). In the late afternoon, they may become muddy. Thirty to 45 minutes below are several other good camp sites: Pamiri; and Shokshogeen, with some dilapidated huts.

Day 4: Perchodwask to Wariben (4½ to 5 hours) Descend the beautiful Boesam Pass valley, and reach the settlement of Mandikshlak and the Ghujerab Valley in two hours. The route over the long Mai Dur Glacier and the Mai Dur Pass joins the trail down the Ghujerab Valley here. One hour west of Mandikshlak lies Avduji (3871m) with its huts and a clear stream. Beyond Avduji along an easy trail lies Wariben (3597m), the main summer settlement in the Ghujerab Valley. Yaks cannot cross the Chapchingol Pass, so locals do not take them beyond Wariben.

From Wariben, an option is to continue down the Ghujerab Valley through juniper to the summer settlements of Dīh and Spesyngo. From Dīh, go south up a side valley to the pastures of Dīh Dasht where ibex and blue sheep are said to be plentiful. Beyond these summer settlements, no trail goes down the Ghujerab Valley. The route to Sost over high, extreme passes is definitely not advisable for trekkers.

Day 5: Wariben to Chapchingol Base Camp (4 to 5 hours) Cross the Ghujerab River, wading if the water is low or crossing by an existing steel cable if it is high, and enter the Chapchingol gorge. The country here is high desert with crumbly, desert varnished granite and juniper trees.

On warm, sunny days, the several fords of the Chapchingol stream are difficult because of the high water levels, requiring a fixed rope and proper technique. If it is cloudy, the cold water will be no more than knee deep. Once through the gorge, the trail thins to a track, rising above the stream and crossing scree slopes to descend to Targeen (the place where tamarisk grows), where a small cramped hut sits by the stream (3870m), two to three hours from Wariben. Beyond

Targeen is the junction of a stream coming from the west and a stream coming from the glaciers at the head of the Chapchingol. Ford the western stream and continue to the base of Chapchingol Pass (4084m) and a camp site with some low stone wall shelters, about two hours from Targeen. There is clear water near the river.

Day 6: Chapchingol Base Camp to Koksil Valley (6 to 7 hours) It is a long, arduous day, so start early. The ascent over scree to the permanently snow-covered Chapchingol

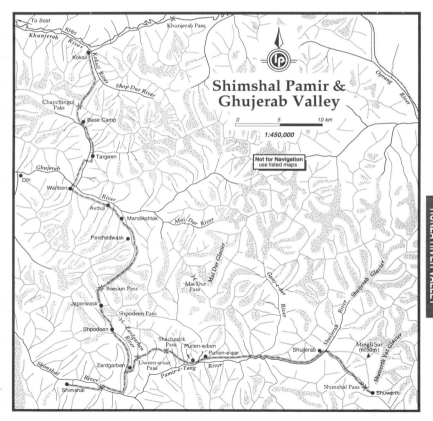

Shimshal Pamir & Ghujerab Valley

0   5   10 km

1:450,000

Not for Navigation
use listed maps

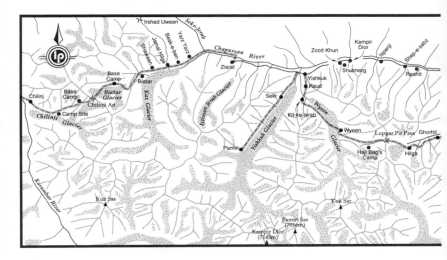

Pass (5100m) takes four hours. It is steep 2nd-class rock near the top, and the rock is loose. The pass is marked by a large cairn and is glaciated on its north side. The slope is steep and requires a fixed rope and careful probing for crevasses, especially for the large bergschrund at the west margin of the glacier. This snow descent is preferable to descending the rock cliff on the west side of the glacier, where a short rapel (abseil) is required.

Once off the glacier, cross the Chapchingol stream to its true left bank. A small rocky area provides a spot to make tea or camp if it becomes too long a day. From this spot, follow the Chapchingol stream down to its confluence with the Shop Dur and Koksil rivers (4420m) and camp along the river.

Day 7: Koksil Valley to Koksil on KKH (3 hours) From this junction it takes two to three hours to walk to the KKH, the KSF check post, and shepherds' huts at Koksil (4410m).

BOIBER VALLEY

(2 to 3 days; mid-June to September)
The Boiber Nala valley runs east from Morkhun village on the KKH. This valley

was the original settlement of the Wakhi people living in the five villages from Ghalapan to Sost. The old route to Shimshal also ran up the Boiber Valley, crossed the Karūn Pir Pass (4873m) and descended 2100m of treacherous scree to reach the Shimshal River at Dūt. The Boiber Nala area has old-growth juniper trees and at the head of the valley is Karūn Koh (7164m).

Map Notes

The Swiss map labels the river Murkhun, but locals call it Boiber. The glacier at the head of the valley labelled Murkhun is called the Karūn Koh Glacier by locals. Maidūn is not named, but its general location is shown by a triangle on the map.

Route Description

Day 1: Morkhun to Boiber (3½ to 4½ hours) Morkhun (2743m) receives more rain than other Gojal villages, as its name suggests (*mor* means 'rain'; *khun*, 'a house'). From Morkhun, walk to adjacent Jamalabad (2789m), named for the late Mir of Hunza, Mohammad Jamal Khan, on the north bank of the Boiber Nala. Follow the trail up river, crossing it twice over bridges. Beyond the

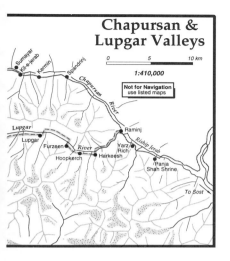

Chapursan & Lupgar Valleys

0   5   10 km

1:410,000

Not for Navigation use listed maps

minutes further. These grassy meadows with good water make a fine base camp for exploring the upper Boiber. The Tupopdan Glacier flows down a southern side valley here. From Maidūn, ascend 1½ hours past yellow rock outcrops to Zardgarben, a grassy pasture. The pass cairn is visible here. Continue, walking to the right of the black moraine of the large Karūn Koh Glacier, to the base of the pass. Ascend a scree gully and traverse to the Karūn Pir Pass (4873m) in one hour. Lupgar Sar (7200m), Trivor (7728m), and Disteghil Sar, rise in front. Legend has it that Mamu Singh, the founder of Shimshal, saw the green meadows along the Lupgar Glacier from this point and so decided to take his livestock to the Shimshal Valley. From the pass, the difficult scree descent to Dūt along the Shimshal River is the reason this route is no longer used. Return from the pass to Maidūn.

Day 3: Maidūn to Morkhun Return down the Boiber Valley to Morkhun.

CHAPURSAN VALLEY

Chapursan is a long west-east valley running parallel to Pakistan's border with China and Afghanistan (see the Chapursan & Lupgar Valleys map). Floods have devastated much of the allegedly once green valley, leaving the upper section a wasteland of huge boulders amid which the Wakhi inhabitants plant wheat and potatoes. Locals say the name derives from Persian *chi pursan* meaning 'What is needed?', implying that all needs are met in Chapursan. Potatoes, a recent introduction, grow so well here (as in the rest of Gojal) that Chapursan farmers now earn enough money selling potatoes to buy all they need, with some money left over. This has alleviated the former local food shortage.

Most Wakhi people who live here have migrated from lower in Gojal, but at least one village, Shutmerg, was settled by migrants from the Wakhan. Raminj was settled by Burusho from Hunza. Chapursan's dramatic landscape of small fields amid red and yellow cliffs topped by snow peaks is strikingly beautiful. The area only opened to

second bridge ascend Yasin Band, a narrow gully with steps made of juniper logs, to the terrace above the north side of the river.

Continue through fields to Abgerch, two hours from Jamalabad. Abgerch (3200m) is the original settlement of the Wakhi people living in the five villages who refer to themselves as 'Abgerchi'. A small fort sits atop the central building, a reminder of the constant battles with Qirghiz people who also used the upper Hunza Valley until the 19th century. From Abgerch, continue up, then cross the river via a bridge to reach Boiber (3505m), a barren summer settlement 1½ hours from Abgerch. Boiber huts sit in a southern side valley, which has a small glacier. Above is the dramatic north face of Tupopdan peak (6106m), 'the mountain of the early morning light'.

Day 2: Boiber to Karūn Pir Pass to Maidūn (6 to 7 hours) From Boiber, continue one hour to a cold spring called Xunza Kuk, then 30 minutes to Periyar. The upper limit of juniper is reached at these overgrazed pastures. Many junipers have been cut, but some of those remaining are over 1000 years old. Maidūn pastures (4000m) are 30

Baba Ghundi Ziarat

Ziarat, called *stiman* in Wakhi, is the most important shrine in Hunza-Gojal and is even visited by people from Baltistan. The current shrine was built by Mir Ghazin Khan in 1924. Inside is said to be the sword of the saint who is not buried here. The shrine is a *yadgah* (memory place) rather than a *mazar* (tomb). Baba Ghundi performed several miracles in Chapurson. His main miracle is a tale of sin and retribution, very similar to other tales in Pakistan and Kashmir. When Baba Ghundi first came to Chapurson, it was a wealthy and green valley where the people lived in sin. He went from house to house, asking for alms, but only one old woman offered him food. Baba Ghundi told her to leave her house and climb the hill. As she did, she saw Baba Ghundi riding at the head of a great flood that wiped out the valley and its people in punishment for their sinful ways. Evidently a great outburst flood from the Yishkuk Glacier did cover most of the valley with boulders and mud as far down as the village of Kampir Dior.

The saint's main blessing is to bestow children on childless couples. The main time for pilgrimage to this shrine is in late September and early October, when agricultural work is done and animals are back from the summer pastures. Religious songs are sung throughout the night. Goats are offered as prayers, and the meat is distributed, imbued with the *barakat*, or spiritual power of the saint. ∎

foreigners after the Russians left Afghanistan.

A 70-km-long jeep road leaves the KKH just north of Sost and goes the length of the Chapurson Valley to Ziarat and the drive is quite interesting. Thirty-five to 45 minutes from Sost, the shrine of Panja Shah with many colored flags sits along the road. Inside is a rock with three long scrape marks, as through made by claws. A saint, Panja Shah, is said to have made these marks, and ghee is poured on them as an oblation. Raminj village sits well above the road, one hour from Sost. Only jeeps can make it up the steep road to Raminj. The three villages col-

lectively known as Kermin are 1½ hours from Sost. The third village, Nurabad, has the only post office and dispensary in Chapursan Valley. Reshit village, where there was an old fort, is a 30 minute drive past Kermin. Ten minutes beyond Reshit is the shrine called Jamal Khan Istan. The imprint of a fist and of a riding crop are said to be in the rock inside. This Jamal Khan is no relation to the late Mir of Hunza. When the British archaeologist Aurel Stein came in the early 1900s, he was told the shrine was called Roshtigar and the marks were the footprints of Baba Ghundi.

After this are the villages of Ispenji, Kampir Dior, Shutmerg, and Zood Khun in close succession. Zood Khun is the highest permanent village in Chapursan. Half an hour's drive from Zood Khun is Ravai Jhui, or Ravai Lake, in which lived a dragon that Baba Ghundi killed. 'Dragon's bones' are found in the dry lake bed. Ziarat, the shrine of Baba Ghundi, is at the end of the road. Close to the main shrine, near the river, is a spring, whose mineral water, called *ab-e-shafa*, bestows health on those who drink it.

LUGPAR PIR PASS & VALLEY
(6 days; June to late September)

This trek follows a 45 km west-to-east route, parallel to and south of the main Chapursan Valley. The trek begins at Yishkuk six km west south-west of Zood Khun, crosses the nonglaciated Lupgar Pir Pass (5190m) into the Lupgar Valley and ends at Raminj, which lies above the confluence of the Lupgar and Chapursan rivers. Early in the season, or in cold years, snow lies on the Lupgar Pir Pass. In warmer years, this pass is completely free of snow by mid-July. The Lupgar Valley features striking red, yellow, and brown rock formations.

You could also trek in the reverse direction from Raminj up the Lupgar Valley and cross the Lupgar Pir Pass, from east to west, descending into the upper Chapursan Valley. This direction entails more ascending, since Raminj is 300m lower than Yishkuk, and the eastern side of the Lupgar Pir Pass is longer and steeper with more scree than the west side. However, this direction allows for better acclimatisation. When starting from Yishkuk, you must be already acclimatised.

Little has been written about this beautiful route. To the best of our knowledge, no other foreigners have crossed the Lupgar Pir Pass. Locals do not use this pass either. No one, not even the oldest grey beards, could recall anyone crossing it. The renowned mountaineer Nazir Sabir, who is from Raminj, thought we might be the first people in 50 years to cover this route. He was enthusiastic that we had 'opened' the route again and hopes others will visit.

Guides & Porters

Route-finding beyond Kit-ke-jerab is difficult and you must hire someone who knows the way. Crossing the Kit-ke-jerab Glacier, finding the pass itself, and crossing the glacier on the east side of the pass are tricky. On the west side of the pass, shepherds from Zood Khun take their animals up to summer pastures as far as Banafshayeen. Herders from Raminj and Khaibar take their animals as far as Wyeen on the east side of the pass. Locals do not know the way over the pass itself, but as more trekkers visit the area, it will become better known. If you agree to pay for your porters' transport back to their village, you are not obliged to pay wāpāsi.

8 stages: only three stages are fixed from Zood Khun to Wyeen, on the west side of the pass. They are Zood Khun to Yishkuk (on the jeep road), half a stage from Yishkuk to Raud, half a stage from Raud to Kit-ke-jerab; and Kit-ke-jerab to Wyeen. It is unfortunate to institute the stage system on a new route, but eight stages is a basis for negotiation.

Map Notes

All maps inaccurately depict the glaciers on both sides of the Lupgar Pir Pass. The Swiss map is the only map to correctly locate the pass. However, many place names are inaccurate. Wyeen (on the west side of the pass) is spelled Wain on the map. Wyeen is between two spurs of the ridge descending from Peak 6006. Locals refer to the glacier

south-east of Kit-ke-jerab as the Wyeen Glacier, not the Kit-ke-jerab Glacier. Kit-ke-jerab is misspelled as Kuk-ki-jerab. The glaciers to the south-west and south-east of the Lupgar Pir Pass are larger and in different positions than drawn on the map. The trail east of the summer settlement of Lupgar is inaccurately drawn. It runs along the river's true left bank until recrossing just above the place mislabelled Hapgurchi. Places names east of here to Raminj are inaccurate; Furzeen, Hoopkerch, and Harkeesh are not shown.

Leomann Map's *Sheet 1: (Gilgit, Hunza, Rakaposhi, Batura Area)* and the U502 *Baltit (NJ 43-14)* are wildly inaccurate for this trek. Glaciers are positioned incorrectly or omitted as are some streams and side valleys. The Leomann map shows a route south from the Lupgar Valley to the Batura Glacier. This is not a trekking route, nor is it the feasible route to the Werthum Nala by which some Passu guides have crossed from the Batura Glacier. Sekr, along the Yishkuk Glacier, is labelled Lal Mitti on maps.

Route Description

Day 1: Yishkuk to Raud (30 minutes to 1 hour) Yishkuk is a well-watered green meadow with some willows. A good spring flows along the road just as you reach Yishkuk (3450m). *Zolg*, a thorny low shrub with edible, tiny blue berries, and wild rose bushes abound here. Leave the jeep road before it begins to climb towards the wooden bridge over the Yishkuk torrent. Walk south up the valley, over moraine rubble, with the Wyeen Glacier river below to the west. Sparse juniper grows along the trail. The trail bends to the south-east and after 30 to 45 minutes, reaches a level area, mostly sandy, next to a large, very cold, clear stream. The stream comes from a spring at the base of a south facing scree slope. This spot, called Raud (3600m), makes a wonderful camp. To the west, across the Yishkuk Glacier, is the unusual red rock called Sekr, at the base of which is a summer settlement. This is a short walk, but most trekkers need to acclimatise before ascending further.

Day 2: Raud to Wyeen (4½ to 5½ hours) Cross the clear stream and walk five minutes along its true left bank to cross the two-part wooden bridge over the large glacial torrent. Ascend 30 minutes above the river's true left bank amid juniper, on a small, clear shepherds' trail to the huts and goat pen at Kit-ke-jerab (3690m). From the huts, reach the small Kit-ke-jerab stream from the south in five minutes. Cross it and continue up the narrow, rocky ablation valley 45 minutes to a side stream called Shōt Dur (avalanche valley) (3780m). This is the last water until on the glacier. Continue up the ablation valley, eventually climbing out of it to contour the green hillside, and reach a black talus slope in 45 minutes. Cross the greasy black talus, called Charva Shui (3990m), in 15 minutes. Return to the ablation valley, ascending steadily 30 minutes until the valley curves south.

Across the Wyeen Glacier to the east is a side valley marked by red rock. Wyeen camp, south of it, is the grassy area visible between two small ridges. Cross the glacier in about two hours. The rock on the glacier is mostly stable and the crossing is easy. Stay to the north (left) of two enormous white and tan rubble mounds in the middle of the glacier. At Wyeen (about 4100m) only one or two tents can be pitched next to the huts and a couple more on roof tops. Larger trekking parties may prefer to camp by the glacial stream, which comes from Banafshayeen. Clear water is just above the goat pen.

Day 3: Wyeen to Haji Beg's Camp (4 to 5 hours) Cross the Banafshayeen stream immediately to its true left bank. Go up the lateral moraine of the Wyeen Glacier on loose boulders one hour. Leave the moraine and walk along the edge of the stream. Cross to its true right bank just below the mouth of the Banafshayeen Valley (4200m). A possible camp site for large trekking parties is across the silty stream in an open area next to a small glacial lake. Ascend east up the grassy slope 30 minutes to the level Banafshayeen Valley (4410m). The view of

unclimbed Kuk Sar *(kuk* means 'spring'; *sar,* 'summit'), and its 3000m vertical face is extraordinary. Banafshayeen means 'the place where *banafsha* grows'. Banafsha is a blue member of the poppy family *(Meconopsis grandis)* that is used as a cold remedy in Ayurvedic medicine. This is the highest pasture area used by Wyeen shepherds.

From this point, no trails or cairns exist. Continue steadily up the true right bank of the stream. One hour above the Banafshayeen pasture is the mouth of a glacier (4650m), which fills the valley. This glacier is not shown on the Swiss map; it shows two small glaciers higher in the valley. These have merged and now descend to below where their stream junction is shown on the map. Skirt the glacier on the slope high above its north margin. Walk on black lateral moraine 45 minutes to a small side valley, where a clear stream comes down. Continue another hour, high above the glacier, to a second side valley with a larger, clear stream tumbling down. Ascend along this stream five to 10 minutes to a large flat area where the remains of a square enclosure next to a large, prominent boulder indicates that others have been this way. This is Haji Beg's camp (4680m), which we named after our travelling companion who embodies the spirit of these mountains. The pass is visible at the head of this side valley. The views from this high camp are remarkable.

Day 4: Haji Beg's Camp to Wyeen (4 to 5 hours) Follow the stream north-east one to two hours to its head (5100m), then east north-east 30 minutes up steeper scree to the Lupgar Pir Pass (5190m). Pamiri Sar (7016m) is visible beyond Kuk Sar to the south-west. Descend steep, loose scree, bearing left to a scree knoll, then continue over the knoll left and down to a glacier. This 300m descent takes 15 to 30 minutes. Head out on to the white glacier, zig-zagging to avoid open crevasses.

Continue working across and slightly down the glacier, which has a 15 to 20° slope, for 30 minutes to a narrow black medial moraine. Follow it down onto terminal moraine where there are a few pools. Some 500m below the mouth of the glacier, more pools are visible. Do not descend to the mouth. Rather, stay high and traverse right on scree, well above the river 30 minutes to a clear stream and another 15 minutes to a grassy yak pasture called Wyeen (4530m).

Day 5: Wyeen to Hoopkerch (5 to 6 hours) Descend to the main river bed and pick up a faint trail. In 15 minutes, reach the large stream from the big glacier to the south. Ford its several knee-deep, cold channels. Across the stream, continue about one hour to Hilga (4380m), a pasture with some old, now unused huts. The water from a hanging glacier is especially silty in the afternoon. On the north side of the valley are spectacular snow-capped spires with scree cascading from their base to the river. On the south side of the valley are fantastic red crags.

Descend 20 minutes to Ghōrhil (*ghor* means 'boulder field'; *hil*, 'a goat and sheep fold'), a natural animal pen amid the boulders. The water is silty. Descend 15 minutes through sharp boulders to a river from the south. Cross the river and continue to Lupgar (*lup* means 'big'; *gar* 'rock') (4140m), the main summer settlement for Khaibar and Raminj shepherds who share pasture rights in this valley. Here the men tend the livestock. A tiny spring at the base of a cliff to the south provides water. Keep close to the cliffs leaving Lupgar, and reach a southern side valley. Cross this over a stone bridge, 15 minutes from Lupgar, then descend along the true right bank of this stream 30 minutes to the main Lupgar River. A huge spring is on the left two-thirds of the way down. Fill water bottles here; this is the last reliable clear water until Raminj.

Cross the river over an interesting bridge and follow the trail along the true left bank through Khuda Khair Charjeshan ('God help us slides'). Rock fall along this section is deadly in wind or rain, and the trail is thin and exposed. Forty-five minutes later, the trail comes to a natural bridge. The gorge is so deep and narrow here that you cannot see the river below. Cross to the true right bank

and continue on a thin loose trail with tricky footing.

Continue down valley, crossing two side streams. The water in one is red, and in the other, white. Descend one hour to a sandy area along the river, passing through Furzeen, a birch grove, then ascend and enter a juniper forest. Ahead and below 15 minutes is the hut called Hoopkerch (*hoop* means 'seven'; *kerch*, 'a hunter's shelter'), where a glacial side stream comes in from the south. A small spring is below the goat pen.

Day 6: Hoopkerch to Raminj (3½ to 4 hours) Cross the bridge over this muddy stream and continue through beautiful ancient juniper forest one hour to Harkeesh (3360m). Harkeesh (*har* means 'a plough'; *keesh* 'to cultivate') is the only Burushashki place name in the Lupgar Valley, named by Burusho from Raminj who tried to farm here. The hut is well-built of stone and wood. The route from the Batura Glacier and Werthum Nala over the Werthum Pass comes out here (see Werthum Nala to Lupgar Valley in this section). Water from the side stream can be quite muddy.

From Harkeesh descend steeply 15 minutes to the river and cross to its true left bank via a sturdy bridge. Birch and juniper are abundant here. The trail is considerably better, though still exposed in places as it goes up and down above the river. After 1½ to two hours, reach the headworks for the Raminj irrigation channel. Follow this willow-lined canal, past several gushing clear springs 45 minutes to Raminj (3150m). The canal, built during the reign of Mir Muhammad Jamal Khan, is a marvel of construction, with several tunnels through the cliff. Raminj is a beautiful, well-tended east and south facing village. Its abundant apricots make a tasty treat on a hot day. From Raminj, it is a 15 minute-walk down the link road to the main Chapurson jeep road.

CHILINJI AN
(6 days; June to September)
The Chilinji An (5160m) is a pass linking the Chapursan Valley with the Karambar Valley

to its west. The east side of the pass is glaciated, whereas the west side is steep, generally dry scree. Proper gear is necessary for travelling through the crevasse field on the glacier. Early in the season, you can expect to find much snow on both sides of the Chilinji An. We describe the route going from east to west, although many trekkers coming from Chitral cross from west to east. The trail head at Ziarat (3660m) is too high to drive directly from Gilgit in one day and the pass is too high to tackle on the third or fourth day of a trek unless you are previously acclimatised.

Guides & Porters

Hire someone from Chapursan who knows the route, if your guide does not. When you trek east to west, you use Chapursan porters, whose relatives occupy the pastures in upper Chapursan and in the remote and fascinating Broghil area. Having Wakhi porters will open doors for you in those areas. When you trek over the Chilinji An from west to east, you will most likely use Chitrali porters.

Some trekking companies have set a precedent to pay 'drop' fees to porters who travel by vehicle from their village to Ziarat, which porters may ask you to pay. Since the porters carry no load and you already pay for their transport, it makes no sense to pay an additional 'drop' fee.

6 stages: Ziarat to Yarz Yarz, Yarz Yarz to Biatar, Biatar to Chilinji An base camp, base camp to Chilinji An, Chilinji An to Chilinji Glacier ablation valley, and Chilinji Glacier ablation valley to Chilinj

Map Notes

The Swiss and Leomann maps properly locate the Chilinji An. However, the Leomann map does not show the correct route on the west side of the pass. The U502 *Baltit (NJ 43-14)* sheet does not accurately depict the terrain on the west side of the pass. All maps give inaccurate place names and locations. In particular, Biatar, an important camp, is actually on the true right side of the river flowing east from the Chilinji An. The glacier on the east side of the Chilinji An,

above Biatar, is unnamed on maps. We refer to it as the Biatar Glacier, because the glacier on the west side of the pass is the actual Chilinji Glacier. The Swiss and the Leomann maps both end at the Karambar River.

Route Description

Day 1: Ziarat to Yarz Yarz (2 hours) There is plenty of room to camp at Ziarat (3660m). Clear springs are across the bridge on the true left bank of the river. Spend one or two nights here to acclimatise. Wakhi and Qirghiz from the Wakhan come to Ziarat to trade livestock for supplies such as flour, tea, salt, and cigarettes. Throughout the year, pilgrims arrive on Thursday to offer prayers on Friday.

From Ziarat, cross the bridge and walk one hour on a good trail to Sekr-jerab (*sekr* means 'red'; *jerab* 'stream') (3720m). Ford this deep stream. Across the main river to the south are the huts of Shpod Kut ('rhubarb on the roof'), called Shikarkuk on the Swiss map. Continue one more hour to Yarz Yarz (*yarz* means 'juniper'). There is not much juniper left. The construction of the road to Ziarat and the tractor trail beyond to Yarz Yarz has converted this once fine stand into firewood and timber. There are huts on either side of a small clear stream and room for a few tents.

Day 2: Yarz Yarz to Biatar (3 hours) Twenty minutes along the alluvial fan, reach the base of a reddish cliff called Besk Rui. A larger camp site called Targeen (*targ* means 'tamarisk') is below, along a tamarisk-lined clear stream just before the terminal moraine of the Kuz Glacier. The camp here is called Besk-e-ben. The trail works up the cliffs 45 minutes, easing off near the top (3900m), then contours for 15 minutes to Jamal Hilga (3810m), a livestock pen and huts below the trail to the south. From here, a trail leads north to Jhui Werth (*jhui* means 'lake'; *werth*, 'a millstone'), which lies above Jamal Hilga out of view, and a pass called Irshad Uween.

This pass leads to Afghanistan's Wakhan corridor and is off-limits to foreigners. Thirty minutes beyond Jamal Hilga, a stream bars the trail where a bridge washed away. Descend to the Kuz Glacier and cross the moraine rubble to avoid fording the deep, swift stream that disappears under the glacier. The trail continues along the true right bank of this stream for another hour to the huts and large animal pen of Biatar (4020m) with large, clear springs and grassy areas for camping amid boulders.

Day 3: Biatar to Chilinji An Base Camp ($3\frac{1}{2}$ to 4 hours) Ascend the rocky pasture directly above Biatar 45 minutes to the base of a large cliff on the east side of the valley. The valley is filled by the Biatar Glacier descending from Chilinji An. Follow a faint trail for 30 minutes to the top of the lateral moraine of the Biatar Glacier (4260m). Cross the glacier over terminal moraine rubble, fording a glacial stream running over the ice. Reach the ablation valley where yaks graze on the west margin of the glacier in about 45 minutes. Late in the season, water is scarce. Ascend the ever-narrowing ablation valley for $1\frac{3}{4}$ hours, climbing steadily to reach the base camp (4620m), with four tent platforms and five rock circles. Water comes from a nearby snow bank. This camp site has some rock-fall danger.

Day 4: Chilinji An Base Camp to Chilinji Glacier Ablation Valley (5 to 6 hours) Walk up the crest of the moraine ridge to a large cairn, which marks the location of the base camp for those coming west to east. Follow the lateral moraine one hour along the glacier's northern margin. As the moraine diminishes and bends right, cross on to the level snow-covered glacier. The pass is directly ahead. Head towards the yellowish rocky crag that marks the northern side of the pass. Some medial moraine descends from this crag. Follow this moraine a short way, until one hour after coming onto the glacier, you encounter black moraine, and the slope steepens to about 30°. From this point, use a rope, as crevasses are frequent. Head up the middle of the glacier towards the pass. Reach the top in one hour, zig-zagging to avoid

crevasses. A tall cairn marks the Chilinji An (5160m), where strong winds are common.

Put away your rope, and head down scree, traversing north (right) to a small ridge. Follow the crest of this ridge for 10 to 15 minutes until you can descend right on scree to the valley below where the west side base camp (4560m) is found. A few small tent platforms on rock are near a clear stream. The 600m scree descent takes 45 minutes.

Follow the stream over very steep, loose scree. Be careful of rock fall. It takes about one hour to descend almost 1000m of scree to the gentler slopes and forest below. Head for the lateral moraine of the Chilinji Glacier 15 minutes ahead through dense willow and birch. In this lovely ablation valley, stop near the obvious bend in the clear stream in the forest and camp.

If coming from Chitral, heading west to east, you can avoid the arduous 1000m scree ascent. Beginning from the Chilinji Glacier ablation valley, follow the stream from the Chilinji An (west side) base camp. Move up out of the forest into a more open area. As the stream enters a gorge-like area with a cliff on its true right bank, head left and away from the stream and up a yellowish gravel area between two cliffs to the top of the ridge. Then traverse right to the base camp. This slightly longer route to the base camp is easier and safer than ascending the scree.

Day 5: Chilinji Glacier Ablation Valley to Chilinj (1 to $1\frac{1}{2}$ hours) Follow the stream through the forested ablation valley of the Chilinji Glacier, crossing it several times. Tall junipers grow further down this enchanting sheltered valley, and a waterfall cascades from cliffs above. After one hour, reach the Gujar summer settlement of Chilinj (3450m) along the Karambar River.

From Chilinj, you have two options. You can cross the Chilinji Glacier and head south along the true left bank of the Karambar River to the road head near Bort. Or, you can cross the Karambar River to its true right bank to the Karambar An and Broghil (see the Ishkoman Valley section in the Ghizar chapter).

OTHER ROUTES
Kamaris, Andra Fort & Gulmit Glacier

From behind Gulmit, follow the jeep track one hour to Kamaris village. A side trip goes 30 minutes north-east to the ruins of Andra Fort, built about 200 years ago to protect against Nagyr raiders. From Kamaris, a trail heads north to Ghulkin village and another heads west to the base of Gulmit Glacier in one hour. From here, follow the south margin of the Gulmit Glacier to the summer pastures of Rajabhil. Allow two or three days to explore them. From Ghulkin, you can walk along the north side of the Gulmit Glacier to Dash Hil, a summer pasture.

Ghulkin Glacier

From Borit Lake (see the Passu & Batura Glaciers map), it is a two to three hour walk along the north side of Ghulkin Glacier to Minal Hil, a summer pasture and the base camp for Shishpar (7611m) and Ghenta (7090m) peaks.

Khaibar Nala

Khaibar village is on the KKH between Passu and Morkhun (see the Passu & Batura Glaciers map). A clear river valley behind Khaibar to the west has a large ibex population, and should offer good viewing opportunities. The high southern ridge (4571m) can be crossed to reach Yashpirt on the Batura Glacier.

Pamiri

Pamiri is a summer pasture used by shepherds from Zood Khun in Chapursan (see the Chapursan & Lupgar Valleys map). The four day walk to Pamiri begins from Yishkuk and goes south-west along the north-west margin of the Yishkuk Glacier. This walk is good for acclimatisation when you plan to cross either the Lupgar Pir Pass or Chilinji An. The trail head (3450m) is on the west side of the bridge over the Yishkuk River. As the road bends to the right near old lateral moraine rubble, climb along the river's true left bank.

Continue past the mouth of the Yishkuk Yaz, along the ablation valley on the west side of the glacier to Kuk Chasham, a shepherds' settlement with a good spring. The next day pass Sekr (marked Lal Mitti on maps), the prominent red rock, just beyond Kuk Chasham. Continue in the ablation valley to Dush Jhui, a small lake with clear water in a green, open area. The trail continues up the ablation valley, ascending gradually to Pamiri, a lovely place to rest and enjoy the views. The stream is called Pamiri, which locals refer to as Banafshayeen because banafsha grows here. From Pamiri, you can either retrace your steps back to Yishkuk or cross the Yishkuk Glacier and walk back along the opposite side of the glacier, crossing the low ridge to join the trail down from Kit-ke-jerab. The route has six stages: Yishkuk to Kuk Chasham, Kuk Chasham to Dush Jhui, Dush Jhui to Banafshayeen, and three return stages.

Baltistan

Baltistan, called Balti-yul by its inhabitants, encompasses the highest peaks and the largest glaciers of the Karakoram. The mighty Indus River sweeps through the land, augmented by the glacial Shigar and Shyok rivers. Baltistan's western boundary with Gilgit is at Shengus village, downstream from the Rondu gorge of the Indus River. To the east and south is the line of control with India, and to the north, along the crest of the Karakoram, is the border with China. Centred on Skardu, Baltistan is home to the Balti-pa, an Islamicised Tibetan people, whose language is the spoken form of classical literary Tibetan. Baltistan, with its Tibetan cultural roots, sharply contrasts with the Hindukush and Karakoram areas to the west. The folklore of the Balti-pa is not that of shamans and fairies, but rather tells of the Tibetan hero-king Kesar. The Balti-pa follow Shia Islam. Hunza and Nagyr are much influenced by Baltistan, with apricots and polo both probably from Baltistan.

REGIONAL HISTORY

Baltistan received Buddhism when the Kushan and Gupta empires spread across the Karakoram and Hindukush during the 1st to 5th century AD, and Kashmir was the main centre of Mahayana Buddhism. The kingdom of Great Balur, as Baltistan was then known, sent emissaries to China in the early 8th century, but by the middle of the 8th century, Tibetan power became preeminent. Many Tibetan people probably moved into the area during this period. Lhasa's power declined towards the end of the 9th century, but Baltistan remained Buddhist until around 1400 AD when missionaries from Kashmir brought the Nur Bakhshiya sect of Shia Islam to Baltistan.

Baltistan had three main kingdoms: Shigar, Khapalu, and Skardu. The Amacha dynasty of Shigar is said to have been founded around 1000 AD by a Hunza prince,

Highlights – Baltistan
Centre of the Karakoram. Most heavily glaciated region with the greatest concentration of high peaks and granite spires. Balti culture has Tibetan origins. Villages are oases in vertical wilderness of rock and ice.

who crossed the Hispar La to the Shigar Valley. Tradition tells of Hunza and Nagyr men crossing the Hispar and Biafo glaciers to play polo with Shigar men near Askole village. The Yagbu dynasty of Khapalu is said to have been founded around 850 AD. Yagbu is a Turkish title, indicating that Turkic adventurers may have crossed the Karakoram from Central Asia and established themselves as rulers over the Tibetan population. The Khapalu Raja's palace stands today. The Maqpon dynasty of Skardu began around 1500, and soon became the most powerful kingdom in Baltistan. The greatest of the Maqpons, Ali Sher Anchan, forged ties with the Moghul emperors of Delhi, who also ruled Kashmir. During the zenith of the Maqpon dynasty, Skardu became caught up in the intrigues of the Moghul court but by the 18th century, fighting among the Maqpon princes led to a decline in Skardu's importance.

The Sikhs, who inherited much of the Moghul empire, including Kashmir, conquered Skardu and Khapalu in 1841. When Gulab Singh became Maharaja of Kashmir, he strengthened his hold on Baltistan and the

Balti kingdom's sovereignty ended. Baltistan retained strong trade and cultural links with Ladakh until the dissolution of the Kashmir state. A Kashmiri governor, supported by a garrison of Dogra troops, administered Baltistan from Skardu until Independence. When the Maharaja of Kashmir declared the state would join India in 1947, the Gilgit Scouts marched on Skardu and besieged the Kashmiri garrison until they surrendered in 1948. Baltistan then became part of the Northern Areas of Pakistan, with the UN administered ceasefire line

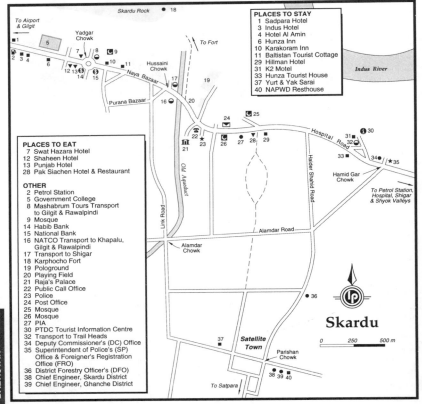

PLACES TO STAY
1 Sadpara Hotel
3 Indus Hotel
4 Hotel Al Amin
6 Hunza Inn
10 Karakoram Inn
11 Baltistan Tourist Cottage
29 Hillman Hotel
31 K2 Motel
33 Hunza Tourist House
37 Yurt & Yak Sarai
40 NAPWD Resthouse

PLACES TO EAT
7 Swat Hazara Hotel
12 Shaheen Hotel
13 Punjab Hotel
28 Pak Siachen Hotel & Restaurant

OTHER
2 Petrol Station
5 Government College
8 Mashabrum Tours Transport to Gilgit & Rawalpindi
9 Mosque
14 Habib Bank
15 National Bank
16 NATCO Transport to Khapalu, Gilgit & Rawalpindi
17 Transport to Shigar
18 Karphocho Fort
19 Pologround
20 Playing Field
21 Raja's Palace
22 Public Call Office
23 Police
24 Post Office
25 Mosque
26 Mosque
27 PIA
30 PTDC Tourist Information Centre
32 Transport to Trail Heads
34 Deputy Commissioner's (DC) Office
35 Superintendent of Police's (SP) Office & Foreigner's Registration Office (FRO)
36 District Forestry Officer's (DFO)
38 Chief Engineer, Skardu District
39 Chief Engineer, Ghanche District

Skardu

to the south marking the Indian border. In 1984, Indian troops moved onto the Siachen Glacier in eastern Baltistan, and this military confrontation continues today.

SKARDU

Skardu (2200m) is the administrative centre and transportation hub of the Skardu district. The town lies along the south side of the Indus River in a broad valley, about 40 km long and 10 km wide.

Karphocho

Karphocho (fort of the *cho*) is a 16th-century fort perched on the east end of the Skardu rock. Probably built by Maqpon Bokha, later rulers added to it, though the Dogras destroyed and later rebuilt it. The trail to the fort starts at the aqueduct. It takes 45 minutes to climb to it for excellent valley views. The fort is open from 9 am to noon and 1.30 to 4.30 pm. The route to the summit of the rock and other fortifications is steep and tricky. It starts near the Sadpara Hotel and scrambles up the west end of the rock for two to three hours. From the pologround there is also a trail around the base of the rock.

Segregation of Women

Skardu has a purdah bazaar and local women do not go into the bazaar. Foreign women are tolerated there, but it is preferable to be accompanied by a man and to dress appropriately. When travelling alone, ask someone from your hotel or a jeep driver to accompany you.

Places to Stay & Eat

The bazaar is extensive and holds enough supplies to outfit treks. The NAPWD Chief Engineers for Skardu (☎ 2788) and Ghanche (☎ 2406 and 2433) districts have offices in Skardu's Satellite Town where rest houses can be booked.

Places to Stay & Eat – bottom end *Rondu Hotel & Restaurant* has charpoys for Rs 10. It costs Rs 20 to pitch your tent at the *Pak Siachen Hotel & Restaurant* or Rs 30 to sleep in one of its tents. Ghulam Rasul runs the

village-style *Hillman Hotel*. Doubles cost Rs 50/100 without/with bathroom. It costs Rs 10 per tent to camp.

Baltistan Tourist Cottage (☎ 2707) has dorms/singles/doubles for Rs 50/100/150 and good food. All rooms have cold-water attached bathrooms. Doubles/triples with hot running water cost Rs 200/250. At the friendly *Hunza Inn* (☎ 2570) cold-water doubles/triples cost Rs 150/250. *Hotel Al Amin* (☎ 2798), west of Yadgar Chowk, has carpeted rooms with attached bathrooms and hot running water. Singles/doubles/triples cost Rs 120/300/400. Some rooms have views out the back of the hotel. At the *Karakoram Inn* (☎ 2442 and 2122) singles/doubles/triples cost Rs 150/200/300. *Sadpara Hotel* (☎ 2951), west of Yadgar Chowk, is upstairs and behind the old PIA building. Hot-water doubles/triples cost Rs 300/350.

Places to Stay & Eat – middle *Indus Motel & Snack Bar* (☎ 2608) is a good bet. Cold-water singles/doubles cost Rs 200/300. Deluxe singles/doubles cost Rs 350/450; the VIP deluxe room costs Rs 500. *Hunza Tourist House* (☎ 2515, 3491), across from the K2 Motel, has clean singles/doubles for Rs 385/495. The *Karakoram Inn* has deluxe (carpeted) doubles with views from Rs 500. The *Yurt & Yak Sarai*, in Satellite Town, has yurts with electricity, private toilets and hot showers, and a common dining room. It was damaged by storms in the winter of 1994-5.

Places to Stay & Eat – top end PTDC's *K2 Motel* (☎ 2946) has excellent views, spacious gardens and is quiet. It caters to trekking parties and mountaineering expeditions and offers secure sheds to store gear and plenty of room to pack and sort loads. Singles/doubles in the old wing cost Rs 500/600 and those in the new wing cost Rs 700/800; meal prices are fixed. The *Pioneer Hotel* is across from the airport 15 km west of town.

Getting Around

Suzukis go through the bazaar for Rs 2, but

only until dark. Taxis to and from the airport and the bazaar cost Rs 200. Taxis to and from the K2 Motel and the bazaar cost about Rs 20. The rare Suzuki to and from the airport costs about Rs 10.

Special hires anywhere are most easily arranged directly with jeep contractors. There are often some in the parking lot of the K2 Motel. Wazir Jaffer Shigri of Alexander Transport Service (☎ 3346, 2946, 2146; fax 3322) in Kazimi bazaar is helpful, as is Aga Abbas. Many cargo jeeps leave from an alley off Hussaini Chowk near the aqueduct.

GETTING THERE & AWAY
Treks throughout Baltistan usually begin or end in Skardu town (see Getting Around for more information). PIA schedules a daily Boeing 737 flight Islamabad-Skardu and the fare costs Rs 690. PIA also schedules once weekly Fokker F-27 flights Islamabad-Skardu that cost Rs 600 and continue Skardu-Gilgit for Rs 395.

From Skardu, the 230 km Skardu-Gilgit road follows the Indus River down valley, and crosses a bridge over the Gilgit River, north of the junction of the Indus and Gilgit rivers, where it joins the KKH. North on the KKH is Gilgit and south is Islamabad/ Rawalpindi.

Basha, Tormik & Stak Valleys

The Basha, Tormik, and Stak valleys offer excellent alternatives to more frequently visited areas of Baltistan. Most trekkers going north up the Shigar Valley turn east into the Braldu Valley. Those that head north and east into the Basha Valley encounter traditional Balti villages comparatively unaffected by expeditions and tourism. Above the last villages is the immense Chogo Lungma (big valley) Glacier with several first-class treks, including the challenging Haramosh La. To the west and south of the Basha Valley are the Tormik and Stak valleys. The Ganto La connects the Basha Valley with the Tormik Valley, and the Stak La links the Tormik and Stak valleys. These valleys are infrequently visited and the passes rarely crossed, making for unspoiled and adventurous trekking.

INFORMATION
Maps
The best map is the 1:250,000 orographical sketch map *Karakoram: Sheet 1* published by the Swiss Foundation for Alpine Research. Other useful maps are the US AMS *India and Pakistan Series U502* 1:250,000 *Mundik (NI 43-3)* and *Gilgit (NI 43-2)* sheets and Leomann's *Karakoram Trekking and Mountaineering* 1:200,000 *Sheet 2: (Skardu, Hispar, Biafo).*

Regulations
Foreigners are allowed to trek anywhere in this open zone. Neither a permit from the Tourism Division nor a licensed mountain guide is required.

Accommodation & Supplies
Only basic supplies are available, so bring everything from Skardu or Gilgit.

Chu Tron Beyond Tissar is the village of Chu Tron, meaning 'hot springs' in Balti. This excellent spring is around 39° C, has almost no sulphur smell, and gushes forth in a large flow. The villagers have constructed several enclosed bath houses with doors, open ceilings, and cement walled knee-deep pools. This is a wonderful place to relax and soak on your way back down the Basha Valley or before crossing the Ganto La. The *NAPWD Rest House* costs Rs 75 for the standard room or Rs 100 for the VIP room. It is reasonably clean with a large compound for camping. The chowkidar can cook simple meals.

Doko As you head north up the Basha Valley, Doko has the last shop with basic supplies.

Stak Nala A restaurant and general store where the Skardu-Gilgit road crosses the

Basha, Tormik & Stak Valleys

Stak Nala is a standard stop for vehicles travelling between Skardu and Gilgit. Charpoys are available.

GETTING THERE & AWAY
Doko

From Skardu, the small town of Haiderabad with its two popular restaurants lies three hours north up the Shigar Valley. At Haiderabad, jeeps to the Basha Valley turn west, leaving the main Braldu Valley road, and cross the Braldu and Basha rivers. From Haiderabad it is about 35 km to Doko village. The first village in the Basha Valley is Tissar,

from where many men who porter up the Braldu come. Beyond Tissar, landslides occasionally block the road. From Skardu, cargo jeeps to Doko cost Rs 60 and special jeeps cost Rs 1500. From Haiderabad, cargo jeeps cost Rs 50 and special jeeps cost Rs 1000. Jeeps from Tissar to Skardu also run down the true right (west) bank of the Shigar River. This road is not as good as the main road on the true left (east) bank.

Villages on Gilgit-Skardu Road

Sassi, Stak, Dassu, and Bagicha are trailhead villages on the Gilgit-Skardu road. The daily NATCO or Mashabrum Tours buses between Gilgit and Skardu pass through them. Vehicles usually stop at the petrol pump in Sassi 1½ hours from Gilgit and at the popular Stak Nala lunch spot 2½ hours from Skardu. A jeep road goes up the Stak Valley as far as Stak village, leaving the main road about one km east of the bridge over the Stak Nala. For cargo jeeps to Stak, ask at the shop next to the restaurant. Dassu and Bagicha are at the mouth of the Tormik Valley, 1½ hours from Skardu. Special hires from Gilgit or Skardu are expensive.

GUIDES & PORTERS

The maximum low-altitude porter's wage is Rs 120 per stage plus food rations. Porters in the Basha Valley ask for a flat Rs 200 per stage and bring their own food. However, be sure they have sufficient food for the number of days you plan to be out. Porters in the Basha Valley want more trekkers to come, so they do not ask to be paid for wāpāsi, the clothing and equipment allowance, or rest days.

CHOGO LUNGMA GLACIER

(5 days; late June to early September)
Godfrey Vigne, who essentially discovered the Karakoram in 1835, called the snout of the Chogo Lungma Glacier the grandest spectacle that he saw on the whole of his travels. The infrequently visited Basha Valley has bridges made of birch and willow fronds and tight compact settlements constructed of woven willow plastered with mud. The villages nestle amid mud fields shaded by poplar, apricot, apple and walnut trees. Women wear broad black *nathing* (hats) with a red rim, and men's nathing are distinctively broad-rimmed also. The hot springs at Chu Tron are the nicest in Baltistan and probably all the Karakoram. The valley is especially picturesque above Doko with green terraced fields beneath granite Mango Brak peak, and low-angle granite slabs, hundreds of metres high, rising above Gon and Arandu. The walking is easy, and the ablation valleys along the north margin of the Chogo Lungma Glacier are lush with trees and flowers, with

excellent views of Spantik (7027m) and Malubiting (7458m). Expeditions to these two peaks and Laila (6986m) follow this route to the base camps. Trekkers crossing the Haramosh La proceed south-west from Laila base camp.

Two mountaineering routes head north out of the Basha Valley. A technical route over the Sokha La leads east to the upper Biafo Glacier. Occasionally crossed by experienced mountaineers, it offers quick access to Snow Lake. Another technical route over the Nushik La (called Nashkura La by Arandu villagers) leads in five days from Doko to Hispar village. It is heavily corniced with a steep ice slope on the north side. The Haigutum Glacier, a branch of the Hispar Glacier, has enormous crevasses, which can only be crossed early before the snow bridges melt. None of the Arandu porters have crossed this pass. Reportedly, Burusho men used to cross this pass to raid Shigar.

Guides & Porters

Hiring a local guide is highly recommended. From Doko to Arandu, hire porters from the lower villages in the valley. At Arandu, select those porters who are most fit and familiar with the route and send back any porters who are not. Arandu villagers are the best porters because they use the pastures along the Chogo Lungma Glacier.

10 stages: Doko to Arandu, Arandu to Churzing, Churzing to Chogo Brangsa, Chogo Brangsa to Kurumal, Kurumal to Bolocho, and return via same route. The distance from Arandu to Bolocho was traditionally three stages: Arandu to Buqon; Buqon to Kurumal, and Kurumal to Bolocho. However, porters now ask for four stages.

Map Notes

Tsibirri village is rendered as Tissa Birri on the Swiss map. It labels Churzing as Churtsinks, Chogo Brangsa as Chohob Langsa, Kurumal as Khurumal, and Wung as Gongon. It does not show Buqon, Manfi Kuru, Gareencho, Bolocho, Skari Byanga, or Sharing. It locates Spantik and Laila base camps, and Mani camp with triangles. It renders the glacier Khilburi Gang as Kilwuri

Gans. It shows both the Khilburi and Bolocho glaciers as being connected directly to the Chogo Lungma Glacier. They have receded, and now rivers flow from these side glaciers into the main Chogo Lungma Glacier.

Route Description

Day 1: Doko to Arandu (5 to 6 hours) A grassy camp site, on the northern outskirts of Doko, is just above the trail under the shade of several large walnut trees near a clear stream. The road between Doko and Arandu is passable for jeeps only during the spring and autumn when the water level in the Basha River is low, but it makes a good, wide walking trail. Ford a large side stream 20 minutes from Doko. Several more clear streams descend from granite cliffs along the western side of the Basha Valley. As the valley begins to turn westward, the trail climbs and then descends to the river. It finally rounds the bend in the valley 2½ to three hours from Doko and heads north north-west over a large plain next to the river. Across the river is the village of Bisil, which is reached via a wooden basket suspended from a steel cable. Bisil is at the mouth of the Berelter River. The route to the Sokha La is up this valley.

Continue 45 minutes to one hour to the village of Gon. Fractured granite slabs tower above Gon and Arandu, which is 45 minutes to one hour ahead. Just west of Arandu is a small camp site. Villagers can show you where the clear springs are. Otherwise, the only water is silty irrigation water from the large glacier behind Arandu. North of Arandu is the Kero Lungma Glacier, and the route to the Nushik La.

Day 2: Arandu to Chogo Brangsa (4 to 5 hours) The trail heads towards the mouth of the Chogo Lungma Glacier, along the true right bank of the river. Ascend the terminal moraine in about 30 minutes. A herders' trail crosses the fairly stable glacier in 45 minutes to one hour to the ablation valley along the glacier's northern margin. The first clear stream is a few minutes along the trail in the ablation valley. Cross another stream, amid willows and wild roses, and 30 minutes after leaving the glacier, reach Churzing, where some huts cluster against the hillside. A rocky, sloping camp site five minutes further along makes a good lunch spot. Continue through dense willow and rosewood thickets to the end of the ablation valley. Contour the hillside, and in 45 minutes to one hour descend into another small, well-wooded valley. Here are the huts of Buqon.

A level camp site is in front of and below the huts, amid willows. However, water is often scarce. Continue 45 minutes to one hour to Manfi Kuru where shepherds' huts perch on a small dung-covered knoll, overlooking the glacier. The large stream coming from the side valley tends to be silty. The only level ground for camping is next to the stream on sand. From Manfi Kuru are the first views of Spantik. Continue 30 to 45 minutes to Chogo Brangsa (big pasture). The stream here is clear, and level camp sites are amid willows along the stream. Shepherds' huts cluster against the hillside further up this pretty side valley, which overlooks the glacier and has a good view of Spantik.

Day 3: Chogo Brangsa to Gareencho or Bolocho (4 to 6 hours) Continue up the ablation valley, with its abundant flowers, one hour to Shing Kuru. *Shing* means 'wood' in Balti, and this is the last camp where juniper is found. The side stream here tends to be silty, and is prone to high water in the afternoon. From the moraine ridge are striking views of the Chogo Lungma Glacier ice and rock, and Malubiting (called Malupiting by locals) first comes into view. Thirty minutes further is upper Shing Kuru with its smaller, clear stream descending from a waterfall on the cliff. This would also be a nice camp site. Fifteen minutes beyond Shing Kuru, the Kurumal area starts. This wide alluvial area has a big clear stream at its eastern end, but no good camp sites. A silty brown pool often covers much of the flat area here. At its far west end, a 15 minute walk, are four porter shelters, and a grassy area for about six tents. Water here is slightly silty. Just beyond these porter shelters is a larger flat area where you can pitch more tents on sand and grass.

From Kurumal, the trail descends 15 minutes and heads out onto the Chogo Lungma Glacier to get around the torrent from the Khilburi Gang (*gang* means 'glacier' in Balti; *khil*, 'pool'). Apparently, there used to be a glacial lake at this spot. It takes about 20 minutes to detour this, and another 10 minutes to climb back to the grassy hillside. A trail continues up the ablation valley, over snow pack at times, and after 30 minutes reaches Wung. A single shepherd's hut lies against the hillside on the eastern end of the alluvial fan. Snow melt provides clear water.

Continue 30 to 45 minutes to the broad, grassy area of Gareencho. The water here has some sediment, which quickly settles. Excellent views of Malubiting, the Polan La, and Spantik, and level camp sites on grass beside the stream make this a nice spot for a rest or acclimatisation day. If going to either Laila base camp or the Haramosh La, camp here. Gareencho is more comfortable than the next camp site, Bolocho. However, if you are going to Spantik base camp (see Other Routes below), you may want to camp at Bolocho, as it is a long walk the next day from Bolocho to Spantik base camp.

Beyond Gareencho, the trail crosses difficult terrain. Descend over scree to the edge of the glacier. Continue along the glacier's margin, through broken areas, where the trail is hard to find. Reach Bolocho after 45 minutes to one hour of toilsome walking from Gareencho. Bolocho is a sandy area, with water from the glacier, and many porter shelters. A large mineral spring lies a few minutes to the right of camp. Locals say it is warm so they do not drink it, but it does feel cold to the touch.

Days 4 & 5: Gareencho or Bolocho to Doko
Retrace the route down to Doko.

LAILA BASE CAMP & HARAMOSH LA
(10 days; late July to early September)
The Haramosh La is a pass connecting the Haramosh and Chogo Lungma glaciers on the north-east with the Haramosh Valley on the south-west. The pass is enclosed by Laila (6986m), which towers over the juncture of the Haramosh and Chogo Lungma glaciers, Mani (6685m) and Haramosh (7409m) peaks.

The route over the Haramosh La begins from Doko in the Basha Valley and ends at Sassi where the Haramosh Valley meets the Gilgit-Skardu road. It follows the trek route up the Chogo Lungma Glacier as far as Bolocho. From Bolocho, it heads south and west up the Haramosh Glacier, passing through the base camp for Laila peak.

It is one of the most formidable trekking routes in the Karakoram, and is probably crossed only once every few years. The upper Haramosh Glacier is crevassed and there is some avalanche danger near the pass. The west side is steep, with avalanche danger, and requires use of rope for the descent. The route is suited to experienced trekkers with mountaineering experience. You need 150m to 300m of rope and crevasse rescue gear.

Guides & Porters
To attempt to cross the Haramosh La without a qualified guide who knows the route and its dangers would be foolhardy. Arandu porters know the route, but do not know where or how to fix ropes, judge avalanche or rock-fall danger, or make crevasse rescues if necessary. Ask to see their letters of recommendation from past trekkers or expeditions. Be sure to equip porters properly for sleeping and cooking on snow.

14 stages: Doko to Arandu, Arandu to Churzing, Churzing to Chogo Brangsa, Chogo Brangsa to Kurumal, Kurumal to Bolocho, Bolocho to Laila base camp, Laila base camp to Sharing, Sharing to the Haramosh La, the Haramosh La to Mani, Mani to Kutwal Lake, Kutwal Lake to Kutwal village, Kutwal village to Iskere, Iskere to Dassu, and Dassu to Sassi.

Map Notes
See Chogo Lungma Glacier route description above.

Top: Springtime apricot blossoms decorate Machulu village along the jeep road to Hushe village.
Bottom: The upper Biafo Glacier offers relatively easy glacier walking amid spectacular mountains.

The unclimbed spires above Tsino village in the closed Saltoro Valley are typical of the high-quality granite towers in eastern Baltistan.

Route Description

Days 1 to 3: Doko to Gareencho See the Chogo Lungma Glacier route description above.

Days 4 & 5: Gareencho to Laila Base Camp (4 to 5 hours) Continue to Bolocho from where the route crosses the Chogo Lungma Glacier, turns west onto the Haramosh Glacier, and reaches the grassy northern ablation valley and Laila base camp. Take a rest day here to acclimatise.

Day 6: Laila Base Camp to Sharing (5 to 6 hours) Rope up to reach Sharing, the level glacial basin at the base of the Haramosh La. Stronger parties may prefer to combine days 6 and 7 by leaving Laila base camp before dawn to ascend Haramosh La the same day, reaching the top by mid-morning.

Day 7: Sharing to Haramosh La (4 hours) Frequent crevasses require a rope and careful probing. Keep to the western side of the glacier where it is less steep and fix a rope at the steepest section near the top. Camp on top of the level, open pass (4800m).

Days 8 & 9: Haramosh La to Kutwal Lake (7 to 8 hours) Depending on snow conditions, you may need as much as 300m of fixed line to descend the steep snow slope on the west side of the pass. Beware of avalanche and rock-fall danger as you descend steep scree lower down. Mani, at the bottom, is a possible camp. Usually, trekkers continue to Kutwal Lake (3260m) to camp and rest for a day if exhausted.

Days 10 & 11: Kutwal Lake to Sassi Continue down valley on a good trail with views of high peaks all around, camping at Iskere en route. When you prearrange a jeep, the vehicle can meet you in Dassu, at the end of the jeep road. Otherwise, follow the road along the Phuparash River to Sassi.

OTHER ROUTES
Spantik Base Camp

Spantik, at the head of the Chogo Lungma Glacier, is usually climbed from the Chogo Lungma Glacier via the relatively easy, long south-east ridge. Fanny Bullock-Workman, in her long skirt and laced knee boots, came within a few hundred metres of the summit some 90 years ago. Nagyr and Hunza people call it Golden peak because of its golden granite north face.

See Chogo Lungma Glacier above for route description from Doko to Bolocho. From Doko you can reach Bolocho in three long days. If you take four days, camp in Arandu, Buqon, Kurumal, and Bolocho, or take a rest day at Gareencho. From Bolocho the trail heads onto the Chogo Lungma Glacier. You can break up the seven to nine hour hike from Bolocho to Spantik base camp by stopping to camp at Skari Byanga, a sandy place along the northern margin of the glacier. *Byanga* means 'sand', and *skari* refers to a minuscule weight used for weighing gold or silver. Apparently, a local villager once found a tiny amount of gold here. Villagers say ibex are abundant above grassy Spantik base camp (marked by a triangle (4300m) on the Swiss map). Allow 10 days from Doko to base camp and back, including a day to explore the area surrounding base camp. From Bolocho it is four stages: Bolocho to Skari Byanga (not marked on maps), Skari Byanga to Spantik base camp, and return via the same route.

Ganto La

The Ganto La makes an interesting, but steep, exit from the Basha Valley, thereby avoiding the 70-km-long jeep ride down the Shigar Valley. The trek begins from Hemasil in the Basha Valley, just across a stream north of Chu Tron. It takes two or three days to cross the Ganto La to Harimal in the Tormik Valley from where you can head south down valley to reach Dassu or Bagicha on the Gilgit-Skardu road in one easy day, or head north to cross the Stak La (see below).

From Hemasil, ascend steeply 1000m to the ridge above Chu Tron. Camp in a meadow near the huts of Matunturu. The next day, continue steeply to the Ganto La (4606m), with a permanent steep snowfield below the pass. It is a steep descent to a pleasant meadow camp site called Pakora. Harimal is a short day's walk further. The pass is usually open from late June to early September.

Stak La

The Stak La links the Stak Nala to the green upper Tormik Valley, both of which have road heads on the Gilgit-Skardu road. The trek makes a three-day loop and can be combined with the Ganto La trek (see above). From the road head at Dassu, head north-east up the Tormik Valley. (At Harimal, not shown on the Swiss map, the route over the Ganto La branches off to the north-east.) Continue up the Tormik Valley to Dunsa and camp near the pologround by shepherds' huts. At the head of the valley cross a small glacier and reach the Stak La (about 4500m). Descend the west side of the pass to a camp, about 900m below the pass. Follow the river valley as it makes a bend to the south 20 km to Stak village, which is connected by a jeep road to the Gilgit-Skardu road.

Deosai Mountains & Plains

The Deosai Plains, a vast high-altitude plateau south and west of Skardu, borders on Indian Kashmir. Nowhere lower than 4000m, this uninhabited alpine grassland has numerous clear streams with unusual snow trout, a large brown bear population, and a multitude of golden marmots. Its remarkable biodiversity has recently earned it recognition as a national wilderness park (see Ecology – Protected Areas in the Facts about the Region chapter). Because of its elevation, the Deosai is snow-covered most of the year, enabling enjoyable spring ski touring. Its brief summer brings out intense July-August mosquito swarms, which are relieved by strong daytime winds. Early September frosts restore peace to the plateau making trekking pleasurable.

A jeep road crosses the Deosai Plains between Skardu and the Astor Valley at the base of Nanga Parbat. From Skardu, the road heads south up the Satpara Valley, passing Satpara Lake and village. It continues west across the Deosai plateau, crossing large clear streams via bridges. As it leaves the Deosai, it skirts the northern shore of a charming lake, then crosses the Chhachor Pass (4266m) to the Das Khirim Gah and upper Astor Valley. You can walk along the jeep road over the plains or explore the side valleys and passes through the Deosai mountains from the Astor Valley, Mendi or Kachura on the Skardu-Gilgit road, or Skardu.

INFORMATION
Maps
The US AMS *India and Pakistan Series U502* 1:250,000 *Mundik (NI 43-3)* sheet shows the Harpo, Banak, Alampi, Dari, Burji, and Katichu passes. The *Gilgit (NI 43-2)* sheet shows the areas west of these passes to the Astor Valley. Leomann's *Karakoram Trekking and Mountaineering* 1:200,000 *Sheet 2: (Skardu, Hispar, Biafo)* only shows the Shigarthang Valley, Banak La, and the valley above Mendi leading to the Harpo La.

Regulations
Foreigners are allowed to trek anywhere in this open zone. Neither a permit from the Tourism Division nor a licensed mountain guide is required. Fishing licences for Satpara can be obtained from the Fisheries office on the Link Rd in Skardu.

Accommodation & Supplies
Once you leave road head villages, nothing is available, so bring everything you need from Skardu or Gilgit.

Astor Valley Astor village is along both banks of the Rama Gah. The bazaar is on the north side; the road continues on the south side. The *Dreamland Tourist Inn* at the top of the bazaar has dorms for Rs 50 and a garden for camping; doubles with shared toilet cost Rs 200. Other hotels are cheaper; the *Rama* and the *Tourist Cottage* have doubles with toilet for about Rs 70, and basic restaurants. The *NAPWD Rest House* in Astor can be booked with the Executive Engineer in Astor or in Gilgit.

Kachura Thirty km west of Skardu, Kachura is known mostly for the *Shangri-La Tourist Resort* with a DC-3 fuselage by a small lake. Doubles cost from Rs 3000 per night. Across the lake is the *Tibet Hotel* where doubles cost about Rs 300. Further west is the larger Kachura Lake.

Satpara The *PTDC Motel* has two doubles that cost Rs 300. At the *Satpara Lake Inn* doubles cost Rs 100 and it costs Rs 50 to camp. The *Lake View Motel* is nearby.

GETTING THERE & AWAY
Astor Valley
At Jaglot the road to Astor leaves the KKH, crosses a bridge over the Indus River and heads 40 km south-east up the narrow Astor Valley. Vehicles for about Rs 20 go all day from Gilgit's general bus stand to Jaglot, from where passenger jeeps go regularly to Astor. Occasionally vehicles go direct

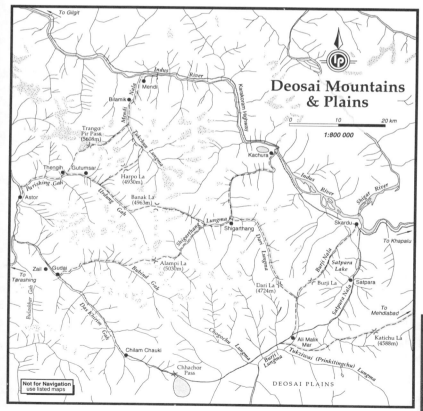

BALTISTAN

Gilgit-Astor and cost about Rs 50. Special hires Gilgit-Astor cost Rs 1600. Astor is about six hours from Gilgit.

Deosai Jeep Traverse
A special hire for a two-day 165-km jeep ride Skardu-Astor, with an overnight en route, costs about Rs 6000. The driving time totals 16 to 18 hours.

Mendi
Mendi, once the capital of the old kingdom of Rondu, is on the true left (south) bank of the Indus River, about 2½ hours from Skardu. Get off any Gilgit-Skardu vehicle across from Mendi and cross the bridge.

Kachura
Get off any Gilgit-Skardu vehicle at Kachura, about 30 km west of Skardu. Taxis from Skardu cost up to Rs 300.

Satpara
Special hires to Satpara, eight km south of Skardu, cost Rs 350 return.

Mehdiabad
A special hire from Skardu is the easiest way to reach Mehdiabad, formerly called Parkutta.

GUIDES & PORTERS
The maximum low-altitude porter's wage is Rs 120 per stage plus wāpāsi and food rations. All of these routes are infrequently used, so you should hire a guide or knowledgeable porter.

BURJI LA
(3 days; mid-June to mid-October. Expect much snow on the pass and on the Deosai Plains early in the season.)

The Burji La (4816m) is a snow-covered north-south pass between the Skardu Valley and the Deosai Plains. From the pass, K2 and Masherbrum are distantly visible. Only 16 km south of Skardu, but some 2600m above, the pass is easiest to cross from the Deosai Plains south to north, descending to Skardu (see the Deosai Mountains & Plains map).

For an excellent three day loop from Skardu, walk up the Satpara Valley along the jeep road, and turn north into the grassy valley that leads to the pass. Fit, acclimatised trekkers can walk up the Burji Nala from Skardu. This approach makes for a stimulating start to a longer trek from Skardu to Nanga Parbat's Rupal Valley trek (see Nanga Parbat in the Gilgit, Diamir & Kaghan Valley chapter). We describe the trek in the north-south direction.

Route Description
Day 1: Skardu to Wozal Hadar The Burji Nala is the first valley west of the large, wide Satpara Nala. From Skardu, follow the road towards the airport. Once across the bridge over the Satpara stream, head for the obvious narrow opening of the Burji Nala. Follow a herders' trail along the clear stream, inexorably ascending past stands of birch and willow. Shepherds' huts and a spring at Pindobal offer a camp site three to four hours up the valley for those not yet acclimatised. The treeless camp site of Wozal Hadar is one to 1½ hours further.

Day 2: Wozal Hadar to Burji Lungma Higher up the valley opens into a wide basin. The Burji La is the obvious snow saddle on the eastern side of the ridge above the upper basin two to three hours from Wozal Hadar. A broad snowfield lies below the pass. If crevasses are visible, ascend the rocky spur just west (right) of the snowfield to the saddle, marked by a cairn. The giant peaks at the head of the Baltoro Glacier rise above the lower ridges in a grand panorama. To the south, several icy blue lakes nestle below a small ridge. Descend south to the valley below, and follow it to its junction with a larger, clear stream and camp in grass along its banks. Up this stream to the north-west is the Dari La, over which lies the Dari Lungma and Shigarthang village (see Other Routes – Kachura to Astor Valley below).

Day 3: Burji Lungma to Skardu Follow the stream south about 10 km to reach the Deosai Plains and the jeep road. Follow the jeep road back to Satpara and Skardu or head west to the Astor Valley. If coming from Skardu and the Satpara Valley, the Burji Lungma, as it is called, is the first clear stream from the north.

Side Trip to Nanga Parbat View
Nanga Parbat can be seen distantly from hilltops on the Deosai Plains. However, if heading north-west down the Das Khirim Gah from the Deosai Plains, cross a bridge below Gudai village to Zail village and follow a trail to pastures above. From the pastures, ascend to the ridge for a stunning, never-to-be-forgotten view of Nanga Parbat. The entire massif stretches before you. From the dry ridge, continue down roughly to the Bulashbar Gah and follow it to the main Astor Valley. From here, it is a one day walk to Tarashing, the road head for the Rupal Valley (see Nanga Parbat in the Gilgit, Diamir & Kaghan Valley chapter).

OTHER ROUTES
Mendi to Astor Valley
Mendi, also called Shoat, is a village on the true left (south) side of the Indus River in the region called Rondu where the Indus River flows through a deep gorge. From Mendi, the Tukchun Lungma heads south. This valley has a sizeable markhor population and should offer viewing opportunities. Two difficult passes from the Tukchun Valley cross the Deosai mountains to the Parishing Gah, an eastern tributary of the Astor River. From Mendi to Astor is a four day trek. The first camp beyond Mendi is usually near Bilamik. Higher up, the valley divides. The south-west branch leads to the extremely high and glaciated Trango Pir Pass (5608m). The south-east (left) branch is the main Tukchun Lungma, which leads to the Harpo La (4930m). There are several summer settlements in the upper Tukchun Lungma. Continue up the valley and camp at the huts of Baltal, where the route to the Harpo La turns south up a side stream. The north side of the pass is glaciated and steep and the descent is steep and rocky. Follow the Harpo Nala down from the pass and camp about four km above the main valley along the

stream. The next day continue down the main valley, called the Urdung Gah, and follow it about 10 km to Thengih village, where the valley becomes the Parishing Gah. A jeep road goes about 10 km down valley to Astor village in the Astor Valley. This route is best done from July to August; take a local porter to show the way.

Kachura to Astor Valley
Kachura Lake and village are 30 km west of Skardu on the Gilgit-Skardu road. Kachura is marked Katzarah on the U502 *Mundik (NI 43-3)* sheet. From Kachura Lake, the Shigarthang Lungma heads south-west. Shigarthang villagers are Brokpa Shina-speakers, who came from Astor. A jeep road goes as far as Tsok. From Shigarthang village, two routes lead over high passes, the Banak La and Alampi La, to the Astor Valley. Another leads east up the Dari Lungma over the Dari La (about 4724m) to the Deosai Plains. Camp in the upper Dari Lungma below this pass, which appears glaciated on the north-east side. This route over the Dari La can be combined with the Burji La as a four to five day loop.

To reach the Astor Valley from Shigarthang village, continue west up the main Shigarthang Valley. The route to the Banak La (4963m) follows a side stream west south-west about six km above Shigarthang village. The valley ascends steeply and becomes rocky. Camp above the treeline at Urdukas (about 3962m), 20 km from Shigarthang. Continue up across a glacier to the pass, six km from camp. Crevasses on the glacier are covered by snow bridges until late summer, but use a rope for safety. Descend steeply eight km to Chumik (3657m) and the Urdung Gah. The next day, continue down the valley to Astor.

The route to the Alampi La (5030m) follows the main Shigarthang Valley 10 km to the huts of Thlashing Spang. Continue up the rocky valley and camp where the upper valley bends south-west. The ascent to the pass is over snow. The descent is extremely steep, at first at an angle of over 35°. It continues more gently over snow to the

BALTISTAN

meadows (about 4000m) in the basin below the pass. Continue five km down this side valley into Bubind Gah, which joins the Das Khirim Gah and the jeep road from the Deosai Plains at Gudai. From Gudai, a side trip for views of Nanga Parbat is possible.

These routes take about six to seven days. The passes are best crossed from mid-June to August. Hire a local to show you the way.

Katichu La

The Katichu La (4588m) is a pass linking Mehdiabad (formerly called Parkutta) on the Indus River east of Skardu to the Deosai Plains. The pass is usually snow-free July to late September and the trek takes about three days. Reportedly, a distant K2 is visible from the pass. When crossing from east to west, this trek is easily combined with the trek over the Burji La (see above), or return to Skardu via the jeep road down the Satpara Valley.

Biafo, Hispar & Baltoro Glaciers

Out of the centre of the most extensively glaciated terrain on the planet outside the polar regions flows the Braldu River, which starts at the junction of the Biafo River flowing from the Biafo Glacier and the Biaho River from the Panmah and Baltoro glaciers. The Biafo Glacier descends from Lukpe Lawo, named Snow Lake by Sir Martin Conway in 1891, and the Sim Glacier, two vast glacial basins beneath spectacular granite peaks, including Baintha Brak (7285m). Above Snow Lake is the Hispar La (5151m), which connects the Biafo Glacier with the Hispar Glacier. Pastures along the Hispar Glacier are used by Burushashki-speaking Nagyrkutz. The Panmah Glacier descends from the eastern side of Baintha Brak. Pastures along the Biafo and Panmah glaciers are used by Braldu Valley Balti villagers.

The Baltoro Glacier remains the number one trekking destination in Pakistan. Out of all the permits issued by the Tourism Division, over 70% are for the Baltoro Glacier. The amazing granite towers and sheer walls along the lower Baltoro yield to the incomparable giants above Concordia. Above all rises K2 (8611m), so massive yet so ethereal, the ultimate mountain of mountains. This entire region is in the Central Karakoram National Park (see Ecology – Protected Areas in the Facts about the Region chapter).

INFORMATION
Maps

The Swiss Foundation for Alpine Research 1:250,000 orographical sketch map *Karakoram: Sheet 1* shows the Braldu Valley, the Biafo and Hispar glaciers, and the lower Baltoro Glacier west of Urdukas. *Sheet 2* shows the upper Baltoro Glacier to Concordia and K2 base camp.

The US AMS *India and Pakistan Series U502* 1:250,000 *Mundik (NI-43-3)* sheet shows the Braldu Valley, the Biafo Glacier to Snow Lake, and the lower Baltoro Glacier west of Goro II, while the *Shimshal (NJ 43-15)* sheet shows the Hispar La and Hispar Glacier to its mouth. The *Chulung (NI 43-4)* sheet shows the upper Baltoro Glacier and Concordia. Leomann's *Karakoram Trekking and Mountaineering* 1:200,000 *Sheet 2: (Skardu, Hispar, Biafo)* depicts the Biafo and Hispar glaciers, but like the U502 series, is of little use for trekking. Leomann's *Sheet 3: (K2, Baltoro, Gasherbrum, Masherbrum, Saltoro Groups)* shows the entire Baltoro Glacier, but does not include the Braldu Valley.

Two excellent and highly reliable maps of the Baltoro Glacier itself are: 1:100,000 *Ghiacciaio Baltoro* published by the Italian Instituto Geografico Militaire; and the out-of-print 1:100,000 *The Baltoro Glacier* published by Yama To Kei Koku Sha of Japan. The latter is the only map to accurately depict the upper Vigne Glacier and the Gondogoro La.

Regulations

The Biafo and Hispar glaciers are in an open zone, where foreigners are allowed to trek.

Neither a permit from the Tourism Division nor a licensed mountain guide is required. However, local authorities may expect trekkers to have a guide or porters. The Baltoro Glacier, the Panmah Glacier and its two upper arms, the Nobande Sobande and the Choktoi glaciers are in a restricted zone, where trekkers must have a permit and a licensed mountain guide.

Check Posts Trekkers must register at police check posts in Shigar, Dassu, and Thungol along the road up the Braldu Valley. Thungol is also the trail head for the Baltoro and Panmah glaciers, which are in a restricted zone. Occasionally trekkers planning to go up the open-zone Biafo Glacier have not been allowed to proceed. Trekkers may want to first request a letter from the DC in Skardu stating that they have permission to go up the Braldu Valley and the Biafo Glacier.

Shigar Failing to register at this check post can create problems later on. Police in Thungol have been known to go as far as Snow Lake to drag trekkers back to register at Shigar. Here police may also ask for your guide's name.

Dassu Just before the bridge over the Braldu River, police at this check post have been known to shake down trekkers, particularly those in small parties, looking for a bribe to allow legitimate trekkers to proceed.

Thungol In 1995, the check post was moved from Askole to Thungol where most trekkers camp. In the past, police have refused to allow unaccompanied backpackers to proceed up the Biafo Glacier and may insist you hire someone locally for your own safety.

Accommodation & Supplies
There are *NAPWD Rest Houses* in Shigar and Dassu. During the summer, a few 'restaurants' spring up at Thungol where tea, soft drinks, and local food are available. Camping here costs Rs 25 per tent. In Askole,

trekkers camp in a walled compound with grassy terraces, trees, a water tap, a latrine, and bath houses. The trees were planted by the Himalayan Green Club, a Japanese organisation. The camping ground was planned by Doug Scott, a veteran British climber, and Haji Mahdi, the village headman who collects Rs 25 per tent.

A shop in Paiju sells basic supplies (eg, flour, sugar, and kerosene). Unfortunately beverages in plastic bottles and aluminium cans have made their way here, adding to the already out-of-control rubbish problem. Buying supplies here is more expensive than buying them in Skardu and paying porters to carry them up. However, it provides an option to resupply or to supply porters with food above Paiju, which can reduce the number of porters' loads to Paiju. Porters going down can buy food here to get back to Askole.

GETTING THERE & AWAY
Thungol/Askole – Braldu Valley
All jeeps going up the Braldu Valley stop at Thungol, below Askole. The road is frequently blocked by high water, rock fall, and landslides. In May and June, the road is usually open and the 185 km trip takes seven to eight hours. As the summer progresses (mid-July to August), expect road blocks, which can make it a two day trip and easily add Rs 1000 to transport costs. When you reach a road block, you leave your jeep and carry your gear across the block to another jeep. This jeep takes you as far as the next block, where you repeat the process. We have seen as many as five blocks, necessitating six jeeps. Normally, special jeeps from Skardu cost Rs 2500 to Rs 3000.

From Thungol, either walk on the jeep road along the river to Askole, or stroll two hours through Thungol and Surungo villages to Askole. This upper trail is more shaded and enjoyable, and crosses two streams in steep, but not large ravines.

When road blocks force your party to walk, you pay porters for the portions of stages over which they carry loads. It takes two or three days to walk the three traditional

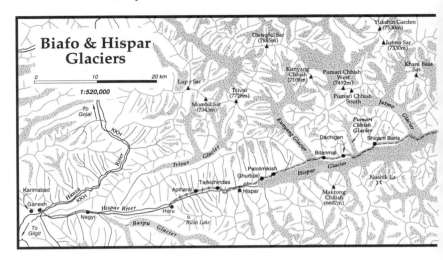

stages between Dassu and Askole. These stages are: Dassu to Chakpo; Chakpo to Chongo; and Chongo to Askole. It is half a stage from Thungol to Askole. The jeep road crosses to the true left bank before Chakpo, avoiding the steep climb to that village, and recrosses beyond Hoto before Chongo.

Huru – Hispar Valley

A jeep road follows the Hispar River from the KKH to Hispar village, but the road is subject to blockage by high water, rock fall and landslides. From June to September, you can only rely on transport to and from Huru and must plan to walk the 16 km between Hispar and Huru. When your trek ends in Huru, either prearrange a special jeep to meet you or walk to the KKH. Some parties send a 'runner' to the KKH to bring a jeep to Huru. Jeeps here are typically VIP jeeps (where drivers allow only four passengers) and not passenger jeeps (where you pile on as many people and as much gear as will fit). A special jeep Huru-KKH takes about 1¼ hours and costs Rs 1200. When the road is open to Hispar, special jeeps Hispar-Nagyr cost Rs 1500.

The 26 km walk from Huru to the KKH is hot and dry, so carry water from Huru. When porters carry loads from Huru to the KKH, you pay them an additional two stages. This can equal the cost of a jeep, so you may as well hire one and enjoy the ride. Porters with no loads are not paid for walking from Huru to the KKH.

Shigar

Passenger jeeps leave Skardu for Shigar in the morning and return the same day. The 32 km trip takes 1¼ hours and costs Rs 20. Special jeeps cost Rs 600 one way and Rs 700 return.

GUIDES & PORTERS

The maximum low-altitude porter's wage is Rs 120 for Balti porters and Rs 160 for Nagyr porters per stage plus wāpāsi, food rations, and the Rs 200 clothing and equipment allowance. Typically the DC in Skardu sets a lump-sum wage per stage each season for Balti porters that supersedes the maximum set by the government. You can hire porters in several places: Skardu, the Naib Tehsildar's office in Shigar, Haiderabad, and villages around Askole. Hiring porters in Skardu is the best bet. Porters are responsible

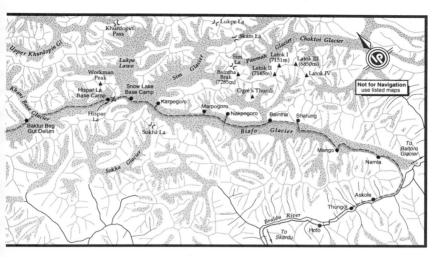

for paying for their own transport to meet you at the trail head. All parties going through the Shigar Valley must hire at least half their porters from Shigar, which includes porters from the Shigar, Basha, and Braldu valleys. The rest can come from elsewhere in Baltistan. Askole's village headman, Haji Mahdi, is in charge of porter hire there and sells goats.

BIAFO-HISPAR TRAVERSE

(12 days; June to September, but by September snow can close the pass and some camp sites are dry)

The Biafo and Hispar glaciers form the largest continuous stretch of glacier (114 km) in the Karakoram, and are connected by the Hispar La (5151m). About 200 trekkers each year cross this difficult pass through what both Francis Younghusband and HW Tilman called the finest mountain scenery in the world, scenery that 'attracts by its grandeur, but repels by its desolation'. Tradition holds that Nagyr men used to travel this route, bringing horses to play polo at Kesar's pologround near Askole. The trail must have been better then. The 130 km trek from Thungol in Baltistan to Huru in Nagyr

crosses very demanding, occasionally dangerous glaciers. Over two-thirds of the walking is actually on glacier. Both the Biafo and Hispar have chaotic, debris-covered lower sections. Their upper sections are crevassed ice fields. This should not be your first Karakoram trek. You must be prepared for the rigours and risks of serious glacier travel. These include camping on snow and ice, knowing crevasse rescue, and roped travel through large crevasse fields.

The granite spires and snowy summits above the Biafo, such as Lukpe Lawo Brak (6593m), Lukpe Brak (6029m), and Baintha Brak, form a magnificent cathedral of mountain architecture. The green ablation valleys and meadows along the glaciers are unused except by wildlife. Bears occasionally appear (raiding camp sites), as do ibex and eagles. For mountain scenery and wildlife, this is probably the best trek in Baltistan (see the Biafo & Hispar Glaciers map).

Guides & Porters

Even though this is an open-zone trek, take an experienced guide who is familiar with the route. Trekkers who attempt this trek on their own are likely to become lost, which can be life threatening. If you are experienced in glacier travel and trekking in Pakistan, you can reduce costs by hiring experienced porters to show the way, rather than a guide. But you cannot expect porters to know how to locate and avoid crevasses, or how to use a rope safely! If at all unsure, hire a guide.

Qualified guides can be hired through trekking companies in Skardu. The length and difficulty of this trek necessitates hiring porters to carry gear and supplies. The ratio of porters to trekkers typically ranges from 3:1 (for smaller scale lower budget treks) to 6:1 (for trekking parties outfitted by a trekking company). Ensure porters have adequate clothing and equipment. Whether they bring their own gear or you provide it for them, keep in mind that they will be walking, sleeping, and cooking on snow and ice for days.

Balti Porters The traverse is usually done from east to west using Balti porters. If you need more than three or four porters, hire them in Skardu. Otherwise hire them in Haiderabad or in Askole. Porters are responsible for paying for their own transport to the trail head. As supplies are consumed and loads eliminated, porters are dismissed. Porters can be released along the Biafo Glacier up to the Hispar La base camp. Never dismiss just one porter. It is dangerous for a porter to return down the glacier alone and irresponsible of any trekker to insist on it. You are committed to take porters who cross the Hispar La all the way to Huru.

Some confusing exceptions to standard porter wages apply to this trek. Porters bring their own food to Baintha I. For these four stages you pay the maximum low-altitude porter's wage of Rs 120 per stage, wāpāsi, and food rations, which totals Rs 200 per stage. It is customary to sacrifice a goat in Baintha. Animals are purchased in Askole, and cost up to Rs 2500. For the remaining stages from Baintha I to Huru, you provide all food and fuel for porters and pay a maximum per stage of Rs 120 plus wāpāsi, which totals Rs 180 per stage. Wāpāsi is

paid, despite the fact that porters never walk back over the glaciers to Baltistan. Porters instead walk to the KKH and take local transportation via Gilgit back to Skardu. You are not responsible for paying for their transport, unless you can get porters to agree not to be paid wāpāsi. Other trekking parties may negotiate lower wages per stage or fewer stages (we have heard as low as 18 stages), but they also pay a lot of baksheesh or face porter strikes. Balti porters expect to receive at least Rs 4000 total for the entire trek.

Nagyr Porters Trekking parties used to begin from Nagyr, but because of difficulties with Nagyr porters, they now begin from Baltistan. However, Nagyr porters are now eager for work and welcome trekkers to do this route from west to east. Reportedly, porters would work for a maximum of Rs 160 per stage plus Rs 60 food rations and would provide their own food for the entire trek. Additionally, Nagyr porters would not ask to paid wāpāsi. Instead, they would want to be paid for the cost of local transport, food, and accommodation to get from Skardu back to Nagyr. Before hiring anyone, see Amir Hamza, the *nambardar*, or village headman, in Hoper. We have been told Nagyr porters promise to behave!

22 stages: Askole to Namla; Namla to Mango I, Mango I to Shafung, Shafung to Baintha I, Baintha I to Nakpogoro, Nakpogoro to Marpogoro, Marpogoro to Karpogoro, Karpogoro to Hispar La Base Camp, Hispar La base camp (Biafo Glacier side) to Hispar La, Hispar La to Hispar La base camp (Hispar Glacier side), Hispar La base camp to first glacier to north; glacier to the west side of the Khani Basa Glacier, Khani Basa Glacier to Hagure Shangali Cham; Hagure Shangali Cham to west side of the Jutmo Glacier, Jutmo Glacier to Shiqam Baris, Shiqam Baris to Pumarikish, Pumarikish to Bitanmal, Bitanmal to Palolimikish, Palolimikish to Ghurbūn, Ghurbūn to Hispar village, Hispar to Apiharai, Apiharai to Huru

Map Notes
The Swiss map marks camp sites and a route over the glacier. A tributary of the Hispar Glacier, labelled Yutmaru Glacier, is called the Jutmo Glacier by Hispar villagers. Apiharai is marked as Aplahara. The trail

head at Huru is not shown. Huru is 150m above the true left bank of the Hispar River, west of the two streams shown flowing north from Rush Lake.

The U502 *Mundik (NI 43-3)* sheet and the Leomann *Sheet 2: (Skardu, Hispar, Biafo)* have routes vaguely drawn in the middle of the glaciers. No trails are drawn to and from ablation valleys and camp sites, rendering them useless for routefinding. If you followed these maps, you would probably end up in trouble.

According to the Italian alpine-scientific expedition 'Biafo 77', the Swiss map reverses the position of Latok I and II. The Italians also determined different altitudes. Latok I, the westernmost summit, is 7151m. Latok II is 7086m and Latok III, correctly located on the Swiss map, is 6850m.

Route Description

Day 1: Askole to Namla (5 to 7 hours) Walk through Askole village (3000m) and follow the irrigation canal 30 minutes to its source at a clear stream. Continue past the confluence of the Biafo and Biaho rivers, following the true right bank of the Biafo River 1½ hours to Kesar Shaguran (3090m), which means 'Kesar's pologround'. A small clear stream is five minutes before this large flat area. After crossing the broad level area, the trails to the Biafo and Baltoro glaciers divide.

The Baltoro trail continues below the rock buttress to the east. The Biafo trail turns north-east up a rock gully between a cliff on the left and a rock buttress on the right. Ascend amid boulders 15 minutes to a large cairn (3360m) and the first view of the Biafo (*biafo* means 'rooster') Glacier. Continue on a trail through the ablation valley, descending to the broken white rock at the glacier's margin in 45 minutes. Move onto the moraine-covered glacier where water lies in shallow pools. Toil gradually up past occasional cairns. After about 4.5 km or three hours on the glacier, head west (left) 15 minutes to the margin. Off the glacier, continue 15 minutes to the grassy area of Namla (3690m) with porters' shelters and sandy camp sites. Get water from the glacier or from the silty Namla stream.

Day 2: Namla to Mango I (5 to 6 hours) Leave Namla on a sandy trail and descend quickly to the glacier. Head straight out over broken, crevassed glacier 1¼ hours to the medial moraine. Cross a medial moraine ridge and a white ice band to a second medial moraine band. This eastern moraine is more level and easier to walk on. In 45 minutes, Janping Chekhma (3734m), a large, green side valley, is visible to the west. This side valley is very hard to reach, blocked by black ice towers and difficult broken glacier.

Continue along the medial moraine, passing occasional cairns made by Askole villagers who bring their yaks as far as Mango. Continue two hours from the point on the glacier opposite Janping Chekhma, until directly opposite a side valley to the west, marking the southern end of the green Mango area. Cross the white ice, the western moraine band, and then broken rock-covered ice to reach Mango I in 45 minutes. Head for the ablation valley above the side valley. High water in this side stream makes an impassible barrier to approach from below. Two camps exist, Mango I and Mango II. Mango I (3660m), at the southern end of this two-km-long ablation valley, is the better camp site with great views, a pond, profuse wildflowers, and porters' shelters.

Day 3: Mango I to Baintha I (4½ to 5½ hours) Walk up the ablation valley 30 minutes to Mango II, a large camp site, but less scenic with silty water. From Mango II, it takes about 2½ hours to cross 6.5 km of alternating bands of white ice and medial moraine to the opposite (east) margin of the Biafo Glacier, with good views of the Latok peaks. Descend onto the glacier and head straight out 30 minutes over broken black rubble-covered ice to a band of white ice. Follow its western (left) edge up 45 minutes, jumping occasional small crevasses.

As the white ice levels out, cross it to the east (right) then climb over a medial moraine ridge and descend to a larger white ice stream. Work east across that white ice, and ascend another, larger medial moraine ridge. Here you are directly opposite the Pharosang Glacier, an eastern tributary of the Biafo. Descend the medial moraine east and onto a third white ice stream. Cross it and the medial moraine beyond, to a broad white ice flow. Follow this ice highway up 30 minutes, then cross one last medial moraine ridge (4054m), opposite the Gama Sokha Lumbu Glacier and ice fall with snowy Gama Sokha Lumbu (6282m) at its head. Cross the broken ice on the eastern margin of the Biafo Glacier at its narrowest point, aiming for a faint trail visible on the grassy hillside ahead.

Enter the dry ablation valley along the north-east margin of the Biafo Glacier and climb the short, steep trail along the hillside. Contour through grass and flowers, pass a small rock shelter, and after one hour descend into a large ablation valley with a broad alluvial fan. Below is Shafung (3930m), a camp site at the base of a large boulder. Warm, clear water flows by this pretty spot. Follow the true left bank of the stream to another side valley, crossing the stream where it braids into many channels. The water may be high on a warm afternoon. Continue north-west passing a small glacial pool and a possible camp site to Baintha I (3990m), 1¼ hours from Shafung. Baintha, a lush, green meadow, is a delightful camp and a good place for an acclimatisation day.

Day 4: Baintha I to Marpogoro (5½ to 6½ hours) Stroll up the green ablation valley 45 minutes to Baintha II (4050m), a less desirable camp site marked by a triangle on the Swiss map at the junction of the Biafo and Baintha Lukpar glaciers. To the east, up the Baintha Lukpar Glacier, is the base camp for Latok I. The northern arm of the Baintha Lukpar, the Urzun Brak, leads to the base camp for Baintha Brak (The Ogre). Move onto the Biafo Glacier, crossing broken ice 20 minutes to the smooth central ice floe. Head up the glacier, working around crevasses and ascending steadily several hours. Early in the season, this section may be snow-covered, necessitating use of a rope.

After walking about eight km in three to 4½ hours on the ice highway, you are opposite the first of the three 'rock' (*goro* means 'rock') camps named for the colour of the rock above them: *nakpo* means 'black'; *marpo*, 'red'; and *karpo*, 'white'. Nakpogoro (4380m) is a large area in an ablation valley on the eastern margin of the Biafo with clear water, some vegetation, and room for many tents. From the main Biafo Glacier, a stream from a side glacier tumbling onto a white alluvial fan is visible. A prominent yellow rock spire towers above Nakpogoro. Access to this camp is through broken ice. You must be directly opposite it and head straight in. Nakpogoro is used by larger trekking parties, as the higher 'rock' camps are smaller. But, camping at Nakpogoro leaves a very long distance the next day if you intend to reach the base camp for the Hispar La.

Continue up the ice highway in the middle of the glacier 3.5 km. Beyond Nakpogoro 1½ hours, you are just below Marpogoro. This small camp site with six or seven tent platforms and stone circles for porters' shelters is just above a side valley with a large ice fall. The rock on the northern side of the camp is distinctly red, hence the name. Angle towards the red rock, working cautiously though the large crevasse field that guards the approach to this camp.

A few flowers bloom and a bit of grass grows at Marpogoro (4410m), but the lush vegetation of Baintha is now behind. The tent sites on a moraine ridge are cold and exposed to wind, but dramatic amid the glaciers and snowy peaks. (Marpogoro is the camp site indicated by a black square on the Swiss map.)

Days 5 & 6: Marpogoro to Hispar La Base Camp (5 to 6 hours) Leaving Marpogoro is not as difficult as reaching it. Head out, angling north 15 minutes, detouring around occasional crevasses to the broad, white ice highway of the main Biafo. A steady breeze constantly blows down the glacier, making the ascent colder and more tiring. A two-hour 6.5 km walk up the white ice brings you opposite the third rock camp, Karpogoro

(4680m). The 22 km from Baintha I to Karpogoro can be covered in one long day, if you are fit and acclimatised. Brown bears occasionally raid Karpogoro, which can be disastrous if they get your food. The camp is at the eastern margin of the glacier, where the Sim and Biafo glaciers meet. It is guarded by a crevasse field and must be approached carefully. To the west is the route to the technical Sokha La first crossed by Tilman in 1937.

If you are not going east to camp at Karpogoro, bear west (left) to avoid broken, crevassed ice. The glacier's surface here moves about 300m per year. The glacier broadens as the Sim and Biafo glaciers meet, and the ascent is gradual. Measurements here show the ice to be almost 1.5 km thick. With permanent snow cover, gaiters are needed and a rope is mandatory.

Continue five km in three to 3½ hours to the area at the base of the Hispar La (4770m). Be careful to avoid setting up camp in a crevasse field. The usual snowy camp site is marked by litter, and has a large pool of water next to it, some 30m below. Some trekkers may want a day here to acclimatise or to explore Lukpe Lawo, the so-called Snow Lake (see Other Routes below).

Day 7: Hispar La Base Camp to Hispar La
(3 to 6 hours) Start before the sun hits the snow and softens it. The four km ascent to the Hispar La is steady, up a 20° to 30° slope to the obvious pass. The route keeps to the middle, detouring to avoid numerous wide crevasses. Many are hidden under snow, so a rope is mandatory. The top of the pass (5151m) is broad and flat and in good weather makes a magnificent camp for acclimatised trekkers. Sir Martin Conway, the first European to cross the pass, called the view to the east of Lukpe Lawo and Baintha Brak (ie, Snow Lake and The Ogre) 'beyond all comparison the finest view of mountains it has been my lot to behold'. Just north of the pass is Workman Peak, climbed by the indomitable Fanny Bullock-Workman. Far to the west are the Ultar peaks above Hunza.

Day 8: Hispar La to Baktur Baig Gut Delum
(6 to 8 hours) Start down before the morning sun hits the snow (see the Hushe Valley map). It takes 45 minutes to one hour to cross the 2.5-km-long flat pass, and another hour to descend the middle of the lower angle snow ramp, skirting yawning crevasses with ice falls on either side. The Hispar Glacier side of the pass is more crevassed than the Biafo side. Once onto the lower Hispar Glacier (5040m), wend around the fissures and sink holes 30 minutes. It is possible to camp here on the glacier near the pools. Continue 1½ hours until even with the first large ice fall to the north. The crevasses decrease and a rope becomes optional. Reach some red rock moraine after 45 minutes, and 45 minutes further, the Khani Basa Glacier (4511m), the first of four major glaciers pushing into the Hispar Glacier from the north.

Climb 15 minutes over the moraine and cross two white ice sections of the Khani Basa Glacier in about 30 minutes, staying right. Kanjut Sar (7760m), at the head of the Khani Basa Glacier, is the 29th highest peak in the world. Enter the ablation valley along the north margin of the Hispar Glacier and ascend 30m of talus to the grassy hillside above. Pass two small possible camp sites. Thirty minutes further along, at the end of the ridge descending from point 5198 on the Swiss map, reach a large and splendid camp called Baktur Baig Gut Delum (4470m), which is Burushashki for 'Baktur Baig pitched his tent here'. Here are a side stream, wildflowers, shelters for porters, and splendid views of the Bal Chhīsh peaks soaring above the Hispar Glacier and The Ogre peering over the Hispar La.

Day 9: Baktur Baig Gut Delum to Shiqam Baris
(7 hours) Cross a stream from the small tributary glacier just beyond camp and descend steeply to the ablation valley along the northern margin of the Hispar Glacier. Move onto boulder-covered medial moraine 30 minutes from camp. On either side of this level moraine band are heavily broken sections. Although a trail hugs the grassy

hillside above the glacier from Baktur Baig Gut Delum five km to the Jutmo Glacier, this trail is sporadically obliterated by mud slides and avalanches and may not be open.

A camp site called Hagure Shangali Cham is on the hillside. If it is not open, move out onto the Hispar Glacier working towards its centre to avoid the broken eastern margin of the Jutmo Glacier where it impacts the Hispar Glacier. After two hours on the Hispar Glacier, cross onto the very convoluted Jutmo floe (4320m). Work around high ice walls and after two tedious hours, reach the cliff at the north-west corner of the Jutmo-Hispar junction.

A thin, steep trail ascends loose, powdery cliffs 15 minutes to the grassy hillside above (4680m). Traverse the hillside, passing several small camp sites along the trail. Each of these camp sites has excellent views and clean water. The largest camp, Shiqam Baris (4170m), is about 1½ hours down the trail at the end of the grassy hill. A large stream descends from a side glacier onto an alluvial plain. Shiqam Baris means 'a green canyon' in Burushashki.

Day 10: Shiqam Baris to Dachigan (7 hours) Continue about one hour on a good trail to another possible camp, Ulum Burum Bun (white rock ahead). Shiqam Baris is a preferable camp as Ulum Burum Bun is colder, with no morning sun, and water is further away. Cross the large stream just beyond Ulum Burum Bun in the morning when the water is low. Beyond the stream, the trail along the hillside towards the Pumari Chhīsh Glacier is occasionally obliterated by rock fall and avalanches. Locals will know if it is possible.

The alternative is to descend the loose moraine cliff to the northern margin of the Hispar Glacier and to follow it to the junction with the Pumari Chhīsh Glacier (4080m). This exhausting, awkward route takes three hours. The hillside trail above, if open, is preferable. Cross the Pumari Chhīsh Glacier in 1½ to two hours. This glacier is much less broken than the Jutmo Glacier, and not as wide. Head for the distinctive red lateral moraine of the Pumari Chhīsh Glacier, which bends west beneath cliffs as it merges with the larger Hispar Glacier. Where the red moraine ends and meets the white moraine of the Hispar Glacier (4020m), climb up the powdery cliff above the north margin of the glacier on a thin, loose 2nd-class trail 15 minutes to the hillside above (4080m). After 30 minutes on a trail, reach a camp site with unreliable water (ie, dry from midsummer on).

The trail climbs above and around this dry camp site and joins the trail from the western side of the Pumari Chhīsh Glacier. Continue 45 minutes to Dachigan (3960m), one of our favourite camp sites. Dachigan (*dachi* means 'wall'; *gan*, 'trail') refers to a wall blocking the trail to prevent animals from straying. A large clear stream waters this beautiful grassy area with grand views of the wall of 6000m peaks south of the Hispar Glacier.

Day 11: Dachigan to Hispar Village (6½ hours) Follow a gentle four km trail 45 minutes to Bitanmal, an expanse of tall, lush grasses used as a pasture by Hispar villagers in late summer. Near the huts and pens is a large rock and shrine. Lofty Makrong Chhīsh (6607m) rises across the Hispar Glacier. Bitanmal means the 'place of the shaman'. Bring water from Bitanmal (3660m) as it is scarce for the next few hours. From Bitanmal, walk 15 minutes across the meadow and descend steep talus to the edge of the Kunyang Glacier. A faint trail crosses the stable, rock-covered Kunyang Glacier in about one hour. The 15 minute climb to the grassy hill (3900m) on the far side (called Daltanas on the Swiss map) is the hardest exit from a glacier yet. It requires careful balance and frequent use of small handholds.

With no more glaciers to cross, enjoy the stroll through junipers and ephedra down the ablation valley. After an hour, reach Pal-olimikish (3630m), a field of tall noxious plants named *palolin*. Continue 30 minutes to a large stream, which must be forded amid tamarisk shrub. Another such stream is 30 minutes beyond. A cluster of stone huts called Ghurbūn are 30 minutes further. The final stream before Hispar village is often difficult to cross in the afternoon. If the water is too high, descend steeply to the true right bank of the Hispar River and ford the side stream where it braids out through more level ground. Pass a large spring and cross the bridge over the Hispar River. Climb steeply about 100m in 15 minutes to Hispar village (3383m), about two hours from Ghurbūn. You will be asked to pay a Rs 15 per person 'bridge toll'. Trekking parties stay in the compound of the dilapidated rest house for Rs 30 per tent. For about Rs 50 your porters can cook and sleep in the single small, intact building. Water here is silty.

Day 12: Hispar Village to Huru (4½ to 5 hours) Follow the jeep road about one hour to a bridge to the true right bank of the Hispar River. A well-known slide here, called Tar-kichindas, causes road blocks. Watch for falling rock. Pass a side stream, with the first water since Hispar, and reach Apiharai (grandmother's pasture), a small grassy camp site with trees in a walled compound. Continue along the true right bank, passing two more slide areas, and reach the second bridge about 2½ hours from Apiharai. Cross the jeep bridge to the true left bank, which marks the end of Hispar village's territory. Climb 150m in 45 minutes to reach pleasant Huru (2972m) (*huru* means 'narrow water channel'), with its grass, apricot orchard, spring, and clear willow-shaded pool. From Huru, a trail leads to Rush Lake via Gutens and to Barpugram (see Nagyr in the Hunza River Valley chapter).

ASKOLE TO CONCORDIA

(15 days; June to September)
The trek to Concordia is indeed a trek into the throne room of the mountain gods, as Galen Rowell proclaimed. The 70 km walk takes seven or eight days. Completion of the jeep road in the Braldu Valley to Askole and improved trail conditions beyond, both results of the Pakistan army's year-round deployment along the Baltoro, have shortened this trek by about a week from the old itinerary. Starting in June when water levels

are low is preferable. The road through the Braldu Valley is less likely to be blocked and river crossings along the trail are easier. By mid-July, water levels rise dramatically and delays and difficulties increase. Most expeditions travel up the Baltoro in June, making that the most crowded month on the trail.

The Baltoro Glacier is a fragile ecosystem whose carrying capacity is overextended. When you look up, you see beautiful mountain scenery in every direction, but when you look down it is another matter. Litter is indiscriminately thrown along the trails and around camp sites. Human faeces are an eyesore and health hazard at every camp site. Do not litter and carry out all non-burnable rubbish. Use the existing cement pit toilets at Thungol, Korophon, Paiju, Liligo, Khoburtse, and Urdukas and encourage your guide, cook, and porters to do the same. (See Ecotourism in the Facts for the Trekker chapter for ways you can minimise your impact on the environment.)

The impact of trekkers, climbers, and porters is most concentrated at camp sites. On the glacier, however, the continuing military presence remains a major environmental problem. Rubbish pits announce each army post as you approach, and the occasional donkey skeleton shows the well-worn trail used to ferry supplies to the soldiers. A telegraph wire links all the army camps. Overhead, daily good-weather helicopter flights serve to remind visitors of the long simmering confrontation between India and Pakistan over the adjacent Siachen Glacier.

Despite the ecological problems today, this remains an incomparable trek through probably the finest mountain scenery on the planet.

Guides & Porters

Every licensed trekking company has experienced guides and cooks who know the route well. Porters are essential on this trek and it is difficult to deviate from the expeditionary-style trekking that has developed. The ratio of porters to trekkers typically ranges from 3:1 (for smaller scale lower-budget treks) to 6:1 (for trekking parties

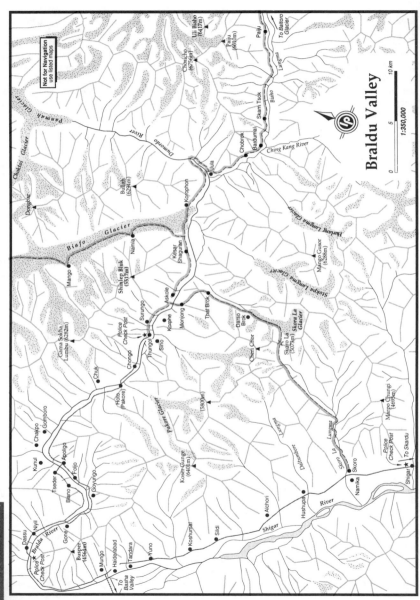

Braldu Valley

1:350,000

0   5   10 km

outfitted by a trekking company). We have seen frustrated budget-conscious trekkers with light-weight gear and freeze-dried food who planned to backpack wondering why they need so many porters. They usually are unsuccessful in negotiating (with their guide or porters) to significantly reduce the number of porter loads. Because a guide is required, you usually have to hire a cook since guides do not cook. Then you need a porter to carry the kitchen, a porter for the kerosene, porters for the guide's and cook's food, and porters to carry the food for those porters. It all adds up. Try to find a cook who also carries a full load.

Some confusing exceptions to standard porters' wages apply to this trek. Porters bring their own food for the first four stages to Paiju. For these four stages, pay a maximum Rs 200 per stage, which includes the per stage wage, wāpāsi, and food rations. For the remaining stages from Paiju to Concordia and back, provide all food and fuel for porters and pay a maximum of Rs 150 per stage. It is customary to sacrifice a goat in Paiju. Animals are purchased in Askole and cost up to Rs 2500. Smaller parties opting not to buy a goat pay each porter a one-time additional Rs 50 meat ration. Porters expect to receive either clothing and equipment as per Tourism Division guidelines or to be paid Rs 200. It is cheaper to buy all of the required items in Skardu at a cost of about Rs 140. Although it takes extra effort, you then know your porters have adequate gear. Whether they bring their own gear or you provide it for them, keep in mind that they will be walking and sleeping on snow and ice for many days.

Pay porters for one rest day, at half-wage, after every seven stages. For example, you pay three rest days if you start in Askole, go to Concordia and return to Askole (which is 18 stages) or cross the Gondogoro La to Hushe (also 18 stages). If you take more than three rest days on either route, you pay a full stage wage for the fourth and subsequent rest days.

18 stages: Askole to Korophon, Korophon to Jula,

Jula to Bardumal, Bardumal to Paiju, Paiju to Liligo, Liligo to Urdukas, Urdukas to Goro I, Goro I to Goro II, Goro II to Concordia, and return via the same route

Round trip from Concordia to K2 base camp four stages: Concordia to Broad Peak base camp, Broad Peak base camp to K2 base camp, and return via the same route. From Concordia to Gasherbrum I base camp and back is also four stages: two stages to Gasherbrum I base camp, and two stages to return via the same route.

Map Notes
The Swiss map is reliable, but Thungol, Jula, Skam Tsok, and Khoburtse are not marked. On the U502 *Mundik (NI 43-3)* sheet Thungol, Jula, Skam Tsok, Liligo, Khoburtse, and Goro II camp sites are omitted. Leomann's *Sheet 3* omits and misplaces several camp sites and draws an inaccurate route up the glacier.

Route Description
Day 1: Askole to Korophon (4 to 5 hours)
When you arrive in Thungol (2850m) spend one night before starting the trek (see the Braldu Valley map). Undoubtedly, your guide and porters will need to get organised, sort out loads, and bake bread. The next day, either walk one hour along the jeep road to Askole or stroll two hours through Thungol and Surungo villages to Askole.

Walk through Askole village (3000m) and follow the irrigation canal 30 minutes to its source at a clear stream. Continue past the confluence of the Biafo and Biaho rivers, following the true right bank of the Biafo River 1½ hours to Kesar Shaguran (3090m), which means 'Kesar's pologround'. A small clear stream is five minutes before this broad, level area. Beyond it, the trail divides. The trail to the Biafo Glacier heads north and up between a cliff to the left and a rock buttress to the right. The trail to the Baltoro Glacier continues east below the rock buttress.

About 30 minutes past the trail junction reach large rocks and climb 15 minutes onto the terminal moraine of the Biafo Glacier. Cross the glacier in 45 minutes on an easy, obvious trail passing above its mouth.

BALTISTAN

Korophon (3000m) is a huge plain on the north-east margin of the Biafo Glacier with dusty camp sites amid a few willows. The area was more heavily wooded, but is suffering from the many porters chopping wood to cook. Water flows from the glacier and becomes silty in the afternoon. About 20 minutes beyond the camp site is a spring and an enormous boulder *(koro* means 'bowl'; *phon*, 'boulder'), which gives Korophon its name.

Day 2: Korophon to Skam Tsok (4½ to 5½ hours) Pass the boulder on a good trail and about one hour from camp come to a spring at the river's edge. Walk along the sandy river bed and then climb about 15 minutes to a cairn. Here the trail turns east north-east towards the Dumordo River coming from the Panmah Glacier. The Dumordo River can be a formidable obstacle. When the water is low (ie, before 1 July) a cable crossing is set 15 minutes up the true right bank of the Dumordo. A wooden box hangs from the cable and local men charge Rs 15 per trip to pull people and gear across. Traffic jams occur when large expeditions take several hours to cross. When the water is high, the cable crossing is moved so much further up river that it adds a half-day detour. To reach the high-water cable, follow an exposed trail across the cliff above the river for about two hours. Cross the river on the cable, and walk down its true left bank to Jula in about 1¼ hours. Jula is Urdu for 'swing' (ie, the cable over the river). This broad plain at the confluence of the Dumordo and Biaho rivers is exposed, with little shelter for porters and silty water from the distant river. Korophon is a better camp site.

Follow the trail along the true right bank of the Biaho Lungma through fragrant tamarisk and ephedra about two hours to a side stream with clear water. This is a good lunch spot called Chobrok. Continue 15 minutes to the confluence of the Ching Kang and Biaho rivers, where the Biaho bends east. Beyond the bend is Bardumal, a now unused camp site with a porter's grave. The preferred camp site, 30 to 45 minutes further amid

tamarisks at the first clear side stream, is called Skam Tsok (3300m) (*skam* means 'dry'; *tsok*, 'a thorny bush'). Between Jula and Skam Tsok are several sections with low-water and high-water trails. The low-water trail is quicker and easier with less climbing.

Days 3 & 4: Skam Tsok to Paiju (3 to 3½ hours) The trail alternates between the river bed and the terraces above, crossing boulder fields and side streams until coming to the stream from the Paiju Glacier (see the Baltoro Glacier – Paiju to Concordia & K2 map). It is easy to ford when the water is low, when the water is high, you may need a rope for safety here. The first glimpses of Paiju peak and Cathedral Towers are from here. Continue around a rocky cliff and drop to the low-water trail along the river; the high-water trail stays high. From the river side, ascend to the terrace and pass through groves of trees to Paiju (3450m), about one to 1½ hours from the Paiju Glacier stream crossing. A small tree-lined stream passes through Paiju, and tent platforms are carved out all over the hillside. Paiju is often crowded and noisy, and always dirty. The tent platforms higher along the stream are quieter with good views. The entire dry area across the stream has become an open toilet.

Some parties reach Paiju in two days, camping at Jula en route. However, the camp sites are better when you take three days. Regardless, almost all parties take a full day in Paiju for acclimatisation. Tradition also dictates a party and a goat feast for porters. Paiju is the last source of wood. Despite kerosene and stoves, and signs urging porters not to cut wood, they do so in order to bake bread for the coming days.

Day 5: Paiju to Liligo or Khoburtse (4½ to 5½ hours) Walk one hour to the mouth of the Baltoro Glacier where an obvious trail leads up the terminal moraine. The trail crosses the glacier angling gently about 3.5 km to the south-east margin in about 2½ hours. Continue up the ablation valley 15 minutes to Liligo. The original camp site with a clear stream below a grassy hillside was wiped out by rock fall and is no longer used. Just around the bend is the new Liligo camp with stone rounds cramped into a boulder field. Water comes from the glacial lake below the camp. The incredibly sheer granite towers of the Baltoro northern wall dominate the view, separated by steep, broken ice floes. Ibex still wander the grassy slopes above.

For the next 1½ hours the trail alternates several times between the lateral moraine and the glacier, finally heading out on the glacier to avoid the outflow from the advancing Liligo Glacier. Khoburtse (3930m), an alternative camp site to Liligo, lies just past the Liligo Glacier. This camp has clear water and a few level tent sites. *Khoburtse* is a bitter, but fragrant green sage eaten by animals. A white sage found in the area is brewed in tea to cure upset stomachs. The tent sites nearest the toilets are subject to rock fall, so pitch tents on the opposite side of the ridge away from the hillside. From these flower-covered hillsides are extraordinary views of Paiju peak (6610m), Uli Biaho (6417m), Great Trango Tower (6286m), Lobsang Spire (5707m) and Cathedral Towers. The scenery is so magnificent, it is worth walking shorter days to enjoy the views from this and the next camp site.

Day 6: Liligo or Khoburtse to Urdukas (2 to 3 hours) Between Khoburtse and Urdukas, two glaciers from the south-east join the Baltoro. The trail along the lateral moraine moves onto the glacier to skirt these side glaciers. Continue 30 minutes more on moraine rubble to an army camp with a large glacial lake below. On the grassy boulder-strewn hillside 50m above is Urdukas (3450m), named for the obvious split boulder (*urdwa* means 'boulder'; *kas*, 'a crack') above camp. Two small streams provide water at Urdukas; the lower (western) one is more frequently used (and polluted), the higher (eastern) one a few minutes beyond camp is better. The trail between Paiju and Urdukas is now so improved that what was always a two day walk now can be done by acclimatised trek-

kers in one day. Urdukas, though heavily used, is much larger than Paiju. The meadows above Urdukas offer one of the finest panoramas in the Karakoram. All the Trango Towers are visible, including Nameless Tower, which has the longest granite face in the world.

Day 7: Urdukas to Goro II (6 to 7 hours) Head north from Urdukas passing several porters' graves. The trail descends and goes straight out to the middle of the glacier. The trail from here to Concordia, though still obvious, is less of a highway, and remains on the glacier. Masherbrum's sheer granite north face and snow-crowned summit (7821m) comes into view as you walk east up the Baltoro. After 3½ to four hours, stop for lunch near the little-used camp site of Shakspoon (*shak* means 'little stones'; *spoon* 'a big pile'). Towering white seracs rise to the right of the trail, which is marked by occasional cairns. This section is more rugged with occasional jumps over small streams. Goro II (4380m), 2½ to three hours further, is just beyond an army camp in the middle of the glacier. Tent platforms and porter circles are fashioned on the ice and rock. Here in mid-glacier, wind blows from the Biange Glacier and Muztagh Tower (7273m). Water comes from the glacier just north of camp. Gasherbrum IV's unique squared-off summit (7925m) beckons towards Concordia and Masherbrum's dramatic summit cap soars behind.

Days 8 to 10: Goro II to Concordia (5 to 6 hours) From Goro II, follow the black medial moraine up the centre of the glacier. The trail marches steadily towards Concordia, working right and close to the Biarchedi Glacier, bounded by a sheer wall of fluted snow. As you approach Concordia, the immense bulk of Broad Peak (8047m) emerges. Concordia (4650m) where the Godwin-Austen Glacier meets the Baltoro, has an army camp. Beyond the army camp 10 minutes is a large level area with many porter shelters and superb views of the colossal pyramid of K2 (8611m). Mitre Peak

(6025m) to the south stands watch over this place of sublime and awesome beauty. Concordia, exposed as it is, receives strong winds and is the coldest camp on the Baltoro. Trekkers usually spend three nights to savour its majesty. The route over the Gondogoro La to Hushe leaves the Baltoro Glacier here (see Concordia to Hushe via Gondogoro La below).

Days 11 to 15: Concordia to Thungol Most trekkers retrace their route down the Baltoro in five days, camping at Goro II, Urdukas, Paiju, Korophon, and Thungol.

Side Trip: Concordia to K2 Base Camp
The route to K2 base camp and back to Concordia can be covered in one long, tiring day. Most trekkers take a more leisurely pace and move camp from Concordia to K2 base camp for one or more nights. As you walk towards K2, and it grows even larger, its incredible size becomes apparent. Leave the Concordia trail 10 minutes beyond (east) of the army camp. Head north, cross a snow bridge, and follow a faint trail through jumbled moraine onto the large light brown medial moraine of the Godwin-Austen Glacier. This moraine runs straight towards K2 with occasional cairns marking the route. It takes 2½ to 3 hours to reach the Broad Peak base camp (5000m), which extends about 30 minutes up the moraine. It is easy to tell when you are there by the old rubbish heaps. About 15 minutes after the highest base camp site, leave the moraine, as it is easier to walk on the white ice to the west (left). Follow this for one hour, then pass through broken glacier and moraine 15 minutes to K2 base camp (5135m). Here, directly below K2's immense bulk, the mountain appears strongly foreshortened, yet completely fills your view. Camps are located on either side of the broken glacier, though most are on the eastern side. The Gilkey memorial lies 100m up the rock slope at the very base of K2. Names of climbers who died on the mountain have been inscribed on steel dinner plates with some

more ornate plaques. A few bodies are also interred here.

Side Trip: Concordia to Gasherbrum I Base Camp
The base camp for Gasherbrum I, also called Hidden Peak, is along the Abruzzi Glacier. From Concordia follow the upper Baltoro Glacier to the south-east, skirting the base of the other Gasherbrum peaks. Head north-east up the Abruzzi Glacier to the base camp. This is too far for a day hike, so plan on spending at least one night here.

CONCORDIA TO HUSHE VIA GONDOGORO LA
(5 days; late June to August)
In 1986 a trekking route was established that connects the Baltoro Glacier to the Hushe Valley over a pass called the Gondogoro La (5940m). Since then, this challenging pass has attracted trekkers and climbers alike. This route enables you to avoid retracing your steps down the Baltoro Glacier and the pass has one of the most overwhelming mountain panoramas anywhere in the world, with four of the five 8000m peaks of Pakistan close at hand.

The Gondogoro La, though popular with trekkers, involves 4th-class climbing. The north side is a 50° snow slope where three pitches must be fixed. The south side is a continuous 50° slope where up to 300m of rope must be fixed. This high, technical pass requires good judgment, commitment, fitness, prior acclimatisation, and basic mountaineering skills of all members of a trekking party. In addition to proper equipment, wearing helmets is prudent.

Parties cross the pass in both directions. The south side of the Gondogoro La is extremely long, with avalanche and rock-fall danger once the sun softens the snow. Therefore, parties must be on top of the Gondogoro La at sunrise to avoid these dangers. Larger parties may prefer to approach from Hushe in order to reach the Gondogoro La before the sun makes the south side dangerous. Such parties must then slog across the crevassed West Vigne Glacier in soft, treacherous snow. We recommend crossing from north to south, or from Concordia to Hushe for four reasons. Firstly, the longer approach up the Baltoro Glacier permits better acclimatisation. Secondly, the objective dangers of the not-straightforward route up the north side are more easily seen. Thirdly, if conditions do not permit crossing the pass, you do not miss out on the Baltoro Glacier and Concordia. Occasionally, especially late in the season, the crevasses on the north side of the Gondogoro La are unbridgeable, and parties must turn back. Fourth, the road from Hushe to Skardu is usually free of road blocks, unlike the road from Askole to Skardu.

Misleading and inaccurate information about three passes between the Baltoro Glacier and the upper valleys of Hushe has been published. These passes are the Gondogoro La, the Masherbrum La, and the Vigne Pass (also called Mazeno La). Of these, only the Gondogoro La can be crossed by trekking parties. The other two present very serious technical difficulties. The Masherbrum La (5364m), between the Yermanendu Glacier, a southern arm of the Baltoro, and a northern arm of the Gondogoro Glacier, has an enormous ice fall on the southern side. The Vigne Pass connects the northernmost section of the Gondogoro Glacier with the head of the West Vigne Glacier, to the north-west of the Gondogoro La. The Vigne Pass, although lower than the Gondogoro La, has more rock-fall danger and some technical sections. Porters are unable to cross this pass. Some maps show the Gondogoro La crossing the ridge between the Biarchedi and Gondogoro glaciers. However, one look at the steep, corniced wall above the Biarchedi Glacier with its multiple avalanche flutes shows that any crossing of this ridge is dangerous and highly technical. The Gondogoro La links the large eastern branch of the Gondogoro Glacier to the West Vigne Glacier.

The pass is easier to cross earlier in the season and can be attempted as early as the last few days in June. By August, objective dangers from crevasses, avalanches, and rock fall increase substantially as the snow cover melts. Rock fall on the southern side of the pass is particularly dangerous late in the season.

Guides & Porters

It is essential to hire an experienced guide who knows the pass. It is very helpful to have strong porters who have also been over the pass. Guides and porters from the Hushe Valley may have more experience crossing the Gondogoro La than those from other regions of Baltistan. Having a strong, experienced team helps ensure success and enables all to enjoy it. Coming from Concordia, pay a total of Rs 150 per stage and continue providing food for porters.

A responsible trekking party should equip each porter with a swami or sling, one carabiner, instep crampons, and gaiters (eg, you can provide them with plastic and string to fashion something useful) for one day. Porters cannot ascend or descend this pass without a fixed rope. The minimum length rope you need to bring for porters' use is 100m, although 300m is better, especially for larger parties.

9 stages: Concordia to corner of Mitre Peak, corner of Mitre Peak to Ali camp, Ali camp to Gondogoro La, Gondogoro La to Gondogoro high camp, Gondogoro high camp to Xhuspang, Xhuspang to Daltsampa, Daltsampa to Gondogoro camp, Gondogoro camp to Shaishcho, and Shaishcho to Hushe

Tough bargainers may be able to negotiate eight stages, eliminating the stage at the corner of Mitre Peak. Reportedly some porters have asked for and been paid double stages/wages going over the pass. Do not follow this precedent, which has no legitimate basis.

Map Notes

The Gondogoro La is misplaced on most maps and is at 35° 39' 18.0" N and 76° 28' 22.0" E. The Swiss map misrepresents the relationship of the Gondogoro Glacier to the West Vigne Glacier, as well as the shape of these glaciers. On Leomann's *Sheet 3: (K2, Baltoro, Gasherbrum, Masherbrum, Saltoro Groups)* no routes or camp sites are shown. However, this map represents the West Vigne

Not for Navigation
use listed maps

Gasherbrum III (7952m)
Gasherbrum II (8035m)
Gasherbrum IV (7925m)
(7133m)
(7300m)
(7774m)
(7004m)
Abruzzi Glacier
Broad Peak (8047m)
(8006m)
K2 Base Camp (5135m)
Snow Dome (7160m)
Chogolisa (7665m)
Vigne (6874m)
K2 (8611m)
Angel (6858m)
Savoia Glacier
Khal-Khal Glacier
Goodwin-Austen Glacier
Baltoro Glacier
Vigne Glacier
Broad Peak Glacier
Marble (6256m)
Cristal (6252m)
Concordia
Mitre (6025m)
Gl
Nuasting
Ali Camp
W Vigne Glacier
Gondogoro La (5940m)
Gondogoro Glacier
Xhuspang
Biange Glacier
Goo II (4380m)
Burchedi Glacier
Dahsampa (4380m)
To Hushe
Muztagh Tower (7273m)
Lhungka Gl
Blanchedi (6751m)
Masherbrum La (5364m)
Vermanandu Glacier
Baltoro Glacier
Lobsang (6225m)
Lobsang Spire (5707m)
Muztagh Glacier
Bialé Glacier
Urdukas
Yermanendu Glacier
Mandu Glacier
IV (5900m)
IIn (6130m)
III (6280m)
II (6320m)
Masherbrum (7821m)
Biale (6729m)
Cathedral (5828m)
Dunge Glacier
Khobutse
Liligo
Liligo Glacier
Liligo (5601m)
H Trango (6239m)
Great Trango (6286m)
F Trango (6763m)
Trango Glacier
Uli Biaho (6417m)
Uli Biaho (6417m)
Uli Biaho Gl
Paiju
Lungma
Uli Biaho Gl
Paiju Glacier
Paiju (6610m)
Biaho
Choricho (6756m)
Skam Tsok
To Askole

Baltoro Glacier– Paiju to Concordia & K2

1:350,000
0   5   10 km

Continued on Braldu Valley Map

Glacier and its relationship to the Gondogoro Glacier more accurately than other maps of the same scale.

Route Description

Day 1: Concordia to Ali Camp (3½ to 5 hours) The route to Ali camp is up the snow-covered Vigne Glacier, so start before the sun softens the snow. From Concordia, head south towards Mitre Peak, crossing the broken south margin of the Baltoro Glacier. Follow lateral moraine around the base of Mitre Peak, parallelling the ridge south from its summit. After four km or about two hours, reach the Vigne Glacier and rope up. Head south south-west up the snow-covered Vigne Glacier 5.5 km to Ali camp. Firmer snow towards the centre of the glacier offers easier walking and avoids crevasses along the west margin. You pass three valleys on the west side of the Vigne Glacier. The first, 15 minutes up the glacier, has a camp site called Miksus *(mik* means 'eye'; *sus,* 'pain'), marked by a cairn along the glacier's margin. 'Snowblindness' camp is infrequently used. Be sure everyone in your party wears sunglasses.

In the second small side valley is an alternative Ali camp. The actual Ali camp is just beyond the third and largest side valley, three hours up the Vigne Glacier at the junction of the Vigne and West Vigne glaciers (ie, the base of point 5943 on the Italian and Japanese Baltoro Glacier maps). Crevasses guard Ali camp, so carefully approach it straight from the centre of the Vigne Glacier. Several tent platforms are wedged against the cliff and on a moraine ridge. Painted in red on the cliff is the name of Ali Muhammad Jungugpa, who crossed the Gondogoro La on 20 June, 1986. The camp is apparently named for him. Ali camp is usually warmer than Concordia. Amazingly, birds and bumblebees make their way to this spectacular snowy place.

Day 2: Ali Camp to Xhuspang (7 to 10 hours) From Ali camp, rope up and move over firm snow along the base of the buttress to your right. Turn into the snow-covered

West Vigne Glacier heading west southwest. On firm snow it takes about one hour to cover the 3.5 km to the base of the pass. The angle is gentle, heading diagonally towards a black rock band descending from the ridge above the south side of the glacier. The pass is south-east (left) of this band, and is not visible until just beneath it.

At the head of the West Vigne Glacier is an obvious low point, which is the more difficult Vigne Pass to the upper Gondogoro Glacier. The steep slope east (left) of the Gondogoro La is prone to avalanche. From the base of the Gondogoro La, the 600m snow ascent takes at least two hours. Three steep 50° sections require fixed ropes. The first pitch goes about 60m to a bench. If no steps exist, kick steps. If steps exist, they may be icy. K2's summit begins to emerge above the ridge to the north as you climb. From the bench, the second pitch is about 25m to a second small bench, with large crevasses on either side. From here, head right up lower angle snow to the base of a large icy cornice. The third pitch turns left and ascends 30m passing left of the large cornice. Above, continue up easy low angle snow a short way to the level Gondogoro La (5940m). From Ali camp, it takes four to six hours to reach the pass. Most trekkers need to start walking by 2 am; larger parties take more time and should start by 1 am.

The view from the pass is the most spectacular mountain panorama in Pakistan, and one of the most impressive in Asia. K2 (8611m), Broad Peak (8047m), and the four Gasherbrums, I (8068m), II (8035m), III (7952m), and IV (7925m), are visible. Trinity Peak (6700m) lies along the ridge south (left) of the pass. Laila peak's lovely snow and granite cone rises over the Gondogoro Glacier as you turn to descend.

On the descent, most parties tie a long sling around a 1.5 m diameter boulder on the south side of the pass, a somewhat dubious anchor for the rope, but the only one available. From this point, angle right and down a ramp about 10m to a point in front of an outcrop of exfoliating granite. Here, an ice axe must be used to redirect the rope 90° left,

BALTISTAN

so that it runs down the 50° slope. Early in the season this slope is snow covered, but as the snow cover melts, the exposed loose rock presents serious rock-fall danger. It is from here that Gondogoro gets its name (*gondo* means 'broken pieces of'; *goro*, 'rock'). After the first 250m, begin traversing right and down for an additional 100m to 150m, at which point the angle begins to ease. Continued use of a rope is recommended but may slow the descent. Reach the glacier, 900m below the pass, in about 1½ hours.

Follow along its north (right) margin 45 minutes to a few stone shelters on moraine near a small glacial pool. When approaching the pass from Xhuspang, this is Gondogoro high camp (4800m), also known as Doug Scott camp, after the well-known British mountaineer. Continue another hour along the north (right) side of the moraine in a pretty ablation valley to the junction of two branches of the upper Gondogoro Valley. This pleasant camp site on the hillside called Xhuspang (4680m) has several tent platforms and stone circles for porters. It is named for the colour of flowers that blanket this meadow in summer (*xhu* means 'turquoise'; *spang*, 'a grassy place').

Just below camp, the ablation valley is often covered by water in summer. Behind the camp a flowered hillside rises to a massive steep-walled granite prow. Water comes from nearby streams, and a latrine has been built a short way up the main Gondogoro Valley. No livestock grazes in this valley. Xhuspang is the base for climbing Gondogoro peak (see Gondogoro Valley in the Shyok & Hushe Valleys section in this chapter).

Day 3: Xhuspang to Daltsampa (2½ to 3 hours) Skirt the pond below Xhuspang in 15 minutes and climb onto the moraine where the two branches of the glacier meet. From here no trail or cairns exist as the route changes regularly. Follow the medial moraine of the east (left) branch 30 minutes. The main Gondogoro Glacier is to the west (right) and its lateral moraine is grey-brown and higher. Continue working left over level

ice for 30 minutes to a rust-coloured moraine ridge. Cross this and the brown moraine to its left in 45 minutes to a broken and crevassed ice band. Follow this down until opposite Laila peak's convex north-east granite face. Cross a moraine ridge left to another ice band and head down towards the hillside above the major southern bend of the glacier (4300m). The massive granite prow above Xhuspang remains a visible landmark as you descend the glacier. Across the Gondogoro Glacier, to the north-west, is the awesome ice fall from the Masherbrum La. Exit left off the Gondogoro Glacier through its heavily broken left margin.

Once on the hillside, grazed by yaks, follow a trail around, turning south-west, and after 30 minutes reach Daltsampa (about 4300m). This beautiful camp site is sheltered in a flowered ablation valley with a clear stream and two small lakes with superb views of the ice falls from Masherbrum's ridge. Daltsampa makes an excellent rest camp after the pass.

Days 4 & 5: Daltsampa to Hushe See Gondogoro Valley in Shyok & Hushe Valleys of this chapter for the route description. Camp at Shaishcho en route.

OTHER ROUTES
Skoro La
The Skoro La (5073m) is a little-used pass linking Askole in the Braldu Valley to Namika and Shigar villages in the Shigar Valley (see the Braldu Valley map). This pass was more frequently used before the jeep road was completed up the Braldu Valley to Askole. It offers an alternative two to three day return trek from Askole to Shigar, especially when the jeep road is blocked.

From Askole, cross the Braldu River on a bridge and ascend steeply to Thal Brok, with fine views. Continue up the west bank of the Skoro La Lungma to Darso Brok, a summer pasture at the edge of the Skoro La Glacier, and camp. The next day continue up the glacier, over snow three to four hours, then turn west and climb to the Skoro La. Descend 450m steeply over snow and rock to the steep grassy slopes below. Camp here or descend another 900m to the head of the Skoro Lungma to camp. The next day, follow the stream, crossing it continuously, with several steep sections, to Namika village on the jeep road in the Shigar Valley, 6.5 km north of Shigar village. The Skoro La is in an open zone.

Panmah Glacier

The 42 km Panmah Glacier forms the Dumordo River, which flows into the Biaho Lungma between Korophon and Jula camps (see Askole to Concordia above). Askole villagers use summer pastures along the Panmah Glacier. The old approach to the Baltoro crossed the snout of the Panmah Glacier when the Dumordo was unfordable. This scenic area is in a restricted zone and can be visited by itself, or in conjunction with the Askole to Concordia trek.

Routes lead up both the west and east sides of the Panmah Glacier. The west side leads to the Choktoi Glacier and the base camp of the Latok peaks. Trekkers report this to be a reasonable trek. Beyond the Latok base camp is the difficult Sim La (5833m) to the Sim Gang.

Trekkers can go up the east side as far as Skinmang (ibex field). Beyond Skinmang, the Nobande Sobande Glacier presents a serious obstacle. Younghusband, in 1887, found it inaccessible with ice blocks the size of houses. The Shipton-Tilman expedition of 1937 found it almost impassable, 'broken by gaping crevasses and tumbled masses of ice'. However, in 1929, Ardito Desio found it remarkably smooth and was able to ski to its head. As the Nobande Sobande is evidently subject to considerable change, mountaineers must be prepared for difficult conditions.

Snow Lake

Lukpe Lawo (Snow Lake) is a relatively level, snow-covered glacial expanse at the head of the Biafo Glacier (see the Biafo & Hispar Glaciers map). From the peaks surrounding Lukpe Lawo descend a half-dozen

of the Karakoram's large glaciers: the Biafo, the Hispar, the Khurdopin, the Virjerab, the Braldu, and the Panmah. Also at the head of the Biafo, and just south of Lukpe Lawo, is the Sim Gang, or Sim Glacier. Together, the Sim Gang and Lukpe Lawo form the largest high glacial basin in the world. This icy playground is best explored on skis, which allow for relatively easy cruising and keep one out of hidden crevasses. Mountaineers can set a base on Lukpe Lawo for exploring and for straightforward ascents of peaks under 6000m.

Besides the Hispar La, Snow Lake's only trekkable pass, four other technical passes lead out of Lukpe Lawo and the Sim Gang. These high and steep passes are challenges for qualified mountaineers, experienced at glacier travel through remote regions. The Khurdopin Pass (5790m) leads north from Lukpe Lawo to the 37-km-long Khurdopin Glacier and Shimshal. Although Tilman reached the pass from Lukpe Lawo in 1937, it was first crossed in 1986 by Cameron Wake of Canada, Shambi Khan and Rajab Shah, both of Shimshal. The extremely steep 600m ascent from Lukpe Lawo and the steep descent to the heavily crevassed East Khurdopin Glacier makes this a truly formidable route.

The Lukpe La (about 5700m) leads northeast from the Sim Gang to the Braldu Glacier. First crossed by HW Tilman in 1937, this high rounded saddle (about 5500m) is guarded by wide crevasses. The ascent from the Sim Gang gains about 500m altitude in three km. The 36-km long Braldu Glacier, north of the pass, is very difficult to cross and is extremely remote. Rescue from here is impossible in case of accident or injury.

Leading east from the Sim Gang are the Skam La (5407m), which crosses to the Nobande Sobande Glacier, and the Sim La (5833m), which crosses the north shoulder of Baintha Brak. This pass leads to the Choktoi Glacier, and the north face of the Latok spires. The Nobande Sobande and Choktoi glaciers are the two upper arms of the Panmah Glacier.

BALTISTAN

Shyok & Hushe Valleys

The Shyok River, a major tributary of the Indus, drains an enormous area of the eastern Karakoram, much of which is Indian territory. In Pakistan, the Shyok is fed by the Thalle, Hushe, and Saltoro rivers. This easternmost part of Baltistan comprises the Ghanche District, with headquarters at Khapalu.

Currently, this area is extremely sensitive due to military confrontation with India over the Siachen Glacier, and the beautiful Saltoro and Kondus valleys are closed to foreigners.

The Shyok River joins the Indus River about 40 km east of Skardu near the village of Kiris, which was once the seat of a small kingdom. The two main trekking areas, the Thalle and Hushe valleys, lie north of the Shyok River, near to the town of Khapalu. At the head of the Hushe Valley is Masherbrum (7821m) and five large glaciers: the Aling; the Masherbrum; the Gondogoro; the Chogolisa; and the Tsarak Tsa.

The Thalle Valley offers one of the easiest treks in Baltistan over the Thalle La (4572m) (see the Thalle La & Tusserpo La map). The popular Hushe Valley offers a variety of short, easy treks; a number of not too technical mountaineering peaks; some interesting rock climbs; and an exciting route for competent trekkers to cross to the Baltoro Glacier.

Khapalu (2600m), the most prosperous of Baltistan's old kingdoms, is beautifully situated along the Ganse River above the wide confluence of the Shyok, Hushe, and Saltoro rivers. Khapalu has a civil hospital and Ghanche district's administrative offices. From Khapalu's main bazaar, a 45 minute walk leads past the pologround to the palace of the ex-Raja of Khapalu, with its impressive four-storey wooden balcony above the entrance.

A steep 20 minutes further is Chakchun village, with an old mosque, and fine views across the Shyok River of Masherbrum at the head of the Hushe Valley.

Residents of the Hushe and Saltoro valleys follow the Nur Bakhshiya sect of Shia Islam. In the Kondus Valley, the people are orthodox Shia. Hushe villagers are environmentally conscious and work to keep their area nice. Hushe is the highest village in the once extremely remote and impoverished valley. Hushe men began working as cooks and porters for expeditions only in the 1960s. Reinhold Messner's cook, Rozi Ali, is from Hushe. Now, the sons of these men have turned wholeheartedly to tourism and the Hushe-pa have developed an excellent reputation as guides, cooks, and high-altitude porters. Hushe is no longer the poorest of villages, and its popularity as a trekking and climbing destination continues to increase.

INFORMATION
Maps

The Swiss Foundation for Alpine Research 1:250,000 orographical sketch map *Karakoram Sheets 1 and 2* show all areas north of the Shyok River. The US AMS *India and Pakistan Series U502* 1:250,000 *Mundik (NI 43-3)* sheet shows the Hushe and Thalle valleys and the Thalle La, although it inaccurately represents the Gondogoro, Chogolisa, and Tsarak Tsa glaciers. The *Chulung (NI 43-4)* sheet shows the Saltoro and Kondus valleys, though again, the glaciers are inaccurately represented. *Sheet 2: (Skardu, Hispar, Biafo)* of Leomann's 1:200,000 *Karakoram Trekking and Mountaineering* map series shows the Thalle La and the area west of it. *Sheet 3: (K2, Baltoro, Gasherbrum, Masherbrum, Saltoro Groups)* shows the Thalle, Hushe, Saltoro and Kondus valleys.

Regulations

Neither a permit from the Tourism Division nor a licensed mountain guide is required to trek in this open zone. However, if you cross north to the Baltoro Glacier via any route, you must have a permit and a licensed mountain guide for that restricted zone. The entire

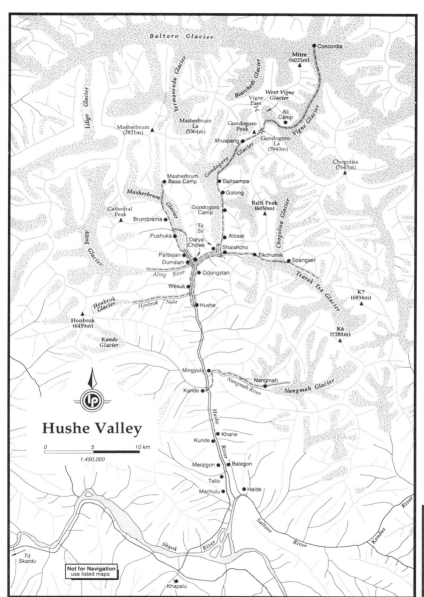

Baltoro Glacier

Concordia

Mitre
(6025m)

Yermanendu Glacier

Biarchedi Glacier

Liligo Glacier

West Vigne
Glacier

Vigne
Pass

Vigne Glacier

Ali
Camp

Masherbrum
(7821m)

Masherbrum
La
(5364m)

Gondogoro
Peak

Xhuspang

Gondogoro La
(5940m)

Gondogoro Glacier

Chogolisa
(7665m)

Masherbrum
Base Camp

Daltsampa

Golong

Balti Peak
(6050m)

Masherbrum Glacier

Cathedral
Peak

Brumbrama

Gondogoro
Camp

Chogolisa Glacier

Pushuka

Tir
Sir

Atosar

Darya
Chowk

Parbisan

Shaishcho

Tikchumik

Spangser

Dumsum

Aling River

Odungstan

Aling Glacier

Tsarak Tsa Glacier

Wesuk

K7
(6934m)

Honbrok
Glacier

Honbrok Nala

Hushe

Honbrok
(6459m)

K6
(7281m)

Kande
Glacier

Mingyulo

Nangmah

Nangmah River

Nangmah Glacier

Kande

Hushe Valley

0   5   10 km

1:450,000

Khane

Kunde

Hushe River

Marzigon

Balegon

Talis

Machulu

Halde

To
Skardu

Not for Navigation
use listed maps

Shyok River

Saltoro River

Kondus River

Khapalu

Saltoro Valley, including the Kondus Valley, is closed.

Accommodation & Supplies

Khapalu The *Ghanche Hotel* and *NAPWD Rest House* are along the river west of town. The Ghanche Hotel has a river view and a garden where you can pitch a tent, and rooms with attached hot-water bathrooms that cost Rs 20. The NAPWD Rest House here is nice. Most hotels are on the main road in town. The *Khaplu Inn* costs Rs 50 per bed. Doubles/triples at the *Siachan Hotel* cost Rs 50/60. At the *New Khaploo Inn Hotel & Restourant* (☎ 62) singles with no toilet cost Rs 50. Singles/doubles with attached hot-water bathrooms cost Rs 150/200. The *K7 Hotel & Restaurant* also has rooms.

Machulu The *NAPWD Rest House* is the only accommodation.

Kande The *K6 Hotel & Restaurant* is above the west side of the jeep road.

Hushe Village Charpoys at the *Mashabrum Inn* cost Rs 50. *Lela Peak Camping*, the small *K6 & K7 Camping Place*, *Ghandoghoro La Camping Place*, and *Ghandughoro Camping Place* serve hot food and let you pitch your tent for Rs 15. Large trekking parties usually camp in fields five minutes north of the village where it costs Rs 10 per tent. There are no toilets. Springs are nearby. The *K2 Shop*, *Aslam Bakery & General Store*, and *Mashebrum Shop* sell and rent mountaineering equipment and basic supplies.

Shaishcho The *Hushe Saitcho Inn/Shop* is the only thing like it in the Karakoram. Opened in 1992 and run by Hakim from Hushe, it stocks a good selection of food and supplies and also rents and sells equipment (sleeping bags, backpacks, tents, jackets, boots, sleeping pads, stoves, ski poles, crampons, ice axes, ropes, ice screws, and snow stakes). It also rents horses. Hakim's kitchen prepares meals from about Rs 30 and camping costs Rs 10 per tent. Use the stylish toilet and rubbish pit behind the tea house. Chopping and burning of wood is not allowed. Hakim keeps this place clean and has created a very relaxing environment.

GETTING THERE & AWAY

Shigar

Passenger jeeps go in the morning from the alley near Hussaini Chowk in Skardu and cost Rs 20. A special hire costs Rs 600 one way and Rs 700 return. The 32 km trip takes 1¼ hours.

Thalle Valley

A jeep road goes up the Thalle Valley to the large village of Khasumik, but trekkers can also get off along the Skardu-Khapalu road at Yugu village, cross the jeep bridge and walk. A new bridge being built to Doghani, the first village on the west side of the Thalle River, will shorten the walk. From Hushe or Khapalu, follow the lesser-used jeep road along the north bank of the Shyok River. From Saling, it is a one day walk to Doghani village at the mouth of the Thalle Valley. A special hire from Skardu to Khasumik costs Rs 1500 one way.

Hushe

The 148 km trip Skardu-Hushe takes about six to seven hours. Cargo jeeps cost Rs 100 and a special hire costs Rs 2500.

Skardu-Khapalu This 100 km trip takes about three to four hours by jeep and five to six hours by bus. A NATCO bus leaves Skardu at 6 am and one leaves Khapalu bazaar after 9 am. The fare costs Rs 45. Cargo jeeps leave from Skardu's Naya bazaar for about Rs 60. They return from Khapalu early the next morning. East of Khapalu the road is closed to foreigners beyond Surmo. A special hire costs Rs 1500 one way and Rs 2500 return.

Khapalu-Hushe The road to Hushe is increasingly reliable, but can be blocked by landslides above Machulu. From Khapalu, a bridge over the Shyok River has replaced crossing the river on a *zak*, the traditional frame raft floated on inflated goat skins. The road crosses the Shyok River just east of Khapalu to Saling and follows the Hushe River north.

Cargo jeeps are infrequent and cost Rs 50. A special hire Khapalu-Hushe costs up to Rs 1200 and takes about 2½ hours. Some trekkers walk the 48 km between Khapalu and Hushe village in two or three days. From Khapalu, it takes about four hours to walk to Machulu, four hours more to Kande, and another four hours to Hushe.

GUIDES & PORTERS
The maximum low-altitude porter's wage is Rs 120 per stage plus wāpāsi and food rations, which total Rs 200 per stage. Porters usually prefer to bring their own food. When you provide porters with food, the maximum wage totals Rs 150 per stage. Porters also expect Rs 200 clothing and equipment allowance regardless of the length of the trek.

THALLE LA & TUSSERPO LA
(3 to 4 days; mid-June to mid-September)
The large and green Thalle Valley leads north-west from the Shyok River, about 15 km west of Khapalu and 85 km east of Skardu (see the Thalle La & Tusserpo La map). The upper valley divides, and the northern branch leads over the infrequently-crossed, high Tusserpo La (5084m), while the southern branch leads over the easier, snow-covered Thalle La (4572m). Both passes lead to the Bauma Lungma, which runs south-west to Shigar, 32 km north of Skardu. The British preferred the Thalle La route between Skardu and Khapalu, as it offered grazing for their pack animals.

The Thalle La is one of the few non-glaciated passes and one of the easiest in Baltistan. Because it takes just three to four days, it lends itself to backpacking. It can be crossed in either direction, and the Shigar trail head is easily reached from Skardu. Because many trekkers use the Thalle La as a return trek from Hushe or Khapalu, we describe the route from east to west. Early in

the season expect much snow on the Thalle La, and even more on the Tusserpo La.

Guides & Porters
The trail over the Thalle La is not hard to find, so a local guide is not necessary. Because the higher and harder Tusserpo La is infrequently crossed, a local guide or porter is recommended. Ask in Khasumik. During the British era the 60 km from Shigar to Doghani over the Thalle La was three stages. Now, porters ask for as many as seven stages. Negotiate carefully; seven is probably too many, but three is not enough.

Map Notes
On the Swiss map, Doghani village is not shown and Khasumik is labelled as Khusumik. The U502 *Mundik (NI 43-3)* sheet depicts the valley west of the Thalle La as steeper than it actually is.

Route Description
Day 1: Khasumik to Thalle Camp (4 to 5 hours) Take a jeep or walk to Khasumik. A wide track continues beyond Khasumik to Bukma, where another route leads south-west over a high pass to the Kiris Lungma and Kiris village along the Shyok River. Continue up the Thalle Lungma from Bukma one hour to Olmo, the last settlement. At Dubla Khan, two hours above Olmo, the path to the Thalle La branches south-west, and the way to the Tusserpo La continues north-west. Dubla Khan, a shepherds' settlement, offers camp sites. One hour beyond Dubla Khan, along the trail to the Thalle La, is another shepherds' settlement. This good camp site along the clear stream leaves less distance to the pass the next day.

Day 2: Thalle Camp to Daserpa (6 to 7 hours) Continue on a good trail through pretty pastures along the stream. As you near the Thalle La, the grass ends and the trail becomes rocky. The pass, about two hours from camp, is marked by a large cairn and has a permanent snowfield on its west side. The east side is snowy early in the season. A steep and snow-covered rocky peak rises

Thalle La & Tusserpo La

0   5   10 km

1:625,000

dramatically south of the pass. Back to the east is a magnificent view of high snowy peaks on the ridge separating the Thalle and Hushe valleys. To the west are the distant peaks above the Shigar Valley. Descend the snow slope (a fine glissade) and continue through dzo pastures to the shepherds' huts of Daserpa, about four hours from the pass.

Day 3: Daserpa to Shigar (5 to 6 hours) Continue down stream about one hour through stands of cedar to the shepherds' huts at Baumaharel, where the stream from the Thalle La joins the main Bauma Lungma and the track from the Tusserpo La. The good trail down the Bauma Lungma leads in about four hours to Shigar and the jeep road to Skardu.

MASHERBRUM BASE CAMP
(5 to 6 days; June to September)
This easy trek leads straight towards the foot of mighty Masherbrum (7821m) with excel-

lent views. It is recommended as a short trek into the heart of the Karakoram or as acclimatisation before tackling the higher destinations in the Gondogoro Valley (see below). The only glacier walking is an easy 30 minutes before the base camp.

Guides & Porters
Beyond Brumbrama, a local guide is recommended for the short glacier crossing.

6 stages: Hushe to Parbisan, Parbisan to Brumbrama, Brumbrama to Masherbrum base camp, and return via the same route

Alternative return route from Masherbrum base camp via Shaishcho to Hushe 5 stages: Mashebrum base camp to Brumbrama, Brumbrama to Darya Chowk, Darya Chowk to Tir Sir, Tir Sir to Shaishcho, and Shaishcho to Hushe.

Map Notes
No place names are shown on the Swiss map except Dumsum, which is misplaced. The

trail beyond Dumsum is not shown. The glacier shown descending from Cathedral Peak, locally called the Drenmo Glacier, does not join the Masherbrum Glacier.

Route Description

Day 1: Hushe to Parbisan (2 to 2½ hours) Cross the Hushe River on either of two bridges (see the Hushe Valley map). The lower bridge, directly west of the village, leads to a trail along the true right (west) bank of the Hushe River. It crosses the Honbrok stream and ascends through fields past stone huts used to store fodder. A rockier trail stays above the east side of the river. In 45 minutes, this trail crosses the higher bridge and joins the trail along the west bank. The huts of Wesuk are 45 minutes further. Cross the Aling River on a bridge 30 minutes from Wesuk, with a shaded clear stream 10 minutes beyond near Dumsum summer village. Follow the stony river bed 45 minutes further to Parbisan (3475m), a pretty willow grove with a clear spring at the base of a talus slope. Across the river from Parbisan cliffs tower overhead. Just south of the cliffs is a small, steep side valley called Kyipotama (in Balti, *kyipo* means 'dog'; and *tama*, 'to send'). The name derives from an abandoned hunting practice. Since the steep walls offer no exit, in the winter hunters used dogs to drive ibex into the valley where they proved easy game.

Day 2: Parbisan to Brumbrama (2 to 2½ hours) Head along the true right bank of the river 30 minutes towards the base of the terminal moraine of the Masherbrum Glacier. Cross a side stream from the west and switchback steeply 60m up a faint trail, marked by an occasional cairn in 15 to 30 minutes. At the top, follow a trail parallel to the lateral moraine 30 minutes, passing a *baghath* (a rock wall built to keep animals from crossing to the other side), to Pushuka, which means 'little river'. Cross to its true left bank via a snow bridge through July, after which you hop rocks. This river is not so little, and parallels the lateral moraine up to the Drenmo Nala.

Climb gently, but steadily 45 minutes to a rise on the lateral moraine ridge covered with flowers and shrubs with excellent views of the upper Masherbrum Glacier and Masherbrum itself. Descend gently 15 minutes to the basin called Brumbrama (4050m), which gets its name from *brama*, an ubiquitous shrub. A stream runs through this flat grassy, and sometimes marshy, ablation valley. Hushe shepherds use these pastures from mid-July to mid-August. Otherwise, unattended male yaks roam the surrounding hillsides. The Drenmo ('bear') Glacier descends the side valley west of the grassy pastures of Brumbrama from Cathedral Peak. On the south margin of the glacier where the river issues from its mouth is a large mound with scattered juniper called Drenmo Saspoon said to have been made by a very large bear.

Day 3: Brumbrama to Masherbrum Base Camp (1½ to 2 hours) Follow a trail up the ablation valley. Contour the hillside and cross the outflow stream from an upper ablation valley 15 minutes from Brumbrama. Climb the Masherbrum Glacier's lateral moraine on a good trail for 10 minutes to the huts of Chogospang (big meadow). Continue up the ablation valley 15 minutes, contouring along the lateral moraine ridge to another meadow. Climb the moraine ridge of a side glacier and descend to the glacier. Cross the glacier covered with white rock in 30 minutes. Masherbrum base camp (4280m) is just beyond in a meadow with a small pool along the moraine.

Days 4 & 5: Masherbrum Base Camp to Hushe Return to Hushe via the same route.

Alternative Days 4 to 6: Masherbrum Base Camp to Hushe via Shaishcho Use this route when continuing up the Gondogoro Valley or on to K7 base camp.

Day 4: Masherbrum Base Camp to Darya Chowk (4 hours) Descend along the west margin of the Masherbrum Glacier to Pushuka. Cross the Masherbrum Glacier to

BALTISTAN

its east margin from just above Pushuka. Descend along the river's true left bank to Darya Chowk, opposite the confluence of the Gondogoro and Aling rivers, where the Hushe River begins.

Day 5: Darya Chowk to Shaishcho (6 to 7 hours) Follow the true right bank of the Gondogoro River to the pastures at Tir Sir. From Tir Sir, cross the Gondogoro Glacier above its mouth as the river is too big to ford, and descend to Shaishcho.

Day 6: Shaishcho to Hushe See the Gondogoro Valley route description below.

GONDOGORO VALLEY
(9 days; July to September)
The Gondogoro Valley was long used for grazing by the Hushe-pa. Now that it is a popular trekking destination, the Hushe-pa no longer use it for grazing, because tourism brings a better economic return. Beautiful camp sites, remarkable mountain views, and the major attractions of Gondogoro peak and the Gondogoro La are the reasons for its popularity. The route up the Gondogoro Valley is steep, but straightforward as far as Daltsampa, from where the Gondogoro Glacier must be traversed to reach Xhuspang, 25 km from Hushe.

Guides & Porters
A local guide is necessary to show the way over the tricky Gondogoro Glacier from Daltsampa to Xhuspang.

8 stages: Hushe to Shaishcho, Shaishcho to Gondogoro camp, Gondogoro camp to Daltsampa, Daltsampa to Xhuspang, and return via the same route

Map Notes
On the Swiss map, Shaishcho is labelled as Chospah. No other camp sites are labelled. The route shown up the middle of the Gondogoro Glacier is incorrect. All maps inaccurately show a side glacier from Peak 6294 flowing west into the Gondogoro Glacier. The glacier has evidently receded

and now only a stream flows into the glacier at Gondogoro camp.

Route Description
Day 1: Hushe to Shaishcho (4 hours) A good trail follows the true left bank of the Hushe River north from Hushe village. About two hours from the village, the Aling and Masherbrum rivers join the combined Gondogoro and Tsarak Tsa rivers to form the Hushe River. The trail, with sheer granite cliffs above, fords a side stream and comes soon to the summer settlement of Odungstan.

Another clear stream is 15 minutes further, and soon the valley bends east. Continue 30 or 45 minutes, cross a bridge to the true right (north) bank, and in 15 minutes reach Shaishcho (*sha* means 'meat'; *cho*, 'a ruler'). Shaishcho was the place where the Raja of Khapalu came and ate ibex, brought to this place by his hunters. Shaishcho (3330m) has good water and lots of flat, sandy camp sites amid tamarisk, wild roses and juniper along the river. It is home to Hakim's popular Hushe Saitcho Inn/Shop.

Day 2: Shaishcho to Gondogoro Camp (2 to 3 hours) From Shaishcho, follow a good trail north one to 1½ hours through the ablation valley on the east side of the Gondogoro Glacier to Atosar (3750m) with a side stream from the east. This flat grassy expanse has lots of water, willows and junipers. Continue gradually through the ablation valley one to 1½ hours to the next side stream and Gondogoro camp (3950m). A big rock marks the spot and a few huts are across the stream. Camp here to acclimatise. Up this side stream and glacier is the distinctive rock spire of Balti peak (point 6050 on the Swiss map).

Days 3 & 4: Gondogoro Camp to Daltsampa (3 to 4 hours) Follow a good trail in the ablation valley one to 1½ hours to Golong, a good lunch spot marked by a large boulder and a stream coming from Golong peak. The spire of Balti peak above Gondogoro camp is prominent to the south.

JOHN MOCK

JOHN MOCK

JOHN MOCK

JOHN MOCK

Top: Roped trekkers approach Hispar Pass base camp on Snow Lake.
Middle: A profusion of wildflowers greets trekkers on reaching Khani Basa camp.
Bottom Left: Author at Top Khana (fort) above Shuwor Sheer, Broghil.
Bottom Right: The shrine at Bitanmal camp, which lies along the Hispar Glacier.

JOHN MOCK

JOHN MOCK

Top: Trekking on Lukpe Lawo (Snow Lake), on the Biafo-Hispar Glacier trek, requires using a rope as protection from hidden crevasses.

Bottom: Dramatic Paiju peak (6610m) is the first of the impressive granite summits lining the lower Baltoro Glacier.

Landslides have wiped out the trail beyond Golong. At the end of the flat area, drop to the edge of the glacier and continue 1.5 km over rubble about one hour. Watch for rock fall. Climb a hillside to a pasture where unattended male yaks graze. Continue 30 to 45 minutes to lovely Daltsampa, sheltered in an ablation valley. A clear stream runs through gorgeous meadows with two small lakes at the southern end. Daltsampa (about 4300m), the most beautiful camp in the Gondogoro Valley, deserves an extra day for acclimatisation and to marvel at the incredible ice fall from the Masherbrum La and enjoy the meadows, stream, and lakes.

Day 5: Daltsampa to Xhuspang (3½ to 4½ hours) The Gondogoro Glacier bends east beyond Daltsampa, and the trail ends at the heavily broken south margin of the Gondogoro Glacier in 30 minutes. The point at which you cross onto the glacier changes from year to year. Once you are on the glacier, the massive granite prow above Xhuspang, five km away, is your obvious landmark. Work up an ice band until opposite Laila peak's convex granite face, then cross a medial moraine band left to a second ice band. Follow this until 1½ to two hours after getting on the glacier. You work left across two moraine ridges, one brown, the other rust-coloured, to a more level ice band. Follow this 45 minutes to the moraine where the Gondogoro Glacier splits. Cross the moraine, and skirt a shallow glacial lake to Xhuspang camp, directly beneath flowered meadows and the large, steep-walled granite prow above the junction of the glacier's two large branches.

Day 6: Xhuspang Spend at least one day here to relax. Xhuspang is also the base for side trips to Gondogoro peak and the Gondogoro La (see Side Trips below). Enjoy the meadows above and the views of Laila peak.

Days 7 to 9: Xhuspang to Hushe Retrace your route down valley, camping at Daltsampa and Shaishcho en route to Hushe.

Side Trip: Xhuspang to Gondogoro Peak

This straightforward technical peak requires a pre-dawn start. The peak lies on the ridge between the two branches of the upper Gondogoro Glacier. The summit (5650m) has excellent views of Masherbrum and Chogolisa, peaks not visible from the Gondogoro La. From Xhuspang, head north (left) around and north of (behind) the granite prow. Work up the slopes, then onto glacier and ascend the snow slope to the summit. Plan to return to camp before noon, otherwise the snow is too soft.

Side Trip: Xhuspang to Gondogoro La

This ascent is higher and harder than Gondogoro peak, requiring climbing gear and an equally early start. Start from Gondogoro high camp (Doug Scott camp). All the giant peaks at the head of the Baltoro are visible from the pass, a view you will never forget. Be careful of rock fall. (See Hushe to Concordia via Gondogoro La below and the Biafo, Hispar & Baltoro Glaciers section in this chapter for more information about the Gondogoro La.)

HUSHE TO CONCORDIA VIA GONDOGORO LA

(8 days; June to August)
The upper Baltoro Glacier and Concordia can be reached from Hushe by crossing the Gondogoro La (see the Hushe Valley map). We have described this route more completely north to south, from Concordia to Hushe, because we think that direction is preferable (see the Biafo, Hispar & Baltoro Glaciers section in this chapter). However, larger trekking parties may choose to cross from south to north in order to pass the objective rock-fall danger on the south side early in the morning when danger is lowest. Some marathon trekkers also cross from south to north to combine this trek with longer traverses of the Baltoro, Biafo and Hispar glaciers. We recommend visiting Masherbrum and/or K7 base camps before trekking up the Gondogoro Valley to permit acclimatisation.

BALTISTAN

Guides & Porters

Be sure to hire an experienced guide and porters who have been over the pass. For the four stages Hushe to Xhuspang, porters provide their own food and the maximum wage totals Rs 200 per stage. When you cross the Gondogoro La, you provide food for the porters and pay Rs 150 per stage beyond Xhuspang. It is customary for parties to sacrifice a goat or sheep either at Gondogoro camp or at Daltsampa. Animals can usually be purchased in Shaishcho or at Gondogoro camp. Sheep cost about Rs 1500 and goats cost up to Rs 2500. If you opt not to buy an animal, porters expect you to pay each porter a one-time additional Rs 50 meat ration.

9 stages: Hushe to Shaishcho, Shaishcho to Gondogoro camp, Gondogoro camp to Daltsampa, Daltsampa to Xhuspang, Xhuspang to Gondogoro high camp, Gondogoro high camp to Gondogoro La, Gondogoro La to Ali camp, Ali camp to corner of Mitre Peak, corner of Mitre Peak to Concordia

Map Notes

The Gondogoro La (misplaced on most maps) links the large eastern branch of the Gondogoro Glacier to the West Vigne Glacier.

Route Description

Days 1 to 5: Hushe to Xhuspang See Gondogoro Valley route description above. Trekkers may also want to spend an extra day in Xhuspang for acclimatisation.

Day 6: Xhuspang to Gondogoro High Camp (1½ to 2 hours) This short, 2.5 km stage helps acclimatisation and puts the party in a better position to cross the pass. Gondogoro high camp (4800m), also known as Doug Scott camp, has a few stone rounds for porters and a reliable water source. The camp can be snow-covered until early July.

Day 7: Gondogoro High Camp to Ali Camp (8 to 10 hours) Start early and plan to be on top of the pass by 6 am. Larger parties should start by 1 or 2 am; smaller or very fit

parties could start by 3 am. The 900m 50° ascent over two km to the Gondogoro La can take up to four hours and may be snow-covered through early July; later in the year it is snow-free and choked with loose rock. Do not attempt the pass on windy days. Descend the steep snow on the north side with three 50° pitches in 1½ to two hours. Continue down the West Vigne Glacier to its junction with the Vigne Glacier. Ali camp faces south-east at the base of the spur at the junction of the West Vigne and Vigne glaciers. An early start avoids post-holing through soft snow from the top of the pass all the way to Ali camp (5010m). If things go well, you could be in Ali camp by 10 am.

Day 8: Ali Camp to Concordia (4 hours) Rope up and head straight out to the middle of the snow-covered Vigne Glacier. Descend easily down the Vigne Glacier to the upper Baltoro Glacier and Concordia (4650m). (See the Biafo, Hispar & Baltoro Glaciers section in this chapter for the more-detailed route description from Concordia to Askole.)

K7 BASE CAMP

(5 days; June to September)
K7 (6934m) and Link Sar (7041m) form a ridge north-east of the upper Tsarak Tsa Glacier. K6 (7040m) is on the ridge south of the upper glacier. The area between Spangser and K7 base camp is a climbers' paradise, with ascents possible on several peaks and many rock climbs.

Guides & Porters

A local guide is helpful for crossing the Chogolisa Glacier.

8 stages: Hushe to Shaishcho, Shaishcho to Tikchumik, Tikchumik to Spangser, Spangser to K7 base camp, and return via the same route

Map Notes

Tsarak Tsa is the Balti name for the glacier labelled as Charakusa Glacier on the Swiss map. Spangser is labelled Supanset and Tikchumik as Techmic.

Route Description
Day 1: Hushe to Shaishcho (4 hours) See the Gondogoro Valley route description above.

Day 2: Shaishcho to Spangser (4 hours) From Shaishcho, head east into the ablation valley north of the large Tsarak Tsa Glacier. The sharp spires of K7 and Link Sar are visible ahead. Tikchumik (*tik* means 'small'; *chumik* 'a spring'), in the ablation valley at the base of the ridge west of the Chogolisa Glacier, has good water. Continue along the base of the ridge to the western margin of the Chogolisa Glacier. Cross this glacier to the green and flowered Spangser above the junction of the Chogolisa and Tsarak Tsa glaciers. Spangser (*spang* means 'meadow'; *ser* 'a place to walk about') is the last pasture and is only used from mid-July to mid-August. Granite slabs rise above Spangser and Namika peak (6325m) towers across the Tsarak Tsa Glacier.

Day 3: Spangser to K7 Base Camp (4 hours) Continue through the ablation valley north of the Tsarak Tsa Glacier, at times over difficult terrain to K7 base camp.

Days 4 & 5: K7 Base Camp to Hushe Follow the trail via Shaishcho to Hushe.

OTHER ROUTES
Honbrok
Picturesque Honbrok summer pastures, high above the Hushe River west of Hushe village, are easily visited on a day hike. It takes four hours to climb steeply to the pastures and 1½ to two hours to return to Hushe village. From Hushe, cross the Hushe River on the lower of the two bridges to its true right bank. Walk up 15 to 30 minutes to Honbrok Nala. Cross it on a sturdy wooden bridge. The trail ascends the true left (north) bank of the stream all the way to the pastures. Honbrok has reliable spring water. From June to October is the best season. Honbrok is labelled Honboro on the Swiss map. Hushe-pa also refer to Honbrok peak (6459m) as Cigarette Peak.

Aling Glacier
The Aling Glacier, the westernmost of the Hushe Valley glaciers, is very large with multiple upper branches. Two under-6000m summits above the upper glacier, Mitre (5944m) and Sceptre (5800m), have been climbed. Hushe-pa have 14 stages up the Aling Glacier, but no one goes beyond the 7th stage. These stages are: Hushe to Dumsum, Dumsum to Shatonchen, Shatonchen to base camp, base camp to Drenmogyalba, Drenmogyalba to Sampibransa, Sampibransa to Khadanlumba, and Khadanlumba to Tasa.

From Hushe, cross the river to its west bank and reach the bridge over the Aling River in two hours. Across the bridge, the trail turns west into the Aling Valley to Dumsum, a summer village with a two-storey mosque. Continue west along the north side of the Aling River to Shatonchen pastures, and along the north side of the Aling Glacier to base camp and Drenmogyalba, which means 'royal bear'. It is the highest pasture used by the Hushe-pa.

K6 Base Camp
K6 (7281m), also called Baltistan peak, is usually approached from Kande village, about midway up the Hushe Valley. From Kande, cross a footbridge over the Hushe River, then cross the Nangmah River to its true right (north) bank to Mingyulu village (labelled Minjlu on the Swiss map). Continue up the north bank of the river to Nangmah summer pastures and on to K6 base camp along the north-west margin of the Nangmah Glacier. Steep granite walls line the Nangmah Valley, including the Great Tower (5800m) south of the summer pastures. It is six stages: Kande to K6 base camp is three stages, and you return via the same route.

Saltoro & Kondus Valleys
This beautiful area will remain closed as long as the dispute between Pakistan and India over the Siachen Glacier remains unsettled. Climbers and explorers always travelled to the peaks along the Siachen Glacier via

either the Sia La, at the head of the Kondus Glacier, or the Bilafond La at the head of the Bilafond Glacier. The southern approach to the Siachen, up the Nubra Valley, was impossible in summer due to high water and quicksand. Villagers in the Saltoro and Kondus valleys no longer see expeditions and so lose the opportunity to earn much-needed income. These eastern valleys have some of the finest clean granite towers in Baltistan, rivalling the Trango Towers for size and sheerness. The towers above Karmading village can be approached without traversing a glacier. These ascents remain for another generation of climbers.

From Halde village, across the Hushe River from Machulu, a jeep road runs along the north bank of the Saltoro River through Tsino (Chino on the Swiss map) with its magnificent granite towers to Brakhor. If you are going up the Kondus Valley, head north-east along the west bank of the Kondus River, and cross a bridge to the east bank at Thang (Kondus on the Swiss map) to reach Karmading, a long day's walk from Brakhor.

A few hours' walk above Karmading to the north-east is the village of Khorkondus. A waterfall tumbles over granite cliffs behind the village, and a small hot spring is 15 minutes north. Above, the Sherpi Gang descends from Sherpi Kangri (7380m) and Saltoro Kangri (7742m). Above the pastures called Lisar (hunting ground) are clean granite walls, a climbers' delight. From Karmading, a trail leads up the main valley for several hours to the snout of the Kondus Glacier. It is two stages to the highest pasture, Rahout Chen, passing through Byangeparo en route. The Kondus Glacier is perhaps the most difficult and chaotic glacier in the Karakoram, but beautiful clean granite pinnacles rise above its upper reaches.

From Brakhor in the Saltoro Valley, a bridge crosses to the south bank. The road up the Saltoro Valley follows the south bank to Goma, the last village. Women in the Saltoro Valley wear unique red-dyed raw-wool hats with brown beaver-like tails. At Goma, the Bilafond, Gyang, and Chulung streams meet, descending from the glaciers above. Beyond the passes above these glaciers are Indian troops.

Glossary

AIG – Assistant Inspector General (of Police)
an – a mountain pass (Khowar)
asalam aleikum – universal Muslim greeting for 'peace be with you' (Arabic)
azad – free

bagh – garden
baksheesh – a tip or donation
bar – river, valley or stream (Burushashki)
bashali – a women's birthing or menstrual house (Kalashamun)
bazaar – market area; a market town is called a bazaar
bergschrund – the giant crevasse found where movement of the glacier breaks it away from the snow slope above
bowl – a basin, sometimes glacial
burqa – a long tent-like garment that completely hides the body shape and face, worn in public by conservative Muslim women who observe purdah

cairn – a heap of stones that marks a route or pass
chador – lightweight blanket often worn as a shawl by men, which doubles as a blanket or pillow, and the shawl worn by women
chai – tea
chapatti – flat, unleavened wheat bread cooked on a griddle
charpoy – a simple bed made of ropes knotted together on a wooden frame
chowk – intersection
cornice – deposits of wind-drifted snow on the lee edge of ridges
crag – an arete
crampons – lightweight alloy 12-pointed snow and ice-climbing aids that are fitted onto boots
crevasse – a deep crack in a glacier

DC – Deputy Commissioner of a district in NWFP and in the Northern Areas
DFO – District Forestry Officer
dakini – female messenger of Buddha realm
dal – lentil soup usually served with rice

dewa – a god (Kalashamun)
dupatta – light scarf often worn by Muslim women to cover their hair in public
dzo – a cross between a cow and a yak

ford – crossing a river by wading because there is no bridge or cable
fork – the place where a trail or river divides into branches

gah – river, valley, or stream (Shina); place (Persian)
gali – a mountain pass (Shina)
gang – a glacier (Balti)
glacier – a large mass of ice and snow flowing down a mountain or valley
gol – river, valley, or stream (Khowar)
gomukh – a glacier (Shina)
gree – a col (Khowar)

haghost – a mountain pass (Burushashki)
hammam – public bath house and barber shop
haqūq ul-ibād – community spirit (Arabic)
hijrah – the flight of the Prophet Mohammad from Mecca to Medina in 622 AD; this is the reference for dates in the Muslim calendar (designated AH, ie, after hijrah)

IG – Inspector General (of police)
Imam – leader; title of one of 12 descendants of the Prophet Mohammad who, according to orthodox Shia belief, succeeded him as temporal and spiritual leader of Muslims
inshallah – 'God willing' (Arabic)

jerab – river, valley, or stream (Wakhi)
jestak – the female deity of hearth and home (Kalashamun)
jestak han – the house in a Kalasha village of the female deity of hearth and home (Kalashamun)

kafir – Muslim term for non-Muslim
khayaban – boulevard or avenue
kucheri – civil courts of law

la – a mountain pass (Balti)
lungma – river, valley, or stream (Balti)

markaz – commercial centre
Mehtar – title of the former rulers of Chitral
memsahib – respectful title for a woman, used alone (ie, like 'Madam') (Urdu)
Mir – title of the former rulers of Hunza and Nagyr
moraine – mass of rocks left by a glacier; along a glacier's margins (a lateral moraine), in its centre (a medial moraine), and at its mouth (a terminal moraine)
muztagh – mountain (Turkic)

nala – river, valley, or stream (Urdu)
nambardar – the head man of a village (also called lambardar)
nan – thick bread rounds baked in a tandoori oven

parāo – a traditional stage or length of a day's march used to calculate porters' wages
peri – magical female spirit beings
punji – cairn (Burushashki)
purdah – segregation and veiling of post-pubescent women from all men outside the immediate family in orthodox Muslim communities

qannat – conservation ethic (Arabic)

Ramadan – the Islamic month of sunrise-to-sunset fasting
route – a course for travelling where no visible trail exists
rui – magical, usually malevolent, female spirit beings
rupee – the currency in Pakistan

SP – Superintendent of Police
SSP – Senior Superintendent of Police
saddle – a low place in a ridge
sahib – respectful title for a man, used alone (ie, like 'Sir') or after a surname or title (ie, like 'Mr') (Urdu)
sar – summit, the head of (Persian)

sarai – a caravan stopping place, now used for a motor-transport staging place
scree – small rock accumulated on a slope, usually collected in a gully which spreads into a fan-shaped cone
serac – a large ice block on a glacier
shahrah – male markhor (Khowar)
shalwar kameez – traditional men's and women's clothing, consisting of a knee-length long-sleeved shirt worn over very loose trousers gathered at the waist
shikar gah – hunting grounds (Urdu)
sirdar – boss or headman of porters on a trek or expedition
switchback – route that follows a zigzag course up a steep grade

talus – large boulders accumulated on a slope, fanning out at its base
tehsil – administrative zone within a district in a province
Tham – title of the former rulers of Hunza and Nagyr
trail – a visible path
true left – the actual left bank of a river when facing downstream
true right – the actual right bank of a river when facing downstream

urs – anniversary of the death of a saint
uween – a mountain pass (Wakhi)

wālā – the person in charge or with experience (eg, a hotel-wālā runs a hotel) (Urdu)
wāpāsi – portion of porter's wage equal to one half of a stage wage, which is paid when a porter is released at a place that is different from the place where the porter was hired and the porter must walk back to the place where he was hired

yak – long-haired member of the ox family kept for dairy and as a beast of burden at high altitude
yaz – a glacier (Wakhi)

ziarat – a shrine to a saint

Index

THANKS

Kimberley O'Neil and John Mock wish to thank:

the Secretary of the Ministry of Sports & Tourism and the Deputy Chief of Operations of the Tourism Division of the Government of Pakistan; Amir Ahmed Qureshi, the Managing Director of Pakistan Tourism Development Corporation (PTDC); Tayyab Nisar Mir, Assistant Tourism Officer PTDC Information Centre, Islamabad; Rehmat Ullah Khan Niazi, Assistant Tourism Officer at PTDC Motels booking office in Islamabad; Dr Syed Rifaat Hussain, Press Minister and Ms Naila Chawdri at the Embassy of Pakistan in Washington, DC; Haider Jalal, General Manager for The Americas and Rasheed Khan, Interline Supervisor at Pakistan International Airlines (PIA) in New York; Muazam Shaikh, PIA District Sales Manager in San Francisco; and Anna Marie Kruizinga and Colleen Raher; and the US Educational Foundation and the staff at Lodgings Guest House, both in Islamabad.

In Chitral we would like to thank: Haider Ali Shah, the gracious host of the Mountain Inn and his wonderful staff; Babu Mohammad, for sharing his unsurpassed Chitral trekking experience; Maqsood ul Mulk and his father Kush Ahmed ul Mulk for true Chitrali hospitality; Abdul Faraz, DFO (Wildlife) – Chitral and his staff, especially Imtiaz Hussain, Range Officer, Deputy Range Officers Altaf Ali Shah and Mehtarjao, and game watchers Akhtar ud Din, Ishfaq Ahmed, Mohammad Safdar Ali Khan, Akram Jan, Aziz Mohammad, and Shafi Ahmed for showing us Chitral's protected areas; Saifullah Jan and Washlim Gul of Balanguru; Jinnah Kalash of Anish; Saeed Akbar Khan and Parsal Khan of Batrik; Sher Beg of Birir; Master Ghulam Nabi and Tata Shah of Uthool; Rahman Nabi, Saiful Rehman, and Gaffar Beg of Shagrom; Sher Qayum Beg of Iwatch, Khot; Rehmat Akbar Khan Rehmat of Chapali; Pholok Khan of Shunup, Gazin; and Mirza Rafi of Broghil.

Everyone who walked with us in Ghizar: Sonak of Haringolshal, Bahushtaro; Mohammad Ali Shah of Nialthi, Thui; Gumburi Khan of Gamelti, Darkot; Bashiruddin of Pakora; and Maiun Jan of Ghotulti for his family's hospitality. In Diamir, special thanks go to: Rehmat Nabi and Raji Wali of Chilas; and Inamullah Khan of Raikhot.

Many friends throughout Hunza, Nagyr, and Gojal helped us. In particular we'd like to thank: Ikram Beg, who has always been the best of friends, FA Khan Changazi and Muhammad Jamal of Hunza Tourist House in Gilgit and their staff; Kalbi of the Tourist Park Hotel, Karimabad; Shafi Ahmed of Nagyr, and Ahmed Hussain, Hadi Ali, and Shaban Ali of Hakalshal; Ashraf Khan of Ghulkin; Izzatullah Beg of the Batura Inn, Qamar Jan, Rasul Khan, and Aziz Khan, all of Passu; the entire village of Shimshal, especially Qurban Ali and family, Dr Farman, Aziz Ullah, Hasil Shah and his wife, Laili Shah, Sabziq, Mehman Khan, Ali Dad, and Saeed Mohammad; and from Chapursan, Alam Jam of Zood Khun who knows his way on glaciers, Rahmat Baig, Javed, Momin Hayat, Shahid Ali, and Haji Beg who intuitively understood what we were doing better than anyone.

In Baltistan, we wish to thank: Ali Mohammad of Arandu, Ma Jan of Karmading, Ghulam Nabi of Halde; Hassan of Kande; Hanefa of Hushe; Noor Ali and Yousef of Gomastokji; the incomparable Ghulam Abbas, Ghulam son of Mehdi, Ali son of Mohammad Ali, Alichu, and Haider, all of Tissar; Ghulam Rasul of Satpara; and Wazir Jaffer Shigri. A very special thanks to Baltistan Tours guide, Sher Ali of Hushe, and his father Ghulam Hassan.

Several trekking companies supported our project: Nazir Sabir, Abdul Quddus, Sultan Ahmed, Mohammad Shifa, Ghulam Sarwar, and Haji Beg of Nazir Sabir Expeditions; Maqsood and Siraj ul Mulk of Hindukush Trails; Mohammad Iqbal and his staff of Baltistan Tours; and S Anwar ul Hassan of Sitara. A special thanks to Shirin and Iqbal Walji of Travels Waljis and Waljis Adventure Pakistan and their staff, especially: Noonihal Shah, Amjad Ayub, Akbar, Abbas Ali Khan and the staff and drivers in Gilgit; Beg Rehamtullah Beg; Shabbir Hussain in Karimabad; Jamil in Islamabad; Mohammad Moinuddin in Peshawar; and Noori Hayat of Baltit, Ali Murad of Maiun, and Sanjar Beg of Passu, guides supreme.

Many other friends contributed much to the book. Many heartfelt thanks to: John King who got us started on this project; Dr David Shlim of the CIWEC Clinic in Kathmandu; Richard Harrison for Kalash architecture information; Michael Speaks for sharing his rafting and kayaking expertise; Vicki Mattice; Dudley Blauwet for gem information; Dan Blumstein, biologist and king of the marmots; Kelly Rich, climbing and trekking pal; Norman Silver, global traveller; and photographers Jonathan Blair, Nancy Shanahan, and Vassi Koutsaftis; and Ben Ailes.

Many companies helped make our many months on the trail more comfortable. We're especially grateful to: Dana Gleeson, owner Dana Design of Bozeman, Montana who donated two Terraplane backpacks and Big Zap battery recharger; Tom Myers of Cascade Designs for Therm-Rest sleeping pads and chair kits; Sara Hysjulien at PUR of Minneapolis, Minnesota for a PUR Explorer water purifying system; Mountain Safety Research of Seattle, Washington for stoves and fuel bottles, pots and pans, and repair kits; and Trimble Navigation of Sunnyvale, California for their Trimble Scout GPS.

PLANET TALK

Lonely Planet's FREE quarterly newsletter

We love hearing from you and think you'd like to hear from us.

When...is the right time to see reindeer in Finland?
Where...can you hear the best palm-wine music in Ghana?
How...do you get from Asunción to Areguá by steam train?
What...is the best way to see India?

For the answer to these and many other questions read PLANET TALK.

Every issue is packed with up-to-date travel news and advice including:

- a letter from Lonely Planet co-founders Tony and Maureen Wheeler
- go behind the scenes on the road with a Lonely Planet author
- feature article on an important and topical travel issue
- a selection of recent letters from travellers
- details on forthcoming Lonely Planet promotions
- complete list of Lonely Planet products

To join our mailing list contact any Lonely Planet office.

Also available: Lonely Planet T-shirts. 100% heavyweight cotton.

LONELY PLANET ONLINE

Get the latest travel information before you leave or while you're on the road

Whether you've just begun planning your next trip, or you're chasing down specific info on currency regulations or visa requirements, check out the Lonely Planet World Wide Web site for up-to-the-minute travel information.

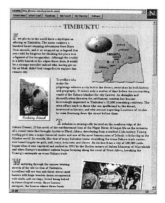

As well as travel profiles of your favourite destinations (including interactive maps and full-colour photos), you'll find current reports from our army of researchers and other travellers, updates on health and visas, travel advisories, and the ecological and political issues you need to be aware of as you travel.

There's an online travellers' forum (the Thorn Tree) where you can share your experiences of life on the road, meet travel companions and ask other travellers for their recommendations and advice. We also have plenty of links to other Web sites useful to independent travellers.

With tens of thousands of visitors a month, the Lonely Planet Web site is one of the most popular on the Internet and has won a number of awards including GNN's Best of the Net travel award.

http://www.lonelyplanet.com

LONELY PLANET PRODUCTS

Lonely Planet is known worldwide for publishing practical, reliable and no-nonsense travel information in our guides and on our web site. The Lonely Planet list covers just about every accessible part of the world. Currently there are eight series: *travel guides, shoestring guides, walking guides, city guides, phrasebooks, audio packs, travel atlases* and *Journeys* – a unique collection of travellers' tales.

EUROPE

Austria • Baltic States & Kaliningrad • Baltic States phrasebook • Britain • Central Europe on a shoestring • Central Europe phrasebook • Czech & Slovak Republics • Denmark • Dublin city guide • Eastern Europe on a shoestring • Eastern Europe phrasebook • Finland • France • Greece • Greek phrasebook • Hungary • Iceland, Greenland & the Faroe Islands • Ireland • Italy • Mediterranean Europe on a shoestring • Mediterranean Europe phrasebook • Paris city guide • Poland • Prague city guide • Russia, Ukraine & Belarus • Russian phrasebook • Scandinavian & Baltic Europe on a shoestring • Scandinavian Europe phrasebook • Slovenia • St Petersburg city guide • Switzerland • Trekking in Greece • Trekking in Spain • Ukrainian phrasebook • Vienna city guide • Walking in Switzerland • Western Europe on a shoestring • Western Europe phrasebook

NORTH AMERICA

Alaska • Backpacking in Alaska • Baja California• California & Nevada • Canada • Hawaii • Honolulu city guide • Los Angeles city guide • Mexico • Miami • New England • Pacific Northwest USA • Rocky Mountain States • San Francisco city guide • Southwest USA • USA phrasebook

CENTRAL AMERICA & THE CARIBBEAN

Central America on a shoestring • Costa Rica • Eastern Caribbean • Guatemala, Belize & Yucatán: La Ruta Maya • Jamaica

SOUTH AMERICA

Argentina, Uruguay & Paraguay • Bolivia • Brazil • Brazilian phrasebook • Buenos Aires city guide • Chile & Easter Island • Colombia • Ecuador & the Galápagos Islands • Latin American Spanish phrasebook • Peru • Quechua phrasebook • Rio de Janeiro city guide • South America on a shoestring • Trekking in the Patagonian Andes • Venezuela

Travel Literature: Full Circle: A South American Journey

ALSO AVAILABLE:

Travel with Children • Traveller's Tales

AFRICA

Arabic (Moroccan) phrasebook • Africa on a shoestring • Cape Town city guide • Central Africa • East Africa • Egypt & the Sudan • Ethiopian (Amharic) phrasebook • Kenya • Morocco • North Africa • South Africa, Lesotho & Swaziland • Swahili phrasebook • Trekking in East Africa • West Africa • Zimbabwe, Botswana & Namibia • Zimbabwe, Botswana & Namibia travel atlas

MAIL ORDER

Lonely Planet products are distributed worldwide. They are also available by mail order from Lonely Planet, so if you have difficulty finding a title please write to us. North American and South American residents should write to Embarcadero West, 155 Filbert St, Suite 251, Oakland CA 94607, USA; European and African residents should write to 10 Barley Mow Passage, Chiswick, London W4 4PH; and residents of other countries to PO Box 617, Hawthorn, Victoria 3122, Australia.

NORTH-EAST ASIA

Beijing city guide • Cantonese phrasebook • China • Hong Kong, Macau & Canton • Hong Kong city guide • Japan • Japanese phrasebook • Japanese audio pack • Korea • Korean phrasebook • Mandarin phrasebook • Mongolia • Mongolian phrasebook • North-East Asia on a shoestring • Seoul city guide • Taiwan • Tibet • Tibet phrasebook • Tokyo city guide

Travel Literature: Lost Japan

MIDDLE EAST & CENTRAL ASIA

Arab Gulf States • Arabic (Egyptian) phrasebook • Central Asia • Iran • Israel • Jordan & Syria • Middle East • Turkey • Turkish phrasebook • Trekking in Turkey • Yemen

Travel Literature: The Gates of Damascus

ISLANDS OF THE INDIAN OCEAN

Madagascar & Comoros • Maldives & Islands of the East Indian Ocean • Mauritius, Réunion & Seychelles

INDIAN SUBCONTINENT

Bengali phrasebook • Bangladesh • Delhi city guide • Hindi/Urdu phrasebook • India • India & Bangladesh travel atlas • Indian Himalaya • Karakoram Highway • Nepal • Nepali phrasebook • Pakistan • Sri Lanka • Sri Lanka phrasebook • Trekking in the Indian Himalaya • Trekking in the Karakoram & Hindukush • Trekking in the Nepal Himalaya

Travel Literature: Shopping for Buddhas

SOUTH-EAST ASIA

Bali & Lombok • Bangkok city guide • Burmese phrasebook • Cambodia • Ho Chi Minh city guide • Indonesia • Indonesian phrasebook • Indonesian audio pack • Jakarta city guide • Java • Laos • Lao phrasebook • Malaysia, Singapore & Brunei • Myanmar (Burma) • Philippines • Pilipino phrasebook • Singapore city guide • South-East Asia on a shoestring • Thailand • Thailand travel atlas • Thai phrasebook • Thai audio pack • Thai Hill Tribes phrasebook • Vietnam • Vietnamese phrasebook • Vietnam travel atlas

AUSTRALIA & THE PACIFIC

Australia • Australian phrasebook • Bushwalking in Australia• Bushwalking in Papua New Guinea • Fiji • Fijian phrasebook • Islands of Australia's Great Barrier Reef • Melbourne city guide • Micronesia • New Caledonia • New South Wales & the ACT • New Zealand • Northern Territory • Outback Australia • Papua New Guinea • Papua New Guinea phrasebook • Queensland • Rarotonga & the Cook Islands • Samoa • Solomon Islands • South Australia • Sydney city guide • Tahiti & French Polynesia • Tasmania • Tonga • Tramping in New Zealand • Vanuatu • Victoria • Western Australia

Travel Literature: Islands in the Clouds • Sean & David's Long Drive

THE LONELY PLANET STORY

Lonely Planet published its first book in 1973 in response to the numerous 'How did you do it?' questions Maureen and Tony Wheeler were asked after driving, bussing, hitching, sailing and railing their way from England to Australia.

Written at a kitchen table and hand collated, trimmed and stapled, *Across Asia on the Cheap* became an instant local bestseller, inspiring thoughts of another book.

Eighteen months in South-East Asia resulted in their second guide, *South-East Asia on a shoestring*, which they put together in a backstreet Chinese hotel in Singapore in 1975. The 'yellow bible', as it quickly became known to backpackers around the world, soon became *the* guide to the region. It has sold well over half a million copies and is now in its 8th edition, still retaining its familiar yellow cover.

Today there are over 180 titles, including travel guides, walking guides, language kits & phrasebooks, travel atlases and travel literature. The company is one of the largest travel publishers in the world. Although Lonely Planet initially specialised in guides to Asia, we now cover most regions of the world, including the Pacific, North America, South America, Africa, the Middle East and Europe.

The emphasis continues to be on travel for independent travellers. Tony and Maureen still travel for several months of each year and play an active part in the writing, updating and quality control of Lonely Planet's guides.

They have been joined by over 70 authors and 170 staff at our offices in Melbourne (Australia), Oakland (USA), London (UK) and Paris (France). Travellers themselves also make a valuable contribution to the guides through the feedback we receive in thousands of letters each year.

The people at Lonely Planet strongly believe that travellers can make a positive contribution to the countries they visit, both through their appreciation of the countries' culture, wildlife and natural features, and through the money they spend. In addition, the company makes a direct contribution to the countries and regions it covers. Since 1986 a percentage of the income from each book has been donated to ventures such as famine relief in Africa; aid projects in India; agricultural projects in Central America; Greenpeace's efforts to halt French nuclear testing in the Pacific; and Amnesty International.

'I hope we send the people out with the right attitude about travel. You realise when you travel that there are so many different perspectives about the world, so we hope these books will make people more interested in what they see. These are guidebooks, but you can't really guide people. All you can do is point them in the right direction.'
– Tony Wheeler

LONELY PLANET PUBLICATIONS

Australia
PO Box 617, Hawthorn 3122, Victoria
tel: (03) 9819 1877 fax: (03) 9819 6459
e-mail: talk2us@lonelyplanet.com.au

USA
Embarcadero West, 155 Filbert St, Suite 251,
Oakland, CA 94607
tel: (510) 893 8555 TOLL FREE: 800 275-8555
fax: (510) 893 8563
e-mail: info@lonelyplanet.com

UK
10 Barley Mow Passage, Chiswick,
London W4 4PH
tel: (0181) 742 3161 fax: (0181) 742 2772
e-mail: 100413.3551@compuserve.com

France:
71 bis rue du Cardinal Lemoine, 75005 Paris
tel: 1 44 32 06 20 fax: 1 46 34 72 55
e-mail: 100560.415@compuserve.com

World Wide Web: http://www.lonelyplanet.com